TWELFE NIGHT,

OR WHAT YOU WILL

A NEW VARIORUM EDITION

OF

SHAKESPEARE, *william*

EDITED BY

HORACE HOWARD FURNESS

TWELFE NIGHT,
OR, WHAT YOU WILL

with a Supplementary Bibliography

by LOUIS MARDER
editor of *The Shakespeare Newsletter*

NEW YORK
AMERICAN SCHOLAR PUBLICATIONS · INC.
1966

FIRST PUBLISHED IN 1901
Reissued 1966 by American Scholar Publications, Inc.
L. C. Catalog Card No.: 63-13369
© 1966

PRINTED IN THE UNITED STATES OF AMERICA
by SENTRY PRESS, NEW YORK, N. Y. 10019

IN MEMORIAM

CONTENTS

PREFACE

THERE is the attempt, in this Edition, to make each volume complete in itself and independent of the others; this renders unavoidable a certain amount of repetition, which is irksome to us all, but, I trust, pardonable.

Of the present play, there is no Quarto Edition; which means, that no copy of it was printed during SHAKESPEARE's lifetime. Of this we are assured by the terms on which the *Stationers' Company* granted a license for the printing of the Folio, in 1623. The plays included in that license are only those which had not before been printed; *Twelfth Night* is among them; it is clear, therefore, that it was then licensed for the first time.

A transcript of the entry of the First Folio is as follows, in the *Stationers' Registers :**

8° Novembris 1623

| Master Blounte Isaak Jaggard | Entred for their Copie vnder the hands of Master Doctor Worrall and Master Cole warden Master William Shakspeers Comedyes Histories, and Tragedyes soe manie of the said Copies as are not formerly entred to other men.   vizt.   **vij^s.** |

	The Tempest
	The two gentlemen of Verona
	Measure for Measure
	The Comedy of Errors
Comedyes	As you like it
	All's well that ends well
	Twelfe night
	The winters tale

| Histories | The thirde parte of Henry ye Sixt |
| | Henry the Eight |

---

* Arber's *Transcript of the Stationers' Registers,* vol. iv. p. 107.

	Coriolanus
	Timon of Athens
	Julius Cæsar
Tragedies	Mackbeth
	Anthonie and Cleopatra
	Cymbeline.

In many another play the lack of a Quarto would prove more unfortunate than in the present. Where the text of the Folio has been obscured by a compositor, a Quarto may shed light; but if the Quarto itself be misprinted, then we have but a dim twilight, whereunder discussions may wax fast and certainly furious. I am not altogether sure that it is not a source of congratulation that our sole authority for *Twelfth Night* lies in the Folio. It is to be feared that in many a case a Quarto might have obtrusively disturbed the tranquillity of the Folio, whereof the text is here so unusually correct that a majority of the editors do not even allude to it, beyond the statement of its source. The most puzzling passage of the play, or at least that which has caused the most discussion, is Malvolio's reference to the 'lady of the 'Strachy, who married the yeoman of the wardrobe,' where 'Strachy' has been conjectured to be a misprint for 'Trachy,' 'Astrachan,' 'Thracy,' 'Duchy,' 'Stitchery,' 'Starchery,' and half a dozen other titles near or far fetched. Possibly a Quarto might have disclosed the personality of this Lady with more precision; but I rather prefer the shadowy outline of a haughty dame whom love forces from her grandeur to wed a humble retainer in a department so very convenient and feminine as the wardrobe. I am not of those who demand a solution of every puzzle; a certain mystery, like Lord Bacon's 'lie,' doth ever add pleasure. Feste's proud argosy of the Vapians riding the waves without vailing its high top as it passes the equinoctial of Queubus is a vision as delightful as any true picture in the voyages of Sir Walter or of Drake. The question of *Text*, then, may be happily dismissed with the assurance, from which there is no dissenting voice among editors, that, with the exception of errors wholly typographical, and to be expected, the Text in *Twelfth Night* is of remarkable purity.

It has been deemed, in mouths of wisest censure, of the utmost importance to know the order in which SHAKESPEARE composed his plays. We must distinguish, so it is urged, his earliest plays from his latest; we shall then be enabled, so we are told, to perceive the growth of his mind; though how this is to help the growth of our minds is not evident; possibly, it is assumed that our minds, being fully grown, can watch with genial smile his early struggles; under such circumstances, who can resist the charm of suggesting that the young poet does very well now, but he will do better when he grows older and wiser? In order thus to marshall the plays in their due order, it is essential to know the *Date of Composition* of each play. To determine this date, there are two resources : first, facts drawn from evidence external to the play, such as references to it in contemporary literature ; and secondly, facts drawn from evidence within the play itself, such as allusions to certain facts whereof the date is readily ascertained. Of *external* evidence of the *Date of Composition* of the present play, we have but two assured items, namely, the *Stationers' Registers*, quoted above, and the *Diary*, or commonplace book of a London barrister, to be quoted hereafter. STEEVENS did, indeed, before the existence of this *Diary* was known, attempt to make out a third ; he imagined that Ben Jonson, ‘who,’ as he said, ‘takes ‘every opportunity to find fault with SHAKESPEARE,’ intended to ridi- cule this comedy, when he makes Mitis say, in *Every Man out of his Humour*, III, i: ‘That the argument of his comedy might have ‘been of some other nature, as of a duke to be in love with a count- ‘ess, and that countess to be in love with the duke’s son, and the son ‘to love the lady’s waiting-maid ; some such cross-wooing, with a ‘clown to their serving-man, better to be thus near, and familiarly ‘allied to the time.’ This play of JONSON was acted by the Company at The Globe, albeit SHAKESPEARE was not one of the actors in it, in 1599 ; so that chronologically a reference to *Twelfth Night* is not impossible ; more than one editor places its date in that same year: 1599. But in *Twelfth Night* there is no countess in love with a duke’s son, nor any duke’s son in love with a waiting-maid ; and as for the ‘cross-wooing,’ GIFFORD says that it was ‘probably to be found ‘among the old trash which has long since perished,’—an expeditious and comfortable way of silencing a troublesome question. I have no faith whatever in the supposition that JONSON here aimed such petty criticism at a play which not only had authority so irreproachably classic as Plautus and Menander for its cross-wooing, but was also written by one whom he ‘loved this side of idolatry.’

As regards *internal* evidence, the present play affords a warning which all who deal in this species of evidence should lay to heart. Some items of it, as conclusive as any that ever were offered, have been utterly disproved by *external* evidence subsequently discovered. For instance, in the Second Scene of the Third Act, Sir Toby insti- gates Sir Andrew to send a challenge to Cesario, and tells him to ‘taunt him with the license of ink ; if thou thou’st him some thrice, 'it shall not be amiss.' All who have read Sir Walter Raleigh's trial will remember the low abuse heaped on him by the Attorney General, Coke. When the latter was denouncing Cobham's treason, Sir Walter remonstrated, saying, 'If my Lord Cobham be a traitor, what is that 'to me?' Whereupon Coke replied: 'All that he did was by thy 'instigation, thou viper; for I thou thee, thou Traitor!' THEOBALD wrote to WARBURTON that there could be no doubt that Sir Toby alluded to this incident, and intended thereby to show his respect for Sir Walter and his detestation of his prosecutors. Moreover, in Coke's speech, is not 'thou' used just thrice, — the very number prescribed by Sir Toby? Could any sane man demand clearer evidence? Raleigh's trial took place in November, 1603; therefore THEOBALD concluded that *Twelfth Night* was written in 1604; and, moreover, found corroborative evidence in Viola's words 'West-'ward ho!' when Olivia tells her her way lies due west. This phrase is the title of a play by Dekker and Webster, which we know was acted in 1605, and presumably written as well as acted much earlier. That THEOBALD could have been beguiled into the belief that in 'Westward ho!' there lies a reference to a play, rather than to the cry familiar to every citizen of London who came within earshot of the watermen plying their trade on the Thames, shows how weak strong men may sometimes be, and how easily a good scholar may be misled when in pursuit of the *ignis fatuus*, internal evidence. Nay, even cautious, conservative CAPELL asserted that unless Viola here referred to Dekker's play, her words 'would have no salt.' CAPELL's own contribution to the internal evidence was hardly less far fetched. Because Sir Andrew 'delighted in masques and revels,' weakly adding 'sometimes altogether,' this Editor inferred that herein lay a reference to 1607; in that year, 'the rage for masques was predominant,' and to represent the weak knight as delighting in them was, as CAPELL choicely phrased it, 'a wipe undoubtedly.'

To the ingenuity of THOMAS TYRWHITT, the editor of Chaucer, the next item is due, and such was the respect in which TYRWHITT's learning was held, that for many years the date of composition was accepted which he had detected lying concealed under the word 'undertakers,' although this date involved the undesirable conclusion that *Twelfth Night* was the last play SHAKESPEARE had written. When the sea-captain, Anthonio, intervenes in the duel between Viola and Sir Andrew, and takes up the quarrel for Viola, whom he mistakes for her twin-brother, Sebastian, Sir Toby exclaims 'Nay, if you be an 'undertaker, I am for you!' In 'undertaker' TYRWHITT perceived an allusion to parliamentary 'undertakers,' who were thus stigmatised because they had *undertaken* in James's time so to manage the elections that a majority favourable to the Court was returned to Parliament. But this violent opposition to 'undertakers' arose in 1614, a date somewhat late for SHAKESPEARE, who died only two years later. But the reference is so unmistakable that there was no help for it; the date of the composition of *Twelfth Night* must be placed in 1614. For many years MALONE accepted this date; but, under the influence of sundry allusions which seemed to point to an earlier one, the significance of 'undertakers' grew less and less pointed until at last it was decently laid to rest, as became its modern calling. MALONE's final judgement is in favour of 1607; in that year, Marston's play of *What you will* was entered on the *Stationers' Registers* in August, and this clearly points to the alternative title of the present play. Furthermore, the 'Sophy' is twice mentioned in *Twelfth Night*. Who can doubt that SHAKESPEARE had here in mind the remarkable career in Persia of the Shirley family, one of whom, Sir Robert, had come to England as the Sophy's ambassador? 'The history of Shirley,' says MALONE, 'was well known 'in England in 1607, and a play written on the subject, called *The* '*Travels of Three English Brothers*, appeared in that year.' Blind indeed must he be, who cannot see that these items of internal evidence point to 1607 as the year of *Twelfth Night*'s birth. But in the meantime, between MALONE's first and last opinion, there appeared CHALMERS, that daring free-lance, who would persist in knowing as much about Elizabethan times as STEEVENS or MALONE, and would not shut his eyes and open his mouth to take what his betters administered. In the 'affair' between Cesario and Sir Andrew, CHALMERS asserts * that SHAKESPEARE meant to throw the duello into a ridiculous light; and, inasmuch as King James, in 1613, issued 'An Edict and Censure 'against Private Combats,' which was designed to put a stop to duels, nothing can be plainer than that the present comedy was written in that year.

There is still another item of internal evidence which is really respectable, and stands on a basis firmer than any of the others. In the Second Scene of the Third Act, Maria says of Malvolio, 'he does 'smile his face into more lines than is in the new Map, with the aug- 'mentation of the Indies.' Here we have a specific map, designated as 'new.' Wherefore, the date of any map bearing an 'augmentation 'of the Indies' must be close enough to the date of *Twelfth Night* to permit Maria to term it 'new.' In 1860, JAMES LENOX, the founder of *The Lenox Library*, suggested that a certain map, extolled

---

* *Supplemental Apology*, etc. 1799, p. 442.

by HALLAM, was the veritable map alluded to by Maria.* Eighteen years later, in the *Transactions* of *The New Shakspere Society*, Mr C. H. COOTE learnedly maintained that in this same map all requirements were fulfilled; it was a map on a 'new' plan, with a record of all the newest news in geographical discovery, whereon the Indies were augmented and more rhumb-lines added than on any previous map; it had been published to be bound up with Hakluyt's *Voyages*, in 1599. Inasmuch as this date harmonises with the external evidence afforded by Manningham's *Diary* (to be hereafter mentioned), it may well be accepted as narrowing the term of years within which *Twelfth Night* was written. Where external evidence corroborates internal evidence, the latter is worthy of all respect.

Finally, two of the songs in the play furnish items which partake both of external and internal evidence. Sir Toby, in the Third Scene of the Second Act, sings snatches of a song beginning: 'Farewell, 'dear heart,' etc. 'This ballad,' says HALLIWELL-PHILLIPPS,† 'had 'first appeared in the *Booke of Ayres* composed by Robert Jones, '1601. Jones does not profess to be the author of the words of this 'song, . . . but there is every reason to believe that the ditty was 'first published in this work, a collection of new, not of old, songs.' This date, 1601, is not opposed to our positive external evidence, and may well be accepted. Jones may have included it in his *Booke*, owing to its popularity as sung in *Twelfth Night;* or it may have been a popular song, familiar to the actor of Sir Toby, and may or may not have been written by SHAKESPEARE.

The second song is that of Feste, beginning, 'O Mistress mine, 'where are you roaming?' CHAPPELL says that this song is contained in Morley's *Consort Lessons*, 1599; 'which proves either that *Twelfth* '*Night* was written in or before that year, or that, in accordance with 'the then prevailing custom, *O Mistress mine* was an old song, intro- 'duced into the play.' ‡ 'This latter supposition,' DYCE observes, 'is 'doubtless the true one.' I do not forget how common is the practice in SHAKESPEARE, and in the Elizabethan drama, to introduce old or familiar songs; I bear in mind that the Gravedigger's song in *Hamlet* was written by Thomas Lord Vaux; I recall that in the present play there stands the stage-direction '*Catch sung,*' where the catch is left to the musical resources of the actors,—and yet in full memory of all this, oxen and wainropes cannot hale me from the belief that this song is SHAKESPEARE's very own. Its phraseology, its histrionic quality (it is a drama in miniature), its sententiousness ('Journeys end in lovers meet-

---

* *Nicolaus Syllacius, De Insulis Nuper Inventis*, New York, 1860, p. xiii.
† *Outlines*, etc. 2nd ed. p. 264.   ‡ *Popular Music of the Olden Time*, i, 209.

'ing,' 'Youth's a stuff will not endure,'—the very word 'stuff' is SHAKE-
SPEARIAN), its interrogation 'What is love?' (like 'Tell me where is
'fancy bred?'), its defining love by what it is not rather than by what
it is,—all these proclaim its author to be either SHAKESPEARE—*aut
Diabolus*.

Among the items of internal evidence thus far dealt with, there are
seven which are not corroborated by external evidence, and these are
they which afford a sad warning to all who indulge in speculations
and theories based on allusions within a play. If these allusions
would only all point to the same date, there might be some comfort
yet, but they do not, and will not; we, the while, poor feeble victims,
eager for the beneficent knowledge of the very year, month, day, and
hour when SHAKESPEARE composed his plays, must abide in depressing
bewilderment. At the very time, however, that THEOBALD, CAPELL,
MALONE, and the rest, were proclaiming each a different date, and
each the true one, there was lying unheeded among the Harleian
MSS (No. 5353) of the British Museum a little unpretending *Diary*,
containing an entry which scatters, like the chaff that it is, all uncorroborated internal evidence.

To whom belongs the right of discovery in regard to this *Diary*, I
find it impossible to determine. HUNTER says that he discovered it in
1828, and mentioned the fact to two literary friends, one of whom was
B. H. BRIGHT, the other is nameless, and that 'up to the period,' he
adds,* 'when it fell into my hands, I have reason to think that no eye
'had fallen on this unobtrusive volume that could perceive its curiosity
'and worth.' COLLIER, on the other hand, speaks of having been 'fortu-
'nate to meet with it' and remarks that 'excepting by the maker of the
'Catalogue, it seems to have remained entirely unexamined.'† Furthermore, in a small book, written in the form of a letter addressed to
HUNTER, COLLIER speaks of 'having discovered the entry' relating
to *Twelfth Night*,‡ which he would not have said had his correspondent had a prior claim. It is pleasant always to bear in mind that
'*suum cuique* is our Roman justice,' but in this case the claims are so
shadowy that it is impossible now to substantiate them. The fact
remains, that COLLIER was the first to publish the existence of the
Diary with its decisive entry concerning *Twelfth Night*. It was
HUNTER, with brilliant skill and unwearied pains, who discovered the
name, and even the history, of the diarist, who was, it appears, 'no
'other than John Manningham, then studying in the Middle Tem-

---

* *New Illustrations*, etc. 1845, i, 369.
† *History of English Dramatic Poetry*, etc. 1831, i, 321.
‡ *Farther Particulars regarding Shakespeare*, etc. 1839, p. 10.

'ple, but in a few years to be removed from London to take pos-
'session of a house and lands at East Malling [in Kent], which were
'given him by a collateral relative ; . . . we do not find his name in
'any other way connected with either the lighter or graver liter-
'ature of the country but through this single manuscript, so that it is
'probable for the remainder of his life he lived the life of a country
'gentleman, cultivating acres of his own, and in due time was gathered
'to his fathers, leaving his inheritance to his children.' *   The *Diary*
has been reprinted by *The Camden Society*, and is now accessible to
all.   It extends from Christmas, 1601, to the fourteenth of April,
1603 ; and is not a continuous journal, but has many intervals, and is
interspersed with facts and fancies, concise reports of Law cases and
voluminous reports of sermons, scandals of the court and gossip of
the buttery bar, whatever, in short, the writer desired to remember,
and some things which he would, we may charitably suppose, vehe-
mently desire to forget.   In his company we may draw nearer, I
believe, than in any historian's, to Queen Elizabeth's death-bed.   He
was in the palace at Richmond the night she died, and learned the
particulars of her state from his friend, Dr Parry, who was with her to
the last.

The entry, however, which fixes a date before which *Twelfth Night*
must have been composed is as follows :— †

'FEBR. 1601.

'Feb. 2.   At our feast wee had a play called "Twelue Night, or What
'"you Will," much like the Commedy of Errores, or Menechmi in
'Plautus, but most like and neere to that in Italian called *Inganni*.
'A good practise in it to make the Steward beleeve his Lady wid-
'dowe was in love with him, by counterfeyting a letter as from his
'Lady in generall termes, telling him what shee liked best in him,
'and prescribing his gesture in smiling, his apparaile, etc., and
'then when he came to practise making him beleeue they tooke
'him to be mad.'

All uncorroborated internal evidence may now flutter away into
space.   How much earlier than January, 1601, *Twelfth Night* was
composed is still undetermined.   The benchers of the Middle Temple
certainly would not select an untried play for their Candlemas festivity.
MERES in his *Wits Commonwealth*, published in 1598, does not mention
Twelfth Night.   This barrier checks those who believe that MERES mentions all of SHAKESPEARE'S plays which had been publicly acted at the

---

* *New Illustrations*, etc. i, 375.   † *Camden Society Reprint*, p. 18.

time he wrote.   But really two years is a field quite spacious enough
wherein critics may frolic in conjecture.   Unhappily, into these very
years they have to squeeze: *Henry the Fifth*, *Much Ado about Nothing*,
As You Like It, and, possibly, *The Merry Wives of Windsor;* but
their embarrassment is of their own seeking.   We who have free souls,
and, as far as the plays themselves are concerned, care as little for the
hour when SHAKESPEARE wrote them as for the quality of his ink, can
smile benignantly.

   Mr FLEAY, whose prodigious work in the dramatic and SHAKE-
SPEARIAN fields entitles him always to a respectful hearing, asserts that
the present play was written at two separate times, and that the earlier
portion was composed in 1593.   The proof of this he finds in what he
asserts to be the fact, that the plot and the under-plot are not so inex-
tricably interwoven that they cannot be disentangled and separately
presented.*   The characters which he considers as belonging to the
early play are the Duke, Sebastian, Antonio, Viola, Olivia, Curio, Valentine, and the Captain.   He specifies the scenes and 'parts' of scenes
in which they enter, and adds that these ' can be so cut out as to make
'a play of itself, entirely independent of the other characters, which is
'an infallible sign of priority of composition.'   On turning to the play,
we find that the 'parts' of scenes, to be thus ' cut out,' are the identical
places where SHAKESPEARE interlaces the two plots ; and with such skill
are they interwoven that a separation could not but be felt as a grievous
mutilation.   Assuredly, in order to carry on the play, other characters
must be introduced to take the place of those eliminated.   A lady
of exalted rank, like Olivia, cannot enter without an attendant.   If
Mr FLEAY discharge poor Maria, he must engage another attendant to
take her situation ; and I greatly fear he will find it somewhat difficult to secure at any 'Intelligence Office' a 'chamber maid,' as Sir
Toby calls her, quite as attractive or quick-witted.   Again, it is
surely a dramatist's duty to impart dignity to his characters of high
rank, by suggesting the grandeur of their establishment and the
number of their retinue.   To this end, are not a sedate Steward,
with his silver chain, and a Fool of choice wit, legitimate attendants of the Countess Olivia?   A palace, darkened by the unalterable
gloom of her who rules it, would prove a background too sombre for
the picture of a joyous comedy ; on the score of dramatic necessity,
therefore, in Olivia's unprotected state, the presence of a man of near
kinship is needed in the household ; and if Uncle Toby raises the
night owl with a catch that will draw three souls out of one weaver,

* See *Appendix*, pp. 324, 325.

between his exuberant merriment and Olivia's lugubrious seclusion a fair average may be struck. And as for Feste,—he is the solvent for all the mirth and pathos of the whole play; next to Viola and Malvolio, he is *the* character of the comedy.

After all, there is cheer for us. The unwelcome gap which separates us from Mr FLEAY is lessening. We can detect signs of his relenting. He wavers in the number of the years of separation. In 1876 he concludes that the 'Viola story' was written in 1594.* In the next year, 1877, he believes that it was written in 1595; † and in 1886, he thinks that the date is 1593.‡ In this vacillation, surely there is justification for the hope that eventually the years dividing the two stories, the plot and the under-plot, will disappear altogether, and that to his eyes, as to ours, *Twelfth Night* will stand revealed a perfectly constructed dramatic unity.

To me, personally, an investigation of the sources whence SHAKE-SPEARE drew the plots of his plays is a subject of inquiry far more interesting than seeking after the date when he wrote them. Into the latter quest, there must, of necessity, enter much that can be never known. Dates belong to history and to biography; I cannot perceive what possible charm they can impart to the play, *Twelfth Night*. Does it add one doit to its value or one ray to its brilliance to know that the Koh-i-noor was presented to Queen Victoria in June, 1850?

In the *Appendix* will be found at length, adequately full, all the sources which have been surmised to be those whence the chief plot of the present play has been derived. All it behooves me here to give is a brief summary.

Down to the discovery of Manningham's *Diary*, there had been suggested but four of these sources. The earliest suggestion is by GERARD LANGBAINE, who found in the resemblance of Sebastian to his twin sister, and in the mistakes arising therefrom, a loan from the *Amphitruo*, or the *Menœchmi* of Plautus.§

Next follows our countrywoman, Mrs CHARLOTTE LENNOX, whose sad old age of penury softens all asperity of judgement on her earlier writings; while granting that SHAKESPEARE might have taken a hint from Plautus, Mrs LENNOX decided‖ that he 'had a much more ample 'supply for the Fable of this Comedy' in a Novel of Bandello; she

---

* *Shakespeare Manual*, p. 231.
† *Introduction to Shakespeared Study*, p. 25.
‡ *Life and Work of Shakespeare*, p. 220.
§ *Account of the English Dramatic Poets*, 1691, p. 446.
‖ *Shakspear Illustrated*, 1753, i, 242.

hints, rather timidly, that possibly SHAKESPEARE could not read Italian, yet does not relinquish the belief that it is the Italian novelist to whom the English poet is indebted for his plot. And assuredly decided parallelisms may be traced between the novel and the play. In Bandello's story Nicuola and Paolo Nanni were twins, identical in features; when about fifteen years old they were separated by the fortune of war, and their father took Nicuola to his estate near Ancona. In the town where they resided there was a youth of great wealth, named Lattanzio Puccini, between whom and Nicuola a vehement love sprung up. Before this love had ripened into a betrothal, Nicuola's father was obliged to go to Rome on business, and confided his daughter to the care of a cousin, Sister Camilla, the abbess of a convent. Lattanzio, ignorant of Nicuola's change of abode, was at first in a despair so profound that he did not answer Nicuola's letters; but he soon transferred his affection to a beautiful damsel named Catella. It now appears that he was wont to go to this very convent to have his shirts made, and one day, when he was there, the disconsolate Nicuola, who had become convinced of his faithlessness, listened at the keyhole (though this is more elegantly expressed in the Italian as 'a place where, with-'out being seen of Lattanzio, she saw him and heard what he said') and learned that he had just lost by fever an efficient page. At once, Nicuola went to an old nurse of hers, and, donning the clothes of a son of the old woman, proceeded to Lattanzio's house, and was there engaged as a page, under the name of Romolo. Lattanzio had her bravely clothed all in white, and was so greatly pleased with her that he confided to her his absorbing love for Catella, and sent her with most loving messages to his mistress. Though with a breaking heart, Romolo loyally and faithfully fulfilled her duty. But Catella, at the first sight of the page, became violently enamoured of him, even to the extent of kissing him. Romolo was surprised and very naturally embarrassed. (Bandello, with the warmth of an Italian imagination, and heedless of optics, says that Romolo 'turned a thousand colours.') At last, Catella said to him: 'I know not what thou hast done to me; 'methinks thou must have bewitched me!' (Compare Olivia's words to Cesario: 'After the last enchantment thou didst here.') Catella asseverates that she never will, nor can, love Lattanzio; and when Romolo endeavours to console her master for this discouraging rebuff, Lattanzio tells her that all damsels are not equally cruel; for, not many months before, one of the fairest of maidens had been in love with him, but he had given her up when she left the city and had not answered her letters. Hereupon, Romolo reproaches him. 'Who 'knoweth,' she asks, 'but this fair damsel yet loveth you and liveth in

'sore affliction for your sake? More by token that I have many a time
'heard say that girls, in their first loves, love far more tenderly and
'with much greater fervour than do men.' (Compare what Cesario
says to the Duke: 'We men may say more, sweare more, but indeed
'Our shewes are more than will: for still we prove Much in our vowes,
'but little in our loue.') Nevertheless, Lattanzio wishes Romolo to go
again to Catella, but on the way thither Romolo catches sight of her
father, who is just arriving from Rome, and she flies to seek counsel
of her old nurse, who persuades her to resume her maiden's clothes,
and stay within doors till a good excuse can be given to her father for
her absence. Lattanzio, fretting over the failure of his page to return,
sets out to seek him, and is guided to the house of the old nurse, to
whom he unburdens his heart; she responds by scolding his obstinacy
in pursuing an obdurate mistress, while Nicuola is all the time constant
to him. Lattanzio protests that, if that be the case, he will cast off
Catella and be the most blest of mortals in the renewal of his first and
truest love. Nicuola hereupon appears and they betroth themselves in
the presence of the nurse. Only a few hours before this happy event,
Paolo, the twin brother, had reached his native town, habited, for a
vow he had taken, all in white, and had been mistaken for Romolo by
Catella's maid and summoned to Catella's presence. When the lovely
damsel greeted him as Romolo, Paolo saw that there was some mistake,
but was too much struck with Catella's beauty to remonstrate. He
yields, and plights to her his troth; when he again appears on the
street, he is recognized by his father; and the story ends with marriages
all round.

Unquestionably, there are here the outlines of a story closely resembling the plot of *Twelfth Night*:—there are twins; similarity of costume; an enamoured girl disguised as a page; sent as a messenger to
an obdurate beauty; who falls at once in love with the messenger; a
brother, mistaken for his disguised sister; invited to the house of an
unknown lady; and there immediately betrothed. The untying of the
knot is entirely different. I have purposely omitted an under-plot which
represents Catella's old father as in love with Nicuola. This merely
widens the gap between SHAKESPEARE and Bandello. But in the main
plot, there is a parallelism which cannot be ignored; in default of a
better source, we must adopt the Italian novel.

To avoid the shuddering acknowledgement that SHAKESPEARE was
cultured enough to be familiar with the fashionable language of his
day, many editors, following the lead of CAPELL, suggest that the plot
of *Twelfth Night* was derived from BELLE-FOREST, whose French translation of Bandello's novel was supposed to be more within SHAKE-

SPEARE'S limited capacity. It is doubtful, I think, that that those who thus adopt CAPELL'S suggestion have ever compared Belle-Forest's translation with Bandello, or even read it. The polished Frenchman evidently prided himself on his talent for writing beautiful poetry and languishing love-letters. (We find this same display in his version of *Much Ado about Nothing.*) Accordingly, in the French version, no sooner have Nicole and Lactance fallen in love, than the lover writes to his mistress an ardent letter, signed 'Vostre esclaue, L. Puccini.' To which the girl replies under the signature 'Vostre bonne amie, 'Nicole de Nanni.' When Nicole is deserted by her lover, her poor heart finds relief in verse, beginning: *S'il y a au monde peine Qui le cœur des hommes geine, S'il y a quelque douleur Qui suyue nostre naissance Pour luy donner cognoissance De sa misere et malheur,* and so on, for more than four pages.

Whatever may have been the original of *Twelfth Night,* I am sure it was not Belle-Forest's version of Bandello. And I am more sure that it was not a story of BARNABE RICHE, called *Apolonius and Silla,* printed in 1581, which COLLIER was the earliest to announce as the 'indisputable source of *Twelfth Night.*' * In this opinion of COLLIER, there has been, however, a general acquiescence. Possibly, the fact that Riche's story is in English, and of SHAKESPEARE'S own day, may have in some degree affected this acquiescence. I venture to dissent; not on the score that there are no incidents common to both story and comedy, because there are such, but I cannot believe that SHAKESPEARE was ever in the smallest degree influenced by Riche's coarse, repulsive novel. I doubt that SHAKESPEARE ever read it,—at least, I hope he never did; his hours were more precious to us all than those of any poet who ever lived; it would be grievous to think that he wasted even half a one over *Apolonius and Silla;* but we, whose time is of no value to anybody, can pause over Riche's story long enough to note some of the discrepancies between it and *Twelfth Night:*—Silla (Viola) and Silvio (Sebastian) are brother and sister, but not twins, although, however, Riche takes care to emphasize their great resemblance in feature to each other. Silla meets Apolonius (Orsino) as a guest under her father's roof, and makes violent love to him, which he rejects, and departs. At this point in Riche's story we find an observation, from which we may draw a fair inference that he had at least read Belle-Forest. Be it remembered that in the French novel, after Lactance's desertion, Nicole indulges in versified grief throughout four pages and more.

---

* *Poetical Decameron,* 1820, ii. 161.

At this same point Riche says: 'I will here for brevities sake, omit 'to make repetition of the long and dolourous discourse recorded by 'Silla for this sodaine departure of her Apolonius.' It is only in Belle-Forest that a 'dolourous discourse' is found. Silla determines to pursue Duke Apolonius; accordingly, accompanied by a servant, she sets sail for Constantinople; the captain of the ship is of a base nature, and Silla escapes dishonour by shipwreck, and is saved from the wreck by clinging to a chest, wherein, when she opens it on land, she finds money and male garments; she pockets the one and dons the other. (All clothes fitted everybody point device, in those happy days!) Thus arrayed, Silla, who adopts the name of her brother Silvio, reaches the palace of Duke Apolonius in Constantinople, enters his service as page, and is entrusted by him with love-messages and love-tokens to Dame Julina, a very rich widow. After many interviews, Julina falls in love with the page. At this point Silvio, the brother, reaches Constantinople, and is met in the street by Julina, who mistakes him for Silvio, the page; she invites him to her house, and, after an interview with her, the youth leaves the city the next morning. This interview wrecks the reputation of Julina, and eventually forces Silla in self-defence to throw off her disguise. The Duke recognises her, marries her, and the fame of the wedding festivities attracts the wandering Silvio, who revisits Constantinople and marries Julina.

The attentive reader can hardly fail to note how few in number are the points where the story and the play coincide:—a shipwreck; a disguised, enamoured page who carries love-messages to his master's mistress, and with whom the latter falls in love; and a brother who is mistaken for his disguised sister. Let nothing induce us to contaminate the spotless Viola and the haughty Olivia by the remotest hint of a kinship with the weak Silla and the brazen Julina.

To the record in Manningham's *Diary* of a performance of *Twelfth Night*, we are indebted in more respects than one. In the search for SHAKESPEARE'S plots, there had long been a recourse to Italian novels, but until Manningham had said that the present comedy was 'most 'like and neere' to the *Inganni* (or *The Deceits*), no one had ever turned to the Italian drama. HUNTER was the earliest to follow the clue, and we are now the heirs to his intelligent and indefatigable labours. Had HUNTER rested content in a comparison of the *Inganni* with *Twelfth Night*, Manningham's assertion would have led to little or no result. The Italian play was written by Nicolo Secchi, or Secco, and acted, so says the title-page, at Milan, in 1547. In it, we have a brother and sister, twins, separated from their father by corsairs; the girl, Ginevra, is dressed like a boy, and is called Ruberto; at the opening of the play, both are known to each other and are living in Naples, in the same street, the boy, Fortunato, as a servant to a light o' love, named Dorotea; and Ruberto (Viola) as a servant to a master who has a son, Gostanzo (Orsino), and a daughter, Portia (Olivia). Ruberto is in love with Gostanzo, who in turn is in love with Dorotea; Portia is in love with Ruberto, whom, of course, she believes to be a man. Gostanzo sends Ruberto to Dorotea with love-messages, but Dorotea does not fall in love with the messenger. Herein lies the essential, the fatal difference between the *Inganni* and *Twelfth Night*. Ruberto finally weans Gostanzo from his love for the purely mercenary Dorotea, and, when she has doffed her disguise, wins it to herself. The old father turns up at the right moment, a rich man with sixty thousand scudi, and Ruberto (Ginevra) is married to Gostanzo, and Fortunato to Portia.*

COLLIER gives a scene which, as he says, ' distantly, and only dis-' tantly, reminds us of SHAKESPEARE'; and HUNTER thinks that SHAKE-SPEARE may have read the play. It is impossible to contradict either of these opinions, but I should never have thought of expressing them.

There is another play, also called *Gl' Inganni*, written by Curtio Gonzaga, printed at Venice, 1592.† This I have not seen, but HUN-TER leads us to suppose that it varies but very slightly from that by Secchi; the only difference which he notes is, that the girl in disguise assumes the name *Cesare*, which suggests 'Cesario' in *Twelfth Night*.

Thus far our gratitude to Manningham, as far as his reference to the Italian drama is concerned, is small. It has really led us nowhither. No serious claim can be set up for *Gl' Inganni* as the source of *Twelfth Night*. But HUNTER was not discouraged; a further search discovered another and an earlier play, called *Gl' Ingannati*, composed and acted in Siena, in 1531, by a Society, or Academy, named *Gl' Intronati*, that is, *The Thunderstruck*, one of those innumerable societies which appear to have been, at that period, the rage in Italy,—a catalogue of the names of more than five hundred has been preserved; some of the titles are quite as fantastic as *The Thunderstruck*, and, presuma-bly, far more descriptive; for instance, there were *Gl' Insipidi*, whereof, I fancy, the roll of members was long.

A reason why this comedy of the *Ingannati* had escaped notice is the misleading title of the little volume wherein it is to be found. Its title runs *Il Sacrificio, Comedia de gl' Intronati;* and the *sacrifice* con-sists of a series of sonnets and madrigals, sung or chanted by each ' Thunderstruck ' as he casts into a sacred flame on an altar some love-

---

* See *Appendix*, p. 339. † HUNTER, *New Illustrations*, etc. i, 391.

token of a mistress who had proved unkind, such as a ring, a glove, a white flower, a copy of verses (why have we not, alas! a modern *sacrificio?*), a handkerchief bathed in tears; and 'Messer Agnol Maleuolti' (whose name, HUNTER thinks, SHAKESPEARE converted into 'Malvolio,' but I much doubt,) deposits 'a sculptured Cupid, the gift of his Fair.' When this depressing rite was over, the comedy of *Gl' Ingannati* began. Here, at last, though HUNTER does not note it, we have, beyond question, in this comedy, the original of—Bandello. *Il Sacrificio* was performed, as it says in the bastard-title, in Carnival week in Siena in 1531; it was reprinted in 1537, again in 1538, and again in 1550, so that there were at least four editions of it in circulation before Bandello's novel was printed in 1554. Apart from mere priority of date, the play itself reveals Bandello's indebtedness to it. In the *Ingannati*, the time of the story is laid in 1527, it is so also in Bandello; the catastrophe which overwhelms the father is the sacking of Rome,—so also is it in Bandello; the father has a friend, an old man named Gherardo, thus it is also in Bandello; the brother and sister dress in white, and the father has a cousin, a nun, named Camilla,—all this is in Bandello, including the name, Camilla. For the pretty name, however, of the heroine, Lelia, he substituted Nicuola. The plot of *Ingannati* may be given in a few lines; it will be readily seen that it is the same as Bandello's novel. Fabrizio and Lelia are the children of an old man who was ruined in the sack of Rome in May, 1527. Fabrizio's fate is unknown to the father, but Lelia is taken by him to Modena, where lives Flaminio, who had in old Roman days exchanged love-vows with Lelia, but had now forgotten her and is in love with Isabella, the daughter of an old man named Gerardo. Lelia is placed in charge of her aunt, Camilla, a nun in a convent, where she obtains a disguise and serves as a page to the fickle Flaminio, who sends by her his passionate love-messages to Isabella. Isabella rejects Flaminio, but falls in love with the page. Fabrizio appears unexpectedly, and is mistaken by Isabella for the page. In the end recognitions are made all round, and Fabrizio weds Isabella, and Flaminio Lelia. It is said in the Prologue (p. 15, *verso*) that 'the story is new, never before 'either seen or read, nor drawn from any other source save from their 'industrious pates [*i. e.*, of the Intronati], just as you draw your lots 'on Twelfth Night.' HUNTER opines that 'in perusing this Prologue 'the eye of SHAKESPEARE would fall upon' this passage, and that he thence derived the title of the present comedy. This is not impossible; but I believe that SHAKESPEARE had no need to go to the Italian original.*

---

* A translation of *Gl' Ingannati* will be found in the *Appendix*, p. 341.

The *Ingannati* was evidently an extremely popular play; there were nine, probably ten or even more, editions of it before 1600. But it is a far cry from Siena to London, and a cry, moreover, in Italian. We must remember, however, that there was an Italian troupe of players, under the management of one Drousiano, in London in 1577–78, who acted before the Queen at Windsor. Although this date is somewhat too early to suggest any personal knowledge of them on the part of SHAKESPEARE, yet it shows a connection between the two national theatres which is not without significance. Assuredly, these Italians would not act unpopular plays. (I prefer to assert what they undeniably would *not* do, rather than to say what, 'probably,' they would do. If the use of the adverb 'probably,' in connection with all statements regarding SHAKESPEARE, were legally forbidden on pain of death without the benefit of clergy, I think the world would be the happier, certainly the wiser.) *Possibly* thanks to these Italian comedians, this popular play, the *Ingannati*, was brought into England. And on English soil we find it, within three years of the public performance of *Twelfth Night* which John Manningham saw, and recorded in his *Diary;* and even closer yet to SHAKESPEARE, if we suppose that *Twelfth Night* was already a popular play when it was acted at the Readers' Feast in the Middle Temple Hall.

In that invaluable storehouse of SHAKESPEARIAN investigations, the *Year-Books* of *The German Shakespeare Society* (has there been a monument erected to SHAKESPEARE more august or enduring than its thirty-six volumes?), there is a recent noteworthy contribution by GEORGE B. CHURCHILL (a fellow-countryman of ours) and WOLFGANG KELLER, giving an account of twenty-eight Latin MS Dramas, performed at English universities in the time of Queen Elizabeth.* Among these MSS is one preserved in Lambeth Palace, called *Laelia*, which was acted in Queen's College, Cambridge, in 1590, and again in 1598. Under this title, *Laelia*, the name of the heroine, we recognise a translation of the *Ingannati*,—faithful in retaining the names of the *Dramatis Personæ*, faithful in every main feature, to the original comedy. That it was in Latin is but of trifling moment. Ben Jonson acknowledged that SHAKESPEARE knew some Latin, albeit he pronounced the extent to be 'small.' Were it many times smaller, it would still have been large enough to read and easily comprehend *Laelia*.

Happy among SHAKESPEARE'S plays is *Twelfth Night!* A source of its main plot is thus traced to England, and close to SHAKESPEARE'S door, immediately before an assured date of its composition.

---

* Vol. xxxiv, 1898, pp. 286, 291. See *Appendix*, p. 359.

Next to the interest which is awakened by observing the alchemy wherewith SHAKESPEARE converts dross into gold, when dealing with the sources of his plots, is, I think, a study of his consummate skill in unfolding before us the *Duration of the Action*. His most remarkable achievement in this regard is to be found in *Othello*, where the whole action, with all its gradual growth of jealousy and developement of character, is comprised within thirty-six hours. Next in wonder is *The Merchant of Venice*, where a three-months' bond expires by limitation in three days. Possibly, the present play stands next in rank. While listening to a performance of *Twelfth Night*, do we not know that we are watching the love of Viola for Orsino grow stronger day by day? Have we not noted the continued firmness with which she represses Olivia's passion for her? Do we not carouse for many an evening with Sir Toby, and is not Malvolio for ever obtruding his aversion to all mirth? Does not Sir Andrew postpone his departure week after week? There has been no haste; time has advanced steadily, ripening all events. Malvolio, poor gentleman! languishes so long in ' hideous ' darkness' that Feste is scolded for having talked to him. The song that Feste sings one evening he must repeat to the Duke the next day. The Duke broods over his disprized love when canopied with bowers through summer afternoons, and in his confiding talks with Viola, she tells him ' a thousand times she never could love woman as she loves ' him.' Under this gramarye of SHAKESPEARE we sit, and accept the truth when Orsino says that for three months Viola had tended upon him. But if we shake off the spell, and, with the book before us, note the sequence of events, and mark off the morning and the evening of the first day and of the next, we find that the time involved in the scenes which have passed before our eyes is exactly three days! Such helpless victims are we of SHAKESPEARE's art, that in the last Act we accept, without a shade of mistrust, as perfectly natural, that within two hours (we have the Priest's watch for a witness) Sir Toby has had a second desperate fight with Sebastian, is become extremely drunk, and has yet found time withal to woo, win, and marry Maria.

It is too late a day to say that this treatment of the *Duration of the Action* is mere accident, or that SHAKESPEARE referred haphazard to the flight of time. The effect is so unquestionable, and so necessary withal to dramatic art, that a sufficing cause must have been intentional. And when we find ÆSCHYLUS employing the same art, should not imputations of accident be silenced?

H. H. F.

July, 1901.

TWELFE NIGHT,

OR WHAT YOU WILL

Dramatis Perfonæ.

Orsino, *Duke of* Illyria.   2

Sebastian, *a young Gentleman, Brother to* Viola.

Antonio, *a Sea-Captain, Friend to* Sebastian.

Valentine, ⎫
         ⎬ *Gentlemen attending on the Duke.*   5
Curio,   ⎭

Sir Toby Belch, *Uncle to* Olivia.

Sir Andrew Ague-cheek, *a foolish Knight, pretend-*
    -ing to Olivia.   9

Dramatis Personæ] This list is not in the Folio, but is first given by ROWE, with, as DR JOHNSON says, 'all the cant of the modern stage.'

2. Orsino] SARRAZIN (*Jahrb.* xxxii, 168): In the winter of 1600–1 a certain Duke Orsino attracted the attention of London. Virginio Orsino, Duke of Bracciano, 'the most brilliant nobleman of his day,' was at that time ambassador to the English court, and was entertained by Queen Elizabeth and her nobility with elaborate festivities, among others on Twelfth Night. Possibly, this suggested to Shakespeare the present name. [The date of Duke Orsino's presence at the English court is somewhat too late for the composition of *Twelfth Night*, if it were already a popular play when Manningham saw it in February, 1601–2.—ED.]

7, 8. Sir] It is not easy to comprehend the 'anfractuosities' of the German mind when it deals with the names of Shakespeare's *dramatis personæ*. German translators, from the highest to the lowest, assume the permission, wherever a name seems to be a clew to the character, to change Shakespeare's nomenclature, and herein they are probably right; but unfortunately they do not always restrict themselves to this limit. Thus here, the knighthood of Sir Toby and Sir Andrew is not without its meaning; the contrast between the dignity of the title and the inferiority of the man is sharp enough to create a sense of mild amusement, and it also elevates the bearer somewhat in the social plane. Both of these effects are lost when these characters are presented, as they always are, to a German audience as *Junker*. Nor is the effect restored when, instead of the familiar nickname, 'Toby,' we have the sonorous, somewhat Puritanic *Tobias*, given in full. Whatever humour there is in *Junker* is silenced in *Tobias*. But what is to be said of SCHLEGEL's change of 'Sir Andrew' into *Junker Christoph*, a change which is still retained by DR SCHMIDT in his revision, for *The German Shakespeare Society*, of Schlegel's translation? Is it one of the anfractuosities that to German ears *Christoph* is funnier than 'Andrew' or *Andreas* as other translators have it? That 'Belch' should be translated *Rülp*, and 'Ague-cheek' *Bleichwangen* is harmless enough, probably right; as President Lincoln was wont to say: 'for those who like this kind of thing, this is just the kind of thing those people would like.' I doubt, however, that any such palliation will cover the translation of an historic name like Hotspur into *Heisssporn;* or

A *Sea-Captain, Friend to* Viola   10
Fabian, *Servant to* Olivia.
Malvolio, *a fantastical Steward to* Olivia.   12

---

even 'Juliet' into *Julia*, which is, I think, universal in Germany. The indignant
derision would be *kolossal* which Germans would heap on an English translator who
should convert 'Gretchen' into *Peggy*.—ED.

7. **Uncle**] Inasmuch as Sir Toby in the very first words that he utters styles
Olivia his 'niece,' ROWE and others call him her 'uncle' here and throughout;
possibly, overlooking the fact that Maria, in her reply to Sir Toby, says 'your
cousin, my lady.' Olivia herself never speaks of Sir Toby as her uncle, but
addresses him as 'cousin,' and, in IV, i, in her vehement anger at his attack on
Sebastian, she calls him, not only plain 'Toby,' but 'Rudesby,' 'ungracious wretch,'
and 'ruffian,'—terms barely consonant with the respect due from a niece to her
uncle. Readers of Shakespeare will recall many instances of the vagueness with
which the word 'cousin' is used to denote degrees of relationship, and if their
memory halt, Schmidt's *Lexicon* will abundantly jog it. Possibly, Sir Toby was
Olivia's nearest male relative, and so near of an age, that it is only by assuming the
closer and more august relationship of uncle that he can magnify in the eyes of Sir
Andrew and Fabian (who alone accept his claim) the influence which he would fain
have them believe he possessed over his wealthy relative.—ED.

11. **Fabian**] HUNTER (i, 396): The name of Fabian was probably suggested
by the name of Fabia, which Lelia in [*Gl' Ingannati*] assumed in her disguise.
[Hunter believed that the present play was founded on *Gl' Ingannati;* nay, he
could almost persuade himself that Shakespeare had used the identical copy which
he had then before him. To him, therefore, this suggestion was 'probable,' but to
me, who cannot thus circumscribe Shakespeare's resources, the suggestion is unlikely.
Moreover, *Fabia* is not the name which Lelia assumes, but *Fabio;* this, however, is
hardly material.—ED.]

12. **Malvolio**] FARMER : This name seems to have been formed by an accidental
transposition in the word *Malivolo.*—HUNTER (i, 396) : Malvolio is a happy adaptation from Malevolti, a character in the *Il Sacrificio*. [*Il Sacrificio*, be it observed,
is a so-called 'Comedia,' which precedes *Gl' Ingannati*, the comedy whereon Shakespeare, as Hunter believes, founded the present play. (See *Preface*, or *Appendix :
The Source of the Plot*.) Hunter's remark in regard to Malvolio's name conveys
the impression that *Il Sacrificio* is a comedy in the ordinary acceptation of the word,
which it certainly is not. It appears that in 1531 there existed in Siena a society who
called themselves *Gl' Intronati*, or *The Thunderstruck*, and that during the festivities of the Carnival in that year they performed this 'Comedia' of *Il Sacrificio*,
wherein the members of the Society, under the leadership of the 'sodo dignissimo
Archintronato,' sacrificed to the flames the mementoes of their love, singing madrigals
the while to the accompaniment of a lyre. The offerings are eminently sentimental,
such as 'a handkerchief bathed with tears,' 'a lock of hair,' 'a silver love-knot,'
'a glove of his Donna,' etc. Nowhere do the performers appear under their own
names, but as 'The Sad One,' 'The Stunned One,' 'The Fantastical One,' etc.
The solitary exception is the instance mentioned by Hunter, where the madrigal is
entitled : *Messer Agnol Maleuolti un Cupido scolpito, dono della sua donna ;* and in
the madrigal itself Messer Malevolti reproaches the little sculptured god with the
loss of those joys which he had foretold him, and recalls the fair promises given by

Clown, Servant to Olivia.   13

Olivia, *a Lady of great Beauty and Fortune,*
       belov'd by the Duke.   15
Viola, *in love with the Duke.*
Maria, *Confident to* Olivia.

Priest, Sailors, Officers, and other Attendants.   18

13. Clown,] Feste, a clown. Cam.   17. Confident...] Olivia's *Woman*
14. a...Fortune,] a rich Countess.   Rowe ii.   Olivia's Waiting-woman
Steev.   Wh. i.
   16. in...Duke.] sister to Sebastian.   18. Officers,] two Officers of Justice.
Cap.   Cap.

---

his mistress when she made him this present; and how bitterly those promises had failed. Wherefore, Cupid is no longer worthy to be called a god; but shall expiate in the fire the numberless wounds he has caused, and shall prove in his own image how sweet is the flame. The likelihood is extremely small, I think, that Shakespeare, even granting that he had ever read *Il Sacrificio*, took the trouble to coin 'Malvolio' out of *Malevolti*, when he had before him, on Hunter's own supposition, the long list of Dramatis Personæ of *Gl' Ingannati*. There is nothing whatsoever in Malevolti's madrigal which corresponds to the character which Shakespeare gives to Malvolio.—ED.]

13. **Clown**] As we learn from II, iv, 13, this Clown's name is Feste (a disyllable). WALKER (*Crit.* i, 2), on the analogy of *Anselme* for *Anselmo*, thinks that, perhaps, this name should be *Festo*. The COWDEN-CLARKES remark that it is a name, aptly invented by Shakespeare, 'from the Italian *festeggiante* which Florio explains: "Feasting, merrie, banqueting, pleasant, of good entertainment."'

14. **Olivia**] C. ELLIOT BROWNE (*Athenæum*, 20 June, 1874): Shakespeare was, probably, indebted for the names of the heroines of *Twelfth Night* to the first part of Emanuel Forde's *Parismus, the Renowned Prince of Bohemia*, London, 1598, for neither Olivia nor Viola occurs in the *Ingannati*. In the romance, Olivia is Queen of Thessaly, and Violetta the name of a lady, who, unknown to her lover, disguises herself as a page to follow him, and she, also like Viola, is shipwrecked. If this conjecture is founded on fact, the negative evidence that *Twelfth Night* was written after 1598, afforded by its omission in Meres's list, is confirmed. [I have no sympathy with an estimate of Shakespeare's originality which would send him a-field or to any one particular authority for the names of his heroines. If, in the sources of his plots, the names were euphonious, he retained them; if they were not, he changed them. Euphony guided his choice, wheresoever the names were found. To say that he took 'Olivia' from Forde's *Parismus* would be paralleled by saying that Tennyson took from the present play the name of his heroine in *The Talking Oak*.—ED.]

16. **Viola**] STEEVENS: Viola is the name of a lady in the fifth book of Gower *de Confessione Amantis*.—GENÉE (*Klass. Frauenbilder*, 79): The name Viola is given to her because of her exquisite grace, and because of her concealment, under

SCENE *a City on the Coast of* Illyria.   19

19. a ... Illyria.] a City of Illyria,   coast near it. Cap.
Residence of the Duke ; and the Sea-

---

cover whereof she could cherish, like a secret treasure, the longings of her loving
heart.

19. **Scene**] W. WINTER (*Shadows of the Stage*, iii, 28) : It is even more difficult
to assign a place and a period for *Twelfth Night* than it is to localise *As You Like It*.
Illyria,—now Dalmatia, Croatia, and Bosnia,—was a Roman province, a hundred
and sixty-seven years before Christ. In Shakespeare's time, Dalmatia was under the
rule of the Venetian republic. The custom has long prevailed of treating the piece
as a romantic and poetic picture of Venetian manners in the seventeenth century.
Some stage managers have used Greek dresses. For the purposes of the stage, there
must be a 'local habitation.' For a reader, the scene of *Twelfth Night* is the elusive
and evanescent, but limitless and immortal, land of dreams.

Twelfe Night, Or what you will.

Actus Primus, Scæna Prima.

Enter Orſino Duke of Illyria, Curio, and other
Lords.

Duke.

 F Muſicke be the food of Loue, play on,　　　　4
Giue me exceſſe of it : that ſurfetting,
The appetite may ſicken, and ſo dye.
That ſtraine agen, it had a dying fall :　　　　7

Twelfe Night,] Twelfe-Night F₃.
Twelf-Night F₄.
　1. Primus,] Primus. Ff.
　　Scæna] Scena F₃F₄.
　　The Palace. Rowe et cet. (subs.)
　2. Enter...] Enter the Duke, Curio,
and Lords. Rowe.　Musick attending.
Cap.
4–10. As mnemonic, Warb.
4. on,] on ; Theob.
5. *ſurfetting*] *ſurfeiting* F₄.
7. *agen*] *again* Rowe.

1. **Twelfe Night**] FARMER : A very ingenious lady, with whom I have the
honour to be acquainted, Mrs Askew of Queen's-Square, has a fine copy of the
Second Folio, which formerly belonged to King Charles I. and was a present from
him to Sir Thomas Herbert.　Sir Thomas has altered five titles in the list of plays,
to Benedick [*sic*] and Beatrice,—Pyramus and Thisby,—Rosalinde,—Mr Paroles,—
and Malvolio.—STEEVENS : Dr Farmer might have observed that the alterations of
the titles are in his Majesty's own hand-writing, materially differing from Sir Thomas
Herbert's, of which the same volume affords more than one specimen.　The book is
now in my possession.　[HALLIWELL : It is now in the library of her present Majesty
at Windsor Castle.]　THEOBALD (*Nichols*, ii, 354) acknowledged to Warburton that
he could not decide whether or not this title 'arose from the time of year at which it
was performed.'　'There is no circumstance,' he goes on to say, 'that I can observe
in the Play to give occasion to this name ; nothing either to fix it down particularly
to *Twelfth Night*,—or to leave it so loose and general a description as *What You
Will.*'　Possibly the same uncertainty beset subsequent editors, or it may have been
indifference, or it may have been acquiescence in the plain meaning of the words
without seeking for any hidden meaning.　KNIGHT was the first to break silence.
He speaks of the '*neutral* title of *Twelfth Night*,' whereby, I suppose, he means
that the title indicates neither a purely poetic nor a purely comic work.　'This
neutral title,' he says (p. 185) '—conveying as it does a notion of genial mirth,—

[1. **Twelfe Night.**]

might warrant us in thinking that there was a preponderance of the comic spirit.
Charles I. appears to have thought so, when, in his copy of the Second Folio, he
altered the title with his own pen to that of *Malvolio*. But Malvolio is not the predominant idea of the comedy ; nor is he of that exclusive interest that the whole
action, even of the merely comic portions, should turn upon him. When Shakespeare means one character to be the centre of the dramatic idea, he for the most
part tells us so in his title :—*Hamlet, Othello, Lear, Macbeth, Timon.* Not one of
the comedies has such a personal title, for the evident reason that the effect in them
must mainly depend upon the harmony of all the parts, rather than upon the absorbing passion of the principal character. The *Twelfth Night* is especially of this
description. It presents us with the golden and silver sides of human life,—the
romantic and the humourous. But the two precious metals are moulded into one
statue.' HUNTER, who skillfully detected the author of an anonymous Diary
kept by a member of the Middle Temple (see *Preface*, or *Appendix, Date of the
Play*), believed that Shakespeare took his plot from an Italian comedy, *Gl' Ingannati.* 'A phrase occurring in a long prologue or preface prefixed to this play in the
Italian appears to me,' says Hunter (i, 396), 'to have suggested the title *Twelfth
Night*, which has no kind of propriety or congruity when looked at in connection
with the play ; and this must have been evident to Shakespeare himself, since he
adds to it *or What You Will*. It might be called *Twelfth Night* or by whatever
other name. In perusing this prologue or preface the eye of Shakespeare would
fall upon the following passage : " The story is new, never seen or read, and only
dipped for and taken out of their own industrious noddles as your prize-tickets are
dipped for and taken out on Twelfth Night [*la notte di Beffana*], by which it appears
to you that the Intronati might have answered you so much upon this part of the
declaration," etc.' This supposition of Hunter that Shakespeare was led to the
choice of his title by the revels of Epiphany (apparent in the Italian 'Beffana') is accepted by B. NICHOLSON (*N. & Qu.* VI, ix, 165) and 'reinforced by
the suggestion that this humourous play, being one in every way fitted for the
season and revels then held, was written for and first produced by Shakespeare at a
representation on that night, and that he thence so named it. It was a Twelfth
Night, or what you will for Twelfth Night, just as for Christmas our writers and
managers have for many years produced pantomimes. Jonson and other authorities
could be quoted for plays and masques on these Twelfth-Night festivities.' Nicholson then proceeds to quote an illustration in point from the less known *Diary of
Henry Machin* (*Cam. Soc.* p. 222). But this meaning does not suit ULRICI,
who, in the alternative title, verily sees 'fantasies, more than cool reason ever comprehends.' 'This *What You Will*,' says Ulrici (ii, 5), 'refers indeed to the relation
between the public and the play, but not, as has been supposed, in the sense quite
inadmissible, that the piece was to give and to represent whatever the spectators
wished. This is not the case ; the play rather creates what *it* wishes, and the better
it is the less can that which it gives be different from what it is. The title is rather
intended to signify that that which men all like to see represented is ever the same ;
namely, a chequered, a varied life, rich in incidents and crossed by misfortunes and
complications, one that excites interest and keeps up a state of suspense, but which,
nevertheless, does not exceed the bounds of ordinary human life, even though it
leads to a happy and harmonious ending through unusual, strange and winding paths.
We are, in reality, all as little fond of an existence which passes with nothing

[1. Twelfe Night.]

unusual, surprising, or exciting to the imagination, where everything happens according to well-considered aims and objects, as we are of the reverse, a life governed solely by chance, whim, and caprice. We would all prefer the greatest possible equality in the mixture of the usual and unusual, of accident and intention, of whim and reflection, imagination and reason. It is not merely the experiencing such a life, the very beholding it produces that gaiety, that inward contentment, at which we are all aiming. And thus Shakespeare could with justice,—especially of this one of his comedies,—maintain that it represented "What You (all) Will." ' Thus far Ulrici. Let the corrective be happily administered by a fellow-countryman. At the close of an article in the *Preussische Jahrbücher*, (July, 1887,) CONRAD says (p. 35) : 'Assuredly, when Shakespeare gave a title to the ripest fruit of his comic Muse, he had no intrusive, covert meaning ; he wished to say merely,—"Herein are to be found comicalities of all kinds, braggadocios, and chickenhearted simpletons, roistering and revelling, ill-conditioned hypocrisy and intolerance, false love and true love, disguises and delusions and mad pranks. What to call it, I know not. Call it 'a masquerade,' 'a Twelfth Night,' or 'Whatever you Like.'"' To any deeper meaning which posterity might find underlying this title, he gave never a thought. Here in this drama we have on one canvas a realistic picture of the life of the Renaissance, with its splendour and its joyousness, with its weaknesses and its follies, with its life of lofty developement of mind and spirit,—such as hardly a second picture in that time affords. In it we find every comic element united in an artistic harmony, whereof the strength and beauty stand unparalleled ; in it we find all things soever that are to be asked for in a comedy,—*absolutely What you will*.' MALONE (*Var*. '21, ii, 442) notes that 'the Comedy of *What You Will*, which was entered at Stationers' Hall, August 9, 1607, was certainly Marston's play.' HALLIWELL (p. 247) adds : 'In Tatham's *Ostella, or the Faction of Love and Beauty*, 1650, mention is made of a play called *The Whisperer, or What you Please*, which is an instance of a double title formed on that of *Twelfth Night*.'—RUGGLES (p. 15) : The title evidently has reference to the subject of the play, which is Man in his relations to Pleasure and Pastime. This title, though suggestive of license, involves morality. As the play gives us a phase of life in which excess seems to be the rule, and moderation the exception, Shakespeare, who is ever loyal to morality, notifies us by the title that it is merely a mirthful, comic entertainment, which looks at life as it is seen under its most genial aspect ; an ideal picture, from which all view of serious affairs is excluded. [It is almost superfluous to add that Conrad's view seems to be the true one.—ED.]

1. **Actus Primus**] For SPEDDING'S division of Acts, see I, iv, 46.

1. **Scæna Prima**] COLERIDGE (p. 209) : Of more importance [than the significancy of the title, and] so, more striking, is the judgement displayed by our truly dramatic poet, as well as poet of the drama, in the management of his first scenes. With the single exception of *Cymbeline*, they either place before us at one glance both the past and the future in some effect, which implies the continuance and full agency of its cause, as in the feuds and party-spirit of the servants of the two houses in the first scene of *Romeo and Juliet ;* or the degrading passion for shews and public spectacles, and the overwhelming attachment for the newest successful war-chief in the Roman people, already become a populace, contrasted with the jealousy of the nobles in *Julius Cæsar ;*—or they at once commence the action so as to excite a curiosity for the explanation in the following scenes, as in the storm of wind and

[1. Scæna Prima.]

waves, and the boatswain in *The Tempest*, instead of anticipating our curiosity, as in
most other first scenes, and in too many other first Acts ;—or they act, by contrast of
diction suited to the characters, at once to heighten the effect, and yet to give a
naturalness to the language and rhythm of the principal personages, either as that
of Prospero and Miranda, by the appropriate lowness of the style,—or as in *King
John*, by the equally appropriate stateliness of official harangues or narratives, so
that the after blank verse seems to belong to the rank and quality of the speakers,
and not to the poet ;—or they strike at once the key-note, and give the predominant
spirit of the play, as in *Twelfth Night* and in *Macbeth ;*—or finally, the first scene
comprises all these advantages at once, as in *Hamlet*.

4–6. **If Musicke . . . so dye**] WARBURTON : There is an impropriety of expression in the present reading of this fine passage. We do not say, *that the appetite
sickens and dies thro' a surfeit ;* but the subject of that appetite. I am persuaded,
a word is accidentally dropt ; and that we should read, and point, the passage thus :
' that, surfeiting The app'tite, Love may sicken, and so die.'—JOHNSON : It is true,
we do not talk of the *death of appetite*, because we do not ordinarily speak in the
figurative language of poetry ; but that *appetite sickens by a surfeit* is true, and therefore proper.—MRS GRIFFITH (p. 119) : The duke is made to wish his passion were
extinct ; which, I believe, the most unhappy lover never yet did. We wish to
remove every uneasy sensation it afflicts us with, by any means whatever ; sometimes even by death itself ; but never by the extinction of the affection.—W. A.
WRIGHT : Compare *Ant. & Cleop.* II, v, 1 : ' Give me some music ; music,
moody food Of us that trade in love.' [Wherever this passage has been paraphrased, the interpretation of Warburton and of Mrs Griffith has been followed,
namely, that ' the food of love ' is the food on which love feeds, and that 'appetite'
refers to *love ;* the conclusion follows that Orsino longs to be freed from his thraldom
to Olivia. I do not so understand the passage. It is not to be believed that Orsino
wishes his love for Olivia to die. His words and deeds throughout contradict it. He
by no means wishes music to diminish his love, a result, as Mrs Griffith justly says,
no lover ever prayed for, but to increase it to the very utmost. Not till music has
exhausted its power, must its services in the cause of love cease. This interpretation
is justified, I think, if we understand music to be, not that on which love feeds, but,
that which feeds love ; in this sense, Orsino says in effect : Give me excess of music,
let it feed love beyond measure, even to a surfeit of itself ; so that when it has done
all that it can, and love is full-fed, the appetite or desire for music sickens and ceases.
—ED.]

5. **surfetting**] It is hardly worth while to pay much attention to the spelling, in
the Folio, of ordinary words where there is no question of obscurity. It is not
Shakespeare's spelling, but a printer's, and one, who, to judge by his performance, is
not altogether worthy of our idolatry. We have ' surfetted to death ' in *Oth.* II, i, 56,
and ' the never surfeited sea ' in *Temp.* III, iii, 76 ; ' the surfeit of sweetest things '
in *Mid. N. D.* II, ii, 143, and ' surfet with too much ' in *Mer. of Ven.* I, ii, 6.
The plays were set up by various compositors, and each one followed his own
spelling.—ED.

7. **That straine agen**] This is addressed to the Musicians, as is also, ' Enough,
no more,' in line 10. In both instances there should be, I think, in a modern text, a
period after them, with a dash before and after, to indicate a change of address.—ED.

7. **a dying fall**] HOLT WHITE : Hence Pope in his *Ode on St. Cecilia's Day :*

O, it came ore my eare, like the ſweet ſound   8
That breathes vpon a banke of Violets ;
Stealing, and giuing Odour. *E*nough, no more,   10

8. *ſound*] Ff, Rowe ii, Knt, Hal. Sta. Wh. Hunter, Cam. Glo. Rlfe, Wrt, Verity, E. Lee, Innes, Cholmely. *Wind* Rowe i, *South-wind* Ktly. *South* Pope et cet. *ſou'wind* or *ſough* Anon. ap.

Cam. *ſcent* MS Dent ap. Hal.
9. *Violets ;*] *Violets*, F₄, Rowe et seq.
10. *Enough,*] *Hush !* Pope, Han. [*Musick ceases.* Cap.

'The strains decay, And melt away, In a dying, dying fall' [lines 19–21]. Again, Thomson, in his *Spring*, line 722, speaking of the Nightingale : '—Still at every dying fall Takes up again her lamentable strain Of winding woe.' KNIGHT gives a general reference to *Comus*, as containing 'fall' thus used. In the passage, beginning with line 251, we find : ' How sweetly did they flote upon the wings Of silence, through the empty vaulted night, At every fall smoothing the raven downe Of darknesse till she smil'd.'—*Facsimile of the MS of Milton's Minor Poems*, p. 14.—ED.

8–10. **sound . . . Odour**] THEOBALD in his correspondence with Warburton (*Nichols*, ii, 354) expresses a preference for Rowe's reading *wind*, and adds that he does not know that Shakespeare 'anywhere expresses an opinion of the sweetness of the *South*,' which is Pope's reading and afterward adopted by Theobald in his own edition. This change of 'sound' to *South* maintained its place in the text without question for nigh a hundred and twenty years, from Pope to Knight. STEEVENS, in the meantime, suggested that the thought may have been borrowed from Sidney's *Arcadia*, 1590 : ' her breath is more sweete then a gentle South-west wind, which comes creeping ouer flowrie fieldes and shadowed waters in the extreame heate of sommer, and yet is nothing, compared to the hony flowing speach that breath doth carrie ; no more all that our eyes can see of her . . . is to be matched with the flocke of vnspeakable vertues, laid up delightfully in that best builded fold.' (ed. 1598, lib. i, p. 2. A longer extract is here given than that given by Steevens, in order to bring in certain phrases, wherein subsequent editors have found proofs that Shakespeare had here in mind this passage in the *Arcadia*. Furthermore, in reference to 'Stealing . . . odour,' Steevens (Var. '85) observes that, ' Milton has very successfully introduced the image : " —now gentle gales Fanning their odoriferous wings dispense Native perfumes, and whisper whence they stole Those balmy spoils." ' —(*Par. Lost*, Bk. IV, line 156.)—KNIGHT, the first editor to recall the Shakespearian world to the grey and venerable authority of the Folio, thus pleads for ' sound ': ' Let us consider whether Shakspere was most likely to have written " sound " or *south*, which involves the question of which is the better word. In the quotation given by Steevens from the *Arcadia*, the comparison is direct. The sweet breath of Urania is more sweet than the gentle southwest wind. Sidney adds, " and yet is nothing, compared to the honey-flowing speech that breath doth carry." The music of the speech is not here compared with the music of the wind ;—the notion of fragrance is alone conveyed. If in the passage of the text we read *south* instead of " sound," the conclusion of the sentence, " Stealing and giving odour," rests upon the mind, and the comparison becomes an indirect one between the harmony of the dying fall and the odour of the breeze that had passed over a bank of violets. This, we think, is not what the poet meant. He desired to compare one *sound* with another

[8–10. sweet sound . . . Stealing and giuing Odour.]

sound. Milton had probably this passage in view when he wrote [the passage quoted above by Steevens]. The image in Milton, as well as in Shakspere, combines the notion of sound as well as fragrance. In Shakspere "the sound that breathes,"—the soft murmur of the breeze playing amidst beds of flowers,—is put first, because of its relation to the "dying fall" of the exquisite harmony; but in Milton the "perfumes" of the "gentle gales" are more prominent than "the whisper,"—because the image is complete in itself, unconnected with what precedes. Further, Shakspere has nowhere else made the *south* an odour-breathing wind; his other representations are directly contrary. In *As You Like It*, Rosalind says, "Like foggy south, puffing with wind and rain" [III, v, 54]. In *Rom. and Jul.* we have the "dew-dropping south" [I, iv, 103]. In *Cym.*, "The south-fog rot him" [II, iii, 136]. We prefer, therefore, on all accounts to hold to the original text.' Knight's arguments were lost on COLLIER, the next editor, who in his First Edition pronounces *south* 'a manifest improvement of the passage; and as "sound" for *south* was an easy misprint, we have continued the alteration, being of opinion, that it is much more likely that the printer should have made an error, than that Shakespeare should have missed so obvious a beauty.' In his Second Edition Collier's opinion was confirmed by finding that 'sound' had been erased and *south* substituted in the corrected Folio of 1632.—HALLIWELL [upholding 'sound']: The Duke intends the imagery to refer to the *strain*, which 'had a dying fall,' and came o'er his ear like the sweet low hum of the summer air, without allusion to any particular quarter whence the wind may come.—STAUNTON: If *south* were the poet's word, he must have employed it, not in the sense Pope intended of *south-wind*, but as *south, sowth,* or *sough* is used in the North, to signify the soft whisper of the breeze: 'The soft south of the swyre, and sound of the stremes,' etc.—*Dunbar, Maitland's Poems*, p. 64. DYCE adopts *south* in all three of his editions and ignores discussion.—R. G. WHITE: It is not easy to discover the supposed difficulty in the original text, in which the effect, that is, the sweet sound, is by a beautiful metonymy put for the cause, the wind. Knight remarks that the question between 'sound' and *south* is, 'which is the better word.' There is no such question admissible. If in the place of 'sound' there were some word without meaning, or even with a meaning incongruous with the tone of the passage, and 'sound' and 'south' were proposed as substitutes, then, indeed, there would be a question as to which is the better word. But 'sound' appears in the authentic text, and, to say the least, is comprehensible and appropriate, and is therefore not to be disturbed, except by those who hold that Shakespeare must have written that which they think best. But did Pope, or the editors who have followed him, ever lie musing on the sward at the edge of a wood, and hear the low, sweet hum of the summer air, as it kissed the coyly-shrinking wild flowers upon the banks, and passed on, loaded with fragrance from the sweet salute? If they ever did, how could they make this change of 'sound' to *south?* and if they never did, they are unable to entirely appreciate the passage, much less to improve it. WALKER (*Crit.* iii, 82) proposed *wind* as an emendation for 'sound,' not knowing that he had been anticipated by Rowe. He then continues: 'In the passage of the Arcadia quoted by [Steevens] the wind is not the [south] but the *south-west;* and I suspect that [Sidney] had a passage of some Greek or Roman poet in view, were it merely on account of the very different character of our English south-wester.' Of this note of Walker, LETTSOM says: 'I can scarcely agree with what [Walker] says on the passage from the Arcadia. A south-wester is a *heavy gale* from the south-west; but

[8–10. **sweet sound . . . Stealing and giuing Odour.**]
we often have genial, bright, and growing weather from that quarter as well as from
the south.   Such was the weather that Shakespeare probably had in view when he
put this speech into the mouth of the lovelorn Orsino.   One verse in particular,—
"it had a *dying* fall," seems inspired by the soft, balmy, but somewhat moist,
relaxing, and languor-breathing air, which is peculiar to the two winds in question.
. . . It is utterly impossible that Shakespeare could have described a *sound* as stealing and giving *odours*.   Sounds sometimes tickle, and sometimes torture, our ears;
but they are incapacitated by nature from affecting our noses.'—The Cowden-
Clarkes: *South* has always had so perfectly the effect to our ear and feeling of
having been Shakespeare's word here, that we cannot bring ourselves to doubt its
being the right one in this passage.   We cannot believe that he would have employed
the expression 'sound' to imply that which '*gives* odour'; whereas 'the sweet
south' at once suggests that balmy air which Shakespeare elsewhere places in
extremity of contrast with the fierce 'septentrion' and 'frozen bosom of the north.'
Not merely do we fancy that Shakespeare may have been thinking of the extract
from the Arcadia quoted by Steevens,—especially of the expression, 'the flock of
unspeakable virtues' which is paralleled by Shakespeare's 'the flock of all affections'
in line 41,—but we also believe that he may have had before his mind Bacon's sentence of similar beauty, 'the breath of flowers is far sweeter in the air (where it
comes and goes like the warbling of music) than in the hand.'—Keightley (*Exp.*
174): A sound breathing is pure nonsense.   Even Pope's correction does not remove
the difficulty, for *south* alone, no more than *north*, *east*, or *west*, is never used for the
wind.   [See Knight's references *supra* to *As You Like It*, III, v, 54 and *Rom. and
Jul.* I, iv, 103.   'Never' and 'always' are extremely dangerous words, in a Shakespearian note.—Ed.]   It seems to me then that the poet wrote *south-wind*, and as
the *th* was usually suppressed in *south*, *north*, etc., as *sou'-west*, *sou'-east*, the printer
pronounced *sou wind* or, it may be, *sou' ind*, which easily became 'sound' in his
mind, and so he printed it.   It is rather remarkable that this very correction is made
by an *Anon.* in the Cam. Edition.   Rolfe (after quoting the notes of Knight and
of R. G. White, continues): When the Folio reading can be so eloquently defended
we do not feel justified in departing from it; but we nevertheless have our doubts
whether Shakespeare wrote *sound*.   It is a serious objection to *south* that he always
refers to that wind as bringing fog and rain.   If he employed the word here, it may
have been, as Staunton suggests, in the sense of *south*, *sowth*, or *sough*.   If we retain
sound, we must make it refer, as Knight and White do, to the sweet murmur of the
breeze.   This was doubtless what Pope understood to be the meaning of the simile.
It is not likely that, in substituting *south*, he intended to make the comparison
between the effect of music on the ear and that of fragrance on the sense of smell.
Why then did he think it necessary to make any change in the *expression* of the
simile?   Because as a poet he felt that it was more poetical to refer to the wind, the
personified source of the sound, as breathing on the bank of violets, than to speak
of the 'sound' itself.   The difference seems to us *almost* that between poetry and
prose.   We cannot agree with Knight that the substitution of *south* gives too much
prominence to the 'indirect' comparison of the harmony to the odour.   Whichever
word we adopt, the main and direct comparison is between the music and the murmur
of the wind; this is at once strengthened and beautified by the reference to the odour.
It will be noticed that the poet dwells on this secondary comparison; he is not satisfied with describing the wind as breathing on the *bank of violets*, but adds the

[8–10. **sweet sound . . . Stealing and giuing Odour.**]

exquisite *stealing and giving odour*. Milton has a *direct* comparison of sound to
fragrance in a very beautiful passage in *Comus*, 555 fol. : ' At last a soft and
solemn-breathing sound Rose like a steam of rich distill'd perfumes, And stole
upon the air.'—HUDSON : Pope's change is most certainly right. For with what
propriety can a *sound* be said to ' breathe upon a bank of violets, stealing and giving
odour'? Moreover, in the old reading, we have a comparison made between a thing
and *itself!* It is as much as to say, ' The sweet sound came o'er my ear like the
sweet sound.' The Poet evidently meant to compare the music to a sweet breeze
loaded with fragrance ; the former coming over the ear as the latter comes over
another sense. So that the old reading is simply absurd. Knight and Grant
White waste a deal of ingenious and irrelevant rhetoric in trying to make it good ;
but nothing of that sort can redeem it from absurdity. And by the methods they
use we can easily read almost any sense we please into whatever words come before
us. In this case, they but furnish an apt illustration of how a dotage of the old
letter, and a certain exegetical jugglery, may cheat even good heads into an utter
dereliction of common sense. [It is not unlikely, I think, that Hudson will prove,
to be the last editor to adopt Pope's change. The excellent text of the *Globe
Edition* bids fair to become the accepted standard ; in the present instance it has
judiciously followed the Folio. The difficulty here, where a sound is said to give
forth an odour, is parallel to that where Hamlet speaks of ' taking arms against a
sea of troubles,' and is due, I think, to the thick-coming fancies of a poetic imagination rather than to a common confusion of ideas, or to a blameworthy mixture of
metaphors. We must remember that we are dealing with poetry, not prose ; and,
surely, in poetry, when imagination is once on the wing, a man may be supposed
to take up arms, the shield of faith and the sword of the spirit, against troubles
which come wave on wave upon him like a sea. Similarly, in the present line, one
sense, that of hearing, may be, with the swiftness of thought, supplemented or
endued with the functions of the other senses. Who can define the infinitely
subtle laws of association? Both in and out of Shakespeare innumerable instances
are to be found of this blending, this identity even, of all the senses. Is it not
a prerogative of poetry? Bassanio tells Antonio that from Portia's eyes he received
speechless messages. Iago says that Desdemona's eye sounds a parley. Ulysses
says of Cressida that her foot speaks. In the twenty-third *Sonnet*, Shakespeare speaks of hearing with the eyes. Ariel says of Stephano and Trinculo
that they lifted up their noses as though they smelled music. And in this present
play Sir Toby speaks of hearing by the nose. And in V, i, 113, Olivia says that
the Duke's words are ' as fat and fulsome to mine ear as howling after Musick'
where the sense of taste is referred to the hearing. What more familiar expression is
there than ' the language of the eye'? In *Exodus* (x, 21) we have ' darkness which may
be felt.' A better example can be hardly found than the passage in *Comus*, quoted by
Rolfe, which is worth recalling, because, so it seems to me, Milton was there, quite
possibly, influenced by this very passage in *Twelfth Night*, which, by the way, he
could have read only in the first three Folios, wherein the word ' sound' was as yet
uncorrupted by Rowe or Pope. In Milton's MS, lines 555, 556 of *Comus* read :
' At last a soft & sollemne breathing sound rose like a steame of rich distill'd perfumes,' and it is unusually interesting to note that Milton deliberated over the use of
soft, *still*, or *sweet* (Shakespeare's own word) as applied to ' sound,' and finally
decided on ' soft'; and again he hesitated between *rich* and *slow*. (For this

'Tis not fo fweet now, as it was before.   11
O fpirit of Loue, how quicke and frefh art thou,
That notwithftanding thy capacitie,
Receiueth as the Sea.   Nought enters there,
Of what validity, and pitch fo ere,   15

12. *thou,*] *thou!* Rowe.   14. *there,*] *thee* Daniel.
   Loue,] *love!* Coll.   15. *pitch*] *pith* Gould.
  13, 14. *That ... capacitie, ... Sea.*   *fo ere*] *fo e're* F_3F_4, Rowe. *soever*
Nought] *That,...capacity...sea, nought*   Cap. Rann.
Rowe ii, et seq.

---

glimpse into his mind we are indebted to the inestimable *Facsimile* of his MS, prepared with minutest care by Dr W. Aldis Wright.)   Again, Shelley, in *The Sensitive Plant*, Part i, has, ' And the hyacinth purple, and white and blue, Which flung
from its bells a sweet peal anew Of music so delicate, soft, and intense, It was felt
like an odour within the sense.'   And also in Part iii, ' —the sensitive plant Felt
the sound of the funeral chant.'   Lastly, in the immortal *Ode*, Wordsworth apos-
trophises ' thou eye among the blind, That, deaf and silent, read'st the eternal deep.'
Both R. G. White and W. A. Wright explain the present use of ' sound ' as an
instance of metonymy, where the effect is put for the cause.   A wind strong enough
to produce a sound would have to be, I fear, more boisterous than the summer air
which breathes upon a bank of violets.   However, the name whereby we classify the
figure is of small consequence, if the examples just gathered be considered parallel.
Under their influence the ears of the deafest of us may be blest by hearing a sweet
sound that steals and gives odour.—ED.]

   10. **Stealing**] MALONE : Here Shakespeare makes the wind steal odour from
the violet.   In his 99th *Sonnet*, the violet is made the thief.

   10, 11. **no more . . . before**] HEUSSER (*Sh. Jahrbuch*, xxviii, 223) observes that
this rhyme strengthens the supposition that in Shakespeare rhymes supplied the place
of stage-directions ; its present use is an intimation to the musicians to cease.   [The
supposition is well-founded, but is hardly applicable here, inasmuch as the Duke had
just commanded the music to cease.   The rhyme is probably accidental.—ED.]

   12. **spirit**] WALKER (*Crit.* i, 193) says that it may be safely laid down as a canon
that this word, in our old poets, wherever the metre does not compel us to pronounce
it disyllabically, is a monosyllable.   See *Mer. of Ven.* V, i, 96 ; *Macbeth*, IV, i, 127 ;
Mid. N. D. II, i, 32, of this edition.

   12. **quicke**] This, of course, means *living, vigorous.*

   13. **That**] For other examples where ' that ' means *in that*, see ABBOTT,
§ 284.

   14. **Sea.   Nought**] If the punctuation of the Folio were right, ' Receiveth '
should be *Receivest.*   ROWE properly changed the period after ' sea ' to a comma.

   14. **there**] W. A. WRIGHT : This refers grammatically to the sea, to which love
is compared.   The writer's mind passed to the figure from the thing signified.   [Does
not ' there ' refer grammatically to ' capacitie ' ?—ED.]

   15. **validity**] MALONE : Here used for *value.*   [Compare, ' more validity, More
honourable state . . . lives In carrion-flies than ' Romeo,' III, iii, 33 (where note
the absorption of *in* in the final *n* of ' than ').—ED.]

   15. **pitch**] MADDEN (p. 201) : This word, signifying in falconry the height to

But falles into abatement, and low price   16
Euen in a minute ; fo full of fhapes is fancie,
That it alone, is high fantafticall.   18

17. *minute ;*] *minute !* Coll.
   is fancie] *in fancy* Theob. Warb.
Johns.   *it's fancy* Upton.
   18. *That it alone, is*] *And thou all
o'er art* Han.

18. *alone*] *all o'er* Quincy MS.
   high fantaftical] *high-fantastical*
Var. '78 et seq. (except Hal. Glo. Rlfe,
Wh. ii. Wrt, Dtn).

---

which a falcon soars or towers (*1 Hen. VI:* II, iv, 11 ; *2 Hen. VI:* II, i, 6 ;
Jul. Cæs. I, i, 78), was used figuratively (*Rich. II:* I, i, 109 ; *Tit. And.* II, i, 14 ;
Rom. & Jul. I, iv, 21 ; *Sonn.* lxxxvi, 6), and came to mean height in general
(*Twel. N.* I, i, 15 ; *1 Hen. VI:* II, iii, 55 ; *Rich. III:* III, vii, 188 ; *Sonn.* vii,
9). [In *Hamlet*, III, i, 86, we have, in the Ff, 'enterprises of great *pith* and
moment,' where the Qq give *pitch*,—a better reading ; as, I think, the present
passage shows.—ED.]

   17, 18. is fancie . . . high] WARBURTON : This complicated nonsense should
be rectified thus : ' So full of shapes *in* fancy, That it alone is *hight* fantastical.'
That is, love is so full of shapes *in fancy*, that the *name* of *fantastical* is peculiarly
given to it alone.—COLERIDGE (p. 120) : Warburton's alteration of 'is' into *in* is
needless. 'Fancy' may very well be interpreted 'exclusive affection,' or 'passionate preference.' Thus, bird-fanciers, gentlemen of the fancy, that is, amateurs of
boxing, etc. The play of assimilation,—the meaning one sense chiefly, and yet
keeping both senses in view, is perfectly Shakespearian. [Inasmuch as Coleridge
rejects only one of Warburton's changes, it might be inferred that he accepted the
other. But it is not likely. Warburton is so dogmatic that it is not easy to listen
to him with equanimity, but, out of justice to him, we should remember that he
held the printed text merely as proof sheets, and careless proof sheets in addition ; he was not, therefore, let us charitably suppose, criticising Shakespeare, but
the printers.—ED.]

   18. alone] ABBOTT (§ 18) classes this with, 'That must needs be sport alone,'
Mid. N. D. III, ii, 123 ; 'I am alone the villain of the earth,' *Ant. & Cleop.* IV, vi,
30, and interprets 'alone' as equivalent to *above all things*, which does not strike
me as of the happiest. In *Mid. N. D.* I prefer *unparalleled ;* in *Ant. & Cleop.
beyond comparison*, and in the present instance, *to the exclusion of all others*, as
W. A. WRIGHT interprets it.—ED.

   12-18. To understand these lines, which are somewhat obscure, I think we should
observe their intimate connection with the first lines of the Duke's speech. The
Duke asks for music, and, while listening to it, one strain so touches his love-sick
soul that he longs to hear it repeated, and yet, after its repetition, he is instantly
satiated, and, perfect though it was in itself, it has lost all sweetness and the Duke
wishes to hear no more. Then follow the present lines which are the explanation and justification of this fickleness. In a poor paraphrase, but the best I can
offer, the Duke says that the spirit of Love, that is, love in its perfection, is so
full of life and fresh energy in growth, that it receives the whole world, as the
sea receives the waters of the heavens and the earth ; there is nothing which may
not minister to it, and yet no sooner is a new element absorbed, (no matter how
fair and lovely in itself, like music, for instance, this new element may be,) but
immediately, even in a minute, it becomes poor and shallow in comparison with

Cu. Will you go hunt my Lord?
Du. What *Cnrio*?   20
Cu. The Hart.
Du. Why fo I do, the Nobleft that I haue :
O when mine eyes did fee *Oliuia* firft,
Me thought fhe purg'd the ayre of peftilence ;
That inftant was I turn'd into a Hart,   25
And my defires like fell and cruell hounds,

---

20. Cnrio] F₁. Curia F₄.
23. *mine*] *my* Pope ii, Theob. Warb. Johns. Var. Mal.

24. In parenthesis, Cap. Knt, Sing. ii, Del. Dtn.
Me thought] *Methought* Rowe.

---

love's full sea ; hence, love, with its ever-varying shapes, is never for a moment the same, but becomes the very type of what is purely imaginative.—ED.

18. **high**] Inasmuch as this qualifies 'fantastical' and not 'it,' there should be, I think, a hyphen after it. How fond Shakespeare is of 'high' as an intensive, Bartlett's *Concordance* will abundantly show.—ED.

19. **go hunt**] See 'go look,' I, v, 136; 'go see,' III, iii, 22 ; 'go tell,' *Mid. N. D.* I, i, 260 ; 'go seeke,' *Ib.* II, i, 13 ; 'go and see,' *Wint. Tale*, III, ii, 220,— all in this edition. Or ABBOTT, § 349.

22. **the Noblest**] For the sake of the threadbare pun on *hart* and *heart*, the Duke gets his metaphor confused. In this line, he hunts his heart, the noblest part of him ; in the 27th line, he is himself the hart and his desires hunt him.—ED.]

24. **Me . . . pestilence**] CAPELL (p. 140): The only mention of seeing Olivia causes the speaker a starting from his begun subject, and the matter of [this present line] is extraneous ; it's sense,—that she had something so sweet about her, that the air was purg'd by it. [Accordingly, Capell placed this line in parenthesis ; wherein he was followed though with some reluctance by KNIGHT, who, after quoting Capell's remark that the matter of the line is 'extraneous,' says] Of this we are not sure. The Duke complains that when he first saw Olivia he was 'turn'd into a hart'; but he had thought, mistakingly, that she 'purg'd the air of pestilence,'—removed those malignant influences from the air which caused his transformation. In this sense 'pestilence' has the same meaning as the 'taking airs' in *Lear*. Whether this be the sense or not, the line is decidedly parenthetical. [Happily, Capell's followers in the use of a parenthesis are few. The punctuation of the Folio can be improved only by a comma after 'methought,' and an exclamation mark after 'pestilence.' I doubt that the latter word has any hidden meaning. Orsino speaks with the ecstatic exaggeration of a lover. Olivia's purity purged from all impurity the wide cope of heaven.—ED.]

25. **That . . . Hart**] DYCE: Compare Petrarch : 'Vero diro, forse e' parrà menzogna, Ch' i' senti' trarmi della propria immago, Ed in un cervo solitario, e vago Di selva in selva, ratto mi transformo, Ed ancor de' miei can fuggo lo stormo.' —*Canzone I.*

26. **fell**] BRADLEY (*N. E. D.*): An adopted form of Old French *fel* = Provençal *fel*, Italian *fello*, fierce, cruel, savage, the extant representative of the popular Latin *fellō*, nominative of *fellō-em*, substantive.

Ere fince purfue me.   How now what newes from her ?   27

Enter Valentine.

Val.   So pleafe my Lord, I might not be admitted,
But from her handmaid do returne this anfwer :   30
The Element it felfe, till feuen yeares heate,

27. *Ere*] *E'er* Rowe.
28. Enter...] After *me* Dyce, Cam. Sta.
29. *pleafe*] *please you* Ktly.
30. *handmaid*] *hand-maid* F_3F_4, Rowe, +, Cap.
31. *yeares heate*] *yeares heat,* F_3.

years heat F_4, Rowe i, Dtn. *years hence* Rowe ii, +, Cap. Var. Ran. Dyce ii, iii, Coll. iii, Huds. *years' heat* Harness, Knt, Coll. i, ii, Hal. Dyce i, Wh. Sta. Cam. Glo. Rlfe. *years heat 'em* Ktly. *years heat it* Id. conj.

27. **since pursue**] ABBOTT, § 62 : We [here] find the present tense after ' since,' to denote an action that *is* and *has been* going on *since* a certain time. [Does not the continuousness of the action here depend on the ' E'er,' meaning *always ?*—ED.]

27. **pursue me**] JOHNSON : This image evidently alludes to the story of Acteon, by which Shakespeare seems to think men cautioned against too great familiarity with forbidden beauty.   Acteon, who saw Diana naked, and was torn to pieces by his hounds, represents a man, who, indulging his eyes, or his imagination, with the view of a woman that he cannot gain, has his heart torn with incessant longing.   An interpretation far more elegant and natural than that of Sir Francis Bacon, who, in his *Wisdom of the Ancients,* supposes this story to warn us against enquiring into the secrets of princes, by showing that those, who knew that which for reasons of state is to be concealed, will be detected and destroyed by their own servants.— MALONE : Our author had here undoubtedly Daniel's *Sonnet V.* in his thoughts : ' Which turn'd my sport into a Harts dispaire, Which still is chac'd, while I haue any breath, By mine owne thoughts, set on me by my Faire : My thoughts (like Houndes) pursue me to my death.'—*Delia* [1592, p. 40, ed. Grosart].   Daniel, however, was not the original proprietor of this thought.   He appears to have borrowed it from Whitney's *Emblems,* 1586, p. 15.   And Whitney himself should seem to have been indebted in this instance to a passage of the Dedication of Adlington's Translation of Apuleius.   [Malone errs in thinking that Whitney was indebted to Adlington.   GREEN (p. 276) shows that Whitney followed Sambucus, 1564, even using the same woodcut ; and probably Sambucus followed Alciatus, 1551.   Thus we have Shakespeare, the vile plagiarist, drawing his inspiration from Daniel, Daniel from Whitney, Whitney from Sambucus, Sambucus from Alciatus,—a pleasing and instructive series,—' thus naturalists observe a flea Has smaller fleas that on him prey ; And these have smaller still to bite 'em, And so proceed *ad infinitum.*'   Let our souls be instructed by the words of W. A. WRIGHT : ' The story of Acteon was in fact a commonplace of the time. Shakespeare, as we know from an allusion in *The Merry Wives of Windsor* [and in *Tit. And.* also] had read the story in Golding's *Ovid,* and did not require others to teach him how to apply it.'—ED.]

29. **So . . . Lord**] DEIGHTON : An apologetic preface to a statement : ' If I may be pardoned for saying so.'

29. **might**] For other examples of the past tense of *may* in the sense of *was able* or *could,* see ABBOTT, § 312.

31. **Element**] Here, and in III, i, 58, used for *the sky.*   But in III, iv, 127,

Shall not behold her face at ample view : 32
But like a Cloyſtreſſe ſhe will vailed walke,
And water once a day her Chamber round
With eye-offending brine : all this to ſeaſon 35

34. *Chamber*] *chambers* Ff, Rowe, Pope, Han.

where Malvolio says : ' I am not of your element,' it means, of course, *sphere
of life.*

31. **yeares heate**] MALONE : ' Heat ' for *heated.*   The air, till it shall have been
warmed by seven revolutions of the sun, shall not, etc.—STEEVENS : Thus, too,
Chapman, *The Nineteenth Odyssey :* ' When the sun was set, And darkness rose,
they slept, till day's fire het Th' enlightened earth.' [l. 593.]—HARNESS [see
Text. Notes] : Surely here Shakespeare uses the word, ' heat,' as a substantive, in
the sense of *course,* or *race.*—DYCE : Whether we take ' heat ' as a participle or as a
substantive, it is equally absurd.   [He therefore reads, *hence.*   As a Cambridge
Editor W. A. WRIGHT agrees with Harness that ' heat ' is more probably a substantive, and as the Editor of the *Clarendon Edition* he paraphrases the sentence,
' till the heat of seven years have passed.'   SCHMIDT (*Lex.*) also inclines to agree
with Harness.   Were it not so common to find the *-ed* omitted in the past participles
of verbs ending in *-te, -t,* and *-d* (ABBOTT, § 342, gives a list of twenty-three of
these verbs and the list is by no means complete) I should be inclined to follow
Harness ; but the ellipsis demands so much to be supplied, ' till the heat *of* seven
years *has passed,*' that it gives us pause.   Merely to express the passage of time,
winter might have been used instead of summer ; but in cold weather, possibly,
Olivia's face would have been muffled up and then the element could certainly never
have beheld it at ample view ; therefore summer is chosen when Olivia's beauty could
be ' dedicate to the sun.'   Substitute to *cool* for to ' heat,' and I think we shall feel
that the past participle is not quite so absurd as Dyce would have it : ' The Element
itself, till seven years *cool'd.*'   Possibly, therefore, ' heate ' in the sense of *heated,*
may be right.—ED.]

32. **at**] ABBOTT, § 144 : *At,* when thus used [in the sense of *near*] in adverbial
expressions, now rejects adjectives and genitives as interfering with adverbial brevity.
Thus we can say ' *at* freedom,' but not ' at *ample* view.'   [But we certainly say,
' at full view.'—ED.]

33. **vailed**] In opposition to the ' ample view ' in the preceding line.

34. **Chamber round**] It is possible that this unusual phrase was suggested,
through a subtle association of ideas, by the preceding ' cloistress,' which suggests the
enclosed walk about a courtyard of a convent ; as a nun paces these four sides of the
cloisters, so Olivia would daily water with her tears the circuit of her chamber.   I
can find but three similar examples, and these are not exactly parallel : ' We'll drink
a measure the table round.'—*Macb.* III, iv, 11 ; ' The sum of this . . . Y-ravished
the regions round.'—*Per.* III, Pro. 35 (which may not be Shakespeare's) ; and
' She throws her eyes about the paintings round.'—*Lucrece,* 1499.   The printers of
the Ff changed ' chamber ' to *chambers ;* this CAPELL further changed to *chamber's,*
which, he remarks with complacency, ' is in truth a correction ; it has been hitherto
an accusative plural, which ruins poetry.'—ED.

35. **brine . . . to season**] WHITER (p. 141) : When a phrase has once become
familiar to our thoughts, we insensibly forget that the terms, which compose it, are

A brothers dead loue, which ſhe would keepe freſh   36
And laſting, in her ſad remembrance.
   Du. O ſhe that hath a heart of that fine frame
To pay this debt of loue but to a brother,
How will ſhe loue, when the rich golden ſhaft   40

---

36. *brothers dead*] *dead brother's*   Pope, Han. *rememberance* Cap. (errata),
Daniel.   Ktly.

37. *laſting,*] *laſting* F₄ et seq.   38. *that fine*] *this fine* F₃F₄, Rowe i.
remembrance] *remembrance still*

---

appropriate and peculiar. Shakespeare is frequent in the metaphorical application
of the word *season*. ‘ *Seasoning* the earth with showers of silver *brine*.’—*Lucrece*,
796; ‘ *tears* . . . the best *brine* a maiden can *season* her praise in.’—*Alls Well*, I, i,
55; ‘ Is not birth, beauty, good shape . . . the *spice* and *salt* that *season* a man.’—
Tro. & Cress. I, ii, 275; ‘ What a deal of *brine* Hath wash'd thy sallow cheeks for
Rosaline ! How much *salt* water thrown away in waste To *season* love.’—*Rom. &
Jul.* II, iii, 69; ‘ the wide sea Hath . . . *salt* too little, which may *season* give To
her foul tainted flesh.’—*Much Ado*, IV, i, 148. In the present passage we have
brine, season, keep fresh.

36. **brothers dead loue**] At first sight, DANIEL'S conjecture: ‘ a dead brothers
love,’ seems almost an *emendatio certissima*, but further reflection will show, I think,
that it is needless, if not injurious. The love which Olivia wished to season and keep
fresh in her remembrance was not *her* love for her brother, ‘ this debt of love,’ as
Orsino calls it, she pays by her seclusion till seven years heat, but the love which
her brother bore to her, whereof the manifestations were buried in his grave. It was
on the memory of this ‘ dead love’ that Olivia wished to dwell, and season with
eye-offending brine.—ED.

37. **remembrance**] If it gratify any one to pronounce words in an unusual
fashion, he will find authority in Walker, *Vers.* 9, and in Abbott, § 477, for pronouncing this, *rememberance*. Both here and in *Wint. Tale*, IV, iv, 88, Capell goes
so far as to spell it thus in his text. I think such pronunciations should be adopted
only when, without them, a line sounds intolerably harsh, which cannot be affirmed,
in the present instance, should ‘ remembrance’ be pronounced as it is spelled. See
also ‘ Countrey’ in line 23 of the next scene.—ED.

38. **that . . . that**] The presence of two *that*'s in this line, possibly led the
printers of the Third Folio to change the second ‘ that’ to *this*, overlooking the fact
that it is here used for *such*, and followed by ‘ To’ in the next line. See, if need
be, ABBOTT, § 277.—ED.

40. **golden shaft**] DOUCE (i, 84) says that this ‘ golden shaft’ might have been
supplied from a description of Cupid in Sidney's *Arcadia*, Book ii. It is hardly
likely. The only reference there to Cupid's arrows is: ‘ Thus painters Cupid paint,
thus poets do A naked God, blind, young with arrowes two . . . But arrowes two,
and tipt with gold or lead.’—p. 155, ed. 1598. There is no mention of the different
offices of the two arrows. Douce further observes that the source might also have
been Ovid's *Metamorphoses*, Golding's translation. This is more likely. The passage
in Golding is found in The first booke (misprinted ‘ Second booke’ in running title)
fol. 8 *verso*, 1567, as follows: ‘ There from hys quiuer full of shafts two arrowes did
he take Of sundrie workes: tone causeth Loue, the tother doth it slake. That causeth

Hath kill'd the flocke of all affections elfe   41
That liue in her.   When Liuer, Braine, and Heart,
Thefe foueraigne thrones, are all fupply'd and fill'd
Her fweete perfections with one felfe king :   44

43. *Thefe*] *Three* Warb. Han. Johns. *Those* Knt, Wh. i.

    thrones,] thrones F$_4$.

43, 44. *are ... perfections*] *her sweet perfections, Are all supplied and fill'd* Coll. conj. Huds.

43, 44. *fill'd Her fweete perfections*] Ff, Rowe. *fill'd, (O sweet perfection !*)

Warb. *fill'd, (Her sweet perfection*) Cap. Sta. Rlfe. *fill'd Of her sweet perfections* Ktly. *fill'd, Her sweet perfections,* Pope et cet. (subs.)

44. *felfe king*] *selfe fame king* F$_2$. *self same king* F$_3$. *self-same king* F$_4$, Rowe, +, Cap. *self-king* Mal. Ktly.

---

loue, is all of golde with point full sharpe and bright, That chaseth loue is blunt, whose steele with leaden head is dight.'   GREEN (p. 400), on the other hand, says that the epithet 'golden' in the present passage might have been used, 'equally well, and with as much probability, through the influence of Alciat, or adopted from Whitney's very beautiful translation and paraphrase of Joachim Bellay's *Fable of Cupid and Death* [1581]: the two were lodging together at an inn, and unintentionally exchanged quivers; Death's darts were made of bone, Cupid's were 'dartes of goulde.'   See *Mid. N. D.* I, i, 180: 'I sweare to thee, by Cupids strongest bow, By his best arrow with the golden head.'—DOUCE adds: Milton seems to have forgotten that Love had only *one* shaft of *gold*.   See *Par. Lost*, iv, 763: 'Here Love his golden shafts employs, here lights His constant lamp,' etc.   [DR SKEAT has kindly called my attention to *The Romaunt of the Rose*, where, as to the number of arrows, William de Lorris evidently had 'later information' than Ovid.   In Chaucer's translation (line 939 *et seq.* ed. Skeat) we find that Cupid had five 'arowes,' 'Of which five in his right hond were . . . with gold bigoon,' and although these were for five different purposes, and not solely to inspire love, as was Ovid's single arrow, yet Milton is justified in that there were more than one.   'Shakespeare certainly had a copy of Chaucer's *Works*,' says Dr Skeat, 'probably the edition of 1561.' —ED.]

41. **flocke of all affections**] See 'flocke of vnspeakable vertues,' in the extract from Sidney's *Arcadia*, quoted by Steevens, in the note on line 8, above.   R. G. WHITE : 'Flock' is used here merely as a collective noun.

43, 44. **These . . . perfections**] A much-belaboured passage, wherein WARBURTON, whose influence has extended even to our day, gave the first distortion by enclosing 'Her sweet perfections' in a parenthesis; to be sure, he changed it to 'O sweet perfection,' which no editor followed, but his parenthesis remained, and even the conservative Capell adopted his '*perfection*' in the singular, and thus remarks (p. 141) : 'That man is woman's *perfection*, her completion, is a doctrine as old as Adam; and nearly of that age is the opinion that " brain, heart, and liver" are the seats of human affection; it's "thrones" properly, from the dominion it [*i. e.* affection] exercises; that which has it's seat in the *brain, i. e.* rises from judgement, being first in degree; but when all are " fill'd (says this passage) with one self-same king," when love in every stage of it centers in one man, then is love in full sovereignty and woman in her perfection.'   Albeit this interpretation smacks not a little of arrogance on the Duke's part, intimating, as it does, that Olivia needs him as a husband to make her perfect, yet it is better than the later construction which makes

[43, 44. These soueraigne thrones, . . . her sweete perfections.]

the 'sweet perfections' refer to 'liver, brain, heart,' which are already sufficiently qualified as 'sovereign thrones.' It was HEATH (p. 186) who set forth this later construction, as follows: 'The "sweet perfections" are her affections, her judgement, and her sentiments, sufficiently denoted by the preceding mention of liver, brain, and heart, the several seats where they are vulgarly and poetically supposed to have their respective residence.' STEEVENS followed Heath, but evidently with reluctance. After stating that the 'liver, brain, and heart, are admitted in poetry as the residence of the *passions, judgement,* and *sentiments,*' he adds, 'These are what Shakespeare calls "her sweet perfections," though he has not very clearly expressed what he might design to have said.' KNIGHT dissents from Steevens whose interpretation he calls mistaken and recurs to Capell. 'The phrase ought, probably,' he says, 'to be "her sweet *perfection*." The filling of the "sovereign thrones" with "one self king" is the perfection of Olivia's merits,—according to the ancient doctrine that a woman was not complete till her union with a "self king." In Lord Berners' translation of Froissart there is a sentence which glances at the same opinion. The rich Berthault of Malines is desirous to marry his daughter to the noble Earl of Guerles; and he thus communes with himself: "Howbeit, I will answer these messengers that their coming pleaseth me greatly, and that my daughter should be happy if she might come to *so great a perfection* as to be conjoined in marriage with the Earl of Guerles."' COLLIER proposed a change in the order of the lines, in the belief that 'the passage would run better for the sense and equally well for the verse, if we were to read, "when liver, brain, and heart, These sovereign thrones, her sweet perfections, Are all supplied and fill'd," etc.' This conjecture HUDSON adopted (by a slip, he attributes it to Capell) with the remark that, 'sense, logic, grammar, and prosody, all, I think, plead together for the transposition.' R. G. WHITE quotes *3 Hen. VI:* III, ii, 86, for the use of 'perfections' in the sense it has here: 'All her perfections challenge sovereignty.' STAUNTON says that the plural, 'perfections' is 'a slight but unfortunate misprint which totally destroys the meaning of the poet.' He therefore follows Capell in his text, but in his note says that the passage should be read "—all supplied and fill'd With one self king,—her sweet perfection." The "sweet perfection" not being as Steevens conjectured, her *liver, brain, and heart,* but her husband, her "one self (or single) king." According to the doctrine of Shakespeare's time,' Staunton continues, in effect following Knight, 'a female was imperfect, her nature undeveloped, until by marriage she was incorporated with the other sex. "—and as one glorious flame, Meeting another, grows the same:" The writers of the period abound in allusions to this belief: "Marriage their object is; their *Being* then, And now *Perfection*, they receive from Men."—Overbury's *Wife.* See also Donne's *Epithalamium made at Lincoln's Inn,* in which this, the predominating idea on such occasions, is made the burden of every stanza: "To-day put on perfection, and a woman's name."' DEIGHTON gives a better illustration than either of those of Staunton: 'I have read Aristotle's Problems, which saith that woman receiveth perfection by the man.'—Marston, *Antonio and Mellida,* III, ii, 12, Part 2. To Staunton's interpretation of 'perfection' by *husband* DYCE objects that 'surely "*sweet*" is opposed' to it. But Deighton says that this objection falls to the ground if the 'one self-king' be 'explained as "Love"' (not as a husband), which having overcome all rivals, now reigns alone.' ROLFE thinks that possibly Capell's 'perfection' is the better reading, making it refer to the preceding sentence. —W. A. WRIGHT: The order of the words ['fill'd Her sweet perfections'] is

Away before me, to fweet beds of Flowres,   45
Loue-thoughts lye rich, when canopy'd with bowres.

Exeunt

Scena Secunda.

Enter Viola, a Captaine, and Saylors.   2

Vio. What Country (Friends) is this *?*
Cap. This is Illyria Ladie.   4

46. *Loue-thoughts*] *Love thoughts* F_4,   The Street. Rowe. The sea-coast
Rowe.   Cap.

    lye] *lie* F_3. *lies* F_4.   3. *Country*] *Countrey* F_3F_4.
    bowres] *bowers* F_4.   4. *This is*] Om. Pope, +, Steev.
  1. *Scena*] *Scæna* F_2.   Huds.
                                                Illyria] Illyria, F_3F_4.

inverted, but the sense is clear. [I cannot but believe that there would have been very little difficulty here had the simple punctuation of the Folio been observed, with possibly a comma after 'supplied,' although it is not absolutely needed. We should then have seen, I think, that the liver, brain, and heart, sovereign though they be, do not include all of Olivia's capacity of loving ; these thrones are lodged in us all ; but in addition, since 'fancy is full of shapes' Olivia has many another sweet perfection (such as her devotion to a brother's dead love) which needs but to be fill'd by an object in order to show the power in her of a master-passion.—ED.]

43. **These**] WARBURTON : We should read *Three*. This is exactly in the manner of Shakespeare. [The change is perfectly harmless, and perfectly superfluous.—ED.]

44. **perfeCtions**] A quadrisyllable. ABBOTT, § 479 ; *Tion*, when preceded by *c*, is more frequently prolonged, perhaps because the *c* more readily attracts the *t* to itself, and leaves *ion* uninfluenced by the *t*. [Several examples follow. See I, v, 297.]

44. **one selfe**] KNIGHT doubts that this means *self-same* and believes 'that the poet means *king of herself.*' It makes really but little difference what meaning is attached to 'self' as long as the idea of one sole king is retained and that king, Love ; but see ABBOTT, § 20, for many examples, and more could be added, of the use of 'self' as an adjective, in accordance with its old meaning of *same*. HUNTER (i, 400) thinks that the last few lines of this passage can hardly have been written as they have come down to us. KEIGHTLEY reads ' *Of* her sweet perfections with one self-king,' and says, 'We might also transpose, but, I think, with a loss of force.' Of what innumerable passages might not this be said !—ED.

4. **This is**] POPE omitted these words ; probably, as injurious to the metre ; DYCE, too, queries whether they be not an interpolation. I suppose they make the Captain's reply a little less abrupt. As regards metre, if ' Illyria ' be a quadrisyllable, as it is in the next line, lines 3 and 4, read as one line, make fourteen syllables ; omitting ' This is ' they make twelve,—still too long a line, with a touch of

Vio. And what ſhould I do in Illyria?   5
My brother he is in Elizium,
Perchance he is not drown'd : What thinke you ſaylors?
  Cap. It is perchance that you your ſelfe were ſaued.
  *Vio.*O my poore brother, and ſo perchance may he be.
  Cap. True Madam, and to comfort you with chance,   10

---

6. *Elizium*] Elizium F₃F₄.   *Elysium*   7. *you ſaylors*] *you, ſailors* F₃F₄.
Pope.   9. *and ſo*] so Pope, +.
  7. *he is*] *hes is* F₃.   10. *chance,*] *chance.* F₂F₃.

---

surliness imparted to the honest Captain to no purpose. Nor do we treat him much
better if we make him say *Illyr-yah.* If we consider line 4 as a separate line, it
will have only eight syllables—a line which SIDNEY WALKER says is unknown to
Shakespeare. Thus encircled by a lurid horizon, with no chance of escape, our only
course is to imitate the scorpion, retire to the centre and die. The truth is, I think,
that, in a dialogue, where fragments of lines are in themselves rhythmical, it is folly
to attempt to cut them up into orthodox iambic pentameters which can never be
appreciated on the stage.—ED.

  4. **Illyria**] GODWIN (*The Architect,* 24 April, 1875) : Although the action of
this play is directed or described as taking place in a city of Illyria, there are but
few words in the text which give anything like a Dalmatian complexion. If we
accept Illyria, we have a city or seaport of the Venetian Republic under the local
government of a duke, or, more correctly, a count, this last being the title given him
by the law officer who arrests Antonio. Two passages,—one referring to this arrest,
the other to the Count's galleys and a sea-fight in which they were engaged,—are
almost the only things, apart from the proper names, which could interfere with the
action if we preferred to remove it to England ; for the spirit of this play, as compared
with the other Italian plays, is thoroughly English. Although, however, the contrast
between the Earl of Southampton and a boozing English knight might be *really* as
great as that between the polished Italian noble and Sir Toby Belch, yet the *apparent*
contrast is no doubt greater in the latter by virtue of the difference of nationality.

  5, 6. **Illyria . . . Elizium**] DOUCE : There is seemingly a play upon these words.
[I do not forget what Dr Johnson says of 'the malignant power' which a quibble
had over the mind of Shakespeare, to whom it was ' the fatal Cleopatra for which he
lost the world and was content to lose it '; I recall that he could make dying men
play nicely with their names ; and yet with all this in mind, I find it impossible to
believe that a quibble was intended in the present passage, or, if a quibble be inevitable, that there was any intention of thereby raising a smile. A play on words
here, when Viola was almost heart-broken, would be not only unbefitting the occasion, but, what is more vital, utterly out of keeping with Viola's character.—ED.]

  8. **Cap.**] KARL ELZE (p. 174) thinks that this speech should be given to one of
the sailors, to whom Viola has addressed her question. However generally Viola's
question may have been addressed to the group of sailors, it was the Captain's duty
to be the spokesman, not only here, but when Viola addressed the group as 'friends,'
in the first line.—ED.

  8. **perchance**] The Captain echoes Viola's word, but by using it as a predicate
gives it its literal meaning, *by chance.*

Affure your felfe, after our fhip did fplit,   11
When you, and thofe poore number faued with you,
Hung on our driuing boate : I faw your brother
Moft prouident in perill, binde himfelfe,
(Courage and hope both teaching him the practife)   15
To a fttong Mafte, that liu'd vpon the fea :
Where like *Orion* on the Dolphines backe,
I faw him hold acquaintance with the waues,
So long as I could fee.   19

11. *felfe,*] *felf* F₄.
12. *thofe*] *that* Rowe ii, +, Var. Steev. Var. *this* Cap. Mal. Dyce ii, iii, Huds. *the* Anon. ap. Cam.
thofe...faued] *those—poor number !—saved* Elze.
faued] Ff, Rowe, Var. '21, Coll. Hal. Wh. Glo. Rlfe. *sav'd* Pope et

cet. (generally.)
13. *our*] *your* Rowe.
driuing] *droving* F₃F₄.
boate :] *boat*, Cap.
14. *Moft*] *Moff* F₄.
16. *fttong*] F₁.
17. Orion] *Arion* Pope et seq.
18. *faw*] *see* Pope ii.

12. **thoṣe poore number**] If the text is to be tampered with at all, I think CAPELL'S *this* is better than ROWE'S *that*, inasmuch as the former suggests a motion of the hand toward the small group of sailors standing near. In recent days, it is generally supposed that Shakespeare considered 'number' as a plural, and that 'those poor number' corresponds to 'those poor people.' In the present instance, however, I think W. A. WRIGHT gives an explanation which I cannot but regard with favour inasmuch as it occurred to me independently. 'Shakespeare,' he says, 'may have written "poor numbers" and the final *s* disappeared before the initial *s* of the next word.' At the same time it is probable that 'those poor number' can be classed with 'these set kind of fools,' in I, v, 86.—ED.

12. **saued**] R. G. WHITE condemns the contraction *sav'd* introduced by POPE, and continued by the majority of editors, on the ground that the accent is thereby wrongly thrown on 'you' instead of on 'with.' Pope's intention was to make a line of ten syllables.

13. **driuing**] MURRAY (*N. E. D.*): *Driving*, participial adjective. 2. Moving along rapidly, especially before the wind; drifting. [The present line quoted.]

16. **liu'd**] W. A. WRIGHT: To 'live' is still used by sailors in this sense. Admiral Smyth in his *Sailor's Wordbook* gives, 'To Live. To be able to withstand the fury of the elements; said of a boat or ship, etc.' Compare Ralegh, *Discovery of Guiana* (Hakluyt Soc.), p. 106: 'we . . . brought the Galley as neere as we could, but she had as much a doe to liue as could be.'

17. **Orion**] See *Text. Notes* for POPE'S correction. It is hardly necessary to relate to modern readers a story which was familiar to an audience in Queen Elizabeth's time.—W. A. WRIGHT: Shakespeare may have read at school 'Orpheus in silvis, inter delphinas Arion' (Virgil, *Ecl.* viii, 56), but the story was so familiar that it is not necessary to suppose even this. HALLIWELL quotes a note of GREY (i, 224), wherein a passage is given from Shirley's *Imposture* (V, i), in which the story of Arion is turned into ridicule. It has no possible bearing on the present line,—nor on any line where Arion is ever mentioned. It is merely an example of Shirley's ponderous attempt to be funny.—ED.

Uio.   For faying fo, there's Gold: 20
Mine owne efcape vnfoldeth to my hope,
Whereto thy fpeech ferues for authoritie
The like of him.   Know'ft thou this Countrey?
   Cap.   I Madam well, for I was bred and borne
Not three houres trauaile from this very place.   25
   Vio.   Who gouernes heere?

20. *For ... Gold:*] *There's gold for
saying so.* Pope, Han.
   22. *authoritie*] *authority,* Rowe.

23. *Know'ft*] *And knowest* Han.
   25. *place:*] *place?* F₂F₃. *place* F₄.
place. Rowe.

23. **of him**] ABBOTT (§ 174), with this present phrase as an example, remarks
that '*Of* passes easily from meaning " as regards " to " concerning," " about." '
Is it not rather the Greek construction where ' of him ' would be explained as in
apposition with the genitive implied in the possessive pronoun, ' mine own,'—the
escape of myself unfoldeth the escape of him ?—ED.

23. **Countrey**] See for the pronunciation ' remembrance,' line 37 of preceding
scene. Small as the necessity seems to me to be to pronounce ' remembrance ' as a
quadrisyllable, the necessity here is even smaller to pronounce ' countrey ' as a trisyllable : ' count*ery*,' as ABBOTT (§ 477) and several modern editors assert that it is
pronounced. The line is broken. No actress would be tolerated who should so
hurriedly utter it as to indicate that the pronunciation *countery* can alone make it
rhythmical. Viola is trying to master her emotion, and the pause is long between
the thoughts of her brother and her inquiries about the country. In this pause, all
memory of the preceding rhythm is lost, so much so that were it retained, and the
accent thrown on ' thou,' it would be wrong ; it would imply that Viola cared only
for the Captain's own personal knowledge, and nothing for information from any one
else. The stress must fall on ' Know'st '; ' country ' will then remain a land to
be found in Geographies.—ED.

24. **bred and borne**] W. A. WRIGHT : It is remarkable that no one has proposed
to read ' born and bred,' in order to preserve the true sequence of events. [Probably,
the cause may be found in the fact that Shakespeare uses ' bred ' in the sense of
begotten (see many examples in Schmidt's *Lex.*). At the same time it is possible
that the phrase before us was mere carelessness on Shakespeare's part ; it is curiously
parallel to one of the examples given by Puttenham of what he calls *The Preposterous:*
' Ye haue another manner of disordered speach, when ye misplace your words or
clauses and set that before which should be behind, *et è conuerso,* we call it in English prouerbe, the cart before the horse, the Greeks call it *Histeron proteron,* we
name it the Preposterous, and if it be not too much vsed is tollerable inough, and
many times scarce perceiueable, vnlesse the sence be thereby made very absurd. . . .
One describing his landing vpon a strange coast, sayd thus preposterously, " When
we had climbde the clifs, and were a shore." Whereas he should haue said by good
order, " When vve vvere come a shore and clymed had the cliffs." For one must
be on land ere he can clime. And as another said : " My dame that bred me vp and
bare me in her vvombe." Whereas the bearing is before the bringing vp.'—*Arte
of English Poesie,* 1589, p. 181, ed. Arber. See also ' lack'd and lost.'—*Much
Ado,* IV, i, 228.—ED.]

Cap.   A noble Duke in nature, as in name.   27
Vio.   What is his name?

---

27. *A ... nature,*] Closing line 26,   27. *as in name.*] *As in his name* Han.
Han. Cap. Var. '03, '13, '21, Coll.   Cap. Var. '03, '13, '21.

27–37. In the division of these lines, KNIGHT's text conforms to that of the First Folio, for which Knight thus claims a superiority over the arrangement of Hanmer and the *Variorum* (see *Text. Notes*): 'We request the reader to look particularly at this part of the dialogue, beginning "Who governs here?" Is it not strictly metrical, and do not the three or four short lines that are thrown in render the question and answer rapid and spirited? It is printed exactly as in the original. But the passage has been jammed into the Procrustean bed of Steevens.' Knight is wise in submitting the question to 'the reader,' who is 'to look' at the passage. Such arrangements or division of lines are solely for 'readers' and for eyes, not for ears or for the stage.—ED.

27. **Duke**] WALKER (*Crit.* ii, 280) has an instructive Article on the *Confusion in sense of king, duke, and count:* In *Love's Lab. L.* II, i, 37, 'Who are the votaries, my loving lords, That are vow-fellows with this virtuous *duke?*' Everywhere else, I believe, he is styled by his proper title, *king.* So in *Twelfth N.* [in the present passage] Orsino is called *duke,* but in several,—perhaps in all,—other places, *count.* [Throughout the rest of the play, it is uniformly 'count,' but the prefixes of his speeches remain, as in the first scene, *Duke.*—ED.] In the *Two Gent.,* the personage who, throughout the rest of the play, is styled the *duke* of Milan, is in I, iii, 28, the *emperor,*—'his companion, youthful Valentine, Attends the emperor in his royal court:' [line 38 :—] 'I will dispatch him to the emperor's court': and II, iii, 5,—'I am going with Sir Proteus to the Imperial's court': for it is futile to attempt to distinguish between the two personages. [LETTSOM, Walker's Editor, has here the following footnote : 'The *emperor* is peculiar to the scenes laid at Verona, the *duke* to those laid at Milan. *Verona* occurs *twice* and *Padua* once for Milan. These negligences I suspect to be the author's.'] In III, i, 163, the duke says,—'But if thou linger in my territories Longer than swiftest expedition Will give thee time to leave our *royal* court.' *Tit. And.* III, i, 154, 'chop off your hand, And send it to the *king,*' in IV, iv, 81, 'King, be thy thoughts imperious, like thy name.' Here, however, the error was easy ; in the latter instance, hardly an error. By the way, III, i, 160, 'With all my heart, I'll send the emperor my hand': *qu.,*—'I'll send the *king* my hand.' *Emperor* occurs three times before. *Hamlet,* III, ii, dumb show,—'Enter a *King* and a *Queen,*' etc. *Ib.,* 'Gonzago is the *duke's* name';—Hamlet is here speaking ; and in the very same speech follows almost immediately,—'This is one Lucianus, nephew to the *king.*' Instances of the same in contemporary dramatists, and others : Beaumont and Fletcher, *Cupid's Revenge,* III, ii, speaking of Duke Leontius and his consort, 'the *duke* and *queen* will presently come forth to you.' In I, i, Leucippus, the heir to the dukedom of Lycia, says, 'I do not wish to know that fatal hour, That is to make me *king.*' In the latter part of Sidney's *Arcadia,* Basilius is called sometimes *king* and sometimes *duke. King, count,* and *duke* were one and the same to the poet, all involving alike the idea of sovereign power ; and thus might be easily confounded with each other in the memory. [This note of Walker silences, I think, Fleay's argument, (founded in part on this confusion of titles,) in favour of a twofold date of composition of the present play.—ED.]

Cap. Orſino.

Vio, Orſino : I haue heard my father name him. 30
He was a Batchellor then.

Cap. And ſo is now, or was ſo very late :
For but a month ago I went from hence,
And then 'twas freſh in murmure (as you know
What great ones do, the leſſe will prattle of,) 35
That he did ſeeke the loue of faire *Oliuia.*

Vio. What's ſhee ?

Cap. A vertuous maid, the daughter of a Count
That dide ſome tweluemonth ſince, then leauing her
In the protection of his ſonne, her brother, 40
Who ſhortly alſo dide : for whoſe deere loue

30. Orſino ·] Orſino ! Ff.
31–37. *He was ... ſhee ?*] Six lines, ending *now,...month...fresh...do,...seek ...she ?* Steev. Hal.
34. *murmure*] murmur F₄.
know] know, Theob.

39. *dide*] di'd Ff.
tweluemonth] twelve months Rowe, +.
41. *loue*] *loss* Walker, Dyce ii, iii, Huds.

29. **Orsino**] JOHNSON : I know not whether the nobility of the name is comprised in *duke*, or in *Orsino*, which is, I think, the name of a great Italian family.—HUNTER (i, 401) : It is plain that Shakespeare was acquainted with the antiquity of the Orsini family, which had recently been illustrated in a large work, devoted to the subject, by Sansovino. [See *Dramatis Personæ*, note on line 2.]

30, 31. THE COWDEN-CLARKES : Here is one of Shakespeare's subtle touches in dramatic art. By the mention of Viola's father having spoken of the duke, we are led to see the source of her interest in Orsino ; and by the word 'bachelor' we are made to see the peculiar nature of that interest. By the delicate indication of an already existing inclination on the part of the heroine for the hero of the play, the circumstance of her at once falling so deeply in love with him, on coming to know him personally, is most naturally and beautifully introduced. [But see Spedding's finer interpretation in note on line 59.—ED.]

32. **late**] For this adverbial use, see III, i, 38 ; V, i, 228.

34. **murmure**] DEIGHTON : The idea in 'murmur' is of their speaking with bated breath of a matter so much above their personal concern.

35. **great ones . . . the lesse**] It is by the evident reference to rank in this passage that we infer the same reference, and not to that of numbers, in the phrase 'more and less' in *Macb.* V, iv, 12, and elsewhere. See, if need be, ABBOTT, § 17.

37. **What's shee ?**] See also I, v, 115 : 'What is he at the gate, Cosin ?'—ABBOTT (§ 254) : In the Elizabethan and earlier periods, when the distinction between ranks was much more marked than now, it may have seemed natural to ask, as the first question about anyone, ' of what condition or rank is he ?' In that case the difference is one of *thought*, not of grammar. [It is a relief to find lines so stubbornly refractory to all rules of rhythm that they are allowed, perforce, to remain unmolested and are dubbed 'interjectional.' See ABBOTT, § 512.—ED.]

41. **deere loue**] WALKER (*Crit.* i, 285) : Read 'dear *losse*.' DYCE (ed. ii)

(They fay) fhe hath abiur'd the fight   42
And company of men.
   Vio.   O that I feru'd that Lady,
And might not be deliuered to the world   45

42, 43. *the fight And company*] Ff,
Rowe, +, Var. '73, '78, Knt, Hal. *the
company And fight* Han. et cet.
  42. *hath*] had Ff, Rowe.
  44. *O*] *o* Cap (corrected in Errata).

45. *deliuered*] Ff, Var. '03, '13, '21,
Coll. Wh. Cam. Rlfe, Dtn.   *deliver'd*
Rowe et cet.
  world] *world*, Rowe et seq.

adopted this change, and affirmed that it was 'made certain by other passages of
Shakespeare,' namely : ' and, portable To make the *dear loss*,' etc., *Temp.* V. i, 146 ;
' Were never orphans had so *dear* a *loss*,' *Rich. III:* II, ii, 77 ; ' Their *dear loss*,
The more of you 'twas felt,' etc., *Cymb.* V, v, 345. [If ' dear love ' were unintelligible, *dear loss* would be accepted with gratitude, but inasmuch as ' dear love ' is
almost irreproachable, the use by Shakespeare of *dear loss* in a hundred passages
ought not to justify its substitution here.—ED.]

  42, 43. **sight And company**] The anticlimax here, coupled with the defective
metre, led HANMER to transpose these words ; and he has been therein followed by
almost every modern editor. But the recollection of ' bred and born ' only a few
lines distant, and of ' lack'd and lost ' in *Much Ado* might reasonably give us pause.
The chiefest obstacle in the way of retaining the Folio text is the metre, which Hanmer's transposition certainly cures. WALKER, who doubts Hanmer's change, asks,
' Is there not something lost in ' line 42 ?—ED.

  45-47. JOHNSON : This is : I wish I might not be *made public* to the world, with
regard to the *state* of my birth and fortune, till I have gained a *ripe opportunity* for
my design. Viola seems to have formed a very deep design with very little premeditation ; she is thrown by shipwreck on an unknown coast, hears that the prince
is a bachelor, and resolves to supplant the lady whom he courts.—MALONE : In the
novel on which Shakespeare founded this play, the Duke Apolonius being driven by
a tempest on the isle of Cyprus, Silla, the daughter of the governor, falls in love
with him, and on his departure goes in pursuit of him. All this Shakespeare knew,
and probably intended in some future scene to tell, but afterwards forgot it. If this
were not the case, the impropriety censured by Dr Johnson must be accounted for
from the poet's having here, as in other places, sometimes adhered to the fable he
had in view, and sometimes departed from it. Viola, in a subsequent scene, plainly
alludes to her having been secretly in love with the duke. [See ' My Father had a
daughter,' etc., II, iv, 114, etc.]—BOSWELL : It would have been inconsistent with
Viola's delicacy to have made an open confession of her love for the Duke to the
Captain.—R. G. WHITE (*Sh.'s Scholar*, 282) : Malone's supposition, that Viola's
beautiful allusion to herself in the story which she tells the Duke of her pretended
sister, is an allusion to her ' *having been* secretly in love with him,' that is, of course,
in love with him before the play opens,—is too absurd to merit notice. Indeed,
indeed, the best part of Shakespeare was written in an unknown tongue to these
learned gentlemen. If there ever were an ingenuous, unsophisticated, unselfish
character portrayed, it is this very Viola,—Dr Johnson's ' excellent schemer,' who,
wretched and in want, forms that ' very deep design ' of supplanting a high-born
beauty, of whom she has never heard, in the affections of a man of princely rank,
whom she has never seen. [Johnson's paraphrase of these lines would have been

Till I had made mine owne occaſion mellow   46
What my eſtate is.
   Cap. That were hard to compaſſe,
Becauſe ſhe will admit no kinde of ſuite,
No, not the Dukes.   50
   Vio. There is a faire behauiour in thee Captaine,
And though that nature, with a beauteous wall
Doth oft clo ſe in pollution : yet of thee
I will beleeue thou haſt a minde that ſuites   54

---

46. *mellow*] Ff, Rowe, +, Wh. Ktly.   Cam. *show* Gould.
mellow, Han. et cet. *fellow* Anon. ap.   53. *clo ſe in*] *close-in* Dyce ii, iii.

---

fair enough had not his judgement been distorted by his assumption that Viola was a 'schemer,' therefore it is that he paraphrased 'made mine own occasion mellow' by 'a ripe opportunity for my design.' The occasion to be mellowed was not a design upon the Duke, but a proper time for revealing her birth and estate. Attention has been called to the recurrence of the same phrase in *Love's Lab. L.* IV, ii, 72 : 'These are begot in the ventricle of memory . . . and delivered upon the mellowing of occasion,' or, in other words, delivered when the time was exactly ripe ; just as Antonio tells Bassanio to 'stay the very riping of the time' at Belmont.—*Mer. of Ven.* II, viii, 43. Thus here, Viola has no intention of remaining always a page, but only until in her own judgement the time was ripe for disclosing her true station. ABBOTT (§ 290), in a list of verbs formed from nouns and adjectives, gives 'mellow,' in the present passage, as a transitive verb, which, unless it means that its object is the phrase 'What my estate is,' I do not understand. It appears to me that 'mellow' is no verb but a simple predicate adjective ; and the construction of 'What my estate is' (that is, *as to* what my estate is) is the same as in *Hamlet*, I, i, 33 (pointed out by W. A. WRIGHT) : 'And let us once again assail your ears, That are so fortified against our story, What we two nights have seen.' Again I must refer to Spedding's excellent vindication of Viola's character ; line 59, below.—ED.]

45. **And might**] HANMER reads 'And '*t* might,' which is good. Possibly, it is unnecessary to insert the '*t ;* it may be faintly but sufficiently heard in the final *d* of 'And.'—ED.

45. **deliuered**] R. G. WHITE (ed. i) objects to the contracted form *deliver'd*, whereby 'the variety of a rhythm, often introduced by Shakespeare in the third foot, is lost.'

52. **though that**] See 'If that,' I, v, 308 ; 'Least that,' III, iv, 349 ; 'If that,' V, i, 387 ; 'When that,' V, i, 409 ; and for additional examples, where 'that' is a conjunctional affix, see, if needful, ABBOTT, § 287.

52, 53. **nature . . . pollution**] W. A. WRIGHT : The same sentiment occurs again in III, iv, 370, 371. [Compare, also, *Sonnets* 93 and 95.]

54. **will**] WALKER (*Crit.* iii, 83) : *Well*, I imagine. [Walker calls attention to what he considers the same misprint, in the Folio, of 'will' for *well*, twice in *Mer. Wives*, I, iii, 56 : 'He hath studied her will, and translated her will,' etc. In a note on this passage DYCE adds : 'Since what I *will* intend,' etc., *Lear* I, i, 224 ; and 'If but as *will* I other accents borrow,' *Ib.* I, iv, 1. As to the passage from the *Mer. Wives*, editors are by no means agreed that 'will' is a misprint ; and as to the present passage, Walker's change, good as it is, seems to have commended itself to no one but Hudson.—ED.]

With this thy faire and outward charra&ter.   55
I prethee (and Ile pay thee bounteoufly)
Conceale me what I am, and be my ayde,
For fuch difguife as haply fhall become
The forme of my intent.   Ile ferue this Duke,   59

57. *ayde,*] *aide.* F$_3$F$_4$.

---

57. Conceale me what I am] See, also, ' I see you what you are,' I, v, 247.
In WALKER'S Article VI. (*Crit.* i, 68) many examples are given of a construction
similar to this, such as : ' I know you what you are,'—*Lear*, I, i, 268 ; ' I will proclaim myself what I am.'—*Mer. Wives*, III, v, 146, etc.—ABBOTT (§ 414) : Instead
of saying ' I know what you are,' in which the object of the verb ' I know ' is the
clause ' what you are,' Shakespeare frequently introduces before the dependent clause
another object, so as to make the dependent clause a mere explanation of the object.

59. Ile . . . Duke] JOHNSON : Viola is an excellent schemer, never at a loss ;
if she cannot serve the lady, she will serve the duke.—HALLAM (iii, 561) : Viola
would be more interesting, if she had not indelicately, as well as unfairly towards
Olivia, determined to win the Duke's heart before she had seen him.—SPEDDING
(*Fraser's Maga.* Aug. 1865) : To us the words convey no such meaning, but imply
rather the very contrary.   And the question is worth examining ; for our conception
of Viola's very nature, and with it the spirit of every scene in which she subsequently appears, and the complexion of the whole play, depends on the answer.
How then stands the case ?   Viola has just escaped from shipwreck, having lost her
twin brother,—her only natural protector,—and everything else except her purse
with a little money in it.   A beautiful, high-bred girl, alone in a strange country,—
what is she to do ?   Where is she to lodge ?   How to procure food ?   The captain
and the sailors are kind and respectful, but they are poor men, and have been
wrecked as well as she.   But she has sense and courage and character and accomplishments, and addresses herself at once to meet the difficulty.   For a lady of her
birth and breeding, the court was the natural place to look to for shelter and sympathy ; and she asks who is governor.   Duke Orsino.   Orsino !   She remembered
the name ; she had heard her father speak of him.   But ' he was a bachelor then,'
she adds ; thinking no doubt that if he were still a bachelor there would be no
female court ; therefore no fit place for her.   Hearing that he was not married, but
going to be, her next most natural resource would be the lady he was going to marry,
—a lady, it seemed, well suited to her case ; for she also was an orphan maid, mourning the recent loss of an only brother ; and it was only on learning that there was no
chance of obtaining access to her, that she resolved to disguise her sex and seek service
at the court in the character of a page.   This would provide for her immediate
necessity ; and for her next step she would wait till she saw her way.   There is not the
shadow of a reason for supposing that in wishing to serve either Olivia or the Duke
she had any other motive or design ; the suggestion of which is the more unjustifiable
and unaccountable, because in all her subsequent intercourse between them (though
she had *then* come to have a very deep and painful interest of her own in the matter)
she shows herself as fair and loyal, as unselfish, as tenderly considerate towards both,
as it is possible for a woman to be.   Three days of confidential communication in so
tender an argument as unrequited love had kindled indeed in her own breast a love
which could not hope and did not ask for requital.   But where are the traces of

Thou ſhalt preſent me as an Eunuch to him,   60
It may be worth thy paines : for I can ſing,
And ſpeake to him in many ſorts of Muſicke,
That will allow me very worth his ſeruice.
What elſe may hap, to time I will commit,
Onely ſhape thou thy ſilence to my wit.   65
   Cap.   Be you his Eunuch, and your Mute Ile bee,
When my tongue blabs, then let mine eyes not ſee.
   Uio.   I thanke thee : Lead me on.   *Exeunt*   68

design, or intrigue, or endeavour to use opportunities for her own advantage? Out
of the experience of her own sad and hopeless passion she borrows imagery and
eloquence to set forth her master's; and the sincerity with which she does it is
proved by the effect. . . . What she had to do she did with perfect loyalty and
good faith; her own love,—though restlessly struggling to utter itself,—remaining to
the last her own sad secret.

60. **Eunuch**] MALONE: The first regular opera, as Dr Burney observes to me,
was performed at Florence in 1600: 'Till about 1635, musical dramas were only
performed occasionally in the palaces of princes, and consequently before that time
eunuchs could not abound. The first eunuch that was suffered to sing in the Pope's
chapel, was in the year 1600.' Compare *Mid. N. D.* V, i, 51: 'The battell with
the Centaurs to be sung By an Athenian Eunuch, to the Harpe.'

62. **speake**] DEIGHTON: Compare *Hamlet*, III, ii, 374, 'it will discourse most
eloquent music.'

63. **allow**] W. A. WRIGHT: That is, approve, cause to be acknowledged. So
'allowance' is used in the sense of acknowledgement or approval in *Tro. & Cress.*
II, iii, 146: 'A stirring dwärf we do allowance give Before a sleeping giant.' The
two senses of 'allow,' to assign, and to approve, are due to the different sources from
which it is derived: the former being from the Low Latin *allocare*, the latter from
allaudare. See IV, ii, 60.

66. **Mute**] SCHMIDT (*Lex.*): In Turkey a dumb officer acting as executioner.
[It is not easy to see the appropriateness of such an officer on the present occasion.—ED.]—DEIGHTON: The mention of 'eunuch' brings into the Captain's
mind the thought of the 'mutes,' dumb attendants in the Turkish harems, and he
promises to perform her behest as faithfully as the mutes performed those of the
sultan. [It is not so much fidelity in service that Viola requires, as concealment of
her disguise. I doubt that the employment of mutes is restricted to the harem. We
all of us remember our *Talisman.*—ED.]

68. There is, to me, something very touching in this submissive appeal, 'Lead me
on,' although it is not an uncommon phrase.—ED.

Scæna Tertia.

Enter Sir Toby, and Maria.   2

Sir To. What a plague meanes my Neece to take the
death of her brother thus ? I am ſure care's an enemie to
life.   5

Mar. By my troth ſir *Toby*, you muſt come in earlyer
a nights : your Coſin, my Lady, takes great exceptions
to your ill houres.

To. Why let her except, before excepted.   9

2. Olivia's House. Rowe.

7. *a nights*] Ff. *a-nights* Rowe ii, +.
o' nights Cap. et seq.

your] *youe* F₂.

7. *Coſin*] *Neice* Rowe ii, +.   *cousin*
Cap. et seq.

9. *except, before*] Ff, Rowe, +, Cap.
Cam. Dtn.   *except before* Han. et cet.

3. **a plague**] ABBOTT (§ 24) : In the expressions 'What a plague ?'—*1 Hen.
IV :* I, ii, 51 ; 'What a devil ?'—*Ib.* IV, ii, 56 ; 'A God's name,' *Rich. II :* II, i,
251, and the like, we must suppose *a* to mean *in, on,* or *of.* [See ' I love a ballet
in print, a life,'— *Wint. Tale,* IV, iv, 288, which is, however, hardly to be placed
in the same list with the foregoing.]

4, 5. **I am . . . life**] Possibly, Sir Toby's anxiety for his niece's life is not
altogether unselfish.—ED.

7. **a nights**] Ever since Capell's edition, this 'a nights' has been changed,
needlessly, I think, to *o' nights.* In the eighth division under *A,* as a preposition,
DR MURRAY (*N. E. D.*) gives : ' Time : in, on, by ; as *a day, a night, an eve, a
morrow, a Monday, a doom's day.* Occasionally prefixed to Old English adverbial
genitives, giving *a nights, now-a-days.*' Among the quotations, is given, ' Let me
haue men about me . . . such as sleepe a nights.'—*Jul. Cæs.* I, ii, 193, where, as
here, Capell led the change to *o' nights.* For *o' nights,* see, if need be, ABBOTT,
§ 182.—ED.

7. **Cosin**] See note on line 7 of *Dramatis Personæ.*

9. **except, before excepted**] FARMER (*Var.* '78) : This should probably be ' *as*
before excepted.' [This emendation would have been hardly worth the noting here in
the Commentary, had not HUNTER (i, 401) approved of it, and RANN, SINGER, and
KEIGHTLEY adopted it.] A ludicrous use of the formal law phrase. RITSON (*Rem.*
63) : The ingenious critic might have spared his remark ; the ' formal law phrase '
being more usually as in the text.—MALONE : It is the usual language of leases :
' To have and to hold the said demised premises, etc. with their and every of their
rights, members, etc. (except before excepted).'—W. A. WRIGHT : Sir Toby's
drunken repartees are intentionally not much to the point. BULLOCH (p. 109) :
An alteration of punctuation, and the addition of the definite article in an elided
form will throw all the light necessary for the due understanding the meaning of
the witty knight :—'let her except—before th' excepted.' Sir Toby wishes to speak
his mind, but not so as to offend his niece ; he pauses, and then blurts out a cut at the
position of his interlocutor, a servant ! In conformity with these remarks, the meaning of his answer will be,—Why let her say so—and to myself. [Had Bulloch's

Ma. I, but you muſt confine your ſelfe within the   10
modeſt limits of order.

To. Confine? Ile confine my ſelfe no finer then I am :
theſe cloathes are good enough to drinke in, and ſo bee
theſe boots too : and they be not, let them hang themſelues in their owne ſtraps.   15

Ma. That quaffing and drinking will vndoe you : I
heard my Lady talke of it yeſterday : and of a fooliſh
knight that you brought in one night here, to be hir woer

To. Who, Sir *Andrew Ague-cheeke* ?

Ma. I he.   20

To. He's as tall a man as any's in Illyria.

Ma. What's that to th'purpoſe ?

To. Why he ha's three thouſand ducates a yeare,   23

---

10. *I...the*] Line spaced to full width in Ff.

14. *and*] Ff, Rowe. *if* Pope, Han. *an* Theob. et cet.

18. *woer*] *wooer.* F₂. *wooer ?* F₃F₄, Rowe, Pope.

19. Ague-cheeke] *Aguecheek* Dyce, Cam. Sta. Rlfe, Huds.

21. *any's*] *any* Pope, Han.

22. *th'*] Ff, Rowe,+, Wh. i. *the* Cap. et cet.

23. *ha's*] *has* F₃F₄.

---

emendation been restricted to the *Text. Notes*, his meaning could not have been understood. Hence the sole reason why his explanation is given here in full.—ED.]

11. **modest**] That is, moderate. See IV, ii, 35.

16. **quaffing**] W. A. WRIGHT : That is, drinking deep. Palsgrave (*Lesclarcisse-ment de la Langue Francoyse*) has ' I quaught, I drinke all ont. *Ie boys dautant.*' Etymologically it is connected with the Scottish *quaigh* or *quaff*, a drinking-cup.

21. **tall**] In a note on *Every Man in his Humour*, IV, v, p. 124, GIFFORD remarks, 'There is scarcely a writer of Jonson's age who does not frequently use "tall" in the sense of *bold* or *courageous*.' See *Wint. Tale*, V, ii, 164 ; also, 'Jemy, who was, as you have heard, a tall low man,' etc. (*i. e.* a courageous man of low stature).—Armin's *Nest of Ninnies*, 1608, p. 21, ed. Sh. Soc. Again, ' If he can kil a man, and dare rob vpon the highway, he is called a tall man, and a valiant man of his hands,' etc.—Northbrooke's *Treatise against Dicing, Dancing*, etc., about 1577, p. 8, ed. Sh. Soc.—ED.

22. **th'**] After adhering to the Folio in Maria's colloquial ' What's,' is there any good reason for deserting it in the equally colloquial ' to th'purpose '?—ED.

23. **three thousand ducates**] KARL ELZE (p. 157) calls attention to the fact that this is also the amount of Shylock's bond ; and, again, the same amount is offered as a reward for the discovery of the murderer of Ferdinando in *Soliman and Perseda*, 1599, Act II, p. 308, ed. Hazlitt-Dodsley. [Of course the identity of the sums is merely haphazard. Possibly, alliteration may have had some influence in the choice of the numeral.—ED.]

23. **ducates**] MURRAY (*N. E. D.* s. v.) : Used as the name of a silver coin issued in 1140 by Roger II. of Sicily, as Duke of Apulia, bearing the inscription R DX AP, i. e. *Rogerus Dux Apuliæ ;* according to Falcone de Benevento ' monetam suam intro-duxit, unam vero, cui Ducatus nomen imposuit ' (Du Cange, s. v.). In 1202, it

Ma. I, but hee'l haue but a yeare in all thefe ducates :
He's a very foole, and a prodigall.   25

*To.*Fie,that you'l fay fo : he playes o'th Viol-de-gamboys, and fpeaks three or four languages word for word
without booke,& hath all the good gifts of nature.

Ma. He hath indeed, almoſt naturall : for befides that   29

26. *o'th*] Ff. *o'th'* Rowe,+, Ran.
Mal. Wh. i. *o'the* Cap. et cet.

26, 27. *Viol-de-gamboys*] *Viol-de-
gambo* Rowe, Pope, Theob. i, Han.
Cap. Var. Ran. Mal. Steev. *Viol-*

degambo Theob. ii. Warb. Johns.

29. *indeed, almoſt*] *indeed,—all most*
Upton, Coll. ii, iii (MS), Dyce ii, iii,
Huds.

---

appears (Pappadopoli, *Moneta di Venetia*, 1893, 81) as the name of a Venetian silver
coin, usually known as the *grosso*. In 1284, the first gold ducat, also called *zecchino
d'oro*, was struck at Venice under the doge John Dandolo. This coin, worth about
9s., bears on one side figures of St. Mark and the Doge, and on the other a figure of
Christ with the legend 'Sit tibi Christe datus quem tu regis iste ducatus'; this,
though it did not originate, may have contributed to spread the name, which was
subsequently applied to the gold coins of various European countries.—HALLIWELL
quotes from Roberts's *Marchant's Mapp of Commerce*, 1638, At Venice there were
'two sorts of duccats, the one currant in payment, which may bee valued ster. about
3s. 4d., and the other of banco, which may be valued about 4s. or 4s. 2d., as the
exchange will admit, the one being twenty per cent. better than the other.'—W. A.
WRIGHT : Cotgrave says of 'all foraine coynes . . . no certaine interpretation can
be giuen, other than that they hold a rate much about v. or vjs. sterl. the peece.'
Coryat, who visited Venice in 1608, tells us that the ducat was worth 4s. 8d.—*Crudities*, ed. 1611, pp. 228, 253. [Lastly, ROLFE tells us that 'the value of the Venetian
silver ducat was about that of the American dollar.' Even this assertion is somewhat vague ; in these times, the 'American dollar' needs the qualification of gold or
silver. The exchangeable value of money is so fluctuating from age to age that it is
fairly impossible to give any precise modern equivalent of any given coin. It ought
surely to suffice us, at least in reading Shakespeare, to take Shylock's word for it
that 'three thousand ducats' is 'a good round sum.'—ED.]

26, 27. **Viol-de-gamboys**] GIFFORD (*Every Man out of his Humour*, III, iii,
p. 125) : It appears, from numerous passages in our old plays, that a viol de gambo
(a bass-viol, as Jonson calls it, in a subsequent passage) was an indispensable piece
of furniture in every fashionable house, where it hung up in the best chamber, much
as the guitar does in Spain, and the violin in Italy, to be played on at will, and to
fill up the void of conversation. Whoever pretended to fashion, affected an acquaintance with this instrument.—W. A. WRIGHT : A base-viol, or violoncello. Florio
(*Italian Dict.*) has : 'Viola di Gamba, a Violl de Gamba, because men hold it
betweene or vpon their legges.'

29. **almost**] UPTON'S suggestion of *all, most* is to me an *emendatio certissima*.
Sir Toby has just said that Sir Andrew 'hath *all* the good gifts of nature,' 'he hath
indeed,' retorts Maria, '*all*, most natural,' that is, in effect, all, most like a natural,
an idiot. Would it accord with the drift of Maria's speech, to represent her, after
pronouncing, in line 25, Sir Andrew 'a very fool,' as saying here that he was 'almost
a fool'? We have a misprint precisely similar, in the Qq and Ff of *Mid. N. D.*
IV, i, 47 (of this ed.) : 'Fairies be gone, and be alwaies away ' where every modern

he's a foole, he's a great quarreller : and but that hee hath   30
the gift of a Coward, to allay the guſt he hath in quarrelling, 'tis thought among the prudent, he would quickely
haue the gift of a graue.

    Tob. By this hand they are ſcoundrels and ſubſtra-
ctors that ſay ſo of him.   Who are they *?*   35

    Ma. They that adde moreour, hee's drunke nightly
in your company.

    To. With drinking healths to my Neece : Ile drinke   38

34, 35. *ſubſtractors*] *subtractors*   36. *that adde moreour*] *add, more-*
Theob. ii, Warb. Johns. Var. '73, '78,   *over, that* Anon. ap. Cam.
Ran. Knt.

---

editor, except WHITE, COLLIER, and HUDSON, has followed THEOBALD in reading,
as it should be, ' *all ways* away.'—ED.

    31. **gust**] E. A. MEREDITH (1863, p. 44) : I venture to propose a slight verbal
emendation, the substitution, namely, of *gift* for ' gust.' Maria is particularising
Sir Andrew's ' gifts ' : ' For besides that he is a fool, he is a great quarreller.'
Quarrelling is plainly one of the gifts. But she goes on to say, the gift of quarrelling is happily qualified by another gift, cowardice. 'And but he hath the *gift* of
a coward to allay the *gift* he hath in quarrelling, 'tis thought among the prudent he would quickly have the *gift* of a grave.' The iteration of ' gift ' is perfectly
Shakespearian. Whereas the introduction of ' gust ' comes in like a discord in a
passage of music and weakens the point of Maria's rejoinder. [TIESSEN, in 1877,
made the same emendation, which is undoubtedly plausible, but, apart from the rule
that where the text makes good sense it must not be molested, there is a difficulty of
construction ; ' gift ' should be followed by ' of ' ; we have ' the gift of a coward,'
' the gift of a grave,' and we ought to have ' the gift *of* quarrelling,' but it is the
' gust *in* quarrelling ' ; which proves, I think, that the text should stand.—ED.]

    33. **gift of a graue**] LOCKE RICHARDSON : What Maria means,—speaking in
the name of ' the prudent ' (provident,—) is that, at the breakneck speed at which
this ' prodigal ' is making ducks and drakes of his patrimony, the fool and his money
will be soon parted, and that, if his quarrelsome temper could only get the start of
his cowardice, he would quickly come to grief in a duel, and, there being no assets
for funeral expenses, be buried as a *pauper*,—at the cost of the *parish*. He would
thus literally have ' the *gift* of a grave.' Maria's gibe is almost an exact parallel to
Gratiano's : ' thy wealth being forfeit to the State, Thou hast not left the value of a
cord ; Therefore thou must be hang'd at the State's charge.'

    34. **By this hand**] Malvolio also swears by his ' hand,' II, iii, **122** ;—a common
oath.

    34, 35. **substractors**] THEOBALD did not show his usual insight if he changed
this spelling intentionally. Were change needed he might as well have spelled it
detractors at once, which is evidently what Sir Toby means. But I doubt that Theobald intended any new reading at all. He calls no attention to it ; it was, I think,
merely a typographical oversight. *Subtractors* has been erroneously attributed to
Warburton, who has quite enough to answer for, without having this in addition.
Both Warburton and Johnson printed from Theobald's Second Edition, wherein
subtractors is found ; they blindly ' followed copy.'—ED.

to her as long as there is a paſſage in my throat, & drinke
in Illyria : he's a Coward and a Coyſtrill that will not   40

39. *there is*] *there's* Pope ii, Theob.   40. *Coyſtrill*] *Kestrel* Han. *Coistrel*
Warb. Johns. Var. Mal. Steev.   Dyce.

---

40. **Coystrill**] Inasmuch as (according to DR MURRAY) *Coistrel* is an obsolete
form of *Kestrel*, the elder commentators were thereby misled, and interpreted 'Coystrill' in the present passage as a worthless coward hawk, unfit for training.   Even
MADDEN accepts this view, and on p. 159 says : 'Shakespeare had a true falconer's
contempt for "kites That bate and beat and will not be obedient,"—(*Tam. of the
Shr.* IV, i, 198) and also for the worthless kestrel or staniel.   This hawk was sometimes trained.   But it was lacking in courage, and was allotted by the old writers to
the knave or servant.'   Hereupon follows, as an example, the present passage.
TOLLET was, possibly, the earliest to detect the meaning which is now generally
accepted.   He defined it as 'a paltry groom, one only fit to carry arms, but not to
use them.'   This meaning he obtained from certain passages, which he quotes from
Holinshed ; but it is not worth while to repeat them here, inasmuch as they are quoted
more fully by W. A. WRIGHT, whose excellent note is as follows : '*a coystrill*, a
knave.   Literally a menial servant or groom ; perhaps from the French *coustillier*,
who was armed with a knife or poniard.   Palsgrave has "Coustrell that wayteth on
a speare—*covsteillier*."   The word appears to have become degraded in meaning,
and in the sixteenth century denoted the lowest kind of camp followers, as will be
seen from the passages of Holinshed to which Tollet refers.   For instance, in Harrison's *Description of England* (Holinshed, i, 162) : "They [esquires] were at the
first *costerels* or bearers of armes of barons or knights."   And in *The Historie of
Scotland* (ii, 89) : "But such coisterels, and other as remained with the Scotish
cariage, seeing the discomfiture of their aduersaries, ran foorth and pursued them
into those marishes."   Again (p. 127) : "Brudus . . . appointed all the horses that
were in the campe, seruing for burden, to be bestowed among the women, lackies,
and coistrels."   In the same book (p. 217) we find enumerated together "cariage-
men, coistrels, women, and lackies."   That "coystrell" was a boy or groom in
attendance upon the horses is clear from Holinshed, iii, 248, where it is said : "A
knight with his esquire, and coistrell with his two horsses, might scarse be com-
petentlie found for two shillings in siluer."   In the Latin of Matthew Paris this is,
"Ita ut quidam jejunus vix poterat miles cum suo armigero et *garcione* et equis
duobus solidis argenteorum competenter sustentari ;" where *garcio* is the French
garçon.   The etymology of the word is doubtful.   If "coustrell" and "coystrill"
are identical, it would appear that Palsgrave derived them from the French *coustillier*,
[see MURRAY *post*.—ED.], but there is another Old French word *costeraux*, a kind
of banditti, with which they may be connected.   Cotgrave has "Costereauls.   A
nickname giuen vnto certaine footmen, that serued the kings of England in their
French warres ; or as Cotereaux ; or Cottereaux."   The former of these equivalents
he defines as "A certaine crue of peasantlie outlawes, who, in old time, did much
mischiefe vnto the Nobilitie, and Clergie."   The Old English *quistron* (Scotch
custroun), which Tyrwhitt defines as a scullion, is a kindred word.   In *The
Romaunt of the Rose*, [line] 886, "This god of love of his fashion Was like no knave
ne quistron," corresponds to the French of the *Roman de la Rose*, "Li Diex d' Amors
de la façon, Ne resembloit mie garçon": which shows that *garçon* and *quistron* are
related as *garcio* and *coistrell* above, and that *quistron* = *coistrell* = *coustrell* = groom

drinke to my Neece. till his braines turne o'th toe, like a
parifh top. What wench? *Caſtiliano vulgo*:for here coms   42

41. *o'th*] *o'th'* F₃F₄. *o'the* Cap. et seq.
42. Caſtiliano vulgo] *Castellano vulgar* Trumbull.

42. vulgo] *volto* Han. Warb. Cap.
Ran. Sing. i, Dyce ii, iii, Coll. iii, Huds.
volgo Johns. Var. '73, '78.

---

or menial servant.'—MURRAY (*N. E. D.* s. v. *Custrel*): This coincides in meaning
with Old French *coustillier, -illeur*, literally a soldier armed with a *coustille*, hence,
'an esquire of the bodie, an armour-bearer vnto a knight, the seruant of a man at
armes; also, a groome of a stable.' (Cotgrave). But the regular English representative of this would be *custeler custlar*, and it is not easy to account for the
metathesis of this to *custrel*. The secondary sense 'knave, base fellow' (commoner
in the variant *coistrel*) is not found with French *coustillier*, and seems to have arisen
from association with *Custron*. [CUSTRON is given by DR MURRAY as 'the adopted
form of Old French *coistron, coestron, quistron, coitron*, in nominative case *questres,
quaistre*, scullion, a regular phonetic descendant of late Latin, *cocistrōnem*, nominative *cocistro* "tabernarius" (Papias); and means a scullion, a kitchen-knave; hence
a boy or lad of low birth, base-born fellow, "cad," vagabond.'
Wherefore, the sum appears to be that *Custrel*, whereof Sir Toby used the commoner variant 'coystrel,' was corrupted by evil communication with *Custron*, and
as Dr Murray has given us the meaning of *custron*, we can, with his help, paraphrase, in the vernacular of today, Sir Toby's assertion: that he who will not drink
to his niece is a coward and a cad.—ED.]
41. **o'th**] It is not easy to decide whether this *o'* is an elision of *on* or *of*. It is,
probably, *on*, I think; on the analogy of 'turning on his heels.'—ED.
42. **parish top**] STEEVENS: A large top was formerly kept in every village, to
be whipped in frosty weather, that the peasants may be kept warm by exercise, and
out of mischief, while they could not work. Compare Fletcher's *Night Walker*,
'And dances like a town-top and reels and hobbles.' [I, iii.]—NARES (s. v.
Parish-top) quotes Fletcher's *Thierry and Theodoret*, 'a boy of twelve Should
scourge him hither like a parish-top, And make him dance before you.' [II, iv.];
Jonson's *The New Inn*, 'A merry Greek, and cants in Latin comely, Spins like the
parish top.' [II, ii.]; and adds, 'Evelyn, speaking of the uses of willow wood,
among other things made of it, mentions "great town-topps."'—*Silva* [Bk. i, xx,
28.—HALLIWELL gives many quotations referring to 'town-tops' and 'parish-
tops,' mainly from the Dramatists of the Restoration. He says, 'an example of
a parish-top has not presented itself'; but he gives us, from an ancient illuminated MS, an enlightening picture of two boys whipping a top.—ED.]—KNIGHT:
This 'parish-top,' provided for the amusement of the peasants in frosty weather,
presents a curious illustration of the mitigating influences of social kindness in an
age of penal litigation. Whilst 'Poor Tom' was 'whipped from tithing to tithing,'
he had his May-games, and his Christmas hospitalities, and his parish-top, if he
remained at home. [After quoting Steevens, as above, Knight proceeds] 'We
rather believe that our ancestors were too much accustomed to rely upon other expe-
dients, such as the halter and the stocks, for keeping the peasants out of mischief.
But yet, with all the sternness which they called justice, the higher classes of society
had an honest desire to promote the spirit of enjoyment amongst their humbler
fellow-men; and they looked not only without disdain, but with a real sympathy,
upon 'the common recreations of the countryfolks.'—LOCKE RICHARDSON, who

[42. parish top]

detected in ' the gift of a grave' an allusion to a burial at the expense of the parish, conceives that by a subtle association of ideas, probably quite unconsciously on Sir Toby's part, Sir Toby here is led to refer to 'the *parish* top'; more especially because in the year 1601, the year when *Twelfth Night* was performed, there was enacted the so-called 'famous statute,'—the earliest under which, by parochial taxation, practical measures for the relief of the poor were adopted, and, consequently, parishes and parish matters were greatly in men's mouths.

42. **Castiliano vulgo**] HANMER (whose text reads *volto*) : By *Castilian countenance* here he means her *best*, her *most civil* and *courtly looks*, which he bids her put on because Sir Andrew is coming. WARBURTON says that *Castiliano volto* means 'grave, solemn looks'; and accuses Hanmer of having 'taken' from him the emendation, *volto*. This claim must rest on Warburton's assertion. Hanmer is, certainly in general, scrupulous in giving credit to the authors of the emendations he adopted, and he makes no mention of Warburton here. The emendation, such as it is, is by no means beyond Hanmer's capacity. CAPELL adopted it, but explains it differently, and, as he affirms, better, thus : ' " What wench ? bridle up your chin and look big, for here comes Sir Andrew Ague-face,'' humorously corrupting the name in this place, as who should say—for here comes one who has no *face* to look big with ; but of this humour editors had no perception.'—STEEVENS : I meet with the word *Castilian* and *Castilians* in several of the old Comedies. It is difficult to assign any peculiar propriety to it, unless it was adopted immediately after the defeat of the Armada, and became a cant term capriciously expressive of jollity or contempt. In *The Merry Devil of Edmonton*, the Host says, 'Ha ! my Castilian dialogues' [p. 226, ed. Hazlitt-Dodsley]. In *Look about You*, 1600, it is joined with another toper's exclamation, very frequent in Shakespeare : 'And Rivo will he cry and Castile too' [Scene xxxiii, *ad fin.* ed. Hazlitt-Dodsley]. Again, in Marlowe's *Jew of Malta*, ' Hey, *Rivo Castiliano!* a man's a man.' [Act IV, p. 325, ed. Dyce.]—SINGER : Warburton proposed *volto*. . . . I have met with a passage in Hall's *Satires*, Bk. iv, Sat. 2, which I think places this beyond a doubt : ' There, soon as he can kiss his hand in gree [*i. e.* kindness] And with good grace bow it below the knee, Or make a Spanish face with fauning cheere,' etc. The Spaniards were in high estimation for courtesy, though the natural gravity of the national countenance was thought to be a cloak for villany. The *Castiliano volto* was in direct opposition to the *viso sciolto* which the noble Roman told Sir Henry Wootton would go safe over the world. Sir Toby seems to parody the phrase intentionally,—as *vulgo* hints rudely at language, and it was Maria's tongue, not her countenance, that he calls on her to restrain. [The attentive reader can hardly fail to note the discrepancy between the first sentences of Singer's note and the last. After having said that Warburton's *volto* was undoubtedly right, he proceeds to remark that Sir Toby said ' vulgo,' and so, in his Second Edition, he retains ' vulgo' in his text. It is not my office to explain such vagaries in editors ; *Davus sum, non Œdipus.*—ED.]—COLLIER : Sir Toby probably uses this as a drinking exclamation.—HALLIWELL : If these words mean anything, and it is hardly necessary to construe all Sir Toby's phrases, they may imply merely a hint to Maria to talk in common Spanish, that is, in familiar language.—STAUNTON observes in reference to the grave looks which Warburton says the phrase implies, ' but Maria appears already to have been more serious than suited Sir Toby's humour.'—W. A. WRIGHT : It is probable that these words have as much meaning now as they had in Shakespeare's time, and that is none at all. They would make a great noise in a drink-

[42. Castiliano vulgo]

ing-bout, and thus serve the only purpose for which they were used.—BR. NICHOL-SON (*N. & Qu.* 7th S. xi, p. 403, 1891) : 'Vulgo' is mere nonsense, while *velo*, seemingly the only other probable substitute, is not as good as *volto*. This change, however,—which, to be still more correct, should be spelt *Castiglione volto*,—would, I think, have been more universally accepted, had the action involved been better understood and made clearer to the reader by a stage-direction and a slight alteration in the punctuation. . . . But granting that [Maria has been, as Staunton says] too serious for Sir Toby, the stage action that seems to me to follow . . . is peculiarly fitted to dispel that seriousness. . . . Sir Toby says, ' He's a coward and a coystrill that will not drink to my niece till his brains turn o'th' toe like a parish top.' Being a man of humour, and it being now late, or more likely early in the morning, and he a man fond of drink, and for both reasons willing to indulge himself with Maria, he seizes the occasion, suits the action to the word, pirouettes o'th' toe, and while so doing places his arm round Maria, turns her also, and while so embracing her, kisses her. I have said that this or some such toying is necessary, because other-wise his ' What, wench !' has no meaning. The phrase points to some attempt on his part, and is in rebuke, loving or otherwise, of her (affected) maidenly coyness. Suddenly, however, espying Sir Andrew in the near distance (off the stage), he stops short, disengages himself, and cries in a lowered tone, ' Castiglione volto, for here comes Sir Andrew Agueface.' That she does put on her Spanish look of sedateness and reserve,—while, perhaps, hastily putting to rights her disordered head-gear,—is shown by Sir Andrew's greeting, ' Bless you, fair shrew !' Sir Toby, too, purposely calls him ' Sir Andrew Agueface,' because he cannot help a chuckle as he thinks how shocked a look this country knight will put on if he have observed these doings of the hitherto, in his presence, reserved, distant, and even shrewish-looking Maria. [Does not Sir Andrew see Maria now for the first time ? This is, apparently, only his second visit to Olivia's house.—ED.] . . . Hence, then, there is required, as seems to me, some such direction after ' parish top' as [*Embracing her while con-tinuing his parish-top gyrations, and after a feigned resistance kisses her*]. Also after ' wench !' a dash, denoting his sudden stop, while the near approach of Sir Andrew requires a comma after *volto*, rather than a colon or a semicolon. [First, it is always perilous to meddle with the speeches of a character like Sir Toby. Sec-ondly, it is very far from likely that the compositors were such masters of Italian as to be able, in case an Italian word were misheard, to substitute another and perfectly correct word in that language,—if they had misheard *volto*, it is not likely that they would have deviated to ' vulgo.' Thirdly, it is an assumption, wholly gratuitous, that *Castiliano volto* means a ' grave, solemn countenance,' or ' most civil and courtly looks '; no other instance of the phrase has been found which will enable us to say what it means. In Singer's quotation from Bishop Hall ' a Spanish face' may be a face which is anything but grave or solemn, or civil or courtly,—it may be a smiling, mocking, deceitful face. Lastly, if *volto* were the true word, but beyond the comprehension of the compositors, as is shown by their mistaking it, it is not likely that it would have been more intelligible to Maria ; and if none of these understood it, is it likely that an audience in the Globe Theatre would have under-stood it ? We have it on the highest authority that a jest's prosperity lies in the ear of him who hears it. There is, however, one argument, slight enough, in favour of *volto*, which, I think, has escaped notice. This is, the name which Sir Toby here gives Sir Andrew ; granting that *volto* is right, Sir Toby says in effect, ' put on a

Sir *Andrew Agueface*.   43
　　　　　　　Enter Sir Andrew.
And.   Sir *Toby Belch*.   How now ſir *Toby Belch*?   45
To.   Sweet ſir *Andrew*.
And.   Bleſſe you faire Shrew.
Mar.   And you too ſir.
Tob.   Accoſt Sir *Andrew*, accoſt.
And.   What's that?   50
To.   My Neeces Chamber-maid.

---

43. Agueface] Ague face F$_2$.   *Ague-*　　Sta. Rlfe.
-cheek Theob. +.   *Agueface* Dyce, Cam.　　44. Scene IV. Pope, +.

Spanish face, here comes Agueface'; possibly, Capell thus understood it.   On the whole, I think that, as has been suggested, 'Castiliano vulgo' is some Bacchanalian phrase, whereof the application is now lost, which rises to Sir Toby's lips at the sight of his boon companion, Sir Andrew.   Possibly, it conveyed to Sir Toby as much meaning as 'paucas palabris' conveyed to Christopher Sly, or 'palabras' to Dogberry,—and, possibly, 'vulgo' is an intentional blunder for *volto*.   Wherefore, under no circumstances, I think, should the text be disturbed.

As to 'What, wench!'—it is impossible to limit the 'business' which an actor may not discern in the phrase.   It may be, as is often the case, merely an exclamation of impatience; Maria is slow to comprehend that her mistress's health ought to be drunk even to the point of intoxication.   It is not to be supposed that Sir Toby utters his speech without moving a muscle, or with his hands at his side.   Whether or not Dr Nicholson has illumined the situation, it is hard to decide.   We should certainly regard his elaborate stage-direction with respect, mindful of our debt to him for his admirable interpretation of Malvolio's words in II, iv, 61.—ED.]

47. Shrew] Pronounced *shrow*.   This familiar address does not necessarily imply any previous acquaintance.   Sir Andrew may have used it at a venture; but, after the opinion, which she had just expressed, it is hardly likely that Maria would wreathe her face in smiles of welcome when she saw the 'very fool' draw near to break up her interview with Sir Toby.—ED.

49. Accost] HALLIWELL observes that it was one of the fashionable terms of courtship current in Shakespeare's time.   Thus, in *Sir Gyles Goosecappe*, 1606: '—tooke time . . . to shew my courtship In the quarter legge, and setled looke, The quicke kisse of the top of the forefinger, And other such exploytes of good Accost.'[IV, ii, p. 64, ed. Bullen.   MALONE, BOSWELL, and many succeeding editors have given us definitions of this word, quoting from Cotgrave and other authorities.   Can we, however, desire a definition better than Shakespeare's own, which he gives us in lines 55, 56, below?—ED.]

51. Chamber-maid] Let not the modern humble duties of making beds, airing rooms, etc., be imputed to Maria, who stóod in relation to Olivia, as a companion, and as an assistant at the toilette.   In I, v, 162, Olivia calls her 'my Gentlewoman,' and Malvolio immediately responds by summoning her, as 'Gentlewoman.'   She can write (II, iii, 154) so 'very like' the Lady Olivia that 'in a forgotten matter we can hardly make distinction of our hands.'   In the end, she marries Sir Toby, and

*Ma.*Good Miſtris accoſt, I defire better acquaintance   52
Ma.   My name is *Mary* ſir.
And.   Good miſtris *Mary*, accoſt.
To,   You miſtake knight : Accoſt, is front her, boord   55
her, woe her, aſſayle her.
And.   *By* my troth I would not vndertake her in this
company.   Is that the meaning of Accoſt?
Ma.   Far you well Gentlemen.
To.   And thou let part ſo Sir *Andrew*, would thou   60
mightſt neuer draw ſword agen.

---

52. Ma.] An. Ff.
    accoſt] *Accost* Rowe.
54. *miſtris*] *Mrs.* Var. '78, Ran.
    Mary, *accoſt.*] *Mary accost.* Rowe
i. *Mary Accost.* Rowe ii, Pope, Han.
Mary Accost,— Theob. et seq.
    55, 56. *boord her*] *board her* Rowe
et seq.
    56. *woe*] *wooe* Ff, Rowe ii,+. *woo*

Cap.
    59. *Far*] *Fare* Ff.
    60, 62. *And*] *If* Pope, Han. *an*
Theob. et seq.
    60. *let part*] F_2. *let her part* F_3F_4,+,
Var. '73, Dyce ii, iii, Coll. iii (MS),
Ktly, Huds.
        would] *'would* Cap. Mal. Steev.
Var. '21, Knt.

---

however disastrous a marriage to so turbulent a husband may prove, we do not feel
that there is any great discrepancy in social rank.—ED.

    52. **acquaintance**] WALKER (*Crit.* iii, 83) : The Folio has no stop after
'acquaintance'; one of its two modes of expressing that a sentence is incomplete ;
the other being, as now, by a ——.   It is an unfinished address,—*subaudi*, 'with
your beauty,' or the like.   The same takes place, III, i, 95.—CAMBRIDGE EDITORS :
The real reason of the omission of the stop in F_1 is that the word occurs so near the
end of the line that there was no room for its insertion.   It is found in all the other
Folios.   [There is another reason for doubting the soundness of Walker's suggestion.   If line 52 be interrupted by Mary, surely line 54 is interrupted by Sir Toby ;
and yet after line 54 there is a stop.   The omission of the stop in III, i, 95, is, I
think, a mere typographical oversight.   Walker makes no attempt there to fill out the
sentence, nor is it easy to imagine that any words are needed.—ED.]

    55. **boord**] WHALLEY conjectured that this should be spelled *bourd*, meaning to
joke, to *jest*, to *toy ;* but STEEVENS supposed that in this case the phrase should be
'*bourd with* her,' and remained unconvinced that 'board,' the naval term, is not the
proper reading.   NARES, with an acrimony unusual to him, says that Whalley was
actuated by the common 'zeal of a critic for a word he had newly discovered.'
HALLIWELL remarks that 'the word is often used with a double entendre, and it is
probable from Sir Andrew's answer that Sir Toby may have here alluded as well to
the more wanton meaning'; and thereupon follow examples from authors other than
Shakespeare.   For those who cannot extract the simple meaning from Sir Toby's
own words, Schmidt's *Lex.* will give six or seven examples of 'board' used in its
figurative sense of to *woo*, to *address*, as here.—ED.

    60. **let part**] The *Text. Notes* show the respectable following which the Third
and Fourth Folios have in reading 'let her part'; this receives additional support
from Sir Andrew's rejoinder, 'And you part so,' etc.   But I doubt that this *her* is

And. And you part fo miftris, I would I might neuer   62
draw fword agen : Faire Lady, doe you thinke you haue
fooles in hand ?

Ma. Sir, I haue not you by'th hand.   65

An. Marry but you fhall haue, and heeres my hand.

Ma. Now fir, thought is free : I pray you bring your
hand to'th Buttry barre, and let it drinke.

An. Wherefore (fweet-heart?) What's your Metaphor ?   70

65. *by'th*] F₂.
66. *hand*] *ha d* F₂.
67. *thought is free*] As a quotation,
Wh. Cam.

68. *to'th*] F₂.
69. *fweet-heart*] *fweet heart* F₃F₄,
Rowe, +.

---

needed ; even if it were not true that an obvious pronoun is frequently omitted
(see ABBOTT, § 244), the phrase may be explained, I think, by the absorption of *it*
in the final *t* of ' let,' where *it* refers to the whole question or the whole subject, just
as we should now say, ' if you let it drop.'   For the eye, therefore, the present
phrase might be printed, I think, ' If thou let' part so,' etc.—ED.

67. **Now sir**] WALKER (*Crit.* iii, 84) : Surely, ' *Nay,* sir.'   [It is a little surprising that Dyce, who, in his Second and Third Editions, was so much under the
influence of Walker and of Walker's editor, Lettsom, did not here adopt this
plausible *Nay,* which seems more appropriate than the didactic ' Now.'   Possibly,
the reason why change is needless, is that ' Now' indicates that Maria has taken Sir
Andrew's hand, and by asserting that ' thought is free' covertly intimates that she
thinks she spoke the truth when, in line 65, she implied that he was a fool.—ED.]

67. **thought is free**] HOLT WHITE : There is the same pleasantry in Lyly's
Euphues, 1581 : 'A noble man in *Sienna* disposed to iest with a gentlewoman . . .
gan thus to salute hir . . . of your wit I cannot iudge, no quoth she, I beleeue you,
for none can iudge of wit, but they that haue it, why then quoth he, doest thou thinke
me a foole, thought is free my Lord quoth she, I wil not take you at your word.' [p.
218, ed. Arber.]—W. A. WRIGHT : A proverbial expression, which is at least as old
as Gower.   See *Confessio Amantis,* B. v (ii, 277, ed. Pauli) : ' I have heard said, that
thought is free.'   And Heywood's *Proverbs* (ed. Spenser Society), p. 47.

68. **Buttry barre**] MURRAY (*N. E. D.*) : *Buttery,*—apparently an adopted form
of Old French *boterie = bouteillerie* (Godef.), extant representative of late Latin
botāria, formed on *bota,* a variant of *butta,* cask, bottle.   The transition from the
sense of ' store-room for liquor' to that of ' store-room for provisions generally' is in
accordance with analogy, but may have been helped by association with Butter.   *Buttery-hatch* is the half-door over which the buttery provisions are served ; *buttery-bar,*
a board or ledge on the top of the buttery-hatch, on which to rest tankards, etc.

69. **sweet-heart**] ROLFE (Note on *Rom. & Jul.* IV, v, 3) says that this combi-
nation is uniformly accented, in Shakespeare, on the last syllable, except in *Wint.
Tale,* IV, iv, 664, ' take your sweet-heart's hat.'   [There is a second exception in
2 Hen. IV : II, iv, 197, ' Give me some sack ; and, sweet-heart, lie thou there.'
For examples from other dramatists, where the accent is on the last word, see
WALKER (*Vers.* 277).—ED.

Ma. It's dry fir.   71

And. Why I thinke fo : I am not fuch an affe, but I can keepe my hand dry. But what's your ieft?

Ma. A dry ieft Sir.

And. Are you full of them?   75

Ma. I Sir, I haue them at my fingers ends: marry now I let go your hand, I am barren.   *Exit Maria*

To. O knight, thou lack'ft a cup of Canarie:when did *I* fee thee fo put downe?

An. Neuer in your life I thinke, vnleffe you fee Ca-   80
narie put me downe : mee thinkes fometimes I haue no

---

76. *fingers ends*] F$_2$, Pope ii, Theob. i, Han. Johns. Var. '73. *finger ends* F$_3$F$_4$, Rowe, Pope i. *finger's ends* Theob. ii, Warb. Var. '85, Steev. *fingers' ends* Cap. et cet.

79. *thee*] *the* F$_3$.
80. *fee*] *saw* Dyce ii, iii, Huds.
81. *put me*] *put* Ff, Rowe.
     mee thinkes] *methinks* Rowe.

---

71. **It's dry sir**] JOHNSON : What is the jest of *dry hand*, I know not any better than Sir Andrew. It may possibly mean, a hand with no money in it ; or, accord-ing to the rules of physiognomy, she may intend to insinuate, that it is not a lover's hand, a moist hand being vulgarly accounted a sign of an amorous constitution.— KENRICK (p. 94) : The 'bringing the hand to the buttery-bar, and letting it drink' is a proverbial phrase among forward Abigails, to ask at once for a kiss and a present. Sir Andrew's slowness of comprehension in this particular, gave her a just suspicion at once of his frigidity and avarice. She, therefore, calls his hand dry ; the moist-ness of the hand being a sign of liberality, as well in matters of love as money. Thus in *Oth.* III, iv, 44, 'This hand is moist, my Lady. . . . This argues fruitfulness and liberall heart : Hot, hot, and moyst.' Dr Johnson need not, therefore, have expressed so much caution of suspecting this to be the truth of the matter. There is one thing, however, he should have attended to ; and this is, that the whole of this insinuation is founded rather on the rules of *palmistry* than *physiognomy*. . . . Maria's finding out anything from Sir Andrew's *palm* by the rules of *physiognomy* is as absurd as if she had read his folly in his *phyz* by the rules of *palmistry*. [For a 'dry hand' as a sign of debility and old age, see *Much Ado*, II, i, 112 ; *2 Hen. IV :* I, ii, 204. See STEEVENS and HALLIWELL for quotations from other sources, in reference to *dryness* and *moisture*, which are more applicable than edifying.—ED.]

72, 73. **I am . . . dry**] MALONE : I suppose, Sir Andrew means that he is not such a fool but that he can keep himself out of the water. [Maria did not say that Sir Andrew was dry, but merely that his hand, which she was holding, was dry. I suppose Sir Andrew means exactly what he says.—ED.]

74. **dry iest**] That is, in one of its meanings, *stupid, tedious ;* Olivia says to Feste, 'Go too, y'are a dry foole.' I, v, 39.

77. **barren**] That is, in one of its meanings, *witless ;* Hamlet refers to 'a quantity of barren spectators.' III, ii, 38.

78. **Canarie**] MURRAY (*N. E. D.*) : A light sweet wine from the Canary Islands. Formerly also in the plural. [The earliest reference, given by Murray, is 1597, *2 Hen. IV :* II, iv, 29 : 'I'faith, you have drunk too much canaries.'

more wit then a Chriſtian, or an ordinary man ha's : but I   82
am a great eater of beefe, and I beleeue that does harme
to my wit.

   To.   No queſtion.   85

   An.   And I thought that, I'de forſweare it.   Ile ride
home to morrow ſir *Toby.*

   To.   *Pur-quoy* my deere knight?

   An.   What is *purquoy?* Do, or not do ? I would I had
beſtowed that time in the tongues, that I haue in fencing   90
dancing, and beare-bayting : O had I but followed the
Arts.

   To.   Then hadſt thou had an excellent head of haire.   93

---

82. *man*] *mans* F₂.   88. Pur-quoy] *Pour-quoi* Rowe ii.
86. *And*] *If* Pope. *An* Theob. et seq.   *Pourquoi* Coll.

---

83. **eater of beefe**] HALLIWELL : ' Beefe is a good meate for an Englysshe man,
so be it the beest be yonge, & that it be not koweflesshe ; For olde beefe and koweflesshe doth ingender melancolye and leporouse humoures.'—Andrew Boorde, *Regy-
ment or dyetary of Helth*, 1542 [p. 271, ed. E. E. Text Soc.].—R. G. WHITE :
' Galen affirmeth yᵗ biefe maketh grosse bloude and engendreth melancholie, espe-
cially if it be much eaten, and if such as doe eat it be of melancholy complexion.'—
The Hauen of Health, 1584, p. 114.—RUSHTON (*Euphuism*, p. 40) : ' As for the
Quailes you promise me, I can be content with beefe, and for the questions they must
be easie, els shall I not aunswere them, for my wit will shew with what grosse diot
I haue been brought vp.'—Lyly's *Euphues and his England*, 1580, [p. 400, ed.
Arber]. Again, *Tro. & Cress.* II, i, 14 : ' Thou mongrel beef-witted lord !' W. A.
WRIGHT (referring to this quotation from *Tro. & Cress.*) : Thersites means that
Ajax's wits were as coarse as his food, not [as Schmidt says in his *Lex.*—ED.] that
he had no more wit than an ox.

92. **Arts**] KARL ELZE (p. 175) suggests that there is here a pun on ' arts' and
hards, coarse tow. But, for reasons too numerous to mention, this is unlikely.—ED.

93. **head of haire**] Unless it be noted that ' tongues' and *tongs* were pronounced
alike, the point of Sir Toby's joke is lost. The credit of discovering this point is
generally given to JOSEPH CROSBY, who announced it in *The American Bibliopolist*, 1875, June, p. 143. But he was certainly anticipated by OTTO GILDEMEISTER
in the Notes to his translation of *Twelfth Night*, in 1869. And I am not sure
that both were not anticipated by RANN, in 1787. Rann's note is brief, so brief,
indeed, as to make it, at first, a little doubtful that he fully appreciated the context,
but, on the whole, the insight must be, I think, conceded to him. His note is on
' by nature,' in lines 95 and 96, and consists of only four words : a dash, which with
him means, ' that is,' and ' without *tongs.* (a pun.)' Surely, by ' a pun' he refers
to ' tongues '; and if so, to him belongs the credit of having first detected Sir Toby's
wit. Gildemeister, who certainly deserves praise for discovering a pun in a language not his own, wrote as follows : ' I know not if, in the 16th century, *tongs* were
used for curling hair ; if they were, we then have, in Sir Andrew's sigh for the
'' tongues,'' a key to a joke which would be otherwise pointless.' Not only were

An. Why, would that haue mended my haire?

To. Paſt queſtion, for thou feeſt it will not coole my   95

*An.*But it becoms we wel enough, doſt not?   (nature

To. Excellent, it hangs like flax on a diſtaffe: & I hope
to ſee a huſwife take thee between her legs, & ſpin it off.

*An.*Faith Ile home to morrow ſir *Toby*, your niece wil   99

---

95. *coole my*] F$_2$. *Cool my* F$_3$F$_4$,   96. *doſt*] Ff. *does't* Rowe et seq.
Rowe, Pope. *curl by* Theob. et cet.   98. *huſwife*] *houſwife* F$_4$. *house-wife*
96. *we*] *me* Ff.   Pope ii, Theob. Warb.

---

the words 'tongues' and 'tongs' pronounced alike, but in one instance, at least,
'tongues' was, in the same sentence, spelled both *tongues* and *tongs*. Thus in
Nashe's *Haue with you to Saffron-Walden*, 1596, we find: 'wheras wittie *Aesope*
did buy vp all the tongues in the market hee could spie, as the best meate hee
esteemed of, they (by all means possible), euen out of the buckles of theyr girdles,
labor to plucke forth the tongs, for feare they should plucke in their vnsatiate greedie
paunches too ſtraight,'—p. 48, ed. Grosart. Again, we find the spelling of 'tongues'
for *tongs*, nigh a hundred years later. That Past-Master in Gossip, JOHN AUBREY,
wrote his *Brief Lives* about 1680, that is, a little before the date of the Fourth Folio.
In his life of Thomas Allen, a great astrologer and reputed conjuror, Aubrey tells
us that on one occasion when Allen was on a visit to 'Mr John Scudamore (grandfather to the lord Scudamor) he happened to leave his watch in the chamber windowe
—(watches were then rarities)—The maydes came in to make the bed, and hearing
a thing in a case cry *Tick, Tick, Tick*, presently concluded that that was his Devill,
and tooke it by the string with the tongues, and threw it out of the windowe into the
mote (to drowne the Devill.) It so happened that the string hung on a sprig of an
elder that grew out of the mote, and this confirmed them that 'twas the Devill. So the
good old gentleman gott his watch again.'—vol. i, p. 28, ed. Clark. In *As You Like
It*, III, ii, 126, we have in the First and Second Folio 'Tonges Ile hang on euerie
tree,' and the Third and Fourth Folios have 'Tongs.' Finally, in Coles's *English
Dictionary*, 1732, there is a list of 'the most usual Words whose *Sound* is the *same*,
but their *Sense* and *Orthography* very *different*'; in this list, we find 'Tongs, *for the
fire*. Tongues, *Languages*.' I have but little doubt that the pronunciation *tungs*
for *tongs* still survives, sporadically, among elderly gentle folk in New England at
this day.—ED.

95. **coole my**] The *Text. Notes* show THEOBALD's admirable emendation. Unfortunately, he missed the pun on 'tongues,' and supposed the point of Sir Toby's
rejoinder lay in the contrast between 'nature' and Sir Andrew's 'arts.' He proposed his emendation in 1729, in a letter to Warburton (*Nichols*, ii, 211), wherein
he says that '*curl by* nature' means 'no more, I think, than, if Sir Andrew had
had art enough in him to tie up his hair, it had not hung so lank as it did by
Nature.'

99. **Ile home**] W. A. WRIGHT: For the omission of the verb of motion, compare *Jul. Cæs.* I, i, 74: 'I'll about'; and *Hamlet*, III, iii, 4: 'And he to England
shall along with you.'

99. **wil**] That is, cannot be persuaded to be seen. Compare 'My eye will scarcely
see it.'—*Hen. V:* II, ii, 104.

not be feene, or if fhe be it's four to one, fhe'l none of me :   100
the Connt himfelfe here hard by, wooes her,

To. Shee'l none o'th Count, fhe'l not match aboue hir
degree, neither in eftate, yeares, nor wit : I haue heard her
fwear t. Tut there's life in't man.

And. Ile ftay a moneth longer. I am a fellow o'th   105
ftrangeft minde i'th world : I delight in Maskes and Reuels fometimes altogether.

To. Art thou good at thefe kicke-chawfes Knight *?*

And. As any man in Illyria, whatfoeuer he be, vnder
the degree of my betters, & yet I will not compare with   110
an old man.

101, 102. *Count,*] *Duke.* Rowe, +.

101. *wooes*] *woes* Cap. *woos* Var. '21.

104. *fwear t*] *fweare* F$_2$. *swear* F$_3$F$_4$, Rowe, Pope, Han. *swear' t* Cap. Wh. i, Dyce, Cam. Sta. Rlfe. *swear it* Theob. et cet.

105. *moneth*] *month* F$_4$.

o'th] *o'the* Var. '73 et seq.

106. *i'th*] *i'the* F$_4$, Cap. et seq.

108. *kicke-chawfes*] F$_2$. *kick-fhawfes*, F$_3$. *kickshawses* Glo. Cam. Rlfe, Huds. Dtn, Wh. ii. *kick-fhaws* F$_4$, Rowe et cet.

111. *an old man*] *an older man* Kinnear.

---

100. **none of me**] ABBOTT (§ 53) : 'None' is still used by us for *nothing*, followed by a partitive genitive, 'I had *none* of it'; and this explains the Elizabethan phrase 'She will none of me,' *i. e.* 'She desires to have nothing from, as regards to do with, me.' So in 'Ile no more of you,' I, v, 39 ; 'satisfaction can be none,' III, iv, 237.

104. **there's life in't**] W. A. WRIGHT : And while there is life there is hope. Compare *Lear*, IV, vi, 206 : 'Then there's life in't.' Similarly, *Ant. & Cleop.* III, xiii, 192 : 'There's sap in't yet.'

106. **i'th world**] In thus imagining himself to be an exception to the rest of mankind, a common trait in weaklings, Sir Andrew furnishes us with the key to his character, or, if not the key, it is at least one of its wards.—ED.

108. **kicke-chawses**] SKEAT (s. v.) : At a later time [i. e. than Shakespeare] *kickshaws* was incorrectly regarded as being a plural form. *Kickshaws* is a curious corruption of French *quelque chose*, literally something, hence, a trifle, small delicacy. This can be abundantly proved by quotations. '*Fricandeaux*, short, skinlesse, and dainty puddings, or *quelkchoses*, made of good flesh and herbs chopped together, then rolled up into the form of liverings, etc., and so boiled.'—Cotgrave. 'Nor shall we then need the *Monsieurs* of *Paris* to take our hopefull Youth into their slight and prodigal custodies and send them over back again transform'd into Mimicks, Apes, and Kicshoes.'—Milton, *Of Education* [vol. iv, p. 393, ed. Mitford].

111. **an old man**] THEOBALD, in his correspondence with Warburton (*Nichols*, ii, 354) conjectured, doubtfully, *a nobleman ;* it was not repeated in his edition, which contains no note on the passage.—WARBURTON : This is intended as a satire on that common vanity of old men, in preferring their own times, and the past generation, to the present.—HEATH (p. 186) : If our poet had this intention, he was

To.   What is thy excellence in a galliard, knight?   112

---

very unhappy in the expressing it ; for the words have not the least tendency to this sense.   And in truth, a satire in the mouth of Sir Andrew would be something very extraordinary, as it would be no less so, that the poet should pitch on him as the organ to convey his own sentiments.   The sense seems to be, And yet I took on myself as above being put on a level with an old man in this matter, how superior soever he may be to me in other respects.—CAPELL (p. 141) : Sir Andrew's meaning is something obscure ; the play's æra must help us; which from great probabilities, we may place at 1607, or thereabouts [Manningham's *Diary* had not, in Capell's time, been discovered.—ED.] ; in that year, the rage of 'masques' was predominant ; and upon these fooleries, is the making Sir Andrew 'delight' in them a wipe undoubtedly ; and upon some director, or patronizer, who was of years to have more wisdom, are the words in question another wipe.—STEEVENS : Aguecheek, though willing enough to arrogate to himself such experience as is commonly the acquisition of age, is yet careful to exempt his person from being compared with its bodily weakness.—HALLIWELL : The text seems to be correct, being merely one of Sir Andrew's absurdities, and intentional on the part of the author.   The worthy knight's head was none of the clearest.—BADHAM (*Text of Sh.* p. 287) : It is useless to look for the explanation of the editors in so palpable a blunder.   It must be obvious to any ordinary reader that 'an old man' is a false reading for *a nobleman.*   Sir Andrew has just been speaking of the Count Orsino as a rival whom he cannot pretend to cope with, so that the allusion to a nobleman is most natural. [It is not to be supposed that Badham knew he had been anticipated by Theobald. —ED.]—The COWDEN-CLARKES : By the term 'an old man,' the knight means *a man of experience,* just as he has before deferred to 'his betters'; while the use of the word 'old' gives precisely that absurd effect of refraining from competing in dancing, fencing, etc., with exactly the antagonist incapacitated by age, over whom even Sir Andrew might hope to prove his superiority.   [But Sir Toby was not referring to 'dancing' and 'fencing,' when he asked if Sir Andrew were good at these kickshawses, but to 'masks' and 'revels.'—ED.]—DEIGHTON : The former comparison, with his betters, he declines on account of his reverence for them, the latter comparison with old men, because he feels his superiority to them.   [HUDSON is the only editor who has adopted Theobald's emendation.   'Why,' he asks 'should Sir Andrew here speak of comparing himself with "an old man"'?   The whole drift of the foregoing dialogue is clearly against that reading.'   Both ROLFE and W. A. WRIGHT think that the comparison, as irrelevant nonsense, may have been intentional, wherein I agree with them ; and yet it is possible that it may be a clumsy disclaimer of any attempt at rivalry, in any accomplishment, with Sir Toby, who, though not an old man, was certainly older than Sir Andrew ; the latter, with the *gaucherie* of his kind, in trying to pay a compliment, offensively exaggerated the difference in their ages.—ED.]

112. MASON (p. 113) : This line should be pointed thus : 'What is thy excellence ? in a galliard, knight ?'   Meaning, 'In what are you most excellent ? is it in a galliard ?'   [RANN and STAUNTON adopted this punctuation.]

112. galliard] BRADLEY (*N. E. D.*) : An adaptation of Old French and French *gaillard, -art* (modern French *gaillard*) = Provençal, *galhart,* Spanish, *gallardo,* Portuguese, *galhardo,* Italian, *gagliardo,* of unknown origin.   2. *sb.* A quick and lively dance in triple time.—NAYLOR (p. 122) : Cinquepace is the name of the original

And. Faith, I can cut a caper.   113

To. And I can cut the Mutton too't.

And. And I thinke I haue the backe-tricke, ſimply as   115
ſtrong as any man in Illyria.

To. Wherefore are theſe things hid? Wherefore haue
theſe gifts a Curtaine before 'em? Are they like to take   118

---

114. *too't*] *to't* F₃F₄ et seq.

116. [Dances fantastically. Coll. ii. (MS).

118. *'em*] Ff, Rowe, Pope, Theob. i, Han. Wh. Dyce, Cam. Glo. Sta. Rlfe, Huds. Dtn. *them* Theob. ii et cet.

Galliard. Praetorius (b. 1571) says a Galliard has *five* steps and is therefore called *Cinque* Pas. (P. 142) Here are the Steps of the Galliard, consisting of five movements of the feet, and the caper, or 'sault majeur.' 1. Greve (which is explained as a 'coup de pied') gaulche; 2. Greve droicte; 3. Greve gaulche; 4. Greve droicte; 5. Sault majeur; 6. Posture gaulche. 1, 2, 3, 4, 6 are the 'Cinq' pas, and 5 is the characteristic leap or caper. [See, if need be, *Much Ado about Nothing*, II, i, 69, of this ed. where the music of a galliard is given.—ED.]

113, 114. **caper . . . Mutton**] ROLFE: The pun here shows that the association of capers with boiled mutton is as old as that of apple-sauce with roast goose, on which Romeo quibbles in *Rom. & Jul.* II, iv, 85.—HUDSON: A double pun is probably intended here; the meaning being, 'If you can do the man's part in a galliard, I can do the woman's.' *Mutton* was sometimes used as a slang term for a *woman* [of low character, however.—ED.].

115. **backe-tricke**] The COWDEN-CLARKES: Here Sir Andrew is making a discursive allusion to his fencing-feats, meaning by 'back-trick' a back-handed stroke with the sword; and not keeping to the discussion of his dancing powers, meaning by 'back-trick' some retiring step, some elegance of graceful retreat. The word 'strong' makes for the former interpretation. [I am at a loss to know to which of these two different interpretations the Editors give their preference.—ED.]—SCHMIDT (*Lex.*): A caper backwards in dancing; perhaps, here, with a quibble: the trick of going back in a fight. [There seems to be a general agreement that Schmidt is right in his definition, but wrong in his suggestion of a quibble. DEIGHTON, who, in his note on 'galliard,' quoted Heywood, *An Humorous Day's Mirth*, 1599: 'I fetcht me two or three fine capers aloft, and took my leave of them as men do of their mistresses at the ending of a galliard.' thinks that the 'back-trick' is 'the caper backwards in retiring, as exemplified by this quotation from Heywood.' A galliard *may* have ended in a *sault majeur*, but I doubt that gentlemen took leave of their partners in this gymnastic manner. There must have been some courtesy as ceremonious as that for which directions are given in the *basse dance* where 'you must salute the Damoiselle, and keep hold of her hand, and lead her back to where you began.'(—Naylor, p. 141.) By the 'back-trick' I think Sir Andrew means, not one single caper backward, but what is called the *Revers* (Naylor, p. 143), where all five steps are reversed, or taken backward. It appears to have been the proper thing in galliards for the partners to return to the place whence they started. To advance was, *possibly*, comparatively easy; it is quite conceivable that to reverse (Sir Andrew's 'back-trick'), some skill was needed so to strike the feet alternately on the ground as to bring the couple in the right position facing each other, not only at the conclusion of the tune but on the spot whence they set out.—ED.]

duſt, like miſtris *Mals* picture ?   Why doſt thou not goe   119

119. Mals] *Mall's* Rowe et seq.

---

118. Curtaine] MALONE: Thus, in Webster's *The White Devil*, 1612 : 'I yet but draw the curtain;—now to your picture.' [p. 70, ed Dyce.]—HALLIWELL (note on I, v, 230) : In allusion to the custom which prevailed in Shakespeare's time, of oil paintings being protected by curtains, which were only drawn on particular occasions or for exhibition. The application to a woman's face occurs in *Tro. & Cress.* where Pandarus says,—'come draw this curtain, and let's see your picture.' [—III, ii, 49.] Allusions to curtains before pictures are frequently met with. ' Two great tables of the Queenes Majesties pictures, with one curtaine of changeable silck ; two great pictures of my Lord, in whole proporcion, the one in armor, the other in a sute of russett sattin ; with one curtaine to them.'—*Inventory of the Goods at Kenilworth Castle*, 1588. 'Of the pictures which Jack of Newbery had in his house, whereby he encouraged his servants to seek for fame and dignity,—In a fair and large parlor, which was wainscoated round about, Jack of Newbery had fifteen fair pictures hanging, which were covered with curtains of green silk, fringed with gold, which he would often shew to his friends and servants.'—*History of Jack of Newbery*. [Many more quotations are given by Halliwell, but, assuredly, the foregoing are all-sufficient, in illustration of a practice which still survives.—ED.]

118, 119. like to take dust] B. NICHOLSON (*N. & Qu.* 1874, 5th, ii, 283) ventures to explain why the picture should be like to take dust by a passage which occurs in Webster's and Marston's *Malcontent*, V, i, where an old courtesan secures a wide-spread advertisement by trickery as follows : ' she gets all the picture-makers to draw her picture ; when they have done, she most courtly finds fault with them one after another, and never fetcheth them ; they in revenge of this, execute her pictures as they do in Germany, and hang her in their shops ; by this means she is better known . . . . than if she had been five times carted.' It is to this story that Nicholson supposes that Sir Toby alludes, ' when the exposed and uncared-for pictures were somewhat dust-covered as compared with the other specimens of each portrait painter's art.'

119. mistris Mals] STEEVENS: The real name of the woman, whom I suppose to have been meant by Sir Toby, was Mary Frith. The appellation, by which she was generally known, was Mall Cutpurse. On the *Stationers' Registers*, August 7, 1610, is entered : ' Henry Gosson. Entred for his Copye vnder thandes of master Edward Abbott and master Adames warden A booke called, The Madde pranckes of mery Mall of the Banckside, with her walkes in mans apparell, and to what purpose, written by John Day.' [—Arber's *Transcript*, iii, 441.] Middleton and Dekker wrote a comedy of which she is the heroine ; its title is as follows : ' The Roaring Girle. Or Moll Cut-Purse. As it hath lately beene Acted on the Fortune-Stage by the Prince his Players. 1611.' The frontispiece to it contains a full length picture of her in man's clothes, smoking tobacco. Nathaniel Field [has introduced her as one of his *Dramatis Personæ*] in his *Amends for Ladies*, and there gives [a character of her, which may be found in I, i, p. 111, ed. Hazlitt-Dodsley]. A Life of this woman was published in 1662.—MALONE: Mary Frith was born in 1584 and died in 1659. In a MS letter in the British Museum from John Chamberlain to Mr Carleton, 11 Feb. 1611-12, the following account is given of this woman's doing penance : ' This last Sunday Moll Cutpurse, a notorious baggage that used to go in man's apparel, and challenged the field of diverse gallants, was brought to the same place

[119. mistris Mals picture]

[Paul's Cross,] where she wept bitterly, and seemed very penitent; but it is since doubted she was maudlin drunk, being discovered to have tippel'd of three quarts of sack before she came to her penance. She had the daintiest preacher or ghostly father that ever I saw in the pulpit, one Radcliffe of Brazen-Nose College in Oxford, a likelier man to have led the revels in some inn of court, than to be where he was. But the best is, he did extremely badly, and so wearied the audience, that the best part went away, and the rest tarried rather to hear Moll Cutpurse than him.' [The curious reader may learn in HALLIWELL'S note *ad loc.* and in DYCE'S *Introduction* to Middleton's *Roaring Girl* many further particulars of Mary Frith's career, and may find her *Life*, told by CHARLES ANDREWS, in admirable Fielding-esque style, in *Lives of Twelve Bad Women*, London, 1897, p. 49. The incurious reader will doubtless find the foregoing extracts from Steevens and Malone quite ample, more especially as the drift of modern opinion is tending greatly to doubt that Sir Toby's 'mistris Mal' has any reference at all to Moll Cutpurse. SINGER (ed. ii) was the earliest to mistrust this reference. 'It has been supposed,' he says in his note *ad loc.*, 'that the allusion here is to Mall Cutpurse. . . . But "Mistress Mall" is no doubt a mere impersonation, like "my lady's eldest son" in *Much Ado about Nothing*. She is merely a type of a lady solicitous for the preservation of her charms even when transferred to canvas.' In the following year, R. G. WHITE observed that Mistress Moll's picture 'appears to be named merely as a type of female portraits which were carefully preserved from dust,—Mary being the commonest of all names for women. . . . It is possible that Moll Cutpurse is referred to though there appears to be no necessity for supposing this to be the case; and her portrait would hardly be painted in a style to require the protection of a curtain, or she be referred to as *Mistress* Moll.' DYCE next hinted a doubt. At the conclusion of his note (*Gloss.*) on the present passage, wherein he quotes at length the notes of Steevens and Malone, he asks, 'After all, can it be that "Mistress Mall's picture" means merely *a lady's picture?* So we still say "master Tom" or "Master Jack" to designate no particular individual, but of young gentlemen generally.' SCHMIDT (*Lex.*) finds an objection to Moll Cutpurse on grounds more substantial than any hitherto urged, namely, on the score of her youth at the time this present play was written. He says that she was born in 1589, which would make her but twelve or thirteen years old when Sir Toby was speaking. Malone's date, however, of Moll's birth, 1584, is more likely to be correct, inasmuch as she died in 1659, and all accounts agree in stating that this was in the seventy-fifth year of her age. Yet this hardly weakens Schmidt's argument; were five years added to twelve or thirteen, her precocity and notoriety would be still incredible. Moll herself says in her *Life* that it was for her first putting on of man's clothes that she was forced to do penance at Paul's Cross; and this we know was in 1611–12, and it may well have been the beginning of her wide-spread notoriety. Wherefore, I think, Schmidt's argument is well founded. Had the Lexicographer stopped there, his note would be entirely satisfactory; unfortunately, he proceeds to say : 'Perhaps Sir Toby only means to say : like a picture intended for a beauty, but in fact representing Mall the kitchen-wench.' What possible connection this meaning can have with the modest conceal-ment of Sir Andrew's accomplishments I cannot, try as I may, discover. ROLFE, influenced by this same fact of Moll's youth at the time *Twelfth Night* was written, 'inclines to agree' with Singer. W. A. WRIGHT believes that the date of John Day's book in the entry in the *Stationers' Registers*, August, 1610, indicates the period when to Church in a Galliard, and come home in a Carranto?   120

120. *Carranto*] *Coranto* Rowe ii et seq.

' the virago appears to have flourished '; ' so that,' he goes on to say, ' I am inclined to think the Mistress Mall of the present passage was some notoriety other than Mary Frith.' In *N. & Qu.* (1878, 5th, x, 3) J. F. MARSH notes an entirely new allusion. He believes that Mistress Mall's portrait is not that of Moll Cutpurse, but of Maria : ' Pictures in general, or any picture in particular, would have served Sir Toby's turn, but he gives force to the expression by specifying the portrait of Olivia's gentlewoman, Maria, with whom Sir Andrew and he have just been having a wit combat, and who was therefore present to his thoughts, if her picture was not hanging before his eyes.' B. NICHOLSON (*Ib.* p. 182) finds three objections to this interpretation of Marsh : First, Maria is never called Mal, or Mistress Mal, or Moll elsewhere in the play. Secondly, it cannot be shown that Maria ever had her portrait taken, or, if she had, is it at all probable that Olivia would have permitted her chambermaid's portrait to be hung up in her public rooms.   Thirdly, if the passage be looked into it will show that Mistress Mal's picture had no curtain. ' Why,' says Sir Toby, ' have these gifts a curtain before them? [when exposed] are they likely to take dust, like Mistress Mal's [exposed] picture ?' Nicholson then refers to his own quotation from *The Malcontent* (in the foregoing note on ' like to take dust ') as likely to show that Shakespeare and Marston and Webster all refer to the same story.   Of course Marsh replied (*Ib.* p. 423) and, to his own satisfaction, swept clean aside all three of these objections, and concluded his note with the emphatic assertion that, ' if the name in Marston's play had been Mall, or even if the exposure of a picture of Moll Cutpurse in a broker's window had been an ascertained fact instead of a conjecture, it would not have shaken my opinion that Shakespeare's text is plain and intelligible with reference to Maria, and that all applications of it to courtesans or others outside of the play are mischievous excecences.'   Marsh seems fixed in the belief that the picture was hanging on the walls in Sir Toby's very presence.   I can find nothing to warrant it.   BARNETT thinks that the allusion is, ' probably, to Mary Ambrée, who fought at the Siege of Ghent, in 1584,' and refers to   Hudibras : ' A bold virago, stout, and tall, As Joan of France, or English Mall.'   (Part I, canto ii, line 367, where GREY asserts that this refers to ' Mary Carleton, or, as she was more commonly distinguished, Kentish Moll, or the German Princess.'   This RITSON denies and says the reference is to Moll Cutpurse.)   Possibly, Barnett was misled by a note which first appeared, according to Furnivall, in the fourth edition of Percy's *Reliques*, edited by Percy's nephew.   Lastly, VERITY inclines to think that Moll Cutpurse is referred to, because ' a casual allusion like this may well have been inserted some time after the *first* production of the play '; of course, this door of escape stands always open, but we should be wary of using it.   Steevens, in spite of the express reason given by Sir Toby why the picture should be curtained, suggested another, drawn from his own prurient imagination.   I have but small belief that any particular Mistress Mall is here referred to, and none at all, that, if there be one, it is Mary Frith, against whose claim chronology is fatal.   It is almost inconceivable that, in ' the fierce light that beats ' upon that period, a Mistress Moll, familiarly enough known to be recognised in a passing allusion, could have escaped detection.   When now-a-days we say ' Jack Robinson,' do we refer to any particular John of that family ?—ED.]

120. **Carranto**] The following extract is taken from a translation by RYE (p. 123)

My verie walke fhould be a Iigge : I would not fo much   121
as make water but in a Sinke-a-pace : What dooeft thou

122. *Sinke-a-pace*] F₂. *cinque-pace*   122. *dooeft*] *doft* F₃F₄.
Han. *Sink-a-pace* F₃F₄ et cet.

---

of a very rare Spanish pamphlet in the British Museum, wherein is found an account
of a Banquet and Entertainment given by James I. to the Constable of Castile, Juan
Fernandez de Velasco, on Sunday, August 19, 1604 : 'After a little while the Prince
[Henry] was commanded by his parents to dance a galliard, and they pointed out to
him the lady who was to be his partner ; and this he did with much sprightliness and
modesty, cutting several capers in the course of the dance. The Earl of Southampton
then led out the Queen, and three other gentlemen their several partners, who all
joined in dancing a *brando*. [What this is, I know not. It is not in Percival's
Spanish Dict., 1622, nor in Florio's *Worlde of Wordes*, 1598. Murray (*N. E. D.*)
refers *brandon* to Littré, who gives it as the name of a kind of rustic dance, or rather
race, with lighted wisps of straw, which is hardly conceivable at this present entertainment.—ED.] . . . After this they began a galliard, and in it a lady led out the
Prince, who then led out another lady whom their Majesties pointed out to him.
After this a *brando* was danced, and that being over, the Prince stood up to dance a
corrента, which he did very gracefully. The Earl of Southampton was now again
the Queen's partner, and they went through the *correnta* likewise. Hereupon the
ball ended.'—NAYLOR (p. 122) : The old English name was ' current traverse,' and
Morley (1597) speaks of the Courant step as 'travising and running,' which would
appear to connect the Italian word with *curro*. Sir John Davies (1570–1626), in
his poem *Orchestra*, identifies Rounds, Corantos, Measures, and some other dances
with Country Dances. That is, whatever the rhythm or speed of the actual time
used, these variously named Country Dances could be performed to it. Sir Roger
de Coverly, our typical English Country Dance, is in *form* almost the same as the
Brawl, Coranto, Galliard, or Measure. A Courant by Frescobaldi (1591–1640) is
in triple time. As for its ' step,' Davies says it is ' on a triple dactile foot,' ' close
to the ground with sliding passages.' According to Sir Toby, it would be a quicker
and gayer dance than the Galliard, for he compares the walk to church to the latter ;
but the more light-hearted journey back to dinner he likens to the Coranto. The
Jig would be even faster, for Sir Andrew's ' very walk,' that is, his *week-day* gait,
was to be ' a jig.'

121. **Iigge**] See *Much Ado about Nothing*, II, i, 70, of this ed.—NAYLOR
(p. 124) : The name comes from *Giga* (*Geige*), a sort of fiddle in use during the
12th and 13th centuries. The oldest jigs are Scottish, and were ' round dances ' for
a number of people. . . . It was a lively dance.

122. HAZLITT (*Age of Elizabeth*, p. 63) : The standard of delicacy varies at
different periods, as it does in different countries, and is not a general test of
superiority. The French, who pique themselves (and justly, in some particulars)
on their quickness of tact and refinement of breeding, say and do things which we,
a plainer and coarser people, could not think of without a blush. What would
seem gross allusions to us at present, were without offence to our ancestors, and
many things passed for jests with them, or matters of indifference, which would
not now be endured. Refinement of language, however, does not keep pace with
simplicity of manners. The severity of criticism exercised in our theatres towards

meane? Is it a world to hide vertues in? I did thinke by 123
the excellent conftitution of thy legge, it was form'd vnder the ftarre of a Galliard. 125
  And, I, 'tis ftrong, and it does indifferent well in a
dam'd colour'd ftocke. Shall we fit about fome Reuels? 127

---

123. *thinke*] *not think* Rowe.
126. *in a*] *in* Warb. (misprint?)
127. *dam'd colour'd*] *damask-colour-*
ed Knt, Wh. i. *flame-colour'd* Rowe
ii et cet. *damson-colour'd* Phelps ap.
Hal. *dove-coloured* Anon. ap. Cam.

paned coloured Nicholson ap. Cam.
claret-coloured Joicey.
127. *ftocke*] *ftocken* F_3F_4, Rowe.
stocking Pope, +, Cap. *stock* Var. '78
et seq.
  fit] *set* Rowe ii et seq.

---

some unfortunate straggling phrases in the old comedies, is but an ambiguous compliment to the immaculate purity of modern times.

  125. starre] See also Beatrice's reference (*Much Ado,* II, i, 319) to the dancing
star under which she was born. DEIGHTON calls attention to the contempt with
which Edmund (*Lear,* I, ii, 112) treats this 'excellent foppery of the world, that
when we are sick in fortune, we make guilty of our disasters the sun, the moon, and
stars.'

  127. dam'd colour'd stocke] KNIGHT : 'Stock' is *stocking.* We have ventured
to read '*damask*-coloured'; for it is evident that, if the word *damask* were written
as pronounced rapidly, *dam'sk,* it might easily be misprinted 'dam'd.' In Drayton
we have 'the damask-coloured dove.' The name of the colour is derived from the
damask rose.—COLLIER (*Notes,* etc., 172) : The Manuscript-Corrector informs us
that this ought to be '*dun*-colour'd.'—DYCE (*Few Notes,* 75) : That Sir Andrew, a
gallant of the first water, should ever dream of casing his leg in a '*dun*-coloured
stock' is not to be supposed for a moment. The epithet *flame-coloured* was frequently applied to dress. Thus, *1 Hen. IV:* I, ii, 11, 'a wench in flame-coloured
taffeta.'—COLLIER (ed. ii) : It would have been more to the point if [Dyce] had
produced some instance in which 'flame-coloured stocks' were mentioned ; such
proof is still wanted, and were it forthcoming, all dispute would be at an end.—
B. NICHOLSON (*N. & Qu.* 1879, 5th, xi, 124) : Granted that 'flame-coloured' was
a common phrase, and twice used by Shakespeare, how does that justify the substitution ? There is no special circumstance requiring 'flame-coloured,' nor any *ductus
literarum,* unless *am* be accounted such. Nor is there such a certainty of error as
to require such a change. 'Damn'd-colour'd' is an easily understood epithet, and
there is nothing against it, beyond our ignorance of the use by any one of a similar
phrase in English. . . . Why cannot Sir Andrew be allowed the imitative affectation
of a word very likely to have been used,—even if it were uncommon,—among the
fashion-mongers of the day? Pope [Rowe?] not improbably substituted 'flame-
colour'd' as a more refined synonym. But it is not a synonym. Devils to this day
are held to be not flame-coloured but black. . . . I venture to think that dark or black
nether garments were well fitted to show off a good leg, especially when in contrast
with the bright and glittering colours then worn. Lastly, I would add that no one
can doubt but that fashions and phrases were then as now freely imported from the
Continent ; and though we have not yet found 'damn'd-coloured' in English, we
can find it in French. Corresponding with my friend Mr Furnivall he turned up
Cotgrave. There under 'Couleur' and 'Enfer' are to be found, *Couleur d'enfer* as

To.   What fhall we do elfe : were we not borne vnder   128
Taurus ?

And.   Taurus? That fides and heart.   130

To.   No fir, it is leggs and thighes : let me fee thee caper. Ha, higher : ha, ha, excellent.   *Exeunt*   132

Scena Quarta.

Enter Valentine, and Viola in mans attire.   2

Val.   If the Duke continue thefe fauours towards you
Cefario, you are like to be much adu anc'd, he hath known
you but three dayes, and already you are no ftranger.   5

128. *elfe :*] *else ?* Pope et seq.
130. *That*] *That's* F₃F₄ et seq.
132. [Sir And. dances. Dyce ii.
    ha, excellent] *ha !—excellent*

Theob.
1. Scena   Quarta]   Scene   V.
Pope, +.
    The Palace. Rowe.

---

much as *Noir-brun enfumè*; '*Enfer. Couleur d'enfer.* A dark and smoakie
brown.'—R. M. SPENCE (*Ib.*, p. 204) : Shakespeare would never have made a vain
coxcomb like Sir Andrew show the good taste to choose so unpretending a colour as
black. By 'a dam'd colour'd ftocke' I understand checkered hose. To this day old
people among the peasantry of Scotland speak of any checkered garment as being of
the 'dam-brod,' *Anglicè* 'draught-board,' pattern. [Does not *dam-brod* relate merely
to *form*, without reference to colour ?—ED.]—W. A. WRIGHT : It is by no means certain what the true reading should be. In the dialogues given in Eliot's *Fruits for the
French* (1593) p. 31, we find, 'Show me a Peach colourd Netherstocke.'   A bright
colour of some kind was intended, and therefore the reference to [Cotgrave's] *couleur
d'enfer* is out of place. [Rowe's emendation has the largest following ; but then
there are eminent critics who dispute it.   There is such a difference, however, both
to the eye and to the ear, between 'dam'd' and *flame* that, until some happier substitute be found, I think the text should remain undisturbed ; and surely, Sir Andrew's
character is not so exalted as to be seriously lowered by a little profanity.—ED.]

130. **sides and heart**] JOHNSON : Alluding to the medical astrology still preserved in almanacks, which refers the affections of particular parts of the body to
the predominance of particular constellations.—DOUCE (i, 85) : Both the knights
are wrong in their astrology according to the almanacs of the time, which make
Taurus govern the neck and throat.   Their ignorance is perhaps intentional.—
ROLFE : In that classic annual *The Old Farmer's Almanac* may still be seen the
ancient astrological figure of the human body with lines radiating from its various
parts to the symbols of the zodiacal signs. [This astrological figure still makes its
appearance annually in other almanacs in this country besides *The Old Farmer's*.
Douce says that *perhaps* Sir Toby's and Sir Andrew's ignorance was intentional,
and B. NICHOLSON (*N. & Qu.* 1878, 5th, x, 283) actually proposed to substitute
the correct signs. Sir Andrew's ignorance was genuine, but Sir Toby wanted merely
a pretext for a coarse allusion.—ED.]

Vio. You either feare his humour, or my negligence,   6
that you call in queſtion the continuance of his loue.   Is
he inconstant fir, in his fauours.   *Ual.* No beleeue me.
                 Enter Duke, Curio, and Attendants.
Vio.   I thanke you : heere comes the Count.   10
Duke.   Who faw *Cefario* hoa ?
Vio.   On your attendance my Lord heere.
Du.   Stand you a-while aloofe.   *Cefario,*
Thou knowſt no leſſe, but all : I haue vnclaſp'd
To thee rhe booke euen of my ſecret fouie.   15

8. *fauours.*] *favours ?* Ff.
9. *Enter...*] Enter Duke, attended.
(after line 10) Cap. Dyce, Cam.
10. *Count*] *Duke* Rowe, +.
11. *hoa*] *ho* Cap.
12. *attendance*] *attendants* F₄.
        my Lord heere] *here, my Lord*
K. Elze.

13. [To Attend. Wh. ii.
        a-while] *a while* F₃F₄, Rowe, +,
Theob. i, Han. Cap. Cam. Dtn. *awhile*
Steev. Var. '21, Knt, Coll. Sta. Rlfe.
        aloofe] *aloof*. [Curio, etc. retire.
Coll. MS.
15. *rhe*] F₁.

6. **humour**] W. A. WRIGHT : That is, caprice, fancy ; or, perhaps, simply disposition ; as in *2 Hen. IV:* II, iv, 256 : ' Sirrah, what humour's the prince of ?'
[Inasmuch as Viola is here directly referring to Valentine's uncertainty as to the
constancy of the Duke's favour, it seems to me that ' humour ' must mean something more than ' simply his disposition.' She asks immediately, ' is he inconstant
in his favours ?'   I rather prefer the interpretation here of ' humour ' as *capricious-
ness.*—ED.]

7. **that**] For other instances where ' that ' is used for *in that*, see ABBOTT, § 284.

9. As in stage-copies, the entrance of the Duke is here marked a little in advance
of his appearance. CAPELL properly transferred this stage-direction to follow line 10.

12. **On your attendance**] W. A. WRIGHT : That is, in attendance upon you.

14. **no lesse, but all**] Compare *Oth.* I, i, 137 : ' with no worse nor better guard,
But with a knaue.' See ABBOTT (§ 127) foro ther examples of ' but ' in the sense
of *than* after negative comparatives. Both in the quotation from *Oth.* and in the
present line the comma of the Folio, before ' but,' is not in accordance with modern
punctuation.—ED.

14, 15. **vnclasp'd . . . booke**] STEEVENS : So, in *1 Hen. IV:* I, iii, 188 :
' And now I will unclasp a secret book.'—WHITER, in his valuable criticisms
founded on Locke's doctrine of *The Association of Ideas*, has gathered many examples (pp. 108–115), including the present, of Shakespeare's fondness of metaphors
drawn from a book, its binding, its clasps, and its margins. Thus, *Rom. & Jul.*
I, iii, 81 : ' Read o'er the volume of young Paris' face. . . . And what obscur'd
in this fair volume lies Find written in the margent of his eyes. This precious
book of love, this unbound lover. . . . That book in many's eyes doth share
the glory ; That in gold clasps locks in the golden story.'   Again, *Ib.* III, ii, 83
(where Juliet speaking of Romeo, says) : ' Was ever book containing such vile
matter So fairly bound.' Thus, *R. of L.* 101 : ' But she, that never coped with
stranger eyes. . . . Nor read the subtle-shining secrecies Writ in the glassy mar-

Therefore good youth, addreſſe thy gate vnto her,   16
Be not deni'de acceſſe, ſtand at her doores,
And tell them, there thy fixed foot ſhall grow
Till thou haue audience.

    Uio.   Sure my Noble Lord,   20
If ſhe be ſo abandon'd to her ſorrow
As it is ſpoke, ſhe neuer will admit me.

    Du,   Be clamorous, and leape all ciuill bounds,
Rather then make vnproſited returne,

    Vio.   Say I do ſpeake with her (my Lord)what then?   25

    Du.   O then, vnfold the paſſion of my loue,
Surprize her with diſcourſe of my deere faith ;
It ſhall become thee well to act my woes :
She will attend it better in thy youth,
Then in a Nuntio's of more graue aſpect.   30

16. *gate*] *gait* Cap.   Rowe, Pope, Mal. Cam. Glo. Wh. ii.
30. *Nuntio's*] F₂F₃. *Nuncio's* F₄, *nuntio* Cap. *nuncio* Theob. et cet.

---

gents of such books.' Again, *Much Ado*, I, i, 308 : 'Thou wilt be like a lover presently And tire the hearer with a book of words.' *Ib.* line 325 : 'And in her bosom I'll unclasp my heart.' Again, *Tro. & Cress.* IV, v, 60 : 'That give accost-ing welcome ere it comes, And wide unclasp the tables of their thoughts To every ticklish reader.' Again, *Love's Lab. L.* IV, ii, 113 : 'Study his bias leaves and makes his book thine eyes.' *Mid. N. D.* II, iii, 120 : 'Reason . . . leads me to your eyes, where I o'erlook Love's stories written in love's richest book.' *King John*, II, ii, 484 : 'If that the Dauphin there, thy princely son, Can in this book of beauty read, "I love."' Whiter's list does not pretend to be at all complete ; Bartlett's *Concordance* will doubtless enlarge it. Whiter's main purpose is to show that there was, in Shakespeare's mind, some subtle association, whatever might be its strange cause, between a book and love and the eye of beauty.—ED.

17. **Be not deni'de**] DELIUS : The Duke is thinking of Valentine's failure to gain admittance.

18. **fixed foot**] Viola obeys this injunction of the Duke, when she tells Malvolio (I, v, 148) that she will ' stand at the door like a Sheriffs post.'—ED.

22. **As it is spoke**] See ABBOTT (§ 200, p. 134) for other examples of this phrase used for '*tis said*.

29. **attend it**] ABBOTT (§ 200, p. 134) : In some cases, as in [the present], the derivation may explain the transitive use.

30. **Nuntio's**] DELIUS : Perhaps this stands for *Nuntius ;* just as the Folio has ' Antonio's ' for *Antonius.*—W. A. WRIGHT : Theobald reads ' nuntio,' but this would require to be preceded by ' in thee' instead of ' in thy youth.' Delius's sup-position, *Nuntius*, can scarcely be. The construction is not strictly grammatical, but is according to the sense of the passage, as if the Duke had said, ' She will attend it better in thy youthful person than in that of a nuncio of more grave appearance.'

30. **aspect**] The accent is uniformly on the last syllable in Shakespeare. See

Vio. I thinke not fo, my Lord.　　　　　　　　　31
　Du. Deere Lad, beleeue it ;
For they fhall yet belye thy happy yeeres,
That fay thou art a man : *Dianas* lip
Is not more fmooth, and rubious : thy fmall pipe　　35
Is as the maidens organ, fhrill, and found,
And all is femblatiue a womans part.
I know thy conftellation is right apt
For this affayre : fome foure or fiue attend him,
All if you will : for I my felfe am beft　　　　　40
When leaft in companie : profper well in this,

33. *belye*] *be-ly* F₄.
34. Dianas] F₂.　Dianaes F₃F₄.
36. *and found*] *in sound* Wh. Dyce
ii, iii, Ktly, Huds.　*of sound* Huds.

conj.
37. *femblatiue a*] *semblative—a* Johns.
semblative to a Ktly.

ABBOTT (§ 490) for a list of words similarly accented on the last syllable, which are now accented on the first.

33. **yet**] By this particle, the idea is conveyed that Viola's extremely youthful appearance will last for many a day to come.—ED.

34. **Dianas**] Diana's lip was never kissed by man, and is, therefore, a type of the choicest purity.—ED.

36. **and sound**] R. G. WHITE (ed. i) : The error '*and* sound' for '*in* sound,' has been hitherto most strangely left uncorrected. The Duke has no occasion to remark upon the soundness of Viola's voice ; but rather the contrary. [This 'contrary' I do not understand.—ED.] He tells her that the sound of her voice is shrill, like that of a maiden's.—DYCE (ed. ii) : Mr W. N. Lettsom thinks the Folio is right, understanding 'sound' to mean 'clear, not cracked.'—The COWDEN-CLARKES : They who alter this to 'shrill *in* sound' surely impair the full meaning of the sentence. To our thinking, the Duke is intended to say, 'Thy slender voice is like a maiden's voice, high in key and at the same time uncracked.' A boy's voice is 'shrill,' high, of treble quality, but not 'sound' or uncracked ; while a girl's is of the same shrillness, or high pitch, and yet perfectly 'sound,' or pure in tone.—W. A. WRIGHT : If 'and sound' be the true reading, 'sound' must signify 'not cracked,' as Hamlet (II, ii, 448) salutes the boy, who among the players acted the woman's part, with, 'Pray God, your voice, like a piece of uncurrent gold, be not cracked within the ring.' [Unquestionably, the Folio is right. There was no indication whatever of manhood in the page's happy years. Is it not clear, that the Duke is proving for his own satisfaction that there is no risk in sending, as his messenger to Olivia, a boy of as dangerous a beauty as Viola's ?—ED.]

37. **is**] TIESSEN (*Archiv f. d. n. Spr.*, 1877, lviii, 14) : Some editions have *its ;* [I have never seen them.—ED.] possibly we should read *thy*.

37. **semblatiue**] W. A. WRIGHT : That is, resembling, like. A word of Shakespeare's coinage.

37. **a womans part**] JOHNSON : That is, thy proper part in a play would be a woman's. Women were then personated by boys.

38. **constellation**] See I, iii, 125.

And thou ſhalt liue as freely as thy Lord,   42
To call his fortunes thine.

   Uio. Ile do my beſt

To woe your Lady : yet a barrefull ſtrife,   45
Who ere I woe, my ſelfe would be his wife.   *Exeunt.*

45, 46. *woe*] *wooe* F₂F₃. *woo* F₄.
45. *Lady:*] *lady;* [Exit Duke.] Johns.
45, 46. *yet...wife*] [Aside] Cap. Mal.
et seq.
45. *a barrefull*] *a barful* F₄, Rowe,
Johns. Var. '21. *O baneful* Pope, Han.

O barful Coll. ii, iii (MS). *a baneful*
Gould. *a woeful* Daniel ap. Cam.
46. *Who ere*] F₂. *who e're* F₃F₄.
Who-e'er Rowe, +. *Whoe'er* Cap. Steev.
Var. '21.

---

42. **as freely as thy Lord**] For many other examples of the transposition of phrases (here, the present phrase should follow line 43), see WALKER (*Crit.* i, 160) and ABBOTT, § 419 *a.* See, also, 'This is a deere Manakin to you Sir Toby.'—III, ii, 54.

45. **a barrefull strife**] STEEVENS : That is, a contest full of impediments. P. A. DANIEL (p. 42) would read 'yet (Ah ! barful strife !).'

46. **Exeunt.**] SPEDDING (*New Sh. Soc. Trans.*, 1877–9, p. 24) : The division of the Acts in *Twelfth Night* is of less importance than in *King Lear* and *Much Ado about Nothing ;* for the movement of the piece is so light and rapid, and the several actions mix so naturally, without perplexing or confusing each other, that if it were played from beginning to end without any pause at all, the spectator would feel no harshness. Nevertheless, though the inter-Acts might in that case be omitted altogether without injuring the dramatic effect, the effect is materially injured on two occasions by the interposition of them in the wrong place.

At the end of the first Act Malvolio is ordered to run after Cesario with Olivia's ring ; in the second Scene of the second Act he has but just overtaken him. 'Were you not *even now,*' he says, 'with the Countess Olivia?' 'Even now, Sir' (she answers), 'on a moderate pace I have arrived but hither.' Here, therefore, the pause is worse than useless. It impedes the action, and turns a light and swift movement into a slow and heavy one.

Again, at the end of the third Act, Sir Andrew Aguecheek runs after Cesario (who has just left the stage) to beat him ; Sir Toby and Fabian following to see the event. At the beginning of the fourth, they are all where they were. Sir Andrew's valour is still warm ; he meets Sebastian, mistakes him for Cesario, and strikes. Here again the pause is not merely unnecessary ; it interrupts what was evidently meant for a continuous and rapid action, and so spoils the fun.

The first of these defects might be sufficiently removed by continuing the first Act to the end of what is now the second scene of the second. The other by continuing the third Act to the end of what is now the first scene of the fourth. But such an arrangement would leave the fourth Act so extremely short that it cannot be accepted for the true one.

I have little doubt that the first Act was meant to end with the fourth scene,—the scene between the Duke and Viola : 'Whoe'er I woo, myself would be his wife'; the second with Viola's soliloquy upon receiving Olivia's ring, II, ii, 43. The third might end where, according to the received arrangement, the second does ; only that the underplot would in that case become rather too prominent, and the main action

46. Exeunt.]

stand still too long.   To avoid this, I would not have the curtain fall till after the second interview between Olivia and Viola, in which Olivia declares her passion.

The fourth Act may end where it now does, with the contract between Olivia and Sebastian ; and the fifth will remain as it is.

I am not aware of any objection that can be made to this arrangement, or of any point which requires further explanation.   Imagine the play properly represented (I say properly ; for on the stage it is always so deformed with burlesque that no true judgement can be made of it from seeing it acted), with the divisions which I have proposed, and I think it will be felt that the arrangement recommends itself. . . . I have seldom seen a piece *acted* for the first time, however bad the acting, and however familiar I had been with the play on paper, without seeing much of it in a new light and with more vivid effect.   And in reading these things, though we may piece out the actor's imperfections with our thoughts as much as we please, imagining everything presented to our mind to seem as real and natural as the thing itself would seem,—real kings and queens, real gentlemen and ladies, real soldiers and real fighting,—we must not forget that we are supposed to be witnessing a succession of scenes passed within our sight and hearing, and so arranged to produce their effect upon the imagination under that condition.   Without a clear perception of the *periods* of action and repose, we cannot enjoy the full benefit of such arrangement ; and therefore, if we wish to have complete enjoyment of Shakespeare's art, we must always take notice of the points which mark these periods,—namely, the intervals between the Acts.   [Spedding's arrangement is, therefore, as follows :—

First Act   = I, i—iv.
Second Act = I, v; II, i, ii.
Third Act = II, iii—v ; III, i.
Fourth Act = III, ii—iv ; IV, i—iii.
Fifth Act   = V; *ad fin.*

SIR HENRY IRVING'S acting-version, according to F. A. MARSHALL, divides, and combines the Acts and Scenes as follows :—

First Act   = I, i—iv.
Second Act = I, v; II, ii, II, iii.
Third Act = II, iv, II, i; II, v, III, i.
Fourth Act = III, iii, III, ii; III, iv ; IV, i, ii.
Fifth Act   = IV, iii; *ad fin.*

See Marshall's notes at the beginning of the respective Scenes.—ED.]

Scena Quinta.

Enter Maria, and Clowne.   2

Ma. Nay, either tell me where thou haſt bin, or I will
not open my lippes ſo wide as a briſsle may enter, in way   4

---

1. Scene VI. Pope, +.   Act II, i,   3. *bin*] F_2F_3.   *been* F_4.
Spedding.   4. *briſsle*] *bristle* Rowe.
     Olivia's House. Rowe.

---

2. **Clowne**] DOUCE (i, 118) : The Clown in this play is a domestic or hired fool,
in the service of Olivia.' He is specifically termed 'an *allowed* fool,' and 'Feste, the
jester, a fool that the lady Olivia's father took much delight in.'   Malvolio likewise
speaks of him as 'a set fool.'   Of his dress it is impossible to speak correctly.   If
the fool's expression, 'I will [did] *impeticoat* thy gratility,' be the original language,
he must have been habited accordingly.   Mr Ritson has asserted that he has neither
coxcomb nor bauble, deducing his argument from the want of any allusion to them.
Yet such an omission may be a very fallacious guide in judging of the habit of this
character on the stage.   It must, however, be admitted that where this happens
there can be no clue as to the precise manner in which the fool was dressed.
[Douce's caution is justified by some of the statements in his own excellent essay
on *Clowns and Fools*, vol. ii, p. 325,—where, speaking of their costume, he says,
'We may suppose that the same variety of dress was observed on the stage which
we know to have actually prevailed in common life.   The fools however, did not
always appear in a discriminative habit, and some of their portraits still remaining
confirm this observation.   A very fine painting by Holbein, in Kensington Palace,
represents Will Somers, the Fool of Henry VIII. in a common dress. . . . In the
celebrated picture of Sir Thomas More's family, by Holbein, Patenson, the Fool,
is not distinguished by any peculiarity of dress; and, in one instance at least, the
same remark applies to Archy, the Fool of James I.'   Wherefore, on Douce's own
showing, it must be acknowledged that Ritson was probably right in his assertion
that Feste neither wore a coxcomb nor carried a bauble, and that in all likelihood
there was no distinction in dress between him and, say, Fabian.   For my own part,
I am sure from what we learn of Feste, that he was dressed with nicest care and
was quite point-device in his apparel.   Douce has given (ii, 311) what he pronounces 'the picture of a real hireling or artificial fool,'—the class to which Feste,
as he says, belongs; it is drawn from Lodge's *Wits Miserie*; as the passage has
been copied and adopted by subsequent editors of Shakespeare, it is proper to
insert it here.   But I am convinced that Lodge's picture is no picture of a Fool at
all, and that when Lodge speaks of a 'jeaster' he means a mere joker, a man of
vulgar and uproariously high spirits, and does not refer at all to a professional Fool.
It is to be remembered that Lodge's tract is written in an extremely exaggerated style.
The extract is as follows : 'The second fiend of this race is IMMODERATE and DIS-
ORDINATE IOY, and he became incorporate in the bodie of a ieaster, this fellow in
person is comely, in apparell courtly, but in behauiour a very ape, and no man ; his
studie is to coine bitter ieasts, or to show antique motions, or to sing baudie sonnets
and ballads : give him a little wine in his head, he is continually flearing and making

of thy excufe : my Lady will hang thee for thy abfence. 5

   Clo. Let her hang me : hee that is well hang'de in this
world, needs to feare no colours. 7

7. *needs to*] *needs* F_3F_4, Rowe, +, Var.   7. *colours*] *collars* Anon. ap. Cam.
'73, '78, Ran.

---

of mouthes : he laughes intemperately at euery litle occasion, and dances about the
house, leaps over tables, out-skips mens heads, trips vp his companions heeles, burns
Sacke with a candle, and hath all the feats of a Lord of misrule in the countrie : feed
him in his humor, you shall haue his heart, in meere kindnesse he will hug you in
his armes, kisse you on the cheeke, and rapping out an horrible oth, crie Gods Soule
Tum [Lodge's name was Thomas.—ED.] I loue you, you know my poore heart,
come to my chamber for a pipe of Tabacco, there liues not a man in this world that
I more honor ; In these ceremonies you shall know his courting, and it is a speciall
marke of him at the table, he sits and makes faces : keep not this fellow company,
for in iugling with him your Wardropes shall be wasted, your credits crackt, your
crownes consumed, and time (the most precious riches of the world) vtterly lost.'—
p. 84, ed. Hunterian Club. It is difficult to see how Douce or Staunton could have
been misled into the belief that this description, possibly drawn from life, referred
or applied to professional Fools.—ED.

   5. **hang thee**] The punishment for Fools, as we all know, was whipping, (Lear's
Fool was threatened with it,) possibly, in obedience to the Biblical Proverb, 'a
rod is for the back of fools.' It is incredible that Olivia should possess the power
of life and death over her servant. We must, therefore, believe either that 'hang'
does not here mean 'sus. per col.,' but some temporary punishment whereof the signification is now lost to us (which is improbable), or that it is still in keeping with
Maria's character to indulge, with the Fool, in this playful exaggeration. This
willingness to intercede for him after his pranks, shows how fond she was of him—
and who could help being so ?—ED.

   7. **feare no colours**] STEEVENS : This expression occurs frequently in the old
plays. Thus, Jonson's *Sejanus*, 'And those [ladies] that would be [fair], physic
soon can make them : For those that are, their beauties fear no colours.'[I, ii,
p. 27, ed. Gifford.] Again, Porter's *Two Angry Women of Abington*, 1599, 'Are
ye disposed, sir? *Nicholas.* Yes, indeed, I fear no colours ; change sides, Richard.'
[p. 359, ed. Hazlitt-Dodsley.]—NARES : Probably at first a military expression,
to fear no enemy. So Shakespeare derives it, and though the passage be comic, it is
likely to be right.—DYCE (*Gloss.*) quotes this, and this only, in explanation of the
phrase.—KNIGHT : It probably meant, I fear no deceptions. Holofernes says,
'I do fear colourable colours.'—*Love's Lab. L.* IV, ii, 154.—HALLIWELL quotes
Cotgrave : '*Aduentureux.* Hazardous, aduenturous ; that feares no colours,' which
repeats the phrase, but hardly advances our knowledge of its derivation. He
also quotes, 'and then pell mell, all alone haue amongst them, if there were
ten thousand of them. *Carneades.* Faith well said, I perceiue thou fearst no
colours.'—Nashe's *Haue With you to Saffron-Walden*, 1596, [p. 46, ed. Grosart.
This is the earliest instance of the phrase given by MURRAY, *N. E. D.*; albeit Halliwell furnishes one from *The Trumpet of Fame* by H. R. 1595, 'Then fear no
colours, set the chance on Christ ! He is your load-star, God of power highest.'
It is more likely that there is a misprint in Halliwell's date than that Murray should
have overlooked it. The many post-Shakespearian examples further given by Halli-

Ma. Make that good.   8

Clo. He fhall fee none to feare.

Ma. A good lenton anfwer : I can tell thee where ẙ   10
faying was borne, of I feare no colours.

Clo. Where good miftris *Mary* ?

Ma. In the warrs, & that may you be bolde to fay in
your foolerie.

Clo. Well, God giue them wifedome that haue it : &   15
thofe that are fooles, let them vfe their talents.

Ma. Yet you will be hang'd for being fo long abfent,
or to be turn'd away : is not that as good as a hanging to
you ?   19

10. *lenton*] *Lenton̦* F$_4$. *lenten* Rowe.

15. *it*] *it not* Gould.

17, 18. *abfent, or to be turn'd away :*] *abfent, or be turn'd away :* F$_2$, Rowe ii, +, Cap. Var, Ran. *abfent, or be turn'd away,* F$_3$F$_4$, Rowe i. *absent ; or, to be turn'd away,* Mal. Wh. Coll. ii, Cam. Glo. Rlfe, Dtn. *absent : or, to be turn'd away ;* Steev. Var. '21, Knt, Coll. i, iii, Hal. *absent ; or, to be turned away,*— Dyce, Sta. Ktly, Huds.

18. *not that*] *not this* Rowe i.

---

well are hardly of moment].—STAUNTON : The allusion is lost to us, here and in other instances, of this 'skipping dialogue.'—W. A. WRIGHT : There is, of course, a pun upon 'colours' and *collars*, as we find elsewhere upon 'dolours' and *dollars*. [There is the same pun upon 'colours' and *collars*, and the same phrase, 'fear no colours,' in *2 Hen. IV :* V, v, 91. In all likelihood the phrase was a 'winged word' long before Nashe used it in his farrago of low abuse ; and so old by Maria's time that she thought it needful to explain its origin to the Clown.—ED.]

10. **lenton**] JOHNSON : A *lean*, or as we now call it, a *dry* answer.—STEEVENS : Surely, it rather means a *short* and *spare* one, like the commons in *Lent.* So, in *Hamlet*, II, ii, 329, 'if you delight not in man, what lenten entertainment the players shall receive from you.' [Cotgrave : '*Amoreux de Quaresme.* A Lenten louer ; a bashfull, modest, or maidenly, woer.']

11. **of**] W. A. WRIGHT : *Of* is used to connect words or phrases in apposition, the saying here being 'I fear no colours.' So in *Coriol.* II, i, 32, 'a very little thief of occasion,' where the occasion is the thief.

16. **talents**] NARES (quoted by Halliwell) : Heaven give real wisdom to those that are called wise, and a discreet use of their talents to fools or jesters.—HALLI-WELL : Perhaps, however, the Clown is perpetrating a joke on 'talents' and *talons*, a quibble which occurs with greater distinctness in *Love's Lab. L.* [IV, ii, 65 : 'If a talent be a claw, look how he claws him with a talent'; where, indeed, the quibble is so distinct that it is not easy to see wherein it is applicable to the present passage.—ED.]—DEIGHTON : There seems to be here a profane allusion to the parable of the talents, *Matthew*, xxv. [Very doubtful.—ED.]

18. **or to be**] W. A. WRIGHT : I am not sure that the punctuation of Malone, now generally followed, is right. The insertion of 'to' before the second of two infinitives connected with the same auxiliary verb is very common, and the construction here appears to be the same as that in *As You Like It*, V, iv, 25, 26 : 'Keepe your word, Phebe, that you'*l marrie* me, Or else refusing me, *to wed* this shepheard.'

Clo. Many a good hanging, preuents a bad marriage :   20
and for turning away, let ſummer beare it out.

20. *Many*] *Marry* Theob. Warb.   21. *let ſummer beare*] *let's summer-*
Johns. Var. '73, '78, Ran.   *sault* Gould.

It might be maintained that in this instance ' to wed ' is in apposition to ' word'; but this cannot be the explanation in *Pericles*, II, v, 17 : ' She tells me here, she'*ll wed* the stranger knight, Or never more *to view* nor day nor light.' The following instances are from the Prayer-book Version of the Psalms : ' Let their habitation be void : and no man to dwell in their tents,' lxix, 26. ' That we should not hide them . . . but to shew . . .,' lxxviii, 4. ' That they might put their trust in God ; and not to forget the works of God, but to keep his commandments ; and not to be as their forefathers,' etc., lxxviii, 8, 9. [See notes in this ed. on the quotation above, from *As You Like It.* Also, on *Ib.* III, ii, 152, 153 : ' Heauen would that she these gifts *should haue*, and I *to live* and die her slaue.' See, too, ABBOTT, § 416.—ED.]

20. **Many . . . marriage**] GREY (i, 225) : The story is well known, of a criminal, whose life was begged by a female, in case he would marry her. Who, upon viewing his intended bride, when upon the cart, and ready to be turn'd off, all he said upon the occasion was, ' drive on, carter.' [This story is told with apparent seriousness by DR A. SCHMIDT, in the notes to his translation of the present play. It is a little surprising that in none of the German translations is this line rendered literally ; the gentle fun in extolling the providential character of good hangings in preventing bad marriages is lost in the statement of a dry fact : ' Gut gehängt ist besser als schlecht verheirathet.'—ED.]—INNES : Montaigne has two stories of a Picard and a Dane, who were going to be executed, and were each offered a reprieve on condition of marrying a girl who in one case was lame and in the other plain. In each case the offer was declined. The stories may have been common property ; Florio's translation of Montaigne was not published till after this play was produced. [Montaigne's story of a Picard is in Manningham's *Diary*, p. 102.—ED.]

21. **turning away**] STEEVENS states that he found the following observation among some papers of ' the late Dr Letherland': ' This seems to be a pun from the nearness in the pronunciation of *turning away* and *turning of whey.*' [The name of the author of this interpretation may be spelled ' Letherland,' but it is to be strongly suspected that it was pronounced *Steevens.*—ED.] Steevens then continues : It is common for unsettled and vagrant serving-men to grow negligent of their business towards summer ; and the sense of the passage is : ' If I am turned away, the advantages of the approaching summer will bear out, or support all the inconveniences of dismission ; for I shall find employment in every field, and lodging under every hedge.'—WILLIAM H. SMITH (*N. & Qu.* 1859, 2nd, vii, 337) : ' Turning away ' should be pronounced ' turning aw-ay '—*i. e.* ' turning *o' hay.*' [' " God bless me !" said my uncle Toby.'—ED.]—JOHN ADDIS, JUN. (*N. & Qu.* 1867, 3rd, xi, 252): The words in their plain sense mean that in summer a homeless person suffers fewer hardships than at other seasons. Accordant with this view I subjoin a passage from the Interlude of *Jacke Jugler :* ' I neuer vse to rune awaye in wynter nor in vere But all wayes in suche tyme and season of the yere When honye lyeth in the hiues of Bees And all maner frute falleth from the trees As Apples, Nuttes, Peres, and plummes also Wherby a boye maye liue a brod a moneth or two.' [E. ii, *verso*, Ashbee's Facsimile.]—W. A. WRIGHT : But perhaps the Clown, having been

Ma.　You are refolute then?　　　　　　　　　　　　　22

Clo.　Not fo neyther, but I am refolu'd on two points

Ma.　That if one breake, the other will hold: or if both
breake, your gaskins fall.　　　　　　　　　　　　　　25

Clo.　Apt in good faith, very apt: well go thy way, if
fir *Toby* would leaue drinking, thou wert as witty a piece
of *Eues* flefh, as any in Illyria.

Ma.　Peace you rogue, no more o' that: here comes my
Lady : make your excufe wifely, you were beft.　　　　30

---

22. *You*] *Your* F₂.　　　　　　　　26. *very*] *vety* F₃.
25. *gaskins*] *gaskings* F₄, Rowe,　28. *in*] Om. Rowe i.
Pope.　　　　　　　　　　　　　　30. [Exit. Pope et seq.

---

frequently threatened with dismissal, simply means, Wait till summer comes, and see
if it be true.

　23. **points**] BLACKSTONE : 'Points' were metal hooks, fastened to the hose or
breeches, (which then had no opening or buttons,) and going into straps or eyes
fixed to the doublet, and thereby keeping the hose from falling down.—STEEVENS :
So in *1 Hen. IV:* II, iv, 238 : ' *Falstaff.* Their points being broken— *Poins.* Down
fell their hose.' Again, *Ant. & Cleop.* III, xiii, 157 : 'To flatter Cæsar, would you
mingle eyes With one that ties his points ?' [Blackstone's definition of 'point'
appears in the *Var.* of 1821, and may be therefore supposed to have been approved
by Steevens, Malone, and Reed ; yet I think it is hardly correct. 'Points' are
always spoken of as *trussed*, or *tied ;* it is not easy to see how ' metal hooks' could
ever have been tied. Over the shirt, our ancestors wore a tight vest or doublet,
which might or might not have sleeves, and is, in fact, the progenitor of our modern
waistcoat ; from its lower edge depended a number of strings or laces (how many,
I do not know), and these strings had metal points, like our modern shoe-laces ;
these *points* it was which gave the name to the strings. There were corresponding
points on the slops or breeches, or hose, or, as Maria here calls them, the 'gaskins.'
When the points on the doublet and the points on the hose were trussed or tied, the
man was dressed, and needed but his cloak, his boots, and his girdle to jet it abroad.
—ED.]

　25. **gaskins**] BRADLEY (*N. E. D*) : Of uncertain origin ; perhaps due to a false
analysis of Galligaskin, to which the 'gallant gaskins' of the quotation [from
G. Harvey, see *infra*] comes close in point of sound. On the other hand, as Cotgrave explains French *grègues* by ' wide slops, Gregs, Gallogascoines, Venetians ; a
great Gascon or Spanish hose,' it seems possible that such hose were actually worn in
Gascony ; if so, this word may have been a special use of *Gascon*, and have existed
earlier than *galligaskin*. A kind of breech or hose. Chiefly plural. G. Harvey
(1573) *Letter-bk* (Camden) 6 : 'His oun gai gallant gaskins, his kut dublets, his
staring hare.'

　27, 28. **thou wert . . . Illyria**] Does not the Clown pretend to whisper this in
Maria's ear ?—ED.

　30. **you were best**] W. A. WRIGHT : That is, it were best for you. Originally
the pronoun in this phrase was in the dative case, but by the time of Shakespeare it
had come to be regarded as the nominative. Similarly, the phrase ' if you please'

Enter Lady Oliuia, with Maluolio.   31

Clo. Wit, and't be thy will, put me into good fooling :
thofe wits that thinke they haue thee, doe very oft proue
fooles : and I that am fure I lacke thee, may paffe for a
wife man. For what faies *Quinapalus*, Better a witty foole,   35
then a foolifh wit.   God bleffe thee Lady.

Ol.   Take the foole away.

Clo.   Do you not heare fellowes, take away the Ladie.

Ol.   Go too, y'are a dry foole : Ile no more of you:be-   39

31. Scene VII. Pope, +.

    Enter...] After '*foolifh wit,*' line
36, Dyce, Cam. Sta. Glo. Rlfe, Huds.
Dtn.

    32. *and't*] *an't* Han. Cap. Var. '21,
Coll. Wh. Dyce, Cam. Rlfe.

    good] *a good* Theob. ii, Warb.

Johns. Var. '73.

    35. Quinapalus,] *Quinapalus ?* Han.
Cap. et seq.

    38. *fellowes,*] *fellows ?* Theob. ii. et
seq.

    39. *y'are*] Ff, Rowe, +, Wh. ii.
you're Cap. et cet.

---

was originally ' if it please you,' the pronoun being in the dative.   [See ' she were
better,' II, ii, 22 ; 'your Ladyship were best,' III, iv, 13 ; or, if need be, ABBOTT,
§§ 230, 352. Or *As You Like It,* I, i, 143 ; *Mid. N. D.* I, ii, 5 ; *Wint. Tale,* v,
ii, 132 ; all of this ed.—ED.]

    31. Enter . . . Maluolio] BR. NICHOLSON (*N. & Qu.* 1892, 8th, i, 370) :
This stage-direction has been generally followed down to the last Cambridge Edition.   Staunton, however, gave, more correctly, '*Enter* Olivia, Malvolio, *and
Attendants,*' for the Clown says, line 38, ' Do you not hear, fellows '; and again,
line 69, ' Take away the fool, gentlemen.'   But these very passages show that even
this stage-direction is insufficient, for in our day we naturally expect that a lady will
be accompanied only by female attendants.   Olivia, however, was a peeress in her
own right, and would be attended by a retinue, or guard, of armed gentlemen servi-
tors.   Shakespeare here, true to the custom of his times, and also that he might at
once set before his spectators,—the full rank of Olivia and the fact that the Duke
was in no way demeaning himself in his love,—the absurd vanity of Malvolio that
is to be hereafter depicted,—and the great good fortune of Sebastian,—provides that
Olivia's first entrance should be made in her usual state, attended both by her women
and her armed retainers ; Malvolio taking his place, not as her confidential friend,
but simply as the steward of her household. . . . A note somewhat to the effect
I have spoken of being made, the direction might run : '*Enter* Olivia *in state,* with
Attendants, female and male, Malvolio *among the latter.*' [Nicholson possibly
overlooked Capell's edition, where the stage-direction implies, I think, what Nicholson, with much reason, has urged : '*Enter* Olivia, *attended, and* Malvolio.'—ED.]

    35. Quinapalus] One of the leaders of the Vapians when they passed the
equinoctial of Queubus.—ED.

    35, 36. Better . . . wit] JOHNSON : Hall, in his *Chronicle,* speaking of the
death of Sir Thomas More, says that, ' he knows not whether to call him a foolish
wise man, or a wise foolish man.'   [Be it not forgotten that ' witty ' is not here used
in its modern sense.—ED.]

    39. dry] See I, iii, 74.

ſides you grow diſ-honeſt.   40

   Clo. Two faults Madona, that drinke & good counſell
wil amend : for giue the dry foole drink, then is the foole
not dry : bid the diſhoneſt man mend himſelf, if he mend,
he is no longer diſhoneſt; if hee cannot, let the Botcher
mend him : any thing that's mended, is but patch'd : vertu   .45
that tranſgreſſes, is but patcht with ſinne, and ſin that a-
mends, is but patcht with vertue. If that this ſimple
Sillogiſme will ſerue, ſo : if it will not, vvhat remedy ?   48

   40. *diſ-honeſt*] F$_2$.   Ran. Mal. et seq.
   41. *Madona*] *Madonna* Var. '78,

---

   39. **Ile no more of you**] See I, iii, 100.

   40. **dis-honest**] RANN : That is, indecent. SCHMIDT gives these additional
examples of the use of the word in this same sense : In *Merry Wives*, III, iii, 196,
Mrs Page, speaking of Falstaff, says, ' Hang him, dishonest rascal '; and again she
applies the same adjective to him in IV, ii, 104 : ' Hang him, dishonest varlet.'
Again, *Hen. V:* I, ii, 49 : ' Who, holding in disdain the German women For some
dishonest manner in their life, Establish'd then this law.' Of course, in all cases the
context must decide the meaning. In III, iv, 387, Sir Toby uses ' dishonest' in its
ordinary sense, *dishonourable*. W. A. WRIGHT calls attention to the use of ' honest '
in the sense of virtuous in Hamlet's interview with Ophelia, III, i, 103 and 123 :
' Are you honest ?' ' I am myself indifferent honest.'

   41. **Madona**] *Madonna*, mistres, mistres mine, madam. Also taken for our
ladie.—Florio, *Worlde of Wordes*, 1598.

   42, 43. **dry . . . dishonest**] In thus interpreting these two words in a sense
different from that in which Olivia had just used them, Feste proves his right to be
the Countess's ' corrupter of words.'—ED.

   44. **Botcher**] ' BOTCHARE of olde thinges. *Resartor.'—Promp. Parv.* (where, in
a foot-note, WAY quotes from Palsgrave : ' to botche, or bungyll a garment as he dothe
that is nat a perfyte workeman, *fatrouiller.*' [I suppose a botcher held the same
relation to a tailor that a cobbler holds to a shoemaker.—ED.]

   45. **patch'd**] MALONE : Alluding to the *patched* or particoloured garment of the
fool. [See line 2 above, where Feste's dress is discussed.—ED.]

   48. **Sillogisme**] RUGGLES (p. 35) : The Clown's whimsical wit invests itself in
the forms of logic. He is the logician of the play,—' a corrupter of words.' His
more elaborate witticisms are arguments that lack but little of regular syllogistic
form.—HUTSON (*Southern Maga.* 1875, May, p. 483) : The logical forms are sound
enough, whatever may be said of their fruit ; and in their formal statement the
propositions run thus :—

        Major Premiss—All mended things are patched things ;
        Minor Premiss—Broken virtue is virtue sin-mended ;
        Conclusion—Therefore broken virtue is sin-patched.

   This is the categorical form ; now let us put the other proposition into the conditional :—

        Major Premis—If sin amends, then sin is mended ;
        Minor Premis—But mended things are patched things ;
        Conclusion—Then sin is patched.

As there is no true Cuckold but calamity, fo beauties a
flower ; The Lady bad take away the foole, therefore I 50
fay againe, take her away.

 Ol. Sir, I bad them take away you.

 Clo. Mifprifion in the higheft degree. Lady, *Cucullus* 53

---

49. *Cuckold*] *counsellor* Han. *dis-*   49. *beauties*] *beautie's* F$_2$. *beauty's*
honour Huds.   F$_3$F$_4$.

The unexpressed fact, upon which both syllogisms rest, is, of course, that human
nature is neither absolutely good nor absolutely bad ; that the man of virtue sometimes sins, and the man of sin sometimes amends ; and hence, whether virtue or sin
be present in any, it must needs be patched with its opposite. That the whole thing
is nonsense, as an argument for maintaining that virtue and vice are things indifferent, is only an additional bell to the fool's cap. His *Cucullus non facit monachum*
is another stone to be added to my theory of his having had a clerical education.
[In this truly delightful essay Prof. Hutson has previously expressed his suspicion
that Feste had been ' educated for the Church and had ruined his prospects by some
wild prank '; he did not, however, notice, in the present instance, what did not escape
W. A. WRIGHT, that Feste is ' talking against time and sense in order to escape the
reprimand he deserves.']

 49. **Cuckold, etc.**] CAPELL (p. 142) : Apothegms in such a mouth as this
speaker's are of themselves laughable, and the Poet has made them doubly and
trebly so : by giving him such as have no relation whatever one to other, and yet
putting them argument-wise ; by corrupting one of them oddly, ' cuckold' for *school*
or else (which is the Oxford text) *counsellor ;* and by both these methods obscuring
their little pertinency to what is in hand, and making shew as they had none : but
this is not the case absolutely ; his first murder'd apothegm squints at his ' turning
away,' and his latter is a memento to his lady. [Which, interpreted, means that
' calamity' refers to the Clown himself, and ' flower' to Olivia. W. A. WRIGHT says
here, justly, that in using the word ' cuckold' the Clown 'purposely blunders.'
Let it be repeated that he is purposely rattling off bewildering nonsense.—ED.]

 52, etc. **Sir, I bad, etc.**] LAMB (ii, 367) : Mrs Powel (now Mrs Renard), then
in the pride of her beauty, made an excellent Olivia. She was particularly excellent
in her unbending scenes with the Clown. I have seen some Olivia's,—and those
very sensible actresses, too,—who in these interlocutions have seemed to set their
wits at the jester, and to vie conceits with him in downright emulation. But she
used him for her sport, like what he was, to trifle a leisure sentence or two with, and
then to be dismissed, and she to be the Great Lady still. She touched the imperious
fantastic humour of the character with nicety.

 53. **Misprision, etc.**] RUSHTON (*Lex Scripta*, p. 84) : Coke says, ' compassings
or imaginations against the King by word, without an overt act, is a *high misprision.*'
—3 *Institute*, cap. lxv. But although the Clown here speaks of misprision in the
highest degree, I think he plays upon the word, using it also in the sense of contempt.
—SKEAT (*Dict.*) : A mistake, neglect. See Blount's *Nomolexicon*, ed. 1691 : ' *misprision* of clerks (Anno 8 Hen. VI. c. 15) is a neglect of clerks in writing or keeping records. . . . *Misprision* also signifies a mistaking.' Old French, ' *mesprison,*
mïsprision, error, offence, a thing done, or taken, amisse.'—Cotgrave. . . . 2. It is
tolerably certain that *misprision* was ignorantly confused with *misprise*, and wrongly

non facit monachum : that's as much to fay, as I weare not
motley in my braine : good *Madona*, giue mee leaue to   55
proue you a foole.

    Ol. Can you do it ?

    Clo. Dexteriouſly, good Madona.   58

---

54. *that's as much to fay,*] Ff. *that's
as much to say* Knt, Dyce, Cam. Sta.
Glo. Rlfe, Dtn, Wh. ii. *that as much
as to say* Rowe i. *that's as much as to
say* Rowe ii et cet.

    as I weare] F₂. *as I wear* F₃,

Cam. Glo. Rlfe, Dtn, Wh. ii. *as I were*
F₄, Rowe i. *as, I wear* Knt, Dyce, Sta.
I wear Rowe ii et cet.

    58. *Dexteriouſly*] *Dexterously* F₄,
Rowe, +, Knt, Sta. Coll. iii.

---

used in the sense of contempt. Thus Blount, in the article already cited, says :
' *misprision* of treason is a neglect or light account made of treason '; and he derives
the word from French *mespris*, contempt. This easy error has probably resulted in
false law. [A quotation by Rushton from Coke shows that the error had received
an authority which no lawyer in those days dare question. ' Misprisio,' says Coke,
3 *Inst.* cap. iii, ' cometh of the word mes, pris, which properly signifieth neglect
or contempt.' I doubt that the Clown knew the precise legal signification of ' misprision '; but by its present use he indirectly imputes to his mistress an offence against
his own superior majesty. Of course, to say that the word here means simply *a mistake*
may be true enough ; but I think the Clown intended to convey much more than
this, when he used such a high-sounding phrase in the superlative degree.—ED.]

    53, 54. **Cucullus . . . monachum**] W. A. WRIGHT : Cotgrave gives the French
proverb, ' L' habit ne fait pas le moine : Pro. The Cowle makes not the Monke ;
euerie one is not a souldier that weares armor ; nor euerie one a scholler thats clad
in blacke.' In the same form it appears in all the languages of Europe. See *Meas.
for Meas.* V, i, 263.

    54. **that's as much to say**] DYCE : Thus, in *2 Hen. VI :* IV, ii, 18 : ' and yet
it is said, labour in thy vocation ; which is as much to say as, let the magistrates be
labouring men.' Both forms [the present and *as much as to say*] were used.—W. A.
WRIGHT : Compare Florio's *Italian Dict.:* ' Madornale, as much to say as lawfully
borne, and of a true and lawfull Mother.' Again, in Holland's *Plutarch*, p. 723 :
' For where wee faile to give reason of a cause, there begin we to doubt & make
question, & that is as much to say, as to play the philosophers.'

    58. **Dexteriously**] W. A. WRIGHT : This may possibly be an intentional cor-
ruption, but it actually occurs in Bacon's *Advancement of Learning*, ii, 22, § 15
(p. 214, ed. Wright) : ' He [the sophist] cannot form a man so dexteriously, nor
with that facility to prize and govern himself, as love can do.' Here the editions of
1605, 1629, and 1633 all read ' dexteriously,' although in another passage the word
is spelt as usual. Again, in Naunton's *Fragmenta Regalia* (ed. Arber), p. 28 : ' We
take him [Leicester] as he was admitted into the Court, and the Queens favour, where
he was not to seek to play his part well, and dexteriously.' [This is generally considered a corruption whether intentional or not. But Wright's quotations suggest that
it was an allowable pronunciation, on the analogy of ' prolixious,' in *Meas. for Meas.*
II, iv, 162 : ' Lay by all nicety and prolixious blushes '; or ' robustious,' in *Hamlet*,
III, ii, 10 : ' It offends me to hear a robustious periwig-pated fellow,' etc.; and in
Hen. V : III, vii, 159 : ' the men do sympathize with the mastiffs in robustious and

Ol. Make your proofe.

Clo. I muſt catechize you for it Madona, Good my   60
Mouſe of vertue anſwer mee.

Ol. Well ſir, for want of other idleneſſe, Ile bide your
proofe.   63

61. *Mouſe*] *Muse* Anon. ap. Cam.   62. *bide*] *bid* F₄. *abide* Var. '85,
mee] Om. F₃F₄, Rowe.   *'bide* Var. '03, '13, '21, Knt, Coll.

rough coming-on.' Thus also in Stubbes, *Anatomie of Abuses*, we find, 'giue the
King to vnderstand the inormious abuse thereof.' (p. 47, ed. New Sh. Society, Series
vi, No. 4.) Lastly, in *Othello*, although the Qq generally have 'jealious,' the First
Folio almost invariably prints it 'jealous.' (See *Othello*, III, iv, 179, of this ed.
Also 'studient,' IV, ii, 10; 'jealious,' IV, iii, 30, *post.*) Walker (*Vers.* 154) quotes
'grevious' from Butler, and calls attention to the present vulgarisms *mischevious*
and *tremendious*. Wherefore, I doubt that Feste intended, or that Olivia noticed,
anything unusual in 'dexteriously.'—ED.]

   60, 61. Good my Mouse of vertue] ABBOTT (§ 13) says that this is formed by
analogy from such phrases as 'good my lord,' 'good my girl,' 'good my knave,'
etc., where the possessive pronouns are so unemphatic that they are transposed and
really combine with the nouns, like the French *monsieur*. If the phrase were merely
'good my mouse,' I think Abbott would be entirely right, and the phrase equivalent
to 'my good mouse,' but we have 'mouse of virtue,' and to say 'my good mouse
of virtue' sounds a little tautological. Wherefore, I think that 'Good' is here
emphatic, and should have a comma after it, with somewhat of the meaning of 'Now,
then,' 'Come, then'; much like Marcellus's 'Good, now sit down, and tell me,'
Hamlet, I, i, 70. There is a pause of a second or two after 'Madonna,' while the
Clown is marshalling his logic. Then he begins, 'Good, my mouse of virtue,
answer me.'—ED.

   61. Mouse] Bartlett's *Concordance* gives the two or three instances where Shakespeare has used this as a term of endearment. The most familiar to us all is
Hamlet's 'Pinch wanton on your cheek, call you his mouse,' III, iv. 183.—W. A.
WRIGHT: In applying this term to Olivia the Clown was stretching to the utmost his
privilege as an allowed fool. He does this purposely to prevent her from referring
to his past misdeeds.

   62. idlenesse] That is, trifling. Or, as ROLFE says, 'pastime, means of whiling
away an idle hour.' The interpretation of *idle* should be always approached with
fear and trembling, 'all that makes wet the pores and lifts the hair.' It is the most
fatal single word in dramatic literature, possibly, in all literature. Owing to Macready's interpretation of it, in Hamlet's 'I must be idle,' twenty-three persons were
killed outright, and as many more horribly mutilated. Over this ensanguined scene
the thoughtful philanthropist can but lament that it was the harmless readers of Shakespeare who were the victims and not the emenders of his text. See *Account of the
Terrific and Fatal Riot at the New York Astor-Place Opera House, May 10th, 1849*,
p. 28.—ED.

   62. bide] Needlessly changed to *'bide* by REED. 'Bide,' says MURRAY (*N. E.
D.*), 'is mostly replaced in modern English by its compound *abide*, but regularly
preserved in northern English and Scotch; and also employed by 19th century
poets, partly, perhaps, as an archaism, partly as an aphetized form of *abide*.'

Clo. Good Madona, why mournſt thou?

Ol. Good foole, for my brothers death.   65

Clo. I thinke his foule is in hell, Madona.

Ol. I know his foule is in heauen, foole.

Clo. The more foole (Madona) to mourne for your
Brothers foule, being in heauen. Take away the Foole,
Gentlemen.   70

Ol. What thinke you of this foole *Maluolio*, doth he
not mend?

Mal. Yes, and ſhall do, till the pangs of death ſhake
him : Infirmity that decaies the wife, doth euer make the
better foole.   75

Clow. God ſend you ſir, a ſpeedie Infirmity, for the
better increaſing your folly : Sir *Toby* will be ſworn that
I am no Fox, but he wil not paſſe his word for two pence
that you are no Foole.

Ol. How ſay you to that *Maluolio*?   80

Mal. I maruell your Ladyſhip takes delight in ſuch
a barren raſcall : I ſaw him put down the other day, with   82

68. *foole*] F₂. *fool you* F₃F₄, Rowe, +,
Cap. Var. Mal. Hal. Ktly.
69. *foule, being*] soul being Rowe et
seq.

74, 75. *the better*] better the Rowe
ii, +, Var. '73.
77. *increaſing*] encreaſing Cap. Var.
Steev. Var.

---

69. **soule, being**] W. A. WRIGHT : This comma changes the construction without materially altering the sense.

74. **decaies**] For the active use of this word, see, ' When rocks impregnable are not so stout, Nor gates of steel so strong, but Time decays.'—*Sonn.* lxv, 8; and ' every day that comes comes to decay A day's work in him.'—*Cymb.* I, v, 56.

76, 77. **the better increasing**] Compare ' With viewing of the town,' III, iii, 46; ' for tainting of my love,' V, i, 144. See ABBOTT (§ 93) for other examples of a verbal noun followed by an object, with or without the definite article before it.

81. **Ladyship**] WALKER having stated (*Crit.* ii, 141) that *Ladiſhip* is always so spelled in the Folio, LETTSOM, in a footnote, subjoins : Walker is not quite correct here. *Ladiſhip* is far more frequent in the Folio than *Ladyſhip*, but the latter occurs fifteen times. The two modes of spelling rarely occur in the same play; never, I believe, but in *All's Well*. *Two Gent. of Verona* has ' Ladiſhip ' sixteen times; *Ladyſhip* never. *Twelfth Night* has ' Ladyship ' five times, and once ' Ladieship '; never *Ladiſhip*. [What is this but poring over the work of a compositor to whom the obligation to preserve uniformity in spelling was of the lightest? —ED.]

82. **barren**] See ' barren,' I, iii, 77, if need be.

82. **with**] For very many examples of this instrumental *with*, equivalent to *by*, see, if need be, ABBOTT, § 193.

an ordinary foole, that has no more braine then a ſtone.   83
Looke you now, he's out of his gard already : vnles you
laugh and miniſter occaſion to him, he is gag'd. I proteſt   85
I take theſe Wiſemen, that crow ſo at theſe ſet kinde of
fooles, no better then the fooles Zanies.   87

83. *braine*] *brains* F₃F₄, Rowe, Pope,
Han.
84. *gard*] *guard* F₄.
86. *theſe*] *those* Han.
Wiſemen] F₂. *Wiſe men* F₃F₄

87. *no better*] *to be no better* Cap.
Wh. i, Coll. ii, iii (MS), Ktly, Huds.
for no better Kinnear.
fooles] *fools'* Theob. ii et seq.

83. **ordinary foole**] STAUNTON : An *ordinary* fool may mean a *common* fool ; but more probably, as Shakespeare had always an eye to the manners of his own countrymen, he referred to a jester hired to make sport for the diners at a public ordinary. [Staunton's suggestion receives some corroboration from what follows : 'that *has* no more brain than a stone,' as though the reference were to a class and not to one particular instance ; in the latter case, we should have expected, 'that *had* no more,' etc. Still, I am not sure that this might not apply equally well to the class of *common* fools.—ED.]

84. **out of his gard**] DEIGHTON : We should now say, *off* his guard, that is, not in a position to defend himself, not prepared to continue the combat. Compare, for a similar metaphor, *Love's Lab. L.* V, i, 62, 'Now by the salt wave of the Mediterranean, a sweet touch, *a quick venue of wit!* snip, snap, quick and home,' 'venue' being a technical term in fencing for a thrust, hit. [I am not sure that *off his guard* is an equivalent of the present phrase. Perhaps Malvolio means that the Clown has exhausted his means of defence. It is not unfair to press a man until he is out of means to guard himself ; it is unfair to attack him when he is off his guard.—ED.]

86. **Wisemen**] I doubt that this word should be separated into its compounds ; at most, there should be merely a hyphen between them ; not because the printers have so transmitted the word, but because it probably represents the pronunciation of the time, when *men* in such compounds had merely an enclitic force. We have it in such proper names, now-a-days, as *Goodman, Chapman,* etc. Moreover, the sense needs the compound ; for instance, 'editors are not wise men in separating a compound which wisemen retain.' WALKER (*Crit.* ii, 136) has gathered examples where the rhythm requires this compound to be retained in such words as *richman, youngman, oldman, deadman,* etc. He would go so far as to read *tameman* in *Mid. N. D.* III, ii, 269, of this ed. The present prose instance, 'Wisemen,' is not included in his list, but, I think, his general rule certainly applies to it.—ED.

86. **crow**] Who will not recall Jaques and his 'My lungs began to crow like chanticleer'?

86, 87. **these set kinde of fooles**] See I, ii, 12, 'those poor number'; here 'kind' like 'number' may be considered a plural. Or, as ABBOTT (§ 412) suggests, the two nouns connected by *of* may be regarded as a compound noun with a plural termination, thus, 'these set *kind-of-fools.*' Or, as W. A. WRIGHT surmises, the pronoun may be attracted into the plural by the plural substantive which follows. Compare *Lear,* II, ii, 96, 'These kind of knaves, I know'; *As You Like It,* II, iii, 11, 'to some kind of men Their graces serve them,' etc.

87. **the fooles Zanies**] DOUCE : That is, *fools' baubles,* which had upon the top

[87. the fooles Zanies]

of them the *head of a fool*. [This erroneous definition caused a trifling skirmish between Collier and Dyce. COLLIER copied it in his First Edition without comment and, therefore, presumably with approval. DYCE (*Rem.* 74) quoted Collier's note with the comment 'Douce's explanation is strangely wrong. "The fools' zanies" is equivalent to "the buffoons, or mimics, of the fools." *Zany*, both as a substantive and verb, is commonly used in that sense by our early writers; "Thou art the Fowler, and doest shew vs shapes, And we are all thy Zanies, thy true apes."— *Verses on Coryate* by *Drayton*, in the *Odcombian Banquet*, etc., 1611; "Laughes them to scorne, as man doth busy apes When they will zanie men."—Marston's *Antonios Reuenge*, 1602.' COLLIER, in his Second Edition, quoted Dyce's remark that Douce's definition was 'strangely wrong,' and then added, somewhat disingenuously, I cannot but think, that it was for that purpose only that he had quoted it in his First Edition. 'Mr Dyce is, however,' he goes on to say, 'quite as much in error as Mr Douce, when he says that in the passage in the text "the fools' zanies" means the *mimics* of the fools; it means those who are silly enough to applaud fools, and thereby become the fools of the fools. If Mr Dyce had here consulted Richardson, he would have seen that "zany" is applied to half-witted people; hence it is used for a fool by nature.' HALLIWELL has gathered a list of quotations illustrating the true meaning of the word, in a note, as follows : ' *Zane*, the name of Iohn. Also a sillie Iohn, a gull, a noddie. Vsed also for a simple vice, clowne, foole, or simple fellowe in a plaie or comedie.'—Florio, *Worlde of Wordes*, 1598. 'Zany, or foolish imitator.'—Minsheu. [This quotation I cannot find in Minsheu, search how I may.—ED.] The term zany was generally applied in England to an inferior fool or buffoon attending on and imitating another, and in this sense the word is used in the text. 'He's like the zany to a tumbler, That tries tricks after him, to make men laugh.' Jonson's *Every Man Out of his Humour* [IV, i, p. 132, ed. Gifford] ; 'The other gallant is his zany, and doth most of these tricks after him; [sweats to imitate him in everything to a hair,'—Ib. *Cynthia's Revels*, II, i, p. 265]. 'Your Inne-a-court-man is Zany to the Knights, and (mary very scuruily) comes likewise limping after it.'—Dekker's *Guls Horn-booke* [Chap. VI, p. 251, ed. Grosart]. 'As th' English apes and very zanies be Of everything, that they do hear and see, [so imitating his ridiculous tricks, They speak and write, all like meer lunaticks.']— Drayton, [*Elegies. To Henry Reynolds, Esq.*] In some of the above instances, and in many others that might be adduced, the term *zany* seems to be merely used in the sense of *imitator*, a metaphorical use derived from the interpretation above given. The fool or attendant on a mountebank was also called a zany. In Jonson's *Fox*, when Volpone is disguised as a mountebank doctor, he addresses his attendant as his zany. [Halliwell gives more than a folio page of additional quotations, but they yield nothing new, and, moreover, are all post-Shakespearian. Whatever credit is due for the elucidation of the meaning of 'zany,' belongs first to Halliwell, and next to Dyce, but they were both overlooked, doubtless inadvertently, by the late Professor BAYNES in his valuable Article on *Shakespearian Glossaries* (*Edin. Rev.* July, 1869) ; wherein it is said that 'no critic has yet explained what "zany" really means, or pointed out the special relevancy of Shakespeare's allusions to the character.' Baynes then gives his own definition, which is, in effect, merely an amplification of Halliwell's interpretation given above. 'The *zany* in Shakespeare's day,' he observes, 'was not so much a buffoon and mimic as the obsequious follower of a buffoon, and the attenuated mime of a mimic. He was the

Ol. O you are ficke of felfe-loue *Maluolio*, and tafte   88
with a diftemper'd appetite. To be generous, guitleffe,
and of free difpofition, is to take thofe things for Bird-   90
bolts, that you deeme Cannon bullets : There is no flan-
der in an allow'd foole, though he do nothing but rayle ;   92

89. *guitleffe*] F$_2$. *guileless* Tiessen, Gould.

---

vice, servant, or attendant of the professional clown or fool, who, dressed like his master, accompanied him on the stage or in the ring, following his movements, attempting to imitate his tricks, and adding to the general merriment by his ludicrous failures and comic imbecility. It is this characteristic not merely of mimicry, but of weak and abortive mimicry, that gives its distinctive meaning to the word, and colours it with a special tinge of contempt.' Were the zanies of the Elizabethan age really 'weak and abortive mimics'? Surely, an abortive zany would create but little laughter. The loudest merriment would be evoked, I should think, when the mimicry of tones, of bearing, of looks, of gestures was most pronounced and successful. See quotation above from *Cynthia's Revels*. Baynes's definition was too much influenced, I fear, by the Clowns in the modern Circus. Indeed, he asserts that 'this feature of the early stage [the zany] has descended to our own times, and may still occasionally be found in all its vigour in the performances of the circus.' To this he was led, I think, by his solitary quotation, in illustration of the present class of zanies, from Ben Jonson's *Every Man Out of his Humour*, given above by Halliwell, wherein the zany is mentioned, not of a Fool, but of a *tumbler*,—a very different character. It was this quotation, coupled with too narrow a range, that gave a bias to Baynes's remarks, which mainly apply to only one class of zanies, and, possibly, the lowest. It is to be borne in mind that *mimicry, ex vi termini*, involves a tinge of contempt, in that it is the attempt to imitate, in a grotesque way, for the purpose of boisterous laughter, the actions of another. Some discussion, on this and other points in Baynes's Article, arose in *Notes & Queries*. But nothing new was called forth. In the issue for 8th of Jan., 1890 (4th, v, 39) Baynes reiterated his definition of zany, just given.—ED.]

88. **sicke of selfe-loue**] In his Article on *Proverbs in Shakespeare*, WALKER (*Crit.* ii, 169) quotes this with the remark, 'This, too, would seem to be a proverbial expression, from its occurring also in Jonson, *Staple of News*, V, i, p. 297, ed. Gifford, 'As if my testimony were not twenty, Balanced with thine ! *Picklock.* So say all prodigals, Sick of self-love.' [Gifford gives the date of *The Staple of News* as about 1625. Any post-Shakespearian phrase should be, therefore, received with caution. So deep was the impression which Shakespeare made on his contemporaries, that even his light expressions may have been caught up and perpetuated like proverbs. If 'sick of self-love' were a proverb, Shakespeare may have started it. —ED.]

90, 91. **Bird-bolts**] In *Much Ado*, I, i, 43, this is spelled, as it was probably pronounced, *Burbolt*. In a note *ad loc.* (in this edition) STEEVENS defines 'bird-bolt' as a 'short, thick arrow without a point, and spreading at the extremity so much as to leave a flat surface, about the breadth of a shilling.'

92. **an allow'd foole**] HALLIWELL : A licensed fool, a fool permitted to say anything. In Hollyband's *Dictionarie*, 1593, mention is made of 'an allowed cart or chariot.'

nor no rayling, in a knowne difcreet man, though hee do   93
nothing but reproue.

 Clo. Now Mercury indue thee with leafing, for thou   95
fpeak'ft well of fooles.

      Enter Maria.

 Mar. Madam, there is at the gate, a young Gentleman, much defires to fpeake with you.

 Ol. From the Count *Orfino*, is it?   100

 Ma I know not (Madam) 'tis a faire young man, and
well attended.

 Ol. Who of my people hold him in delay *?*

 Ma. Sir *Toby* Madam, your kinfman.   104

---

95. *indue*] *endue* Var. '03.
 leafing] *learning* Rowe, Han.
pleasing Warb.
96. *fpeak'ft*] *speakest* Var. '03, '13,
'21, Knt, Coll. Hal. Dyce, Cam.

98, 99. *Gentleman, much*] Ff, Theob.
Warb. Johns. Cap. Mal. Steev. *gentleman much* Rowe et cet.
100, 107. *Count*] *Duke* Han.
104. *kinfman*] *Uncle* Rowe ii, +.

 93, 94. **discreet man . . . reproue**] Is not this what Capell would call 'a
wipe' on Malvolio, in payment for his reproof (almost amounting to insolence) of
Olivia for laughing at Feste's jokes?—ED.

 95. **leasing**] HEATH (p. 187): Olivia had been making a kind of apology for
fools; and the Fool in recompense prays Mercury, the god of cheats and, consequently, of liars, to bestow upon her the gift of leasing, or lying; humourously intimating that, whoever undertook the defence of fools would have plentiful occasion
for that talent.—KNIGHT: Is it not rather,—since thou speakest the truth of fools
(which is not profitable), may Mercury give thee the advantageous gift of lying?—R.
G. WHITE: As Olivia undertakes the defence of his calling, the Clown prays Mercury,
the god of liars, to enable her to push her defence beyond the bounds of truth.
'Leasing' appears to have been used to convey the idea of falsehood without malice.
It was measurably synonymous with 'gabbling,' which is apt to run into lying.
'Gabbynge, or lesynge, *Mendacium, mendaciolum.*'—*Prompt. Parv.* [But 'Gab-
bing' in the *Prompt.* has in it no trace of *gabbling.* That there is a difference
between *lying* and *leasing* seems clear; possibly, about the same as between
lying and *fibbing.* In a letter written by Robert Armin, and printed in the *Introduction* to his *Nest of Ninnies* (p. xvi, ed. Sh. Soc.), we find, 'It is my qualitie to
add to the truth, truth, and not leasings to lyes.' Heath has given, I think, the
best interpretation of the present passage; DR JOHNSON has a note to the same
effect.—ED.]

 99. **much desires**] For this very common omission of the relative, see line 184,
below; II, i, 24; II, iv, 91, 114; III, iv, 220. Or ABBOTT, § 244.

 101-108. WALKER (*Crit.* i, 17) endeavoured to convert these lines into verse, but
inasmuch as he himself confessed to a comparative failure in the latter portion,
we need spend no time over his process, beyond noting that he had to squeeze 'I pray
you' into *pray,* 'the Count' into *th' Duke* (which shows that he used Hanmer's text), and 'I am sicke' into *I'm sick.*—ED.

Ol. Fetch him off I pray you, he fpeakes nothing but   105
madman : Fie on him.   Go you *Maluolio* ; If it be a fuit
from the Count, I am ficke, or not at home.   What you
will, to difmiffe it.   *Exit Maluo.*

Now you fee fir, how your fooling growes old, & people diflike it.   110

Clo. Thou haft fpoke for vs (Madona) as if thy eldeft
fonne fhould be a foole : who fe fcull, Ioue cramme with
braines, for heere he comes.   *Enter Sir Toby.*
One of thy kin has a moft weake *Pia-mater.*   114

---

106. *him.*] *him !* [Exit Maria.] Cap.
109. *Now you*] *Now* Rowe, Pope,
Han.
113, 114. *for heere he comes.   One*]
Ff, Rowe i.   *for here comes one* Rowe
ii, +, Cap, Var. '73, '78, Ran. Wh. i,

Dyce ii, iii, Huds. *for,—here he comes,—
one* Cam. Glo. Rlfe, Dtn, Wh. ii.   *for
here he comes, one* Mal. et cet.
113. Enter...] After line 114 Rowe
et seq.
114. Pia-mater] Pia mater F$_4$, et seq.

105, 106. **speakes . . . madman**] Compare, ' She speakes poynyards,' *Much
Ado*, II, i, 236; ' I will speake daggers,' *Hamlet*, III, ii, 414; ' He speaks plain
cannon fire, and smoke, and bounce,' *King John*, II, i, 462; ' Drunke?   And
speake Parrat ?' *Othello*, II, ii, 308.

113, 114. **heere . . . kin**] See *Text. Notes.*—DYCE (ed. ii) : The Cambridge
Editors, unwilling to part with a blunder of the old copy, give the passage in a
fashion which would have surprised Shakespeare.—W. A. WRIGHT : In common
with other modern editors from the time of Rowe, Dyce read ' here comes one of
thy kin,' etc., which yields a certain sense, but has no particular point.   The Clown
hints that folly ran in Olivia's family, and illustrates this by pointing to Sir Toby,
who was just entering.   In the sentence as printed by Rowe and his successors,
' for ' has no meaning, being connected with ' here comes,' and not with ' one of thy
kin,' etc.   [The Cambridge text is, I think, the only correct one, and Wright's vindication of it conclusive.   R. G. WHITE (ed. i) asserts that ' he ' can refer to no
one but to Olivia's prospective son, and that it was, therefore, absurdly wrong.
He overlooked the fact that Olivia had just sent for Sir Toby, and that it was to
him that the Clown refers.   It is to be feared that Collier's MS Corrector also failed
to catch the meaning ; he has inserted *that* before ' has.'—ED.]

114. **Pia-mater**] ' The braine . . . is closed and conteined within two thinne
skinnes, which be named the milde and harde mother ; . . . The second web and
skinne is called *Pia mater*, the meeke mother, that is set vnder the hard mother,
and is nesher [i. e. more delicate] and softer then the hard mother, & compasseth the
substance of the braine, and departeth asunder the foresayd cells.   And the milde
mother is not superfluous neither to much : for it harboureth & holdeth togethers the
veines of the braine within.   And keepeth & knitteth the braine togethers, that it
flow not neither faile by ÿ fleeting and softnesse thereof.   Also this milde mother
helpeth and beclippeth the braine, and defendeth it from the harde mother.   Also by
veines that it hath, it nourisheth the braine, and by the organe and small veines that
it conteineth, it sendeth spirit thereto.'—Batman *vppon Bartholome*, Lib. Quintus,
Chap. 3, p. 37.   Of course, ' pia-mater ' is here put for the brain itself.   The med-

Ol. By mine honor halfe drunke.   What is he at the   115
gate Cofin?
To.   A Gentleman.
Ol.   A Gentleman? What Gentleman?
To.   'Tis a Gentleman heere.   A plague o'thefe pickle
herring : How now Sot.   120

115. Scene VIII. Pope, +.
By...drunke.] Aside. Ed. conj.
116. *Cofin*] *Coufin* F₃F₄. *Uncle* Rowe
ii, +.
119. *Gentleman heere. A*] Ff (subs.)
Rowe, Pope. *gentleman. Here,—*
[belches.] *A* Theob. Han. *gentleman-*
heir,—A Warb. *gentleman here.—A*

Johns. Coll. i, ii.   *gentleman :*—[hic-
cups] *A* Cap. *gentleman here*—[hic-
cuping]—*A* Ran. *gentleman here—A*
or *a* Var. '73 et cet. *gentleman neece.*
A Gould.
120. *herring :*] *herring !* Theob. +.
herrings ! Mal. Steev. Var. Knt, Coll.
Hal. Wh. i. *herring' !* Dyce ii, iii.

ical work of Shakespeare's day, which best set forth the latest knowledge of anatomy, is probably *Microcosmographia : A Description of the Body of Man*, etc., by
Helkiah Crooke, Doctor in Physicke. London, 1615. On p. 444, in describing the
membranes of the braine, we read : 'The *Arabians* called them *Matres* the Mothers,
and so now they are commonly tearmed. . . . The one of these which is the outward
is thicke and called *dura mater* the hard Mother, the other inward and thinne called
Pia mater, the deere or neere Mother, because it immediately incompasseth and
imbraceth the substance of the braine.' In 1888, a question was started in the
columns of *The Lancet* in regard to the source of Shakespeare's knowledge, in the
present play, of the 'pia mater.' The editor of *The Asclepiad*, B. W. RICHARD-
SON, M. D., replied that inasmuch as the printer of Crooke's large folio was William
Jaggard, 'the same man who was printer for Shakspere, . . . to that office the indefatigable playwright would often be drawn by his own business, and there he would
hardly fail to see unfolded before him the anatomy of man from a sure source.'—
vol. v, p. 387. The printer of the First Folio was *Isaac* Jaggard, and Crooke's
Microcosmographia was not published until at least thirteen years after *Twelfth Night*
was performed.—ED.

115. **What is he**] See I, ii, 37, if need be, for the construction.

119. **Gentleman heere**] In mercy to the very small number of readers who
ever look at the *Text. Notes* and may be therefore lost in bewilderment over Warburton's emendation *gentleman-heir*, be it explained that Warburton means 'some
lady's eldest son just come out of the nursery ; for this was the appearance Viola
made in men's clothes.' Coleridge, in one of his notes, speaks of 'the ever
thought-swarming, but idealess, Warburton !'—ED.

119. **heere**] CAPELL (p. 142) : This word appears to be a corruption of some
interjectory particle that directed a drunken *hiccuping ;* follow'd, perhaps, by something for which the 'herrings' are blam'd. [The stage-directions inserted by several
editors are adequately enlightening.—ED.]

120. **herring**] ROLFE : This is a legitimate plural, like *trout, salmon*, and other
names of fishes. Compare *Lear*, III, vi, 33 : 'two white herring.' The regular
form of the plural is also used, as in the case of some other nouns of this class.
See III, i, 35, below. [It will be remembered that it was a surfeit of pickled herrings
and Rhenish wine that caused poor Greene's death in 1592.—ED.]

Clo.   Good Sir *Toby*.   121

Ol.   Cofin, Cofin, how haue you come fo earely by
this Lethargie?

To.   Letcherie, I defie Letchery : there's one at the
gate.   125

Ol.   I marry, what is he?

To.   Let him be the diuell and he will, I care not: giue
me faith fay I. Well, it's all one.   *Exit*

Ol.   What's a drunken man like, foole?

Clo.   Like a drown'd man, a foole, and a madde man :   130
One draught aboue heate, makes him a foole, the fecond
maddes him, and a third drownes him.

Ol.   Go thou and feeke the Crowner, and let him fitte
o'my Coz : for he's in the third degree of drinke : hee's
drown'd : go looke after him.   135

Clo.   He is but mad yet Madona, and the foole fhall
looke to the madman.

Enter Maluolio.

Mal.   Madam, yond young fellow fweares hee will
fpeake with you. I told him you were ficke, he takes on   140
him to vnderftand fo much, and therefore comes to fpeak
with you. I told him you were afleepe, he feems to haue
a fore knowledge of that too, and therefore comes to   143

121. Toby.] Ff, Rowe, Pope, Han.
Toby !— Dyce, Sta. *Toby !* Cam. Rlfe.
Toby,— Theob. et cet.

122. *Cofin*] *Uncle* Rowe ii, +.

124. *Letcherie,*] *Letchery !* Theob.
Letchery ? Cap.

127. *and he*] Ff, Rowe, +, Var. '73.
an he Han. et cet.

130. *madde man*] *mad man* Ff. *mad-man* Rowe.

131. *heate*] *mark* Gould.

133. *Crowner*] Ff, Knt, Wh. Dyce,
Cam. Sta. Rlfe, Dtn. *Coroner* Rowe
et cet.

134. *Coz*] *Uncle* Rowe ii, +. *cousin*
Cap. conj. Var. '73.

135. *go looke*] *go, look* Theob.

137. [Exit Clown. Rowe.

139. *yond*] *yon'* Cap. *yond'* Coll.

143. *fore knowledge*] *foreknowledge*
Hal. Wh. Dyce, Cam. Rlfe. *fore-
-knowledge* F_3F_4 et cet.

124-128. In spite of Sir Toby's drunken state, there is a thread of logical sequence
in his befogged brain ; 'defie' suggests the 'devil,' and the 'devil' suggests 'faith.'
Toby's drunkenness is here a dramatic necessity. Maria has been sent to 'fetch
him off,' and Malvolio to dismiss the Duke's messenger. Some time must be given
to Malvolio's altercation with Viola at the gate ; Sir Toby must obey the summons,
but must not anticipate any portion of Malvolio's report. This is attained by representing him as so intoxicated that he can tell nothing.—ED.

131. **heate**] STEEVENS : That is, above the state of being warm in a proper
degree.

135. **go looke**] For the construction, see I, i, 19.

ſpeake with you.   What is to be ſaid to him Ladie, hee's
fortified againſt any deniall.   145

   Ol.   Tell him, he ſhall not ſpeake with me.

   Mal.   Ha's beene told ſo : and hee ſayes hee'l ſtand at
your doore like a Sheriffes poſt, and be the ſupporter to
a bench, but hee'l ſpeake with you.

   Ol.   What kinde o'man is he ?   150

---

144. *him Ladie,*] F₂.   *him, Lady,*
F₃.   *him? Lady.* F₄.   *him, Lady?*
Rowe et seq.
  147. *Ha's*] Ff, Rowe.   *Ha's* Wh. i,
Sta.   *Has* Dyce i, Cam. Dtn, Wh. ii.
'Has Dyce ii. iii.   *He has* Pope et cet.

148. *and be*] *or be* Han. Coll. MS,
Wh. i, Ktly.
       to] *of* Var. '03, '13, '21, Knt.
  150. *o'*] Ff, Rowe, +, Cap. Var. '73,
Dyce, Cam. Sta. Rlfe, Dtn.   *of* Var. '78
et cet.

---

  147. **Ha's**] Of course, the full form is 'He has'; but inasmuch as in familiar
speech the 'he' (or possibly 'a' which sometimes stands for 'he') was reduced to
a mere aspirate, I suppose the printer believed he had reproduced the full phrase
by giving the 'Ha' in full and then putting an apostrophe to represent the *ha* in
'has.' Be this as it may, 'has,' 'is,' and 'was' are often to be found without a
nominative.   Sometimes a nominative in the second person is omitted, as in 'then
cam'st in smiling,' V, i, 368, if that reading be correct ; see also 'hadst it?' II, iii,
28.—Ed.

   148. **Sheriffes post**] HALLIWELL : The houses of Mayors and Sheriffs of towns
were distinguished by large posts set up before the doors.   These posts were often
elaborately carved, and were generally repainted on an accession or re-election to the
office. 'Their lips are so lauishly red, as if they vsed to kisse an okerman euery
morning, and their cheeks suger-candied & cherry blusht so sweetly after the colour
of a newe Lord Mayors postes, as if the pageant of their wedlocke holiday were
harde at the doore; so that if a Painter were to drawe any of their counterfets on a
Table, he needes no more but wet his pencill, and dab it on their cheekes, and he
shall haue vermillion and white enough to furnish out his worke.'—Nashe's *Pierce
Penilesse* [p. 43, ed. Grosart.   Halliwell gives a wood-cut of one of these posts
'taken from a specimen at Norwich, the original being' about eight feet and a
half high, of the time of Elizabeth.   KNIGHT also gives a picture (p. 147) of
the same post.   It is generally supposed, on Warburton's authority, that to these
posts were affixed proclamations and public notices.   But this, Knight doubts, and
inclines to believe that 'they were only tokens of authority, to denote the residence
of a magistrate.'   Certainly, the dozen or more quotations given by Halliwell seem
to justify Knight's doubt.   It seems hardly likely that so much pains would be taken
in carving and painting, if the posts were to be afterward concealed under proclamations and temporary notices.—Ed.].

   149. **but**] Here used in its original meaning, namely, *out-take*, or *except*.   See
'But you should pittie me,' line 275 *post*, or see ABBOTT, § 120.—Ed.

   150. **What**] See 'What time we will our celebration keep,' IV, iii, 33 ; or, for
other examples of the omission of prepositions, ABBOTT, § 202.   Note the encour-
aging sign that a majority of the best modern editors adhere to the old text in
reading 'o' ' for *of*.

Mal.   Why of mankinde.   151

Ol.   What manner of man?

Mal.   Of verie ill manner : hee'l fpeake with you, will
you, or no.

Ol.   Of what perfonage, and yeeres is he?   155

*Mal.*Not yet old enough for a man, nor yong enough
for a boy : as a fquafh is before tis a pefcod, or a Codling
when tis almoft an Apple : Tis with him in ftanding wa-   158

---

151. *Why*] Why, F₃F₄.
    mankinde] F₂, Rowe, +, Knt,
Wh. Cam. Rlfe, Dtn. *man kind* F₃F₄,
Cap. et cet.
    153. *ill manner*] ill manners F₃F₄,

Rowe, +.
    157. *pefcod*] peascod Rowe.
    158. *him in*] Ff, Rowe, +, Knt, Dyce,
Cam. Sta. Rlfe. *him e'en* Cap. et cet.
him Coll. MS, ap. Cam.

151, 153. mankinde . . . ill manner] Very respectfully be it spoken, but I
cannot think that this quibbling is in keeping with Malvolio's sedate character.
It is true to his nature that he should say, with precision, 'will you or no,' instead
of 'will ye, nill ye'; and that he should be non-committal in drawing the exact
line between a peascod and a squash, or between boy and man,—but this dallying
with words, which merely irritates his mistress, and is like the Clown's talk, which
he has just been condemning,—I do not understand.—ED.

155. personage] Thus, in *Mid. N. D.* III, ii, 306 : 'And with her personage,
her tall personage, Her height (forsooth).'

157. squash] Divesting our American minds of the belief that a squash (an
Indian word) can only be a large melon, we shall find the best definition of an Elizabethan 'squash' in the line before us.   See, if needful, *Mid. N. D.* III, i, 193,
and *Note.*—ED.

157. Codling] W. A. WRIGHT : This appears to have been a small unripe apple.
So much is evident from the present passage, and the notes of commentators have
added nothing to our knowledge.—MURRAY (*N. E. D.*) : From the beginning the
name seems to have been applied to a hard kind of apple, not suitable to be eaten
raw ; hence to any immature, or half-grown apple.   In the beginning of the 17th
century, it was applied to a variety suitable to be cooked while still unripe.

158, 159. in standing water] CAPELL (p. 143) : What conception moderns
have had of ['in standing water'] the editor knows not ; but having none himself,
he has look'd on 'in' as an error, and substituted for it what all will comprehend at
first sight [*e'en*].—W. A. WRIGHT : The phrase, if the reading be correct, must
mean 'in the condition of standing water.'   So 'in Pyramus' (*Mid. N. D.* IV, ii,
24) signifies 'in the character of Pyramus' (compare *Ib.* V, i, 220, 'in a man and
a lion').   It is not clear that Capell's alteration is necessary, although 'in' is to be
found as a misprint for *e'en ;* as, for example, in *Ant. & Cleop.* IV, xv, 73, where
the Folios have, 'No more but in a woman.'   And again in *All's Well*, III, ii, 20.
[Capell's emendation is, I think, wrong ; it throws too much emphasis on the
phrase.   *Possibly*, the simile was drawn from the tides at London Bridge.   In the
Tempest, II, i, 236, Sebastian says, 'I am standing water,' where, as the context
shows, he means just at the turn of the tide, neither ebbing nor rising.   But
whencesoever the simile be drawn, Wright's interpretation of 'in' is essential.—ED.]

ter, betweene boy and man.   He is verie well-fauour'd,
and he fpeakes verie fhrewifhly : One would thinke his   160
mothers milke were fcarfe out of him.

  Ol.   Let him approach : Call in my Gentlewoman.
  Mal.   Gentlewoman, my Lady calles.   *Exit.*

          Enter Maria.

  Ol.   Giue me my vaile : come throw it ore my face,   165
Wee'l once more heare *Orfinos* Embaffie.

          Enter Uiolenta.

  Vio.   The honorable Ladie of the houfe, which is fhe ?
  Ol.   Speake to me, I fhall anfwer for her : your will.
  Uio.   Moft radiant, exquifite, and vnmatchable beau-   170
tie.   I pray you tell me if this bee the Lady of the houfe,
for I neuer faw her.   I would bee loath to caft away my
fpeech : for befides that it is excellently well pend, I haue
taken great paines to con it.   Good Beauties, let mee fuftaine no fcorne ;   I am very comptible, euen to the leaft   175
finifter vfage.

164. Scene IX. Pope, +.
165. *come throw*] *come, throw* Rowe.
167. Uiolenta] F₁.
    Enter...] Enter...and Attend-
ants. Cam.
169. *will.*] *will ?* F₄.
170. *radiant*] *radient* F₄.

170, 171. *beautie.*] beauty. F₂F₃, Coll. beauty, F₄, Knt. beauty ! Wh. i. beauty— or beauty,— Rowe et cet.
173. *pend*] F₂. *penn'd* F₃F₄. *pen'd* Cap. *penned* Coll. Cam.
175. *comptible*] prompt Han. easy cowed, liable Orger.

---

161. were] See 'my outside have not charmed her,' and, if need be, for similar subjunctives, ABBOTT, § 368.

167. Violenta] This is the name of a character in *All's Well that Ends Well*, who does not, however, speak throughout the play.   From the occurrence of the name here, together with 'Capilet,' both as the family name of Diana in *All's Well* and as the name of Sir Andrew Aguecheek's horse, FLEAY (*Life*, etc., p. 217) infers that *Twelfth Night* is later in date than *All's Well*.   The fact may well be true ; but it is not quite clear that a mere repetition of names can prove a sequence in time in favour either of one play or of the other.   We have no assurance that 'Violenta' occurred in Shakespeare's MS.   It sounds suspiciously like *Viola enter* which the compositor misheard and transformed into its present shape, after having already carelessly set up '*Enter*' before it.—ED.

171. I pray you tell me, etc.] It cannot be that Viola could not tell which was Olivia ; there must have been, between the highborn mistress and the attendant, a marked difference in the elegance of dress, which Viola's quick woman's eye would have instantly detected,—the veil alone was a sufficient indication,—but Viola was burning with impatience to see the face with which Orsino was enamoured, and, to gain this end, thus pleaded her embarrassed ignorance.—ED.

175. comptible] WARBURTON : That is, ready to call to account.—HEATH

Ol. Whence came you fir?   177

Vio. I can fay little more then I haue ftudied, & that
queftion's out of my part. Good gentle one, giue mee
modeft affurance, if you be the Ladie of the houfe, that   180
may proceede in my fpeech.

Ol. Are you a Comedian?

Vio. No my profound heart : and yet (by the verie
phangs of malice, I fweare) I am not that I play. Are you
the Ladie of the houfe?   185

181. *my*] Om. F₃F₄, Rowe i.   184. *phangs*] *pangs* Rowe i, *fangs*
                                            Rowe ii.

(p. 188) : The meaning is plain, I am very apt to take to heart, and to make account
of, the least sinister usage.—M. MASON : There is no such word as 'comptible.'
. . . If we are to adopt a new word, let us rather borrow one from the French,
which will clearly express what Viola means, and read *domptable*, that is, apt to be
subdued or tamed. Yet I am not satisfied with this conjecture. [It would be discourteous here to disagree.—ED.]—STEEVENS : Viola begs she may not be treated
with scorn, because she is very submissive, even to lighter marks of reprehension.—
HARNESS : The meaning here intended appears to be *susceptible*.—MURRAY (*N. E.
D.* s. v. *Countable*, where, under the third subdivision, the present passage is the only
quotation) : Liable to answer *to*, sensitive *to*. [I prefer Harness's definition, and if
to it be added Murray's *sensitive*, an ample meaning is obtained. Both HALLI-
WELL and W. A. WRIGHT furnish examples of *comptable*, which seem to me to
mean *accountable*, but this is assuredly not Viola's meaning.—ED.]

180. **modest assurance**] W. A. WRIGHT : That is, moderate assurance, only
enough to satisfy me. [In other words, pray lay aside your veil, and let me see
your face.—ED.]

181. **may**] This begins p. 259 in the Folio. The catchword 'I' at the bottom
of p. 258 has been overlooked.—ED.

182. **Comedian**] The COWDEN-CLARKES : Olivia's sarcasm at the *acting a part*
which the delivery of a *set speech* implies. [Every phrase of Viola intimated that
she was 'acting a part'; her words were all tinged with the stage : her 'speech'
was 'well penn'd,' she had 'conned' it, and she had 'studied' her 'part.' There
could be but little sarcasm in taking her at her own valuation. Did not the sting
lie in the word 'Comedian'? The social brand thereby implied was almost of the
lowest. In *Sonnet* cxi, Shakespeare is supposed to bewail the degradation to which
his profession subjected him.—ED.]

183. **profound heart**] W. A. WRIGHT : The epithet 'profound' is applied to
Olivia in bantering compliment to her sagacity. DEIGHTON, however, thinks that
these words are 'merely a continuation of the euphuistic style in which Viola had
begun her address, "most radiant, exquisite," etc.'

183, 184. **by the verie phangs of malice**] W. A. WRIGHT : Viola appears to
challenge the most malicious construction which could be put upon her conduct, and
it would amount only to this, that she was not what she seemed. [Viola invokes
the very bitterest malice, its very fangs, to vouch for the truth that she was not
what she played. There is a parallel passage in *Othello*, where Desdemona asks

Ol. If I do not vſurpe my ſelfe, I am.   186

Uio. Moſt certaine, if you are ſhe, you do vſurp your
ſelfe : for what is yours to beſtowe, is, not yours to re-
ſerue. But this is from my Commiſſion : I will on with
my ſpeech in your praiſe, and then ſhew you the heart of   190
my meſſage.

Ol. Come to what is important in't : I forgiue you
the praiſe.

Vio. Alas, I tooke great paines to ſtudie it, and 'tis
Poeticall.   195

Ol. It is the more like to be feigned, I pray you keep
it in.I heard you were ſawcy at my gates, & allowd your
approach rather to wonder at you, then to heare you. If
you be not mad, be gone : if you haue reaſon, be breefe :   199

---

187. *you do*] *yo do* F₃.

196. *feigned,*] *feigned.* Rowe, +.
feign'd; Cap.

197. *& allowd*] *and I allow'd*
Pope, +.

199. *not mad*] *mad* Mason, Ran.
Dyce ii, iii, Huds. Dtn. *but mad* Sta.
conj. Coll. ii, iii.

gone] *gon* F₂.

Iago, 'what praiſe could'ſt thou beſtow on a deſeruing woman indeed? One, that
in the authorithy of her merit, did iuſtly put on the vouch of very malice it ſelfe.'—
II, i, 170, of this ed. where see *Notes.*—ED.]

184. **not that I play**] See, for omission of relative, line 99 above.

186. **vsurpe my selfe**] That is, counterfeit. See V, i. 265.

187–189. **Most certaine . . . yours to reserue**] This somewhat obscure and
elliptical sentence may be, I think, thus paraphrased : if it be in your power to give
away the lordship of this house (Portia said she was the *lord* of her fair mansion,
master of her servants) it is so rightfully your duty to do it, that, if you do not do
it, you are a usurper of the lord on whom you should bestow it, that is, of course,
on Orsino. In thus earnestly pleading Orsino's cause, Viola was here, I think, for a
moment, betrayed into seriousness. She instantly sees, however, that this tone is
premature, and apologises, 'But this is *from* my commission.' Her bearing is forced
and unnatural, even flippant, until Maria has retired, then it becomes serious and
every word comes from her heart.—ED.

189. **from**] See 'Write from it,' etc., V, i, 351, or ABBOTT, § 158, for other
examples of 'from' used in the sense of *away from*, without a verb of motion.

189. **I will on**] See ABBOTT (§ 405) for ellipses of verbs of *motion*, or of *purpose* after 'will' and 'is.' Compare, 'Your store is not for idle markets,' III,
iii, 50.

196. **feigned**] Compare *As You Like It*, III, iii, 17, where Touchstone tells
Audry that the 'truest poetrie is the most faining.'

199. **you be not mad**] M. MASON (p. 114) : The sense evidently requires that
we should read : 'If you be mad,' etc. For the words 'be mad,' in the first part
of the sentence, are opposed to 'reason' in the second. [DYCE and DEIGHTON
adopted this emendation.]—STAUNTON : We should perhaps read : 'If you be *but*

'tis not that time of Moone with me, to make one in fo   200
skipping a dialogue.

Ma. Will you hoyft fayle fir, here lies your way.

Vio. No good fwabber, I am to hull here a little longer. Some mollification for your Giant, fweete Ladie ;   204

---

200. *that time of Moone*] *the time of
the moon* Rowe. *that time of the moon*
Pope. +, Var. Ran.

202. *fir,*] *sir ?* Pope et seq.
204. *mollification for...Giant*] *modification of...taunt* Gould.

---

mad,' etc., that is, 'If you are a mere madman, begone,' etc. No two words are
more frequently confounded in these plays than *not* and *but.* [This emendation
DYCE (ed. ii) pronounced 'very unsatisfactory'; COLLIER (ed. ii) thought differently; it is in his text.]—The COWDEN-CLARKES thus paraphrase, 'If you are not
quite without reason, begone; if you have some reason, be brief, that you may be
soon gone.'—W. A. WRIGHT : There is quite as much contrast as that which Mason
finds, between a state of mind which is a little short of madness, and that which is
distinguished by the possession of clear reason, and Olivia seems to imply that
Viola may not be actually mad, but only going mad, and in that case bids her
begone. [The paraphrase of the Cowden-Clarkes seems adequate. Had Olivia
supposed it possible that the Page might be downright mad, as Mason's emendation
implies, she could hardly have imagined that an appeal to him to go would have
any effect; I am inclined to think that she would herself have left the room as
quickly as possible. In what I have said above, I do not wish to imply that Collier
adopted Staunton's emendation, without acknowledgement. Staunton's edition and
Collier's Second Edition were issued almost simultaneously, and as the former was
issued in monthly Numbers, beginning with November, 1857, it is almost impossible,
at this late day, to know which edition was the predecessor.—ED.]

200. **time of Moone**] 'The Moone when he is in the second signe after the
ascendent, betokeneth discomfort, wo, sorrow, & losse of cattel by theeues & robbers.
Also in the fourth signe, & in the sixt, and in the eight, he betokeneth wrath,
anguish, withdrawing & changeablenesse of the people, & betokeneth in the tenth
signe, that who that then beginne to rebell shall be soone set down : and in the
twelfth, he betokeneth let, strife, hardnesse & prison of friends. And in all other
houses & signes he hath good effect, and betokeneth good.'—Batman *vppon Bartholome*, Lib. VIII, Cap. 30, p. 134 verso. This is quoted merely as an illustration
of the belief in the influence of the times of the moon. It is possibly superfluous ;
the belief cannot be said to have even yet died out. In the *Wint. Tale* we have
'These dangerous lunes of the King.'—ED.

201. **skipping**] JOHNSON : That is, wild, frolic, mad.—MALONE : Again, in *Mer.
of Ven.* II, ii, 132 : 'allay with some cold drops of modestie Thy skipping spirit.'

203. **to hull**] MURRAY (*N. E. D.*): To float or be driven by the force of the
wind or current on the hull alone ; to drift to the wind with sails furled. [Among
the quotations are *Rich. III:* IV, iv, 438, and the definition in Capt. Smith's *Sea-
man's Grammar*, 1627, ix, 40 : 'If that split . . . then hull, which is to beare no
saile.' *Ibid.* 'They call it hulling also in a calme swelling Sea, which is commonly
before a storme, when they strike their sailes lest she should beat them in peeces
against the mast by Rowling.']

204. **Giant**] JOHNSON : Ladies, in romance, are guarded by giants, who repel

tell me your minde, I am a meffenger.   205

205. *tell...meffenger*] Oli. *Tell me*   Var. Knt, Sta. Coll. ii, Dyce, Ktly,
your mind. Vio. *I am a messenger.*   Huds. Dtn.
Warb. Han. Johns.Var. Ran. Mal. Steev.

---

all improper or troublesome advances.   Viola, seeing the waiting-maid so eager to
oppose her message, entreats Olivia to pacify her giant.—STEEVENS : Viola likewise
alludes to the diminutive size of Maria, who is called, on subsequent occasions,
' little villain,' ' youngest wren of mine,' etc.—MALONE : So, Falstaff to his page,
' Sirrah, you giant,' *2 Hen. IV :* I, ii, 1.

205. tell . . . messenger] WARBURTON : These words must be divided between
the two speakers. [See *Text. Notes.*] Viola growing troublesome, Olivia would
dismiss her, and therefore cuts her short with this command, ' Tell me your mind.'
The other taking advantage of the ambiguity of the word ' mind,' which signifies
either *business* or *inclination*, replies as if she had used it in the latter sense, ' I am
a messenger.'—HEATH (p. 188) : It is extremely odd that Mr Warburton should
understand these words to express Viola's inclinations, not her business.—M.
MASON : As a *messenger*, she was not to speak her own mind, but that of her
employer.—CAPELL (who adhered to the Folio): Viola's ' tell me your mind ' may
stand well enough for—shall I have this favour from you ? alluding to what she had
just ask'd ; and her ' I am a messenger' follows such question aptly ; but, to speak
the truth, the passage were best without those first words ; which, among other
objections to them, cause the speech to end metrically.—COLLIER was the first, after
Capell, to restore the old text, but he recanted in his Second Edition, and was a ' convertite' to the Folio again, in his Third.   In his First Edition he remarks, ' Viola
asks Olivia to tell her her mind, because she is a messenger, and wishes to take
back an answer.   Olivia could hardly say to Viola, "Tell me *your* mind," when
she knew that Viola only brought a message from the Duke.'   But how can Viola
expect to carry back an answer, and ask Olivia to tell her her mind, when she has
not yet delivered any message ?   Collier failed to see the good interpretation of
Capell ; but HUNTER, (who applauded Collier for restoring the Folio,) saw it, and
remarked (i, 402) : ' Viola evidently appeals to Olivia whether she will suffer Maria
to turn her out of the house so unceremoniously, and claims the privilege of an
ambassador to be courteously treated, and allowed to deliver his message.'   This
interpretation was lost on DYCE, who suspected corruption in the whole passage,
and that ' perhaps something more than prefixes' had dropped out ; ' I adopt here,'
he goes on to say, ' Warburton's distribution of the dialogue ; what has been urged
against it by Mr Collier and Mr Hunter having only tended to strengthen my conviction that "Tell me your mind " cannot possibly belong to Viola.'   Hereupon,
Collier, in his Second Edition, acknowledged that he was ' convinced, on reconsid-
eration,' that Warburton was right.   But, as I have said, Collier's conviction was
not steadfast when he issued his Third Edition.   ROLFE and W. A. WRIGHT both
express a belief in a possible corruption or omission here.   It is not impossible ; but
with Capell's and Hunter's interpretation at hand, there seems to be little need of
resorting to this rather ignominious retreat.   We must bear in mind that this
dialogue was not carried on by actors with hands hanging at their sides.   It is not
extravagant to picture Maria's zeal as so warm that she attempts to force Viola from
the apartment.   ' Mollification,' for which Viola pleads, implies somewhat more
of vehemence than is expressed in merely ' Will you hoist sail, sir.'   Possibly, a

Ol. Sure you haue fome hiddeous matter to deliuer,　206
when the curtefie of it is fo fearefull. Speake your office.

Vio. It alone concernes your eare : I bring no ouer-
ture of warre, no taxation of homage; I hold the Olyffe
in my hand : my words are as full of peace, as matter.　210

Ol. Yet you began rudely. What are you?
What would you?

Vio. The rudeneffe that hath appear'd in mee, haue I
learn'd from my entertainment. What I am, and what I
would, are as fecret as maiden-head : to your eares, Di-　215
uinity; to any others, prophanation.

Ol. Giue vs the place alone,
We will heare this diuinitie. Now fir, what is your text?

Vio. Moft fweet Ladie.　219

---

209. *taxation*] *Taxations* F₄, Rowe i.
Olyffe] *Oliff* F₄. *olive* Rowe.
211, 212. Continuous line, Pope et
seq.
215. *as maiden-head*] *as a maiden-*
-heard F₂. *as a maiden-head* F₃F₄,
Rowe, Pope, Han. *as maidenhood*
Coll. MS, Huds.

216. *others*] *other's* Pope ii, Theob.
Warb. et seq.
218. [Exit Maria. Rowe. Exeunt
M. and Attendants. (after *diuinitie*)
Cap.
219. *Ladie.*] *Lady,*— Theob. Warb.
et seq.

---

repugnance to accepting any emendation at Warburton's dogmatic hands may have
some influence with me; yet I cannot but think that, wherever the words of the
Folio admit of a dramatic explanation, the text should be retained.—ED.

208. **alone**] This word in the present passage is marked by ABBOTT as coming
under his Paragraph (§ 420) on *The Transposition of Adverbs;* several editors have,
consequently, remarked that this 'alone' is transposed and that it does not qualify
'It' or 'concerns,' but 'ear.' Herein, they seem to overlook that this makes
Viola virtually assert that her message does not concern Olivia's mouth, or hands,
but her 'ear alone.' *Possibly*, it was to avoid this very awkwardness that
Shakespeare put 'alone' just where it is,—the only place where it can be put
while the present phrase is retained. A purist, so-called, would change the
phrase and write : 'It concerns the ear of you alone.' But even this expression is erroneous; no change is necessary if 'alone' be regarded as parenthetical : 'It (alone) concerns your ear'; this suggests the full phrase : 'This
concerns your ear, when we are alone.' (Viola may have glanced at Maria as
she uttered the word.) This alleged 'transposition of adverbs' is common in
Shakespeare, but in many a case, I think, we are inclined to accept it too
readily.—ED.

209. **taxation**] That is, claim, demand.

215. **secret as maiden-head**] This is, as always, maidenhood.—THEOBALD
(Nichols, *Illust.* ii. 355): The context seems rather to persuade, 'as sacred as maid-
hood.' And this afterwards Olivia swears by, 'By maid-hood, honor, truth, and
euery thing.' [III, i, 154].

Ol. A comfortable doctrine, and much may bee ſaide   220
of it. Where lies your Text?

Vio. In *Orſinoes* boſome.

Ol. In his boſome? In what chapter of his boſome?

Vio. To anſwer by the method, in the firſt of his hart.

Ol. O, I haue read it: it is hereſie. Haue you no more   225
to ſay?

Vio. Good Madam, let me ſee your face.

Ol. Haue you any Commiſsion from your Lord, to
negotiate with my face: you are now out of your Text:
but we will draw the Curtain, and ſhew you the picture.   230
Looke you ſir, ſuch a one I was this preſent: Iſt not well
done?   232

---

221. *your*] *the* Rowe, Pope, Han.
222. Orſinoes] Orſino's F$_3$F$_4$.
231. *ſuch a one I was this preſent:*] *ſuch a one I wear this present:* Warb. Theob. Han. *such as once I was, this presents:* Mason, Ran. Harness. *such a one as I was this present:* Var. '03, '13, '21. *such a one I was, this presents;* Becket. *such a one as I was this presents.*

Jackson. *such a one I was as this presents;* Sing. conj. Clarke. *such a one I am at this present;* Coll. MS. *such a one as I with this* [unveiling] *present:* Anon. (1814) ap. Cam. *such a one I was, as this present...* Ktly. *such a one, I, as this presents.* Daniel. *such a one I'm, as this presents* K. Elze.
232. [Unveiling, Rowe et seq.

---

220. **A comfortable doctrine**] That is, a comforting doctrine. Thus Juliet says, 'O comfortable friar.'—DEIGHTON: It is a phrase used in religious or theological language.

224. **method**] That is, to keep the theological style.

225. **heresie**] DEIGHTON: In 'text,' 'comfortable doctrine,' 'chapter,' 'first of his heart,' 'heresy,' Olivia is merely carrying on the idea suggested by Viola's use of 'divinity' and 'profanation.'

230. **Curtain**] See 'Curtaine,' I, iii, 118.

231. **such a one . . . present**] WARBURTON: This is nonsense. The change of 'was' to *wear*, I think, clears all up, and gives the expression an air of gallantry. Viola presses to see Olivia's face; the other at length pulls off her veil, and says, 'We will draw the curtain and show you the *picture*.' I wear this complexion today, I may wear another tomorrow; jocularly intimating that she *painted*. —CAPELL (p. 143): A pleasantry upon herself most undoubtedly; and its meaning,—when you make your report of me, you may say I *was* such and such when you saw me, but can't answer for what I may be at the time you are talking: the intimation is both genteeler in this way, and juster-worded, than by [Warburton's emendation.] For who talks of *wearing* a 'picture,' yet that is the predicate, and to that the terms after should be accommodated.—STEEVENS (*Var.* 1785): I am not satisfied with [Warburton's] emendation. She says, 'I *was* this present,' instead of saying 'I *am*,' because she has once shown herself, and personates the beholder, who is afterwards to make the relation. [It is to be feared that Steevens took the hint from Capell.—ED.] IBID. (*Var.* 1793): We may read, 'Such a one I was. This *presence*, is 't not well done?' *i. e.* this mien, is it not happily represented?

Uio.   Excellently done, if God did all.   233

—M. MASON : This passage is nonsense as it stands, and necessarily requires some emendation.   That proposed by Warburton would make sense of it ; but then the allusion to a picture would be dropped, which began in the preceding part of the speech, and is carried on through those that follow.   If we read *presents*, instead of ' present,' this allusion will be preserved, and the meaning will be clear.   I have no doubt but the line should run thus : ' such *as once* I was, this *presents*.'   *Presents* means *represents*.—MALONE : I suspect, the author intended Olivia should again cover her face with her veil before she speaks these words.—KNIGHT [adopting Malone's suggestion]: The Folio text appears clear enough.   Olivia unveils her face for an instant only ; and says, ' Look you, sir, such a one I was this present,'—such I was this moment.—HUNTER (i, 402): Olivia is not speaking in print, as if her words were to be like the words of a professed orator, but engaged in a lively dialogue, and any words more appropriate to the act of unveiling than those which the poet has assigned her [in the Folio] cannot be conceived.   ' This present ' is a common phrase, often occurring at the close of letters.—DYCE (ed. ii): Mr Lettsom's [alteration is] ' such a one as I this presents,' *i. e.* ' this picture represents my poor person.'—DEIGHTON : It is probably nothing more than an affectation by Olivia of legal preciseness : this is what I was just now, though hidden by my veil ; different from what you saw me, but not changed.   [Her question, ' *Is't* not well done ? ' weakens the suggestion of Malone and Knight that she restores her veil.   I think her words are an attempt to be jocular to hide the embarrassment caused by removing her veil to allow an exceedingly handsome young man to gaze on her face, and she says in effect, ' Such a one I was an instant ago,' before she removed her veil, and, of course, such she still remains.—ED.]

233. **Excellently . . . all]** C. SCOTT (p. 271) : Few will forget the surprising effect Miss Terry made in [the present line].   It was the very conceit of graceful impudence.   [I doubt the propriety of ' graceful impudence.'   Olivia had invited the suspicion that her beauty was fictitious by asking, ' is it not *well done ?* ' and there is more of tragedy than comedy in Viola's reply.   She knew that God had done all, but replied merely in Olivia's vein while her admiration was gathering itself into that earnest tribute, which follows, to the exquisite beauty of her rival. —ED.]

233. **if God did all]** See ' Is he of God's making ?'—*As You Like It*, III, ii, 201, and notes in this ed.   Possibly, painting and other artificial aids to beauty were more prevalent in Shakespeare's time than is generally supposed.   It is unsafe to trust satire ; we must take, therefore, for what it is worth, the following from Lodge's *Wits Miserie*, 1596 : ' Beleeue me, I thinke in no time Ierome had better cause to crie out on pride then in this, for painting now adaies is grown to such a custome, that from the swartfaste Deuil in the Kitchen to the fairest Damsel in the cittie, the most part looke like Vizards for a Momerie, rather than Christians trained in sobrietie.' p. 15, ed. Hunterian Club.   See also, where is no satire, but apparently a plain statement of facts, albeit in Italy, Guazzo, *The ciuile Conuersatiòn*, trans. by G. pettie, 1586, Third booke, p. 125 : ' We ought to thinke also, that those which use artificiall meanes, displease God much, in altring his image, & please men neuer a whit, in going about to deceiue them.   I know no man of judgement, but setteth more, by ods, by a naturall beautie that sheweth but meanlie, then by a painted artificiall beautie that shineth most gallantlie : And I would wish those

   Ol. 'Tis in graine fir, 'twill endure winde and weather.   235

dawbed, pargetted, and vermilion died faces, to consider what scoffes and mockes,
men when they are by themselues, giue to these bolstred beauties. . . . For I knew
one once inueigh earnestly against counterfaite women, not perceiuing poore foole
her owne purple died face, whereas some of the coulours stack vpon her gorget :
but such women would be tried in such sort as a great manie were once by an honest Matrone : who at a feast making one at a game wherein euerie one by turnes
commaundeth ouer all the rest, being come to her turne, she caused a basen with
water to be brought, wherwith she forthwith washed her hands & face, command-
ing all the rest to doe as much, whereby a great manie of them with griefe and
shame, made the painting runne downe along their cheekes. I know also a young
woman, whose face two monthes since was like a colliers, and now she ietteth vp
and downe so bewhited, or rather so bepainted, that she seemeth quight another
woman : yet when she wrieth her head a little, there appeareth such blacknesse in
her neck and throate, so different from her face, that you would verelie thinke that
it were a Flemminges head set vppon a Moores necke.' In Jonson's *Sejanus*, II,
i, Eudemus, the physician of Livia, is represented as applying to his royal mistress
various cosmetics and artificial aids to beauty.—ED.

   234. **in graine**] MARSH (p. 67) : The history of the word *grain*, in the sense
of a dye, is this : The Latin *granum* signifies a seed or kernel, and it was early
applied to all small objects resembling seeds, and finally to all minute particles. A
species of oak or ilex, the *quercus coccifera* of botanists, common on all the Mediterranean coasts, is frequented by an insect of the genus *coccus*, the dried body, or
rather ovarium, of which furnishes a variety of red dyes. From its round, seed-like
form, the prepared *coccus* was called in later Latin, *granum*, [which] becomes *grana*
in Spanish, *graine* in French, and from one of these is derived the particular use of
the English word [as in Milton's 'robe of darkest grain']. *Grain*, then, as a col-
oring material, strictly taken, means the dye produced by the coccus insect, often
called, in commerce and in the arts, *kermes*, but inasmuch as the kermes dye, like
that extracted from the murex of Tyre, is capable of assuming a considerable variety
of reddish tones or hues, Milton and other English poets often use *grain* as equivalent to *Tyrian purple*. . . . (P. 72.) The color obtained from kermes or grain was
a peculiarly durable, or as it is technically called, a *fast* or fixed dye, for *fast* used
in this sense is, etymologically, *fixed*. When then a merchant recommended his
purple stuffs, as being dyed in *grain*, he originally meant that they were dyed with
kermes [the Arabic name for the coccus insect] and would wear well, and this
phrase, by a common process in language, was afterwards applied to other colours,
as a mode of expressing the quality of durability. Thus in the *Com. of Err.* III,
ii, 108, to the observation of Antipholus, 'That's a fault that water will mend,'
Dromio replies : 'No, sir, 'tis in grain; Noah's flood could not do it.' And in
Twelfth Night, Olivia replies ''Tis in grain,' etc. In both these examples it is the
sense of permanence, a well-known quality of the purple produced by the *grain* or
kermes, that is expressed. It is familiarly known that if wool be dyed before spin-
ning, the color is usually more permanent than when the spun yarn or manufactured
cloth is first dipped in the tincture. When the original sense of *grain* grew less
familiar, and it was used chiefly as expressive of *fastness* of color, the name of the

Vio. Tis beauty truly blent, whofe red and white,	236
Natures owne fweet, and cunning hand laid on :
Lady, you are the cruell'ft fhee aliue,
If you will leade thefe graces to the graue,
And leaue the world no copie.	240

Ol. O fir, I will not be fo hard-hearted : I will giue
out diuers fcedules of my beautie. It fhalbe Inuentoried
and euery particle and vtenfile labell'd to my will : As,
Item two lippes indifferent redde, Item two grey eyes,
with lids to them. Item, one necke, one chin, & fo forth.	245
Were you fent hither to praife me?

242. *diuers*] *diverse* Theob. Warb. Johns. Var. Ran. Mal.

fcedules] *schedules* Rowe.

It fhalbe] *I shall be* Han.

244. *Item*] *Item,* F₃F₄.

246. *praife*] *'praise* Mal. Var. '78, '85, Steev. Var. Wh. i, Dyce ii, iii, Huds. Coll. iii.

---

effect was transferred to an ordinary known cause, and *dyed in grain*, originally meaning dyed with kermes, then dyed with fast color, came at last to signify, dyed in the wool or other raw material.

238. **shee**] Compare, 'The faire, the chaste, the vnexpressive shee'—*As You Like It*, III, ii, 11 ; 'I am that he, that vnfortunate he,'—*Ib.* line 378. Or, see ABBOTT, § 224, for other examples.

239, 240. **If you . . . copie**] STEEVENS points out an iteration of this idea in *Sonnet* 3 ; and MALONE in *Sonnets* 9 and 13. For 'copy' as here used, see *Wint. Tale*, I, ii, 150, and II, iii, 126.

242. **scedules**] W. A. WRIGHT : Cotgrave gives three forms of this word in French : *Cedule, Scedule,* and *Schedule ;* and in Sherwood's *Eng. and French Dict.* [appended to Cotgrave] we find, '*A Scedule.* Scedule, cedule ; minute, schede, schedule.' [In Hollyband, we find, '*Cédule*, a sedule, a briefe, a handwriting,' and also '*Scédule &* obligation, an obligation, a bill.']

243. **labell'd**] RUSHTON (*Testamentary Language*, p. 9) : The word 'label' has two significations : it signifies a paper annexed by way of addition or explication to a will or testament, which is called a codicil or label (Cowell, *Interpr.*), and in this sense it may be used by Olivia. It also signifies a slip of paper or parchment for an appending seal.

244. **indifferent**] See I, iii, 126, where Sir Andrew says his leg does indifferent well in a dam'd colour'd stock.

244. **grey**] See *Rom. & Jul.* II, iv, 39, 'Thisbe, a grey eye or so.' When applied to the sky or to eyes, this colour is generally accepted as *blue.* See *Much Ado*, V, iii, 28, ' Dapples the drowsy East with spots of grey.'

246. **praise**] MALONE : That is, *appraise*, or *appreciate.* M. MASON and KNIGHT prefer to accept 'praise' in the sense of *extol, applaud ;* COLLIER (and also Knight) maintained that the old word for *appraise* was *apprise*, but in his Third Ed. Collier accepts Malone's spelling, *'praise.* HALLIWELL proves by quotations that Malone's reading is certainly possible. His note is as follows : Olivia is here speaking very satirically, and asks Viola, in ridicule or assumed indignation, whether he (she) was sent to appraise her beauties, like a broker might do furniture. ' *I prayse* a thynge,

Vio. I fee you what you are, you are too proud :   247
But if you were the diuell, you are faire :
My Lord, and mafter loues you : O fuch loue
Could be but recompenc'd, though you were crown'd   250
The non-pareil of beautie.
      Ol. How does he loue me ?
      Vio, With adorations, fertill teares,   253

250. *Could*] *Should* Coll. MS.
251. *non-pareil*] *non-pareill* F$_2$. *non-parill* F$_3$. *non-paril* F$_4$. *nonpareil* Var. '03 et seq.
253. *adorations, fertill*] Ff, Rowe,
Knt, Coll. Hal. Wh. Cam. *adoration's fertile* Han. Ran. Mal. *adoratiöns, with fertile* Huds. *adorations, with fertile* Pope et cet. *faithful adorations fertile* Joicey (*N. & Qu.* 8th, vi, 283).

I esteeme of what value it is. *Je aprise*, prim. conj. I can nat prayse justly howe moche it is worthe, but as I gesse : *je ne le puis poynt apriser combien it vault, mays comme je diuine.'*—Palsgrave, 1530 [p. 664, ed. 1852]. 'Prayse by value, *estimo*,' Huloet's *Abecedarium*, 1552. 'A praiser or valuer,' Baret's *Alvearie*, 1580. [It is a question of interpretation. The word in the Folio may mean either *praise* or *appraise*. The only other quotation given by SCHMIDT, or by the editors, of Shakespeare's use of this word in this sense, is equally ambiguous ; in *Tro. & Cress.* III, ii, 97, we have, 'Praise us as we are tasted, allow us as we prove.' I prefer the sense of *appraise*, but it cannot be said that those who prefer *praise* are wrong.—ED.]

247. **I see . . . you are**] For the construction, compare, 'Conceal me what I am,' I, ii, 58 ; or ABBOTT, § 414.

253. **With . . . teares**] From the days of POPE, the metre of this line has been supposed to be defective. MALONE, at first (1790), would not acquiesce in Pope's *with ;* he pronounced 'adorations' as of five syllables, and 'tears' as of two,—the true scansion, I think, if we are to scan with our fingers ; but he afterward surrendered to Pope. DYCE (ed. i) pronounces the omission of the second *with* (i. e. Pope's *with*) 'a mistake, as the context (to say nothing of the metre) plainly shows.' WALKER (*Crit.* iii, 84) is sure that ' a word or words are lost before "adorations," involving the same metaphor as the rest of the two lines.' Adopting this suggestion, the CAMBRIDGE EDITORS conjecture that 'perhaps the lost word may have been *earthward* or *earthly*, so that all the four elements "of which our life consists" (II, iii, 11) would be represented in the symptoms of Orsino's passion.' *Earthly* would be good, if it did not somewhat degrade 'adorations,' which are generally supposed to be heavenly. ABBOTT (§ 505) ingeniously transposes, to follow 'tears,' the 'With' at the beginning of the next line. This, however, obliges him to pronounce 'gro-ans' as a disyllable, which is no better than Malone's 'te-ars.' Abbott adds, very justly, 'But the *enumerative* character of the verse (§ 509) may justify it as it stands.' This is, I think, the true solution. After 'adorations,' pronounced either as four syllables or five, there is one of those *moræ vacuæ* of the old prosodists, *empty pauses*, which emotion and due dramatic elocution demand, and makes up to the ear the loss of a metric foot. These pauses are for ever stumbling blocks to the silent reader of Shakespeare, but never to the actor.—ED.

253. **fertill**] WALKER (*Crit.* iii, 84) : This is, I think, *copious*, as *e. g. Hamlet*, I, ii, 'No, nor the fruitful river in the eye.'

With groanes that thunder loue, with fighes of fire.

*Ol.*Your Lord does know my mind, I cannot loue him   255
Yet I fuppofe him vertuous, know him noble,
Of great eftate, of frefh and ftainleffe youth ;
In voyces well divulg'd, free, learn'd, and valiant,
And in dimenfion, and the fhape of nature,
A gracious perfon ; But yet I cannot loue him :   260
He might haue tooke his anfwer long ago.

Vio.   If I did loue you in my mafters flame,
With fuch a fuffring, fuch a deadly life :   263

---

259. *the fhape*] *fhape* F₃F₄.   260. *But yet*]¸*yet* Pope, Han.

---

254. thunder] MALONE : Compare, ' O, that forced thunder from his heart did
fly.'—*Lover's Complaint*, 325.

256–260. Yet I suppose . . . I cannot loue him] SPEDDING (*Fraser's Maga.*
Aug., 1865, p. 261) : These lines are left out in the acting, which is surely a great
mistake. As addressed by Olivia to Viola, they have a peculiar and pathetic meaning, and it is strange that the mixed emotions which they must have excited in her
should not have been made one of the ' points ' in the play.

258. voyces well divulg'd] MALONE : That is, well spoken of by the world.—
STEEVENS : So, in *Timon*, IV, iii, 81, ' the Athenian minion, whom the world
Voic'd so regardfully.'—W. A. WRIGHT : By public acclamation held of good
repute. Compare *Coriol.* II, ii, 144, ' the people Must have their voices.' And
Jul. Cæs. II, i, 146, ' And buy men's voices to commend our deeds.'—DEIGHTON :
This seems to me to be connected with the rest of the line, *i. e.* well spoken of by
the world *as being* free (gracious), learned, and valiant. Having first referred to
what she can only assume regarding the Duke, *sc.* his virtue, Olivia goes on to mention what she can knows as facts, viz. that he is of noble birth and fortune, that his
youth has been blamelessly spent, that he is spoken of as gracious, learned, and
valiant, that his personal appearance is handsome. His being free, learned, and
valiant would be a matter of opinion, his being considered so would be a matter of
fact within her knowledge.

258. free] Compare *Othello*, III, iii, 228, ' I would not haue your free and Noble
Nature,' etc. See, also, ' free maides,' II, iv, 53, *post.*

259. dimension] That is, bodily proportion.—ROLFE : See V, i, 252, ' that
dimension,' the only other example of the singular in Shakespeare.

260. gracious] ABBOTT (p. 498) refers to *King John*, ' There was not such a
gracious creature born,' III, iv, 81.

262. in] W. A. WRIGHT : ' In ' is here used very much like the French *en.*

263. deadly life] HUDSON, whose text reads deadly *love*,' thinks ' life ' ' a very
evident misprint ; yet it has waited a good while to be corrected.'—DEIGHTON :
That is, with such a painful and fatal vitality of love ; ' deadly life ' for the sake of
the antithesis ; compare *Hen. V :* IV, ii, 54, ' To demonstrate the life of such a
battle In life so lifeless as it shows itself.' [To me, ' deadly *love* ' is meaningless.
' Deadly ' is the climax of ' suffering '; a ' deadly life ' is a life of suffering extended
even to its last limit, death.—ED.]

In your deniall, I would finde no fence,
I would not vnderſt and it.   265
  Ol.   Why, what would you?
  Vio.   Make me a willow Cabine at your gate,
And call vpon my ſoule within the houſe,
Write loyall Cantons of contemned loue,
And ſing them lowd euen in the dead of night :   270
Hallow your name to the reuerberate hilles,
And make the babling Goſsip of the aire,
Cry out *Oliuia :* O you ſhould not reſt
Betweene the elements of ayre, and earth,
But you ſhould pittie me.   275

266. *Why,*] Om. Han.
  you ?] *you doe ?* F₃F₄, Rowe, +.
267. *Cabine*] *Cabin* F₄.
269. *Cantons*] *Cantos* Rowe ii, +,
Var. '73, '78, Ran. *canzons* Cap.
270. *dead*] *dread* F₃F₄.
271. *Hallow*] *Hollaw* F₂. *Hollow*

F₃F₄, Rowe, +, Cap.   *Holloo* Var. '73.
Haloo Var. '78, Ran. Var. '85.   *Halloo*
Coll. Cam. Rlfe, Dtn, Wh. ii.   *Holla*
Mal. et cet.
  271. *to the*] *to* F₄.
  reuerberate] *reverberant* Theob.
Han. Johns.

267. **willow**] Of course, with the suggestion of the willow as an emblem of forsaken or of rejected love.   It were superfluous to quote Desdemona's song, or the
allusions in *Much Ado.*

269. **Write, etc.**] See LAMB'S note on Mrs Jordan's acting, II, iv, 118.

269. **Cantons**] MALONE : There is no need of alteration. 'Canton' was used
for *canto* in our author's time. So, in *The London Prodigal,* 1605 : 'What-do-you-
call-him hath it there in his third canton.'[III, ii, p. 489, Var. 1780.] Again, in
Heywood's *Preface to Britaynes Troy,* 1609 : '—in the judicial perusal of these
few cantons,' etc.—W. A. WRIGHT notes that this latter work is described in the
title-page as 'A Poem deuided into xvii. seuerall cantons.'

271. **reuerberate**] STEEVENS : Theobald's emendation is unnecessary. Jonson,
in one of his Masques, says : 'which skill, Pythagoras First taught to men by a
reverberate glass.' [*Masque of Blackness,* p. 15, ed. Gifford.]—HOLT WHITE, in
support of 'reverberate' quotes the following line from Heywood's *Troja Britannica,* 1609, canto xi, st. 9 : 'Give shrill reverberate echoes and rebounds.' RICH-
ARDSON (*Dict.*) quotes from Drayton's *Polyolbion,* Song ix, 55 : 'The loftie Hills . . .
Sent forth such ecchoing shoutes (which every way so shrill With the reuerberate
sound the spacious ayre did fill)'; and also from Bacon's *Naturall Historie,* § 261 :
'Both audibles and visibles will be reverberate ; as in mirrours and in ecchos.' But,
as W. A. WRIGHT observes, in regard to the quotations from Heywood and from
Drayton (and the same is true of that from Bacon also) that in these cases 'reverberate' is passive and not active. Ben Jonson, however, uses the word actively, and
this is sufficient. 'Similarly,' says Wright, 'in *Coriol.* I, i, 106, "participate"
is equivalent to *participant;* and in *Hamlet,* I, i, 83, "emulate" has an active
sense.'—ED.

275. **But**] See line 149, above.

Ol. You might do much :   276
What is your Parentage *?*

Vio. Aboue my fortunes, yet my ſtate is well :
I am a Gentleman.

Ol. Get you to your Lord :   280
I cannot loue him : let him ſend no more,
Vnleſſe(perchance) you come to me againe,
To tell me how he takes it : Fare you well :
I thanke you for your paines : ſpend this for mee.

Vio. I am no feede poaſt, Lady; keepe your purſe,   285
My Maſter, not my ſelfe, lackes recompence.
Loue make his heart of flint, that you ſhal loue,
And let your feruour like my maſters be,
Plac'd in contempt : Farwell fayre crueltie.   *Exit*

Ol. What is your Parentage ?   290
Aboue my fortunes, yet my ſtate is well ;
I am a Gentleman.   Ile be ſworne thou art,
Thy tongue, thy face, thy limbes, actions, and ſpirit,
Do giue thee fiue-fold blazon : not too faſt : ſoft, ſoft,
Vnleſſe the Maſter were the man.   How now ?   295

276, 277. Two lines, Ff, Rowe, +, Var. '73, Wh. Cam. Rlfe, Dtn. One line, Cap. et cet.

285. *no feede poaſt*] *no feede-poaſt* F₂. *no-feed poſt* F₃. *no feed-poſt* F₄, Pope. *no feeʼd-post* Rowe. *no feeʼd post* Theob. et seq.

288. *feruour ... maſters*] *fervour,... masterʼs,* Theob.

294. *ſoft, ſoft,*] *soft ;* Cap. Separate line, Dyce ii, iii, Huds.

295. *Maſter were the man*] *man the master were* (ending lines 294–297, *fast ...were...catch...perfections*) Han.

285. **feede poaſt**] That is, hired messenger. The compositors of the Folios seem to have been puzzled over it.

287. **his . . . that**] For the construction, see 'their . . . that,' II, iv, 103–105 ; or ABBOTT, § 218, for other examples of possessive pronouns as antecedents to relatives.

290, 292. **your . . . thou**] Note the dawning of love in this change from *you* to *thou.*—ED.

294. **blazon**] A description, according to the rules of Heraldry, of armorial bearings ; hence the transferred sense of a record or description of any kind. See *Much Ado*, II, i, 282, with *note*, in this ed. if needful.

294. **soft, soft**] DYCE made a separate line of these words ; K. ELZE prefixes them to the next line, and makes 'How now ?' a separate line,—both equally efficacious in relieving the eye from the dread sight of an Alexandrine, which the ear does not, or should not, hear.—ED.

295. **the Master . . . man**] CAPELL (p. 143) : These words are rang'd contrary to expectation ; 'man' is look'd for where 'master' stands now : the sense is much the same either way ; but by this arrangement the speaker contrives to cheat

Euen fo quickly may one catch the plague ?   296
Me thinkes I feele this youths perfeƈtions
With an inuifible, and fubtle ftealth
To creepe in at mine eyes.   Well, let it be.
What hoa, *Maluolio.*   300
    Enter Maluolio.
 Mal.   Heere Madam, at your feruice.
 Ol.   Run after that fame peeuifh Meffenger
The Countes man : he left this Ring behinde him
Would I, or not : tell him, Ile none of it.   305
Defire him not to flatter with his Lord,

---

299. *it be.*] *it be—* Rowe, +.
300. *hoa*] *ho* Theob.·
301. Maluolio.] *Malvolio,—* Theob.
Warb. Johns.

304. *Countes*] *Counts* Ff.   *Duke's*
Rowe, +.   *Count his* Ktly.   *County's*
Cap. et cet.
    left] *left here* Han.

---

herself into an opinion that the declaration is less humiliating ; ' were the man ' is—
were like the man.—MALONE : Unless the dignity of the master were added to the
merit of the servant, I shall go too far, and disgrace myself.   Let me stop in time.—
STEEVENS : Perhaps she means to check herself by observing,—'This is unbecoming
forwardness on my part, unless I were as much in love with the master as I am with
the man.'—ROLFE : Olivia evidently wishes that the master and man could change
places, but just what she would have said if she had not checked herself we need
not trouble ourselves to guess.—W. A. WRIGHT (in reference to Hanmer's text) :
But Olivia does not wish that the man had the rank and dignity of the master, but
that the master had the attractiveness of the man.   [In ' unless ' there lies a train
of thought which passes through Olivia's mind ' as swift as meditation or the thoughts
of love.'   The word ' blazon,' with its suggestion of high nobility, recalls the Duke
to her.   She instantly remembers that she has utterly rejected him.   Was she therein
true to herself?   Could she really never love him?   No, she could not—unless—
unless he were like his man.   By this flash of light she perceives that she has caught
the ' infection of the eye.'—ED.]

 297. **perfeƈtions**] See I, i, 44.

 299. **To creepe**] As to the construction, see ABBOTT (§ 349) for examples of the
insertion, and of the omission, of ' to ' after verbs of *perceiving*, and after *have need*,
and after *let* in the sense of *suffering* and of *hindering*.   The following examples
occur in the present play : ' Thou hadst need send,' II, iii, 176 ; ' I had rather hear
you to solicit that,' III, i, 110 ; ' I my brother know Yet living,' III, iv, 381 (see
Abbott, p. 251) ; ' If nothing lets to make vs,' V, i, 264.

 303. **peeuish**] DYCE (*Gloss.*) : This appears to have generally signified, during
Shakespeare's days, *silly*, *foolish*, *trifling*, etc.; though, no doubt, the word was formerly used to signify, as now, *pettish*, *perverse*, etc.—COLLIER : In this place Olivia
may wish Malvolio not to perceive that she takes any interest about so insignificant
a person as ' the county's man.'   [Whatever the precise meaning, Malvolio repeats
the word when he delivers the ring.]

 305. **Would I, or not**] For this subjunctive, see ABBOTT, § 361.

Nor hold him vp with hopes, I am not for him :   307
If that the youth will come this way to morrow,
Ile giue him reafons for't : hie thee *Maluolio*.

   Mal. Madam, I will.   *Exit.*   310

   Ol. I do I know not what, and feare to finde
Mine eye too great a flatterer for my minde :
F a te, fhew thy force, our felues we do not owe,
What is decreed, muft be : and be this fo.

                     Finis, Aĉtus primus.   315

Aĉtus Secundus, Scæna prima.

       Enter Antonio & Sebaftian.   2

   Ant. Will you ftay no longer : nor will you not that
I go with you.   4

---

309. *reafons for't : hie thee*]F₂ (subs.) *reafons for't by thee,* F₃. *reafon for't by thee,* F₄, Rowe. *reason for't. Hye thee* Pope, Han. *reasons for't. Hye thee* Theob. et seq.

315. Om. Rowe et seq.

315. primus] primi Ff.
   The Street. Rowe.   The Sea-coast. Cap.

3, 4. *longer ... you.*] *longer :... you?* F₂F₃. *longer ?...you ?* F₄ et seq.

306. **flatter with**] See ABBOTT, § 194, for examples of the use of *with* after verbs, where we should use a different preposition, or even none at all.

308. **If that**] For the construction, see I, ii, 52.

312. **Mine eye**, etc.] JOHNSON : I believe the meaning is : I am not mistress of my own actions ; I am afraid that my eyes betray me, and flatter the youth without my consent, with discoveries of love.—M. MASON : Johnson's explanation is evidently wrong. . . . The true meaning appears to be this : 'She fears that her eyes had formed so flattering an idea of Cesario, that she should not have strength of mind sufficient to resist the impression.' She had just before said that she felt the youth's perfections creep in at her eyes.—MALONE : I think the meaning is, 'I fear that my eyes will seduce my understanding ; that I am indulging a passion for this beautiful youth, which my reason cannot approve.'—HARNESS : Her *mind*, here used for *heart*, had fixed itself on Viola, and her *eye flattered* her *mind* by discovering in the object of affection more than her true merits.—HALLIWELL : This seems to mean, I fear it will turn out that my eye will indulge me in wishes and expectations, so that it will overpower my judgement. W. A. WRIGHT expresses it concisely : 'my mind will be unable to resist the too favourable impression which my eyes have received.'

313. **owe**] That is, own, possess. See Shakespeare *passim*.

2. MARSHALL : This scene in [Irving's] acting-version, becomes scene ii. of Act III. ; thus the action of the play is rendered more consecutive.

3. **nor . . . not**] For double negatives, see ABBOTT, § 406 ; or Shakespeare everywhere.

Seb. By your patience, no : my ſtarres ſhine darkely   5
ouer me ; the malignancie of my fate, might perhaps di-
ſtemper yours ; therefore I ſhall craue of you your leaue,
that I may beare my euils alone.   It were a bad recompence for your loue, to lay any of them on you.

*An.*Let me yet know of you, whither you are bound.   10

Seb. No ſooth ſir : my det erminate voyage is meere
extrauagancie.But I perceiue in you ſo excellent a touch   12

7. *yours*] *your's* Coll. ii.   *'sooth* Cap. Mal. Steev. Var. Knt, Coll.
   I ſhall] *I* Rowe, Pope, Han.   Hal. Ktly.
11. *ſooth*] *in sooth* Johns. Var. Ran.

5. By your patience] DEIGHTON : If you will suffer it to be so.   [It has a
deeper meaning than simply 'by your leave,' which Sebastian uses shortly after ; it
is used in the present sense by the aged Gonzalo when he entreats his companions
to bear with his weariness, *Temp.* III, iii, 3.—ED.]

6. malignancie] The reference to the stars suggests this astrological term, and,
possibly, 'distemper.' Compare *1 Hen. VI*: IV, v, 6 : 'O malignant and ill-boding
stars !' In *Mid. N. D.* II, i, 110, Titania ascribes 'distemperature' to the influence
of the Moon.—ED.

7. craue of you your leaue] Compare for the construction, 'I shall desire you
of more acquaintance,' in *Mid. N. D.* III, i, 188, and only a few lines further on
'I shall desire of you more acquaintance.'   The present text shows that the phrase
in the latter quotation from *Mid. N. D.* is not a possible misprint, as was there too
hastily suggested by the present—ED.

10. bound] MURRAY (*N. E. D.* s. v. 'Bound' participial adjective) : An adopted
form of Old Norse *búinn*, Norwegian *búen* past participle of *búa* to get ready,
appearing first in the north as *bún*, afterwards in Middle English *boun ;* the added
d in the modern form may be due in part to its being regarded as the past participle
of the derived verb BOUN, and in part to confusion with BOUND participial adjective
equivalent to obliged ; but compare other instances as in *Mahound, sound, compound, astound,* for *Mahoun, soun, compoun, astoun,* also the vulgar *gownd,
drownd,* etc. [The definition, which applies to the present word, is under 2 :]
Prepared or purposing to go, starting, directing one's course, destined. [See 'bound,'
III, i, 77.]

11. sooth] The *Text. Notes* show that many an editor has followed Capell's lead
in printing this as though it were a contraction for *in sooth*.   'The full phrase,' says
W. A. WRIGHT, 'is *in sooth* or *in good sooth*, both which are of common occurrence,
and both are used without the preposition.'

11, 12. determinate . . . extrauagancie] W. A. WRIGHT : Sebastian says,
his most settled plan of travelling is mere vagrancy.   [Both words are used in their
derivative Latin sense.   See *Hamlet*, 'The extravagant and erring spirit hies To
his confine.' I, i, 154.]

12. touch] SCHMIDT (*Lex.*) is somewhat astray in defining this present use of
'touch' as 'dash, spice, smack'; 'touch' is more refined than these rude words.
W. A. WRIGHT defines it by 'delicate feeling,' and quotes in proof the following
appropriate examples : *Mid. N. D.* III, ii, 286 : 'Have you no modesty, no maiden

of modeftie, that you will not extort from me, what I am　　13
willing to keepe in : therefore it charges me in manners,
the rather to expreffe my felfe : you muft know of mee　　15
then *Antonio*, my name is *Sebaftian* (which I call'd *Rodo-*
rigo) my father was that *Sebaftian* of *Meffaline*, whom I
know you haue heard of. He left behinde him, my felfe,
and a fifter, both borne in an houre : if the Heanens had
beene pleas'd, would we had fo ended. But you fir, al-　　20
ter'd that, for fome houre before you tooke me from the
breach of the fea, was my fifter drown'd.

　　Ant. Alas the day.

　　Seb. A Lady fir, though it was faid fhee much refem-　　24

16, 17. Rodorigo] *Roderigo* Var. '73,
Coll. Cam. Sta.
　17. Meffaline] *Mettaline* Knt, conj.
　19. *an houre*] *one hour* F$_3$F$_4$,
Rowe, +.

19. *Heanens*] F$_1$.
21. *houre*] *houres* F$_3$. *hours* F$_4$,
Rowe, Pope, Han.
22. *breach*] *beech* Grey (i, 226).
24. *though*] *who, tho'* Han.

---

shame, No touch of bashfulness?'; *Tempest*, V, i, 21 : 'Hast thou, which art but
air, a touch, a feeling Of their afflictions?'; And *Cymb.* I, i, 135 : 'I am senseless
of your wrath ; a touch more rare Subdues all pangs, all fears.'

　　15. expreffe] JOHNSON : That is, to reveal myself.—HALLIWELL : Thus, in
Kendall's *Flowers of Epigrammes*, 1577 : 'When thei had robde hym of his coine.
Quoth one among the reste,—My maisters, let us cutte his throte, For feare we be
expreste.'

　　16, 17. which I call'd Rodorigo] R. G. WHITE (ed. ii): Why, does not appear.
It would seem that there must be an allusion to some story or play of which we know
nothing. Indeed the whole of this scene has the air of one worked up out of another,
particularly in the Captain's speeches, which contain matter superfluous and foreign
to the interest of the play as we have it.

　　17. Messaline] Inasmuch as this locality is unknown to geographers, HANMER
changed it to *Metelin*, (the modern name, as Capell points out, of *Mitylene*,) utterly
regardless of the identity of Sebastian's father, who, we may be very sure, was never
in Metelin in his life. He was 'Sebastian of Messaline,' and if we do not know
where Messaline was, it merely proves that we know less than the Captain of the
ship,—an ignorance which is not humiliating. I *think* Messaline was the chief town
on Prospero's island.—ED.

　　19. in an houre] For this use of *a* or *an* for *one*, see Shakespeare and early
literature *passsim ;* or ABBOTT, § 81.

　　21. some houre] See ABBOTT (§ 21) for examples of 'some' qualifying nouns
of time.

　　22. breach] STEEVENS : That is, what we now call the *breaking* of the sea. In
Pericles, II, i, 161, it is called 'the rupture of the sea.' [It is 'rupture' in the
Qq and F$_3$F$_4$, according to the Cam. Ed., but modern editors follow Rowe ii, in
reading 'rapture.' The 'breach of the sea' is where, as Tennyson says in *Enoch
Arden*, 'the league-long rollers thunder on the beach.'—ED.]

bled me, was yet of many accounted beautiful:but thogh   25
I could not with fuch eftimable wonder ouer-farre be-

26. *fuch*] *much* Cartwright.   26. *ouer-farre*] *overfar* Johns.

24. **though**] For the omission of the relative, see, if need be, I, v, 99. Hanmer inserted it.

26. **such estimable wonder,** etc.] WARBURTON : An interpolation of the players.—JOHNSON : But what did the players gain by it? they may sometimes be guilty of a joke without the concurrence of the poet, but they never lengthen a speech only to make it longer. Shakespeare often confounds the active and passive adjectives. 'Estimable wonder' is *esteeming wonder*, or *wonder and esteem*. The meaning is, that he could not venture to think so highly as others of his sister.— HEATH (p. 188) : That is, with an admiration that held her in as high account as they did who thought her beautiful ; or, in short, with so high a degree of admiration.—CAPELL (p. 144) : The sense is briefly this,—with such wonder in my esteem ; 'tis a peculiarity of the poet's, and his adjective a coinage. [In 1853 COLLIER published his *Notes and Emendations*, etc., from MS Corrections in a copy of the Second Folio ; in this volume, with the pardonable zeal of a discoverer, he set forth the emendations in a somewhat dogmatic tone, which seems to have stirred profoundly the whole Shakespearian world. (May I be pardoned if I here say, parenthetically, that I have entire faith in Collier as an honourable man? If there were any fraud connected with this Folio, or with the State Papers, the Bridgewater, or the Dulwich collections, I believe Collier to have been the victim, and not the perpetrator.) In the present passage, there was, in his Folio, this correction : 'I could not with *self-estimation wander so far to* believe that, yet' etc.; to this he added the following note : 'May we conclude, that this new and self-evident improvement of the absurd old reading was derived from some original source, perhaps from some better manuscript than that employed by the old printer of the Folio, 1623, which was exactly followed in the Folio, 1632? Such an emendation could hardly be the result of mere guess-work.' Five years later, in his Second Edition, Collier was even more emphatic in his approval of this emendation ; he adopted it in his text, and not only pronounced it ' one of the most excellent emendations' in the annotated Folio, but asserted that it 'must inevitably be right.' Other critics, however, did not share Collier's assurance. R. G. WHITE pronounced the change 'most pitifull,' and a Reviewer (said to be LETTSOM, but I doubt) in *Blackwood's Maga.* (Aug., 1853) asserts that it is 'certainly a very bad piece of tinkering,' and asks, 'who can believe that Shakespeare would wander so far in his speech as to write in such a roundabout feckless fashion as this?' In the meantime, the interest excited by Collier's Second Folio aroused SINGER, who found that he possessed two annotated Folios, a Second and a Third, and for the MS corrections therein he claimed consideration. In the present passage, his annotator had made the following change : 'I could not, with such *estimators, wander* overfar *to* believe that, yet,' etc. This emendation Singer pronounced 'a much better rectification of the passage' than Collier's. DYCE (ed. i) agrees with the Blackwood critic that Collier's change is 'a very bad piece of tinkering,' and then adds that Singer's change 'comes under the same description.' Singer's reading, however, 'struck' BAILEY (i, 204) 'as an improvement,' and, after he had changed in it, *estimators* into *estimate*, he considered that it made 'passable sense.'—HALLIWELL : In other words, though I could not altogether agree with such a high degree of admiration.—R. G. WHITE

leeue that, yet thus farre I will boldly publifh her, fhee　　27
bore a minde that enuy could not but call faire : Shee is
drown'd already fir with falt water, though I feeme to
drowne her remembrance againe with more.　　　　　　30

　　Ant.　Pardon me fir, your bad entertainment.

　　Seb.　O good *Antonio*, forgiue me your trouble.

　　Ant.　If you will not murther me for my loue, let mee
be your feruant.　　　　　　　　　　　　　　　　34

---

28. *enuy could not but*] *envy itself*　　　　33. *murther*] *murder* Steev. et seq.
would Cap. conj.　　　　　　　　　　　　(except Knt, Wh. i.)

(ed. i) : When we remember the sense in which Shakespeare uses 'capable impressure,'—*As You Like It*, III, v, 23, 'intenible sieve,'—*All's Well*, I, iii, 208, and
'something that is deceivable,' in this very play, IV, iii, 23, we have no difficulty in
understanding Sebastian, when, with manly modesty, he says of the *beauty* attributed
to the sister who so much resembled him, 'though I could not, with such estimable
(esteeming) wonder, overfar believe *that*,' and adds, 'yet *thus* far I will boldly publish
her ;' etc.—WALKER (*Crit.* i, 187) quotes the present 'estimable' among his examples where ' adjectives in -*able* and -*ible*, both positive and negative ones, are frequently
used by old writers in an active sense.'—DYCE (ed. ii) : The late Mr W. W.
Williams (under the signature W. D.) writes thus in *The Literary Gazette* for
March 29, 1862, p. 310 : 'I would submit that, if Sebastian's speech be read carefully, it will require no long pondering to perceive that he is modestly deprecating
any comparison of himself with such a beautiful girl as his sister.　If this be the
purport of the words,—and there can hardly be a doubt about it,—the simple insertion of the indefinite article will meet all the necessities of the case.　Read as follows, and all difficulty vanishes : 'though I could not, with such *an* estimable
wonder [*i. e.* when compared with such an admirable woman], overfar believe that,
yet' etc.　[HUDSON adopted this emendation.]—W. A. WRIGHT : 'Such estimable
wonder' means 'with the admiration which influenced such a judgement.'　[The
general meaning seems plain to every one, from Johnson downward ; the chief difficulty seems to have been found in accepting 'estimable' in an active sense, and
'wonder' in the sense of *admiration.*—ED.]

　　30. with more] STEEVENS : Compare *Hamlet*, IV, vii, 186 : 'Too much water
hast thou, poor Ophelia, And therefore I forbid my tears.'

　　33, 34. If you . . . seruant] KNIGHT : We think that these words have a latent
meaning, and they allude to a superstition of which Sir Walter Scott has made such
admirable use in *The Pirate*.　Our readers will remember that, when Mordaunt has
rescued Cleveland from 'the breach of the sea,' and is endeavouring to restore the
animation of the perishing man, he is thus reproved by Bryce, the pedlar : 'Are you
mad ? you, that have lived so long in Zetland, to risk the saving of a drowning
man ?　Wot ye not, if you bring him to life again, he will be sure to do you some
capital injury ?'　Sir Walter Scott has a note upon this passage : 'It is remarkable
that, in an archipelago where so many persons must be necessarily endangered by the
waves, so strange and inhuman a maxim should have engrafted itself upon the minds
of a people otherwise kind, moral, and hospitable.　But all with whom I have
spoken agree that it was almost general in the beginning of the eighteenth century,

Seb. If you will not vndo what you haue done, that is   35
kill him, whom you haue recouer'd, defire it not.   Fare
ye well at once, my bofome is full of kindneffe, and I
am yet fo neere the manners of my mother,that vpon the
leaft occafion more, mine eyes will tell tales of me : I am
bound to the Count Orfino's Court,farewell.   *Exit*   40
   Ant.   The gentleneffe of all the gods go with thee :
I haue many enemies in Orfino's Court,
Elfe would I very fhortly fee thee there :
But come what may, I do adore thee fo, -
That danger fhall feeme fport, and I will go.   *Exit.*   45

Scæna Secunda.

   Enter Viola and Maluolio, at feuerall doores.   2
   *Mal.*Were not you eu'n now, with the Counteffe O-
liuia ?   4

<table>
<tr><td>40. Count] Duke Rowe,+.</td><td>2. Enter...] Enter Viola, Malvolio</td></tr>
<tr><td>   farewell] farwel F₄.</td><td>following. Cap. et seq.</td></tr>
<tr><td>41. all the] the F₄.</td><td>3. eu'n] e'en Rowe,+, Wh.   even</td></tr>
<tr><td>42. many] made F₃F₄, Rowe,+.</td><td>Cap. et seq.</td></tr>
<tr><td>   A Street. Cap.</td><td></td></tr>
</table>

---

and was with difficulty weeded out by the sedulous instructions of the clergy and the
rigorous injunctions of the proprietors.   There is little doubt it had been originally
introduced as an excuse for suffering those who attempted to escape from the wreck
to perish unassisted, so that, there being no survivor, she might be considered as
lawful plunder.'   It appears to us, however, if we do not mistake the meaning of
our text, that the superstition was not confined to the Orkneys in the time of Shakespeare.   Why should Sebastian murder Antonio for his love if this superstition were
not alluded to ?   Indeed, the answer of Sebastian distinctly refers to the office of
humanity which Antonio had rendered him, and appears to glance at the superstition
as if he perfectly understood what Antonio meant : ' If you will not undo what you
have done, that is, *kill him whom you have recovered*, desire it not.'   The vulgar
opinion is here reversed.—W. A. WRIGHT : But Antonio seems only to appeal to
Sebastian not to kill him as a reward for his love by abandoning him.—DEIGHTON :
That is, I shall die if you refuse to let me serve you. [I think that Wright and
Deighton give the just interpretation.—ED.]
   38. mother] MALONE : Compare *Hen. V.* IV, vi, 30 : ' But I had not so much
of man in me, And all my mother came into my eyes.'
   2. Enter...] COLLIER : Malvolio may be supposed to be coming out of Olivia's
house, but Viola must necessarily be in the street, having lately quitted the presence
of Olivia.
   3. eu'n] By changing this to *even*, as nearly all modern editors have done, under

Vio. Euen now fir, on a moderate pace, I haue fince a-   5
riu'd but hither.

Mal She returnes this Ring to you (fir) you might
haue faued mee my paines, to haue taken it away your
felfe.She adds moreouer,that you fhould put your Lord
into a defperate affurance, fhe will none of him.And one   10
thing more, that you be neuer fo hardie to come againe
in his affaires, vnleffe it bee to report your Lords taking
of this : receiue it fo.   13

5. *fir, ... pace,*] *sir; ... pace,* Rowe.
sir; ... pace Pope et seq.
    7. *(fir)*] *Sir ;* Rowe. *sir; she will
none of your lord's ring* K. Elze.

10. *into*] *in* F_3F_4, Rowe i.
fhe...him.] *she is not for him.* K.
Elze.
him.] him. Han.

Capell's lead, I think an undue emphasis is given to it. It has escaped notice, I
suppose, that 'you' is the emphatic word, and that 'e'en now' should receive no
stress. When, however, Viola replies, then the 'e'en' becomes emphatic, and is
pronounced, in full, 'Even,' and with deliberation,—a form of assent more courteous
than a blunt 'ay' or 'yes.'—ED.

    5. **sir, . . . pace,**] Pope's punctuation is an improvement on Rowe's.

    5. **on**] See ABBOTT (§ 180, p. 119) for other examples where 'the metaphorical
uses of *on* have now been mostly divided between *of, in,* and *at,* etc.'

    7. **(sir)**] Although Olivia bade Malvolio run after the County's man, with the
ring, and 'tell him I'll none of it,' Malvolio did not repeat these very words of the
message ; he changed 'it' into *him ;* and yet Viola in her soliloquy (line 26) repeats
them substantially : 'None of my Lord's ring?' Wherefore, in order to explain
Viola's knowledge of Olivia's words, HANMER inserted in Malvolio's speech, after
the present 'sir': *for being your Lord's she'll none of it.* I suppose that this was
his object; he has no note of explanation.—ED.

    8. **to haue taken it**] That is, by taking it. See 'conclusions to be as kisses,'
V, i, 22. For many examples of the infinitive thus used indefinitely, see ABBOTT,
§ 356.

    10. **desperate assurance**] This is Malvolio's version, correct enough, of Olivia's
words 'nor hold him up with hopes.'—ED.

    11. **so hardie to come**] Compare 'no woman's heart So bigge to hold,' II, iv,
101 ; 'so much a sinner to be a double dealer,' V, i, 34 ; and for other examples of
the omission of *as* after *so,* see ABBOTT, § 281, p. 192.

    13. **receiue it so**] CAPELL evidently interpreted Malvolio's words 'to report
your Lord's taking of this' as referring to the taking of this, the ring, instead of
referring to the whole message ; he changed 'receive it so' into 'receive it, sir.'
This is ingenious ; because Viola at once refers to the ring, and takes no notice of
the rest of the message ; at the same time, it is quite possible that COLLIER is right
in saying that 'receive it so' is equivalent to *understand* or *take* it so, probably
without reference to the ring. See 'To one of your receiving,' that is, to one of
your capacity for understanding, III, i, 122.—ED.

Vio. She tooke the Ring of me, Ile none of it.   14

14. *the Ring of me, Ile*] Ff (*I'le* F₃F₄), Rowe, +. *the ring of me! I'll* Anon. Mal. Var. '21. *the ring of me.* *I'll* Knt, Wh. i. *the ring of me!—I'll*

Coll. i, ii, Hal. *not the ring of me; I'll* Ktly. *no ring of me;—I'll* Mal. conj. Dyce ii, iii, Coll. iii (MS), Huds. *the ring of me; I'll* Steev. et cet.

---

14. **tooke . . . of it**] MALONE: This passage has been hitherto thus pointed: 'She took the ring of me; I'll none of it' [see Steevens, *Text. Note*] which renders it, as it appears to me, quite unintelligible. The punctuation now adopted: 'She took the ring of me!—I'll none of it,' was suggested by an ingenious friend, and certainly renders the line less exceptionable: yet I cannot but think there is some corruption in the text. Had our author intended such a mode of speech, he would probably have written: 'She took *a* ring of me!—I'll none of it.' Malvolio's answer seems to intimate that Viola had said she had not given any ring. We ought, therefore, perhaps, to read: 'She took NO ring of me!—I'll none of it.' [Thus, Collier's MS.] So afterwards: 'I left *no* ring with her.' Viola expressly denies her having given Olivia any ring. How then can she assert, as she is made to do by the old regulation of the passage, that the lady had received one from her? [To this note, Malone added in his ed. 1790 the following, which he afterward withdrew: 'it has occurred to me that the latter part of the line may have been corrupt, as well as the former; our author may have written: 'She took *this* ring of me! She'll none of it!']—STEEVENS: I do not perceive the necessity of the change recommended. Viola finding the ring sent after her, accompanied by a fiction, is prepared to meet it with another.—KNIGHT: Viola would screen Olivia from the suspicions of her own servant. The lady has said that the ring was left with her; and Viola has too strong a respect for her own sex to proclaim the truth. She makes up her mind during Malvolio's speech to refuse the ring; but not to expose the cause of her refusal. [To the same effect, substantially, R. G. WHITE (ed. i), and also SPEDDING.]—HALLIWELL: A note of admiration after 'me' [Malone's punctuation] best expresses the author's intention, which was no doubt to make Viola utter an exclamation of surprise, equivalent to saying, is it possible any one can say she took the ring of me? Besides, the real truth of the matter is not suspected by Viola until afterwards, and she is too much taken by surprise to imagine a subterfuge that would fit the occasion.—COLLIER (ed. ii): There is no need [of the change made in the MS, which] accords with Malone's suggestion. After Malvolio has gone out, and Viola's surprise is past, she quietly observes, 'I left no ring with her,' and it is immediately followed by the statement of her suspicion regarding Olivia's passion. —DYCE (ed. i): I agree with Steevens and Knight that the old text is uncorrupted. —DYCE (ed. ii, wherein he adopts Malone's punctuation, which is the same as Collier's MS): I formerly retained [the text of the Folio.] I now think it quite wrong, and that what has been said in defence of it is ridiculously over-subtle. [After this conversion of the arch-enemy of Collier's MS, Collier took heart of grace, and adopted, in his Third Edition, the change here made by his MS.]—SPEDDING (*Fraser's Maga.*, August, 1865, p. 265): This passage has always appeared to us one of the finest touches in the play. When Malvolio overtakes Viola with the ring . . . her immediate answer is: '*She took the ring of me :* I'll none of it.' Now, as she had *not* left any ring, it has been thought that there must be some mistake

Mal. Come fir, you peeuifhly threw it to her : and   15
her will is, it fhould be fo return'd : If it bee worth ftoo-
ping for, there it lies, in your eye : if not, bee it his that
findes it.   *Exit.*

Vio. I left no Ring with her : what meanes this Lady?
Fortune forbid my out-fide haue not charm'd her :   20

---

here. . . . But it is plain from Malvolio's reply, 'Come, sir, you peevishly threw it
to her,' etc., that *he* understood her to mean that she *had* left it.   And so no doubt
she did.   For though taken quite by surprise, and not knowing at first what it
exactly meant, she saw at once thus much,—that the message contained a secret of
some kind which had not been confided to the messenger ; and with her quick wit
and sympathetic delicacy suppressed the surprise which might have betrayed it.—
ROLFE (*Literary World*, 8 March, 1884) learns from a friend that Madame Mod-
jeska 'assumes that Viola speaks as one half-bewildered by Malvolio's assurance,
and on the stage utters the sentence interrogatively, "She took the ring of me?"
[Thus also Miss Kate Terry.—*ap.* Spedding] as if in doubt of his meaning.'   She
considers that this interpretation is sustained by Malvolio's answer, and also by
Viola's subsequent soliloquy.   [I prefer the deliberate assertion, and for the reasons
set forth by Knight and Spedding.—ED.]

   15. threw it to her] Thus far Malvolio has acquitted himself, as a messenger,
tolerably well.   But here he oversteps his knowledge.   Olivia had said merely
that the peevish messenger (a qualification which remains in Malvolio's memory)
had *left* the ring behind him,—she uttered no word about *throwing* it.   In thus
filling out the details of an imaginary scene are we to find a forecast of that fantastic
dreamer who could picture, even to a branched velvet gown, his married life with
the Countess ?—ED.

   17. in your eye] That is, in your sight.   Compare, 'Into the eye and prospect
of his soul,' *Much Ado*, IV, i, 238.   W. A. WRIGHT quotes *Hamlet*, IV, iv, 6 :
'We shall express our duty in his eye.'

   19, etc. I left, etc.] HANMER'S changes, which are by way of *improving* Shakespeare, are too elaborate to be comfortably, or, perhaps, intelligently, indicated in
the *Text. Notes.*   First of all, he so transposes line 26, 'None of my Lord's ring?
Why he sent her none,' as to make it Viola's first words, printing 'None of my
Lord's ring' in Italics, as a quotation.   Next, he converts 'my outside have not
charm'd her (line 20) into 'my outside *should have* charm'd her.'   Then in line 22,
'her eyes had lost her tongue' is changed into 'her eyes *did let* her tongue,' that is,
hindered, *tied* her tongue.   Finally, having removed line 26, as just stated, he puts
a full stop after 'messenger,' in line 25.   It is to be always borne in mind that these
changes by Hanmer (for whose text I have much regard) and others like them by
the early editors, were made solely in the interest of Shakespeare, as it was then supposed to be.   See *note* on l. 26.—ED.

   20. haue not] See 'were scarse out of him,'—I, v, 161.—W. A. WRIGHT :
'Not' is frequently found after verbs which contain in themselves a negative idea.
Compare *Pass. Pil.*, 124 : 'Forbade the boy he should not pass those grounds';
Much Ado, IV, i, 13 : 'If either of you know any impediment why you should not
be conjoined,' etc.   Similarly, *Com. of Err.* IV, ii, 7 : 'First, he denied you had in
him no right.'

She made good view of me, indeed ſo much,   21
That me thought her eyes had loſt her tongue,
For ſhe did ſpeake in ſtarts diſtractedly.
She loues me ſure, the cunning of her paſsion
Inuites me in this churliſh meſſenger :   25
None of my Lords Ring? Why he ſent her none ;
I am the man, if it be ſo, as tis,   27

---

22. *That*] Knt, Coll. i, Hal. Dyce i,
Cam. Sta.   *That, as* Dyce ii, iii, Coll.
iii, Huds.   *That ſure* Ff et cet.
      me thought] *methought* Rowe et
seq. *methought that* Ktly.
26. *none ;*] *none ?* Ff.   *none.* Rowe.
27. *I am the*] *I should be* Han.

27. *man, if it be ſo, as tis,*] man, if
it be ſo as tis, Ff.   man—If it be so as
'tis, Rowe, Pope.   man—If it be so, (as
'tis ;) Theob. Warb. Johns. Var. '73,
'78.   man, if it be so ; as 'tis, Han.   man !
If it be so,—as't is,— Sta.   man ;. If it
be so, (as 'tis) Cap. et cet. (subs.)

---

22. **That**] The defective metre in this line is supposed to have been supplied by
sure of the Second Folio. MALONE, however, was not altogether satisfied with it ;
he remarks that '*sure* is not very likely to have been the word omitted in the First
Folio, being found in the next line but one.' Nevertheless it satisfied COLLIER ; and
R. G. WHITE says that it 'suits the place in every respect.' WALKER (*Vers.* 279)
queried 'That, *as* me thought,' etc.? and quoted Browne, *Britannia's Pastorals*,
Bk. ii, song iv : 'The wether's bell . . . Yields, as methinks, this day a deader
sound.' This quotation converted DYCE, who, in his Second Edition, adopted
Walker's conjecture. W. A. WRIGHT thinks that *sure* is not a very happy emendation. If it be the missing word, its repetition two lines further on amounts to but
little, I think ; an objection on this score might lie against the second *sure*, but
hardly against the first. I am, however, certain that a good actress could so speak
the line that the ear could detect no fault in the metre.—ED.

22. **had lost**] It is sufficient merely to record that WARBURTON pronounced this
'nonsense,' and that the word was *crost*, that is, *fascinated ;* whereto HEATH
replied that he had never heard that a 'person, or any part of him, had been fascinated by his own eyes.'—JOHNSON : We say a man *loses* his company when they go
one way and he another. So, Olivia's tongue lost her eyes ; her tongue was talking
of the Duke, and her eyes gazing on his messenger.—KNIGHT : That is, caused her
tongue to be lost.—HALLIWELL : The plain meaning seems to be that her eyes
were so occupied in looking at Viola, her talk was distracted.—W. A. WRIGHT :
Compare *Lear*, I, ii, 125 : 'It shall lose thee nothing.'

26. **None,** etc.] The mention of the 'churlish messenger' recalls to her mind
the scene with Malvolio ; we can now see how great the dislocation which this line
suffered at the hands of Hanmer.—ED.

27. **I am the man**] *Saturday Review* (12 July, 1884) : One fault only we have
thus far to find with Miss Ellen Terry's rendering of the whole part. . . . Miss
Terry gives the words, 'I am the man' with an air of pretty and intense amusement, and follows them by a charming and laughing assumption of a mannish walk.
That this is the right interpretation we cannot believe. Viola, light-hearted and
brave as she was in the midst of trouble, was not the person to be unfeeling towards
the trouble of another woman. Amusement she may very naturally have felt at the
mistake ; but it would not have been unmixed. There would have been some touch

Poore Lady, fhe were better loue a dreame:　　　　　　　28

Difguife, I fee thou art a wickedneffe,

Wherein the pregnant enemie does much.　　　　　　　30

How eafie is it, for the proper falfe

In womens waxen hearts to fet their formes :

Alas, O frailtie is the caufe, not wee,

For fuch as we are made, if fuch we bee :　　　　　　　34

31. *proper false*] *proper-false* M.
Mason, Mal. et seq. (except Coll.)
32. *formes :*] *forms !* Rowe.
33. *O*] *our* Ff et seq.
not wee,] Ff, Rowe, +, Coll. Del.
not we ; or *not we !* Cap. et cet.

34. *we are made, if fuch*] Ff, Rowe
ii, +, Var. Knt, Coll. i, ii. *we are, we
are made, if such* Rowe i. *we are made,
ev'n such* Han. Cap. Ktly, Coll. iii. *we
are made of, such* Tyrwhitt, Ran. et cet.

of pity and of interest, and of this Miss Terry gave no hint.　But this is the one important blemish on a performance which came near being ideal, and may no doubt come nearer when the nervousness inseparable from attacking so difficult a part has disappeared.—IBID. (19 July, 1884): Miss Terry still delivers these words with a most captivating laugh and assumption for a moment of a mannish walk.　But she now gives to the subsequent words, 'poor lady, she were better love a dream,' precisely the touch of pathos which on the first night we missed.

28. **she were better**] See, for the construction, 'you were best,' I, v, 30.

30. **pregnant enemie**] JOHNSON : This is, I believe, the dexterous fiend, or enemy of mankind.—W. A. WRIGHT : That is quick-witted, alert, ready.　[See III, i, 90.]

31. **proper false**] JOHNSON : This is obscure.　The meaning is, 'how easy is disguise to women !' how easily does *their own falsehood*, contained in their *waxen*, changeable *hearts*, enable them to assume deceitful appearances !　The two next lines are perhaps transposed, and should be read [in the order, 34, 33].—TYRWHITT (p. 44) : The sense, I think, is clearly this : '*How easy is it for the proper false* [handsome counterfeits, beautiful outsides] *to set their forms* [to impress themselves] *in women's waxen hearts !*'　It cannot be necessary to prove by quotations that 'proper' signifies *handsome ;* and 'false' alludes to Viola's own case.—STEEVENS : The 'proper-false' is certainly a less elegant expression than the *fair deceiver*, but it seems to mean the same thing.—M. MASON : Viola's reflection, 'how easy it is for those who are handsome and deceitful to make an impression on the waxen hearts of women,' is a natural sentiment for a girl to utter who was herself in love.　An expression similar to 'proper-false' occurs in III, iv, 370, where we find 'beauteous-evil.'　[M. Mason was the earliest to note that these words should be joined by a hyphen.]—MALONE : So, in *R. of L.* 1240 : 'For men have marble, women waxen, minds, And therefore are they form'd as marble will : The weak oppress'd, the impression of strange kinds Is form'd in them by force, by fraud, or skill.'—WELLESLEY (p. 3) : The difficulty of affixing a satisfactory sense to that strange compound 'the proper-false' inclines me to believe it an invention of the compositor, the word which baffled him being *impresses ;* and I would propose to read : 'How easy is it for impresses false,' etc., *i. e.* women are easily *impressible*.　[The interpretation of either Tyrwhitt or Monck Mason suffices.]

33. **O**] A manifest misprint, corrected in the Second Folio.

34. **such as . . . we bee**] TYRWHITT (p. 45) : I incline to read thus, 'such as

How will this fadge? My mafter loues her deerely,   35
And I (poore monfter) fond afmuch on him :

35. *fadge*] *fadg* F₄.   36. *afmuch*] *as much* F₄.
36. *monfter*] *minister* Han.

---

we are made OF, such we be.'—MALONE : *Of* and *if* are frequently confounded in
the old copies.   Thus, in *King John*, II, i, 367, the Second Folio has ' Lord of our
presence, Angiers, and *if* you [instead of : *of* you].   Again, *Mer. of Ven.* III, ii,
18 : ' Mine own, I would say, but, *if* mine, then yours ' in the Quartos is misprinted
' *of* mine ' in the First Folio.   In *As You Like It*, II, vii, 81, we have a construction nearly like the present : ' When such a one as she, such is her neighbor.' —
KNIGHT : If Viola meant to say—we be such as we are made—the particle *of* is
surplusage.   But we think she does not mean this.   She would say ' our frailty is
the cause, not we ourselves, that the proper-false deceive us ; because such as we are
made frail *if* we be frail.'   The poet did not mean the reasoning to be very conclusive.   [I think Knight's meaning would be more clearly expressed if a comma
were placed before and after ' as we ':—' because such, as we, are made frail,' etc.
—ED.]—COLLIER (ed. ii) : [Tyrwhitt's emendation] seems a decided error, for all
that Viola means to say is, that if women are indeed what they are represented to
be, the frailty of the sex is the cause of it.—ABBOTT (§ 299, p. 212) adopts Tyrwhitt's *of*, but retains the original punctuation ; this, combined with his comment
thereon, I do not quite understand.   He reads and punctuates the two lines as follows : ' Alas, our frailty is the cause, not we, For such as we are made, of such we
be.'   He then observes, ' it can scarcely be asserted that " For " is *for that* or
because.'   Note that by placing a comma before and after ' not we ' he connects
' cause,' in construction directly with ' For such,' etc., and yet will not allow us
to interpret ' For ' as *for that*.   He adds : ' It is more probable that the scene
originally ended there, and that Shakespeare used ' be ' in order to get the rhyme,
which so often terminates a scene.'   It is proper to explain that Abbott is discussing
the use of *be* in dependent clauses.   I think that the correct punctuation after ' wee '
is that adopted by every editor, except Collier and Delius, since Capell's time.   The
meaning of the two lines, with Tyrwhitt's good emendation, seems plain.—ED.

35. **fadge**] BOSWELL : '*Andar' a vanga*, to fadge, to prosper with, to go as one
would haue it.'—Florio, *A Worlde of Wordes*, 1598.—BRADLEY (*N. E. D.*) : Etymology unknown ; first found late in 16th century.   The various uses of the word are
substantially identical with those of the older FAY, verb. (extant representative of
Old English *fégan*), of which, however, it can neither be a variant nor a derivative
by any known process.   Possibly it may have been a new type formed unconsciously
on the suggestion of *fay* and some word ending in -*dge*.   The close correspondence
of the senses with those of COTTON, verb, is remarkable.   [4. *intransitive*] To fit
in with or suit the surroundings ; hence to get on, succeed, thrive.   Of an event :
To come off.   Often with an indefinite subject, *It, that, this, matters, things*, etc.

36. **monster**] DELIUS : This refers to her present androgynous state, neither man
nor woman ; just as she afterward says, ' As I am man,' and ' as I am woman.'

36. **fond**] BRADLEY (*N. E. D.*), under the second division of ' fond ' as a verb,
constructed with *on, over, upon*, gives, as its meaning of ' doting upon,' etc., the
following examples : 1530 PALSGRAVE, 553 : ' I fonde, or dote upon a thyng for
inordynate love.'   1567 TURBERVILLE, *Ovid's Epistles*, 154 : ' Whilst thou . . .

And fhe (miftaken) feemes to dote on me :   37
What will become of this ? As I am man,
My ftate is defperate for my maifters loue :
As I am woman (now alas the day)   40
What thriftleffe fighes fhall poore *Oliuia* breath ?
O time, thou muft vntangle this, not I,
It is too hard a knot for me t'vnty.   43

38. *man*] *a man* F₃F₄, Rowe.
39. *maifters*] *mafters* F₄.
40. *woman*] *a woman* Rowe i.

41. *breath*] F₃. Cap. *breathe* F₂F₄.
43. *t'vnty*] Ff, Rowe, +, Coll. Wh. i,
Sta. Dyce. *to unty* Cap. et cet.

did fonde on Phyllis.' 1590 FENNE, *Frutes*, 1, 53 : ' Immoderately fonding over
wife, sonne, daughter.' And, lastly, the present instance.

37. **And she**] DYCE (ed. i) : To this, as far as I am aware, no editor has
objected; but I question if we ought not to read,—'*As* she,' etc. [In his ed. ii,
Dyce adopted this conjecture (and was followed by HUDSON) because 'And' was,
'no doubt, repeated from the line above.']

38. **of this**] For other examples where ' of' means *in consequence of*, see ABBOTT,
§ 168, p. 111.

43. **t'vnty**] Albeit that we have this contraction veritably printed before us in the
Folio, and albeit that ABBOTT (§ 462) gives these words as an example of contraction in pronunciation, I nevertheless hope and trust that *tuntie* is due to the compositor or to his reader, and that such a contraction was never adopted by Shakespeare, or by any one else,—aloud.

From all that I can read or learn, the impersonators of Viola appear to have given
to this soliloquy an air of mirth at the discovery that Olivia had fallen in love with
the page,—an interpretation which I cannot but regard as far astray, not only from
Viola's character in general, but from her present circumstances. At the very first
mention of Olivia, in the second scene of the play, Viola's heart had gone out in
sympathy to one whose profound grief over the loss of a brother was so identical with
her own ; and now when she discovers that Olivia is destined to cherish a hopeless
passion, similar to her own, their twinship in despair again most deeply touches her
heart, and the whole soliloquy is pervaded with a gentle sadness. This interpretation is also Spedding's, who, in his criticism of Miss Kate Terry's acting of
Viola, remarks as follows : ' The messenger being gone, Viola proceeds to consider
what the meaning of it is. And it is in the soliloquy which follows (though delivered with admirable spirit and skill) that Miss Terry seemed to us to commit her
gravest fault. Following again the traditions of the stage,—where " I am the man "
is commonly made the " point " of the speech,—and forgetting how sad Viola's
heart was, and how forlorn her prospects,—she represented her as taking a light
pleasure, as of gratified vanity, in Olivia's mistake, and as rather enjoying the perplexity of the situation ; for she made her exit with a laugh, musical enough in
itself, but terribly out of tune with the sentiment of the play. According to Shakespeare, Viola's sense of the humour of the situation is immediately lost in sympathy
and sad reflection, accompanied with a kind of self-reproach [see lines 27, etc.].
And most certainly it is with a sigh and not with a laugh, that she gives up the
attempt to see how it can all end.'—*Fraser's Maga.* 1865, Aug., p. 265.—ED.

Scœna Tertia.

Enter Sir Toby, and Sir Andrew.   2

To.   Approach Sir *Andrew* : not to bee a bedde after
midnight, is to be vp betimes, and *Deliculo ſurgere*, thou
know'ſt.   5

And.   Nay by my troth I know not : but I know, to
be vp late, is to be vp late.

To.   A falſe concluſion : I hate it as an vnfill'd Canne.
To be vp after midnight, and to go to bed then is early :
ſo that to go to bed after midnight, is to goe to bed be-   10
times.   Does not our liues conſiſt of the foure Elements ?

And.   Faith ſo they ſay, but I thinke it rather conſiſts
of eating and drinking.

To.   Th'art a ſcholler ; let vs therefore eate and drinke.   15
Marian I ſay, a ſtoope of wine.

1. Act III. Scene i. Spedding.
Olivia's House. Rowe.

3. *a bedde*] *a bed* Ff.   *a-bed* Rowe.

4. Deliculo] Diliculo Ff.   *Diluculo*
Rowe et seq. (subs.)

5. *knowſt.*] *know'st,*— Theob. et
seq.

11. *Does not our liues*] Ff, Rowe i,
Ktly.   *Do not our lives* Mal. Steev. Var.

Knt, Coll. Hal. Dyce i.   *Does not our
life* Rowe ii et cet.

15. *Th'art*] Ff, Rowe, +.   *Thou'rt*
Cap. Wh. Dyce, Cam. Sta. Rlfe, Huds.
Thou art Var. '78 et cet.

16. Marian] *Maria* Pope, +, Cap.
Dyce ii, iii, Coll. iii, Huds.

ſay,] *say !* Theob.

ſtoope] *ſtoop* F₄.   *stoup* Cam.

4. **Deliculo surgere**] MALONE : *Diluculo surgere saluberrimum est.* This adage
our author found in Lilly's *Grammar*, p. 51. [' To get up at dawn is most healthy.']

11. **our liues**] R. G. WHITE (ed. i) : That ' liues ' is an error for *life* is shown
not only by the demonstrative ' it ' in Sir Andrew's reply, but by the consideration
that the four elements were supposed to constitute life, not individual lives.

11, 12. **the foure Elements**] MALONE : Thus, in *Hen. V :* III, vii, 22 : ' he is
pure air and fire ; and the dull elements of earth and water never appear in him.'
Again, in *Ant. & Cleop.* V, ii, 292 : ' I am fire and air ; my other elements I give
to baser life.' [' So mans bodie is made of foure Elements, that is to wit, of Earth,
Water, Fire & Aire.'—Batman *vppon Bartholome*, Lib. iv, cap. 1, p. 24.—ED.]

16. **Marian**] WALKER (*Crit.* i, 232) has an Article on the ' Double Forms of
some Proper Names ' ; in it he quotes this passage with the remark, ' Marian occurs
nowhere else in *Twelfth Night.*   Can it ever have been synonymous with *Maria*
and *Mary ?* '

16. **stoope**] W. A. WRIGHT : A *stoup* is a drinking cup, and the word is still
used in our college halls and butteries.   See *Hamlet*, V, i, 68 : ' Fetch me a stoup
of liquor.'   It was a vessel of varying capacity.

Enter Clowne.   17

And. Heere comes the foole yfaith.

Clo. How now my harts : Did you neuer fee the Picture of we three?   20

To. Welcome affe, now let's haue a catch.

And. By my troth the foole has an excellent breaft. I
had rather then forty fhillings I had fuch a legge, and fo   23

17. Enter Clôwne.] After line 18,   20. *we three*] As a quotation, Hal.
Dyce.   Cam. Coll. iii.

---

20. **we three**] HENLEY : An allusion to an old print, sometimes pasted on the
wall of a country ale-house, representing *two*, but under which the spectator reads,
—' *We three* are asses.'—MALONE believes the print or sign represented two wooden
heads, with the inscription under them : ' *We three* loggerheads be.' 'The Clown
means to insinuate that Sir Toby and Sir Andrew had as good a title to the name
of *fool* as himself.'—DOUCE : The original picture seems to have been two *fools*.
Thus in Shirley's *The Bird in a Cage*, Morello, who counterfeits a *fool*, says : 'we
be three of old, without exception to your lordship, only with this difference, I am
the wisest fool.' [IV, i, Douce errs in saying Morello 'counterfeits a *fool*,'—
Morello was 'disguised like a lady.'] Sometimes, as Henley has stated, it was two
asses. Thus, in Beaumont & Fletcher's *Queen of Corinth*, III, i : ' *Neanthes*. He
is another ass, he says ; I believe him. *Uncle.* We be three, heroical prince—
Neanthes. Nay then, we must have the picture of 'em, and the word [motto] *Nos
sumus.*' [p. 438, ed. Dyce.]—HALLIWELL : The sign is still preserved in England,
where a few taverns still exist, the sign consisting of two grotesque or idiotic heads,
and the inscription being : 'We three loggerheads be.' ' Plaine home-spun stuffe
shall now proceed from me, Much like unto the Picture of ,Wee Three.'—Taylor's
Farewell to the Tower-Bottles, 1622. The marginal note to this is,—' The picture
of two fooles, and the third looking on, I doe fitly compare with the two black
bottles and myselfe.' [The Clown referred to the picture of three fools, and Sir
Toby retaliated by referring to the picture of three asses.—ED.]
      21. catch] MURRAY (*N. E. D.*) quotes Grove : 'The catch was for each suc-
ceeding singer to take up or catch his part in time.' [See line 66, below.]
      22. breast] In Nichols's *Lit. Hist.* (ii, 631) there is a number of conjectural
emendations of Shakespeare's text, which were sent to Theobald's printer by an
anonymous correspondent, signing himself ' L. H.'; some of these conjectures are
more than usually ingenious ; among those, however, which are less happy, is that
of *breath* for 'breast,' in the present passage.—MURRAY (*N. E. D.*) gives, in addition to the present passage, the following examples of 'breast' in the sense of
breath, voice in singing : 1547 J. Heywood *Four P's :* 'I have some syght in
syngynge. But is your brest any thynge sweet?' ante 1553 Udall *Roister Doister*, p. 14, ed. Arber : ' So loe, that is a breast to blow out a candle.' 1621
Fletcher's *The Pilgrim*, III, vi. (N.) : ' Let's hear him sing, he has a fine breast.'
1711 Strype *Parker* 9 (N.) : ' Queristers, after their breasts are changed.'—
HALLIWELL gives a folio page of similar examples.—STAUNTON says, the phrase is
so common in our old writers, that it would be superfluous to cite examples of its
use in this sense.
      23. **such a legge**] Precisely what this means, it is difficult to say. A ' leg ' is a

fweet a breath to fing, as the foole has. Infooth thou waft
in very gracious fooling laft night, when thou fpok'ft of   25

24. *Infooth*] *In sooth* Theob. ii. et   25. *fpok'ft*] *spokest* Mal. Knt, Dyce,
seq.   Cam.

---

common term for a *bow*, or an *obeisance;* thus in *How a Man may choose a Gooa
Wife from a Bad*, 'do not come With foolish sonnets to present her with, With
legs, with curtsies, congees, and such like.'—p. 18, ed. Hazlitt-Dodsley. Feste
may have entered with a graceful bow to all the company,—he could do nothing
awkwardly,—and to this Sir Andrew may have referred. Or, Feste may have had
aristocratic small legs, 'a fashionable characteristic of a fine gentleman,' says
Gifford, in a note on Chloe's remark in Jonson's *Poetaster*, that 'a man borne
upon little legs is always a gentleman born.' II, i, p. 417. To this feature, 'there
are,' adds Gifford, 'innumerable allusions in our old writers,' and he proceeds to
give several. I prefer the picture of the conciliatory sweep of Feste's graceful arms
(which Sir Andrew finds so enviable) to that of any legs however fashionably thin
and small. Schmidt gives many examples of 'leg' meaning a *bow.*—ED.

   25. gracious fooling] STAUNTON : All clowns were capable, more or less,
of the biting sarcasms and coarse practical merriment which their vocation
licensed ; but few, probably, had sufficient information, not to say learning, to
garnish their discourse with the mock erudition and the snatches of axiomatical
philosophy exhibited by the jesters of *Twelfth Night* and *As You Like It;* and
from them any reasoning admitting a sensible interpretation must not, of course, be
looked for ; though something may be traced in them which bears a close affinity
to the fantastic extravagance and wild conceits of Rabelais. The source, however,
of their sham sententiousness is of an earlier date than the romance of the great
French satirist. The first known edition of that work is dated 1532; but in the
library of M. de Bure were found two more ancient though undated books, entitled
Les Chroniques de Gargantua, which have much of this peculiar humour. The history of Gargantua, as an enormous giant, was well known too in England during
the sixteenth century, though the romance relating to him contains nothing of the
amusing rhodomontade indulged in by Rabelais and the humourists in question. A
remote resemblance to it may be detected in some parts of the poems of William
Langland, *The Vision and Creed of Piers the Plowman;* and there is extant a genuine specimen of the 'gracious fooling' for which the Clowns of Shakespeare stand
unrivalled, in the form of a mock sermon, in a manuscript of the fifteenth century,
preserved in the Advocates' Library at Edinburgh, which, with other burlesques of
the same date, was printed in 1841 by Mr T. Wright, in the *Reliquiæ Antiquæ*, i,
82. One extract from this effusion, with the orthography partly modernised, will
convey no very imperfect notion of the Clown's 'gracious fooling' with Sir Toby
and his companion knight :—' Why hopest thou not, for sooth, that there stood once
a cook on St. Paul steeple top, and drew up the strapuls of his breech ? How
provest thou that ? By all the four doctors of Wynebere hylles; that is to say,
Vertas, Gadatryme, Trumpas, and Dadyl Trimsert ; the which four doctors say, that
there was once an old wife had a cook to her son ; and he looked out of an old
dove-cote, and warned and charg'd that no man should be so hardy neither to ride
nor to go on St. Paul steeple top but if he rode on a three-footed stool, or else that
he brought with him a warrant of his neck, and yet the lewd letherand lurdon went
forth, and met seven acres of land betwixt Dover and Quicksand, and he brought

Pigrogromitus, of the *Uapians* paſsing the Equinoƈtial of   26
Queubus: 'twas very good yfaith: I ſent thee ſixe pence
for thy Lemon, hadſt it?   28

26. Pigrogromitus] *Pigrogomitus* Var.   *sixpence* Var. '03.
'21 (misprint?)   28. *Lemon*] Ff, Rowe, Pope, Johns.
   26, 27. *Equinoctial of* Queubus] *equi-*   Coll. i.   *leman* Theob. Han. Warb.
noctial; of Queubus; Tiessen.   Cap. et seq.
   27, 34. *ſixe pence*] *six-pence* Theob.

---

an acre in his recke [hand-basket] from the Tower of London unto the Tower of
Babilon; and, as he went by the way, he had a foul fall, and he fell down at the
Castle of Dover into a gruel-pot, and brake both his shins.   Thereof came tripping
to the king of Hongre, that all people which might not lightly come to the Plain
of Salisbury, but the fox and the grey convent, should pray for all the old shoe-soules
that ben roasted in the king's dish on Saturday.'

   26, 27. Pigrogromitus . . . Queubus] LEIGH HUNT (*Wit and Humour*, p. 86):
Not that Shakespeare was habitually melancholy.   He had too healthy a brain for
that, and too great animal spirits; but in running the whole circle of thought, he
must of necessity have gone through its darkest as well as brightest phases; and
the sunshine was welcome in proportion.   Shakespeare is the inventor of the phrase,
'setting the table in a roar'; of the memory of Yorick; of the stomach of Falstaff,
stuffed as full of wit as of sack.   He 'wakes the night-owl with a catch'; draws
'three souls out of one weaver'; passes the 'equinoctial of Queubus' (some glorious torrid zone, lying beyond three o'clock in the morning).—BREWER (*Reader's
Handbook*): 'The Equinoctial of Queubus,' a line in the 'unknown sea,' passed
by the Vapians on the Greek kalends of the Olympiad era B. C. 777, according to
the authority of Quinapalus.   [However settled the conviction that these are mere
nonsense names invented by the Clown on the spur of a convivial moment, it is vain
to deny that a curiosity, almost invincible, possesses us all to know something more
of these Vapians, whose passing of the Equinoctial of Queubus was so infinitely
droll that the humour thereof permeated even the thin and watery wits of Sir
Andrew.   Almost instinctively, we all turn to Rabelais; I am sure that I have
merely followed many editorial predecessors in reading his volumes from the first
line to the last on a keen but futile scent for the possible originals of these fictions
of the Clown.   Wheresoever we may search, of one fact, however, we may rest
assured, and this is, that these names are not precisely those which the Clown used.
Sir Andrew would not be Sir Andrew, if he repeated them correctly.   They must
be ludicrous distortions; *possibly,* readily recognised as such by Shakespeare's
audience, to whom the true names may have been familiar enough in some jest of
the day.   Furthermore, the reference to 'passing the Equinoctial' should show
us, I think, that it is not exclusively to Rabelais that we should look for light, but
also to Astrology and to conjuring.   And this leads to the only feeble little ray
that here dawns on me.   At the risk of being deemed a copesmate of Sir Andrew,
I am willing to confess that in the distorted 'Pigrogromitus' I think we may possibly find Sir Andrew's version of the *Tetragrammaton.*—ED.]

   28. Lemon] THEOBALD: The Clown was neither pantler nor butler.   The poet's
word was certainly mistaken by the ignorance of the printer.   I have restored
leman, i. e. I sent thee sixpence to spend on thy mistress.—STEEVENS: We still
have '*Leman*-street' in Goodman's fields.—HALLIWELL: The spelling 'lemon' is

Clo.   I did impeticos thy gratillity : for *Maluolios* noſe   29
is no Whip-ſtocke   My Lady has a white hand, and the
Mermidons are no bottle-ale houſes.   31

29. *impeticos thy gratillity*] *impeticoat
thy gratility* Var. '73. *impeticoat thy
gratuity* Johns. conj. Var. '78, Ran.
Var. '85. *impeticos thy gratulity* Kinnear.

31. *Mermidons*] *Mirmidons* Rowe,
Pope. *Myrmidons* Theob. et seq.
       bottle-ale houſes] *bottle ale houſes*
F₃. *Bottle-Ale-houſes* F₄, Rowe i, Cap.

a very common form of the word. [Halliwell devotes two folio pages to quotations,
many of them quibbles on *leman* and *lemon*, which are neither witty nor pretty.
Cotgrave gives : *Amie :* f. A loue, a lemman, a she-friend, a sweet-heart.—ED.]
—W. A. WRIGHT : In Middle English the word appears in the forms *leofmon,
lefmon,* and *lefman,* of which *lemman* or *leman* is the abbreviation. It is used of
either sex. See *Merry Wives,* IV, ii, 172 : ‘As jealous as Ford, that searched a
hollow tree for his wife’s leman.’

28. **hadst it ?**] The common omission of the nominative in familiar questions,
like the present, or like ‘Art any more then a Steward,’ line 112, or like Hamlet’s
‘ Didst perceive ?’ III, ii, 275 ; or Lear’s ‘ Wilt break my heart ?’ III, iv, 4 ; or
Touchstone’s ‘ Hast any philosophy in thee, shepherd ?’ III, ii, 22 ; is not precisely similar to such phrases as ‘ Has been told so,’ I, v, 147, or ‘ then cam’st in
smiling,’ V. i, 368 (if this last be the true reading).

29. **impeticos thy gratillity**] HANMER : He means to say, *impocket thy gratuity.*
—JOHNSON : Hanmer is undoubtedly right ; but we must read,—‘ I did *impeticoat*
thy *gratuity.*’ [Thus, too, Collier’s MS.] The fools were kept in long coats, to
which the allusion is made.   There is ·yet much in this dialogue which I do not
understand.—RITSON : It is a very gross mistake to imagine that this character was
habited like an idiot.   Neither he nor Touchstone, though they wear a particoloured
dress, has either *coxcomb* or *bauble,* nor is he by any means to be confounded with the
Fool in *King Lear,* nor even, I think, with the one in *All’s Well.* [See note on I,
v, 2.]—B. NICHOLSON (*N. & Qu.* 3rd, V, 229) : I would read *impiticos* or
impiticose.   In Florio’s *Queen Anna’s New World of Words,* we find the following :
—‘ *Pitocare,* to beg up and down for broken pieces of meat or scraps.   Also to
dodge and patter.   *Pitocco,* an old crafty beggar, a micher, a patchtcoat beggar, a
dodger, a patterer, a wrangler. [Nicholson goes on to assert that begging is a distinctive characteristic of the Clown, and that seeing how much money Sir Toby
extracted from Sir Andrew, the Clown had endeavoured to do the like, but had
received for his pains only a paltry sixpence.]   With a covert sneer, therefore, he
coins a diminutive to express the smallness of the gift, and acknowledges the
gratillity, and in the same vein coins *impiticose,* (*s* being the usual causative, and
im the usual intensive augment) ; and says, I did make a great ‘ begging up and
down,’ and after much ado and importunity, I received ‘ a scrap’ of your bounty, a
crumb from Dives—I did *impiticose* thy gratillity. [This is ingenious, but not con-
vincing.—ED.]

29-31. **Maluolios nose . . . bottle-ale houses**] STEEVENS : The Clown says
he did *impeticoat* the gratuity, *i. e.* he gave it to his *petticoat companion ;* for (says
he) ‘ Malvolio’s nose is no whip-stock,’ *i. e.* Malvolio may smell out our connection,
but his suspicion will not prove the instrument of our punishment.   ‘ My mistress
has a white hand, and the myrmidons are no bottle-ale houses,’ *i. e.* my mistress

An. Excellent : Why this is the beſt fooling, when   32
all is done.   Now a ſong.

To. Come on, there is ſixe pence for you.   Let's haue
a ſong.   35

An. There's a teſtrill of me too : if one knight giue a

33. *ſong.*] song— Var. '73.   36. *giue a*] give a- F$_2$.   give a- - F$_3$.
give a— F$_4$.

---

is handsome, but the houses kept by officers of justice are no places to make merry
and entertain her at.   Such may be the meaning of this whimsical speech.—HUT-
SON (p. 484) : This reply of the Clown is apparently a whimsical series of incon-
secutive ideas ; but, examined closely, it will be found not to lack continuity :—' I
pocketed thy trifling gratuity [for he seems to me to mean a hidden sneer by his
diminutive], because Malvolio would soon nose me out if I abstracted wine from
the steward's stores ; my lady [not Olivia, but the girl Sir Andrew sent him the
sixpence for] has too white a hand to condescend to common tipple, and the tavern
called The Myrmidons, where I would regale her, is no place for cheap drink.'

30. **Whip-stocke**] STEEVENS says he ' believes ' that this is ' the handle of a
whip ' and quotes two or three examples from old dramas.   As ROLFE remarks, it
has survived in this sense, in this country, and is still in common use.—ED.

31. **bottle-ale**] WEISS (p. 200) : This phrase occurs once more in *2 Hen. IV:* II,
iv, 140, to express contempt,—' Away, you bottle-ale rascal !'   Was the bottling of
ale just coming in, to the immense disgust of the loyal Briton, who thought nobly
of the ancient brew and would not have it save, mightily, on tap ?

36. **testrill**] W. A. WRIGHT : A sixpence ; like ' tester,' which occurs in *2 Hen.
IV:* III, ii, 296, a corruption of ' teſton,' which was borrowed from the French.   It
may be that ' testril ' is a diminutive of ' tester.'   Cotgrave defines ' Teston : m. . . .
a Testoone ; a piece of siluer coyne worth xviij d. sterling.'   It was struck by Louis
XII. and so called because it had a head (*teste*) stamped upon it.   See Ruding's
Annals of the Coinage, ii, 86.   In England testoons were first struck by Henry
VIII. in 1543, going for twelve pence a piece, the pound of silver being ten ozs. fine
and two ozs. alloy.   In the reign of Edward VI. the coinage was so far debased that
a testoon was only current for sixpence, and in 1560 the better sort were marked
with a portcullis and passed for 4½ d., while the inferior were marked with a greyhound, and passed for 2¼ d.   See Stow's *Annals* (ed. 1580), p. 1115.

36. **of me**] Compare ' She tooke the Ring of me,' II, ii, 14, or see ABBOTT,
§ 165, p. 110.

36. **knight giue a**] COLLIER'S MS Corrector supplies a line, which the hyphen
(in the Second Folio) seems to indicate had been carelessly omitted, as follows :
' if one knight give a-*way sixpence, so will I give another : go to, a song.*'   In his
Second Edition, Collier remarks, ' The new words are in themselves of comparatively
little value, but they are a recovery of what, in all human probability, must have
come from Shakespeare's pen, and therefore ought to be studiously preserved.'—
SINGER (*Shakespeare Vindicated,* etc., p. 65) : The Corrector's addition is an
improbable one which I cannot hail as *welcome* [Collier, in his *Notes and Emendations,* had termed the line a ' welcome addition.'—ED.] ; and what would fully answer
all the purposes of filling up the hiatus, should it be thought necessary, would be to
complete the sentence thus : ' if one knight give a-*nother should.*'   This avoids

   Clo. Would you haue a loue-fong, or a fong of good   37
life ?

   To.   A loue fong, a loue fong.

   An.   I, I. I care not for good life.   40

                               Clowne fings.

    O Miſtris mine where are you roming ?   42

40. *I, I,*] *Ay, ay.* Rowe.   42. mine] mine, F_3F_4.

supplying too many words to the poet.—DYCE (ed. i) : Mr Collier ought to have
said, 'an addition welcome to those who *will* have the speech filled up.'—EDIN-
BURGH REVIEW (*Collier and Singer*, April, 1856, p. 372) : We need scarcely intimate the trouble which the mutilated text has given the critics [This is somewhat of
an exaggeration ; every critic and editor from Rowe to Collier accepted the line,
without comment, as an interrupted one.—ED.] ; or how far every one of them, we
believe, has been from guessing that a line had *dropt through*. And yet, how self-
evident the change appears when suggested ; and what incredible boldness of conception, as well as neatness of execution, such an alteration *on conjecture* would
evidence. Were we inclined to rest the Corrector's reputation for authority on any
single passage, there is none we would sooner fix on. Mr Singer's objection, as he
must needs object, simply is, that the Corrector being a guesser, ought not to have
guessed so boldly,—which is only one instance in a hundred of his practice of
taking the point in issue for granted,—and he proceeds to insinuate a most innocent
conjecture of his own ; which he is not ashamed again to propose in his new edition
of the plays, without even noticing the Corrector's line at all !—BOWEN (p. 495) :
He who was capable of inventing [the MS Corrector's addition], so perfectly in
keeping with Sir Andrew's character and manner, might have written without effort
the whole comic portion of *The Twelfth Night*. [Can it be possible that Professor
Bowen meant this seriously?—ED.] In mercy to Mr Singer, we forbear to quote his
comment, and the way in which *he* proposes to fill up the gap. [I much prefer to
believe that Feste interrupts Sir Andrew's twaddle.—ED.]

   37, 38. **good life**] STEEVENS : I do not suppose that by a song of 'good life,'
the Clown means a song of a *moral turn ;* though Sir Andrew answers to it in that
signification. 'Good life,' I believe, is 'harmless mirth and jollity.'—MALONE : In
The Merry Wives, III, iii, 127, these words are used for a virtuous *character :*
'Defend your reputation, or farewell to your good life for ever.' [The general
opinion seems to hold, with Sir Andrew, that this means a sententious song or a
song of virtuous conduct with a moral in it. But I incline to think that the Clown
knew his company too well to propose any such entertainment at this hour of the
night, and that Steevens more justly interprets it as of 'harmless mirth and jollity'—
possibly, omitting the 'harmless.'—ED.]

   42, etc. **O Mistris,** etc.] CHAPPELL (i, 209) notes that this is contained in both
editions of Morley's *Consort Lessons*, 1599 and 1611. 'It is also found in Queen
Elizabeth's Virginal Book [1603], arranged by Byrd. As it is to be found in print
in 1599, it proves either that *Twelfth Night* was written in or before that year, or
that, in accordance with the then prevailing custom, "O Mistress mine" was an old
song, introduced into the play '—DYCE (ed. ii) : The latter supposition is doubtless
the true one.—CAPELL (p. 145) : This song should be a new composition, and not
borrow'd as are the scraps that come after it ; but excepting that it breaths better

O ſtay and heare, your true loues coming,   43
That can ſing both high and low.
Trip no further prettie ſweeting :   45
Iourneys end in louers meeting,
Euery wiſe mans ſonne doth know.

An.   Excellent good, ifaith.

To.   Good, good.

Clo. *What is loue, tis not heereafter,*   50
Preſent mirth, hath preſent laughter :
What's to come, is ſtill vnſure.
In delay there lies no plentie,
Then come kiſſe me ſweet and twentie :   54

---

43. and heare,] *for here* Coll. MS.
       true loues] *true Love's* Rowe.
true-love's Cap. Dyce, Sta. Huds.
   46. louers] Ff, Rowe, Pope, Theob.
i, Han. Cam. Rlfe, Dtn, Wh. ii. *lovers'*
Theob. ii et cet.
   47. wiſe mans] *wise man's* Rowe.

   50. loue,] *love ?* Pope et seq.
   53. In delay] Indelay F₂. *In decay*
Warb.
   54. ſweet and twentie] *sweet, and
twenty* Theob. +, Cap. Var. '73. *sweet-
and-twenty* Var. ' 03, '13, '21, Hal.
Dyce, Sta. Ktly, Huds. Wh. ii.

---

sense than those old ballads, it has all the cast of them. [See *Preface* to the present
play.   For the music, see *Appendix*, p. 323.—ED.]

   54. sweet and twentie] CAPELL (p. 145) : What we are to conceive by it is
this,—then give me a kiss, sweet, give me twenty kisses.—JOHNSON : This line is
obscure ; we might read : 'Come, a kiss then, sweet and twenty.'   Yet I know not
whether the present reading be not right, for in some counties 'sweet and twenty,'
whatever be the meaning, is a phrase of endearment.—STEEVENS : So in *Wit of a
Woman*, 1604 : 'Sweet and twenty ; all sweet and sweet.'   Again in *The Life
and Death of The Merry Devil of Edmonton*, by T. B., 1631 : '—his little wanton
wagtailes, his sweet and twenties, his pretty pinckineyd pigsnies, etc., as he himself
was wont to call them.'—NARES (*s. v.* 'sweet and twenty') : Without a change of
the reading, it cannot be otherwise explained than as a term of endearment.   If we
read as suggested by Johnson, or, 'Then a kiss, my sweet, and twenty' all would
be easy.—MALONE : Compare *Merry Wives*, II, i, 203 : 'Good even and twenty,
master Page.'—STAUNTON : A proverbial endearment ; thus in *The Merry Devil
of Edmonton* [Staunton then gives the same quotation as Steevens, above].—
HALLIWELL : That is, twenty times sweet.   There is no necessity for alteration.   It
may be worth observation that *twain-ty* occurs in the Devonshire dialect as a term of
endearment to little children, possibly in the sense of, double sweet.—WALKER
(*Crit.* iii, 84) : Does the Clown mean, 'Then come kiss me, sweet, and twenty,'
subaudi, kisses ?   Compare *Merry Wives* [as above].   Beaumont and Fletcher,
Wit at Several Weapons, III, i, ' *Sir Gregory*. Good morrow, mistress !   *Niece.*
An ill day and a thousand, come upon thee !   *Sir Gregory.* 'Light, that's six hundred more than any almanack has.'[p. 45, ed. Dyce.]   Reversing the common form ;
a little below, ' Good morrow, niece.   *Niece.* Many fair ones to you, sir.'   Peele,
Old Wife's Tale, 'Neighbour, farewell.   *Lampriscus.* Farewell, and a thousand.'

[54. sweet and twentie]

p. 217, ed. Dyce. . . . The passage quoted by Steevens from *The Merry Devil of Edmonton*, . . . is perhaps decisive. [Dyce's note on Peele, *ad loc. cit.* adds two more examples : Middleton, *A Trick to catch the old one*, 1608, Sig. G. 4 : 'let me hug thee farewell, and a thousand.' And Rowley, *When you see me you know me* [p. 26, ed. Elze], 'God ye god night and Twenty, sir.']—DYCE (*Gloss.*) : That is, twenty times sweet ; A term of endearment ; Steevens cites, from *The Merry Devil of Edmonton*, etc.—DEIGHTON : A term of endearment, said to mean twenty times sweet. Steevens quotes *The Merry Devil of Edmonton*, etc.—W. A. WRIGHT : That is, sweet kisses and twenty of them, twenty being used as a round number. . . . To read 'sweet and twenty' as a vocative with Boswell [qu. Reed?] is certainly wrong. Compare *Merry Wives*, II, i, 203, and Rowley [as above], and *Two Noble Kinsmen*, V, ii : ' *Wooer.* I told her presently, and kiss'd her twice. *Doctor.* 'Twas well done ; twenty times had been far better.' And again in the same scene, '*Daughter.* And shall we kiss too ? *Wooer.* A hundred times. *Daugh.* And twenty ? *Wooer.* Ay, and twenty.' [These lines are omitted in the eds. of Knight, Simms, Skeat, and Rolfe. Steevens's quotation, which many of those, who have accepted it as decisive, assert is to be found in *The Merry Devil of Edmonton*, is not in that play. Editors, as careful and exact as Dyce even, have been led into this erroneous assertion. They overlooked the fact that Steevens quotes from *The Life and Death of The Merry Devil of Edmonton*,—another play. I regret that I cannot verify Steevens's quotation. I do not own the play, nor do I know where in this country it is to be found. It is not in the Catalogue of *The Barton Library* in Boston, nor in Allibone's Catalogue of the Shakespeare Department in *The Lenox Library* in New York; nor is it among the *Spurious Plays* (wherein *The Merry Devil of Edmonton* is sometimes reckoned) in the Shakespearian Catalogue of the British Museum. Certain it is, that it is not the same as *The Merry Devil of Edmonton*. In the *Stationers' Registers*, under the date ' 22 Octobris' (1607), we find entered, 'A plaie called the Merry Devill of Edmonton.' (—Arber's *Transcript*, vol. iii, p. 362.) Then on the '5ᵗᵒ Aprilis' (1608) there is entered ' a booke called. the lyfe and deathe of the Merry Devill of Edmonton with the pleasant prankes of Smugge the Smythe. Sir John. and myne Hoste of the George about their stealynge of Venson. by T. B.' (—*Ib.* p. 374, where Arber adds after the initials T. B. ' [*i. e.* Thomas Brewer],' on what authority he does not state.) These are the same characters as those in *The Merry Devil*, and what is strange is that their poaching expedition after venison is an essential feature in the plot of the earlier play, which looks as though the later work were an enlargement or a revision of the earlier ; and it may not have been a play at all. The Stationer's entry terms it a ' booke'; but no great stress can be laid on this ; the clerk was by no means scrupulously exact in his definitions. No author would willingly let die, so good a character as Sir John, the Priest, with his solvent for every circumstance whether good or ill, 'ahem,—grass and hay,—we're all mortal,—let's live till we die, and be merry, and there's an end'; he would be tempted to revive him in a second play, as Shakespeare continued Falstaff. (See *Appendix*, p. 418.)

Many of the foregoing quotations are not, I think, exactly parallel to the present phrase ; the 'twenty' or the 'hundred' or the 'thousand' is repeated directly after a noun, such as 'evening,' 'day,' 'night,' 'farewell,' 'times.' Thus here, had the expression been, 'give me kisses sweet and twenty' the meaning would have been clear and Theobald's punctuation inevitable. But in the text before us I can-

Youths a ſtuffe will not endure.   55

An.   A mellifluous voyce, as I am true knight.

To.   A contagious breath.

An.   Very ſweet, and contagious ifaith.

To.   To heare by the noſe, it is dulcet in contagion.

But ſhall we make the Welkin dance indeed? Shall wee   60
rowze the night-Owle in a Catch, that will drawe three
ſoules out of one Weauer? Shall we do that?   62

55. Youths] Youth's F_3F_4.   '78, Ran.
56. *true*] *a true* Rowe,+, Var. '73,   59, 60. Line runs on, Rowe et seq.

---

not but see a vocative term of endearment, and find therein the indescribable charm
which differentiates poetry from prose.—ED.]

57–59. **contagious . . . contagion.**] DEIGHTON : By a misuse of 'contagious'
Sir Toby ridicules Sir Andrew's 'mellifluous voice,' and Sir Andrew echoes the
expression as though it were an apt description. Then, punning on the word
'breath,' which he had just now used in the sense of *voice*, and perhaps imitating
the Clown's fooling, so highly commended by Sir Andrew, Sir Toby says, 'judging
of the merit of his breath (*i. e.* his singing) by the nose, as we judge of scent, it is
sweet in contagion, not foul as contagious breath (in its ordinary sense) usually is.'
[Sir Toby may use 'contagious' as a high-sounding word to match Sir Andrew's
'mellifluous,' but I doubt that he misuses it, or that he intends it otherwise than as a
compliment to Feste. He uses 'breath' for the song (or the tune), and pronounces
it *catching* or, in modern slang, 'catchy.' (Helena in *Mid. N. D.* (I, i, 198) says
'sickness is catching,' *i. e.* contagious, 'O were favour so . . . My tongue should
catch your tongue's sweet melodie.') When Sir Toby sees that Sir Andrew has
not perceived his meaning but takes 'contagious' in its ordinary sense, then he
replies, in effect, 'ay, if a tune be contagious, or catching, then it must be caught,
like contagion, through the nose, and this song is, in truth ['is' is the emphatic
word] sweet in its contagiousness.' 'It' refers to song, not to the whole preceding
clause.—ED.]

60. **Welkin dance**] JOHNSON : That is, drink till the sky seems to turn round.
—STEEVENS : So, in *Ant. & Cleop.* II, vii, 124 : 'Cup us, till the world go round.'

61, 62. **three soules . . . Weauer**] WARBURTON : The expression of the power
of music is familiar with our author. *Much Ado*, II, iii, 61 : 'Now is his soul ravished. Is it not strange that sheeps' guts should hale souls out of men's bodies?'
—Why he says, '*three* souls,' is because he is speaking of a catch of *three parts ;*
and the peripatetic philosophy, then in vogue, very liberally gave every man three
souls. The *vegetative* or *plastic*, the *animal*, and the *rational*. To this, too, Jonson alludes in his *Poetaster :* 'What! will I turn shark upon my friends? or my
friends' friends? I scorn it with my three souls' [V, i, p. 513, ed. Gifford]. By the
mention of these *three*, therefore, we may suppose it was Shakespeare's purpose to hint to us those surprising effects of music, which the ancients speak of,
when they tell us of Amphion, who moved *stones* and *trees ;* Orpheus and Arion,
who tamed *savage beasts ;* and Timotheus, who governed, as he pleased, the *passions
of his human auditors.* So noble an observation has our author conveyed in the
ribaldry of this buffoon character. [I have squandered the space for this note of
Warburton in order to give the comment on it by] COLERIDGE (p. 120) : O genuine,

And. And you loue me, let's doo't : I am dogge at a   63
Catch.

Clo. Byrlady fir, and fome dogs will catch well.   65

An. Moft certaine : Let our Catch be, *Thou Knaue.*

---

63. *And*] *An* Pope et seq.   Rowe, +, Var. '73, '78, Ran. Var. '85,
    am dogge] *am a dog* F₃F₄,   Wh. i, Coll. ii.

---

and inimitable (at least I hope so) Warburton ! This note of thine, if but one in
five millions, would be half a one too much.—FARMER : In Carew's translation of
Huarte's *Triall of Wits*, 1594, there a curious Chapter concerning the three souls.
[The heading of Chap. IIII. is ' It is prooued that the soule vegetatiue, sensitiue,
and reasonable, haue knowledge without that any thing be taught them, if so be
that they possesse that conuenient temperature, which is requisite for their operation.'
p. 32.—ED.]—MALONE : I believe Shakespeare here only means to describe Sir
Toby's catch as so harmonious that it would hale the soul out of a weaver (the
warmest lover of a song) *thrice over ;* or in other words, give him thrice more
delight than it would give any other man.—HALLIWELL quotes from *Batman vppon
Bartholome*, 1582 : ' If we take heed to the soule in comparison to his working, wee
finde three manner of vertues, *Vegetabilis*, that giueth lyfe, *Sensibilis*, that giueth
feeling, *Racionalis*, that giueth reason,' etc. [Liber Tertius, Chap. 7, p. 14.]—W.
A. WRIGHT : That Shakespeare had in mind the three souls given to man by the
peripatetic philosophers, as Warburton suggests, is open to serious doubt. To draw
three souls out of one starved weaver can be nothing more than a humorously exaggerated consequence of the power exerted by music, and to bring this about by a
drinking song was a greater triumph still, for weavers were given to psalms. Compare *1 Hen. IV :* II, iv, 147 : ' I would I were a weaver ; I could sing psalms or
anything.' See also Jonson, *The Silent Woman*, III, ii : ' He got this cold with
sitting up late, and singing catches with cloth-workers.'—DEIGHTON : An allusion
to the peripatetic philosophy would spoil the point of the joke, and if it had been
intended, we should have had ' *a* weaver' instead of ' *one* weaver.' A like fondness for singing is ascribed, *1 Hen. IV :* III, i, 264, to tailors whose occupation
like that of weavers is a sedentary one. [*Hotspur.* Come sing. *Lady Percy.* I will
not sing. *Hotspur.* 'Tis the next way to turn tailor.']

    63. **I am dogge**] HALLIWELL : There does not appear, from the annexed exam-
ples, to be a necessity for the particle [' a ' supplied in the Third and Fourth Folios] :
' I remember my great grandfather's grandmother's sister's coosen told mee, that
pigges and French-men speake one language, *awee*, *awee ;* I am dogg at this,'—
Englishmen for my Money. [Written in 1598, by William Haughton.] ' I myselfe
have knowne many old women old dogge at this kind of divination.'—Melton's
Astrologaster, 1620. ' *Jane.* No, no, we'll have a bout at blindmans-buff and a
dance first. *Jobson.* Ay, ay, come, I'm old dogg at that.'—*The Devil of a Wife*,
1686. [Thus also Lodge's *Wits Miserie :* ' He is dog at recognisances and statutes.'
p. 33, ed. Hunterian Club.—ED.]

    65. **Byrlady**] In *Tit. And.* IV, iv, 48, this is spelled ' ber Lady ' in the First
Folio ; and in *Hamlet*, II, ii, 406, it appears as ' Berlady ' in the Second, Third, and
Fourth Folios. WALKER (*Vers.* 191) says it was pronounced ' beer lady,' but
possibly, he has given too long a sound of *e*.—ED.

    66. **Thou knaue**] HAWKINS : A ' catch ' is a species of vocal harmony to be

Clo. Hold thy peace, thou Knaue knight. I fhall be con-   67
ftrain'd in't, to call thee knaue, Knight.

An. 'Tis not the firft time I haue conftrained one to
call me knaue. Begin foole : it begins, *Hold thy peace.*   70

Clo. I fhall neuer begin if I hold my peace.

67. Knaue *knight.*] *knave, knight.*   '78 et seq. (subs.)
Rowe, +, Var. '73.   *knave knight?*   71. *I fhall*] Shall *I* F₃F₄.
Cap. (Errata).   *knave, knight?* Var.

---

sung by three or more persons ; and is so contrived, that though each sings precisely
the same notes as his fellows, yet by beginning at stated periods of time from each
other, there results from the performance a harmony of as many parts as there are
singers. Compositions of this kind are, in strictness, called *Canons in the unison ;*
and as properly *Catches,* when the words in the different parts are made to *catch* or
answer each other. One of the most remarkable examples of a true *catch* is that of
Purcell, *Let's live good honest lives,* in which, immediately after one person has
uttered these words, 'What need we fear the Pope?' another in the course of his
singing fills up a rest which the first makes, with the words 'The devil.' The
'catch' to be sung by Sir Toby, Sir Andrew, and the Clown, from the hints given
of it, appears to be so contrived as that each of the singers calls the other *knave* in
turn ; and for this the Clown means to apologise to the knight, when he says he
shall be constrained to call him *knave.* I have here subjoined the very catch, with
the musical notes to which it was sung in the time of Shakespeare, and at the original performance of this comedy. The evidence of its authenticity is as follows :
There is extant a book entitled, 'Pammelia, Musickes Miscellanie, or mixed Varietie
of pleasant Roundelays and delightful Catches of 3, 4, 5, 6, 7, 8, 9, 10 Parts in one.'
Of this book there are at least two editions, the second printed in 1618. In 1609,
a second part of this work was published with the title of *Deuteromelia,* and in this
book is contained the catch here given. [Instead of the antiquated notes reproduced
by Sir John Hawkins, Knight's setting is here given, 'put into the treble clef, instead
of the contratenor,'—

COLLIER : A performance of the same character, where the singers call each other
'fool,' (the music by John Bennett,) is in Ravenscroft's *Briefe Discourses,* etc.,
London, 1614.

An. Good ifaith : Come begin.   *Catch fung*   72
               Enter Maria.

Mar. What a catterwalling doe you keepe heere ? If
my Ladie haue not call'd vp her Steward *Maluolio*, and   75
bid him turne you out of doores, neuer truft me.

To, My Lady's a *Catayan*, we are politicians, *Maluolios*
a Peg-a-ramfie, and *Three merry men be wee*. Am not I   78

---

72. Catch fung] Catch fing. F₃F₄.   74. *catterwalling*]   *catterwauling*
They sing a catch. Rowe.   Theob.
  73. Scene IV. Pope, +.   77. Maluolios] Maluolio's F₃F₄.

---

77. **Catayan**] More than a hundred and twenty years ago STEEVENS said that it
is in vain to seek for the precise meaning of this term of reproach, and the remark,
unfortunately, still holds good. DR MURRAY (*N. E. D.*) is reduced to quoting NARES,
whose definition is founded on what Steevens had said in a note on the word in *The
Merry Wives*, II, i, 148: 'I will not believe such a Cataian, though the priest o'
the town commended him for a true man,' where Steevens suggests that, the contrast with 'true man' shows that 'Cataian' means a thief. THEOBALD (Nichols,
Illust. ii, 276) suggested as a cause of its obnoxious signification the lamentable failure on the part of Frobisher to make good his golden promises of treasure from
his voyages to China, or Cataia, as it was then called ; hence a 'Cataian' became a
byeword for one who promised more than he could perform, and therefore a liar.
STEEVENS notes that 'Catain' is found in D'Avenant's *Love and Honour*, and
NARES adds, in the sense of *sharper*. The whole passage, not given by Steevens, is
as follows : 'Hang him, bold Cataian, he indites finely ; And will live as well by
sending short epistles, Or by sad whisper at your gamester's elbow . . . as any bash-
ful Gallant of 'em all.'—II, i. 'Cataian' may here bear the meaning Nares ascribes
to it, but it is somewhat doubtful ; the Cataian referred to by his detractor, was a
valiant high-souled Prince of Parma. It is, perhaps, not difficult to see how Sir
Toby happens to call his niece a 'Cataian'; he was in that stage of drunkenness when mere sounds connect words having no relationship to each other ; he
had heard Maria accuse the whole party of 'caterwauling,' and straightway the
sequence was clear to him that if he was a '*cater*wauler' his niece was a '*Cat*aian.'
—ED.

77. **politicians**] Shakespeare generally uses 'politician' in a derogatory sense ;
it is possible, therefore, that its present use by Sir Toby may be intended to show that
the knight was too drunk to know that his epithet was by no means complimentary.
See Sir Andrew's use of the word, III, ii, 32.—ED.

78. **Peg-a-ramsie**] CHAPPELL (p. 218) : There are two tunes under the name
of *Peg-a-Ramsey*, and both as old as Shakespeare's time. The first is called *Peg-a-
Ramsey* in William Ballets Lute Book, and is given by Sir John Hawkins as the
tune quoted in *Twelfth Night*. Ramsey, in Huntingdonshire, was formerly an
important town. [The music is given by HAWKINS, in the *Variorum;* by KNIGHT,
in his *Illustrations;* and by NAYLOR, p. 188 ; it is superfluous to repeat it here.
Sir Toby does not allude to 'Peg-a-Ramsey' as a song, and no words are given
with the music, indeed, they could not be with propriety, if, as it is alleged,
they are the same as a coarse Song in D'Urfey's *Songs Compleat*, etc., v, 139.
I cannot see that Chappell's note, quoted at greater length by Dyce, Halliwell, and

confanguinious? Am I not of her blood : tilly vally. Ladie, *There dwelt a man in Babylon, Lady, Lady.*   80

---

79. *Am I not*] *Am not I* F_3F_4, Rowe, Ff. *vally, Lady!* Rowe, +. *vally!*
Pope, Han.   *Lady!* Cap.
 79, 80. *vally. Ladie,*] *vally. Lady!* 80. *Lady.*] *Lady* [Singing] Rowe.

---

others, throws any illumination whatever on the text. Why Sir Toby called Malvolio a Peg-a-Ramsey, or wherein consisted the opprobrium, no one, I suppose,
but Sir Toby can tell.—ED.]

 78. Three ... wee] STEEVENS : The fragment of some old song; perhaps the
following, in *The Old Wiues Tale* by Peele, 1595, may be the original. Anticke,
one of the characters, says : '—let us rehearse the old proverb : Three merry men,
and three merry men, And three merry men be we ; I in the wood, and thou on the
ground, And Jack sleeps in the tree.'[I, i, p. 208, ed. Dyce.] I find it repeated in
Dekker and Webster's *Westward Ho*, 1607, [V, iii, p. 125, ed. Dyce] ; and by
Beaumont & Fletcher, in *The Knight of the Burning Pestle*, [1611, II, viii, ed.
Dyce,] ; again, in *The Bloody Brother*, of the same authors : ' Three merry boys,
and three merry boys, And three merry boys are we, As ever did sing in a hempen
string Under the gallow-tree' [III, ii, ed. Dyce] ; again, in *Ram Alley*, 1611
[II, i].—HAWKINS : This is a conclusion common to many old songs. One of the
most humourous that I recollect, is the following : ' The Wisemen were but seven,
nere more shall be for me ; The Muses were but nine, the Worthies three times three ;
And three merry boyes, and three merry boyes are we. The Virtues were but seven,
and three the greater be ; The Cæsars they were twelve, and fatal Sisters three ;
And three merry girles, and three merry girles are we.'[*Antidote against Melancholy*,
1661, p. 85, Collier's *Reprint.*]—CHAPPELL (p. 216) : The tune is contained in a
MS commonplace book, in the handwriting of John Playford, the publisher of *The
Dancing Master.* [The following arrangement, which is somewhat simpler than
Chappell's, is given from NAYLOR (p. 188).

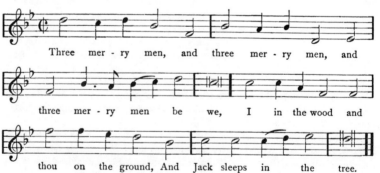

 79. tilly vally] JOHNSON : An interjection of contempt, which Sir Thomas
More's lady is recorded to have had very often in her mouth.—STEEVENS : It may
be a corruption of the Roman word (without a precise meaning, but indicative of
contempt) *Titivilitium.* See the *Casina* of Plautus. [' Non ego istuc verbum
emissim titivillitio '—II, v, 39. One can never be sure that Steevens is in earnest.
The *Century Dictionary* pronounces the origin obscure.—ED.]—NARES : The

Clo. Beſhrew me, the knights in admirable fooling.   81

An. I, he do's well enough if he be diſpos'd, and ſo
do I too : he does it with a better grace, but I do it more
naturall.   84

81. *knights*] *knight's* Ff.

Hostess corrupts it to 'tilly-fally' in *2 Hen. IV:* II, iv, 90 : 'Tilly-fally, Sir John,
ne'er tell me ; your ancient swaggerer comes not in my doors.' We read, in the
life of Sir Thomas More, that his wife, who was a loquacious troublesome woman,
was much addicted to the use of this expression ; of which two remarkable instances
are given. One when Sir Thomas had resigned the seals, she said : 'Tillie vallie,
tillie vallie, what will you do, Mr. More, will you sit and make goslings in the
ashes?' The other, when he was in prison in The Tower, where, when he asked,
'Is not this house as near heaven as mine own?' she answered, after her custom,
'Tillie vallie, tillie vallie.' Both these are in Dibdin's *Introd.* to *Utopia*, p. xv.
—HEATH says it corresponds to *fiddle faddle*.

79, 80. **vally. Ladie**] From ROWE to CAPELL the words 'tilly vally. Ladie'
are printed in Italics, as though part of the song ; (Caulfield actually gives the music
for them). STAUNTON prints 'Lady' in Italics, apparently for the same reason that
Rowe so printed the whole phrase. It was CAPELL who first perceived that they
were part of Sir Toby's speech, and punctuates, as I think, properly. 'Lady'
might be, possibly, in quotation marks ; it refers, I think, to Maria's use of it to
intimidate Sir Toby into better behaviour. This it is, which rouses his indignation,
that she should be 'Lady' to him who was consanguineous, one of her blood ; and
he pronounces the word contemptuously. Again, as before in 'caterwauling,'
'Lady' here suggests the Babylonian song.—ED.

80. **There dwelt**, etc.] T. WARTON : The ballad whence this line is taken was
licensed by T. Colwell, in 1562, under the title of 'the godly and constante Wyfe
Susanna' [Arber's *Transcript* (i, 210) reads 'wise Susanna.—ED.]—PERCY (i,
187) : This old ballad is preserved in the Pepys Collection, but is so poor a performance that it will be sufficient here to give the first stanza : 'There dwelt a man in
Babylon Of reputation great by fame, He took to wife a faire woman, Susanna she
was callde by name ; A woman fair and vertuous ; Lady, lady ; Why should we not
of her learn thus To live godly?'—TYRWHITT : A song with the same burthen is
alluded to in Jonson's *Magnetic Lady*, 'Compass. As true it is, lady, lady, in the
song.'[IV, iii.]—MALONE : The oldest song that I have seen with this burden is
in the old Morality, entitled *The Trial of Treasure*, 1567.—COLLIER : In the
volume of *Old Ballads*, printed for the Percy Society, 1840, is one by Elderton to
the same tune, printed as early as 1559. It is entitled, '*The Panges of Love, and
Lovers' Fittes.*'—HALLIWELL : Sir Hugh, in the original sketch of the *Merry Wives*,
ed. 1602, quotes the first line of this ballad. There are several known black-letter
editions of the ballad, varying slightly from each other. The burden 'Lady, lady' is
very common in old ballads.—NAYLOR (p. 189) gives a musical setting of this ballad
which is anonymous, and, he remarks, 'most probably later than Shakespeare's time.'

81. **Beshrew me**] W. A. WRIGHT : Literally, may mischief befall me. It was
used merely as a strong asseveration, as similar expressions are still by persons whose
vocabulary is limited.

84. **natural**] Inasmuch as a 'natural' means an idiot, ABBOTT (p. 497) thinks
that there is here 'a pun.'

To.   O the twelfe day of December.   85
Mar.   For the loue o'God peace.
                Enter Maluolio.
Mal.   My mafters are you mad? Or what are you?
Haue you no wit, manners, nor honeftie, but to gabble
like Tinkers at this time of night? Do yee make an Ale-   90
houfe of my Ladies houfe, that ye fqueak out your Cozi-
ers Catches without any mitigation or remorfe of voice?
Is there no refpeƈt of place, perfons, nor time in you?
    To.   We did keepe time fir in our Catches. Snecke vp.   94

85. O] *Oh!* Ktly.
    the twelfe] F₂.   twelf F₃F₄.
twelfth Rowe, Pope. *the twelfth* Theob.
et seq.
    December.] *December.* [Singing]
Rowe et seq. (subs.)   *December,—*
Theob. Warb. et seq.
    89. *gabble*] *gobble* Coll. MS, ap. Cam.
    91. *ye*] *you* Han. Huds.

91, 92. *Coziers*] *Cosiers'* Han. Dyce.
Cottiers Warb.   *Clothiers'* Quincey
MS.
    94. *Snecke vp.*] F₂. *Strike up.* Rowe
ii, Pope, Han. *Sneck up!* [Hiccoughs.]
Theob. Warb. Johns.   *Sneck-up!* Cap.
Sta. *sneak-cup?* Cap. conj. Ran. *Snick
up!* Coll.   *Snick-up!* Dyce, Huds.
Sneck up. or *sneck up!* F₃F₄ et cet.

85. **O the twelfe**] WALKER (*Crit.* i, 104): Read 'O' th' twelfth,' etc. It is
the first line of a narrative ballad.—COLLIER (ed. ii.): No other trace remains of
this ballad. Opposite these words, in the MS, we find written '17 Nov.,' which
may mean that in the time of the annotator a song on the 17th Nov. (the anniversary of Elizabeth's accession) was substituted for the then perhaps forgotten piece
'O! the twelfth day of December.'
    89. **but to gabble**] ABBOTT (§ 122): That is, to prevent you from gabbling.
[Where see other examples of this 'but' signifying prevention.]
    90. **Tinkers**] SCHMIDT (*Lex.*): Proverbial tipplers and would-be politicians.
[That tinkers were of the lowest order, classed with gipsies and vagabonds, and
their trade a noisy one, are sufficient reasons for Malvolio's application of the word.
It is their gabbling like tinkers, not their drinking like tinkers that he denounces.
—ED.]
    91, 92. **Coziers**] MURRAY (*N. E. D.*): A Cobbler; an adaptation of the Old
French *cousere* seamster, tailor, accusative *couseor, -eur*, formed on *coudre, cousant,*
to sew; cf. Spanish *coser*, to sew.
    94. **keepe time**] NAYLOR (p. 87): To 'keep time' is almost the only virtue a
catch singer *must* have.
    94. **Snecke vp**] STEEVENS: The modern editors seem to have regarded this
unintelligible phrase as the designation of a *hiccup* [See *Text. Notes*]. It is, however, used in Beaumont & Fletcher's *Knight of the Burning Pestle:* 'No, Michael,
let thy father go sneck up.' [II, ii, 'snick-up,' ed. Dyce.] Again, in the same play:
'give him his money, George, and let him go sneck up.' [III, ii, 'snick-up,' ed.
Dyce.] Again, in *Wily Beguiled:* 'An if my mistress would be ruled by him,
Sophos might go snick-up.' [p. 285, ed. Hazlitt-Dodsley.] Again, in *Two Angrie
Women of Abington,* 1599: 'his men be good fellows, so it is; if they be not, let
them go snick up.' [p. 272, ed. Hazlitt-Dodsley.] Again, in Heywood's *Fair Maid*

Mal. Sir Toby, I muſt be round with you. My Lady   95
bad me tell you, that though ſhe harbors you as her kinſman, she's nothing ally'd to your diſorders. If you can
ſeparate your ſelfe and your miſdemeanors, you are welcome to the houſe : if not, and it would pleaſe you to take
leaue of her, ſhe is very willing to bid you farewell.   100

---

96. *that though*] *that* F₃F₄, Rowe,   96, 97. *kinſman*] *Uncle* Rowe ii, +.
Pope, Han.   99. *and it*] *an it* Pope et seq.

---

of the West : ' 1 *Drawer.* Bess, you must fill some wine into the Portcullis ; the
gentlemen there will drink none but of your drawing. *Spencer.* She shall not rise,
sir. Go, let your master snick-up. 1 *Draw.* And that should be cousin-german to
the hick-up.' [p. 12, ed. Sh. Soc.] In *1 Hen. IV :* III, iii, 99, Falstaff says, ' How !
the prince is a Jack, a sneak-cup,' *i. e.* one who takes his glass in a sneaking manner.
I think we might safely read *sneak-cup*, at least, in Sir Toby's reply to Malvolio.
[Capell's conjecture ; see *Text. Notes.*]—MALONE : This cant phrase occurs in
many of the old comedies. From the connection in all of them, it seems to have
been synonymous to the modern expression, ' Go hang yourself.'—CROFT (p. 10)
would omit all punctuation in the line, and interpret it, ' We did keep time in our
catches close together.'—BOSWELL : Weber, in a note on the passage from *The
Knight of the Burning Pestle*, has clearly shown that ' snick up ' meant go hang
yourself, by the following very apposite quotation from Taylor, the Water Poet's
Praise of Hempseed : ' To end this matter, thus much I assure you, A Tiburne
Hempen-caudell well will cure you. It can cure Traytors, but I hold it fit T'apply 't
ere they the treason doe commit ; Wherefore in Sparta it ycleped was, Snickup,
which is in English Gallow-grasse.' [p. 552, ed. Spenser Soc.—*ap.* Wright.]—' R. R.'
(*N. & Qu.* Ist, i, 467, May, 1850) quotes from Halliwell's *Archaic Dict. :* ' *Sneck*,
that part of the iron fastening of a door which is raised by moving the latch. To *sneck*
a door is to latch it ' ; and, therefore, concludes that Sir Toby means, *close up, shut
up.*—HALLIWELL : A phrase of great indignation and contempt, equivalent to, be
hanged ! It was possibly a corruption of, *his neck up !* A rural charm for the
hiccough commences ' hick-up, snick-up.' The phrase *snick up* is still used in the
eastern Counties in England in the sense of *begone, away with you !* [Halliwell
here adds two or three examples to those given above, of the use of the phrase, but
none more conclusive than that from Taylor the Water Poet, nor better than the following from CHAPPELL (p. 289), quoted by Staunton ; it is somewhat late in date,
but ' 'twill serve ' ; it is from a song ' by Patrick Carey, a loyal cavalier, on bidding
farewell to his hospitable entertainers at Wickham, in 1651] : ' And now, helter-
skelter, to th' rest of the house ; The most are good fellows, and love to carouse ;
Who's not, may go sneck-up ; he's not worth a louse That stops a health i' th'
round.'

95. **round**] W. A. WRIGHT : That is, plainspoken, straightforward. So in *Hen.
V :* IV, i, 216 : ' Your reproof is something too round.' And *Hamlet*, III, ii, 191 :
' Let her be round with him.' Again in Bacon, *Essay i*, p. 3 : ' It will be acknowledged, even by those, that practise it not, that cleare and Round dealing is the Honour of Mans Nature.'

99, 100. **it would . . . she is**] See ABBOTT, § 371, for other examples where
' the consequent does not answer to the antecedent in mood or tense.'

To.   Farewell deere heart, ſince I muſt needs be gone.   101
Mar.   Nay good Sir *Toby.*
Clo.   His eyes do ſhew his dayes are almoſt done.
Mal.   Is't euen ſo?
To.   But I will neuer dye.   105
Clo.   Sir *Toby* there you lye.
Mal.   This is much credit to you.
To.   *Shall I bid him go.*
Clo.   *What and if you do?*
To.   *Shall I bid him go, and ſpare not?*   110
Clo.   *O no, no, no, no, you dare not.*

101. As a quotation, Theob. et seq. [Singing. Han.
102. Mar.] Mal. Pope, +, Var. Ran. Mal. Steev. Sta.
103. As a quotation, Theob. et seq.
105. As a quotation, [singing] Han. [Falls down drunkenly. Hal.

105. *neuer*] *nevery* F$_2$.
108. go.] goe? Ff. *go?* [Singing] Rowe.
109. and if] *an if* Theob. et seq.
111. no, no, no, no,] no, no, no, F$_4$, Rowe, +.

101–106. It will be noticed that the snatches of the Song are not printed in Italics, as they should be, until we come to line 108.   For this I know of no explanation other than that, owing to the interspersed prose, the compositor did not at first recognise, from his reader's voice, that they were lines of a song.   From Maria's remonstrance, 'Nay, good sir Toby,' it is to be inferred that the knight addressed his 'Farewell, dear heart' personally to her, accompanied with some tipsy demonstrations of affection.   In the Clown's, 'Sir Toby there you lye,' CAPELL (ii, 146) detects 'a waggish remark in tune upon a great stumble of Sir Toby's which brings him almost upon his nose.'   See Halliwell's stage-direction in *Text. Notes.*—ED.

101–111. **Farewell deere heart,** etc.] PERCY (i, 187): *Corydon's Farewell to Phyllis*—is an attempt to point a lover's irresolution, but so poorly executed, that it would not have been admitted into this collection, if it had not been quoted in *Twelfth Night.*   It is found in a little ancient miscellany intitled *The golden Garland of princely delights,* 12 mo. bl. let. [The 'Farewell' extends to five stanzas; it is only from the first two, here given, that Sir Toby and Feste sing snatches]:

> Farewell, dear love; since thou wilt needs begone,
> Mine eyes do shew, my life is almost done.
> > Nay I will never die, so long as I can spie
> > There be many mo, though that she doe goe.
> > > There be many mo, I fear not;
> > > Why then let her goe, I care not.

> Farewell, farewell; since this I find is true,
> I will not spend more time in wooing you;
> > But I will seek elsewhere, if I may find **love there;**
> > Shall I bid her goe? what and if I doe?
> > > Shall I bid her goe and spare not?
> > > O no, no, no, I dare not.

To. Out o'tune fir, ye lye : Art any more then a Stew-   112

112. *tune fir,*] *tune, sir,* Rowe, Pope, Han. Cap. Var. '78, '85. *time, sir?* Theob. Wh. i, Dyce, Rlfe, Huds. *time, sir,* Warb. Johns. Var. '73, Ran. Mal. Wh. ii. *time? sir,* Steev. Var. '03, '13, '21, Knt, Hal. *tune!—Sir,* Coll. i, ii, Ktly. *tune, sir?* Sta. *tune, sir:* Glo. Cam. *time!—sir,* Coll. iii.

112. *Art*] *Art thou* Rowe, +.

HALLIWELL-PHILLIPPS (*Outlines*, etc., p. 264): This ballad first appeared in the *Booke of Ayres* composed by Robert Jones, 1601. Jones does not profess to be the author of the words of this song, for he observes,—'If the ditties dislike thee, 'tis my fault that was so bold to publish the private contentments of divers gentlemen without their consents, though, I hope, not against their wils'; but there is every reason to believe that the ditty referred to in *Twelfth Night* was first published in this work, a collection of new, not of old, songs. [The music in the *Booke of Ayres*, I am not able to give ; I do not know that it has been ever reprinted. It is not in Chappell. The following is from John Caulfield's *Collection of the Vocal Music of Shakespear's Plays* . . . *Chiefly from the Collection of W. Kitchener, Esq* M. D. . . . *Arranged by Mr. Addison.* n. d.

Fare well dear heart, since I must needs be gone   His eyes do

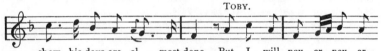

shew his days are al - most done.   But   I   will nev - er, nev - er

nev - er die.   Oh there Sir   To - by, there, oh   there you   lie.

This is reprinted by Naylor (p. 190), who adds that it 'can hardly be the original tune of *Corydon's Farewell to Phillis.*'—ED.]

106. **you lye**] R. G. WHITE (ed. i) : The original has 'there *thou* lie,'—a mistake caused by the common use of *y* for *th* in monosyllables. [This may possibly be an illustration of the fact that copies of the First Folio, like many other books printed at that time, vary in trifling particulars. The word is 'you' in my own copy of the Folio ; it is 'you' in Booth's inimitable *Reprint;* also in Staunton's *Photolithograph*, and the CAMBRIDGE EDITORS have no record of any other reading. If White had access to a First Folio, and spoke from personal knowledge, the variation would be undoubted, but, I think, he must have consulted Vernor & Hood's *Reprint*, of 1807, where the word in question is printed 'thou.' In a MS list (made by UPCOTT, and now before me) of errors in this *Reprint, thou* in the present line is marked as a misprint for 'you.'—ED.]

112. **Out o' tune**] THEOBALD silently changed 'tune' to *time*, presumably to bring it into accord with what Sir Toby had said in line 94 ; he has been followed

ard? Doſt thou thinke becauſe thou art vertuous, there   113
ſhall be no more Cakes and Ale?

Clo.   Yes by *S.*Anne, and Ginger ſhall bee hotte y'th   115
mouth too.

---

115. S. *Anne,*] S. Ann, F$_4$. *Saint Anne,* Ran. Cam. Rlfe. *Saint Anne;* Rowe
et cet.

---

by the majority of editors.—MALONE: In the MSS of our author's age, *tune* and
time are often quite indistinguishable; the second stroke of the *u* seeming to be the
first stroke of the *m*, or *vice versâ.* Hence, in *Macbeth,* IV, iii, 235, in the First
Folio we have 'This time goes manly' instead of 'This *tune,*' etc. [See also
'untunable' in *As You Like It,* V, iii, 36, 37, where the context makes it doubtful
that the true reading be not *untimeable.*—ED.]—COLLIER (who adhered to 'tune'
in two editions, but silently adopted *time* in his third): All that Sir Toby means is,
that the Clown had sung out of tune. 'Sir, ye lie!' is addressed to Malvolio for
the purpose of affronting him.—DYCE: The whole of this line is obviously spoken
to Malvolio. *The Clown* would hardly *sing out of tune;* he is *the* singer of the play.
—R. G. WHITE (*Shakespeare's Scholar,* p. 285): Theobald's correction, *time,* is
manifestly demanded. . . . The intoxicated knight reverts, in the true revolving style
of drunken thought, to the remark [of Malvolio in line 93] to which he had first
replied; and again, with comical earnestness, defends the party against the supposed or assumed attack upon their musical accuracy. The text [of the First Folio]
destroys one fine exhibition of the poet's knowledge of the workings of the mind
under all circumstances.—STAUNTON: Very needlessly changed to 'out of *time!*'
in most editions. Sir Toby desires an excuse for insulting the Steward, and finds it
in pretending he had decried their singing. [I think the Folio is exactly right, and
that the words are addressed to Feste. Throughout the singing both Sir Toby and
Feste have changed the sex in the original Song from 'her' to *him,* in order to make
it fit the hour and Malvolio. To Sir Toby's question, 'Shall I bid him go and spare
not?' Feste gives a more emphatic denial than the metre allows; the original has
only three 'noes,' Feste adds a fourth, this extra 'no' of course demanded an extra
note (possibly sung *fortissimo*), which Sir Toby detects and says 'Out o' tune, sir!'
then, resenting this most pronounced imputation on his courage, that he dare not bid
Malvolio go, he adds 'ye lie.' Whereupon, to prove his courage he turns on Malvolio with, 'Art any more,' etc.—ED.]

112. **Art**] See line 28, above.

114. **Cakes and Ale**] LETHERLAND: It was the custom on holidays and saints'
days to make cakes in honour of the day. The Puritans called this superstition.
See Quarlous's account of Rabbi Busy in Jonson's *Bartholomew Fair.* [The scene
referred to, is as follows: '*Winwife.* What call you the reverend elder you told me
of, your Banbury man? *Littlewit.* Rabbi Busy, sir; he is more than an elder, he
is a prophet, sir. *Quarlous.* O, I know him! a baker, is he not? *Lit.* He was
a baker, sir, but he does dream now, and see visions; he has given over his
trade. *Quar.* I remember that too; out of a scruple he took, that, in spiced conscience, those cakes he made, were served to bridales, may-poles, morrices, and
such profane feasts and meetings. His christian-name is Zeal-of-the-land. *Lit.*
Yes, sir; Zeal-of-the-land Busy.' I, i, p. 385, ed. Gifford.]

115. **S.Anne**] Why Feste and Christopher Sly should both swear by Saint

To.   Th'art i'th right.   Goe fir, rub your Chaine with   117
crums.   A ftope of Wine *Maria.*

Mal.   Miftris Mary, if you priz'd my Ladies fauour
at any thing more then contempt, you would not giue   120
meanes for this vnciuill rule ; fhe fhall know of it by this
hand.   *Exit*   122

---

117. *Th'art*] *Thou'rt* Rowe et seq.   121. *this*] *his* Ktly.
118. *ftope*] Ff.   *stoup* Cam. Rlfe,   *of it by*] *of it, by* Rowe et seq.
Dtn, Wh. ii.   *stoop* Rowe et cet.

Anne, I do not know.   In Chambers' *Book of Days* (ii, 389) a 'whimsical satire of
the sixteenth century' is given, wherein we find : 'St. Anne gives wealth and living
great to such as love her most, And is a perfect finder out of things that have been
lost.'   In *The Two Angry Women of Abington*, Mall Barnes says, 'Now, by Saint
Anne, I will not die a maid.' p. 292, ed. Hazlitt-Dodsley.—ED.

115. Ginger] Gerarde (*Herball*, p. 62) classes ginger, 'canded, greene, or con-
dited,' among the aphrodisiacs.—ED.

117, 118. Chaine with crums] JOHNSON : I suppose it should be read, 'rub
your *chin* with crums,' alluding to what had been said before that.   Malvolio was only
a steward, and consequently dined after his lady.   [This emendation continued to
appear in the Variorums of 1773 and 1778, but in the Variorum of 1785, the first
after Dr Johnson's death, it was mercifully suppressed.—ED.]—STEEVENS : Stewards
anciently wore a chain as a mark of superiority over other servants.   Thus, in
Love's Cure by Beaumont & Fletcher, ' *Piorato.* Is your chain right ?   *Bobadilla.*
It is both right and just, sir ; For though I am a steward, I did get it With no man's
wrong.'[III, ii.   Again in the same Play, II, ii, Clara says, 'Thou false and per-
emptory steward !   For I will hang thee up in thine own chain'; Dyce thereupon
remarks : 'That in great families, a gold chain was worn by stewards appears from
innumerable passages of our early writers.'   It is needless, therefore, to multiply
examples.   The following apt quotation will suffice, it not only confirms the wearing of chains, but also the mode of cleaning them recommended to Malvolio ;
Steevens quotes from Webster's, *Dutchess of Malfi*, '*Fourth Officer.* How scurvy
proud he would look, when the treasury was full ! well, let him go.   *First Officer.*
Yes, and the chippings of the buttery fly after him, to scour his gold chain.' III, ii,
p. 241, ed. Dyce.   There is a reference to a 'usurer's chain' in *Much Ado*, II, i,
183.—ED.]

121. vnciuill rule] JOHNSON : 'Rule' is method of life ; so *misrule* is tumult
and riot.—STEEVENS : 'Rule' on this occasion is something less than common
'method of life.'   It occasionally means the arrangement or conduct of a festival or
merry-making, as well as behavior in general.   So, in Drayton, *Polyolbion*, *The
twenty-seventh Song*, 'Cast in a gallant round about the hearth they go, And at each
pause they kiss, was never seen such rule In any place but here, at bonfire, or at
Yule.' [p. 375, ed. 1748.] Again, in Jonson's *Tale of a Tub*, ' *Puppy.* —— let
them go Into the barn with a warrant, seize the fiend, And set him in the stocks for
his ill rule.' [IV, v, p. 217, ed. Gifford.]—HALLIWELL quotes from Calthrop's
Reports, 1670 : 'No man shall after the hour of nine at night, keep any rule
whereby any such sudden outcry be made in the still of the night, as making any affray
or beating his wife, or servant, or singing, or revelling in his house,' etc.—DYCE

Mar. Go fhake your eares.   123
An. 'Twere as good a deede as to drink when a mans
a hungrie, to challenge him the field, and then to breake   125
promife with him, and make a foole of him.

123. Mar.] Mal. F₄.

125. *a hungrie*] *hungry* Var. '21.
a-hungry Coll. Dyce, Cam. Ktly.

125. *the field*] Ff, Rowe i, Knt, Coll.
ii, Hal. Dyce, Cam. Sta. Rlfe, Huds.
Dtn, Wh. ii. *to the field* Rowe ii et cet.

(*Gloss.*) : I believe ['rule'] is equivalent to 'revel, noisy sport': Coles has 'Rule
(stir), *Tumultus.'—Lat. and Eng. Dict.;* and compare *night-rule.*

121, 122. **by this hand**] See I, iii, 34.

123. **shake your eares**] HALLIWELL : In the Epitaph of the worthie knight Sir
Henrie Sidney, Lord President of Wales, 1591, we read,—'Hence, therefore, Death !
go shake thine eares.' Again, in Howell's *Familiar Letters,* 1650, 'This being one
day done, they shut their gates against him, and made him go shake his ears, and
to shift his lodging,' etc.—WALKER (*Crit.* iii, 85) : See Beaumont & Fletcher's
Coxcomb, II, iii,—' *Servant.* Cannot I deliver it [a letter] ? *Antonio.* No, by my
trot and fait, canst thou not, man. *Servant.* Well, sir, I'll call her to you ; pray,
shake your ears Without a little.'—RUSHTON (*N. & Qu.* IVth, x, 369) calls attention
to the use of the phrase in Lyly's *Euphues and his England:* 'Philautus was glad
he slept so long, and was awaked in so good time, beeing as weary of the seas, as
he that neuer vsed them. Euphues not sorrowfull of this good newes, began to
shake his eares, and was soone apparailed.'[p. 251, ed. Arber.]—W. A. WRIGHT :
Compare *Jul. Cæs.* IV, i, 26 : 'And having brought our treasure where we will,
Then take we down his load, and turn him off, Like to an empty ass, to shake his
ears, And graze in common.' [Thus, Stubbes (*Christall Glasse,* etc., 1591, p. 205,
ed. New Sh. Soc.) reports the words of his wife which she addressed to Satan,
shortly before her death, in a conflict for her soul : 'thou maist get thee packing,
thou damned dog, & go shake thine eares, for in me hast thou nought.' The present
passage is frequently interpreted as equivalent to calling Malvolio an ass. But in
view of the seriousness with which the phrase is used in the foregoing quotations,
the reference to an ass is by no means certain. It is quite probable that the phrase
might have been originally derived from that animal, but long usage had obscured
its origin and rendered it respectable. At the same time, it is not prudent to put
limits to Maria's contempt.—ED.]

125. **him the field**] COLLIER (ed. ii) : The authentic expression in cases of the
kind.—SCHMIDT (*Lex.* s. v. *challenge*) : Perhaps ' *to* field.' Compare *Rom. & Jul.*
III, i, 61, 'go before to field.' [Not an editor gives a parallel instance of this use
of 'field' without a preposition. DYCE notes that the phrase has here been changed
to 'to the field' and adds 'improperly, I believe.' MURRAY (*N. E. D.* s. v. *challenge,* †c) gives but three examples, one is doubtful, another is the present line, and
the third is of the year 1693 ; the first and the last are as follows : '[1556 *Chron. G.
Friars* (1852) 7 'Roberte of Vere chalynched them in the field and was ouercome.]'
'1693 W. Robertson, *Phraseol. Gen.* 477 'The disagreement grew so high, that they
challenged the field one of another.' [*Ibid.* 601, To challenge one into the field :
in arenam provocare.] The foregoing brackets are Dr Murray's, and indicate, I presume, that the example thus enclosed is, possibly, of doubtful application. If this
be so, there then remains but one parallel example, and this example is nearly a

To. Doo't knight, Ile write thee a Challenge : or Ile   127
deliuer thy indignation to him by word of mouth.

Mar. Sweet Sir Toby be patient for to night : Since
the youth of the Counts was to day with my Lady, ſhe is   130
much out of quiet. For Monſieur Maluolio, let me alone
with him : If I do not gull him into an ayword, and make
him a common recreation, do not thinke I haue witte e-
nough to lye ſtraight in my bed : I know I can do it.

To. Poſſeſſe vs, poſſeſſe vs, tell vs ſomething of him.   135
Mar. Marrie ſir, ſometimes he is a kinde of Puritane.

---

129. *Sweet Sir Toby*] *Sweet, Sir Toby,*   Rowe et seq. (subs.) *a bye-word* L. H.
Rowe i.   ap. Nichols, *Illust.* ii, 633.
  130. *the youth*] *that youth* Coll. MS.   135. To.] Sir And. Walker, Dyce ii,
    Counts] *Duke's* Rowe, +.   Huds.
  131. *Monſieur*] *Mounſieur* Ff.   136. *Puritane*] F₂. *a Puritane* F₃F₄,
  132. *an ayword*] Ff. *a nayword*   Rowe, +.

---

century later. Under the circumstances, (albeit that 'challenge him the field'
sounds idiomatic,) I think an editor would be excused, should he yield to temptation and add a *to* before 'the field.' On the other hand, INNES remarks,
'Considering that Sir Andrew is so drunk as to talk of "a-hungry" when he means
"thirsty," it is very unnecessary to follow the commentators who desire to correct
his grammar and read "to the field."' I have always supposed that Sir Andrew
thus confused the two appetites because he was Sir Andrew.—ED.

132. **an ayword**] STEEVENS : This has since been called a *byeword*, a kind of
proverbial reproach.—COLLIER : 'Ayword' may be the true reading, the meaning
being 'an *everlasting* word'; 'ay' is *ever*.—DYCE (*Remarks*, 75): The explanation
of Steevens is right. Forby, in his *Vocabulary of East Anglia*, gives ' Nay-word . . .
A bye-word ; a laughing-stock.'—HALLIWELL : *Nayword* is probably a crasis for *an
aye-word*, a word that may be always used, a proverbial reproach. I doubt whether
Forby had heard the term used, there being a possibility that this word, with some
others from Shakespeare, were merely inserted in his MS, with the view of ascertain-
ing whether he could recover a provincial example of it. The dialectical glossaries
are unfortunately not always to be implicitly relied upon.—W. A. WRIGHT : In the
Merry Wives, II, ii, 131, a 'nay-word' is used for a password : 'In any case have
a nay-word, that you may know one another's mind, and the boy never need to
understand anything.' And again, V, ii, 5 : 'We have a nay-word to know one
another.' Possibly a 'nay-word' may have been a word which had no meaning to
anyone but the persons using it. . . . It is included by Canon Forman in his *Upton-
on-Severn Words and Phrases* (Eng. Dialect Soc.). [To the ear of the compositor
'an ayword' and *a nayword* were indistinguishable.—ED.]

135. **To.**] WALKER (*Crit.* ii, 188) : Surely Sir Toby needed no information
respecting Malvolio. Rather *Sir Andrew*. Note, too, Maria's reply,—' Marry, *sir*,
sometimes,' etc.

135. **Possesse vs**] JOHNSON : That is, inform us, tell us, make us masters of
the matter.

136. **Puritane**] HALES (*Contemporary Rev.* Jan., 1895, p. 65): The play in

An. O, if I thought that, Ide beate him like a dogge.   137

To. What for being a Puritan, thy exquifite reafon,
deere knight.

An. I haue no exquifite reafon for't, but I haue reafon   140
good enough.

Mar. The diu'll a Puritane that hee is, or any thing
conftantly but a time-pleafer, an affection'd Affe, that
cons State without booke, and vtters it by great fwarths.   144

---

138. *Puritan,*] *Puritan?* F₄, Rowe
et seq.
139. *knight.*] *knight?* Cap. et seq.
(except Coll. who has *knight!*)

143. *affection'd*] *affected* Han. Ran.
Var. '85.
144. *fwarths*] *swaths* Coll. Wh. i,
Dyce ii, Huds.

---

which Shakespeare most nearly approaches,—but only approaches,—the subject of
Puritanism is unquestionably *Twelfth Night*. There is a touch of the Puritan in
Malvolio, but the merest touch. Fabian's remark, 'You know he brought me out
o' favour with my lady about a bear-baiting here' (II, v, 8), cannot but remind one
of the Puritan disapproval of popular sports; and the stiff and ungenial respecta-
bility, and the acrid manner of the Steward were certainly features vulgarly associated with those unpopular pharisees, who often enough seemed, rightly or wrongly,
to 'the man in the street' to cultivate the art of being disagreeable.—ROLFE (*Poet-
lore*, July, 1898, p. 420): Malvolio at no time talks like a Puritan, as he would
naturally have done if he had been one, when he came in to reprove the midnight
roysterers. It is the noise and disturbance they are making at that unseasonable hour
for which he reproaches them, not the sin of their drunken revelry, against which a
Puritan would have inveighed. Falstaff was a better Puritan when he played the
part of one at The Boar's Head (*1 Hen. IV:* II, iv, 421) and lectured Prince Hal
on his profligate habits.

137. *if . . . dogge*] W. A. WRIGHT: Sir Andrew anticipates The Shortest
Way with the Dissenters.—HALES (*Contemporary Review*, Jan., 1895, p. 65):
Surely the notion that Puritanism *quâ* Puritanism deserved only kicks and lashes is
sufficiently exposed and censured by putting it into the mouth of such an arrant fool
as Sir Andrew Aguecheek, who also informs us he had 'as lief be a Brownist as a
politician.' Even the reckless Sir Toby has misgivings as to its justifiableness.
However this may be, the quick-witted Maria at once revokes a term which she is
not slow to see she has hastily misapplied.

142. *The diu'll*] When Maria is trying to smooth a rough asseveration into a
'sarcenet surety,' is it fair, is it courteous to disregard her delicacy, as do all editors,
and make her blurt out *devil*, when she uses only an equivalent to the modern and
innocent 'de'il'?—ED.

143. *affection'd*] W. A. WRIGHT: That is, affected, full of affectation. In
Hamlet, II, ii, 464, 'nor no matter in the phrase that might indite the owner of
affectation,' is the reading of the folios, while the quartos have 'affection.' Compare
Love's Lab. L. V, i, 4: 'Witty without affection'; which is the reading of the first
folio, changed in the later editions to 'affectation.'

144. *cons . . . booke*] W. A. WRIGHT: That is, learns by heart, as an actor his
part. A word of the theatre, as 'without book' that follows. See *Rom. & Jul.*

The beſt perſwaded of himſelfe : ſo cram'd (as he thinkes)   145
with excellencies, that it is his grounds of faith, that all
that looke on him, loue him : and on that vice in him, will
my reuenge finde notable cauſe to worke.

To.   What wilt thou do?

Mar.   I will drop in his way ſome obſcure Epiſtles of   150
loue, wherein by the colour of his beard, the ſhape of his
legge, the manner of his gate, the expreſſure of his eye,
forehead, and complection, he ſhall finde himſelfe moſt
feelingly perſonated.   I can write very like my Ladie
your Neece, on a forgotten matter wee can hardly make   155
diſtinction of our hands.

To.   Excellent, I ſmell a deuice.

An.   I hau't in my noſe too.

To.   He ſhall thinke by the Letters that thou wilt drop
that they come from my Neece, and that ſhee's in loue   160
with him.

Mar.   My purpoſe is indeed a horſe of that colour.

An.   And your horſe now would make him an Aſſe.   163

---

145. *himſelfe :*] *himſelf,* Cap. et seq.
146. *excellencies*]   *excellences* Knt, Coll. Wh. i.
    grounds] Cap. Dyce, Cam. Dtn. *ground* Ff et cet.
152. *gate*] *gait* Johns.
153. *complection*] F₂. *complexion* F₃F₄, Rowe et seq.

159. *Letters*] *letter* Coll. MS.
160. *they come*] *it comes* Coll. MS.
    ſhee's] F₂F₃, Wh. Dyce, Cam. Sta. Rlfe, Huds.   *ſhe is* F₄ et cet.
163. *An.*] Sir Toby. Tyrwhitt, Harness, Dyce ii, iii, Huds.
    horſe now] *horse, now,* Coll.

I, iv, 6: 'Nor no without-book prologue, faintly spoke After the prompter.'   In Ben Jonson's *Every Man out of his Humour* it is said in the description of Shift, 'He waylays the reports of services, and cons them without book.'   For 'cons state without book' it has been proposed to read 'cons stale wit out of books.'   But Malvolio's affectation was not wit, but deportment.

144. **swarths**] STEEVENS : A 'swarth' is as much grass or corn as a mower cuts down at one stroke of his scythe.—COLLIER : This word occurs again in the same sense in *Tro. & Cress.* V, v, 25 : 'And there the strawy Greeks, ripe for his edge, Fall down before him, like the mower's swath'; but there, in the old copies, it is spelled 'swath.'—W. A. WRIGHT : More properly *swath.*   The spelling 'swarth' indicates the pronunciation.

145. **best perswaded of himselfe**] That is, having the best opinion of himself.

146. **grounds**] Needlessly changed to *ground* in the Ff.

152. **expressure**] Compare 'impressure.' II, v, 91.

162. **horse of that colour**] Compare, 'boyes and women are for the most part, cattle of this colour.'—*As You Like It,* III, ii, 393.

163. **An.**] CAPELL (p. 146) says that words are here put into Sir Andrew's

Mar. Affe, I doubt not.

An. O twill be admirable.   165

Mar. Sport royall I warrant you : I know my Phy-
ficke will worke with him, I will plant you two, and let
the Foole make a third, where he fhall finde the Letter :
obferue his conftruction of it : For this night to bed, and
dreame on the euent : Farewell.   *Exit*   170

To. Good night *Penthifilea.*

An. Befo re me fhe's a good wench.

To. She's a beagle true bred,and one that adores me :
what o'that?   174

164. *Affe, I*] *Ass—I* Cap. *Ass I*
Ran. Coll.
167. *with him,*] *him him.* Rowe ii.
with him. Rowe i et cet.

169. *his*] *this* Ff.
170. Exit] After line 171, Dyce.
171. Penthifilea] *Penthesilea* Johns.

mouth 'that are something too good for him, but the temptation was strong.'
TYRWHITT goes even further. 'This conceit,' he observes, 'though bad enough,
shews too quick an apprehension for Sir Andrew. It should be given, I believe,
to Sir Toby ; as well as the next short speech : " O, 'twill be admirable." Sir
Andrew does not usually give his own judgement on any thing, till he has heard
that of some other person.' WALKER (*Crit.* ii, 188) proposed the same arrangement,
not knowing that he had been anticipated by Tyrwhitt. 'This seems,' he says,
'too witty for Sir Andrew ; I think it belongs to Sir Toby.' DYCE (ed. ii) adopted
the change.—W. A. WRIGHT : The mistake in assigning it might easily have arisen
from the first word 'And' being supposed to indicate the speaker.—HALLIWELL :
The objection to this [change], otherwise a probable one, consists in the reply of
Maria, who evidently intends to be witty at the expense of Sir Andrew, although
she very possibly alludes at the same time to Malvolio. A practical actress would
have no difficulty in aiming at both.

164. **Asse, I doubt not**] It is strange that WALKER, with his noteworthy acuteness, should have had a doubt concerning this pun, as palpable as it is poor. 'Is
there a pun here, he asks (*Crit.* iii, 85), "*As* I doubt not" ?' W. A. WRIGHT calls
attention to a similar play on 'As' and 'Ass' in *Hamlet*, V, ii, 43 : 'And many
such-like "As'es" of great charge.'

168. **Foole make a third**] For some reason or other, this intention of Maria,
was not carried out ; Fabian takes the place of Feste. Of this change I do not see
the cause. Fleay would doubtless find in it a proof of patchwork due to the different
times at which Shakespeare wrote the play. I think it likely that it arose from some
exigencies in the staging.—ED.

171. **Penthisilea**] As we all know, the Queen of the Amazons, slain by Achilles.
If Maria was of a diminutive size, and there seem to be several indications of it,
the incongruity between her figure and the heroic mould of Penthesilea, must have
been comic enough, to Shakespeare's audience.

172. **Before me**] A conversion of 'Before God !' into a 'pretty oath that is not
dangerous.'

173. **beagle true bred**] Again an allusion to Maria's small size. MADDEN

An.   I was ador'd once too.   175

To.   Let's to bed knight : Thou hadſt neede ſend for
more money.

An.   If I cannot recouer your Neece, I am a foule way
out.

To.   Send for money knight, if thou haſt her not i'th   180
end, call me Cut.

181. *Cut*] *cut* Theob. Warb. Cap. Coll. Dyce, Cam.

(p. 179) : I cannot, therefore, say for certain that the Justice kept, in addition to
his kennel of running hounds suitable for every chase, a pack of beagles devoted
exclusively to the hunting of the hare.   I know, however, that they were in high
favour with Gloucestershire sportsmen.   The sordid pot-hunter, when he uncouples
at his game, may care only to 'score their backs, And snatch 'em up, as we take
hares, behind.' (*Ant. & Cleop.* IV, vii, 12.)   But the true sportsman took delight in
the music of a pack composed of 'the little beagle which may be carried in a
man's glove, and bred in many countries for delight onely, being of curious scents,
and passing cunning in their hunting ; for the most part tyring (but seldom killing)
the prey except at some strange advantage.' (Gervase Markham, *Country Contentments.*)   Thus when Sir Toby said of Maria, 'she is a beagle true-bred,' he meant
to compliment her keenness and sagacity.

176. **send**] See I, v, 299 ; or ABBOTT, § 349, p. 249.   Iago's similar advice to
Roderigo will occur to every one.

178. **recouer**] SCHMIDT (*Lex.*) furnishes many examples of this verb with the
meaning *to get, to gain.*

178, 179. **a foule way out**] SCHMIDT (*Lex.*) defines 'out' in the present passage
as 'on the wrong scent, aiming or going a wrong way.'—W. A. WRIGHT defines it,
'out of my reckoning.'   But I agree with DEIGHTON that it means 'out of pocket,'
—a use of 'out' still current in this country.—ED.

181. **Cut**] STEEVENS : So, in *A Woman's a Weathercock*, 1612, 'and for pleasure, if I help you not to that as cheap as any man in England, call me cut.'
[IV, ii, p. 69, ed. Hazlitt-Dodsley.]   Again, in *The Two Angry Women of Abington*, 1599, 'I'll meet you there ; and I do not call me Cut.' [p. 336. *Ibid.*]   This term
of contempt, perhaps, signifies only—call me gelding.—MALONE : 'Call me Cut' is
'call me horse.'   So, Falstaff in *1 Hen. IV :* II, iv, 215, 'I tell thee what, Hal,
if I tell thee a lie, spit in my face, call me horse.'   That this was the meaning of
this expression is ascertained by a passage in *The Two Noble Kinsmen,* 'He's buy
me a white cut, forth for to ride.' [III, iv, 22.]—RITSON (*Quip Modest,* 8) : This
expression, having induced a suspicion that curtailing or cutting the tail of either
horse or dog, implied some degree of infamy or shame, I was glad to meet with a
passage in Bracton, which may serve to give us a pretty clear idea of the matter.
'Of the punishment of a ravisher,' says this ancient writer, 'according to the laws
of the Romans, Franks, and English, if he were a knight, his horse, to his disgrace,
shall have the skin cut off the upper lip, and the tail ought to be cut off close to the
buttock.   So a dog, if he have one with him, greyhound, or other, shall be disgraced in the same manner.'—L. 3, t. 2, c. 28. . . . [This law] leads one to suppose that, in feudal times the distinction between the horse or dog of a knight

An.   If I do not, neuer truſt me, take it how you will.   182
To.   Come, come, Ile go burne ſome Sacke, tis too late
to go to bed now : Come knight, come knight.   *Exeunt*   184

---

and that of a villain, appeared by the tail ; and hence the word 'cut' might be as
reproachful as the word *villain;* the former implying the *horse* or *dog* of a *clown*,
the latter the *clown himself.*—NARES : A familiar appellation for a common or
labouring horse. [This definition Dr MURRAY (*N. E. D.*) adopts, and adds :] It is
doubtful whether the sense is 'cut-tail horse' or 'gelding.' As 'a term of abuse,
applied to a man or woman' the same authority gives the following examples, in
addition to the present passage : *c* 1490 H. MEDWALL, *Nature,* 'If thou se hym
not take hys owne way Call me cut when thou metest me another day.' 1575
J. STILL, *Gammer Gurton's Needle,* V, ii, 'That lying cut is lost, that she is not
swinged and beaten.' 1605 *London Prodigal,* Cij b, 'And I doe not meete him,
chill giue you leaue to call me cut.' 1820 SCOTT, *Abbot,* xix, ' "You shall call me
cutt if I do go down," said Adam.'—W. A. WRIGHT : A curtal horse was a horse
whose tail had been docked, as a curtal or curtail dog was one who had been treated
in a similar manner ; and as from the latter the abbreviation 'cur' came to be used
as a term of contempt, so 'cut' from 'curtal' was employed in the same way.
[Fanciful derivations have not been lacking. CROFT (p. 10) affirmed that ' "cutt"
was a moss-trooper ; the Cutts were the worst of the Scotch borderers.' J. WETH-
ERELL (*N. & Qu.* IIIrd, vii, 317, 1865) suggests that the phrase may have come
from 'a boyish game still in vogue in Cumberland' wherein lots were drawn by
straws 'cut' in different lengths. HAZLITT in a note in his edition of Dodsley's
Gammer Gurton (p. 216) remarks : 'It appears probable to me that the opprobrious
epithet 'Cut' arose from the practice of cutting the hair of convicted thieves.']

   183. **Sacke**] DYCE (*Gloss.*): 'It seems to be admitted, on all hands, that the term
Sack was originally applied to certain growths of Spain. Dr Percy has the credit of
restoring the original interpretation of the term. In a manuscript account of the dis-
bursements by the chamberlain of the city of Worcester, for the year 1592, he found
the ancient mode of spelling to be *seck*, and thence concluded that "Sack" was
merely a corruption of *sec*, signifying a dry wine. Minshew renders the term *vin sec;*
and Cotgrave gives the same translation. The most satisfactory evidence, however,
in support of this opinion is furnished by the French version of a proclamation for
regulating the prices of wines, in 1633, where the expression *vins secs* corresponds
with the word "sacks" in the original copy (Rymer's *Fœdera*, Tome viii, Part iv,
p. 46). It may also be remarked that the term *sec* is still used as a substantive by the
French, to denote a Spanish wine ("on dit aussi quelquefois absolument du *sec*, pour
dire, du vin d'Espagne."—*Dict. de Trevoux*); and that the dry wine of Xerez is distinguished at the place of its growth by the name of *vino seco*. These several authorities, then, appear to warrant the inference that "Sack" was a *dry* Spanish wine.
But, on the other hand, numerous instances occur in which it is mentioned in conjunction with wines of the sweet class.' [To reconcile this discrepancy a learned
examination here follows of the character ascribed to Sack by the few writers who
have described it, with a side reference to the general custom of the English to add
sugar to their wines, which is generally considered a proof that the wines thus treated
were dry.] 'The conclusion at which we thus arrive is so far satisfactory, as it proves
that the wines formerly known under the name of *Sacks*, though they may, upon
the whole, have been inferior, yet differed in no essential quality from those with

Scena Quarta.

Enter Duke, Viola, Curio, and others.   2
*Du.*Giue me fome Mufick; Now good morow frends.
Now good *Cefario*, but that peece of fong,   4

---

1. Scena...] Scene V. Pope, +. F_2. *friends*— Johns.   *friends;* F_3F_4
   The Palace. Rowe.   et cet.
3. *frends.*] Coll. Wh. Cam. *friends*

---

which we are at present supplied by the same countries which originally produced them, and which are still held in such deserved estimation.   They probably first came into favour in consequence of their possessing greater strength and durability, and being more free from acidity than the white wines of France and Germany ; and owed their distinctive appellation to that sub-astringent taste which characterises all wines prepared with gypsum.'—Henderson, *Hist. of Ancient and Modern Wines*, pp. 298–308.

1. **Scena Quarta**] F. A. MARSHALL : With this scene, in [Irving's] acting-edition, Act III. commences.

3, 4. **Now good . . . Now good**] The awkwardness of this repetition seems to have been perceived, with but one exception, by no editor; at least no attempt has been made greatly to vary the punctuation of the Folio.   The exception is JOHN-SON, of whose text no notice, that I can find, has ever been taken.   He punctuates thus : 'Give me some music now.—Good morrow friends—Now, good Cesario,' etc.   This is, certainly, an improvement ; it avoids the beginning of two consecutive sentences with 'Now,' and it makes the salutation to the Musicians and others a courteous side-remark.   It leads the way, moreover, to an arrangement (which occurred to me, but wherein I have been anticipated. *Pereant qui ante nos*, etc.) recorded in the CAMBRIDGE EDITION (ed. ii), by Mr BLAIR, who has suggested the following punctuation : 'Give me some music. [*To Viola.*] Now,—[*Enter Musicians*] good morrow friends,—Now, good Cesario,' etc.   This is better than Dr John-son's ; it avoids the ending of the Duke's first sentence with a weak 'now,' and makes the second 'Now' a mere repetition of the first, and not the beginning of a new address.—ED.

4. **Cesario**] FLEAY (*Sh. Manual*, p. 228) believes that this play was written at two different times, and the first indication of it is the present passage, 'where Viola was evidently intended to be the singer.'   'Compare, 'he continues, ' "for I can sing, And speak to him in many sorts of music," I, ii, 62.   This was from the first draft ; but in the revised play Curio makes the strange answer (in prose, as all, or nearly all, the later work is in this drama), "He is not here that should sing it," and the Duke says, "Who was it ?" forgetting the singer he had heard the night before.   He afterwards points out the special character of the song (lines 51–56) to Cesario, who had also heard it, and who had just been asked to sing it ; all this, I think, could not have been written at one time.'—WEISS (p. 196) : The Duke has forgotten that Feste and not Cesario was the singer.   Fleay overlooks this touch of nature.   But the Duke is mooning about in his sentimental fashion, and

That old and Anticke ſong we heard laſt night ;   5
Me thought it did releeue my paſſion much,
More then light ayres, and recolleᴄted termes   7

5. *Anticke*] *Antick* F₃F₄, Rowe. *an-*   6. *Me thought*] *Methought* Rowe.
tique Pope.

---

vaguely recollects that Cesario was presented to him as one that could sing and
'speak to him in many sorts of music.' He had done so, no doubt, so that the
mistake was natural to the distraught mind of the Duke who seems to allude to it
when he says immediately to Cesario, 'If ever thou shalt love,' etc., lines 18–23.
His obliviousness is indeed so profound that he blunders in dismissing Feste when
the song is over, saying to him, 'Give me now leave to leave thee.' This, so far
from being an imperfect reading, is a perfect touch of his abstruse mood. [See notes
on line 77 below.] It amuses Feste, who says, aside, 'Now the melancholy god
protect thee,' etc. Every line and word of this beautiful scene is unalterably well
placed.—Elze (p. 179) : It seems evident that according to the poet's intention two
singers were required for the performance of this play : one to sing in Orsino's palace (the performer of Viola) and another to sing in Lady Olivia's house (the
Clown). As, however, at some time or other, the Lord Chamberlain's men could
boast of only a single singer, and that one the Clown, they gave him access to the
Duke's palace and made him do the singing of both parts. [See note on Devrient's
Acting Version, line 59 below.]

5. **old and Anticke**] R. G. White (ed. i) : This is not mere pleonasm ;
'antique' carried, and, perhaps we may say, still carries, the idea of quaintness
added to antiquity.—W. A. Wright : 'Antique' has the accent on the first syllable
as always in Shakespeare.

6. **passion**] W. A. Wright : That is, suffering, grief ; used of strong emotions
of any kind. Compare *Tempest*, I, ii, 392 : 'Allaying both their fury and my
passion With its sweet air.'—Innes : That is, fever of his love, for which Orsino
regards music as a sort of medicine, as in the opening lines of the play. [The
'passion' of Ferdinand weeping for his father is not the 'passion' from which
Orsino suffers. It must be remembered that Orsino was enduring the 'pangs of disprized love,' one of the calamities of life which Hamlet enumerates as justifying a
quietus with a bare bodkin. Wherefore, I think that Wright's definition, 'suffering'
(but not 'grief') is the best.—Ed.],

7. **recolleᴄted**] Warburton : That is, studied.—Johnson : I rather think that
'recollected' signifies, more nearly to its primitive sense, *recalled, repeated*, and
alludes to the practice of composers, who often prolong the song by repetitions.
[Though I cannot accept this definition, it is only fair to suggest that Dr Johnson
might have adduced, as an illustration, Thomas Morley's music, written about 1600,
for the Song in *As You Like It* : 'It was a lover and his lass,' where each stanza
thus ends : 'In the spring time, the spring time, In spring time, the only pretty ring
time, When birds do sing, hey ding a ding-ding, hey ding a ding-ding, hey ding a
ding-ding, Sweet lovers love the spring. In spring time. In spring time, the only
pretty ring time, When birds do sing, hey ding a ding-ding, hey ding a ding-ding,
hey ding a ding-ding, sweet lovers love the spring.'—Ed.]—Knight : 'Term'
forms no part of the technical language of music. Its plural may possibly be
intended by Shakespeare to signify those passages called *phrases ;* but it is more
likely that the word was originally written *tunes*, which would render the expression

Of thefe moft briske and giddy-paced times.   8
Come, but one verfe.

Cur. He is not heere (fo pleafe your Lordfhippe) that   10
fhould fing it ?

Du. Who was it ?

Cur. *Fefte* the Iefter my Lord, a foole that the Ladie
Oliuiaes Father tooke much delight in. He is about the
houfe.   15

Du. Seeke him out, and play the tune the while.
                              Muficke playes.

Come hither Boy, if euer thou fhalt loue   18

---

8. *giddy-paced*] *giddy-pated* Han.   16. *Seeke*] *Go, seek* Cap. Ktly.
giddy-pac'd Var. '85.   *giddy-pac'd*   17. [Exit Curio. Pope et seq.
Dyce.   18. [To Viola. Coll. ii (MS).
  13. Fefte] *Fefte* Ktly.   *loue*] *love*, Rowe.
  14. Oliuiaes] Olivia's F_3F_4.

---

intelligible. In not very clear manuscript 'termes' might easily have been mistaken
by the compositor for *tunes*. We agree with Dr Johnson's *recalled*, if by 'recalled'
is to be understood *known by heart,—by memory.*—R. G. WHITE (ed. i) : 'Terms'
does not, I think, mean musical phrases, nor is it a misprint for *tunes*. A song consists of both music and words ; and this song, which was 'old and plain,' suited the
lover's mood by reason of the simple sweetness of its air and the homely directness
of its phrase, more than the 'light airs' (gay, trivial music) to which the 'recollected terms' (carefully culled expressions) in the songs of those 'most brisk and
giddy-paced times' were set. 'Recollected terms' is a phrase which might well be
applied to the words of a song written under the influence of *Euphues and his
England.*—The COWDEN-CLARKES : The poet probably means what musicians
call 'phrases of repetition,' or 'passages of imitation'; where rapid successions
of notes, and florid ornamentation, produce the effect of liveliness which the Duke's
love-melancholy shrinks from, and contrast with the simplicity he so much prefers.
—SCHMIDT (*Lex.*) : Equivalent to picked, refined? or trivial?—W. A. WRIGHT :
That is, phrases gathered with pains, not spontaneous. Knight proposed *tunes*, but
we have already had the *tunes* in the 'airs,' and the 'terms' must therefore be the
words set to music. So 'festival terms,' in *Much Ado*, V, ii, 41, are 'holiday
phrases.' Compare *Love's Lab. L.* V, ii, 406 : 'Taffeta phrases, silken terms precise.' The sense here given is confirmed by a passage in *Pericles*, II, i, 54 : 'How
from the finny subject of the sea These fishers tell the infirmities of men ; And from
their watery empire recollect All that may men approve or men detect !' [The most
concise definition is given by Warburton, viz : *studied*. This is virtually the same
as both White's and Wright's : 'studied expressions' are 'carefully culled expressions,' and they are also 'phrases gathered with pains, not spontaneous.' INNES
says that 'recollected terms' 'apparently conveys the same sort of idea as "light
airs."' I cannot at all agree with him when he adds, in reference to Wright's
interpretation, that it 'might be true if it did not appear wholly inappropriate.'
On the contrary, it is, I think, exactly in the trending of the true explanation.
—ED.]

In the fweet pangs of it, remember me:
For fuch as I am, all true Louers are,   20
Vnftaid and skittifh in all motions elfe,
Saue in the conftant image of the creature
That is belou'd.   How doft thou like this tune?
    Vio.   It giues a very eccho to the feate
Where loue is thron'd.   25
    Du.   Thou doft fpeake mafterly,
My life vpon't, yong though thou art, thine eye
Hath ftaid vpon fome fauour that it loues :
Hath it not boy?
    Vio.   A little, by your fauour.   30
    Du.   What kinde of woman ift?
    Uio.   Of your complection.
    Du.   She is not worth thee then. What yeares ifaith?
    Vio.   About your yeeres my Lord.
    Du.   Too old by heauen : Let ftill the woman take   35
An elder then her felfe, fo weares fhe to him;

---

19. *me :*] *me ?* F₂F₃.   *me ;* F₄.
21. *motions*] *notions* Theob. conj.
Warb.
24, 25. Mnemonic lines, Warb.
24. *to*] *from* Warb.

30. *fauour.*] *favour,* F₄.
31. *ift*] *is't* F₃F₄.
32. *complection*] *complexion* F₃F₄.
35-37. Mnemonic, Warb.

---

21. **motions**] That is, emotions ; frequently used with especial reference to love.
Thus, 'teach me ... with what art You sway the motion of Demetrius' heart.'—
Mid. N. D. I, i. 204.   Again, 'A maiden ... Of spirit so still and quiet, that her
motion Blush'd at her self.'—*Othello*, I, iii, 113.

24. **to the seate**] WARBURTON : We should read, '*from* the seat,' *i. e.* it reaches
the throne of love and reverberates thence.—HEATH (p. 190) : The tune could not
properly be said to be in the heart, and therefore could not give an echo from it.
The common reading, therefore, is certainly right.   It gives the heart a very echo ;
that is, It is so consonant to the emotions of the heart that they echo it back again.
[The emotion issuing from the heart, is caught up and interpreted by the music which
returns it as an echo.—ED.]

25. **thron'd**] See I, i, 43.

30. **by your fauour**] JOHNSON : The word 'favour' is ambiguously used.—
STEEVENS : 'Favour,' in the preceding speech, signifies *countenance*.   [There is
also a play upon the word 'by,' which, as ABBOTT (§ 145, p. 97) points out, may
be here taken in its original meaning, *near*.]

30, etc.] To this passage COLLIER finds an indistinct parallel in *Gl' Inganni*.
See *Appendix, Source of the Plot*.

36. **An elder then her selfe**] MALONE (*Life*, Var. 1821, ii, 112) : Anne
Hathaway whom our poet married in June or July, 1582, was then in her twenty-
sixth year, that is, seven years and a half older than her husband ; a disproportion

[35, 36. **Let still the woman take An elder then her selfe**]
of age, which seldom fails, at a subsequent period of life, to be productive of
unhappiness, and which . . . perhaps, suggested the judicious precept [in the present
lines].—DE QUINCEY (p. 46) : Shakespeare, looking back on this part of his youthful history from his maturest years, breathes forth pathetic counsels against the errors
into which his own experience had been ensnared.   The disparity of years between
himself and his wife he notices in a beautiful scene in the *Twelfth Night*. . . .
These counsels were uttered nearly twenty years after the event in his own life to
which they probably look back ; for this play is supposed to have been written in
Shakespeare's thirty-eighth year [?].   And we may read an earnestness in pressing
the point as to the *inverted* disparity of years, which indicates pretty clearly an
appeal to the lessons of his personal experience.—KNIGHT (p. 189 : [This passage]
has been supposed to bear upon the domestic history of Shakspere.   We believe
that such conjectures are in general founded on a misapprehension of the dramatic
spirit in which he worked ; and that such notions, especially as that he was himself
jealous, because he has so truly depicted the passion of jealousy,—or that he had
himself felt the bitter pang of filial irreverence, because he had written [certain
passages in *Lear*] are altogether idle and worthless.   The details, however, of
Shakspere's private life are so few, and the facts and traditions which have come
down to us require such careful examination, that we need not be surprised that the
language which he has held to be characteristic of the persons and incidents of his
dramas should have been deemed, with more or less ingenuity, to be characteristic
of himself, his actions, and his circumstances.   Amongst the least overstrained of
these applications is the [present passage]. . . . Upon the general principle which
we have stated,—that is, the wonderful subjection of his conception of what was
individually true to what was universally true,—he would, we think, have *rejected*
whatever was peculiar to his own experience, if it had been emphatically recommended to his adoption through the medium of his self-consciousness.   [Knight
then proceeds to the more immediate purpose of this 'Postscript,'—an extremely
valuable contribution to those who are interested in the *Life* of Shakespeare,—
which is, to prove that the poet's domestic life was not unhappy owing to the disparity in years between himself and his wife, and that the bequest to her of his 'second-
best bed' betokened no neglect, nor lack of affection for her, inasmuch as she had
her right of dower in his freehold property, wherein the bulk of his large estate consisted.]—HALLIWELL : The suggestion that the dialogue was intended to allude in
any way to the poet's domestic unhappiness, not only destroys the independence of
one of his best scenes, but is in itself exceedingly improbable.—COLLIER (ed. ii,
Life, i, 64) : Whether these lines did or did not originate in the author's reflections
upon his own marriage, they are so applicable to his own case, that it seems impossible he should have written them without recalling the circumstances attending his
hasty union, and the disparity of years between himself and his wife.   Such, we
know, was the confirmed opinion of Coleridge, expressed on two distinct occasions in
his Lectures, and such, we think, will be the conclusion at which most readers will
arrive : 'I cannot hesitate in believing,' observed Coleridge in 1811–12, 'that in this
passage from *Twelfth Night*, Shakespeare meant to give a caution, arising out of his
own experience ; and, but for the fact of the disproportion in point of years between
himself and his wife, I doubt much whether the dialogue between Viola and the
Duke would have received this turn.'—IBID. (ed. ii, vol. ii, 638) : It was an opinion
confidently stated by Coleridge in his Lectures in 1818, that this present passage had

So fwayes fhe leuell in her husbands heart :   37
For boy, howeuer we do praife our felues,
Our fancies are more giddie and vnfirme,
More longing, wauering, fooner loft and worne,   40
Then womens are.

40. *worne*] F₂F₃. *won* Han. Ran. Wh. i, Coll. ii, iii (MS), Dyce ii, iii, Ktly,
Huds. *worn* F₄ et cet.

---

a direct application to the circumstances of Shakespeare's marriage with Anne Hathaway. . . . Coleridge took the opportunity of enlarging eloquently on the manner in
which young poets have frequently connected themselves with women of very ordinary personal and mental attractions, the imagination supplying all deficiencies,
clothing the object of affection with grace and beauty, and furnishing her with every
accomplishment.—R. G. WHITE (*Life*, i, xxxiv) : Who can believe that the well-
known counsel in [these present lines] was not a stifled cry of anguish from [Shake-
speare's] tormented, over-burdened soul, though he had left his torment and his
burden so far behind him? It is impossible that he could have written it without
thinking of his own experience ; the more, that the seeming lad to whom it is
addressed is about his years, and the man who utters it about Anne Hathaway's at
the time when they were married.—DYCE (ed. ii, *Life*, i, 33) : It is unfair to conclude, as Malone and others have done, from certain passages in our author's plays,—
each of which passages more or less grows out of the incidents of the play,—that he
had cause to complain of domestic unhappiness : indeed, without taking into account
the tradition of his regular visits to Stratford, we have strong presumptive evidence
to the contrary in the fact, that the wife of his youth was the companion of his latest
years, when he had raised himself to opulence and to the position of a gentleman.
—W. A. WRIGHT : Shakespeare was seldom autobiographical, and did not wear his
heart upon his sleeve.—INNES : Shakespeare was not in the habit of making his
characters mouthpieces ; the Duke's opinion must, in this case as in others, be taken
for what it is worth, as his own view and not necessarily that of the poet.—LEE
(p. 25) : Although it is dangerous to read into Shakespeare's dramatic utterances
allusions to his personal experience, the emphasis with which he insists that a
woman should take in marriage an ' elder than herself,' and that prenuptial intimacy
is productive of ' barren hate, sour-eyed disdain, and discord,' suggest a personal
interpretation.   [Not only do I not believe that Shakespeare was here referring to
his own experience, but I do not believe that Orsino's assertion itself is true.   The
record of marriages where the woman is the elder will prove, I think, that, *as a
rule*, such unions, founded as they are, not on the fleeting attractions of youth, which
is ' a stuff will not endure,' but on the abiding elements of intellectual congeniality,
have been unusually happy.—ED.]

39–41. **Our . . . are**] INNES : This admission hints that Orsino is becoming alive
to the fact that his constitution has more to do with his fitfulness than the ardour of
his passion.

40. **lost and worne**] JOHNSON : Though ' lost and worn ' may mean ' lost and
worn *out*,' yet ' lost and *won* ' being, I think, better, these two words coming usually
and naturally together, and the alteration being slight, I would so read in this place
with Hanmer.   [And yet he did not.—ED.]—CAPELL (p. 146) : *Won* carries strong
marks of genuineness ; it is coupl'd often with ' lost ' in these writings, and seems

Uio.　I thinke it well my Lord.　　　　　　　　　　42

Du.　Then let thy Loue be yonger then thy felfe,

Or thy affection cannot hold the bent :

For women are as Rofes, whofe faire flowre　　　　45

Being once difplaid, doth fall that verie howre.

Vio.　And fo they are : alas, that they are fo :

To die, euen when they to perfection grow.

　　　　　　　Enter Curio & Clowne.

Du.　O fellow come, the fong we had laft night :　　50

Marke it Cefario, it is old and plaine ;

The Spinfters and the Knitters in the Sun,

And the free maides that weaue their thred with bones,　53

42. *well my*] *well, my* Rowe et seq.
46. *that*] *the* F₄ Rowe i.
47. *fo :*] *so.* Rowe i.　*so,* Rowe ii.
so,— Dyce.
50. *night :*] *night.* Rowe, Pope, Han.
Coll. Dyce, Cam. Ktly.　*night,—*

Theob. +, Sta.
　52. *and the*] *and* Vernor & Hood's
Rep.
52-56. Mnemonic, Warb.
53. *the free*] *the fair* Grey.　*thrifty*
J. Addis, Jr. (*N. & Qu.* III, xi, 252).

wanted to sort with 'giddy' and 'longing,' as 'lost' does with the other two.—
MALONE : The text is undoubtedly right, and 'worn' means consumed, worn out.
So Lord Surrey, describing the Spring, says : 'Winter is worn, that was the flowers'
bale.' [*Description of Spring.*]　Again, *2 Hen. VI :* II, iv, 69 : 'These few days'
wonder will be quickly worn.'　Again, in *Wint. Tale,* V, i, 142 : 'and but infirmity Which waits upon worn times.'—WALKER (*Crit.* iii, 85) : It seems wonderful
that any one should have hesitated between this and the true reading *won.*—
LETTSOM (*Footnote to Walker*) : So in the *Mer. of Ven.* I, iii, 50, the Folio has
'well-worne thrift,' and, if it had not been for the Quartos, the corruption might
have deformed modern texts. [W. A. WRIGHT is, I think, a little too emphatic when
he says that *won* 'would have no meaning here'; does not the word 'wavering'
imply now lost now won? but he is altogether right in retaining 'worn'; even
apart from its appropriate meaning of 'lost and consumed,' the very triteness of the
phrase 'lost and won' is against its adoption.　Here, if anywhere, the well-worn
Durior lectio preferenda est should prevail.—ED.]

　　44. bent] MURRAY (*N. E. D. s. v.* Bent, 9) : Extent to which a bow may be
bent, or a spring wound up, degree of tension ; *hence* degree of endurance, capacity
for taking in or receiving ; limit of capacity, etc.　[See *Much Ado,* II, iii, 214 ;
IV, i, 194, of this ed.]

　　48. euen when] ABBOTT (§ 38, p. 42) : This means here, '*just* when.'

　　53. free maides] JOHNSON : That is, perhaps, vacant, unengaged, easy in mind.
—KNIGHT : Upon the passage in Milton's *L'Allegro,*—'But come, thou goddess,
fair and free, In heaven yclep'd Euphrosyne,'—Warton remarks that 'in the
metrical romances these two words, thus paired together, are a common epithet for
a lady,' as in *Syr Eglamour,* 'The erles daughter fair and free.'　'But in these
cases,' observes W. A. WRIGHT, '"free" denotes one of gentle or noble birth.
See I, v, 258.　Thus in the *Romance of Sir Perceval of Galles* (*Thornton Romances,*
Camden Soc.) 521, we find "Percyvelle the free"; and in Robert of Gloucester's

Do vſe to chaunt it : it is ſilly ſooth,
And dallies with the innocence of loue,   55
Like the old age.
    Clo. Are you ready Sir?
    Duke. I prethee ſing.   *Muſicke.*
               The Song.   59

54. *ſilly ſooth,*] silly, sooth, Wh. i.
55. *dallies*] tallies Warb.
58. *I prethee*] Ff, Rowe. *I pr'y thee*

Pope, Han. *Ay ; pr'y thee* (or *prithee*)
Theob. ii et seq.
59. The Song.] Song. Rowe et seq.

Chronicle (ed. Hearne), p. 420, Henry I. is described as "Of fayrost fourme and maners and mest gentyl and fre."' Wright, therefore, defines 'free' in the present instance, as 'free from care, careless, happy,' and therein agrees with Dr Johnson ; among the many meanings which can be properly given to the word, this appears to suit the present context best.—HALLIWELL quotes the following, from Miss Baker's *Northamptonshire Glossary: Lace-songs,* jingling rhymes, sung by young girls while engaged at their lace-pillows. The movement of the bobbins is timed by the modulation of the tune, which excites them to regularity and cheerfulness ; and it is a pleasing picture, in passing through a rural village, to see them, in warm sunny weather, seated outside their cottage doors, or seeking the shade of a neighbouring tree ; where in cheerful groups they unite in singing their rude and simple rhymes.

53. bones] W. A. WRIGHT: In Beaumont & Fletcher's *Scornful Lady,* V, ii, among the accomplishments of a good housewife, it is said, 'She cuts cambric at a thread, weaves bone lace, and quilts balls.'—MURRAY (*N. E. D.*) : Bone-lace is usually of linen thread, made by knitting upon a pattern marked by pins, with bobbins originally made of bone.

54. silly sooth] JOHNSON : That is, it is plain, simple truth.

55. dallies] STEEVENS : That is, play, trifle. So in III, i, 16.

56. the old age] JOHNSON : That is, the ages past, the times of simplicity.—HUNTER (i, 403): Dr Johnson's interpretation is confirmed by what goes before, 'it is old and plain.' The poets have always had their golden age of innocence and truth. In *Sonnet,* cxxvii, we have, 'In the old age black was not counted fair.' [Compare Orlando's speech to Adam ; 'how well in thee appears The constant service of the antique world,' etc., II, iii, 58.—ED.]

59. The Song] CAPELL (p. 146) : This song is undoubtedly ancient, but is not met with as some are of Sir Toby's.—STAUNTON : On comparing the Duke's description of that 'antique song' he heard last night, with this ballad, the difference is so striking, as to beget suspicion that the latter was an interpolation, and not the original song intended by the poet. It appears, indeed, to have been the privilege of the singer formerly, whenever the business of the scene required a song, to introduce one of his own choice ; hence we frequently find in our old dramas, instead of the words of a ballad, merely a stage direction, 'A Song,' or 'He sings.'—INNES : Nevertheless, a song of the woeful fate of a swain who dies of love may very fitly be described as 'dallying with the innocence of love,' especially by the Duke, who would rather like to believe that he is dying of love himself.—HUTSON (p. 489) : The true significance of the great dramatist's putting this wailing dirge into the Clown's mouth seems to me to be that he wishes to indicate his conception

Come away, come away death,   60
And in fad cypreffe let me be laide .
Fye away, fie away breath,
I am flaine by a faire cruell maide :   63

62. Fye away, fie] F$_2$.   Fie away, fie F$_3$F$_4$.   *Fly away, fly* Rowe et seq.

---

of the character as that of one whose culture and native gifts have been both over-borne by some imperious and ineradicable foibles, aided by the force of circum-stances. Capacity for thought, still manifested in metaphysical tendencies of expres-sion, ... and capacity for sentiment, still manifested in his musical ability, and the power with which he evidently rendered this song, indicate versatility of mind and character.   To this we must add the histrionic capacity afterwards shown when he deceives Malvolio by feigned voice and style into mistaking him for the Parson. This versatility might have borne better fruit than the life of a great lady's jester but for the large developement of certain lower tastes and passions, which one can-not help noting in Feste, and also the opportune opening for him in the new pro-fession, when his lively pranks shut him off from the clerical career for which he seems to have been originally destined.   Something in his personal appearance, too, operated against his entering that profession, and fitted him peculiarly for the cap-and-bells and the motley garb. [See IV, ii, 8. In the *Acting Version* of EDUARD and OTTO DEVRIENT this Song is sung by Viola.   In the Introduction to the play, the Editors, who were themselves eminent actors, express the belief that in this dis-tribution of parts they were, in reality, restoring Shakespeare's original intention. That, in the Folio, this Song is sung by Feste, they attribute to the changes which were introduced by the company at The Globe, after Shakespeare had left the stage, —changes which may have been due at first to some temporary expediency and became afterward permanent.   At the very outset of the play we are led to suppose that Viola's chief attraction is her singing ; and yet here at the supreme moment when her singing is to have its most powerful effect, she is silent, and the power to stir the Duke's heart to the inmost is given to the Clown.   The whole sentiment of the Song points to Viola as the Singer ; in it she pours out her soul.   'Is it to be imagined,' they ask, 'that Shakespeare should have allowed our expectations of Viola's singing to be aroused only to have them fulfilled by the Clown ?'   Further-more, they say that 'if we examine the text which sets forth the substitution of the Clown for Viola, we cannot for a moment doubt that we are dealing with an inser-tion by a Stage manager, who has had to meet a sudden and unexpected misadvent-ure,—possibly an attack of hoarseness in Viola, and Feste, ever ready with his songs, must help her out. But why this substitution was permanent, and why Viola was not reinstated, and why the impromptu jokes of the Clown were retained in the Folio are questions as hard to answer as why these noteworthy inconsistencies have not been hitherto noticed.'   The Editors then go on to say that on the stage, in many performances at Carlsruhe, the change from Feste to Viola has been extremely effective.—CONRAD (*Preuss. Jahrb.* July, 1887, p. 17) suggests that when Shake-speare first wrote this play, the boy, who took the part of Viola, had a fresh young voice, but when, at a later date, he enlarged the play the boy had grown up, and the only good tenor in the company was the Clown.—ED.]

61. cypresse] MALONE : In the books of our author's age the thin transparent lawn called *cyprus,* which was formerly used for scarfs and hatbands at funerals, was,

My ſhrowd of white,ſtuck all with Ew,O prepare it.
My part of death no one ſo true did ſhare it .   65

Not a flower, not a flower ſweete
On my blacke coffin, let there be ſtrewne :
Not a friend, not a friend greet
My poore corpes,where my bones ſhall be throwne :
A thouſand thouſand ſighes to ſaue ,lay me ô where   70
Sad true louer neuer find my graue ,to weepe there.

Du.   There's for thy paines.
Clo. No paines ſir, I take pleaſure in ſinging ſir.
Du.   Ile pay thy pleaſure then.   74

64. Ew] Ff.   *Yew* Rowe.
64, 65. O prepare it...did ſhare it]
Separate lines, Pope et seq.
64. O prepare] *Prepare* Pope, Han.
66. flower ſwecte] *flower, sweet,* Anon.
ap. Cam.
70, 71. lay me ô where...to weepe
there] Separate lines, Pope et seq.

70. ô] O Ff.   Om. Pope, Han.
71. Sad] Om. Pope, +, Var. '73.
    true louer] *true-love* Cap. Var.
'78, '85, Dyce ii, iii, Huds.
    neuer] *ne'er* Han. Mal. Steev.
Var. '03, '13, Sta.
72. [Giving money. Coll. ii (MS.)

I believe, constantly spelt *cypress*. So, in the *Wint. Tale*, IV, iv, 251 : 'Cypresse
blacke as ere was Crow,' where undoubtedly *cyprus* was meant. [See note, *ad loc.*
in this ed.] So, again in the play before us, III, i, 123, 'a Cipresse, not a bosome
Hides my heart.' It is from the context alone, therefore, that we can ascertain
whether *cyprus* or *cypress* was intended. Mr Warton has suggested, in his edition
of Milton's *Poems*, that the meaning here is,—'Let me be laid in a shroud made
of *cyprus*, not in a coffin made of *cypress* wood.' But in a subsequent line of this
song the shroud (like that of Polonius), we find, is *white*. There was, indeed, white
cyprus as well as black ; but the epithet 'sad' is inconsistent with white, and,
therefore, I suppose the wood to have been here meant. Coffins being frequently
made of *cypress* wood (perhaps in consequence of *cyprus* being used at funerals)
the epithet 'sad' is here employed with strict propriety. [Malone then quotes from
Speed an incident which occurred at the 'solemne funerals' of Robert de Vere.
Stow, Speed's predecessor, gives the same incident as follows : '[King Richard II.]
caused the Coffin of Cipres, wherein his body being embalmed lay, to be opened,
that he might behold his face, & touch him with his fingers.'—*Annales*, p. 503, ed.
1600.]—KNIGHT : It is difficult, and perhaps unnecessary, to decide the question
[whether a *coffin* or a *shroud* be here meant ;] the sentiment is the same, whichever
meaning we receive.—W. A. WRIGHT : It is, either a coffin of cypress wood or on
a bier strewn with branches or garlands of cypress.

65. **My part . . . share it**] JOHNSON : Though 'death' is a 'part' in which
every one acts his 'share,' yet of all these actors no one is 'so true' as I.

70. ô] This 'ô,' with a circumflex, WALKER (*Crit.* i, 105) notes as frequently
used (though, of course, not here) as the *o* in the forms *o' my truth, o' my life*, etc.

Clo. Truely fir, and pleafure will be paide one time, or   75
another.

Du. Giue me now leaue, to leaue thee.

Clo. Now the melancholly God proteƈt thee, and the
Tailor make thy doublet of changeable Taffata, for thy
minde is a very Opall. I would haue men of fuch conftan-   80

---

76. *another*] *other* Rowe, +, Var. '73,
'78, '85, Ran.

    77. *Giue...thee*] *I give thee now...me.*
Harness, Coll. iii (MS.)

77, 78. *Giue me...Now*] *Give me now
leave. Clo. To leave thee !—Now* Mac-
donald, ap. Cam.

    78. Clo.] Duk. F$_2$.

    75, 76. **pleasure will be paide,** etc.] DEIGHTON : Sooner or later pleasure (*i. e.* indulgence) will be requited by pain, will have to pay the penalty of pain.

    77. **Giue me now leaue,** etc.] HARNESS : There are here two errors of the press : the omission of the preposition [*sic*] *I,* and a transposition of ' me ' and ' thee.'   According to the old reading, the Duke's [speech] is not only contrary to the rank and situation of the characters but to the circumstances which immediately follow. [Harness's text reads : ' I give thee now leave to leave me '; which is also the reading of Collier's MS.]—HALLIWELL, after quoting Harness's note, observes : The Duke is scarcely solicitous to preserve the language belonging to the dignity of his position in his conversation with the Clown.   He is here speaking either jocularly or ironically, or both.—DYCE (ed. ii, asks, concerning the present text) Is not this a courteous form of dismissal ?—W. A. WRIGHT answers that it is, and adds : When Henry says to Worcester (*1 Hen. IV :* I, iii, 20), ' You have good leave to leave us,' it amounts to a command to withdraw. [See WEISS'S note on line 4 above.]

    79. **changeable Taffata**] HALLIWELL : ' —as our changeable silk turned to ye Sunne hath many colours, and turned backe the contrary, so wit shippeth [' sharpeth,' *ap.* Halliwell ; qu. shapeth ?—ED.] it self to euery conceit being constant in nothing but inconstancie.'—Lily, *Euphues and his England,* [1580, p. 320, ed. Arber.]—W. A. WRIGHT : Taffeta was originally any kind of plain silk, but it now denotes many other varieties.   The word is said to be Persian in origin, from *tâftah,* woven, which is the participle of *tâftan,* to intertwine.   It appears in French as *taffetas,* in Italian as *taffeto,* and in Spanish as *tafetan.*   In Chaucer (*C. T.* 442) the Doctor of Physic's robe was, ' Lyned with taffata and with sendal.' The earliest example given by Littré is of the 15th century : ' Une piece de taffetas changeant de Levant.'

    80. **Opall**] ' *Optallio* is called *Oppalus* also, and is a stone distinguished with colors of diuers precious stones, as *Isid.* saith.   Therein is the firie colour of ye Carbuncle, the shining purple of the *Ametistus,* the bright greene colour of *Smaragdus,* and all the colours shine therein, with a manner diuersitie, and hath the name of the Countrie.   This stone breedeth onely in *Inde,* and is deemed to haue as many vertues, as hiewes and colours.   Of this *Optallius,* it is said in *Lapidario,* that this stone *Optallius* keepeth and saueth his eyen that beareth it, cleere and sharp and without griefe, and dimmeth other mens eyen that be about, with a maner clowde, and smiteth them with a maner blindnesse, that is called *Amentia,* so that they may not see neither take heede what is done before their eyen.   Therefore it is said, that

cie put to Sea, that their bufineffe might be euery thing,   81
and their intent euerie where, for that's it, that alwayes
makes a good voyage of nothing. Farewell.   *Exit*

   Du. Let all the reft giue place : Once more *Cefario*,
Get thee to yond fame foueraigne crueltie :   85
Tell her my loue, more noble then the world
Prizes not quantitie of dirtie lands,
The parts that fortune hath beftow'd vpon her :
Tell her I hold as giddily as Fortune :
But 'tis that miracle ,and Queene of Iems   90
That nature prankes her in, attracts my foule.

82. *that's it, that*] *that's it that*
Rowe.
  84. Scene VI. Pope, +.
    place :] *place.* [Exeunt. Johns.
[Exeunt Cur. and Att. Cap.
  85. *yond*] *yon'* Cap. Steev. Var. '73,

'78, '85.   *yond'* Coll.
  87, 88. *lands, ... her,*] *lands, ... her,*
Ff, Rowe. *lands ;...her,* Pope et seq.
  90. *Iems*] *Jems* F_3F_4, Rowe. *gems*
Pope.

---

it is the most sure patron of theeues.'—Batman *vppon Bartholome*, 1582, Lib. xvi,
cap. 73, p. 264.—ED.

  82. **euerie where**] WARBURTON : Both the preservation of the antithesis and the
recovery of the sense, require we should read,—' and their intent *no* where.' Because
a man who suffers himself to run with every wind, and so makes his business every
where, cannot be said to have any *intent ;* for that word signifies a determination of
the mind to something. Besides, the conclusion of ' making a good voyage' of
nothing directs to this emendation.—HEATH (p. 191) : An intent *every* where is
much the same as an intent *no where,* as it hath no one particular place more in
view than another.—M. MASON (p. 116) : We cannot accuse a man of inconstancy
who has no intents at all, though we may the man whose intents are every where ;
that is, are continually varying. [Just as the incomparable Feste had detected
Maria's scheme to capture Sir Toby, (I, v, 27,) so here he shows with what exactness he had read the Duke's character.—ED.]

  86. **world**] That is, the social world.

  87. **dirtie lands**] W. A. WRIGHT : Like Osric, in *Hamlet*, Olivia was ' spacious
in the possession of dirt.'

  89. **giddily**] That is, carelessly, indifferently.

  91. **prankes her in**] WARBURTON : What is ' that miracle and queen of gems,'
we are not told in this reading. Besides, what is meant by ' nature pranking her in
a miracle'? We should read, ' That nature pranks, *her mind*'—i. e. what ' attracts
my soul' is not her ' fortune,' but *her mind,* ' that miracle and queen of gems that
nature pranks,' *i. e.* sets out, adorns.—JOHNSON : The ' miracle and queen of gems'
is her *beauty*, which the commentator might have found without so emphatical an
enquiry. As to her mind, he that should be captious would say, that though it may
be formed by nature, it must be ' pranked' by education. Shakespeare does not say
that nature pranks her in a miracle, but in the miracle of gems, that is, in a gem
miraculously beautiful.

  91. **attracts**] For the omission of the relative, see I, v, 99.

Vio.   But if fhe cannot loue you fir.   92
Du.   It cannot be fo anfwer'd.
Vio.   Sooth but you muft.
Say that fome Lady, as perhappes there is,   95
Hath for your loue as great a pang of heart
As you haue for *Oliuia* : you cannot loue her:
You tel her fo : Muft fhe not then be anfwer'd?
   Du.   There is no womans fides
Can bide the beating of fo ftrong a paffion,   100
As loue doth giue my heart : no womans heart
So bigge, to hold fo much, they lacke retention.   102

92. *fir.*] Ff, Rowe. *Sir,*— Theob.+.   *I* Han. et seq.
sir? Pope et seq.   94. *Sooth*] '*Sooth* Cap. Var. Steev.
   93. *It*] Ff, Rowe, Pope, Theob. Coll. i.   100. *bide*] *abide* F₃F₄.

93. **It cannot**] MALONE : I am not sure that [Hanmer's change '*I* cannot'] is
necessary. The Duke may mean, ' my *suit* cannot,' etc.—COLLIER (ed. i) : That
is, my love cannot be so answered. Viola's reply means, that if your love cannot be
so answered, you must be content with the answer.—DYCE : The Folio is proved
to be wrong by the next speech ; 'Sooth, but *you* must . . . must *she* not, then, be
answer'd ?'—COLLIER (ed. ii) : We have doubts whether the old text should be
altered here. . . . We follow [Hanmer's] example with some hesitation. [Hanmer
is probably right.—ED.]

99. **There is . . . sides**] ABBOTT (§ 335) : When the subject is as yet future,
and, as it were, unsettled, the third person singular might be regarded as the normal
inflection. Such passages are very common, particularly in the case of 'There is.'
—SKEAT (*N. & Qu.* IXth, v, 360, May, 1900) thus excellently formulates the usage
founded on the practice of old authors :—When a verb occurs as the *second word* in
a sentence, and is preceded by such words as *it, that, what, where, here,* and the
like, such a verb is usually employed in the *singular* number, irrespective of the
number of the substantive which follows it. Examples of such usage are common
from the ninth century onwards. Hence a ballad may begin, 'It was a lover and
his lass,' or we may begin a sentence with 'There is tears,' or 'Here is pansies.'
This is the right explanation of the famous line in *The Tempest :* 'What cares these
roarers for the name of king?' If I remember rightly, the form 'cares' has been
explained as 'a Northern plural.' But what had a Warwickshire man to do with 'a
Northern plural'?

102. **to hold**] For the omission of *as,* see II, ii, 11.

102. **retention**] W. A. WRIGHT : That is, the power of retaining. See *Sonnet*
cxxii, 9 : 'That poor retention could not so much hold.'—The COWDEN-CLARKES :
The Duke one moment owns his sex's fickleness, the next maintains its superior
strength of passion ; in one speech, proclaims women's greater constancy ; in
another, accuses them of incapacity for steady attachment.—INNES : The Duke,—
very properly and entirely in character,—makes two flatly contradictory statements
about women in general in the course of a single scene,—consequently there are
plenty of people who will quote one opinion or the other, and say we have not
Orsino's but Shakespeare's authority for taking that view. What Shakespeare

Alas, their loue may be call'd appetite,   103
No motion of the Liuer, but the Pallat,
That fuffer furfet, cloyment, and reuolt,   105
But mine is all as hungry as the Sea,
And can digeft as much, make no compare
Betweene that loue a woman can beare me,
And that I owe *Oliuia*.

   Uio. I but I know.   110
   Du. What doft thou knowe?

103, 104. *appetite,...Pallat,*] F₂. *appetite:...Pallat,* F₃F₄, Rowe,+. *appetite,—...palate,*— Cap. et seq. (subs.)
105. *fuffer*] *suffers* Rowe,+, Ran.
Coll. Dyce ii, iii, Huds. Dtn.

107. *digeft*] *difgeft* F₂.
much, make] *much; make*
Rowe et seq.
110. *know.*] *know*— Rowe et seq.
(subs.)

thought on the subject we may infer from the characters of the women he drew more accurately than from the various opinions expressed by his *dramatis personæ.*

103–105. **their . . . That**] For the construction, see I, v, 287,—if the antecedent of 'That' be 'their,'—which is doubtful.

104. **motion of the Liuer**] That is, no emotion of the liver. That the liver is the seat of love and valour has been the belief from time immemorial. The following from Bartholomæus, who flourished about 1360, is noteworthy merely as showing the prevalence of the belief in the Middle Ages : 'the lyuer is the chiefe foundation of kindly vertue, and gretest helper of the first digestion in the stomacke... and sendeth feeding to all the members, and exciteth loue or bodelye lust, and receiueth diuers passions.'—Batman *vppon Bartholome*, 1582, Lib. V, cap. 39, p. 57.

105. **That suffer surfet**] MALONE : 'Suffer' is governed by *women*, implied under the words 'their love.' The love of women, etc., *who* suffer.—DYCE (ed. ii) : Malone attempts in vain to defend 'suffer.'—DEIGHTON : The line 'No motion . . . Pallat' is parenthetical. The fact that the Duke immediately afterwards contrasts his appetite as never suffering surfeit, etc., with that of women seems to show that 'That' refers to appetite, and consequently we must have the singular verb, *suffers.* The final *s* might be easily omitted before 'surfeit.'—INNES : 'That' refers back to 'their,' not to palate. [In a case like this, where the ear can only with difficulty detect a difference between 'suffer surfeit' and 'suffers surfeit,' it is hardly safe to be dogmatic. The terms : 'surfeit, cloyment' and, especially, 'revolt,' certainly seem more applicable to 'appetite' than to *women.*—ED.]

105. **cloyment**] W. A. WRIGHT : Apparently a word of Shakespeare's own coinage.

106. **hungry as the Sea**] STEEVENS : So, in *Coriolanus*, V, iii, 58 : 'Then let the pebbles on the hungry beach Fillip the stars.'

109. **I owe Oliuia**] I suppose the general pronunciation of 'Olivia' is with a long *O*, which is shortened in the abbreviation, *Olive.* Is it fanciful to infer, from the present phrase, that Shakespeare's pronunciation was the same in both cases, and that he pronounced 'Olivia' with a short *O?* Otherwise it is difficult to suppose that his ear would not have detected the cacophony of the iterated long *o* in 'owe Olivia.'—ED.

Uio. Too well what loue women io men may owe : 112
In faith they are as true of heart, as we.
My Father had a daughter lou'd a man
As it might be perhaps, were I a woman 115
I fhould your Lordfhip.
Du. And what's her hiftory *?*
Vio. A blanke my Lord : fhe neuer told her loue, 118

---

112. *may owe*] *owe* F₃F₄. *do owe*
Rowe i.
117. *And what's*] *What's* Pope, Han.

118–123. Mnemonic lines, Pope,
Warb.

---

114. lou'd] For a similar omission of the relative, see I, v, 99.

118, etc. **A blanke, etc.**] HAZLITT (p. 259): The great and secret charm of *Twelfth Night* is the character of Viola. Much as we like catches and cakes and ale, there is something we like better. We have a friendship for Sir Toby ; we patronise Sir Andrew ; we have an understanding with the Clown, a sneaking kindness for Maria and her rogueries ; we feel a regard for Malvolio, and sympathise with his gravity, his smiles, his cross-garters, his yellow-stockings and his imprisonment in the stocks. [?] But there is something that excites in us a stronger feeling than all this,—it is Viola's confession of her love. What we so much admire here is not the image of Patience on a monument, which has been generally quoted, but the lines before and after it. 'They give a very echo to the seat where love is throned.' How long ago it is since we first learned to repeat them ; and still, still they vibrate on the heart, like the sounds which the passing wind draws from the trembling strings of a harp left on some desert shore !—COLERIDGE (p. 121): After the first line (of which the last five words should be spoken with, and drop down in, a deep sigh), the actress ought to make a pause ; and then start afresh, from the activity of thought, born of suppressed feelings, and which thought had accumulated during the brief interval, as vital heat under the skin during a dip in cold water. —CHARLES LAMB (ii, 366): Those who have only seen Mrs Jordan within the last ten or fifteen years can have no adequate notion of her performance of such parts as Ophelia ; Helena in *All's Well that Ends Well;* and Viola. . . . Her joyous parts, in which her memory now chiefly lives, in her youth were outdone by her plaintive ones. There is no giving an account of how she delivered the disguised story of her love for Orsino. It was no set speech, that she had foreseen, so as to weave it into a harmonious period, line necessarily following line, to make up the music,—yet I have heard it so spoken, or rather *read*, not without its grace and beauty,—but, when she had declared her sister's history to be a 'blank,' and that she 'never told her love,' there was a pause, as if the story had ended,—and then the image of the 'worm in the bud,' came up as a new suggestion,—and the heightened image of 'Patience' still followed after that, as by some growing (and not mechanical) process, thought springing up after thought, I would almost say, as they were watered by her tears. So in those fine lines, 'Write loyal cantons of contemned love,' etc. There was no preparation made in the foregoing image for that which was to follow. She used no rhetoric in her passion ; or it was Nature's own rhetoric, most legitimate then, when it seemed altogether without rule or law. [This description of Mrs Jordan's acting agrees so fully with Coleridge's assertion of the

But let concealment like a worme i'th budde
Feede on her damaske cheeke : fhe pin'd in thought,   120
And with a greene and yellow melancholly,
She fate like Patience on a Monument,
Smiling at greefe.   Was not this loue indeede?   123

122. *fate like*] *sat, like* Knt, Wh. Ktly, Huds. Dtn.

---

way in which the present passage should be acted, that I am inclined to think
that Coleridge must have been, quite unconsciously, drawing on his memory of
this charming actress's performance. He had the same opportunities that Lamb
had of seeing Mrs Jordan, who, as Boaden says, 'long continued to delight the
town in Viola, which she acted for the first time' in November, 1785, and she
retired from the stage only a few years before Coleridge's *Notes* were written, if they
were written, as I think, in 1818.—ED.]

119, 120. **let concealment . . . Feede,** etc.] With this expression HENRY (ii,
553) compares, 'At Regina . . . Vulnus alit venis et caeco carpitur igni.'—*Aeneid*,
IV, 2 ; and strangely enough asserts that Virgil is more correct than Shakespeare,
inasmuch as it is 'not concealment, but the love which is concealed, which feeds on
the cheek.' This form of metonymy is too common for criticism. Henry overlooked
the first clause in the line, where there is a metonymy as marked as Viola's: 'Vulnus
alit venis'; Dido does not foster the wound with her veins, but with the blood in her
veins.—ED.

120. **in thought**] This has been variously defined as *melancholy, grief, sorrow,
sorrowful reflection, sadness,* etc. I think, however, that the best and simplest
paraphrase is given by DEIGHTON : 'in brooding over her love.'

122, 123. **Patience . . . greefe**] THEOBALD (ed. i) suggests that it is not impossible that Shakespeare might have 'borrowed' this 'very fine image' from Chaucer's
Assembly of Fowls, 242, 'Dame Pacience, sittynge ther I fonde, With face pale,
upon an hille of sonde.' Compare, also, *Pericles*, V, i, 138 : 'yet thou dost look
Like Patience gazing on kings' graves, and smiling Extremity out of act.' [Much
of the discussion on this passage, (and it is so voluminous that Boswell transposed
it, in the Variorum of 1821, to the end of the play,) was set abroach by MALONE,
who could not comprehend how Patience could smile *at* grief, unless grief
were actually before her face as an object to smile at. It never occurred to him
that she who smiled, was not Patience but Viola's sister ; he evidently supposed
that all Viola's sister had to do was to sit. In order, therefore, that Patience's
smiles should not be wasted he projected a second monumental figure, Grief ;
and took much comfort in a quotation from *Rich. III.*, which, as he said,
'countenanced' his idea,—'like dumb statuas, or breathing stones, Gaz'd each on
other, and look'd deadly pale.' III, vii, 25. If there were only one figure, he
argues, we cannot suppose that '*at* grief' meant '*in* grief,' because 'no statuary
could form a countenance on which smiles and grief should be at once expressed.'
DR PERCY afforded so much relief by suggesting that 'grief' meant *grievance*, that
Malone finally acknowledged that this interpretation might be the true one, but to
the last would not acknowledge that his objection to *at*, and to the impossibility of
a sculptor's making a face expressing two contrary emotions, was without foundation.
STEEVENS professed himself 'unwilling to suppose that a monumental image of
Patience was ever confronted by an emblematical figure of Grief, on purpose that one

We men may fay more, fweare more, but indeed
Our fhewes are more then will : for ftill we proue   125
Much in our vowes, but little in our loue.
   Du. But di'de thy fifter of her loue my Boy ?
   Vio. I am all the daughters of my Fathers houfe,
And all the brothers too : and yet I know not.
Sir, fhall I to this Lady?   130
   Du. I that's the Theame,
To her in hafte : giue her this Iewell : fay,
My loue can giue no place, bide no denay.   *exeunt*   133

---

124. *more, but*] *more : but* Cap. et seq. (subs.)

128. *I am*] *I'm* Pope, Theob. Warb. Johns. Huds.

128, 129. *I am...all the brothers too : and*] *She's...I am all the sons, but* Han.

129. *too : and...not.*] *too—and...not—* Rowe, +. *too ;—and ... not ;—* Cap. *too ;—and...not.*—Knt.

133. *My*] *Thy* F$_2$. *bide*] *bid* F$_4$, Rowe.

---

might sit and smile at the other ; because such a representation might be considered as a satire on human insensibility'; and concludes his note with the remark, 'that to "smile *at* grief " is as juftifiable an expression as to "rejoice *at* prosperity," or repine *at* ill fortune.' BOSWELL's note, one of the best he ever wrote, is :—' The meaning appears to me to be this : "While she was smiling at grief, or in the midst of her grief, her placid resignation made her look like patience on a monument." The monumental figure, I apprehend, is no more said to have smiled at grief than to have pined in thought, or to have been of a green or yellow hue.' This just interpretation of the passage has been accepted by all editors, I believe, since the year it was published. Knight's punctuation, I think, is the best. Among modern critics, HUNTER (i, 404) alone accepts Malone's *two* monumental figures. W. A. WRIGHT remarks with quiet humour : 'Shakespeare may very well have seen some such emblematical figure on a funeral monument, or he may even have imagined it, as he was not wanting in imagination.' 'Grief,' here, is *suffering.*—ED.]

123. **Was not this loue indeede ?**] GERVINUS (i, 549) : As she utters these words, overcome by tears, she breaks off her speech and leaves. [*'Und gleich darauf bricht sie von Thränen ueberwältigt ihre Rede ab und geht.'*—I repeat the original that there can be no question of the fact that Gervinus believed that the young man, Cesario, bursts into tears and cries before the Duke.—ED.]

129. **and yet I know not**] She is thinking of Sebastian, and of the possibility of his having been saved.

133. **denay**] STEEVENS : That is, denial. To *denay* is an antiquated verb sometimes used by Holinshed. So, p. 620 : ' the cardinall, then being bishop of Winchester, tooke vpon him the state of cardinall, which was naied and denaied him.' [*Henrie the sixt*, ed. 1587.] Again, in Warner's *Albions England*, 1602, 2 booke, chap. 10 : ' The old-wife . . . thus did say : The thing (friend Battus) you demaund not gladly I denay.' [p. 46.]—DYCE (*Gloss.*) : ' Of milde denaies, of tender scornes,' etc. Fairfax's trans. of Tasso's *Gerusalemme*, B. xvi. st. 25.

Scena Quinta.

Enter Sir Toby, Sir Andrew, and Fabian.   2

To. Come thy wayes Signior *Fabian.*

Fab. Nay Ile come : if I loofe a fcruple of this fport,
let me be boyl'd to death with Melancholly.   5

To. Wouldft thou not be glad to haue the niggard‒
ly Rafcally fheepe-biter, come by fome notable fhame?   7

---

1. Scene...] Scene VII. Pope, +.   4. *loofe*] *lofe* Ff.
Olivia's Garden. Pope.

---

3. **wayes**] See ABBOTT (§ 25, p. 35) for adverbs ending in *s* formed from the
possessive inflection of nouns. Compare 'other gates,' V, i, 206.—W. A. WRIGHT :
'Ways' is here the old genitive, used adverbially.—INNES demurs ; 'but surely,'
he says, ' " thy " makes this a very difficult explanation. May it not be the plural,
and object of " come "?'

3. **Fabian**] See II, iii, 168. INNES : Fabian is described as 'a servant of
Olivia,' but he treats the two knights as if he were very much on an equality with
them. [It is Rowe who gives us the Dramatis Personæ, and who first designated Fabian as a ' servant.' Fabian uniformly addresses the two knights with the
respectful ' you ' of an inferior.—ED.]

5. **boyl'd**] GREY (i, 229) calls attention to the fact that there was only one
crime for which the penalty, under English laws, was boiling to death, and that
was, poisoning. This law was enacted in Henry VIII.'s time, and under it two
cases occurred where the culprits were so executed. It was repealed by the first of
Edward VI. Grey thinks it probable that 'boiled' should be here *broiled*, not,
however, on legal, but physiological, grounds, because, as he asserts, 'melancholy'
arises from ' a black bile, which lies broiling upon the stomach.'

7. **sheepe-biter**] RANN, HALLIWELL, DYCE : That is, a thief. Halliwell
quotes from Taylor, the Water Poet, *Works*, 1630 : ' Although it be not found in
ancient writers I finde all mutton-eaters are sheepe-biters, And in some places I
have heard and seene, That currish sheepe-biters have hanged beene.'—R. G.
WHITE (ed. i): Unless this is Sir Toby's phrase for *cur*, or *mutton-eater*,—more
probably the former,—I am at a loss to explain it.—SCHMIDT (*Lex.*) : Evidently
equivalent to a morose, surly, and malicious fellow.—R. G. WHITE (*Studies*,
etc., p. 310) : ' Sheep-biter' does not mean ' a morose, surly, malicious fellow,' nor
anything like that. If Dr Schmidt had said it meant a thief, he would have had
the support of good ' authority' (whatever that may be). It was indeed applied to
thieves, as in this line : ' How like a sheep-biting rogue, taken i' the manner !'—
Fletcher, *Rule a Wife*, etc., V, iv, and so it was to malicious persons, as in the following line : ' His hate like a sheep-biter fleering aside.' Tusser, *Envious and Naughtie
Neighbour*, p. 112, ed. 1610. But it was so applied merely because it was a general term of reproach. It means merely ' mutton-eater.' This I suggested in my
first edition, and afterwards I found the following reference to the phrase by Addison : ' Mutton . . . was formerly observed to be the food rather of men of nice and

Fa. I would exult man : you know he brought me out   8
o'fauour with my Lady, about a Beare-baiting heere.

To. To anger him wee'l haue the Beare againe, and   10
we will foole him blacke and blew, fhall we not fir *Andrew?*

An. And we do not, it is pittie of our liues.

Enter Maria.

To. Heere comes the little villaine : How now my   15

9. *o'fauour*] Coll. Wh. Dyce, Cam.   ii, +.
Sta. *of favour* Ff et cet.   14. Enter...] After *villaine*, line 15,
13. *And*] *An* Pope et seq.   Dyce, Cam.
    it is] *'tis* Rowe i. *it's* Rowe

---

delicate appetites than those of strong and robust constitution. For which reason
even to this day we use the word Sheep-biter as a term of reproach, as we do Beef-
eater in a respectful, honourable sense.'—*Tatler*, No. 148. Addison's testimony
(and he mentions that he had consulted antiquaries—in 1709—on the subject of
his paper) leaves no doubt as to the meaning of the compound, and as to its use as
a general term of reproach. But I venture a dissent from his inference in regard to
delicate appetites. Mutton two and three hundred years ago was looked upon as
very inferior food to venison and to beef ; and ' mutton-eater,' coarsened into ' sheep-
biter,' corresponded to the modern 'tripe-eater.'—W. A. WRIGHT: A term of
reproach, taken from a vicious dog. It usually denotes a niggard. So, in Dekker,
The Honest Whore (*Works*, ii, 121) : ' A poor man has but one Ewe, and this
Grandee Sheepe-biter leaues whole Flockes of fat Weathers (whom he may knocke
downe), to deuoure this.'[Second Part, II, i, p. 162, Middleton's *Works*, ed.
Dyce. It may be doubted that Addison is to be followed as to the use, in his own time,
of words current a hundred years earlier, in Elizabethan times. Among the lower
classes, where such terms of reproach mostly originate, it is hardly conceivable
that an eater of mutton should have been held in disgrace. Given the word, ' sheep-
biter,' and any mind of a humorous turn could have detected, as did Taylor, the Water
Poet, that it is equivalent to *mutton-eater ;* but this does not make it a term of reproach.
There can be little doubt, from the foregoing quotations from Fletcher (supplied by
White himself) and from Dekker that the word was originally applied to a dog that
bit or worried sheep,—a dog that has once indulged in this practice, becomes so
worthless and incorrigible that it has to be incontinently killed (' hanged,' says
Taylor, the Water Poet, *supra*), as every one knows who has had any experience in
the keeping of sheep. A third pertinent quotation is in Nashe's *Pierce Pennilesse*,
1592 : ' What curre will not bawle, & be ready to flye on a mans face, when he is
set on by his master, who, if hee bee not by to encourage him, he casts his taile
betwixt his legges, & steales away like a sheepe byter.' p. 35, ed. Grosart.—ED.]

9. **Beare-baiting**] Every one will recall Macaulay's remark that the Puritans
objected to bear-baiting not because it gave pain to the bear but because it gave
pleasure to the spectators.—ED.

13. **pittie of our liues**] Compare, ' If you thinke I come hither as a Lyon, it
were pitty of my life.'—*Mid. N. D.* III, i, 41.

15. **little**] C. C. CLARKE (*Gentleman's Maga.* 1873, p. 538) : With his usual

Mettle of India?   16

16. *Mettle*] *Nettle* Ff, Rowe, +, Cap. Var. Ran. Steev. Var. Sing. Sta. Ktly. *metal* Mal. Var. '21 et cet.

---

felicity, harmony, and consummate taste, the poet has made Maria a *little* woman, and he constantly keeps that fact fresh and green in the mind of the reader. A woman of Amazonian stature indulging in such pranks would be too horrible an infliction ; no one short of Theseus himself,—that queller of Amazons,—could have fitly coped with her. As she is, Maria is perfection,—in her small-sized way.

16. **Mettle of India**] STEEVENS (who adopted in his text, *Nettle* of F₂) : The poet must here mean a zoophyte, called the *Urtica Marina*, abounding in the Indian seas. ' Quæ tacta totius corporis pruritum quendam excitat, unde nomen *urticæ* est sortita.'—Wolfgangi Franzii *Hist. Animal.*, 1665, p. 620. Perhaps the same plant is alluded to by Greene in his *Carde of Fancie*, 1608 : ' the flower of *India* pleasant to be seene, but who so smelleth to it, feeleth present smart.'[p. 46, ed. Grosart.] Again, in his *Mamillia*, 1593 : ' Consider the hearbe of *India* is of pleassant smell, but who so commeth to it feeleth present smart.'[p. 265, ed. Grosart.] ' Mettle' of the First Folio may mean, my *girl of gold*, my *precious girl.*—M. MASON : '*Nettle* of India,' which Steevens has ingeniously explained, certainly better corresponds with Sir Toby's description of Maria,—' here comes the little villain.' The nettle of India is the plant that produces what is called cow-itch, a substance only used for the purpose of tormenting, by its itching quality.—MALONE (who, in 1790, was the first to restore the present text): So, in *1 Hen. IV:* II, iv, 307 : ' Lads, boys, hearts of gold,' etc.; again *Ib.* III, i, 169 : ' —and as bountiful As mines of India '; again in *Hen. VIII:* I, i, 18 : ' To-day the French, All clinquant, all in gold, like heathen gods, Shone down the English ; and tomorrow they Made Britain India ; every man that stood, Show'd like a mine.' So Lyly, *Euphues and his England*, 1580 : ' I see that *India* bringeth golde, but England breedeth goodnesse.'[p. 311, ed. Arber.] Again, in *Wily Beguiled*, 1606 : ' Come, my heart of gold, let's have a dance at the making up of this match.'[p. 254, ed. Hazlitt-Dodsley.] The person there addressed, as in *Twelfth Night*, is a woman. The two words [*metal* and *nettle*] are very frequently confounded in the early editions of our author's plays.—KNIGHT : If Shakespeare had wished to call Maria a *stinging nettle*, he would have been satisfied with naming the indigenous plant,—as he has been in *Rich. II.* and *Hen. V.*,—without going to the Indian seas.—COLLIER : ' Metal of India ' is merely a paraphrase for gold. The supposition that there was some allusion to the ' nettle of India ' is a mere fancy. Robert Greene, who has been vainly quoted on the point, would never have called a *nettle* of India a ' flower of India.'—HUNTER (i, 406) : Neither phrase has been justified by exhibiting it as used elsewhere by Shakespeare, or by any other writers. So far then the two expressions stand on equal grounds. To me *nettle* appears by far the better reading. Maria was about to sting Malvolio, to be a *nettle* to him. [According to Dyce, it was with LETTSOM a matter of doubt whether *Nettle* of the Second Folio were not a mere misprint for ' Mettle.' I share this doubt to the full. Shakespeare did not need to go to India for nettles, nor is there any proof that the *Urtica Marina* was ever called the *Urtica Indica* or *Urtica Marina Indica*, or even ' nettle of India '; nor does it follow that the ' flower ' or ' the hearbe of India ' is a nettle. To suppose that Sir Toby salutes Maria as a nettle, because she was about to torment Malvolio, is to endow the bibulous Knight with the gift of prophecy. Sir Toby

Mar.   Get ye all three into the box tree : *Maluolio's*   17
comming downe this walke, he has beene yonder i'the
Sunne practiſing behauiour to his own ſhadow this halfe
houre : obſerue him for the loue of Mockerie : for I know   20
this Letter wil make a contemplatiue Ideot of him. Cloſe
in the name of ieaſting, lye thou there : for heere comes
the Trowt, that muſt be caught with tickling.   *Exit*
                    Enter Maluolio.

Mal.   'Tis but Fortune, all is fortune. *Maria* once   25
told me ſhe did affect me, and I haue heard her ſelf come
thus neere, that ſhould ſhee fancie, it ſhould bee one of
my complection.   Beſides ſhe vſes me with a more exalted reſpect, then any one elſe that followes her.   What
ſhould I thinke on't ?   30

To.   Heere's an ouer-weening rogue.

17. *box tree*] box-tree F₄.
18. *has*] ha's F₃F₄.
21, 22. *Cloſe in*] Close, in Rowe.
22. *ieaſting, lye*] Ff, Rowe, Pope.
jesting ! lye Theob.+.   *jesting.* [Men
hide themselves] Cap.
23. Exit.] [Throws down a letter,
and exit.] Theob.   [Drops a letter]

(after *there*, line 22) Han. Cap.
24. Scene VIII. Pope,+.
28. *complection*] F₂. *complexion* F₃F₄.
31, etc. Until M.'s exit, all the
speeches of Toby, And. and Fab. are
marked as aside, by Cap.
        weening] weaning Rowe, Pope,
Theob. Warb.

cannot know Maria's errand before she discloses it.   There may be truth in wine,
but not prophesying.   Steevens's concluding sentence shows that he clearly understood the meaning of the text of the First Folio.—ED.]

   21. **contemplatiue**] ABBOTT (p. 497) refers to *As You Like It*, II, vii, 33 :
'That Fooles should be so deepe contemplatiue.'

   23. **tickling**] STEEVENS : Thus, Cogan, in his *Haven of Health*, 1595, 'This
fish of nature loveth flatterie ; for, being in the water, it will suffer it selfe to be
rubbed and clawed, and so be taken.'—HALLIWELL : '*Grope* or *tickle*, a kind of
fishing, by putting one's hand into the water-holes where fish lye, and tickling them
about the gills ; by which means they'll become so quiet, that a man may take them
in his hand, and cast them to land, or if large fish, he may thrust his fingers into
their gills and bring them out.'—*Dict. Rust.*   Catching trout in this manner is an
old and deadly mode of poaching, but it can only be practised in very dry, sultry
weather, and when the water is exceedingly low ; then the country urchins, early
instructed in this destructive practice, wade into the pools, grope for, and easily take
large trout by tickling them.   'Whoop : fut, how he tickles yon trout under the
gilles ! you shall see him take him by and by, with groping flattery.'—Marston's
Antonio and Mellida. [II, p. 23, ed. Halliwell.]   'This is the tamest trout I ever
tickled.'—Beaumont & Fletcher, *The Humorous Lieutenant.* [III, v.]   Hence the
term *trout* came to be used as applied to a foolish person, easily entrapped.

   26. **she**] This refers, of course, to Olivia.

   27. **fancie**] That is, love.—W. A. WRIGHT : It is used again absolutely in *Tro. &
Cress.* V, ii, 165 : 'Never did young man fancy With so eternal and so fix'd a soul.'

Fa. Oh peace : Contemplation makes a rare Turkey　　32
Cocke of him, how he iets vnder his aduanc'd plumes.

And. Slight I could fo beate the Rogue.

To. Peace I fay.　　　　　　　　　　　　　　　　35

Mal. To be Count *Maluolio.*

To. Ah Rogue.

An. Piftoll him, piftoll him.

To. Peace, peace.

Mal. There is example for't : The Lady of the *Stra-*　40
chy, married the yeoman of the wardrobe.

33. *aduanc'd*] *advan'd* F$_3$F$_4$.
34. *Slight*] *'Slife* Rowe, + . *'Slight*
F$_3$F$_4$ et cet.
　Rogue.] *rogue :*— Cap. et seq.
(subs.)
36. Maluolio.] *Malvolio,*— Theob.
Warb. et seq. (subs.)
40, 41. *the* Strachy] Ff, Johns. Cap.
Var. '73, Knt, Coll. Hal. Wh. Dyce,

Cam. Sta. Rlfe, Dtn. Innes. *the Trachy*
Warb. *the strachy* Var. '78 et cet. *the*
duchy Bailey (ii, 238). *the Tragedy*
Bulloch (110). *the County* Kinnear
(p. 168). *Malfi* Elze (p. 180). *the*
Stracci Lloyd ap. Cam. *the Starosty*
Erfurdt (*Archiv f. d. S. d. n. Sp.* 1862,
xxxi, 92).

33. **iets**] STEEVENS : That is, to strut, to agitate the body by a proud motion.
So, in *Arden of Feversham,* 1592 : ' Is now become the steward of his house And
brauely iets it in his silken gowne.' [p. 2, ed. Bullen.]　Again, in Chapman's
Bussy d'Ambois, 1607 : ' They foolish-proud To jet in others plumes so haughtly.'
[p. 15, ed. 1873.]—HALLIWELL : Palsgrave (1530) has, *I jette* with facyon and
countenaunce to set forthe my selfe, *je braggue.* I pray you, se how this felowe
jetteth : *je vous prie, aduisez comment ce compaignon braggue.* [Hereupon follow
nine or ten quotations from the dramatists and elsewhere, none, however, so good as
that furnished by Shakespeare himself in *Cym.* III, iii, 5 : ' The gates of monarchs
Are arch'd so high that giants may jet through And keep their impious turbans on.']

34. **Slight**] HALLIWELL : A contracted form of the petty oath, *by this light.*
' This morning, being the 9th of January, 1633, the kinge was pleas'd to call mee
into his withdrawinge chamber to the windowe, wher he went over all that I had
crosste in Davenants play-booke, and allowing of *faith* and *slight* to bee asseuera-
tions only, and no oathes, markt them to stande, and some other few things, but in
the greater part allowed of my reformations.　This was done upon a complaint of
Mr. Endymion Porters in December.　The kinge is pleasd to take *faith, death,*
slight, for asseverations, and no oaths, to which I doe humbly submit as my masters
judgment ; but under favour conceive them to be oaths, and enter them here, to
declare my opinion and submission.'—Herbert's *Diary.* [Sir Andrew uses this oath
again at III, ii, 14 ; and another weak one : ' Odd's lifelings,' at V, i, 195.　These
were the kind of oaths that Rosalind considered safe : ' By my troth, and in good
earnest, and so God mend mee, and by all pretty oaths that are not dangerous.'—
As You Like It, IV, i, 179.—ED.]

35, 39. W. A. WRIGHT : These speeches are more appropriate to Fabian than
Sir Toby.

40, 41. **Lady of the Strachy,** etc.] HANMER : It is not easy to conjecture what

[40, 41. **The Lady of the Strachy,**]

'Strachy' should be; perhaps *Stratarch*, which (as well as *Strategue*) signifies a General of an Army, a Commander-in-chief. [In Hanmer's First Edition the foregoing note is signed 'Sir T. H.'; in his Second Edition, it is signed 'Warburton.' —ED.] WARBURTON wrote to Theobald (Nichols, *Illust.* ii, 642) that 'Strachy' should be '*Satrape, i. e.* governor.' In his subsequent edition, we find: We should read *Trachy, i. e.* Thrace; for so the old English writers called it. Mandeville says: 'As Trachye and Macedoigne, of which Alisandre was kynge.' It was common to use the article *the* before names of places; and this was no improper instance, where the scene was in Illyria. [Ashton's admirable edition of Maundeville is a reprint of East's reprint of Pynson's edition, 1568. On p. 15, the foregoing sentence quoted by Warburton reads thus: 'that is to say ... Tracy & Macedony, of which Alexander was king.'—ED.]—CAPELL (p. 146): A great stumbling-block, and like to continue so; for what the editor has to propose, is almost too hardy to expect it will meet with such an assent as shall preclude future guesses. First then, it appears to him that 'Strachy' is not the only corruption, for the multitude of definite articles, and other causes, create suspicion that there is error in them too; 'Strachy' should be the name of some place; the 'example' Malvolio wants, is of a lady having sov'reignty somewhere who had marry'd beneath herself; Thessaly (a neighbour country to his) has a city—*Trachyna*, in English—*Trachyne;* and, to be brief, the editor would read if he might—'the lady of *Trachyne* marry'd the yeoman of *her* wardrobe.'—JOHNSON: What we should read is hard to say. Here is an allusion to some old story which I have not yet discovered.—REV. MR SMITH (*ap.* Grey, i, 230): *Straccio* (see Torriano's and Altieri's *Dictionaries*) signifies *rags, clouts,* and *tatters;* and Torriano, in the Grammar, at the end of his *Dictionary,* says that *straccio* was pronounced *stratchy.* So that it is probable that Shakespeare's meaning was this, that the chief Lady of the queen's wardrobe married a yeoman of the king's, who was vastly inferior to her.—STEEVENS: It does not appear that *strachy* was ever an English word, nor will the meaning given it by the Italians be of any use on the present occasion. Perhaps a letter has been misplaced, and we ought to read *starchy; i. e.* the room in which linen underwent the once most complicated operation of *starching.* I do not know that such a word exists; and yet it would not be unanalogically formed from the substantive *starch.* In Harsnet's *Declaration,* 1603, we meet with 'a yeoman of the sprucery'; *i. e.* wardrobe; and in the Northumberland Household-Book, *nursery* is spelt *nurcy. Starchy,* therefore, for *starchery,* may be admitted. In *Rom. & Jul.,* the place where *paste* was made is called the *pastry.* The *lady* who had the care of the linen may be significantly opposed to the *yeoman, i. e.* an inferior officer of the wardrobe. While the *five different coloured starches* were worn, such a term might have been current. In the year 1564, a Dutch woman professed to teach this art to our fair country-women. 'Her usual price,' says Stowe, 'was four or five pounds to teach them how to starch, and twenty shillings how to seeth starch.' The alteration was suggested to me by a typographical error in *The World toss'd at Tennis,* no date, by Middleton and Rowley; where *straches* is printed for *starches.* I cannot fairly be accused of having dealt much in conjectural emendation, and therefore feel the less reluctance to hazard a guess on this desperate passage.—M. MASON (p. 117): It probably denotes some country; perhaps Austrasia, the ancient name for Lorraine.—MALONE: The place in which candles were kept, was formerly called the *chandry;* and in Jonson's *Bartholomew Fair,* a ginger-bread woman is called 'lady of the basket.' The great

[40, 41. The Lady of the Strachy,]

objection to this emendation [Steevens's] is, that from the *starchy* to the *wardrobe* is not what Shakespeare calls a very 'heavy declension.' The 'yeoman of the wardrobe' is not an arbitrary term, but was the proper designation of the wardrobe-keeper in Shakespeare's time. Thus, Florio, *Worlde of Wordes*, 1598: '*Vestiario*, ... a wardrobe keeper, or a yeoman of a wardrobe.' The story which our poet had in view is perhaps alluded to by Lyly in *Euphues and his England*, 1580: 'assuring my selfe that ... there was a certain season when women were to be won, in the which moment they have neither will to deny, nor wit to mistrust. Such a time I haue read a young Gentleman found to obtaine the loue of the Duchesse of *Millayne;* such a time I haue heard that a poore yeoman chose to get the fairest Lady in *Mantua.*' [p. 273, ed. Arber.]—BOSWELL : ' The dutchesse of *Malphey* chose for her husband her seruant *Vlrico.*'—Greene, *Carde of Fancie*, 1593. [p. 119, ed. Grosart. In Webster's play, the 'servants' name is Antonio Bologna.—ED.]— R. P. KNIGHT : The Governors employed by the Greek Emperors in Sicily and Italy from the sixth to the tenth century, were called Στρατηγοί, *Generals*, or *Prætors*, corrupted by the Italians, partly through their own, and partly through the Byzantine pronunciation, to *stratici*, pronounced *stratichi;* which continued to be a title of magistracy in many states long afterwards ; and this word 'Strachy' is only a further corruption of it acquired in its passage through successive French and English translations of some old Italian novel, in which the widow of one of those magistrates had married an inferior officer of her household. See Giannone *Hist. di Napoli*, l. xi, c. vi. [R. G. WHITE (ed. i) pronounced this suggestion 'somewhat plausible.']— NARES : Whatever becomes of the name 'Strachy,' similar occurrences were never wanting, which might be the subject of allusion. R. Brome produces parallel instances in the song of a servant to his lady : ' Madam, Faire truth have told That queens of old Have now and then Married with private men. A countess was no blusher To wed her usher. Without remorse A lady took her horse-Keeper in wedlock.'—*New Acad.* IV, i. One of these might be a lady of the *strachy*. Such examples were never rare. Lord Bacon's daughter married her gentleman-usher, Underhill ; and, though she was not a countess, her birth was noble. It is also asked by another dramatist, ' Has not a deputy married his cook-maid ? An alderman's widow one that was her turn-broach [*i. e.* turn-spit] ?'—Beau. & Fl. *Wit at Seven Weapons*, III, i.—BECKET (p. 241) : I would read ' the lady of the *stitch'ry*'; this will mean the companion of some distinguished female ; one who sits at needle-work with her, and consequently of a superior situation in life to the 'yeoman.' Thus, in *Coriolanus*, I, iii, 75 : ' Come, lay aside your stitchery.'—COLLIER : 'Strachy' [may have been] the name of some noble family of which one of the female branches had condescended to marry a menial. Possibly that family was the Strozzi of Florence, [which the copyist of Shakespeare's MS converted into] *Strozzi* or *Strozzy*. *Strozzy* in old writing would look like ' Strachy.'—KNIGHT : The context points to some corruption of the name of a *place*. Malvolio would hardly say ' the *lady*' of the governor, for the *widow* of the governor ; but he would say, the *lady* of such a land, for the *princess*. Where the scene of the elevation of ' the yeoman of the wardrobe' was placed is of little consequence. It might be Astrakhan— Astracan—easily enough contracted into *A-strachy*, and as easily metamorphosed by a printer into *the* Strachy.—HUNTER (i, 380), in discussing the Date of the present play, suggests that, in the ridicule which Shakespeare throws on Malvolio, and on the Puritan character in general, he was giving what aid and countenance he could to

[40, 41. The Lady of the Strachy,]

Dr Harsnet, who made a bitter attack on certain Puritans, in his *Discovery of the fraudulent practices of John Darrel*, etc., 1599 ; these 'practices' took place in the house of Nicholas Starkey or Starchy, and Hunter thinks it 'as reasonable a conjecture as is likely to be offered' that Shakespeare introduced the name 'Strachy' on account of its 'near resemblance to the name *Starchy*, and as a kind of intimation to his audience to expect something on a topic which was at that time of no small public interest.' This expectation was afterwards fulfilled in the supposed lunacy of Malvolio, and the ludicrous travestie of exorcism perpetrated by Feste.—HALLI-WELL : That is, the lawyer's or judge's lady or widow. The term is now only preserved in the Russian language, but it was probably taken by Shakespeare from some novel or play, upon which he may have founded the comic incidents of this drama. ' From the list of all the crown servants of Russia, sent every year to the State Secretary of the Home Department at St. Petersburg ; in which, for 1825 and 1826, Procureur Botwinko was reported to be imprisoned at Vilna for the above case, and the *Strapchy* of Oszmiana was acting in his stead as procureur *pro tem.*'— *Household Words*, 15 March, 1851: Various alterations of 'strachy' have been suggested : . . . *saucery, sophy.* Strachy was and is an English family surname. William Strachey published *Lawes*, etc., for Virginia, 1612, and there are verses by him preserved in MS, Ashmol, 781. [See *Tempest*, p. 313, of this ed.] It may be worth notice that one of the characters in *Gl' Inganni*, by Secchi, is described as, ' *Straccia*, Servidor del Capitano,' though there is no probability that the name of this inferior personage could have suggested that found in the present comedy. —Colonel HENRY STRACHEY (p. 5) : I think it may be shown that Steevens was probably right in his conjectural emendation, and failed only to state his own case in a conclusive way. A corroboration of this may be found in the very passage of the old annalist to which he refers,—too briefly,—and I now subjoin it, from Stow's *Annals*, p. 868, ed. 1631 : 'In the year 1563, at which time began the civill dissention in Flanders, and very many Netherlanders fled into this land, with their wives children and whole families.' (Page 869) : 'In the year one thousand five hundred and sixty foure, Mistris Dinghen Van-den-Plasse, born at Teenen in Flanders, daughter to a worshipfull Knight of that province, with her husband, came to London for their better safeties, and there professed herself a Starcher ; wherein she excelled, and [to] whom her own nation presently repaired ; and payed her very liberally for her work. Some very few of the best and most curious wives of that time observing the neatnesse and delicacy of the Dutch for whiteness and fine wearing of linen, made them Cambricke Ruffes, and sent them to Mistris Dinghen to starch ; and after a while they made them ruffes of lawn, which was at that time a stuffe most strange and wonderfull ; and thereupon rose a generall scoffe or byword that shortly they would make Ruffes of spiders' web ; and then they began to send their daughters and neatest [*sic.* qu. *nearest ?*] kinswomen to Mistris Dinghen to learn how to starch. Her usual price at that time was foure or five pounds to teach them how to starch, and twenty shillings how to seethe starch. This Mistris Dinghen was the first that ever taught starching in England.' Here we find that the ' Dutch woman' of Steevens was a Flemish *Lady* of equestrian parentage, and therefore a born gentlewoman ; and there is no ground for supposing that her husband, who accompanied her from Flanders, was anything less than a gentleman of the same country and rank. So that they themselves cannot with any probability be identified with the ' Lady' and the ' Yeoman' of the mesalliance. The Lady we

[40, 41. **The Lady of the Strachy,**]

are in quest of would be more probably one of the English patronesses or pupils of
the Flemish artist; among 'the best and most curious wives of that time'; or one
of 'their daughters or nearest kinswomen'—presumably of the same rank, as 'the
daughter of a worshipfull knight.' We know that new fashions in dress begin at the
upper end of the social scale, and descend afterwards, through old clothes and inferior copies, to 'the lower orders'; and in those days ladies of the higher class put
their own hands to many details of domestic work since relegated to servants. The
'Cambricke' and 'Lawn,' now common enough, but then 'most strange and wonderfull stuffe,' must have been costly materials at that time; and 'the usual price'
charged by the Flemish Professor 'for teaching how to starch' them,—considering
the relative value of money in the middle of the 16th century and the end of the
19th—far exceed the fees now paid by our west-end young ladies for a course of
lectures on cookery or other of the finer arts and sciences at the University of South
Kensington. A *Lady*, 'therefore, may be admitted' for the direction of a Starchery,—
in the early days of the new art,—at that time Queen Elizabeth was in her prime,—
aet. 31,—but (if it may be said without lèse-majesté) her beauty was not like that
of her remote ancestress,—'when unadorned adorned the most,'—nor was Queen
Bess 'the farest of her' subjects; and she certainly was not behind the 'best and
most curious' of her country women, in resorting to the decorations of the new
Flemish art, as testified by the noli-me-osculari chevaux-de-frise of her contemporary portraits. The Starchery would thus become a necessary adjunct to the royal
laundry, of sufficient importance to be placed under the charge of a lady attached
to the Queen's court. Such a person might have been 'the daughter of a Count,'
like 'the fair Olivia,'—or of a 'worshipfull knight,'—as 'Mistress Dingen-van-den-
Plasse' of Brabant,—or as the Queen's own mother Anne, daughter of Sir Thomas
Boleyne,—perhaps some Alice Ford or Anne Page of Windsor, whose 'articles of
gentry' were not to be bartered for 'hack' knighthood. The least of these would
be as far above the Yeoman in social rank as the Countess was to her Steward, who
is repeatedly spoken of as a 'gentleman,' and was superior in manners and education to the two Knights. We cannot positively identify the Yeoman in question;
but indirect evidence of the existence of such a person may be found in the history
of 'the King's wardrobe.' This was formerly a separate department of the royal
household, and the office of *Master of the Wardrobe* was held by a person of high
rank. In the latter part of Elizabeth's reign the Master, Sir John Fortescue, also
held other high offices, and the so-called Wardrobe was also used as a depository for
important state papers. Under such conditions, it is obvious, that the lower duties
of the Wardrobe proper must have been committed to a subordinate of inferior rank,
who, according to the custom of that time, would be called 'the Yeoman'; an indispensable person; though not so important as to claim particular mention in historical
records. The office of the Warbrobe was abolished a hundred years after Elizabeth's
death in 1603, and nothing now remains of the old habitation but its locality and
name. The Starchery, as a distinct department of the royal laundry, would probably disappear with Elizabeth herself; the yeoman still survives in the ranks of the
royal body-guard. . . . The reading *Starchy*, proposed by Steevens, thus becomes
intelligible and appropriate, when applied to the Queen's house-hold. [As to the
English family named Strachey, mentioned by Halliwell, whereof the head and
earliest known ancestor has been brought into an imaginary connection with Shakespeare, Col. Strachey remarks in conclusion that 'this family could not, in any way,

An. Fie on him Iezabel.   42

Fa. O peace, now he's deepely in : looke how imagination blowes him.

Mal. Hauing beene three moneths married to her,   45
fitting in my ftate.

To. O for a ftone-bow to hit him in the eye.   47

43. *in : looke*] *in. Look* Ktly.   46. *ftate.*] *state*— Pope et seq. (subs.)

---

be connected with Shakespeare's "Lady of the Strachy." ' To me the insuperable
objection to all the foregoing emendations is that we are not thereby advanced one
jot. What help is there to be found in hearing that the Lady of the Stracci or of
the Strozzi or of the Starchy married the Yeoman of the Wardrobe, when we know
no more about any of them than we do about the Lady of the Strachy herself?
Unless the instance of some particular Lady, with a story attached, be adduced,
it is merely an exchange of one unknown name for another unknown name ; and,
like Dr Johnson's whirlpool, it becomes motion without progression. In a 'desperate' case like the present, there can be no possible objection to the assumption that
we have here a misprint. No one who has examined Halliwell's *Dictionary of
Misprints*, where we find that 'Juggler' has been misprinted *tailor*, and 'oysters'
misprinted *eye-sores*, will hesitate to agree with Halliwell when he says that 'the
unsettled spellings of our ancestors render almost any emendation, however extravagant, a typographical possibility'; but, first, the misprint must be proved to be a
misprint, and, next, the emendation must be an emendation. Steevens's 'Straches'
for *Starches* undoubtedly suggests the possibility of a misprint here ; this possibility
would become a certainty were there known to history any Lady of the Starchy
who had married beneath her; without this knowledge, *Starchy* is no better than
'Strachy,' and the change can hardly be called a genuine emendation.—ED.]

42. Iezabel] It is sufficient for Sir Andrew that 'Jezebel' sounds insulting.
According to the Cam. Ed., LLOYD conjectured that we should read *her* instead of
'him.' This ingeniously makes Sir Andrew's remark apply to the Lady of the
Strachy. It saves the knight's weak intellect at the expense of two letters. Is it
worth them ?—ED.

43. deepely in] This has been interpreted by DEIGHTON, 'now he's well into
the snare'; but he has not yet been caught in the snare. It rather means, I think,
now he is deeply lost in his wild fancies.—ED.

44. blowes him] STEEVENS : That is, puffs him up. So, in *Ant. & Cleop.* V,
ii, 352 : 'Here on her breast There is a vent of blood and something blown.'

46. state] STEEVENS : This signified a chair with a canopy over it. So, in
1 Hen. IV : II, iv, 416 : 'This chair shall be my state.'—W. A. WRIGHT : The
'state' was properly the canopy itself. Compare Milton, x, 445 : 'Invisible
Ascended his high throne, which, under state Of richest texture spread, at the
upper end Was placed in regal lustre.' [Cotgrave has *'Dais* or *Diaz.* A cloth
of Estate, Canopie, or Heauen, that stands ouer the heads of Princes thrones ; also
the whole State, or seat of Estate; also the boords of a beds teaster whereat the
valances be hanged.']

47. stone-bow] JOHNSON : That is, a cross-bow, a bow which shoots stones.—
STEEVENS : Thus, in Marston's *Dutch Courtezan*, 1605 : 'the drawer . . . knowing
that whosoever will hit the mark of profit must, like those that shoot in stone-bows,

Mal. Calling my Officers about me, in my branch'd   48
Veluet gowne : hauing come from a day bedde, where I
haue left *Oliuia* fleeping.   50

To. Fire and Brimftone.

Fa. O peace, peace.

Mal. And then to haue the humor of ftate : and after
a demure trauaile of regard : telling them I knowe my
place,as I would they fhould doe theirs : to aske for my   55
kinfman *Toby.*

To. Boltes and fhackles.

Fa. Oh peace, peace, peace, now, now.

Mal. Seauen of my people with an obedient ftart,   59

49. *day bedde*] *day-bed* Rowe. (subs.)
50. *fleeping.*] *sleeping :* Cap. et seq. (subs.)
54. *regard :*] *regard,* Rowe et seq. (subs.)
55. *theirs :*] *theirs—* Rowe et seq.
56. *kinfman*] *Uncle* Rowe ii, +. *Toby.*] *Toby—* Rowe et seq. (subs.)
58. *peace, now*] *peace ; now* Rowe ii. *peace ! now* Cap. et seq. (subs.)

wink with one eye.' [I, i.] Again, in Beaumont & Fletcher, *A King and no King :* 'Children will shortly take him for a wall And set their stone-bows in his forehead.' [V, i.]—HALLIWELL : Thus, 'Hailstones full of wrath shall be cast as out of a stone bow.'—*Book of Wisdom*, v, 22.

48. **branch'd**] W. A. WRIGHT : That is, ornamented with patterns of leaves and flowers. Cotgrave gives : '*Fueillage :* m. Branched worke, in Painting, or in Tapistrie.' And, '*Velours figuré.* Branched Veluet.' Compare, Ford, *The Witch of Edmonton*, III, iii : 'Th' other's cloak branch'd velvet, black, velvet-lin'd his suit.'

49. **day bedde**] That is, a couch, or sofa. 'Day-beds' were apparently quite as common formerly as are couches or lounges now. Thus, in Beaumont & Fletcher, *Rule a Wife and have a Wife*, III, i : 'Is the great couch up, the Duke of Medina sent? *Altea.* 'Tis up and ready. *Margarita.* And day-beds in all chambers? *Altea.* In all, lady.'

53. **humor of state**] COLLIER (ed. ii) : Few words have been more frequently printed for each other than 'humour' and *honour ;* here the MS wrote *honour* in the margin and erased 'humour' in the text. The '*honour* of state' must mean the honour due to state ; and the 'humour of state' the airs Malvolio may mean to give himself upon his exaltation. As the case is doubtful, we [retain the original word]. —R. G. WHITE : *Honour* is possibly the right word, as 'humour' might also possibly have been, if 'honour' had been found in the text.—ANON. (*Blackwood*, Aug. 1853, p. 201) : 'Humour of state' means the high airs, the capricious insolence, of authority, which is what Malvolio is glorying that he shall by and by have it in his power to exhibit.

54. **demure trauaile of regard**] That is, scanning his 'officers' gravely one by one.

57. **Boltes and shackles**] Suggestive of a prison.

59. **Seauen of my people**] This extravagant number shows how 'deeply' Malvolio was 'in.'

make out for him : I frowne the while,   and perchance   60
winde vp my watch, or play with my fome rich Iewell :
Toby approaches; curtfies there to me.

   To.   Shall this fellow liue ?

   Fa.   Though our filence be drawne from vs with cars,
yet peace.   65

---

61. *my fome*] F₂, Mal. Var. '21, Knt, Hal. Sing. Dyce i.   *my—some* Coll. Wh. Cam. Ktly, Rlfe, Dtn.   *my handsome* Daniel.   *fome* F₃F₄ et cet.

   62. *curtfies*] *court'sies* Mal.   *courtesies* Knt.

    me.] *me :* Cap. et seq. (subs.)

   64. *with cars*] *with cares* Ff, Rowe, +, Cap. Var. '73.   *by th'ears* Han. Coll. ii,

iii (MS), Dyce ii, iii, Rlfe, Huds.   *with ears* Knt (misprint ?).   *with cats* (*i. e.* whips) Jackson.   *with cords* Wh.   *with screws* Bailey (i, 206).   *with crows* (*i. e.* crow-bars) Orger.   *with cues* Joicey (*N. & Qu.* VIII, vi, 283, 1894).   *with racks* Mitford ap. Cam.   *with curs* Anon. ap. Cam.

---

   61. **watch**] Watches were first brought to England from Germany in 1577. Spring pocket-watches (watches properly so called) have had their invention ascribed to Dr Hooke, . . . he appears certainly to have produced what is called the pendulum watch about 1658.—HAYDN, *Dict. of Dates.*

   61. **with my some rich Iewell**] STEEVENS : This may signify, ' and play with some rich jewel of *my own,*' some ornament appended to *my* person.   He is entertaining himself with ideas of future magnificence.—COLLIER : It is more natural to suppose that Malvolio, having mentioned his watch, then rather a rarity, wishes to enumerate some other valuable in his possession, and pauses after ' or play with my,' following it up with the words ' some rich jewel,' not being able on the sudden to name any one in particular.—DYCE (ed. ii) : ' My ' is an accidental repetition, occasioned by the preceding ' *my* watch.'—B. NICHOLSON (*New Sh. Soc. Trans.* 1875–6, p. 154) : There is here a true touch of nature and a most humorous one.   While Sir Toby is being fetched to the presence, the Lord Malvolio would frowningly wind up his watch or play with—and here from force of habit he fingers [his badge of office], and is about to add ' play with my chain,' but suddenly remembering that he would be no longer a steward, or other gold-chained attendant, he stops short, and then confusedly alters his phrase to—' some rich jewel.' [This explanation carries instant and complete conviction to the present—ED.]

   62. **Toby**] W. A. WRIGHT : Malvolio's ' humour of state ' begins to show itself in this familiarity with Sir Toby's Christian name.

   62. **curtsies**] REED : This word was employed to express acts of civility and reverence by either men or women.   Lord Herbert of Cherbury, in his *Life*, speaking of dancing, recommends that accomplishment to youth, ' that he may know how to come in and go out of a room where company is, how to make courtesies handsomely, according to the several degrees of persons he shall encounter.'

   63. **Shall this fellow liue ?**] Note the ascending degrees of Sir Toby's wrath. First ' rogue,' then ' hit him in the eye,' then ' Fire and brimstone,' next, to clap him in prison, and here, to hang him.   From this point his fury subsides and the humour of the situation begins to have sway.—ED.

   64. **drawne from vs with cars**] JOHNSON : I believe the true reading is : ' drawn from us with *carts.*'   Compare *Two Gent.* III, i, 265 : ' yet I am in love ;

Mal. I extend my hand to him thus : quenching my　　66
familiar fmile with an auftere regard of controll.

To. And do's not *Toby* take you a blow o'the lippes,
then ?　　　　　　　　　　　　　　　　　　　　　　　　　69

67. *controll.*] *controul;* Cap. et seq.　　68. *o'the*] *on the* Rowe i.
(subs.)

but a team of horse shall not pluck that from me.' So, in this play, III, ii, 60 :
'oxen and wainropes cannot hale them together.'—STEEVENS : It is well known
that 'cars' and *carts* have the same meaning.—TYRWHITT (p. 27) : If I were to
suggest a word in place of 'cars,' which I think is a corruption, it should be *cables*.
[COLERIDGE (p. 121) makes the same suggestion.] It may be worth remarking that
the leading ideas of Malvolio, in his 'humour of state,' bear a strong resemblance
to those of Alnaschar in *The Arabian Nights.*—HUNTER (i, 406) : If we must alter
'cars,' I would suggest *cart-ropes*, on the ground that this may be one of the many
allusions to passages of Scripture which are found in these plays. 'Woe unto them
that draw iniquity with cords of vanity, and sin, as it were, with a cart-rope.'—
Isaiah v, 18. [From this same verse of Isaiah, R. G. White subsequently drew his
emendation, *cords.*—ED.]—WALKER (*Crit.* ii, 7) : I believe that the true reading
is *racks*, and that it was written 'cars' by a species of mental confusion, which we
have all at times experienced, the *c* and the *r* changing places in the writer's
thoughts. [In proposing *racks* Walker was anticipated by 'Dent, MS,' according
to Halliwell, and also by Mitford, according to the *Text. Notes* of the Cam. Ed.]
—LETTSOM (Footnote to Walker) approves of Walker's emendation, and remarks
that it 'speaks for itself.'—STAUNTON considered it preferable to any suggestion
that had been previously made.—SINGER (*Sh. Vind.* p. 66) : We should read,
'with *tears*.' Their risible faculties were so excited by the ridiculous conduct of
Malvolio, that to suppress loud laughter brought tears into their eyes.—DYCE
(ed. ii) : Hanmer's reading, I feel convinced, is what the author wrote. Formerly
'bith' was very common as the contraction of 'by the'; and therefore 'bith ears'
might easily be corrupted into 'with cars.'—R. G. WHITE (ed. i) : *Cords* for 'cars'
would seem an obvious correction. [In White's Second Edition the text reads *cords*,
without any note or comment to intimate that it is the Editor's own word, and not
in the Folio. In his general *Preface*, White tells us that 'in determining what
passages were sufficiently obscure to justify explanation [he] took advice of his
washerwoman.' It is evident that he had consulted her on the present occasion, and that she had emphatically decided in favour of *cords*, as synonymous to
lines. It is a little remarkable that her voice did not plead successfully for the
Lady of the Starchy.—ED.]—HUDSON : I have little doubt the text should be
wi' th' ears : for the Poet very often uses *with* in such cases where we should
use *by*, and the double elision of *with* and *the*, so as to make one syllable, is very
frequent with him.—W. A. WRIGHT : Shakespeare may have read of the fate of
Mettus Fuffetius who was torn asunder by chariots for treachery by the orders of
Tullus Hostilius. See Virgil, *Æn.*, viii, 642–5. [Fabian means that they must not
speak even though the greatest imaginable strain were applied to make them break
silence. To express this heavy strain, Shakespeare uses the word 'cars';
therewith I am content ; and do not wish to abridge the happiness of my neighbour
if he find more vigorous agents in *cart-ropes, racks, screws, cords, cats,* or *crows*.
—ED.]

Mal. Saying, Cofine *Toby*, my Fortunes hauing caft   70
me on your Neece, giue me this prerogatiue of fpeech.

To. What, what ? .

Mal. You muft amend your drunkenneffe .

To. Out fcab.

Fab. Nay patience, or we breake the finewes of our   75
plot *?*

Mal. Befides you wafte the treafure of your time,
with a foolifh knight .

And. That's mee I warrant you.

Mal. One fir *Andrew*.   80

And. I knew 'twas I, for many do call mee foole.

Mal. What employment haue we heere ?

Fa. Now is the Woodcocke neere the gin.   83

---

70. *Cofine*] *Uncle* Rowe ii, +.
71. *giue*] *gives* Coll. MS. ap. Cam.
   fpeech.] *fpeech:* Ff. *fpeech—*
Rowe.
76. *plot?*] Ff. *plot.* Rowe.
78. *knight.*] Ff. *knight—* Rowe, +
knight; Cap. et seq. (subs.)

79. *you.*] *you:* Ff.
80. Andrew.]   *Andrew,—* Theob.
Andrew: Cap. et seq. (subs.)
82. *employment*] *implement* Theob.
conj. Han.
   [Taking up a Letter. Rowe. (the
Letter. Theob.)

---

68. **Toby**] Possibly, in a modern text, this might be placed in quotation marks,
as an echo of Malvolio's 'Toby' in line 62.—ED.

68. **take you a blow**] W. A. WRIGHT : Compare *Hen. V:* IV, i, 231 : ' By this
hand, I will take thee a box on the ear.'—DEIGHTON : Compare *Meas. for Meas.*
II, i, 189 : 'he took you a box on the ear'; *Tam. of the Shr.* III, ii, 165 : 'took
him such a cuff.'

74. **scab**] Still in current use in this country, applied to those who refuse to join
in a workman's strike. See *Much Ado*, III, iii, 99 (of this ed.), where it is used in
a double sense.—ED.

82. **employment**] WARBURTON : Equivalent to, ' What's to do here ?' [In V, i,
of Chapman's *Widow's Tears*, Lysander enters with a crow-bar, halter, etc., wherewith to remove from the tomb a corpse which was supposed to be that of himself,—
the plot is the familiar story of the *Matron of Ephesus*,—and says to Cynthia ' my
stay hath been prolong'd With hunting obscure nookes for these emploiments.' In
a note REED says that ' employments ' is here used in the same sense as *implements*,
and that it may be defended by its use by Malvolio in the present passage. WALKER
(*Crit.* iii, 86) quotes the lines from *The Widow's Tears*, with Reed's note thereon';
and observes : ' Surely we should read, in both passages, *implement* and *implements*,
Imploiment—implement.' However needful may be the change in Chapman's
Comedy, it is not so manifest an improvement here. Lysander is not Malvolio.
The steward is still acting the imaginary Lord, and therefore lofty speech is appropriate. I think ' employment ' should stand. Neither Reed nor Walker seems to
have been aware that THEOBALD (Nichols, *Illust.* ii, 356) had proposed *implement*,
and that HANMER had adopted it.—ED.]

To. Oh peace, and the ſpirit of humors intimate rea-
ding aloud to him.   85
Mal. By my life this is my Ladies hand : theſe bee her
very *C's*, her *U's*, and her *T's*, and thus makes ſhee het
great *P's*. It is in contempt of queſtion her hand.   88

84. *and*] *Now* Rowe, +.   *her* U's F$_3$.
85. *him.*] *him!* Rowe ii et seq.   87. *het*] F$_1$.
87, 89. *her* U's] F$_4$.   *her* V's F$_2$.   88. *contempt of*] *contempt to* F$_3$F$_4$.

83, 84. **Fa. . . . To.**] ELZE (p. 181) : A nice discrimination between the characters of Fabian and Sir Toby leads to the suspicion that the prefixes of these two
speeches have been most likely transposed and should be altered.

83. **Woodcocke**] WILLUGHBY (p. 290) : Among us in England this Bird is
infamous for its simplicity or folly ; so that a *Woodcock* is Proverbially used for a
simple foolish person. [The incomparable Feste uses the bird with effect in his
exorcism of Malvolio.—ED.]

83. **gin**] W. A. WRIGHT : An abbreviated form of *engine*, which originally
denoted anything made with skill (Lat. *ingenium*).   So in Chaucer's *Squire's Tale*
(10442) : ' He that it wrought, he cowthe many a gyn'; that is, a skilful contrivance.

87. To understand the *Text. Note*, it is to be observed that the Italic ' *U* ' is one
which is used indifferently for Italic *V* or *U;* as is frequently to be seen in the prefixes to Viola's speeches.   It is the same letter in F$_4$.   It is an Italic *V* in F$_2$, and
an unmistakeable Italic *U* in F$_3$.   As far as the Folio is concerned, we have quite
as much right to say that the letter is a V as a U.—ED.

88. **great P's**] STEEVENS : In the direction of the letter which Malvolio reads,
there is neither a C, nor a P, to be found.—MALONE : This was perhaps an oversight in Shakespeare.   It is remarkable, that in the repetition of the passages in
letters, which have been produced in a former part of a play, he very often makes
his characters deviate from the words before used, though they have the paper itself
in their hands, and though they appear to recite, not the substance, but the very
words.   So, in *All's Well*, V, iii, 312, Helen says, ' here's your letter ; this it says :
" When from my finger you can get this ring And are by me with child," etc.'; yet
in III, ii, 60, she reads this very letter aloud ; and there the words are different and
in plain prose : ' When thou canst get the ring upon my finger, which never shall
come off, and shew me a child begotten of thy body,' etc.   Had she spoken in
either case from memory, the deviation might be easily accounted for ; but, in both
places, she reads the words from Bertram's letter.—RITSON : From the usual custom
of Shakespeare's age, we may easily suppose the whole direction to have run thus :
' To the Unknown belov'd, this, and my good wishes, with Care Present.'—HALLI-
WELL : The usual address of letters, in Shakespeare's time, amongst equals, was
merely, ' to my loving friend give this,' to which the words *with speed* were sometimes added.   Instead of *give this* were sometimes the words, *these be delivered*, or
deliver these.—W. A. WRIGHT : If Ritson's supposition be correct, no more needs
be said on the point ; but I have grave doubts about it.—INNES : It is an obvious
and simple way out of the difficulty to suppose that Malvolio does not read the
whole of the address aloud, but that would not fit well with so precise a character.
Probably Shakespeare merely named letters that would sound well, knowing that no
audience would detect a discrepancy.   [See ' throwne,' V. i, 391.]

An.   Her *C's*, her *U's*, and her *T's*: why that?

Mal.   *To the vnknowne belou'd, this, and my good Wiſhes* :   90
Her very Phraſes : By your leaue wax. Soft, and the im-
preſſure her *Lucrece*, with which ſhe vſes to ſeale : tis my
Lady : To whom ſhould this be?

Fab.   This winnes him, Liuer and all.

Mal.   *Ioue knowes I loue, but who, Lips do not mooue, no*   95
man muſt know.   No man muſt know.   What followes?

89. *her* T's :] *her Ts and Ps !* Ktly.	(reading *Alas ! but who,*) Han. Two
90. [Reads.] Cap. [Reads the super-	lines, Johns. Var. '73, Huds. Four
scription.] Coll. iii.	lines. Cap. et seq.
91. *Soft,*] *Soft !* Rowe. *soft ;* Cap.	95. but who,] *but who ?* Cap. et seq.
93. [Opes the Letter.] Cap.	Lips] *Lips*, Cap. (Errata.) Wh.
95, 100. [Reads.] Cap.	Glo. Cam. Dyce ii, iii, Huds. Dtn.
95, 96. Ioue ... know.] Two lines	96. *know.*] *know—* Rowe, +.

88. **contempt of question**] W. A. WRIGHT : That is, beyond the possibility of
dispute ; so obvious, that to question it is absurd.

91. **wax.   Soft**,] Strangely enough, MALONE supposed that ' Soft' applied to
the wax ; he referred to the custom of sealing letters with soft wax, and, in proof,
quoted from Middleton's *Your Five Gallants*, II, iii : ' Fetch a pennyworth of soft
wax to seal letters'; and also Falstaff's speech in *2 Hen. IV :* IV, iii, 140: ' I have
him already tempering between my finger and my thumb, and shortly will I seal with
him.'—STEEVENS : I do not suppose that ' Soft !' has any reference to the wax ; but
is merely an exclamation equivalent to ' Softly !' *i. e.* be not in too much haste.
Thus, in *The Mer. of Ven.* IV, i, 320 : ' Soft ! The Jew shall have all justice ;
soft ! no haste.'   I may also observe, that though it was anciently the custom (as it
still is) to seal certain legal instruments with soft and pliable wax, familiar letters
(of which I have seen specimens from the time of Henry VI. to James I.) were
secured with wax as glossy and firm as that employed in the present year.

91. **By your leaue**] Thus, also, in *Lear*, IV, vi, 258, when Edgar opens a letter he says, ' Leave, gentle wax.'   And Imogen says, ' Good wax, thy leave.'—
Cym. III, ii, 35.

92. **Lucrece**] WHITER (p. 42, footnote) : Everything that we read in our ancient
authors respecting Lucretia appears to remind us of the source from which it is
derived, and to point out how familiarly her picture or representation is impressed
on the mind of the writer.   She seems to have been a common subject for engraving
on seals. [The present passage is here quoted, and also the reference to ' Lucrece '
in line 100.] Nay, so common were her portraits, that she became the figure on the
Sign of the King's Printer Berthelette in Fleet-street, who flourished about the year
1540.   A cut of her is sometimes to be seen in his books.—HALLIWELL gives an
engraving and a minute description of an antique ring, bearing an engraved head of
Lucretia, in the possession of Lord Londesborough.   But W. A. WRIGHT says that
' it is very doubtful indeed whether it represents Lucretia at all, and being in niello
it could not have been used as a signet ring.'

95, 96. **Ioue . . . mooue, no man must know**] CAPELL'S division of this prose
into four lines of verse has been properly, and almost uniformly, followed.   Unfortu-

The numbers alter d : No man muft know,   97
If this fhould be thee *Maluolio ?*
  To.   Marrie hang thee brocke.
  Mal.   I may command where I adore, but filence like a Lu-   100
      creffe knife :
With bloodleffe ftroke my heart doth gore, M. O. A. I. doth
          fway my life.   103

97. *numbers alter d :*] Ff. *numbers*
alter'd— Rowe i. *number's alter'd*—
Rowe ii, Theob. Warb. Johns. Knt,
Coll. Wh. i. *numbers alter*— Han.
number is alter'd Var. '73. *numbers
alter'd !* Cap. et cet.
  100, 101. Lucreffe knife] F_2. Lucrefs

wife F_3F_4. *Lucrece knife* Rowe ii et
seq. *Lucrece' knife* Walker (*Crit.* ii,
101), Dyce, Huds.
  100–103. Four lines, Han. Johns. et
seq.
  102. bloodleffe] *boldness* Rowe i.

nately, not so uniform has been the adoption of his excellent comma after 'Lips',
which converts the phrase into a command to 'Lips' not to move.—ED.

  97. **The numbers alter d**] That is, the versification. Thus, *Hamlet*, II, ii,
120 : 'O dear Ophelia, I am ill at these numbers.' It will not escape notice that
lines 97 and 98 are printed as a rhyming couplet ; an arrangement which can be
merely the vagary of a compositor. Although Malvolio says, in reference to lines
100–103, that the metre is altered, he does not proceed at once to read these lines,
but is distracted by the enigma in what he has already read.—ED.

  99. **brocke**] RITSON (*Remarks*, p. 64) : That is, a badger. Sir Toby uses the
word as a term of contempt, as if he had said, 'hang thee, *cur !*' 'Out, *filth !*'—
MALONE : That is, thou vain, conceited coxcomb, thou over-weening rogue ! So, in
The Merrie Conceited Jests of George Peele, 1657 : 'This self-conceited brock had
George invited to half a score sheets of paper,' [ii, 289, ed. *Dyce.* As W. A.
WRIGHT says, the epithet here, in this quotation from Peele, 'supplies the sense
which Malone would attribute to "brock."']—HALLIWELL : The word is frequently
used by Jonson, and is of common occurrence in many contemporary writers. As a
term of contempt it is still used in Scotland and in some of the counties of England.

  102. **M. O. A. I.**] HALLIWELL : This 'fustian riddle,' either purposely meaningless, or intended for, My Own Adored Idol, or some such words, or cypher, is
imitated from similar enigmas which were current at the time. An example occurs
in the *Book of Merry Riddles*, 1629 : 'M. and J. made great mone, When C. upon
C. was left alone.—*Solution.* That is, Mary and John made great mone, When
Christ on a Crosse was left alone.'—FLEAY (*Shakespeariana*, 1884, i, 136) : I
believe that Malvolio was a representation of Marston's vanity. . . . At any rate,
there is a singular likeness between the names of Malevole [in Marston's *Malcontent*] and the steward Malvolio, and a still more singular agreement between **IO** :
MA :, Marston's abbreviated signature, and the M. O. A. I. of the letter addressed
to **MAlvolIO.** These anagram conceits are so common in the sixteenth and seventeenth centuries as to need no further notice ; and no satisfactory explanation of
M. O. A. I. has hitherto been given. SMALL (p. 139), while acknowledging the
shrewdness of this suggestion of Fleay, intimates that it is unsound, because, 'unfortunately for Fleay,' 'Malvolio bears not the least resemblance to Malevole except in
name. Malevole, moreover, is clearly not intended to represent Marston himself ;

Fa. A fuſtian riddle.

·To. Excellent Wench, ſay I.   105

Mal. *M. O. A. I.* doth ſway my life. Nay but firſt
let me ſee, let me ſee, let me ſee.

Fab. What diſh a poyſon has ſhe dreſt him *?*

To. And with what wing the ſtallion checkes at it ?

Mal. *I may command, where I adore* : Why ſhee may   110
command me : I ſerue her, ſhe is my Ladie. Why this is
euident to any formall capacitie. There is no obſtruction   112

106, 107. *firſt let me ſee*] *firſt* F₃F₄,
Rowe, +, Var. '73.
108. *What*] *What a* Rowe, +, Cap.
Var. Ran. Var. Mal. Steev. Var. Knt,
Coll. Ktly.

108. *diſh a*] F₂. *diſh o'* Wh. Dyce,
Cam. Rlfe, Huds. *dish a'* Hal. *diſh*
of F₃F₄ et cet.
109. *ſtallion*] *stanyel* Han. et seq.

---

and, lastly, *Twelfth Night*, mentioned by Manningham in February, 1601–2, must
have appeared at least eighteen months before *The Malcontent*, with its imitation
of the version of *Hamlet* acted in 1603 and its allusion to the Scots that came in
with James I.'

102, 103. **doth sway my life**] MALONE: This phrase is seriously employed in
As You Like It, III, ii, 5 : 'Thy Huntresse name, that my full life doth sway.'

108. **drest him ?**] DYCE (ed. ii) : The interrogation-point at the end of this speech
and the next is wrong. The meaning is, 'What *a* dish of poison,' etc.

109. **stallion**] The mention of 'wings' and 'checking' makes HANMER'S
stannyel an *emendatio certissima*.—WILLUGHBY (p. 84) gives a full description of
'The Kestrel, Stannel, or Stonegall, in Latine *Tinnunculus* or *Cenchris*,' and concludes with saying : 'Kestrils are wont commonly with us in England to be reclaimed
and trained up for fowling, after the manner of other Rapacious birds. They catch
not only small birds but also young Partridge. . . . This bird is by some called the
Wind-hover.'—MALONE : Here is one of at least a hundred instances of the transcriber of these plays being deceived by the ear. The eye never could have confounded *stannyel* and 'stallion.'—COLLIER (ed. ii) : This altered to *falcon* in the
MS is decidedly wrong, but probably the word was used on the stage at a time when
'stannyel' was not understood, or considered obsolete. [Malone's remark is eminently just, but had he been familiar with the practice of the early printing estab-
lishments he would have said that it was the ear of the compositor, not of the
'transcriber,' that was deceived.—ED.]—NARES : 'This beautiful species of hawk,'
says Montagu (*Ornith. Dict.*), 'feeds principally on mice,' which accounts for its
not being noticed at all by Latham and other writers on Falconry.

109. **checkes at it**] STEEVENS : 'To checke,' says Latham, *Falconry*, 1633, 'is
when crows, rooks, pies, or other birds, comming in the view of the hawke, she
forsaketh her naturall flight to flie at them.' [See III, i, 64.]

112. **formall capacitie**] STEEVENS: That is, any one in his senses, any one
whose *capacity* is not disarranged, or out of *form*. [Or, as W. A. WRIGHT
expresses it, 'any one of a well-regulated mind.'] So in *Com. of Err.* V, i, 105 :
'Till I have used the approved means I have, With wholesome syrups, drugs, and
holy prayers, To make of him a formal man again.'

in this, and the end : What fhould that Alphabeticall po-   113
fition portend , if I could make that refemble fomething
in me ? Softly, *M.O.A.I.*   115

   To.   O I, make vp that, he is now at a cold fent.

   Fab.   Sowter will cry vpon't for all this, though it bee
as ranke as a Fox.   118

---

113. *this,*] *this*— Rowe et seq. (subs.)
   end :] *end*— Rowe et seq.
(subs.)
   114, 115. *portend,...me ?*] Ff. *portend.
...me ?* Rowe i, *portend ?...me ?* Rowe
ii, +, Var. '73. *portend ?...me.* Han.
portend ?...me,— Cap. et cet.

115. I.] *I,*— Dyce, Cam.
   116. *O I*] *O, I,* F₃F₄. *O, ay!* Rowe
et seq.
   make vp] *make out* Han. *take
up* Anon. ap. Cam.
   117. *it bee*] *it ben't* Han. *it be not*
Johns. Ktly.

---

116. **O I**] Sir Toby's echo of the letters is caught by the eye a little quicker in the Folio than in Rowe's 'O, ay.'—ED.

117. **Sowter**] STEEVENS : A 'sowter' was a cobbler ; it is here, I suppose, the name of a hound. Thus, in Greene's *Carde of Fancie*, 1608 : 'If Appelles that cunning Painter, suffer the greasie Souter to take a view of his curious worke, hee will grow so malapert, as to meddle with his picture.'[p. 102, ed. Grosart.] —MADDEN (p. 52, footnote) : Beckford, in his *Thoughts on Hunting* (1781), includes among the names of hounds in common use, Fury, Tyrant, . . . Echo, Mounter, and Saunter. For these, Shakespeare's Mountain and Sowter may be misprints. All the other names have some meaning applied to hounds ; but Mountain and Sowter (*cobbler*) absolutely none. [But are we certain that 'Souter' (so spelled in the foregoing quotation from Greene) was not pronounced *Shouter ?*— just as *suitor* was pronounced *shooter*. Would there then be absolutely no meaning, as a hound's name, in 'Shouter'? Would it not be as appropriate as Echo ?—ED.]

118. **ranke as a Fox**] CAPELL (p. 147) : The fourth modern [Hanmer] thought a negative was here wanted, but this quest that Malvolio is upon *is* rank as a fox, and to be follow'd without a *cry* (without op'ning) by any dog but a 'Sowter,' and, so taken, a negative lessens the speech's wit.—MALONE : I believe the meaning is : This fellow will, notwithstanding, catch at and be duped by our device, though the cheat is so *gross* that any one else would find it out.—HALLIWELL : The original text seems to be correct. Fabian, comparing Malvolio to a hound, says that he will cry upon it, that is, hunt after it, though it be gross and palpable.—The COWDEN-CLARKES : 'Though it be' seems here to mean *since it is* or *being as it is*.—B. NICHOLSON suggested (*N. & Qu.* VIIth, xii, 63, 1891) *crank ;* that is, 'though it be as twisting or winding as the wiles of a hunted fox. In fact, it would be used in exactly the sense in which Shakespeare uses it in *Ven. & Ad.* when speaking of the hare : "How he outruns the wind, and with what care He cranks and crosses with a thousand doubles." lines 681, 682.'—W. A. WRIGHT : Fabian speaks ironically : 'Malvolio will make it out in time, though it is plain enough.'—INNES : 'Sowter,' literally 'cobbler'; so equivalent to bungler. 'Bungler' (as though Malvolio were a stupid dog named Bungler) 'will open cry' (*i. e.* 'will recover the scent'), 'though a very inferior hound could do that seeing how rank it lies.' [We need here the indicative, *though it is*, not the subjunctive, 'though it be'; and a majority of the preceding paraphrases boldly substitute it. The only way, it seems to me, whereby

Mal.   *M*. *Maluolio*, *M*. why that begins my name.

Fab.   Did not I fay he would worke it out,   the Curre   120
is excellent at faults.

Mal.   *M*. But then there is no confonancy in the fequell
that fuffers vnder probation :   *A*. fhould follow, but *O*
does.

Fa.   And *O* fhall end, I hope.   125

To.   I, or I le cudgell him, and make him cry *O*.

Mal.   And then *I*. comes behind.

Fa.   I, and you had any eye behinde you, you might
fee more detraction at your heeles, then Fortunes before
you.   130

119. M. Maluolio,...*name*] *M,—why*
...*name. M,—Malvolio !* or *M,—M,—*
M,— why...name Cam. conj.
119, 122. M.] *M,—* Cap.
120. *out*,] *out ?* Pope et seq.

122, 123. *fequell that*] *sequel; that*
Rowe et seq.
128. *and you*] *an you* Han. Cap. Var.
'78 et seq.

we can retain the present text is by laying a strong emphasis on 'be,' and thus
impart to it an indicative force. I would paraphrase the passage thus : ' For all this,
that he is now at a cold scent, the dog will find it out, though it *be* as rank as a fox.'
This, I think, helps to make the phrase equivalent to ' because it really *is*.' I can
find no reason why ' Sowter' (or, possibly, *Shouter*, see preceding note) should be
more contemptuous than any other name of a dog ; it is sufficient that it is equivalent to dog, and, *possibly*, there is a play on the words ' Shouter' and ' cry.'—ED.]

121. **at faults**] BRADLEY (*N. E. D.* s. v. *Fault*, 8) : *Hunting*. A break in the
line of scent ; loss of scent ; a check caused by failure of scent. Thus, *Ven. & Ad.*
694 : ' The hot scent-snuffing hounds . . . have singled . . . the cold fault cleanly out.'

123. **probation**] Knowing that ' probation ' means *proof*, it is not hard to translate Malvolio's lordly style. If we retain the punctuation of the Folio by discarding
Rowe's semicolon after ' sequel,' an Anonymous conjecture, recorded in the CAM.
ED., of *suffices* for ' suffers,' becomes plausible. I think Rowe's semi-colon should
be merely a comma.—ED.

125. **O shall end**] JOHNSON : By ' O ' is here meant what we now call a *hempen
collar.*—STEEVENS : I believe he meant only ' it shall end in sighing.' So, in *Rom.
& Jul.* III, iii, 90 : ' Why should you fall into so deep an O ?' [As W. A. WRIGHT
says, ' the jesters never intended to carry their joke as far as' a hempen collar.]

126. **To.**] Does this failure to catch Fabian's joke about ' O,' or, rather, thus repeat
it weakly, sound like Sir Toby ? After having longed for a ' stone-bow,' and invoked
' Fire and Brimstone,' ' Bolts and Shackles,' and after having even questioned whether
Malvolio should live, is it in keeping that Sir Toby should talk of ' cudgels'? The anti-
climax would be hardly more abrupt had he said that Malvolio should be *spoken to*.
In this speech do we not catch the tones of Sir Andrew's weak treble ?—ED.

128. **and you**] CAPELL, in his text, adopted Hanmer's ' *an* you,' but in his *Notes*
(p. 147) he withdraws this *an*, and says ' the reading ought to have been—"Ay, and
if you had "; for " you " is emphatical.'

*Mal. M,O,A,I.*This fimulation is not as the former: 131
and yet to crufh this a little, it would bow to mee, for e-
uery one of thefe Letters are in my name. Soft, here followes profe: *If this fall into thy hand, reuolue.* In my ftars
I am aboue thee, but be not affraid of greatneffe : Some   135
are become great, fome atcheeues greatneffe, and fome
haue greatneffe thruft vppon em. Thy fates open theyr
hands, let thy blood and fpirit embrace them, and to in-
vre thy felfe to what thou art like to be : caft thy humble
flough, and appeare frefh. Be oppofite with a kinfman,   140
furly with feruants : Let thy tongue tang arguments of

---

131. *fimulation*] *similation* Cap. (Errata), Ran.

132. *bow to mee*] *bow me* F_3F_4.

133. *are*] *is* Rowe ii, Var. Ran.

134–148. If this...*Farewell*,] F_2. In Italics F_3F_4 et seq.

134. *ftars*] *state* Lettsom ap. Dyce ii.

136. *atcheeues*] *atcheeve* Ff et seq.

and fome] *and fome, and fome* F_2.

137. *thruft vppon em*] F_2. (reading '*em* Sing. ii, Dyce, Cam. Sta. Ktly, Rlfe.) *put upon em* F_3. *put upon them* F_4, Rowe i. *thruft upon them* Rowe ii et cet.

137. *open*] *upon* F_3F_4.

138, 139. *them,...like to be:*] *them; ...like to be,* Rowe et seq. (subs.)

---

131. simulation is not as the former] That is, this disguise is not so easily detected as 'I may command where I adore.' CAPELL, in his Errata, changed 'simulation' into *similation* on the ground, I suppose, that 'simulation' implies that Malvolio suspected some deceit.—ED.

132, 133. euery one . . . Letters are] The not uncommon plural by attraction ; here, after 'letters.' For many other examples, see ABBOTT, § 412.

136. are become great] This phrase is afterward quoted twice, once by Malvolio, in his interview with Olivia (III, iv, 44), and again by the Clown, in the last scene (V, i, 390) ; in both cases it is given 'some are born great.' ROWE, accordingly, for the sake of uniformity, changed 'become' to *born* in the present passage, and therein has been uniformly followed by succeeding editors.

136. atcheeues] CAMBRIDGE EDITORS : The First Folio here reads 'atcheeues,' but as it has 'atcheeue' in III, iv, 46, and 'atchieue' in V, i, 390, it is plain that the first is a mere misprint. In many other passages, doubtless, the incorrect grammar found in the oldest editions is due to the printer, not to the author.

138. blood and spirit] W. A. WRIGHT : 'Blood' is used metaphorically for passion, or courage and high temper. Thus, in *Hamlet*, III, ii, 74 : 'And blest are those Whose blood and temper are so well commingled,' etc.

140. opposite] MALONE : That is, adverse, hostile. An opposite meant an *adversary*. [See III, ii, 64, where it is so used. Perhaps 'hostile' is too strong ; antagonistic, contradictory, seem more nearly right. It is not easy to see why any note is needed at all ; none would certainly have been recorded here had not so very many editors deemed a note of explanation needful.—ED.]

141. tang] This word occurs again, but not in the First Folio, at III, iv, 74, where the other Folios have 'tang with,' which HANMER adopted here. He has had, however, no followers.—W. A. WRIGHT : 'Tang' appears to be used of a

ſtate ; put thy ſelfe into the tricke of ſingularitie.   Shee   142
thus aduiſes thee, that ſighes for thee.   Remember who
commended thy yellow ſtockings, and wiſh'd to ſee thee
euer croſſe garter'd : I ſay remember, goe too, thou art   145

145. *remember, goe too*] *remember ; go to* Rowe ii et seq. (subs.)

loud dominant sound.   See Fletcher's *Night Walker*, III, iv : ''Tis a strange
noise ! and has a tang o' the justice.'

142. **tricke of singularitie**] W. A. WRIGHT : That is, the affectation of being
eccentric, which has before this done duty for originality.   Compare *Wint. Tale*,
IV, iv, 839 : ' He seemes to be the more Noble, in being fantasticall.'

144. **yellow stockings**] PERCY : Before the civil wars yellow stockings were
much worn.   So in D'Avenant, *The Wits*, [1636] : ' You said, my girl, Mary
Queasy by name, Did find your uncle's yellow stockings in A porringer,' etc. [IV,
ii, p. 236, ed. Maidment.   This passage is to be found only in the ed. 1673, and
is not believed to have been written by D'Avenant.—ED.]—STEEVENS : So, Middleton & Rowley, in *The World Tost at Tennis*, 1620, where the five different-
coloured starches are introduced as striving for superiority, *Yellow Starch* says to
White : ' since she cannot Wear her own linen yellow, yet she shews Her love to 't,
and makes him [her husband] wear yellow hose.' [p. 182, ed. Dyce.   The hose
here referred to are represented as yellow merely because it was the colour of
jealousy,—not because yellow hose were fashionable.—ED.]   Again, in Dekker's
Honest Whore, second part, 1630, Lodovico says, ' What stockings have you put on
this morning, madam? if they be not yellow, change them.' [I, i, p. 134, ed.
Dyce, who, in a footnote, says, ' Lodovico means—it is time for you to be jealous :
" Since citizens wiues fitted their husbands with yellow hose, is not within the memory of man." Dekker's *Owles Almanacke*, 1618, p. 7.   The word "yellows" was
frequently used for jealousy.'   These last two quotations given by Steevens are in
reality pointless, and would not have been repeated here were it not that they have
been quoted by subsequent editors who did not notice that they were inappropriate.
The following quotation is to the point.—ED.] From Henry Goldwell's account of an
entertainment performed before Queen Elizabeth, in 1581, I find that ' The yeomen
attending the Earl of Arundel, Lord Windsor, and Mr Fulke Greville were dressed
in yellow worsted stockings.'—W. A. WRIGHT : ' Yellow stockings ' were apparently a common article of dress in the 16th century, and the tradition of wearing
them survives in the costume of the boys at Christ's Hospital.   They had apparently
gone out of fashion in Sir Thomas Overbury's time, for in his *Characters* he says
of ' A Country Gentleman,' ' If he goes to Court, it is in yellow stockings'; as if
this were a sign of rusticity.   They appear to have been especially worn by the
young, if any importance is to be attached to the burden of a song set to the tune
of *Peg a Ramsey* (Chappell, *Popular Music*, etc., p. 218), in which a married man
laments the freedom of his bachelor days : ' Give me my yellow hose again, Give
me my yellow hose.'   Malvolio may have affected youthful fashions in dress.

145. **crosse garter'd**] STEEVENS : So, in Ford, *The Lover's Melancholy*, 1629
[acted in 1628] : '*Cucullus*. Do I not look freshly, and like a youth of the trim?
Grilla. As rare an old youth as ever walked cross-gartered.'[III, i, p. 48, ed.
Dyce.] Again, in [Field's] *A Woman is a Weathercock* : ''Tis not thy leg, no,
were it twice as good, Throws me into this melancholy mood ; Yet let me say and

[145. crosse garter'd]

swear, in a cross-garter Paul's never show'd to eyes a lovelier quarter.'[IV, ii, p. 70, ed. Hazlitt-Dodsley.] It appears that the ancient Puritans affected this fashion. Thus, Barton Holyday, speaking of the ill-success of his play called *Technogamia*, [1618] says : ' Had there appear'd some sharp cross-garter'd man, Whom their loud laugh might nickname Puritan ; Cas'd up in factious breeches, and small ruffe ; That hates the surplice, and defies the cuffe, Then,' etc. In a former scene Malvolio was said to be an affecter of puritanism.—DOUCE (i, 91) : In the English edition of Junius's *Nomenclator*, 1585, mention is made of 'hose garters, going acrosse, or overthwart, both above and beneath the knee.' In Porter's *Two angry Women of Abington*, 1599, a *serving*-man is thus described : ' Ile tell thee, sirrah, he's a fine neat fellow, A spruce slave ; I warrant ye, he'll have His cruel garters cross about the knee.'[p. 286, ed. Hazlitt-Dodsley.]—NARES : While modes are new, they are confined to the gay or affected ; when obsolete, they are yet retained by the grave and old. In Shakespeare's time this fashion was yet in credit, and Olivia's detestation of it arose, we may suppose, from thinking it coxcombical. Malvolio's puritanism had probably nothing to do with this. Yellow stockings were then high fashion, and so, doubtless, were cross-garters. The following passage proves it : ' All short-cloak'd knights, and all cross-garter'd gentlemen, All pump and pantofle, foot-cloth riders, With all the swarming generation Of long stocks, short pan'd hose, and huge stuff'd doublets,' etc.—Fletcher, *The Woman-hater*, 1607, I, ii. But when Holyday wrote of the ill-success of his *Technogamia*, the fashion was exploded, and was retained only by Puritans and old men.—HALLIWELL gives four wood-cuts of cross-garters. The first is copied from a figure of one of the Magi in the Benedictional of St. Ethelwold, a MS of the tenth century, and much resembles a surgeon's bandage overlapping from the ankle to the knee ; the fourth and fifth represent the cross-gartering depicted on a Tartar, in a book on costume published at Antwerp in 1582, and on the leg of a Guerilla in 1818, respectively ; neither of these is very greatly to the purpose for obvious reasons ; but Nos. 2 and 3 represent ' the front and back views of the knee of a gentleman, from a piece of tapestry of the early part of the sixteenth century ; they very clearly show the mode in which the garter was brought from beneath the knee, and secured in a bow above it, after passing behind the leg.'—FARMER : Thus Sir Thomas Overbury presents a Footman, 'Gards hee weares none ; which makes him live more upright than any crosse-gartered gentleman-usher.'—*Character of a Footman*, 1614.—W. A. WRIGHT : Malvolio was to be cross-gartered, not like a stage bandit, but wearing the garters both above and below the knee, so as to be crossed at the back of the leg. There are frequent references to this fashion. When Ford wrote his *Lover's Melancholy* 'cross-garters' were apparently becoming obsolete. ... The Puritans would naturally be in the rearward of the fashion and would go cross-gartered long after every one else had ceased to do so. And it by no means follows, because 'cross-gartered' was an appropriate epithet for a Puritan some fifteen or twenty years later, that Shakespeare intended Malvolio's Puritanism (which, after all, had its existence only on Maria's sharp tongue), to show itself in this manner. ... Sir Thomas Overbury, when he wrote his *Character of a Footman*, had probably Malvolio in his mind.—DEIGHTON : From the 'villanous' way in which, according to Maria, Malvolio had cross-gartered himself, and from his own admission of the 'obstruction in the blood' caused by so doing, we may perhaps infer that in the present instance the fashion had been exaggerated, travestied.

made if thou defir'ft to be fo : If not, let me fee thee a fte-   146
ward ftill, the fellow of feruants, and not woorthie to
touch Fortunes fingers Farewell, Shee that would alter
feruices with thee, tht fortunate vnhappy daylight and
champian difcouers not more : This is open, I will bee   150
proud, I will reade pollticke Authours, I will baffle Sir
Toby, I will wafh off groffe acquaintance, I will be point
deuife, the very man. I do not now foole my felfe, to let   153

148. *fingers*] *fingers*. Rowe et seq.

149. *thee,   tht   fortunate   vnhappy
daylight*] Ff.   *thee.' The fortunate and
happy Day-light* Rowe, Pope, Theob.
thee the fortunate and happy.' Daylight
Han. Warb. Johns.   *thee, The fortu-
nate-unhappy.' Daylight* Cap et cet.
    tht fortunate vnhappy] Separate
line, Cap. Mal. et seq.

150. *champian*]   *champion*   F₃F₄.
champaign Coll. i, Wh. i.   *champain*

Dyce, Glo. Cam.

150. *difcouers not*] *discovers no* Pope,
+. *discover no* Han.   *discover not*
Dyce ii, iii, Huds.

151. *pollticke*] F₁.

152, 153. *point deuife*] *point de vice*
Johns.   *point-de-vice* Var. '73.   *point-
device* Ktly.

153. *not now*] *now* Ff, Rowe, Pope.
not Han.

149. **fortunate vnhappy daylight**] HANMER was the first to perceive that the
letter ended with 'vnhappy' and that 'daylight' is the beginning of Malvolio's
comment ; but like all the editors from ROWE to JOHNSON, he vitiated his text by
reading 'fortunate and happy.' CAPELL was the first to perceive that 'The fortunate vnhappy' is the subscription.

149, 150. **daylight and champian**] WARBURTON : That is, broad day and an
open country cannot make things plainer.—DYCE : I have not retained the spelling
of the Folio, because in *Lear* I, i, 65, it has 'With shadowie Forrests and with
Champains rich'd.'—W. A. WRIGHT : 'Champian' is the spelling of the word in
the margin of the Authorized Version of *Ezekiel*, xxxvii, 2.

151. **pollticke Authours**] That is, authors on state craft ; so that his tongue may
tang arguments of state.

152, 153. **point deuise**] STEEVENS : Chaucer uses this phrase in *The Romaunt
of the Rose*, l. 1215 : 'Her nose was wrought at point devise.' *i. e.* with the utmost
possible exactness.—SKEAT : A shortened form of the older phrase *at point device*,
equivalent to with great nicety or exactitude, as : 'With limmes [limbs] wrought at
point device.'—*Rom. of the Rose*, l. 830 ; a translation of Old French *à point devis*,
according to a point [of exactitude] that is devised or imagined, *i. e.* in the best way
imaginable.—W. A. WRIGHT : That is, precisely, exactly. The full phrase was
'at point devise,' which we find in Chaucer, *Cant. Tales* (ed. Tyrwhitt), l. 3689 :
'Up rist this jolly lover Absolon, And him arayeth gay, at point devise.' And
l. 10874 : 'So painted he and kempt, at point devise, As wel his wordes, as his
contenance.' Again in *Rom. of the Rose*, l. 830 and l. 1215. In the last-quoted
passages there is nothing corresponding in the French *Roman de la Rose*. Steevens,
by printing the word in the form 'point-de-vice, suggested another etymology which
appears to have no authority. Shakespeare uses point-device,' or 'point devise,' as
an adjective, in the sense of 'precise,' in *As You Like It*, III, ii, 367 : 'You are
rather point deuice in your accoustrements.' And in *Love's Lab. L.* V, i, 21 : 'I

imagination iade mee ; for euery reaſon excites to this,
that my Lady loues me.   She did commend my yellow   155
ſtockings of late, ſhee did praiſe my legge being croſſe-
garter'd, and in this ſhe manifeſts her ſelfe to my loue, &
with a kinde of iniunction driues mee to theſe habites of
her liking.   I thanke my ſtarres, I am happy : I will bee
ſtrange, ſtout, in yellow ſtockings, and croſſe Garter'd,   160
euen with the ſwiftneſſe of putting on.   Ioue, and my

---

158. *iniunction*] *conjunction* F₃F₄,   160. *ſtockings*] *ſtocking* F₂.
Rowe i.

---

abhor such fanatical phantasimes, such insociable and point-devise companions.'—
INNES : The word is used in two other places in Shakespeare apparently in the sense of
superfine.   Perhaps we should here also take it in this sense as an adjective, placing
a comma after it.   Whether it is adverb or adjective, the sense of ' superfine ' rather
than ' precise ' seems to predominate in Chaucer as well as in Shakespeare.   [Here,
' superfine' seems to me to miss the point.   Malvolio is resolving that he ' will
be the very man ' down to the minutest particular that the letter enjoins on him.
HALLIWELL quotes an example from Palsgrave : ' This shyppe is armed or decked
poynte devyse : *ceste nauire est betreschée en tous poynts.*' p. 436.—ED.]
    154. iade mee] That is, to play me, what Shakespeare elsewhere calls, a jade's
trick.   What the precise trick is, it is not easy to define.   W. A. WRIGHT thinks it
means to run away with ; but this seems to me rather too vivacious for a jade.
SCHMIDT (*Lex.*) says it means 'to make appear like a jade,' which is wide of the
mark, but then he adds, ' to make ridiculous and contemptible,' which is better, but
does not explain a jade's agency in the matter.   In *Much Ado*, I, i, 142, it was
suggested that a jade's trick might mean to slip the head out of the collar.   Possibly,
this may approximate the meaning here.   In effect, Malvolio says that he does not
intend to let himself be so led on by his imagination that, when he thinks his position is secure, through his interpretation of the letter, he finds he has been deceiving
himself, and that his substance is a shadow ; that, in short, the jade has slipped her
collar and left him helpless.—ED.
    154, 158. for euery reason . . . kinde of iniunction] CAPELL conjectured that
we should here read : ' for *very* reason ' and ' with a kind injunction '; both conjectures are good, but somewhat too much in the way of improving Shakespeare.
—ED.
    160. stout] DYCE (ed. ii) : Something wrong here, it would seem.—An Anon-
ymous critic conjectures, apud *The Cambridge Shakespeare*, with great violence,
' bestir me, strut *in*,' etc.—CARTWRIGHT (p. 13) : Read *proud;* after reading the
letter Malvolio says, ' I will be proud.'   [Malvolio is repeating the items of the letter
which tells him to ' be opposite with a kinsman,' therefore he will be ' strange ';
to be ' surly with servants,' therefore he will be ' stout.'   To this meaning of ' stout '
SCHMIDT (*Lex.*) gives us a parallel, with the meaning, *proud, overbearing :* ' Oft
have I seen the haughty cardinal. . . . As stout and proud as he were lord of all.'—
2 Hen. VI : I, i, 187.]
    161, 165. Ioue] HALLIWELL (Note on III, iv, 78) : In this, and in most of the
other passages where *Jove* is mentioned in this comedy, the probability is that *God*

ſtarres be praiſed. Heere is yet a poſtſcript. *Thou canſt*   162
not chooſe but know who I am. If thou entertainſt my loue, let
it appeare in thy ſmiling, thy ſmiles become thee well. There-
fore in my preſence ſtill ſmile, deero my ſweete, I prethee. Ioue   165
I thanke thee, I will ſmile, I wil do euery thing that thou
wilt haue me.   *Exit*

   Fab. I will not giue my part of this ſport for a penſi-
on of thouſands to be paid from the Sophy.   169

---

162. [Reads.] Coll.
163. but know] *to know* Rowe i.
   entertainſt] F₂F₃, Cap. Wh. i,
Sing. ii, Ktly, Huds. *entertaineſt* F₄
et cet.

165. deero] deere F₂. dear F₃F₄.
168. *I will*] *I would* Ktly conj.
(withdrawn.)
   part] *patt* F₄.

---

was the original word, which was altered on account of the statute of James I.
Even in a play, it seems to me there is more impropriety in a character solemnly
referring to a fictitious deity than in his using the natural language of thankfulness.
Malvolio, with Puritanical sentiments, would freely use the name of the Almighty.
The change was one frequently made. Thus, in *The Four Prentices of London*,
' in God's name,' in the first edition, is altered to ' in Jove's name,' in the second.
—HUDSON : Malvolio is not a heathen ; he is rather a strait-laced sort of Christian ;
such a one as would be very apt to ascribe his good fortune to the fact of his being
among ' the elect.' So I suspect that ' Jove' was inserted by some second hand in
compliance with the well-known statute against profanation. Halliwell prints as in
[my text] ; and I was fully convinced it ought to be so, long before I knew he
printed it so. [See III, iv, 78.]

   165. deero] DANIEL (p. 43) : Is this a misprint for ' dear, *O* my sweet'? [It is
not improbable ; but its languishing tone might, possibly, impart a shade of exaggeration, which might tend to arouse suspicion. For examples like ' dear my sweet,' see
Shakespeare *passim*, or ABBOTT, § 13.—ED.]

   169. Sophy] STEEVENS : Allusion, as Dr Farmer observes, to Sir Robert Shirley
[or Sherley] who was just returned in the character of ' embassador from the Sophy.'
He boasted of the great rewards he had received, and lived in London with the
utmost splendor.—W. A. WRIGHT : The title of Sophy, by which the Shah of
Persia was most commonly known in the 16th and 17th centuries, was derived from
the Safavi dynasty, founded in 1500 by Sháh Ismail, whose descendants occupied the
throne till 1736, when the power was seized by Nádir Sháh. The attention of
Englishmen had been attracted to Persia, at the beginning of the 17th century,
by the adventures of three brothers, Sir Robert, Sir Anthony, and Sir Thomas
Shirley, whose account of their travels and reception by the Sophy was printed
in 1600. [MALONE (*Var. 1821*, vol. ii, p. 444) gives some further particulars concerning Sir Thomas Shirley ; among them that he arrived as ambassador from the
Sophy in 1611 ; that he and his wife (said to be a niece or sister of the Sophy) at
this time made much noise by their lavish expenditure ; in 1607 a play on the subject, called *The Travells of Three Brothers*, was written by Day, Rowley, and Wil-
kins. See also *Retrospective Review*, ii, 351. Neither the ambassador's return
in 1611 nor the play in 1607 could have been referred to in *Twelfth Night*, which

To. I could marry this wench for this deuice.   170
An. So could I too.
To. And aske no other dowry with her, but fuch ano-
ther ieft.

Enter Maria.

An. Nor I neither.   175
Fab. Heere comes my noble gull catcher.
To. Wilt thou fet thy foote o'my necke,
An. Or o'mine either?
To. Shall I play my freedome at tray-trip, and becom
thy bondflaue?   180

---

170. *deuice.*] Ff, Rowe, +, Coll. Cam. i, Glo. Ktly, Rlfe, Dtn, Wh. ii. *device,*— Wh. i, Dyce, Sta. Huds. Cam. ii. *device ;* Cap. et cet.
171. *So*] *And so* Han.
172. *And*] *—and* Wh. i, Huds.

174. Enter...] After line 175, Cap. [Scene IX. Pope, +.
176. *noble*] *notable* Schmidt (*Lex.*) conj.
177. *necke.*] *necke ?* Ff.
179. *at*] *at a* F₃F₄.

---

was acted in 1602. Malone adduced them when he supposed that the date of the present play was 1617.—ED.]

179. **tray-trip**] STEEVENS: This is mentioned in Glapthorne's *Wit in a Constable,* 1640: 'Meane time you may play at Tray-trip or cockall for blacke puddings.' Again: 'With lanthern on stall, at trea trip we play For ale, cheese, and pudding, till it be day,' etc.—TYRWHITT: The following passage might incline one to believe that tray-trip was the name for some game at tables or draughts. 'There is great danger of being taken sleepers at tray-trip, if the king sweep suddenly.'—Cecil's *Correspondence,* Lett. x, p. 136. Ben Jonson joins tray-trip with mum-chance: 'Nor play with costar-mongers at mum-chance, tray-trip.'—*Alchemist,* V, ii.— REED: We find the following in Machiavell's *Dogge,* 1617: 'But, leaving cardes, lett's goe to dice awhile, To passage, treitrippe, hazarde, or mumchance. ... And trippe without a treye makes had-I-wist To sitt and mourne among the sleeper's rancke.'—NARES: An old game, undoubtedly played with dice, and probably in the tables. Some commentators [Hawkins, Croft] have fancied that it resembled *hop-scotch* or *Scotch-hop;* but this seems to rest merely on unauthorised conjecture. It is joined with *mum-chance,* also a game at dice; though, perhaps, sometimes played with cards. [Reed's quotation from Machiavell's *Dogge*] is decisive as to both games. Success in it depended on throwing a trois.—HALLIWELL: A game at cards, played with dice as well as with cards, the success in which chiefly depended upon the throwing of treys. [DYCE (*Gloss.*) accepts this defintion.]—W. A. WRIGHT: It could not have been the game of tables, that is, backgammon, or draughts, as now played. Torriano (*It. Dict.,* 1656) gives 'Giocare al nove, to play at noven, or tray-trip, also to play at nine-holes.' There appears to be no ground for the assertion of Hawkins that it was a game like hop-scotch, which could hardly be played by watchmen at night [as in Steevens's first quotation from] Glapthorne's *Wit in a Constable.* [But in the second quotation, it will be observed that the watchmen put their lanthern on a stall.—ED.]

An.   Ifaith, or I either ?   181

Tob.   Why, thou haſt put him in ſuch a dreame, that
when the image of it leaues him, he muſt run mad.

Ma.   Nay but ſay true, do's it worke vpon him ?

To.   Like Aqua vite with a Midwife.   185

Mar.   If you will then ſee the fruites of the ſport, mark
his firſt approach before my Lady : hee will come to her
in yellow ſtockings, and 'tis a colour ſhe abhorres, and
croſſe garter'd, a faſhion ſhee deteſts : and hee will ſmile
vpon her, which will now be ſo vnſuteable to her diſpo-   190
ſition, being addiĉted to a melancholly, as ſhee is, that it
cannot but turn him into a notable contempt : if you wil
ſee it follow me.

To.   To the gates of Tartar, thou moſt excellent diuell
of wit.   195

And.   Ile make one too.   *Exeunt.*

                               Finis Aĉtus ſecnndus   197

181. *I*] Om. F₃F₄.   194. *gates of Tartar*] *gates Tartar*
185. *Aqua vite*] *Aqua-vitæ* Ff.   F₄. *gates, Tartar,* Rowe.   *gates of*
191. *to a*] *to* F₃F₄, Rowe, Pope.   *Tartarus* Coll. MS.
193. *me.*] *me.—* Ff.   197. ſecnndus] Secundi Ff.

185. **Aqua vite**] JOHNSON : This is the old name of *strong waters.*   [Cotgrave
has ' Eau de vie. *Aquauite.*']

189. **a fashion shee detests**] ROLFE : I am not aware that any commentator
has noted the inconsistency of Maria's assertion that cross-gartering is a fashion that
Olivia ' detests,' and what she had written in the forged letter : ' Remember who
commended thy yellow stockings and wished to see thee ever cross-gartered '; which
is confirmed by Malvolio : ' She did commend my yellow stockings of late, she did
praise my leg being cross-gartered.' Possibly, Olivia had spoken ironically, and the
conceited steward took it as serious praise ; but more likely it is one of Shakespeare's
inconsistencies in minor matters. [It is doubtful if credence should be placed on any
of Malvolio's assertions in regard to Olivia's demeanour toward him in the past.
He was in such an exalted frame of mind that by the light of memory any absent-
minded glance cast on him haphazard by Olivia would have been interpreted by
him as one of absorbing devotion ; had the look been one even of annoyance, Malvolio would have now recalled it as a struggle to hide her tender affection.—ED.]

191. **addiĉted**] W. A. WRIGHT : This is now generally used in connexion with
some bad habit, but this is a modern sense, for it is said with praise of the house of
Stephanas (*1 Cor.* xvi, 15), that they had ' addicted themselves to the ministry of the
saints.'

194. **Tartar**] Compare, ' If that same demon . . . should with his lion gait walk
the whole world, He might return to vasty Tartar back And tell his legions,' etc.—
Henry V : II, ii, 123.

Actus Tertius, Scæna prima.

Enter Uiola and Clowne.   2

Vio. Saue thee Friend and thy Muſick : doſt thou liue
by thy Tabor?
Clo. No ſir, I liue by the Church.   5
Vio. Art thou a Churchman?
Clo. No ſuch matter ſir, I do liue by the Church : For,
I do liue at my houſe, and my houſe dooth ſtand by the
Church.   9

A Garden. Rowe.   Olivia's Gar-   playing on his Tabor. Coll. iii.
den. Pope.   4. *thy*] *the* Ff, Rowe, Pope, Han.
2. Enter...] Enter... meeting. Cap.   Cap. Var. '73.
Enter... with a tabor. Mal.   Enter...

1. **Scæna prima**] MARSHALL: In [Irving's] acting-edition, this scene forms a
continuation of the previous one and concludes Act III.   The arrangement is perfectly justifiable, as the events of Act II, Scenes iv. and v, and of Acts III, IV,
and V, all take place on the same day.   For stage purposes such a division of the
Acts is preferable, as, with Olivia's declaration of love to the supposed Cesario, an
important step in the more serious interest of the play is reached.

4. **Tabor**] CAPELL (p. 148): Viola's question and salute show that she meets the
Clown playing on the tabor. [This anticipates Malone's stage-direction.]—STEEVENS:
The Clown, I suppose, wilfully mistakes Viola's meaning, and answers as if he had
been asked whether he lived by the 'sign of the tabor,' the ancient designation of
a music shop. [This unfortunate misapprehension by Steevens of Viola's innocent
question as to whether or not the Clown's means of livlihood were the tabor, opened
the way to a display of learning on a subject which adds nothing to the elucidation
of the text.   Malone, Douce, and Boswell learnedly discuss the name of a tavern
kept by Tarleton.—ED.]—HALLIWELL: The tabor and pipe were used by Fools
long before Shakespeare's time. . . . The Clown's equivoque merely turns on the
different meanings of the particle 'by,' and there is hardly a necessity for supposing
that he chooses to take Viola's question in the sense of an enquiry as to whether he
lived by the sign of the tabor.—INNES: If there is any such hidden jest [as that in
reference to an inn], which is extremely doubtful, it might rather be supposed that
the Clown pretends to mistake Viola's pronunciation of 'tabor' for 'tavern.' [For
'tabor' see, if necessary, *Much Ado*, in this ed. II, iii, 15.—ED.]

7. **I do**] CAPELL, in his *Various Readings*, p. 35, conjectures that this should be
'*yet* I do'; in his *Notes*, p. 148, he says '*and yet* must have stood before "I"'; nor
will the reasoning be natural, 'till these words are replac'd.' [With a strong emphasis on 'do,' the 'reasoning' becomes 'natural. —ED.]

9. **Church**] HUTTSON (May, p. 481): We learn that Feste had been 'a fool
that Lady Olivia's father took much delight in.'   He was therefore a long established inmate of that baronial mansion, which we are to imagine Lady Olivia's

Vio.   So thou maiſt ſay the Kings lyes by a begger, if a   10
begger dwell neer him : or the Church ſtands by thy Tabor, if thy Tabor ſtand by the Church.

Clo.   You haue ſaid ſir : To ſee this age : A ſentence is
but a cheu'rill gloue to a good witte, how quickely the
wrong ſide may be turn'd outward.   15

Vio.   Nay that's certaine : they that dally nicely with
words, may quickely make them wanton.   17

10. *maiſt*] *maieſt* F₄.
    Kings] *King* Ff.
    lyes] *lives* Cap. conj. Var. '73,
Wh. Coll. ii, iii (MS), Dyce ii, iii, Huds.
10, 11. *begger*] *beggar* F₄.

13. *ſir :*] *sir.* Steev.
    age :] *age !* Ff.
14. *cheu'rill*] *chev'ril* Rowe. *cheveril*
Var. '73.
    witte,] *wit ;* F₃F₄.

house to be.   He afterwards tells Viola, ' I do live at my house and my house doth
stand by the Church.'   When Shakespeare wrote this, he was probably conceiving
Feste as a retainer of the Lady Olivia's father, settled hard by the Church and with
some hereditary claim to service and preferment in it, but as having missed his vocation in some way, and fallen back upon this, his real vocation as a jester, in lieu of
the other living, greatly helped in the new walk by the clerical training he had
received.

10. **Kings**] This word is quoted, as well as   wisemens,' in line 68, by WALKER
(*Crit.* i, 235) in his valuable chapter on the omission and interpolation, in the Folio,
of the final *s*.   This peculiarity is so strange that Walker would be inclined to think
that it originated in some trick in Shakespeare's handwriting were it not for the
varying degrees of frequency with which it occurs, being comparatively rare in the
Comedies, more frequent in the Histories, and quite common in the Tragedies.
[This variation in frequency exonerates Shakespeare and places the peculiarity
wholly on the compositors, where all such peculiarities in the printing of the Folio
belong.—ED.]

10. **lyes**] MALONE : That is, dwells, sojourns ; as in many other places in old
books.—R. G. WHITE (ed. i) : The context conclusively shows that this is a misprint ; the Clown's speech, ' I do *live* by the Church,' requiring, of course, in Viola's,
' *So* thou may'st say the King *lives*'; not 'the King *lies*.'—DYCE (ed. ii) : ' Lyes '
is well enough for the sense, but the context ('live' occurring *four times* in what
precedes) determines it to be an error. [The short dialogue at the beginning of
Othello, III, iv, where the joke turns on 'lyes,' as equivalent both to lodge and
to deceive, strengthens the presumption that the present text of the Folio is right.
—ED.]

11, 12. **Church stands by thy Tabor**] Again, a double meaning.   ' Stand by '
may be equivalent to uphold, to maintain.—ED.

14. **cheu'rill**] STEEVENS : That is, a glove made of *kid* leather : *Chevreau*,
French.   So in *Rom. & Jul.* II, iv, 87 : ' O, here's a wit of cheveril, that stretches
from an inch narrow to an ell broad.' [It is due to this stretching quality that the
glove can be so quickly turned wrong side outward.—ED.]

16, 17. **dally nicely . . . wanton**] That is, those who play ingeniously with
words may quickly give them a double meaning.   BARNETT says that ' the allusion
is still to the playfulness of the *kid*.'

Clo. I would therefore my fifter had had no name Sir.   18

Vio. Why man ?

Clo. Why fir, her names a word, and to dallie with   20
that word, might make my fifter wanton : But indeede,
words are very Rafcals, fince bonds difgrac'd them.

Vio. Thy reafon man ?

Clo. Troth fir, I can yeeld you none without wordes,
and wordes are growne fo falfe, I am loath to proue rea-   25
fon with them.

Vio. I warrant thou art a merry fellow, and car'ft for
nothing.

*Clo.*Not fo fir, I do care for fomething:but in my confcience fir, I do not care for you : if that be to care for no-   30
thing fir, I would it would make you inuifible.

Uio. Art not thou the Lady *Oliuia's* foole?   32

---

18. *had had*] *had* F₃F₄, Rowe, Pope,
Han.
20. *names*] *name's* Ff.

32. *not thou*] *thou not* Steev. ('corrected in MS' ap. Cam.)

---

22. **words are very Rascals, since bonds disgrac'd them**] HUDSON : This probably alludes to an order of the Privy Council, June, 1600, laying very severe restrictions on the Poet's art.   The order, besides that it allowed only two houses to be used for stage-plays in the city and suburbs, interdicted those two from play-ing at all during Lent, or in any time of great sickness, and also limited them to twice a week at all other times.   If rigidly enforced it would have amounted almost to a total suppression of play-houses.   As the penalty was imprisonment, it might well be said that words were disgraced by bonds.—DEIGHTON : A play upon words in the sense of (1) since they have been disgraced by being put into bonds (into con-finement) and (2) since they were used in money bonds.   Hudson's reference to the Privy Council's order is a very forced meaning to put upon the words.—CHAMBERS'S ED. (1895) : A quibble upon *bonds*, in the sense of limits and of money bonds or contracts to pay.—VERITY (p. vii) : It is thought that this passage alludes to certain restrictions on the stage ordered by the Privy Council in 1600 and 1601. [(Foot-note) In view of the] Order of the Council in June 1600, [and in view of the] fur-ther steps taken by the Council in the next year against the stage, Dramatists might well complain that 'bonds' were laid upon them.—CHOLMELEY : 'Since bonds dis-graced them' by using them in the trickeries of business.   Or it may refer to the restrictions laid upon acting by the Privy Council. [I have given every explanation that I can find of this dark passage ; and I confess that none of them affords me a ray of light.   I cannot see how words are disgraced by being used in contracts, nor can I see how they become rascals by restrictions placed upon Theatres.   The only explanation I can offer, and I fear it is quite as far fetched as the others, is that words are placed in bonds when they are accurately defined.   To have strict, unalterable meanings attached to words could not but have been offensive to Feste, whose delight, and even profession, it was to be a 'corrupter of words.'—ED.]

Clo. No indeed fir, the Lady *Oliuia* has no folly, fhee   33
will keepe no foole fir, till fhe be married, and fooles are
as like husbands, as Pilchers are to Herrings, the Huf-   35
bands the bigger, I am indeede not her foole, but hir corrupter of words.

Vio. I faw thee late at the Count *Orfino's.*

Clo. Foolery fir, does walke about the Orbe like the
Sun, it fhines euery where. I would be forry fir, but the   40
Foole fhould be as oft with your Mafter, as with my Mi-
ftris : I thinke I faw your wifedome there.

Vio. Nay, and thou paffe vpon me, Ile no more with   43

35. *like*] *like to* Ktly.

Pilchers] *pilchards* Cap. et seq.

are] Om. Ktly conj.

35, 36. *husbands*] F₂. *husband's*
F₃F₄.

36. *hir*] F₁.

38. *Count*] *Duke* Rowe, +, Var. '73.

39. *does*] *he does* Rowe i.

39, 40. *Orbe ... Sun,*] *orb ... sun;*
Theob. +. *orb,...sun;* Cap. *orb;...*
sun, Dyce, Huds.

43. *and*] *an* Pope et seq.

35. **Pilchers**] R. G. WHITE (ed. i) : The pilchard is, I believe, unknown in
this country. It is so like the herring that, according to Lord Teignmouth, they
can only be distinguished by the ability of the pilchard to furnish the fat in which it
can be fried, which the herring lacks.—W. A. WRIGHT : The spelling varied even
in Shakespeare's time. In Minsheu's *Spanish Dict.*, 1599, we find, ' Sardina, a
little pilchard, a sardine'; and also, ' a Pilcher, vide Sardina.' So, again, in
Florio's *Worlde of Wordes*, 1598, ' Sardella, a little pickled or salt fish like an
anchoua, a sprat or a pilcher, called a sardell or sardine'; while in his *Italian
Dict.*, 1611, and in Cotgrave, of the same date, the spelling is ' pilchard.'

39, 40. **Orbe . . . Sun,**] I think Dyce's punctuation doubtful.

40. **I would be sorry**] ABBOTT (§ 331, p. 234) : It must be confessed there
seems little reason here for ' would.' Inasmuch, however, as the Fool is speaking
of something that depends upon himself, *i. e.* his presence at the Count's court, it
may perhaps be explained as, ' I *would* not willingly do anything to prevent,' etc.,
just as we can say ' I *would* be loth to offend him,' in confusion between ' I *should*
be loth to offend him,' and ' I *would* not willingly,' or ' I *would* rather not, offend
him.' DEIGHTON pronounces this explanation by Abbott, ' somewhat subtle'; and
in *Much Ado*, II, iii, 114, where Abbott gives a similar explanation of ' I would
have thought,' etc., W. A. WRIGHT denies it altogether, and says ' would' is here
' used for the conditional of *should*.' Inasmuch as a repeated action is spoken of,
namely, that the Fool was to be with Orsino as often as with Olivia, may it not be
that ' would' is here used in the sense of ' it would be my custom to be sorry' or
' I would always be sorry'? just as when Othello says (I, iii, 170, of this ed.) of
Desdemona, ' But still the house Affaires would draw her hence,' *i. e.* were accustomed to draw her hence.—ED.

40. **but**] W. A. WRIGHT : ' But' is here equivalent to *if . . . not.*

42. **your wisedome**] A sarcastic perversion of ' your worship.'

43. **passe vpon**] W. A. WRIGHT : The Clown, being by profession a corrupter
of words, tried some of his word fencing upon Viola ; and to this she seems to refer

thee· Hold there's expences for thee.

Clo. Now Ioue in his next commodity of hayre, fend   45
thee a beard.

Vio. By my troth Ile tell thee, I am almoſt ſicke for
one, though I would not haue it grow on my chinne. Is
thy Lady within?

Clo Would not a paire of theſe haue bred ſir?   50

Vio. Yes being kept together, and put to vſe.

Clo. I would play Lord *Pandarus* of *Phrygia* ſir, to bring
a *Creſſida* to this *Troylus*.

Vio. I vnderſtand you ſir, tis well begg'd.   54

44. *thee.*] F₁.
　　[Gives him a piece of money.
Han.
　48. *though…chinne*] [Aside.] Cam.

Rlfe, Wh. ii.
　54. [Giving him more money. Coll.
ii (MS).

when she uses the expression 'pass upon'; to pass signifying to make a pass in
fencing, and such word-play being elsewhere called 'a quick venue of wit' (*Love's
Lab. L.* V, i, 62). But to 'pass upon' had also the meaning, 'to impose on, play
the fool with,' as in V, i, 371, and it may be so here.]

　44. there's expences] BADHAM (p. 287): As the Clown has not been laying
out money for Viola, it is impossible he should receive 'expenses' from her, even
supposing such a circumstance could justify so strange an expression. It is probable
that he would be rewarded with the same coin he had already got from the two
knights, and that Viola says to him: 'Hold; here's sixpence for thee.' ['Expenses'
here means not money that has been spent, but money that is to be spent.]

　45. commodity] W. A. WRIGHT: The modern mercantile phrase would probably be 'cargo' or 'consignment.' See *1 Hen. IV:* I, ii, 93: 'I would to God
thou and I knew where a commodity of good names were to be bought.' And the
old play of *Sir Thomas More* (ed. Dyce), p. 63: 'What will he be by that time he
comes to the commoditie of a bearde?'

　50. haue bred] MALONE: I believe our author wrote 'have breed.' The Clown
is not speaking of what a pair *might* have done, but what they *may* do hereafter in
his possession; and therefore covertly solicits another piece from Viola. Compare,
Ven. & Ad. 768: 'Foul-cankering rust the hidden treasure frets, But gold, that's
put to use, more gold begets.' [See in *Mer. of Ven.* I, iii, 98, Shylock's reply to
Anthonio's question, 'is your gold and siluer Ewes and Rams?' 'I cannot tell, I
make it breede as fast.' And again, Anthonio says (*Ibid.* 137), 'when did friendship
take A breede of barraine mettall of his friend?' Possibly, Malone intended to
say *breed*, not *have breed*. Hudson adopted *breed* in his text. No change is
needed. The Clown says, in effect, 'Had you given me a pair would they not
have bred?']

　51. put to vse] 'Use' is here interest; as in *Much Ado*, II, i, 267, Beatrice,
speaking of Benedick's heart, says 'hee lent it me a while, and I gave him vse for
it, a double heart for a single one.' See, also, *Sonnet*, vi, 5: 'That use is not forbidden usury Which happies those that pay the willing loan.' Again, in the quotation
from *Ven. & Ad.* in the preceding note: 'gold that's put to use.'

Clo. The matter I hope is not great fir; begging, but a   55
begger : *Creffida* was a begger.   My Lady is within fir.   I
will confter to them whence you come, who you are, and
what you would are out of my welkin, I might fay Element, but the word is ouer-worne.   *exit*   59

55. *begging,*] *begging* Pope.   Wh. ii.
56. *begger*] *beggar* F$_3$F$_4$.   57. *come,*] *come;* Rowe ii et seq.
57. *confter*] *construe* Steev. Var.   58. *are*] *is* Ff, Rowe, +, Var. '73,
Coll. Hal. Dyce, Cam. Sta. Rlfe, Huds.   '78, Ran.

55, 56. **begging, but a begger**] In his preceding speech, Feste has begged for
a Cressida, who was, he now goes on to say, a begger.

56. **Cressida was a begger**] THEOBALD (ed. i) : The Poet in this circumstance
undoubtedly had his eye on Chaucer's *Testament of Cresseid*.   Cupid, to revenge
her profanation against his Deity, calls in the Planetary gods to assist in his vengeance.   They instantly turn her mirth into melancholy, her health into sickness,
her beauty into deformity, and in the end pronounce this sentence upon her : ' This
sall thow go begging fra hous to hous, With cop and clapper lyke ane lazarous.'
[Henryson's *Works*, ed. Laing, p. 87, as quoted by W. A. Wright.]   CAPELL
(p. 148) quotes from the same source : ' And greit penuritie Thow suffer sall, and
as ane begger die.'—*Op. cit.* p. 86.—W. A. WRIGHT : *The Testament of Cresseid*,
once attributed to Chaucer, was really the work of Robert Henryson.   Another
reminiscence of it occurs in *Hen. IV :* II, i, 80 : ' The lazar kite of Cressid's kind.'

57. **conster**] As far as spelling is concerned, Shakespeare's printers used
' conster ' quite as often as *construe*.   To be exact, ' conster ' (including *consture*
and *constured*) is so spelled in the Folios and Quartos eight times, and *construe*,
seven times.   (See note on *Othello*, IV, i, 118, of this ed., where the references are
given.)   It is really a matter of indifference which spelling is adopted.   In the
dramatists of Shakespeare's time, ' conster ' is, I think, the commoner form.   Dyce
(*Remarks*, p. 76) commends Knight for adhering to ' conster ' in this passage, and yet
when Dyce himself came to select his own text he adopted *construe*, with the note
that ' had " conster " been a mere vulgarism, I should have retained it, as perhaps
not inappropriate in the mouth of the Clown ; but it is nothing more than a variety
of spelling.'   Dyce gives an instance of the use of ' conster ' as late even as Pope,
who, in a *Letter to the Duchess of Hamilton* (*Add.* to *Works*, 1776, ii, 2), writes,
' Lord William will conster this Latine, if you send it to Thistleworth.'   In my copy
of Dyce's *Remarks*, Lettsom has written in the margin : ' The word was *pronounced*
conster among schoolboys in the early part of this century.'   The meaning of ' conster ' is here, of course, to explain, unfold.—ED.

57. **them**] HANMER changed this to *her*, to make it correspond to ' My Lady,'
but Feste was thinking, of course, of Olivia and her gentlewoman, Maria, who both
enter shortly afterward.—ED.

58, 59. **Element . . . ouer-worne**] See I, i, 31, and III, iv, 127.—W. A.
WRIGHT : ' Element ' being sometimes used for *sky*, the Clown makes ' welkin '
synonymous with it to avoid the more familiar word.—R. W. BOODLE (*Shakespear-*
iana, March, 1887, iv, 116) : In *Satiro-mastix* [which SMALL dates in 1601, therefore written, possibly, earlier than *Twelfth Night*.—ED.] Dekker repeatedly puts
the obnoxious [word ' element '] in the mouth of Horace (Ben Jonson).   Speaking

Vio. This fellow is wife enough to play the foole,   60
And to do that well, craues a kinde of wit :
He muſt obferue their mood on whom he ieſts,
The quality of perſons, and the time :
And like the Haggard, checke at euery Feather   64

60. *fellow is*] *fellow's* Steev. Var. Coll. Hal. Sing. Sta. Ktly, Huds.

63. *of perfons*] *of the persons* Rowe, +, Var. '73, '78, Ran. Var. '85.

64. *And*] *Not* Johns. conj. Ran. Coll. ii, iii (MS), Sing. Hal. Dyce, Rlfe, Huds. *Nor* Harness. *And not* Ktly.

---

of Captain Tucca, he says, ''tis out of his element to traduce me ; I am too well ranked, Asinius, to be stabbed with his dudgeon wit.' (p. 195, ed. Pearson). Asinius, Horace's friend, also uses the expression as a favourite one with 'his ningle' (*i. e.* Horace) : 'Marry, for reading my book, I'll take my death upon 't (as my ningle says) 'tis out of my element.' (p. 196). Lastly, the words are among the things that Horace is forced to abjure : ' *Sir Vaughan*. Thirdly, and last of all saving one, when your plays are misliked at Court, you shall not ... say you are glad you write out of the courtiers' element. *Tucca*. Let the element alone, 'tis out of thy reach.' If, as seems probable enough, Shakespeare is alluding in [the present passage] to the ridicule bestowed upon the expression in *Satiro-mastix*, additional point is given to the Clown's remark.

60, 61. **play the foole ... craues a kinde of wit**] FEIS (p. 159) says that there is a reference to this passage in the following from Jonson's *Poetaster*, IV, iii : ' I have read in a book that to play the fool wisely is high wisdom.' The reference is extremely doubtful. *The Poetaster* was produced, says Gifford, in 1601, the same year which witnessed the production of *Twelfth Night*, unless the latter was per- formed for the first time, which no one has supposed, at the Readers' Feast in the Middle Temple. Jonson could not use the words ' read in a book ' when in truth it had been only heard on the stage. *Possibly*, the book to which Jonson refers is Guazzo's *Civile Conuersation*, translated by ' G. pettie ' and published in 1586, wherein, on p. 74, is the following : ' To plaie the foole well, it behooueth a man first to be wise.'—ED.

64. **And like the Haggard**] JOHNSON : The meaning may be that he must catch every opportunity, as the wild hawk strikes every bird. But perhaps it might be read more properly, '*Not* like the haggard.' He must choose persons and times, and observe tempers ; he must fly at proper game, like the trained hawk, and not fly at large like the unreclaimed ' haggard ' to seize all that comes in his way. [This emendation is pronounced 'indispensable' by DYCE; 'obvious' by COLLIER; ' essential ' by HALLIWELL.]—W. A. WRIGHT : The text, however, appears to be right. It is part of the fool's wisdom to make a jest of everything, because in that case his jests will not appear directed at any particular person. [To the same effect, INNES. Dr Johnson's interpretation of this passage erred, I think, in supposing that the two clauses, viz. : the regard to moods and the checking at every feather, are opposed to each other, instead of being supplemental. A Fool must have tact, but without a sense of humour he will have nothing wherewith to display tact. His sense of humour must reveal jests to him in every incident of life, there is not a feather that he must not check at. But to see a jest is one thing, to bring it forth with discrimination is another and a very different thing. Dr Johnson seems to

That comes before his eye.   This isa practice,   65
As full of labour as a Wife-mans Art:
For folly that he wifely fhewes, is fit ;
But wifemens folly falne, quite taint their wit.   68

65. *isa*] F₁.

66. *Wife-mans*] *wise man's* Han.
Cap. et seq.

68. *wifemens folly falne, quite taint*]
Wife mens folly falne, quite taint F₂.
wife mens folly faln, quite taint F₃F₄,
Rowe i. *wise mens folly fall'n, quite
taints* Rowe ii, Pope, Johns. Var. '73,
'78, '85. *wise men's, folly fall'n, quite*

taints Theob. *wise men's folly shewn,
quite taints* Han. Wh. Rlfe, Huds. *wise
men's folly-fall'n, quite taints* Warb.
wise men, folly fall'n, quite taint Ran.
wise men's folly, fall'n, quite taints
Mal. Hal. *wise men's folly fall'n quite
taints* Coll. *wise men, folly-faln, quite
taint* Cap. ef cet.   *wise men, folly-
-blown, quite taint* Anon. ap. Cam.

---

think that to check at every feather means to strike at every one.   It rather means,
I think, that materials for jests must be gathered from every possible source, everything mirthful must be stored to be mellowed on occasion ; and this practice of col-
lecting materials, Viola goes on to say, is as full of labour as a wiseman's art.   Over
and above all, a Fool must have address, and know when and where and at whom
to level his shafts, and he must gather a sheaf of shafts by checking, like the
haggard, at every feather he sees.—ED.]

64. **Haggard**] MADDEN (p. 147, etc.) : You may train your falcon in either of
two ways.   You may take from the eyrie the nestling or eyess, rearing and making
it to your use from its earliest days.   Or you may capture a full-grown wild hawk,
after she has been taught to fare for herself by the sternest of taskmasters for man or
bird—hunger.   The lessons learned in this school will not be forgotten, and the
wild hawk or haggard, reclaimed and manned, has learned somewhat to which the
eyess can never attain. . . . If you would have a hawk at once high-spirited, loving,
and tractable, you must man and train a haggard ; that is to say. a wild hawk which
has lived and fared at liberty until she has moulted for the first time and has assumed
her adult plumage.   On this point all the masters of falconry are of one mind. . . .
The haggard falcon that has never learned constancy to her legitimate pursuit will
' check,' or change the quarry at which she is flown for any magpie or crow that
fortune may throw in her way.   ' The peregrine seems often to strike down birds for
his amusement,' says Mr St. John, writing of the male haggard : ' I have seen one
knock down and kill two rooks who were unlucky enough to cross his flight, without
taking the trouble to look at them after they fell.'

64. **checke**] See II, v, 109.

67. **folly that he wisely shewes**] BADHAM (p. 273) : I have no doubt that we
should read : ' For *he that folly* wisely shows is fit '; *i. e.* he that wisely shows folly
is a skilful man.

68. **wisemens folly falne, quite taint**] In 1729 THEOBALD wrote to Warburton : ' I read and point thus : " But wise men, folly-fall'n, quite taint their wit." '
But when he came to print his edition four years later, he unfortunately deserted this
excellent reading, and did not even allude to it.   In 1761 (probably) CAPELL'S text
reads as Theobald, in his private letter, had proposed to Warburton it should be read ;
but of this Capell was, of course, entirely ignorant.   In his *Notes*, which appeared
in 1780, he has the following (p. 148) in reference to the present line : ' The single
error of printers was their converting a comma [which should follow " wisemen "]

Enter Sir Toby and Andrew.

To. Saue you Gentleman. 70

Uio. And you fir.

And. *Dieu vou guard Monfieur.* 72

Scene II. Pope, +.

69. Andrew.] Sir Andrew. Rowe.

70. To.] Sir And. Theob.+, Var. '73, '78, Ran. Var. '85.

72, 74. And.] Sir Tob. Theob.+, Var. '73, '78, Ran. Var. '85.

72. vou guard] *vous guard* Rowe. *vous guarde* Pope. *vous garde* Var. '73.

---

into an *s*; the present copy restores it; and (with it) a sense sufficiently clear, under this restriction, that "taint" is—taint it in man's opinion, call *their wit* into question.' In the meantime, in the *Variorum* of 1778, TYRWHITT proposed the same reading which is to be found in Capell's text. Several years before, in the *Variorum* of 1773, JOHNSON, who adhered to Pope's text, gave the following explanation: 'The folly which he shews with proper adaptation to persons and times *is fit*, has its propriety, and therefore produces no censure; but the folly of wise men, when it *falls* or *happens*, taints their wit, destroys the reputation of their judgement.' This is a good explanation of a text which might be improved. Indeed, the general meaning of the passage is obvious; the difficulty, as in many and many another phrase, is merely to harmonise, with the least possible change, this meaning and the grammatical construction.—HEATH (p. 192): I suppose 'folly-fall'n,' in one word, is an error of the printer, as it destroys the construction, by depriving it of a substantive. The sense is, But wise men's folly, when it is once fallen into extravagance, overpowers their discretion.—R. G. WHITE (ed. i) justifies his adoption of Hanmer's 'folly *shewn*,' in the remark that 'the antithesis is plainly between the folly which the fool shows and that which the wise men show. The former is fit, *i. e.* becoming; but the latter, being unfit, *i. e.* unbecoming, quite taints their wit, *i. e.* intelligence.' There is one point in favour of Hanmer's reading, to which attention was called by M. MASON (p. 117), namely, that the use of 'shewes' in the preceding line seems almost to demand, for the sake of complete antithesis, the use of *shewn* in the present line. Capell's text is to me the best. For the final *s* in 'wisemens,' see Walker's note on 'lies,' in line 10 of the present Scene.—ED.

70, 72. **To. . . . And.**] THEOBALD: I have ventured to make the two Knights change speeches [see *Text. Notes*] in this dialogue with Viola; and, I think, not without good reason. It were a preposterous forgetfulness in the Poet, and out of all probability, to make Sir Andrew not only speak French, but understand what is said to him in it, who in the First Act did not know the English of 'Pourquoi.'—CAPELL (*Notes*, p. 148): What passes within very few lines might have taught [Theobald] that [the French] are words the Knight had got 'ready' (see line 72) instructed by his Sir Toby; and, at III, iv, 218, it had been further learnt by him, had he been so dispos'd, that Sir Toby's form of saluting is in the words which he takes from him.—MALONE: If we are to believe Sir Toby, Sir Andrew could 'speak three or four languages word for word without book.' [The four words of salutation are Sir Andrew's entire stock of colloquial French; when Viola replies to him in the same, he is out of his depth and has to respond in English, after catching the one word, 'serviteur.'—ED.]

Vio.　Et vouz oufie voftre feruiture.　　　　　　　　73

An.　I hope fir, you are, and I am yours.

To.　Will you incounter the houfe, my Neece is defi-　　75
rous you fhould enter, if your trade be to her.

Vio.　I am bound to your Neece fir, I meane fhe is the
lift of my voyage.

To.　Tafte your legges fir, put them to motion.

Vio.　My legges do better vnderftand me fir, then I vn-　　80
derftand what you meane by bidding me tafte my legs.

To.　I meane to go fir, to enter.

Vio.　I will anfwer you with gate and entrance, but we
are preuented.

　　　　　　Enter Oliuia and Gentlewoman.　　　　85
Moft excellent accomplifh'd Lady, the heauens raine O-
dours on you.　　　　　　　　　　　　　　　87

---

73. vouz oufie] vouz aufie Ff.　*vous
ausi* Rowe.　*vous aussi* Pope.
　　voftre feruiture] F₄.　voftre fervi-
teure F₂F₃.　*vostre servitur* Rowe i.
vostre serviteur Rowe ii.
　75, 76. To. *Will*, etc.] Continuation
of preceding speech, Theob.+, Var.

'73, '78, Ran. Var. '85.
　75. incounter] *encounter* Rowe.
　　houfe,] house ? Theob. et seq.
82. go] *go in* Ktly.
83. gate] *gaite* Johns.
85. Gentlewoman] Maria. Rowe.

---

　75. **incounter**] It has been supposed that the elevated language, which continues
in this scene until Viola and Olivia are alone together, is in ridicule of euphuism, but
I doubt it.　Here, of course, it is purposely used by Sir Toby in order to turn Viola
into ridicule, but she returns as good as she gets.—ED.

　76. **trade**] BOSWELL : That is, business or employment of any kind.　Thus, in
Hamlet, III, ii, 346 : 'Have you any further trade with us?'

　77. **bound**] See II, i, 10.

　78. **list**] JOHNSON : That is, bound, limit, farthest point.

　79. **Taste**] STEEVENS : Thus in Chapman's *Odyssey*, Bk. 21st : 'He now began
To taste the bow, the sharp shaft took, tugg'd hard.' [line 211, ed. Hooper, who, in
a footnote, says : ' *Taste.*—The old French verb *taster* (derived from the Teut.
tasten) was to handle, feel, touch, to try by the touch.'　See *1 Hen. IV :* IV, i, 119 :
'Let me taste my horse.'　Compare also, 'taste their valour,' III, iv, 243, of the
present play.—HALLIWELL, after giving many examples of 'taste' in the sense of
test, feeling, etc., makes the remarkable suggestion that 'Sir Toby is perhaps ridiculing the effeminate appearance of Viola, and tells her to taste her legs, they are so
tender and delicate.'—ED.]

　80. **vnderstand**] That is, stand under.

　84. **preuented**] STEEVENS : That is, anticipated.　So, in *Psalm* cxix, 148 :
'Mine eyes prevent the night-watches.'　*Hamlet*, II, ii, 305 : 'so shall my anticipation prevent your discovery.'

　86, etc. **Most excellent**, etc.] The dialogue between Viola and Olivia, when
they are alone, is in verse.　WALKER (*Crit.* i, 18) thinks that the verse begins here,

And. That youth's a rare Courtier, raine odours, wel.   88

Vio. My matter hath no voice Lady, but to your owne
moſt pregnant and vouchſafed eare.   90

And. Odours, pregnant, and vouchſafed : Ile get 'em
all three aJready.

Ol. Let the Garden doore be ſhut, and leaue mee to
my hearing. Giue me your hand ſir.   94

88, 91. [Aside.] Cap. Dyce ii, iii.

88. *odours, wel.*] Ff. *odours ? well.*
Pope, +. *odours ! well.* Rowe et cet.
(subs.)

91. *Odours...vouchſafed*] As quotations, Cap.

92. *already*] F₂. *all ready* Mal. Var.

'21, Knt, Coll, i, ii, Wh. Dyce i, Cam.
Rlfe. *ready* F₃F₄ et cet.

92. [Writing in his table-book. Coll.
ii (MS).

94. [Exeunt Sir T, Sir A, and Maria.
Rowe et seq.

Scene III. Pope, +.

---

and proposes to divide the lines : 'Most excellent-accomplish'd lady, th' heavens Rain
odours on you ! . . . My matter hath no voice, lady, but to Your own most pregnant
and vouchsafed ear.' It can do no harm thus to divide the lines for the sake of the eye,
—for the ear it is a matter of indifference. Walker's hyphen between 'excellent'
and 'accomplish'd' is well placed.—ED.

88. **raine odours,**] I am not sure that, in place of this comma, Pope's interrogation mark is not better than Rowe's exclamation.—ED.

90. **pregnant**] See II, ii, 30.

92. **all three already**] MALONE judiciously changed 'already' into ' *all* ready,'
with the remark that 'the repetition of the word *all* is not improper in the mouth
of Sir Andrew.'—The COWDEN-CLARKES : We have sometimes thought that the
Folio misprinted 'I'll get' for *I've got*, because it gives 'already' instead of ' *all*
ready.' [Sir Andrew desires to have them all ready for future use in conversation.
—ED.]

93. **Let . . . shut**] CAPELL (p. 148), in the belief that this is a line of verse, conjectured that it should read : ' *Maria*, let the garden door,' etc.

94. **Giue me your hand sir**] To understand the scene which now follows
between Olivia and Viola, we must bear in mind that this is only the second time
that Olivia has seen the lovely Page, and that since the first interview she has been
'much out of quiet,' brooding over the 'enchantment' Viola had wrought, and
growing more and more deeply in love, until at last, in imagination, Viola is become
the god of her idolatry, and she the humble worshipper at Viola's feet. It is
almost with timidity that she asks to touch Viola's hand, and when Viola, highly
resolved to discourage the passion of Olivia, which she had detected, coldly offers only
her 'duty and humble service,' Olivia could interpret the action only as springing
from exalted rank, and at once asks Viola's name. When Viola replies, 'Cesario
is your servant's name,' this was an inversion of their position which Olivia at once
resented with the reply, ''Twas never merry world since lowly feigning was termed
compliment,' Viola ought not to pretend, out of mere compliment, to be inferior to
her ; Cesario was servant to the Duke (and a Duke's servants might be of high
rank), but not to her ; in Olivia's imagination Viola was enthroned her lord and
master. This, I think, explains the opening of the dialogue.—ED.

Uio. My dutie Madam, and moſt humble feruice   95
Ol. What is your name?
Vio. *Ceſario* is your feruants name, faire Princeſſe.
Ol. My feruant fir? 'Twas neuer merry world,
Since lowly feigning was call'd complement :
y'are feruant to the Count *Orſino* youth.   100
   Vio. And he is yours, and his muſt needs be yours :
your feruants feruant, is your feruant Madam.
   Ol. For him, I thinke not on him : for his thoughts,
Would they were blankes, rather then fill'd with me.
   Vio. Madam, I come to whet your gentle thoughts   105
On his behalfe.
   Ol. O by your leaue I pray you.
I bad you neuer ſpeake againe of him ;
But would you vndertake another ſuite
I had rather heare you, to folicit that,   110
Then Muſicke from the ſpheares.

95. *feruice*] *feruice.* Ff.
100. *y'are*] Ff, Rowe,+. *you're*
Cap. Coll. Wh. Dyce, Cam. Sta. Rlfe.
you are Var. '73 et cet.
   feruant] *fervaut* F₄.
   Count] *Duke* Rowe,+.
101. *his*] *he* Theob. ii (misprint?)
Warb. *I* Warb. MS, conj. (*N. & Qu.*
VIII, iii, 142).

106. *behalfe.*] Ff, Rowe,+, Coll.
Cam. Ktly, Rlfe, Wh. ii. *behalf :—*
Cap. et cet. (subs.)
107. *you.*] *you;* Rowe et seq.
109. *ſuite*] F₂. *ſuit?* F₃F₄. *suit,*
Rowe et seq.
10. *I had*] *I'd* Pope,+.
   that] *That* Theob. Warb.

95. **seruice**] The lack of a period after this word in the Folio is, I think, merely
accidental. In my copy there is a faint mark, as of an inverted type. See I, iii, 52,
where the same omission occurs.

98. **'Twas neuer merry world**] This phrase occurs again in *Meas. for Meas.*
III, ii, 6, and in *2 Hen. VI :* iv, ii, 9. For the omission of the article both here
and in III, iii, 33 (' you slew great number'), see ABBOTT, § 84, p. 60.

100. **y'are**] Now-a-days we do not slur our personality, and, therefore, say
you're.

103. **For . . . for**] For other examples where ' for ' is loosely used for *as regards,*
see ABBOTT, § 149, p. 100.

110. **heare you, to solicit**] For this grammatical form, see I, v, 299.

111. **Musicke from the spheares**] See Plato's *Republic* (Book x, chap. 14)
where the spheres, wherein the fixed stars and the planets roll, are represented as
eight in number, and are like casks, fitted one within another ; on each sphere sits a
Siren, and when the spheres are set in motion by the distaff of Necessity the Sirens
sing, each one note ; from the heavenly harmony thus produced comes ' the music
of the Spheres.' See *Mer. of Ven.* V, i, 74, of this ed.—ED. —W. A. WRIGHT :
The passage in Milton's *Arcades*, 63–73, is directly taken from [the passage just
cited in Plato's *Republic*]. Milton himself wrote an academical *Essay, De Sphæra-*

Vio. Deere Lady.   112

Ol. Giue me leaue, befeech you : I did fend,

After the laſt enchantment you did heare,

A Ring in chace of you. So did I abuſe   115

My felfe, my feruant, and I feare me you :

Vnder your hard conſtruction muſt I ſit,

To force that on you in a ſhamefull cunning

Which you knew none of yours. What might you think?   119

112. *Deere*] *O dearest* Han.
Lady.] *lady,—* Theob. et seq.
113. *Giue*] *Nay, give* Cap.
befeech] F₂, Knt, Hal. Dyce,
Cam. Sta. Rlfe, Wh. ii. *'beseech* Mal.
Var. '21, Coll. *I befeech* F₃F₄ et cet.
114. *enchantment you did heare*] Ff

(*hear* F₃F₄), Rowe, Pope, Theob. *en-chantment* (*you did hear*) Han. Johns.
Var. '73, '78, '85. *enchantment you did here* Thirlby, Warb. et cet.
115. *chace*] *chafe* F₄.
116. *me*] *me,* F₃F₄.

---

rum Concentu, which is printed among his prose works. See also *Paradise Lost,* V, 625.

   113. **beseech you**] It is hardly worth while to call attention to the superfluous *I* which was prefixed by the Second Folio. Even Malone's apostrophe is as needless as would be apostrophes in the phrase *good-bye.*

   114. **enchantment you did**] For other examples of *do* used transitively, see ABBOTT, § 303, p. 215. Again, V, i, 146.

   114. **you did heare**] The *Text. Notes* reveal the vitality possessed by this mis-print of 'heare' for *here.* None of the editors who followed the Folio vouchsafed any explanation, but when WARBURTON contemptuously called 'hear' 'nonsense' and emended it to *here,* DR JOHNSON winced, and said bluntly : 'The present reading [hear] is no more nonsense than the emendation,' and as long as Dr John-son lived, 'hear' kept its place in the text of the *Variorums.* Of Warburton's emendation, M. MASON (p. 118) observed that 'there is not perhaps a passage in Shakespeare where so great an improvement of sense is gained by changing a single letter.' [This change of 'hear' to *here* was proposed by Thirlby in a letter to Theo-bald (Nichols, *Illust.* ii, 226) dated 7 May, 1729 ; but so little attention did Theobald bestow on it that, in December of the same year, he wrote to Warburton that 'unless the punctuation were wrong' he did not understand the passage. There is no evidence that Warburton had ever seen Thirlby's letter.—ED.]

   115. **abuse**] That is, beguile, impose upon. See V, i, 22 : 'by my friends I am abused.' So also *Macbeth,* II, i, 50 : 'and wicked dreams abuse The curtain'd sleep'; and *Hamlet,* II, ii, 579 : 'the devil . . . Out of my weakness and my melan-choly Abuses me to damn me'; and Lear, when awaking from his trance, 'I am mightily abused,' IV, vii, 53.

   118. **To force**] For other examples of the gerundive use of the infinitive, see ABBOTT, § 356, p. 256.

   118. **shamefull**] COLLIER (ed. ii) : 'In a *shame-fac'd* cunning,' says the MS Corrector ; but Olivia means that the artifice to which she had resorted was full of shame, and put her to the blush upon reflection.

   119. **might**] For other examples, where 'might' is equivalent to *could,* see ABBOTT, § 312, p. 221.

Haue you not fet mine Honor at the ftake,   120
And baited it with all th'vnmuzled thoughts
That tyrannous heart can think?To one of your receiuing
Enough is fhewne, a Cipreffe, not a bofome,   123

121. *th'vnmuzled*] *the unmuzzl'd*
Cap. Var. '73, '78, Dyce, Cam. Sta.
Rlfe, Wh. ii.
   122. *receiuing*] *conceiving* Mason.
   123. *fhewne,*] *shewn ;* Rowe et seq.

123. *Cipreffe*] F₂F₃.   *Ciprefs* F₄.
cypress Rowe, Pope, Han. Cam. Glo.
Rlfe, Dtn, Wh. ii.   *cyprus* Theob. et
cet.

120, etc. **stake . . . baited . . . vnmuzled**] Metaphors taken from the Bear-
garden.

122. **That tyrannous . . . your receiuing**] A line of unmanageable scansion,
as it stands. HANMER, the only editor except HUDSON who has attempted a remedy,
reads 'To your receiving,' omitting 'one of'; but this is only a partial recovery, not
a cure. WALKER (*Crit.* iii, 86) proposes to arrange as follows : '——To one of
your receiving | Enough is shown ; | A ciprus, not a bosom, hides my heart : | So
let me hear you speak. I pity you. | That's a degree to love.' 'At any rate,' he
adds, 'the present disposition of the lines is wrong.—Malone's ears !' Honest
Malone is not responsible for the present disposition, which, as we see, is as old as
the First Folio. If Lettsom has correctly reproduced Walker's note, Walker has
left untouched the present monstrous line—Walker's ears ! DYCE says properly
that this arrangement by Walker seems 'objectionable.' To me, HUDSON's arrangement also seems objectionable ; he divides the line at 'your,' reading as one line
'Receiving enough is shown'; in the rest he follows Walker. ABBOTT (§ 66) gives
still another division, which is what, I think, Walker really intended ; Abbott reads
as one line 'To one of your receiving enough is shown.' To me all these divisions
of lines are of trifling moment ; no ear can detect them ; if it could, the delivery
would be stilted and offensive ; metre is a servant, not a master ; here we are dealing,
not with didactic, or epic, or lyric poetry, but with dramatic, where emotion is all in
all. In the present instance, Olivia is labouring under deep and suppressed excitement ; she is on the point of revealing a secret of her innermost soul. Her words
are in perfect rhythm. Let them be so spoken, and let the lines take care of themselves.—ED.

122. **receiuing**] WARBURTON : That is, to one of your ready apprehension.
[See II, ii, 13.]

123. **Cipresse**] W. A. WRIGHT : Cypress is a fine transparent stuff now called
crape. Compare Milton's *Penseroso*, 35 : 'Sable stole of cypress lawn.' Palsgrave
gives : 'Cypres for a woman's necke—*crespe*'; and Cotgrave : 'Crespe : m. Cipres.
also, Cobweb Lawne.' In Jonson's *Every Man in his Humour*, I, iii, the edition
of 1616 reads : 'And he . . . this man ! to conceale such reall ornaments as these,
and shaddow their glorie, as a Millaners wife do's her wrought stomacher, with a
smokie lawne, or a blacke cypresse ?' The etymology of the word has been considered doubtful. Skinner (*Etymol. Angl.*) regards it as a corruption of the French
crespe, but suggests that it may be derived from the island of Cyprus, where it was
first manufactured. The latter derivation is the more probable. There are many
instances in which articles of manufacture are named from the places where they
were made, or at which they were commonly sold. For example, arras was so called
from Arras, baudekyn from Baldacco or Bagdad, calico from Calicut, cambric from

Hides my heart : ſo let me heare you ſpeake.   124

124. *Hides*] *Hideth* Del. conj. Glo.   Var. Ran. Var. Steev. Sing.
Ktly, Wright, Rlfe, Dtn, Wh. ii. *Con-*   124. *ſo*] *so* ,Cap. (Errata) Coll. Dyce,
ceals or *Covers* Ktly conj. (*Exp.* 179).   Cam.
        my] *my poore* Ff, Rowe, +, Cap.   *me*] *us* Rowe ii, +.

Cambray, cashmere from Cashmere, damask from Damascus, dimity from Damietta, dornick from Tournay, dowlas from Dourlans, lockeram from Locrenan, muslin from Mosul. The probability that cypress (or sipers, as it is also spelt) has a similar origin, is increased by finding that the island of Cyprus is associated with certain manufactures. In the Antient Kalendars and Inventories of the Treasury of the Exchequer, edited by Sir Francis Palgrave (iii, 358), among the goods and chattels belonging to Richard II., and found in the Castle at Haverford, are enumerated : ' Prim'ement xxv. draps d'or de div'ses suytes dount iiii. de *Cipre* les autres de *Lukes.*' Lukes is here Lucca (Fr. *Lucques*), and Cipre is Cyprus. Again, in a list of draperies sold at Norwich in 44 and 45 Elizabeth (quoted by Mr Gomme in *Notes and Qu.* 5th Ser. x, 226, from the *Appendix* to the *Thirty-eighth Report of the Deputy Keeper of the Public Records,* p. 444), we find 'fustyans of Naples . . . Paris clothes . . . sattins of Cipres, Spanish sattins.' Further, in the Nomenclator of Hadrianus Junius, translated by Higins (ed. Fleming, 1585, p. 157), we find, ' Vestis subserica, tramoserica . . . De satin de Cypres. A garment of cypers satten, or of silke grograine.' If therefore there were special fabrics known as ' cloth of gold of Cypres' and ' satin of Cyprus,' it is evident that these were so called, either because Cyprus was the place of their manufacture, or, which is equally probable, because they were brought into Europe from the East through Cyprus. In Hall's account (*Chronicle,* Hen. VIII., fol. 83a) of a masque at the entertainment given to Henry the Eighth by Francis, it is said that three of the performers had ' on their hedes bonettes of Turkay fashyon, of cloth of gold of Tyssue, and clothe of syluer rolled in Cypres kercheffes after the Panyns fashyon,' which points to an Eastern origin for the use of cypress. From denoting the material only, the word 'cypress' came to signify a particular kind of kerchief or veil worn by ladies, as in the present passage [in *Twelfth N.*]. So in Florio's *Italian Dict.* : ' Velaregli, shadowes, vailes, Launes, Scarfes, Sipres, or Bonegraces that women vse to weare one their faces or foreheads to keepe them from the Sunne.' And the pedlar in John Heywood's play of *The Four P's* has in his pack (Dodsley's *Old Eng. Plays,* ed. Hazlitt, i, 350) : ' Sipers, swathbands, ribbons, and sleeve laces.' [This valuable note is quoted in full in *Wint. Tale,* IV, iv, 251. DR MURRAY (*N. E. D.*) cites it as the authority for his statement that Cypress is probably formed on ' Old French *Cipre, Cypre,* the island of Cyprus, from which, in and after the Crusading times, various fabrics were brought.']

123. **a Cipresse, not a bosome**] COLLIER : Meaning, that her heart may be as easily seen as if it were covered only with a cyprus veil, and not with flesh and blood.—GOLLANCZ : The force of these words has, it would seem, been missed ; the point of the ' cypress' is not its blackness, but its transparency. Compare, ' Her riding-suit was of sable hew black, Cypress over her face, Through which her rose-like cheeks did blush, All with a comely grace.' — *Robin Hood, Will. Scadlock and Little John.* ' Bosom' must, I think, be used in this passage in the sense of ' the bosom of the dress,' which conceals the body. Olivia says, ' you can see my heart ; a thin gauze, as it were, hides it, not a stomacher.'

Vio.   I pittie you.   125
Ol.   That's a degree to loue.
Vio.   No not a grize : for tis a vulgar proofe
That verie oft we pitty enemies.
 Ol.   Why then me thinkes 'tis time to fmile agen:
O world, how apt the poore are to be proud?   130
If one fhould be a prey, how much the better
To fall before the Lion, then the Wolfe?
Clocke ftrikes.

The clocke vpbraides me with the wafte of time:
Be not affraid good youth, I will not haue you,   135

---

127. *grize*] Cam. *grice* Ff, Rowe, +.   130. *proud ?*] *proud !* Theob.
grise Steev.   131. *the better*] better F_3F_4, Rowe.
 129. *me thinkes*] *methinks* F_4.   135. *haue you,*] *have you;* Ff.

---

 124. **Hides**] DELIUS : Possibly, we should read *Hideth*. W. A. WRIGHT, who,
in the Globe edition, adopted this conjecture, for the sake of the metre, calls attention to a similar inftance in *Rich. III:* III, vi, 11, 'where the quartos have " sees
not " for " seeth not," while the folios mend the metre by reading " cannot see." '
[Were any emendation needed, almost any one is to be welcomed rather than the
weak, self-commiserating ' My poor heart' of the Second Folio. And yet HUNTER
(i, 407) defends it (Delius's change had not then been proposed), because without this
' excellent reading,' as he terms it, the verse is ' hobbling and almost unpronounce-
able.' Could Hunter, admirable critic as he was, have imagined that Olivia pronounced this line *as* a line? After the words ' Hides my heart' was there not a long
and painful silence? until at last Olivia has to entreat Viola to speak.—ED.]
 124. **so**] ABBOTT (§ 66) : That is, after this confession.
 127. **grize**] MURRAY (*N. E. D.* s. v. *Grece*) : An adoption of Old French, *grez*,
greyz, greis, plural of *gré*, taken as a collective singular in sense of ' flight of steps,
staircase'; contemporaneously a double plural *greces, greeses* was formed and used
with the meaning ' flight of steps' and ' steps in a flight'; whence in the 15th cent.
a singular form *grece* [or as here ' grize'] was deduced,—in the sense of a single
step or stair in a flight.   [That it was not in common use, even in Shakespeare's
own time, we may infer from *Othello*, I, iii, 227, where it is immediately explained :
' lay a Sentence, Which as a grise, or step may helpe these Louers.' It occurs only
once more, in *Timon*, IV, iii, 16 (p. 90, column *a*, in Folio) : ' for euerie grize of
Fortune Is smooth'd by that below.'—ED.]—W. A. WRIGHT : The plural of this
word, ' grisen' or ' grizen,' is the proper name of the steps at Lincoln, which are
known as the Grecian stairs.
 127. **vulgar**] MALONE : That is, it is common proof, the experience of every day.
 135. **I will not haue you**] DYCE (ed. ii) : Mr Lettsom queries *harm ;* and
observes, ' In either case, after this a line or more seems to have been omitted, in
which Olivia tells the supposed youth that he is too young to marry.'   [That any
line is lost, is doubtful ; but it seems to me that Olivia's sentence, owing to her
emotion, is unfinished. To give to these words the meaning ' I will not marry you,'
represents Olivia as refusing an offer before it is made.—ED.]

And yet when wit and youth is come to harueſt,   136
your wife is like to reape a proper man :
There lies your way, due Weſt.
   Vio. Then Weſtward hoe :
Grace and good diſpoſition attend your Ladyſhip :   140
you'l nothing Madam to my Lord, by me :
   Ol. Stay : I prethee tell me what thou thinkſt of me ?   142

---

136. *is come*] *are come* Pope, +, Var.
'73, Hal.
  140. *attend*] Ff, Rowe, +, Cap. Cam.
Rlfe. *'tend* Steev. Var. Knt, Coll. Wh.
Sta. Ktly, Huds. *tend* Dyce ii, iii.
   your Làdyſhip] *you* Han.

141. *me :*] *me ?* Rowe et seq.
  142. *Stay :*] Separate line, Cap. Var.
'78 et seq.
   I prethee] *pr'ythee* Pope, +.
   me ?] *me.* Cap. Var. '78 et seq.

---

136. when wit and youth is come] At the present time, when a verb in the singular is found, in Shakespeare, after two nominatives which together form one composite idea, the cry of 'bad grammar' is no longer raised.

137. a proper man] That is, a very handsome man. In a note on *Much Ado*, II, iii, 177, W. A. WRIGHT quotes from the 'Authorised Version of *Hebrews*, xi, 23 : "By faith Moses, when he was born, was hid three months of his parents, because they saw he was a proper child." Also, Lyly, in his *Euphues* (p. 352, ed. Arber), says of Adam and Eve, "Yet then was she the fairest woman in the worlde, and he the properest man." '

138. due West] W. A. WRIGHT : As the sun of his favour was setting. [But, was it ?—ED.]

139. Westward hoe] STEEVENS : This is the name of a comedy by Dekker and Webster, 1607.—NARES : *Eastward Hoe* was the title of another play by Chapman and Marston. Both must have been current phrases before they became titles for plays. *Eastward Hoe* seems to be equivalent to a trip to the city ; and *Westward Hoe* implies a trip to Tyburn.—STAUNTON : In our poet's time the Thames formed the great highway of traffic, and 'Westward, ho !' 'Eastward, ho !' equivalent to the modern omnibus conductor's 'West-end !' 'City !' were the cries with which the watermen made its shores resound from morn till night. At that period, before the general introduction of coaches, there were not less, according to Taylor, than forty thousand of these clamorous Tritons plying their calling on the river in and near the metropolis ; and their desperate contentions to secure custom sometimes led to scenes of scandalous riot and confusion.

139, 140. WALKER (*Crit.* iii, 87) would arrange these lines : 'Then westward—ho ! Grace and good disposition | Attend your ladyship.' This arrangement is adopted by the THE GLOBE ed. by DEIGHTON, WHITE ii, INNES, and, in general, by those who have used *The Globe* to print from. It has the recommendation that it preserves 'attend' of the Folio. But then THE CAMBRIDGE ed. retains 'attend,' and yet does not follow Walker ; it adheres to the division of the Folio, which gives us a line of excellent and invincible prose.—ED.

142. Stay : I prethee] CAPELL'S scansion, whereby 'Stay' is made an interjectional line, WALKER would reject, and read (*Crit.* iii, 87) as in the Folio, except that 'I prethee' is to be read, with Pope, as *pr'y thee.*

Vio. That you do thinke you are not what you are.   143
Ol. If I thinke fo, I thinke the fame of you.
Uio. Then thinke you right : I am not what I am.   145
Ol. I would you were, as I would haue you be.
Vio. Would it be better Madam, then I am *?*
I wifh it might, for now I am your foole.
Ol. O what a deale of fcorne, lookes beautifull?
In the contempt and anger of his lip,   150
A murdrous guilt fhewes not it felfe more foone,
Then loue that would feeme hid : Loues night,is noone.
Cefario, by the Rofes of the Spring,
By maid-hood, honor, truth, and euery thing,
I loue thee fo, that maugre all thy pride,   155

146. *were, as*] *were as* Pope, Han. Cap. Var. '78 et seq.

147. *am* ?] Ff, Rowe i, Theob. Warb. Johns. Var. '73, Coll. i, Hal. Cam. Sta. Rlfe, Wh. ii.   *am*, Rowe ii et cet.

149. [Aside] Sta. Ktly, Huds.

149, 150. *beautifull ? ... lip,*] *beautiful ?...lip !* F$_4$.   *beautiful,...lip !* Rowe et seq.

151. *murdrous*] *murderous* F$_4$, Rowe, Coll, Dyce, Cam.

143. **That . . . what you are**] That is, that you do think you are not in love with a woman, but you are.

147. **then I am ?**] The interrogation mark seems here indispensable ; without it the construction of ‘ it might ’ in the next line is difficult, perhaps to be relieved only by boldly changing it, with Hanmer, into ‘ *I* might.’

149, 150. **O what a deale . . . anger of his lip**] In so far as that a woman has fallen in love with a woman in disguise, the present situation is similar to that where Phebe falls in love with Rosalind in *As You Like It*. There, as here, anger and scorn merely fan the flame. Phebe says to Rosalind (III, v, 68) : ‘ Sweet youth, I pray thee chid a yere together.’ Very noteworthy, too, is the different treatment which Viola and Rosalind, each true to her own character, bestow on their female adorers. Steevens quotes appositely : ‘ Which bred more beauty in his angry eyes.’ — *Ven. & Ad.* 70.—Ed.

151, 152. **A murdrous guilt . . . is noone**] This seems to be the argument whereby Olivia justifies to herself an avowal of her love. Since passion cannot be hidden, since what is night to a lover is noon to all others, concealment is useless, and she is driven to disclose her love ; thereupon she pours forth her burning words.—Ed.

154. **maid-hood**] This word is also used in *Othello*, I, i, 189 : ‘ Is there not Charmes, By which the propertie of Youth, and Maidhood May be abus’d ?’

155. **maugre**] That is, in spite of. Again, in *Lear*, ‘ I protest,—Maugre thy strength, place, youth, and eminence,’ V, iii, 132 (where the First Quarto has *Maugure*). Cotgrave gives, ‘ *Maulgré eux*. Mauger their teeth, in spight of their hearts, against their wills, whether they will or no.’

155. **thy pride**] COLLIER (ed. ii) : This is injudiciously altered to ‘ *my* pride ’ by the MS Corrector ; Olivia refers to the ‘ contempt and anger ’ she has just above imputed to Viola.

Nor wit, nor reaſon, can my paſſion hide :   156
Do not extort thy reaſons from this clauſe,
For that I woo, thou therefore haſt no cauſe :
But rather reaſon thus, with reaſon fetter ;
Loue ſought, is good : but giuen vnſought, is better.   160
   Uio. By innocence I ſweare, and by my youth,
I haue one heart, one boſome, and one truth,
And that no woman has, nor neuer none
Shall miſtris be of it, ſaue I alone.
And ſo adieu good Madam, neuer more,   165
Will I my Maſters teares to you deplore.
   Ol. Yet come againe : for thou perhaps mayſt moue
That heart which now abhorres, to like his loue.   *Exeunt*   168

157. *thy*] *my* Ktly conj.
158. *For that*] Ff. Rowe, +, Dyce, Cam. Sta. Ktly, Rlfe, Wh. ii. *For, that* Cap. et cet.
159. *thus, with*] *thus with* Rowe et seq.
160. *ſought,…vnſought,*] Ff, Rowe. *ſought…unsought* Pope, Han. Cap. Mal.

Coll. Dyce, Cam. *ſought…given, unſought,* Theob. Warb. Johns.
164, 165. *ſaue…And*] Oli. *Save I alone!* Vio. *And* Han.
168. *heart…abhorres,*] F₂. *heart,… abhorres* F₃F₄, Rowe, Pope, Han. *heart, …abhors,* Theob, et seq.

157, 158. **Do not . . . no cause**] The meaning of these two lines seems to be : From this avowal of mine (this clause) do not extort the excuse that, because I woo, thou hast, therefore, no need to do so. It seems, however, to have puzzled HANMER, who resorted to emendation. His text reads : 'Do not extort 'wry reasons from this clause, For that I woo'; whereof the comprehension must be left to the intelligence of the reader. 'The clause' refers, I think, to what Olivia had just said : 'I love thee so,' etc. But CAPELL understands it as applying to what follows. 'Clause,' says Capell, 'must mean—article, and "thy reasons"—thy reasons for not wooing ; the "clause" being this,—that, because I woo, therefore you need not,—express'd in the line following.'—DEIGHTON : That is, do not endeavour forcibly to release from the sentence in which they are imprisoned reasons which shall seem adequate to you ; 'clause' apparently is used with reference to its literal sense from Latin *claudere*, to shut up, and the metaphor is kept up in 'fetter,' two lines lower.

158. **For that**] That is, because. For other similar instances, see ABBOTT, §§ 151, 288.

163. **nor neuer none**] W. A. WRIGHT : Another instance of such a triple negative will be found in *As You Like It*, I, ii, 27 : 'nor no further in sport neyther.'

164. **saue**] ABBOTT (§ 118, p. 81) : 'Save' seems to be used for *saved*, and 'I' to be the nominative absolute. Thus also in *Jul. Cæs.* V, v, 69 : 'All the conspirators save only he.'

164. **saue I alone**] JOHNSON : These three words Sir Thomas Hanmer gives to Olivia probably enough. [Very improperly, I think.—ED.]

Scœna Secunda.

Enter Sir Toby, Sir Andrew, and Fabian.   2

And.   No faith, Ile not ſtay a iot longer :

To.   Thy reaſon deere venom, giue thy reaſon.

Fab.   You muſt needes yeelde your reaſon, Sir *An-*   5
drew ?

And.   Marry I ſaw your Neece do more fauours to the
Counts Seruing-man, then euer ſhe beſtow'd vpon mee :
I ſaw't i'th Orchard.

To.   Did ſhe ſee the while, old boy, tell me that.   10

And.   As plaine as I ſee you now.

Fab.   This was a great argument of loue in her toward
you.   13

Scene IV. Pope, +. Act IV. Scene
i. Spedding.
 Olivia's House. Rowe.
3. *longer :*] F$_2$. *longer.* F$_3$F$_4$ et seq.
8, 35. *Counts*] *Duke's* Rowe, +.
8. *vpon*] *on* Rowe ii, +, Var. '73.

10. *ſee the*] *ſee thee the* F$_3$F$_4$ et seq.
  boy, ... that.] *boy, ... that ?* Ff,
Rowe, +, Cap. *boy ? ... that* Steev. et
seq.
 12. *toward*] *towards* Theob. ii, Warb.
Johns.

1. **Scœna Secunda**] MARSHALL : In [Irving's] acting-edition this and the following scene are transposed, forming scene i. and ii. respectively, of Act IV.

3. **a iot**] EASTWOOD & WRIGHT (*Bible Word-book*) : In the Hebrew alphabet
yod (corresponding to Greek ἰῶτα) is the smallest letter, and therefore the most
likely to be omitted or overlooked.   Hence it is applied to any small quantity whatever. . . . The origin of the word is seen more clearly in the form in which it appears
in the following quotation : 'But the limits of his power [*i. e.* the devil's] were set
downe before the foundations of the world were laide, which he hath not the power
in the least *iote* to transgresse.'—King James I. *Dæmonologie*, II, i.

3. **longer :**] It is possible that this colon, unnoticed by editors, is intentional, and
indicates Sir Toby's scant toleration of the weak Knight's speeches, and his eagerness to crush at the outset any signs of rebellion.—ED.

4, 5, etc. **To. Thy . . . Fab. You**] Note Sir Toby's familiar second person, in
which he always addresses Sir Andrew, and the respectful, and equally invariable,
you of Fabian.—ED.

10. **the while**] ABBOTT (§ 137, p. 93) : 'While' is originally a noun meaning
'time.'   'The while that,' from a very early period, is used in the condensed form
'the while,' or 'while that' or 'while'; and 'whiles' (genitive of *while*), meaning
'of, or during, the time,' was similarly used as a conjunction.   See 'Whiles you are
willing,' etc., IV, iii, 32.

And. S'light; will you make an Affe o'me.

Fab. I will proue it legitimate fir, vpon the Oathes of　　15
iudgement, and reafon.

To. And they haue beene grand Iurie men, fince before
Noah was a Saylor.

Fab. Shee did fhew fauour to the youth in your fight,
onely to exafperate you, to awake your dormoufe valour,　　20
to put fire in your Heart, and brimftone in your Liuer :
you fhould then haue accofted her, and with fome excellent iefts, fire-new from the mint, you fhould haue bangd
the youth into dumbeneffe : this was look'd for at your
hand, and this was baulkt : the double gilt of this oppor-　　25
tunitie you let time wafh off, and you are now fayld into

---

14. *S'light ;*] F₂. *'Slight ;* F₃F₄.
'Slight ! Rowe ii,+. *'Slight,* Cap.
Dyce, Cam.
　　me.] *me ?* Ff.
15. *I will*] *I* Ff, Rowe, Pope, Han.
17. *grand Iurie men*] F₂. *grand
Jury-men* F₃F₄, Rowe, Pope, Han.
Grand Jury-men Theob. Warb. Johns.

grand-jury-men Cap. *grand-jurymen*
Dyce, Cam.
22, 23. *and with … mint,*] *with …
mint;* Theob. ii, Warb. Johns.
24, 25, 26. *look'd…baulkt…fayld*]
looked…baulked…sailed Var. '03, '13,
'21, Knt, Coll. Hal. Dyce, Cam.

15–17. **Oathes … grand Iurie men**] CASTLE (p. 108) : In comedy we have
Meas. for Meas. full of law and *Twelfth Night* without it, as this play contains, I
think, only two legal references, and both wrong. One where Sir Toby and Fabian
are persuading Sir Andrew not to give up his pursuit of Olivia [in the present pas-
sage]. Of course, this is wrong, witnesses prove matters upon oath. Jurymen find
verdicts or bills. The doubt I have in my mind is whether this mistake is intentional, as in *Meas. for Meas.*, where Elbow considers an action for battery the proper
remedy for slander. The joke does not appear self-evident enough to have been
put in on purpose ; apparently there has been confusion between the duties of a
witness and those of a grand juryman. That Shakespeare … knew what a
juryman was is to be seen in *1 Hen. IV.*, when Falstaff not only assaults and
robs the travellers, but insults them : ' No, ye fat chuffs. . . . On, bacons, on !
What, ye knaves ? young men must live. You are grandjurors, are ye ! We'll
jure ye, 'faith.' [II, ii, 97. See IV, i, 34, *post.*]

19. **Shee did shew fauour**] ' Did ' is here emphatic. Fabian grants the fact of
Olivia's favour, only to make his conclusions therefrom more forcible.—ED.

20. **dormouse**] MURRAY (*N. E. D.*) : Origin obscure : the second element has
been, at least since about 1575, treated as the word *mouse*, with plural *mice*, though
a plural *dormouses* is evidenced in the 16–17th centuries. The first element has also
from the 16th century been associated with Latin *dormīre*, French *dormir*, to sleep
(as if *dorm-mouse ;* compare 16th century Dutch *slaep-ratte, slaep-muys*) ; but it is
not certain that this is the original composition. Skeat suggests for the first element Old Norse *dár*, benumbed ; compare also dialectic ' *dorrer*, a sleeper, a lazy

the North of my Ladies opinion, where you will hang   27
like an yſickle on a Dutchmans beard, vnleſſe you do redeeme it, by ſome laudable attempt, either of valour or
policie.   30
   And.   And't be any way, it muſt be with Valour, for

---

29. *laudable*] Om. Rowe, Pope,   31. *And't*] *An't* Han. Cap. Coll.
Han.   Wh. Hal. Dyce, Cam. Ktly, Rlfe.

---

person' (Halliwell).   The French *dormeuse*, feminine of *dormeur*, sleeper, sometimes suggested as the etymon, is not known before the 17th century.

  27. **the North**] That is, into the region of cold disdain.

  28. **an ysickle, etc.**] C. H. COOTE (*New Sh. Soc. Trans.* 1877–9, p. 94) suggests that Shakespeare derived this reference to the icicles on a Dutchman's beard
from a glance at a·new map whereon was recorded the discovery of Novaya Zembla
by the Dutchman Barentz, in 1596.   'From whence,' asks Mr Coote, 'did Shakespeare obtain this knowledge?   Certainly not from the pages of Hakluyt, as they
are silent respecting it.   That he obtained it as current oral news is, of course, quite
possible ; but be this as it may, the most reasonable and natural explanation of the
matter is, that it was suggested to the mind of Shakespeare by a glance at our " new
map" with many lines, in all probability the earliest engraved map produced in England whereon this important Arctic discovery is to be found.' [See Coote's description
of the 'new map' (line 79 of this scene).   It seems to me more likely that Shakespeare was indebted to some published account of Arctic voyages than to a glance at
a map.   W. A. WRIGHT states that 'a translation of Gerrit de Veer's account of
this voyage [of Barentz] was entered on the books of the Stationers' Company to
John Wolfe on the 13th of June, 1598.'   I do not know that any copy of this translation of this date exists ; if it were ever actually published and a copy of it read by
Shakespeare, it seems to me that this book would be the most likely source of Shakespeare's knowledge.   The entry on the Stationers' Registers is as follows : 'xiii°
Junii [1598]. John wolfe | Entred for his Copie vnder th handes of master Hartwell
and the warden master mans hand | A true description of Three voyages by sea,
whereof the world as yett hath had but small intelligence : Three yeeres one after
another by the Hollanders and Zelanders by north Norwaye, Musovya, and Tar-
taria to the kyngdome of Cattay and Chyna Together with the discoverye of the
Weygattes Nova sembla and of the land of 80 degrees which hath been taken for
Groenland whereas yett there hath no man dwelt | And of the feirce Beares and
other Sea monsters and merveylous could and howe in the last voyage the shippe is
besett in Iyce and thatt our men beinge vnder 76. degrees of Nova sembla built
them a howse and Remayncd there 10 monethes and after that Ryd in little slight
vesselles alongest the sea. CCCl.[350] myles alwaies with verye greate Daunger
and incredible labour | By Jerrett De veer of Amsterdam.'—Arber's *Reprint*, III,
118.   Is it not more likely that Shakespeare found stories of icicles on Dutchmen's
beards, in this book with its accounts of the 'merveylous could' and of ships
'besett in ice,' than that he inferred them from a glance at a map?   I have supposed that no copy of this book dated 1598 is extant from Dr Wright's remark
that 'the reprint of Phillip's translation for the Hakluyt Society is taken from a
copy of 1609, and apparently an earlier edition is known.'—ED.

policie I hate : I had as liefe be a Brownift, as a Politi-   32
cian.

---

32. **Brownist**] STEEVENS : The Brownists seem, in the time of our author, to
have been the constant objects of popular satire. In *Ram-Alley*, 1611, is the following : 'Pandarism ! why, 'tis grown a liberal science, Or a new sect, and the
good professors Will (like the Brownist) frequent gravel-pits shortly, For they use
woods and obscure holes already.'[I, i, p. 283, ed. Hazlitt-Dodsley.]—W. A.
WRIGHT : Earle, in his *Micro-cosmographia* (ed. Arber, p. 64), says of 'A Shee
precise Hypocrite,' ' No thing angers her so much as that Woemen cannot Preach,
and in this point onely thinkes the Brownist erroneous.'   And in the old play of
Sir Thomas More (Shakes. Soc.), p. 51 : 'Heers a lowsie jest ! but, if I notch not
that rogue Tom barbar, that makes me looke thus like a Brownist, hange me !'
[Robert Brown, the founder of the Brownists, was born in 1550. His father obtained,
by a charter of ͵Henry VIII., the singular privilege of wearing his cap in the King's
presence. About the year 1580, he began to promulgate his principles of dissent
from the Established Church.   His assaults upon the Church of England form
of government gained him many followers.   His sect daily increasing, Dr Freake,
bishop of Norwich, with other ecclesiastical commissioners, called him before them.
Being insolent to the court, he was committed to the custody of the sheriff's officer,
but was released at the intercession of his relative, the Lord Treasurer Burghley.
Brown now left the kingdom and settled at Middlebury in Zealand, where he formed
a church of his own.   The removal of persecution, however, broke up the unity of
the party, and Brown soon returned to England. For his indiscreet attempts to gain
proselytes, he was cited by the bishop of Peterborough, and, refusing to appear, was
finally excommunicated for contempt.   The solemnity of this censure immediately
effected his reformation.   He moved for absolution, which was obtained, and from
that time became a dutiful member of the Church of England.   In a short time
afterwards (about 1590) Brown was preferred to a rectory where he might probably
have died in peace ; but having some dispute with the constable of his parish relative to the payment of rates, he proceeded to blows, and was afterwards so insolent
to the justice that he was committed to Northampton jail, where he died in 1630.
Brown boasted on his death-bed that he had been confined in thirty-two different
prisons. Sir Walter Raleigh, in a speech in 1592, estimated the number of Brownists at no less than twenty thousand.   Soon, however, differences of opinion began
to arise ; some became absolute Separatists ; others adopted a milder form of opposition to the Church, which ultimately resulted in Independency. This latter form
prevailed, and the Brownists gave place to the Independents.   The occasion of the
Brownists' separation was not any fault they found with the faith, but only with the
discipline and form of government of the other churches in England.   They condemned the celebration of marriages in the church, maintaining that, as matrimony
was a civil contract, its confirmation ought to come from the civil magistrate.   They
rejected all forms of prayer, and held that the Lord's prayer was not to be recited as
a prayer, having been given only for a rule or model whereon all our prayers are
to be formed.   Their form of church government was democratic. They did not
erect the priesthood into a distinct order.   As the vote of the brotherhood made a
man a minister, so the same power could discharge him from his office, and reduce
him to a mere layman again.   In a word, every church on the Brownists' model is a
body corporate, having full power to do everything which the good of the society

To. Why then build me thy fortunes vpon the baſis of
valour.Challenge me the Counts youth to fight with him   35
hurt him in eleuen places, my Neece ſhall take note of it,
and aſſure thy ſelfe, there is no loue-Broker in the world,
can more preuaile in mans commendation with woman,
then report of valour.

Fab.   There is no way but this ſir *Andrew.*   40

An.   Will either of you beare me a challenge to him?

To.   Go, write it in a martial hand, be curſt and briefe:
it is no matter how wittie, ſo it bee eloquent, and full of
inuention : taunt him with the licenſe of Inke : if thou
thou'ſt him ſome thrice, it ſhall not be amiſſe, and as ma-   45

---

38. *mans*] *mens* F₃F₄, Rowe i.   Pope, Han.
    woman] *women* F₃F₄, Rowe,   39. *then*] *than* Ff.

---

requires, without being accountable to any presbytery, synod, assembly, convocation,
or other jurisdiction whatever.—Condensed from *Encyclopædia Britannica*, Ninth
Ed.—ED.]

32, 33. **Politician**] W. A. WRIGHT : Shakespeare generally uses this word in
an unfavourable sense, as denoting a political intriguer or conspirator. See, for
instance, *1 Hen. IV:* I, iii, 241 : ' this vile politician, Bolingbroke.' And *Hamlet*,
V, i, 86 : ' It might be the pate of a politician, which this ass now o'erreaches ; one
that would circumvent God, might it not ?' Again, *Lear*, IV, vi, 175 : ' Get thee
glass eyes ; And like a scurvy politician, seem To see the things thou dost not.' [See
Sir Toby's drunken use of the word, II, iii, 77.]

34. **me**] The so-called ethical dative ; it occurs again in the next line, ' Challenge me.' It is still in common use. See, if need be, ABBOTT, § 220, or Shakespeare *passim*.

35. **youth . . . with him**] TYRWHITT (*Var.* 1773) : This is nonsense. Read,
' Challenge me the Duke's youth ; go, fight with him.'—RITSON (*Remarks*, p. 65) :
If any alteration be necessary, it should be, ' to fight with you.' The text, however,
is neither nonsensical nor difficult. KEIGHTLEY reads ' with thee.' [But the text
means simply, ' Let your challenge to the Count's youth be to fight with him.']

36. **shall**] That is, must. For other instances, see ABBOTT, § 315.

42. **martial hand**] JOHNSON : This seems to be a careless scrawl, such as shewed
the writer to neglect ceremony. [Possibly, it may mean with heavy-faced, aggressive
flourishes.—ED.]

42. **curst**] JOHNSON : That is, petulant, crabbed. A curst cur is a dog that with
little provocation snarls and bites. DOUCE (i, 99) finds in ' curst' and ' brief' an
allusion to the proverb : ' A *curst* cur must be tied *short*.' [' Except those explanatory of customs, dress, etc.,' says Dyce (*Remarks*, p. 96), ' the notes of Douce are
nearly worthless.']

44. **with the license of Inke**] That is, with all the freedom of speech which the
written word allows.

44, 45. **thou thou'st him**] THEOBALD : These words seem to me directly
levelled at the Attorney-General Coke, who, in the trial of Sir Walter Raleigh,

ny Lyes, as will lye in thy fheete of paper, although the   46
fheete were bigge enough for the bedde of *Ware* in England, fet 'em downe, go about it. Let there bee gaulle e-
nough in thy inke, though thou write with a Goofe-pen,
no matter : about it.   50

     And.   Where fhall I finde you ?

     To.   Wee'l call thee at the Cubiculo : Go.

                                 Exit Sir Andrew.   53

---

48. *go about it*] Ff, Knt, Wh. Hal.
and go about it Rowe, Pope, Han. *go,
about it* Cap. et cet.
49. *write*] *write it* Rowe, Pope, Han.

52. *the*] *thy* Han. Ran. Dyce ii, iii,
Coll. iii, Huds.
53. Scene V. Pope, +.

---

attacked him with the indecent expressions : ' All that he did was at thy instigation,
thou viper ; for I *thou* thee, thou traitor'; ' Thou hast a Spanish heart, and thyself
art a spider of hell,' etc.—CAPELL (p. 149) : The Poet's boldness was great, or his
regard great for the character [Raleigh] so treated, if he ventur'd at producing this
speech as it now stands ; 'tis more probable that 'twas abridg'd [from 'invention' to
' about it '] in its stage exhibition ; at least at first, and 'till things had taken a turn
(which they did shortly) which made adventuring safe. [Raleigh's trial took place
in November, 1603. In 1845, HUNTER discovered from Manningham's *Diary* that
Twelfth Night was acted in February, 1602, which at once disproves Theobald's
reference unless this clause were a later addition, inserted after the trial, and before
this play was printed in the Folio ; this, HUNTER (i, 408) believes, is 'not probable'; on the other hand, J. CHURTON COLLINS (p. 279, *footnote*) asserts that
' nothing is more likely.' In general, I have small faith in these contemporary
allusions. Moreover, Hunter points out that as far as Shakespeare had any connection with a political party, he belonged to the party to which Raleigh was
opposed. Stubbes (*Christal Glasse*, etc., 1591, p. 198, ed. New Sh. Soc.) says of
his late wife that ' she was neuer heard to giue any the lie, nor so much as to thou
any in anger '; we need, however, no quotation better than Coke's language as
given above.—ED.]

    47. **bedde of Ware**] The Frontispiece to HALLIWELL'S seventh volume is an
elaborate engraving of this bed, taken in 1832. His note is as follows : This celebrated bed is formed of oak, curiously and elaborately carved. The date 1460 is
given on the back as the year of its construction, but it is undoubtedly a relic of the
time of Queen Elizabeth. It is 7 ft. 6 in. in height, 10 ft. 9 in. in length, and 10 ft.
9 in. in width. The earliest notice of the bed yet discovered occurs in the Itinerary
of a German prince, Ludwig of Anhalt-Köthen, who came to England in 1596, and
who mentions this renowned piece of furniture as so large that four couples might
conveniently rest in it without any pair incommoding another.—DYCE (*Gloss.*) : At
what inn in Ware it was kept during Shakespeare's days is uncertain ; but, after
being for many years at *The Saracen's Head*, it was sold there by auction in September, 1864, and knocked down at a hundred guineas (the newspapers erroneously
adding that Mr Charles Dickens was the purchaser). W. A. WRIGHT says that it
is now to be seen at the Rye-House.

    52. **Cubiculo**] HANMER'S reading *thy*, commended by WALKER (*Crit.* ii. 234)

Fa. This is a deere Manakin to you Sir *Toby.*

To. I haue beene deere to him lad, fome two thoufand　　55
ftrong, or fo.

Fa. We fhall haue a rare Letter from him; but you'le
not deliuer't.

To. Neuer truft me then : and by all meanes ftirre on
the youth to an anfwer. I thinke Oxen and waine-ropes　　60
cannot hale them together. For *Andrew*, if he were open'd
and you finde fo much blood in his Liuer, as will clog the
foote of a flea, Ile eate the reft of th'anatomy.

Fab. And his oppofit the youth beares in his vifage no
great prefage of cruelty.　　　　　　　　　　　　　　65

Enter Maria.

To. Looke where the youngeft Wren of mine comes.　　67

---

54. *Manakin*] *manikin* Theob. Warb. Johns. Huds.

58. *deliuer't.*] *deliver it.* Mal. Steev. Var. Knt, Coll. Hal. Sta. Ktly. *deliver't ?* Dyce, Cam, Rlfe, Huds. Wh. ii.

61. Andrew] *sir Andrew* Coll. ii (MS).

62. *and*] *an* Walker (*Crit.* ii, 153), Huds.

63. *of th' anatomy*] Ff, Rowe, +, Wh. *o' the anatomy* Cap. *of the anatomy* Var. '73 et cet.

67. *mine*] Ff, Rowe, Pope, Hal. *nine* Theob. et cet.

---

and adopted by DYCE, has much in its favour if 'cubiculo' refer to Sir Andrew's apartment ; but as Sir Toby was apparently lodging in Olivia's house, and Sir Andrew, too, for that matter, it is quite possible that it may refer to some definite common chamber, to which Sir Toby gives a Latin name, either to impress Sir Andrew or to flatter him, as he did at the opening of II, iii, by assuming Sir Andrew's familiarity with that tongue.

54. **a deere Manakin to you**] ABBOTT (§ 419 *a*, p. 309): Unless 'to' is used loosely like 'for,' 'dear' is here transposed. [See I, iv, 42.]

60. **Oxen and waine-ropes**] BOSWELL : So, in Fletcher's *Loyal Subject* [1618] : 'A coach and four horses cannot draw me from it.' [III, ii, p. 57, ed. Dyce.]

62. **blood in his Liuer**] A bloodless liver was a sign of cowardice. See II, iv, 104. Thus, *Macbeth*, V, iii, 15 : 'Go prick thy face, and over-red thy fear, Thou lily-liver'd boy !' And, *Mer. of Ven.* III, ii, 92 : 'How manie cowards . . . Who inward searcht, haue lyuers white as milke.'

64. **opposit**] MALONE : That is, an adversary. 'Opposite' was used as a substantive. [See II, v, 140.]

67. **Wren of mine**] HANMER : The Wren is remarkable for laying many eggs at a time, nine or ten and sometimes more ; and as she is the smallest of birds, the last of so large a brood may be supposed to be little indeed, which is the image intended here to be given of Maria.—WARBURTON : The women's parts were then acted by boys, sometimes so low in stature, that there was occasion to obviate the impropriety by such kind of oblique apologies.—HALLIWELL (the only modern

Mar. If you defire the fpleene, and will laughe your   68
felues into ftitches, follow me; yond gull *Maluolio* is tur-

69. *ftitches*] *side-stitches* Cap.   69. *yond*] *yon'* Cap. Mal. Steev.
                                               yond' Knt, Coll. Wh.

editor who follows the Folio) : That is, my youngest wren, in allusion to the diminutive size of Maria.   The term *wren* is similarly applied to a thin bony person in
How to Chuse a good Wife, 1602.   Theobald's alteration is, I think, unnecessary.
[Halliwell's reference to the use of 'wren' in *How to Chuse a good Wife*, etc., is
hardly parallel, inasmuch as it is there applied to an elderly pedant.   I suppose the
passage he refers to is the following : 'When didst thou see the starveling schoolmaster? That rat, that shrimp, that spindle-shank, That wren, that sheep-biter,
that lean chitty-face,' and so on, in three more lines of opprobrious epithets.—II, iii,
p. 40, ed. Hazlitt-Dodsley.   I am not sure, however, that Halliwell is not, otherwise,
right in discarding Theobald's emendation.   Why should the phrase be the youngest
of *nine?*   The selection of this number seems to me pointless ; nine eggs are no
more characteristic of the wren than seven or eight, or ten or eleven, or any other
number up to eighteen ; these many eggs has the wren been known to lay.   Willughby,
in his Chapter on *The Wren*, says (p. 229) : 'A late English Writer tells us, that he
hath had eighteen Eggs out of one Nest, and sixteen young ones out of another.'
That Sir Toby chose a wren on account of its diminutive size is quite probable,
but possibly there is an additional reason.   At the sight of Maria, he recalls when
and where he had last seen her, it was when she had planted them in the box tree,
which means a hedge, to watch Malvolio ; she had then at once flitted from them ;
as soon as Malvolio leaves, Maria as suddenly reappears.   It was this quick, vivacious flitting to and fro among the hedges and alleys of the garden that reminded
Sir Toby of a wren.   'It creeps about hedges and holes,' says Willughby, 'whence
it is not undeservedly called *Troglodites*.   It makes but short flights,' etc.   If this
characteristic of the diminutive bird be Sir Toby's predominant association, at the
moment, with Maria, Theobald's change is superfluous, and 'mine' of the Folio
becomes Sir Toby's admiring claim to possession in his little 'wren'; and since
youth is the season of vivacity, Maria was the 'youngest' of wrens, because the
most vivacious.—ED.]

68. spleene] This word is used by Shakespeare in more than one meaning.
In *Mid. N. D.* I, i, 156, it means excessive haste : 'Briefe as the lightning in the
collied night, That (in a spleene) vnfolds both heauen and earth.'   In the passage
before us it evidently means mirth in excess.   For this mirthful attribute of the spleen
Shakespeare had authority in the physiology of his times.   In Batman *vppon Bartholome* we find (Lib. Quintus, Cap. 41) : 'The Milt is called *Splen* in Latine . . .
And some men suppose, that the mylt is the cause of laughing.   For by the Splene
we are moued to laugh : by the Gall, we be wroth : by the Heart, we be wise : by
the Braine, we feele : by the Lyuer, we loue.'   And Batman adds : 'The mylt is a
spongeous substance, lieng vnder the short ribbes, in the left side, by which equall
of kinde, man is disposed to mirth, otherwise there follow, the passions of sadnesse.'
—ED.

68. will laughe] That is, desire to laugh.

69. gull] NARES : That is, a dupe, a fool.   When sharpers were considered
as bird-catchers, a *gull* was their proper prey.   In the Dramatis Personæ to the play
of *Every Man in his Humour*, master Stephen is styled 'a country gull,' and master

ned Heathen, a verie Renegatho; for there is no chriftian   70
that meanes to be faued by beleeuing rightly, can euer
beleeue fuch impoffible paffages of groffeneffe. Hee's in
yellow ftockings.   73

70. *Heathen*] *a   heathen* Walker   70. *Renegatho*] *renegado* Rowe et
(*Crit.* i, 91).   seq.

Matthew 'the town gull,' which is equivalent to the dupe of each place. But a ' gull '
is most completely defined by J. D. (supposed to be Sir John Davies) in an epigram
on the subject, about 1598 : 'Oft in my laughing rimes I name a *gull*, But this new
terme will many questions breede ; Therefore at first I will expresse at full, Who is
a true and perfect gull indeed. A gull is he, who feares a velvet gowne, And when
a wench is brave, dares not speake to her ; A gull is he which traverseth the
towne, And is for marriage knowne a common wooer. A gull is he who while he
proudly weares A silver-hilted rapier by his side, Indures the lyes and knockes about
the eares, While in his sheath his sleeping sword doth bide. A gull is he which
weares good hansome cloathes, And stands in presence stroaking up his hayre ; And
filles up his unperfect speech with oathes, But speakes not one wise word throughout the year. But to define a gull in termes precise, A gull is he which seems and
is not wise.—*Ovid's El. by C. M. and Epigrams by I. D.*

    70. **Renegatho**] W. A. WRIGHT : This represents somewhat the pronunciation
of the Spanish word. Minsheu has ' Renegado, an apostata, one that hath forsaken
the faith.' The word appears not to have been thoroughly naturalized till the 18th
century, for, although ' renegade ' is found at the end of the previous century, ' renegado ' is used by Addison. In earlier English the form was ' renegate,' from the
French ' renégat,' and this was corrupted into ' runagate.'

    72. **passages**] In a note on *All's Well*, I, i, 20 : 'O, that " had " ! how sad a
passage 'tis !' JOHNSON remarks : ' Passage ' is anything that passes. So we now
say, a ' passage ' of an author ; and we said about a century ago the ' passages ' of
a reign.—STEEVENS : Thus Shakespeare himself: *Com. of Err.* III, i, 99, ' Now
in the stirring passage of the day.' So, in Shirley's *Gamester*, 1637 : 'I'll not be
A witness of your passages myself,' *i. e.* of what passes between you [II, ii, p. 214,
ed. Dyce]. Again, in *A Woman's a Weathercock*, 1612 : 'I not desire it, sir, Nor
ever lov'd these prying, listening men, That ask of others' states and passages.'
[I, i.] Again, *Ib.*, ' I knew the passages 'twixt her and Scudamore.' [V, i.] Again,
in *The Dumb Knight*, ' *Cyprus*. Ourself and our own soul, that have beheld Your
vile and most lascivious passages.' [V, i.]—NARES : ' Passage ' was currently used
in this sense as late as Swift's time.—W. A. WRIGHT : ' Passages of grossness,'
gross impositions. Compare ' pass upon,' III, i, 43.—DEIGHTON thus paraphrases
the sentence : I say heathen and renegade, for he must be so, since not a Christian
in the whole world, who expects salvation from holding the true faith, can ever
believe such grossly impossible doctrines as Malvolio has embraced in putting faith
in the directions of my letter. ' Passages ' seems to be used in the sense of passages
from Scripture laying down principles of conduct, and 'impossible passages of grossness,' to be put for passages of such gross impossibility. [The interpretation of
' passages ' as *acts*, given by Johnson, Steevens, and Nares seems to be the true one.
In *1 Hen. IV :* III, ii, 8, the King in rebuking the young Prince, says, ' But thou
dost in thy passages of life Make me believe that thou art only mark'd For the hot

To. And croſſe garter'd?

Mar. Moſt villanouſly: like a Pedant that keepes a   75
Schoole i'th Church : I haue dogg'd him like his murtherer. He does obey euery point of the Letter that I dropt,
to betray him : He does ſmile his face into more lynes,
then is in the new Mappe, with the augmentation of the
Indies : you haue not ſeene ſuch a thing as tis: I can hard-   80

76, 77. *murtherer*] Ff, Rowe, +, Wh. *murderer* Steev. et cet.

77, 78. *dropt, to*] *dropt to* Rowe et seq.

79. *then is*] Ff, Rowe, +, Cap. Cam. Rlfe. *than are* Steev. et cet.

80. *as tis:*] *as'tis.* Cam. Rlfe, Wh. ii.

vengeance and the rod of Heaven,' etc. Again, in *Hamlet*, IV, vii, 113, the King says to Laertes, 'love is begun by time, And that I see, in passages of proof, Time qualifies the spark and fire of it.' Thus, here, Maria ſays that it was these almost incredible *acts of absurdity* that were to make them laugh their sides into stitches. —ED.]

75. **Pedant**] Cotgrave gives : '*Pedagogue : m.* A Schoole-master, Instructor, Teacher, Tutor, Pedant.' Also, '*Pedant : m.* A Pedant, or ordinarie Schoole-master.'

76. **Schoole i'th Church**] HALLIWELL: It is curious and worthy of remark, although there is no great probability of there being here a local allusion, that the grammar-school at Stratford was at intervals during Shakespeare's time, probably while the school was under repair, kept in the Church or Chapel of the Guild, which was opposite one side of the poet's residence, New Place. If *Twelfth Night* were composed at Stratford, no improbable supposition, at the very time this passage was written, there may have been 'a pedant that keeps a school in the Church' within a few paces of the author's own house. [Evelyn in his *Kalendarium* records under '1624, I was not initiated into any rudiments till I was four years of age, and then one *Frier* taught us at the church porch of *Wotton*.'—*Memoirs*, etc., vol. i, p. 3, ed. Bray.]

79, 80. **the new Mappe . . . Indies**] STEEVENS: A clear allusion to a Map engraved for Linschoten's Voyages, an English translation of which was published in 1598. This map is *multilineal* in the extreme, and is the first in which the *Eastern Islands* are included.—HUNTER (i, 379) : I would not assert that there is not an allusion to these maps of Linschoten, but I doubt it. The turn of the expression seems to point not to the maps in Linschoten, but to some single map well-known at the time, 'the new map'; and further that the map alluded to had the words in its title 'with the Augmentation of the Indies,' which is not the case with any of Linschoten's maps.—KNIGHT gives an engraving of a portion of the multi-lineal map in Linschoten's Voyages, exhibiting the islands of Malacca and Borneo. —HALLAM (ii, 494) : But the best map of the sixteenth century is one of uncommon rarity, which is found in a very few copies of the first edition of Hakluyt's Voyages. This contains Davis's Straits, Virginia by name, and the lake Ontario. The coast of Chili is placed more correctly than the prior maps of Ortelius. . . . Corea is represented near its place, and China with some degree of correctness ; even the north coast of New Holland is partially traced. . . . The Ultra-Indian region is inaccurate. . . . But upon the whole it represents the utmost limit of geo-

[79, 80. new Mappe, with the augmentation of the . . . Indies]
graphical knowledge at the close of the sixteenth century.—J[AMES] L[ENOX] (*Nicolaus Syllacius De Insulis Meridiani*, etc., New York, 1860, *Int.* p. xiii) : The translation of Linschoten's *Voyages to the East Indies*, published in London in 1598, . . .
contains the map of the *East Indian Islands*, to which Shakespeare is supposed to
refer in *Twelfth Night.* . . . But do not the words ' with the augmentation of the
Indies' refer rather to a map representing a larger portion of the world than merely
the East Indian islands? Such a map of *the World* is given in Hakluyt's Voyages,
published in London in 1598–1600. It has been celebrated by Hallam as the best
map of the sixteenth century. . . . This map embraces both the East and West
Indian islands, and is quite as *multilineal* as that which appears in Linschoten's
Voyages. The observation of Steevens on the passage in *Twelfth Night* . . . would
have been more correct had he called [Linschoten's map] the first in which these
islands were delineated on a large scale, or with any pretensions to accuracy. [The
map in Hakluyt's *Voyages* described by Hallam, and suggested by Lenox as the
'new map' referred to by Maria, was still further identified by C. H. COOTE (*New
Sh. Soc. Trans.* 1877–9, p. 88, 14 June, 1878), who agrees with Lenox that
Steevens's note, quoted above, is wide of the mark, and proves that the multilineal
map reproduced by Knight is no more multilineal than 'any number of maps and
charts reaching back to half a century,' and that it had no claim to be considered a
'new map,' since, in point of fact, it was thirty years old at the time of the appearance of *Twelfth Night*. But as to the map described by Hallam, Coote shows that
'it was a new map on a new projection laid down upon the principles set forth by
Edward Wright'; and that on it 'we find the latest geographical discovery recorded,
namely, that of Northern Novaya Zembla, by the Dutchman Barentz in 1596. The
news of this did not reach Holland until 1598. Allowing one year for this to reach
England and to be worked up into our map, the conclusion is irresistible that this
map had every claim to be regarded as the "new map," in that it was published in
1599, within two years of the performance of *Twelfth Night* in 1601.' 'Now what
was the state of things upon the eastern portion of our "new map" at the close of
the 16th century, as compared with the best maps of the world which preceded it?
A marked development in the geography of India proper, the island of Ceylon, and
the two peninsulas of Cochin China, and Corea. For the first time Japan began to
assume its modern shape. Turning to the S. E. portion of the "new map," there
were to be seen traces of the first appearance of the Dutch at Bantam, synchronizing
almost within a year with that of their fellow-countrymen in Novaya Zembla. . . .
It is this appreciation of the marked improvement and development of the eastern
portion of our map, to which I believe Shakespeare desired to give expression in
his judicious and happy use of "augmentation." ' Coote proves that the maker of
this 'new map' was Emmerie Mollineux, 'possibly with the assistance of Hakluyt.'
'It would be an anachronism,' he continues, 'to associate our "new map" with
the first edition of Hakluyt, 1589; to do so exclusively with the second would be
equally a mistake, as in the latter we find no mention of it or of the discovery of
Barentz. The truth seems to be that it was a separate map well known at the time,
made in all probability for the convenience of the purchasers of either one or the
other of the two editions of Hakluyt.' 'The whole case for our map may be sum-
marized thus : 1. It was a "new map" on a new projection made by one of the
most eminent globe-makers of his time, probably under the superintendence of Hakluyt. 2. It had upon it as many sets of rhumb-lines as were to be found on any that

ly forbeare hurling things at him, I know my Ladie will   81
ſtrike him : if ſhee doe, hee'l ſmile, and take't for a great
fauour.

    To. Come bring vs, bring vs where he is.

Exeunt Omnes.   85

Scæna Tertia.

Enter Sebaſtian and Anthonio.   2

    Seb. I would not by my will have troubled yo u,
But ſince you make your pleaſure of your paines,
I will no further chide you.   5
    Ant. I could not ſtay behinde you : my deſire
(More ſharpe then filed ſteele) did ſpurre me forth,   7

---

81. *at him,*] *at him.* F₄.
  1. Scæna...] Scene VI. Pope, +.
    The Street. Rowe.
  2. Anthonio.] Ff, Rowe, +. *An-*

tonio. Cap. et seq.
    7. *forth,*] *forth;* Theob. et. seq.
(subs.)

---

preceded it, and *four* more than the one of the Moluccas in Linschoten [repro-
duced by Knight]. 3. It showed the whole of the East Indies, including Japan,
which the map of Linschoten did not. 4. [Mr Coote here finds the reference to
Barentz's voyage referred to at line 28 above.] Future research may possibly bring
to light a successful rival to our "new map," but I doubt the probability of it.'—
W. A. WRIGHT, in regard to this 'new map' of Mollineux, is inclined to share
Hunter's doubt as to Linschoten's. Maria's description of the map 'has so much
the appearance of the title under which it was issued, that the absence of it from
the map in question creates in me some misgiving as to whether it is really the map
which Shakespeare had in mind. In all other respects it suits exactly, and the difficulty I have suggested may not be an insuperable one.' [Inasmuch as this 'new
map' was adapted for insertion in both the first and the second editions of Hakluyt,
Hallam's cautious remark that it is to be found in a very few copies of the first edition is evidently correct. If on preceding maps the Indies were already marked,
however imperfectly, on any new map the statement that it had the 'addition of
the Indies,' would have been false ; consequently 'augmentation' was the only
word that could be used ; and this, as Hunter and Dr Wright remark, sounds so
like a title, advertised on the map itself, that one cannot help regretting that this
insignificant link is lacking in Mr Coote's admirably welded chain.—ED.]

  80, 81. **I can hardly forbeare hurling things at him**] O mighty Master !

  82. **strike him**] STEEVENS : We may suppose that in an age when ladies struck
their servants, the box on the ear which Queen Elizabeth is said to have given to
the Earl of Essex was not regarded as a transgression against the rules of common
behaviour.

And not all loue to ſee you (though ſo much   8
As might haue drawne one to a longer voyage)
But iealouſie, what might befall your rrauell,   10
Being skilleſſe in theſe parts : which to a ſtranger,
Vnguided, and vnfriended, often proue
Rough, and vnhoſpitable.   My willing loue,
The rather by theſe arguments of feare
Set forth in your purſuite.   15

   Seb.   My kinde *Anthonio,*
I can no other anſwer make, but thankes,
And thankes : and euer oft good turnes,   18

---

9. *one*] *me* Heath, Dyce ii, iii, Huds.
   voyage)] *voyage.* Rowe ii, Pope.
voyage.) Theob. Warb. Johns. *voyage;*
Han.

10. *rrauell*] *travell* F$_2$.

14. *feare*] *fear*, Pope et seq.

18, 19. Om. Ff, Rowe.

18. *And thankes : and euer oft good
turnes*] Knt.   *And thanks : and ever
oft-good turns* Pope i.   *And thanks :
and ever-oft good turns* Pope ii.   *And
thanks, and ever thanks ; and oft good
turns* Theob. Han. Warb. Johns. Cap.
Del. Dyce i, Sta. Hunter, Rlfe, Verity.
And thanks, and ever.   Oft good turns
Var. '73.   *And thanks, and ever : oft
good turns* Var. '78, '85, Coll. i.   *And
thanks again, and ever.   Oft good turns*
Tollet, Ran.   *And thanks, and ever
thanks : oft good turns* Mal. Perring.
*And thanks, and ever thanks : often
good turns* Steev. Var. '03, '13, '21,
Sing. i, Harness.   *And thanks, still*
thanks ; and very oft good turns Coll.
ii, iii (MS), Dyce ii, iii.   *And ever
thanks : and oft good turns* Sing. ii.
*And thanks, and ever thanks ; though
oft good turns* Lettsom ap. Dyce.   *And
thanks : and very oft good turns* Wh. i.
*And thanks, and thanks ; and very oft
good turns* Wh. i conj.   *And thanks,
and ever oft good turns* Hal. Symons·
*And thanks ; and ever ... oft good
turns* Cam. Glo. Wright, Cholmeley,
Chambers, Gollancz.   *And thanks, and
ever thanks.   Good turns oft* Ktly.   *And
thanks, and ever thanks ; too oft good
turns* Seymour, Huds. Conrad, Innes,
Lee. *And thanks ; and ever thanks. How
oft good turns* Abbott (*Index* p. 497)·
Dtn.   *And thanks, and thanks ; and
ever oft good turns* Wh. ii.   *And thanks
add every hour—though oft good turns*
Bulloch.   *And thanks, and evermore
thanks.   Oft good turns* Orger.

---

8. **not all loue**] CAPELL (p. 149) : These lines are most defectively worded, and
to be supply'd in this manner : ' *Nor was* love to see you all *the cause,* (though so
much *was that love's quantity,* as might, etc.

9. **haue drawne one**] HEATH (p. 192) conjectured ' drawn *me* '; again suggested by WALKER (*Crit.* iii, 87), who cites Dyce, *Remarks,* p. 16, where we read :
' The word " one " is frequently printed by mistake for *me ; e. g.* in Beaumont &
Fletcher, *The Bloody Brother,* I, i, we find, according to 4to, 1639, and folio, 1679 :
" ' Twas not in one, my lord, to alter nature," while 4to, 1640, gives rightly, " ' Twas
not in me, my lord," etc.' [*Me* is better than ' one,' but, inasmuch as ' one ' makes
tolerable sense, the propriety of change is doubtful.—ED.]

10. **iealouſie**] That is, suspicion, apprehension, as in *Much Ado,* II, ii, 45 :
' iealouſie shall be cal'd assurance.'

18. **And thankes : and euer oft good turnes**] THEOBALD : This line is too

Are fhuffel'd off with fuch vncurrant pay :
But were my worth, as is my confcience firme,   20
You fhould finde better dealing : what's to do ?
Shall we go fee the reliques of this Towne ?

   Ant. To morrow fir, beft firft go fee your Lodging ?

   Seb. I am not weary, and 'tis long to night
I pray you let vs fatisfie our eyes   25
With the memorials, and the things of fame
That do renowne this City.

   Ant. Would youl'd pardon me :
I do not without danger walke thefe ftreetes.
Once in a fea-fight 'gainft the Count his gallies,   30

20. *worth*] *wealth* Coll. MS.
23. *Lodging ?*] *Lodging.* Ff.
28. *Would youl'd*] *'Would, you'd* Theob. Warb. Johns.

28. *Would...me :*] *Would you pardon me ?* Coll. MS ap. Cam. *youl'd*] F₂.
30. *Count his*] *Duke his* Rowe, +.

short by a whole foot. Then, who ever heard of this goodly double adverb 'ever-oft,' which seems to have as much propriety as *always-sometimes ?* [The *Text. Notes* furnish twenty-one readings, adopted by fifty-two editors and critics, not counting KNIGHT, who sturdily and in obscurity follows the Folio. The comments are few and scanty; they consist, in the main, of simple statements that the line should be read thus and so. R. G. WHITE pronounces the reading of Collier's MS Corrector the 'best possible emendation' of 'ever,' yet he does not adopt it in his First Edition; and he himself proposes a reading which he does not adopt in his Second. W. A. WRIGHT says that Theobald's reading would be improved by substituting *for oft* instead of 'and oft'; which is virtually Lettsom's emendation. Theobald's text has the largest following, and, with either Lettsom's or Wright's modification, would be, I think, the best that can be done with the line, which, be it noted, the other Folios shrewdly omitted altogether.—ED.]

   20. *worth*] M. MASON : This means, in this place, wealth or fortune.—DYCE (*Note* on 'I know the gentleman To be of worth and worthy estimation.'—*Two Gent.* II, iv, 56) : 'Worth' is often used by our early writers as equivalent to 'substance, wealth'; compare, 'They are but beggars that can count their *worth ;* But my true love is grown to such excess, I cannot sum up half my sum of *wealth.'*—*Rom. & Jul.* II, vi. 'This is the life of the Prigger, who trauailes vp and downe the whole kingdome vpon his geldings of 20 and 40 pound price, and is taken for a man of good worth by his outward show,' etc.—Dekker's *Belman of London,* sig. G2, ed. 1608.

   20. *as is my conscience*] That is, as is my consciousness of what is your due.

   21. *what's to do*] That is, to be done. For other examples of the use of the infinitive active where we should use the passive, see ABBOTT, § 359, p. 259.

   22. *go see*] See, if need be, 'go hunt,' I, i, 19.

   22. *the reliques*] MALONE : These words are explained by lines 25–27.

   30. *Count his gallies*] MALONE : I suspect our author wrote,—'*County's* gallies,' and that the transcriber's ear deceived him. [For 'transcriber's' read *compositor's.*

I did fome feruice, of fuch note indeede,   31
That were I tane heere, it would fcarfe be anfwer'd.
  Seb. Befike you flew great number of his people.
  Ant. Th offence is not of fuch a bloody nature,
Albeit the quality of the time, and quarrell   35
Might well haue given vs bloody argument :
It might haue fince bene anfwer'd in repaying
What we tooke from them, which for Traffiques fake
Moft of our City did.   Onely my felfe ftood out,
For which if I be lapfed in this place   40
I fhall pay deere.

32. *tane*] Ff. *ta'en* Rowe.   *Dyce* ii, iii.   *The offence* Cap. et cet.
33. *people.*] *people?* Dyce, Sta.   35. *of the*] *of* F₃F₄, Rowe i.
34. *Th offence*] Ff, Rowe,+, Wh. i,

—ED.]—WALKER (*Crit.* iii, 87) : The use of 'his' as a separate word,
instead of the termination *s* (now written *'s*) in the genitive singular, is generally
rare in the Elizabethan poets, except in those cases where the substitution does not
increase the number of syllables.   Read, therefore, 'the County's gallies.'   In like
manner, *All's Well*, III, vii,—'the Count he is my husband'; 'the Count he woos
your daughter'; read 'the *County* is,' etc., 'the *County* woos,' etc.—W. A. WRIGHT :
In the Authorised Version of 1611, in the contents of *Ruth* iii, we find : 'By Naomi
her instruction, Ruth lieth at Boaz his feete.'   See ABBOTT, § 217.

  32. **answer'd**] That is, defended.   In line 37, it means compensated.

  33. **great number**] For the construction, see III, i, 98.

  36. **argument**] That is, cause, reason.   Compare *Hamlet*, IV, iv, 54, 'Rightly
to be great Is not to stir without great argument,' etc.

  40. **lapsed**] HUNTER (i, 408) : If authorities could be produced for the use of
lapse in this sense [*i. e.* taken, surprised], which perhaps may be done, no more is
to be said.   But *lapse* is generally understood to mean something which does not in
the least suit this passage, while there was a word *latched*, very like it, the sense of
which is consistent.   Take an example of its use from Golding's *Ovid :* 'A flaming
firebrand from amidst an altar Rhœtus snatch't With which upon the left side of his
head Charaxus lacht A blow that crack't his skull.'—Bk. xii.   So, in Palsgrave :
'If I had latched the pot in time it had not fallen to the ground.'   Again, 'A sound
being made by the clashing of hard things together, and latched by the outward
ear.'—*Gate of Language*, p. 330.   It appears to be nearly the same word with *catch*.
[KEIGHTLEY adopted this change, which is certainly very tempting, but not
absolutely necessary.   Hunter might have added, 'I have words That would be
howl'd out in the desert air, Where hearing should not latch them.'—*Macbeth*, IV,
iii, 195, and notes in this ed.; also, in *Sonnet* 113, 6 : 'For it [*i. e.* the eye] no form
delivers to the heart Of bird, of flower, or shape, which it doth latch.'   The word
'latch't' in *Mid. N. D.* III, ii, 38, is of a different derivation, according to Skeat,
meaning to drip, or cause to drop.   SCHMIDT (*Lex.*) defines 'lapsed' as 'surprised,
taken in the act'; and gives two examples, the present phrase and *Hamlet*, III, iv,
107 ; but to neither does his definition completely apply (the passage in *Hamlet*,
'who lapsed in fume and passion,' is altogether misinterpreted).   The *Century Dict.*

Seb. Do not then walke too open.   42

Ant. It doth not fit me : hold fir, here's my purfe,
In the South Suburbes at the Elephant
Is beft to lodge : I will befpeake our dyet,   45
Whiles you beguile the time, and feed your knowledge
With viewing of the Towne, there fhall you haue me.

Seb. Why I your purfe ?

Ant. Haply your eye fhall light vpon fome toy
You haue defire to purchafe : and your ftore   50
I thinke is not for idle Markets, fir.

Seb. Ile be your purfe-bearer, and leaue you
For an houre.

Ant. To th'Elephant.

Seb. I do remember.   *Exeunt.*   55

45, 46. *lodge ... knowledge*] *lodg ... knowledg* F₄.

46. *the time*] *your time* Theob. ii, Warb. Johns. Var. '73, '78, '85, Ran.

47. *Towne,*] *town ;* Theob. et seq.

52, 53. *Ile...For*] One line, Theob. +,

Cap. Var. Mal. Steev. Var. Dyce, Hal. Wh. i. Prose, Var. '21, Coll.

54. *th' Elephant*] Ff, Rowe, +, Wh. i, Dyce ii, iii, Huds. *the elephant* Cap. *the Elephant* Var. '73 et cet.

---

has no reference to 'lapse' as here used ; but Webster's *International* gives the present passage as an example of the meaning, 'to surprise in a fault or error ; hence to surprise or catch, as an offender.'—ED.]

44. **the Elephant**] HALLIWELL : The Elephant was a well-known sign in London, and Shakespeare was unquestionably thinking of his own country, both in the writing of this passage and in the subsequent one which alludes to the bells of St. Bennet. 'The Elephant and Castle' was, and is, a still more common sign. In MS Ashmol, 334, a medical MS written in 1610 and 1611, mention is made of 'Mr Dee at the signe of the Elephant and Castle by Fleet condyt, an apothecaryes howse.' There was an 'Elephant and Castle' near the Royal Exchange in Cornhill, 1681.—W. A. WRIGHT : If it were not an anachronism, I should like to suggest that Shakespeare might be thinking of the Elephant and Castle at Newington, which is in 'the south suburbs'; but I have been unable to trace that inn further back than the middle of the seventeenth century.

45. **Is best**] For other examples of the ellipsis of 'it,' see ABBOTT, § 404, p. 291 ; also 'that satisfaction can be none,' III, iv, 237, where there is an ellipsis of *there*.

45. **dyet**] W. A. WRIGHT : That is, food or fare generally ; not, as now, prescribed or limited food. In Shakespeare's time it had the sense of 'daily food,' as is clear from Cotgrave, who gives : 'Diete : f. Diet or dailie fare,' supposing it to be from the Latin *dies* instead of the Greek δίαιτα.

47. **With viewing**] See I, v, 76, 77, 'for the better increasing.' Here the definite article is absorbed in the final *th* of 'With': 'With' viewing.'—ED.

51. **is not for**] That is, is not fit for, or full enough. See, 'I will on with my speech,' I, v, 189.

Scœna Quarta.

Enter Oliuia and Maria.   2

Ol. I haue fent after him, he fayes hee'l come:
How fhall I feaft him? What beftow of him?   4

---

1. Scœna...] Scene VIII. Pope, +.   3. *he fayes hee' l*] *say, he will* Theob.
   Olivia's House. Rowe.   Olivia's   *say he will* Han.
Garden. Cap.   4. *of him*] *on him* Pope, +, Var. '73,
   3. [Aside. Sta. Huds.   Ran. Steev. Var.
     him,] *him :* Rowe et seq.

---

3. **he sayes**] THEOBALD : But who [*sic*] did he say so to? Or from whom
could my Lady have such intelligence? Her servant was not yet return'd ; and,
when he does return, he brings word that the youth would hardly be entreated back.
I am persuaded, she was intended rather to be in suspense, and deliberating with
herself ; putting the supposition that he would come ; and asking herself, in that
case, how she should entertain him. I imagine, therefore, the Poet wrote : ' Say,
he will come ' ; so Viola, before, in this play : ' Say, I do speak with her, my lord ;
what then ?' So, Petruchio in the *Tam. of the Shrew :* ' Say, that she rail ; why,
then I'll tell her plain,' etc. And in numberless other passages.—WARBURTON :
That is, I suppose now, or admit now, he says he'll come ; which Mr Theobald,
not understanding, alters unnecessarily to ' say he will come.' [These two notes
are here given in full as a fresh instance of the high-handed treatment which
Theobald received at the hand of Warburton. (Happily, Theobald was dead
when Warburton's edition appeared ; and never knew the bitter unkindness
of him who in correspondence constantly signed himself ' your most affectionate friend.') No attentive reader can fail to note that Warburton deliber-
ately appropriates Theobald's explanation, and then accuses Theobald of failing to understand the passage. It would not have been worth while to call
attention to this incident, were it not that in consequence of the insertion of Warburton's note in the *Variorum* of 1821, while Theobald's was ignored, whatsoever
credit is due to the explanation is given, and to this day, to Warburton.—ED.]
CAPELL (p. 149) gives the same explanation as Theobald : ' Admit his answer be—
that he'll come.'—HUDSON believes that the ' concessive sense ' is required, not the
affirmative ' he says,' and that this sense is obtained ' naturally enough ' by the
simple transposition, ' says he,' ' the subjunctive being often formed in that way.'
And so he reads in his text.—KARL ELZE (p. 183) : These first four lines are evidently spoken aside by Olivia, as confirmed by her own words, ' I speak too loud ' ;
only in the fifth line she addresses Maria. It is, however, in the natural course of
things that she should have conversed with Maria on the subject before, and that the
latter should have tried to console her enamoured mistress. I should, accordingly,
feel no hesitation in reading : ' *Oliv.* [Aside]. I have sent after him ; *she* says he'll
come,' etc. [Theobald's explanation seems to be the true one, and the text, without alteration, will bear it out.—ED.]

4. **bestow of him**] For other examples where ' of ' is equivalent to *on*, see

For youth is bought more oft, then begg'd, or borrow'd.   5
I fpeake too loud : Where's *Maluolio*, he is fad, and ciuill,
And fuites well for a feruant with my fortunes,
Where is *Maluolio* ?
   Mar.   He's comming Madame :
But in very ftrange manner.   He is fure poffeft Madam.   10

6. *I fpeake too loud*] Ff, Rowe, Ktly.
Separate line, Pope et cet.
   Where's] Ff, Rowe, Ktly.   *Where
is* Pope et cet.
9, 10. Prose, Pope i, Var. '21, Knt.
Glo. Cam.   *He's...manner*. One line,
Pope ii, Theob. Warb. Johns. Var. Ran.

Var. Dyce, Coll. Sta.
   9. *He's*] *He is* Han.
   10. *But...poffeft*] One line (reading
in strange manner), Han. Steev. Var.
'03, '13.
   very] *a very* Ktly.
   Madam.] Om. Steev. Var. '03,'13.

ABBOTT, § 175, who points out that 'the connection between *of* and *on* is illustrated
by *Mer. of Ven.* II, ii, 90, where old Gobbo says, "thou hast got more haire *on* thy
chin, than Dobbin my philhorse has *on* his taile"; and Launcelot retorts, "I am
sure he had more haire *of* his taile than I have *of* my face." '—BADHAM, however
(p. 273), 'strongly suspects that confusion has arisen from "of" in one of the transcripts being so written as to appear to belong to the verse preceding its own, and
that "him" was subsequently added to complete the sense. In the original copy
Olivia would have said,—"How shall I feast him, what bestow? for youth Is
bought more oft then begged or borrowed." '
   6. *sad*] That is, grave, serious, as in line 21, below.   Compare, Rosalind's
'Speake sadde brow and true maid.'—*As You Like It*, II, ii, 209.
   6. *ciuill*] MALONE : That is, solemn and grave. So, in *Rom. & Jul.* III, ii, 10,
'Come, civil night Thou sober-suited matron, all in black,' etc.—STEEVENS : So, in
As You Like It, 'Tongues I'll hang on every tree That shall civil sayings show.'
[III, ii, 127, of this ed. where, see Note, if need be.]—STAUNTON : Interpreted to
import *solemn* and *grave*, which is mere tautology.   'Civil' here means *tart, sour,
bitter*.   Thus, in *The Scornful Lady* cf Beaumont & Fletcher : 'If he be civil, not
your powder'd sugar, Nor your raisins, shall persuade the captain To live a coxcomb
with him.'[IV, ii,—a passage wherein it is almost incomprehensible that Staunton
should have supposed the meaning of 'civil' to be *tart, sour*, or *bitter*. The Widow,
whose late husband had been a grocer, and, (as we are expressly told in I, iii,) had
sold powdered sugar, raisins, etc., is trying to make Young Loveless cast off his
boon companions who were not, as she says, fit 'to furnish out a civil house'; she
tells him he 'shall be civil, And slip off these base trappings,' whereupon the Captain, who was one of the 'trappings,' replies, 'He shall not need, my most sweet
Lady Grocer,' and then follows Staunton's quotation, where clearly the reference to
'powdered sugar' and 'raisins' does not apply to 'civil,' as though to sweeten its
tartness, but is merely, as Capell would say, a 'wipe' on the source of the Widow's
wealth.   Staunton, in a note on 'Civil as an orange' in *Much Ado*, urged this same
meaning of 'Civil' as *bitter;* but the notion seemed so wide of the mark that I did
not refer to it in the notes on that passage.   DR MURRAY, in the *N. E. D.*, gives no
such meaning to 'civil' as Staunton here claims for it.—ED.]
   9, 10...12–14. The *Text. Notes* show the lame attempts to convert Maria's honest
kersey prose into verse.

Ol.   Why what's the matter, does he raue?   11

Mar.   No Madam, he does nothing but fmile:your La-
dyfhip were beft to haue fome guard about you, if hee
come, for fure the man is tainted in's wits.

Ol.   Go call him hither.   15

Enter Maluolio.

I am as madde as hee,
If fad and metry madneffe equall bee.
How now *Maluolio*?

Mal.   Sweet Lady, ho, ho.   20

Ol.   Smil'ft thou? I fent for thee vpon a fad occafion.

Mal.   Sad Lady, I could be fad :
This does make fome obftruction in the blood :
This croffe-gartering, but what of that?
If it pleafe the eye of one, it is with me as the very true   25
Sonnet is : Pleafe one, and pleafe all.

11–14. *Why...wits.*] Four lines, ending *Madam,...best...come,...wits.* Cap.
Var. '78, '85, Ran. Mal. Ending,
Madam, ... ladyship ... come; ... wits.
(reading *have guard*) Steev. Var. '03,
'13.

11. *matter,...raue?*] *matter?...rave?*
Cap. et seq.

12–14. Four lines, ending *smile;...
guard...man...wits.* (reading *nothing
else*) Han.

14. *in's*] Ff, Rowe. Pope, Theob. i,
Var. '21, Coll. Wh. Hal. Dyce, Cam.
Rlfe. *in his* Theob. ii et cet.

15–17. *Go...hee*] One line, Cap. et
seq.

15. *hither.*] *hither.* [Exit Maria]
Dyce, Cam.

16. Enter...] After line 18, Cap.

17. *I am*] Ff, Rowe, Var. '21, Knt,
Coll. Wh. Dyce i, Cam. Rlfe. *I'm*

Pope et cet.

18. *metry*] F_1. *mercy* F_2. *merry*
$F_3 F_4$.

19. *How*] Ol. *How* F_2.

20. *ho, ho.*] *ha, ha* Ff, Rowe,+,
Var. '73. Om. Cap.
    [Smile   fantastically.   Rowe
(Smiles, Rowe ii).

21. *I...occafion*] One line, Cap. et seq.

22–24. Prose, Pope et seq.

22. *Sad Lady,*] *sad, lady?* Theob.
et seq. (subs.)

23, 24. *blood: This croffe-gartering,*]
Rowe, Pope. *blood; this cross-gartering;* Theob. Warb. Johns. *blood, this
cross-gartering,* Han. *blood, this cross-
gartering;* Cap. et seq. (subs.)

24. *of that?*] *of it?* Theob. ii, Warb.
Johns. Var. '73. *of that,* Var. '03, '13.

26. *is*] *it* F_2. *has it* Cap. *hath it*
Coll. MS.

---

13. **were best**] For the construction, see I, v, 30.

25, 26. **the very true Sonnet**] HALLIWELL : An allusion to a popular ballad
of the time, originally published in the year 1591–2, according to the following entry
in the Stationers' Registers : 'xviij. die Januarii, 1591, Henry Kyrkham, entred for
his copie under Mr Watkin's hande a ballad intituled the Crowe she sittes upon the
wall : please one and please all.' [Halliwell gives a facsimile of a copy] of one of
the original editions of this ballad, probably the first issued, from the collection of
Mr Daniel. The initials R. T. [at the end] perhaps stand for Richard Tarlton,

Mal. Why how doeſt thou man? 27
What is the matter with thee?
Mal. Not blacke in my minde, though yellow in my 29

27. Mal.] Ol. Ff.   *Why,* Cap. et seq. (subs.)
27, 28. Prose, Pope et seq.   **27.** *doeſt*] *do'ſt* F₃F₄.
27. *Why*] F₂. *Why ?* F₃F₄, Rowe, +.

---

the celebrated actor. If so, the ballad must have been current some time before its publication in 1592, as Tarlton died in 1588.—W. A. WRIGHT: Only one copy is known to exist, in the collection formerly belonging to the library at Helmingham, which was sold at Mr George Daniel's sale, and is now in the possession of Mr Huth.—STAUNTON: It is adorned with a rude portrait of Queen Elizabeth, with her feathered fan, starched ruff, and ample farthingale. The numbers of this relic are not lofty, nor the expression very felicitous; but 'Please One and Please All' is worth preserving, both as an illustration of Shakespeare, and as a specimen of the quaint and simple old ballad literature of our forefathers :—

A prettie newe Ballad, intytuled:
The Crowe sits vpon the Wall,
Please one and please all.
To the tune of, Please one and please all.

Please one and please all,
Be they great be they small,
Be they little be they lowe,
So pypeth, the Crowe,
  sitting vpon a wall :
  please one and please all. [*bis.*]

Be they white be they black,
Have they a smock on their back,
Or a kircher on her head,
Whether they spin silke or thred,
  whatsoeuer they them call :
  please one and please all. [*bis.*]

Be they sluttish be they gay,
Loue they worke or loue they play,
Whatsoeuer be theyr cheere,
Drinke they Ale or drinke they beere,
  whether it be strong or small :
  please one and please all. [*bis.*]

The goodwife I doo meane,
Be shee fat or be she leane,
Whatsoeuer that she be,
This the Crowe tolde me,
  sitting vppon a wall :
  please one and please all. [*bis.*]

Be she cruell be she curst,
Come she last come she first,
Be they young be they olde,
Doo they smile doo they skould,
  though they doo nought at all :
  please one and please all. [*bis.*]

Though it be some Crowes guise,
Oftentimes to tell lyes, .
Yet this Crowes words dooth try,
That her tale is no lye,
  For thus it is and euer shall :
  please one and please all. [*bis.*]

[I have given a selection from the nineteen stanzas as a sufficient taste of their quality,—quite sufficient to please certainly one and please possibly all.—ED.]

27. Mal.] This error was quickly corrected in the Second Folio. COLLIER conjectured that the speech may 'in fact belong to Maria, *Mal.* having been printed instead of *Mar.*'

29. blacke . . . yellow] COLLIER: There was an old ballad tune called 'Black and Yellow,' and to this Malvolio may allude.

legges : It did come to his hands, and Commaunds ſhall   30
be executed.   I thinke we doe know the ſweet Romane
hand.

   Ol. Wilt thou go to bed *Maluolio?*

   Mal.   To bed *?* I ſweet heart, and Ile come to thee.

   Ol. God comfort thee : Why doſt thou ſmile ſo, and   35
kiſſe thy hand ſo oft *?*

   Mar.   How do you *Maluolio?*

   Maluo. At your requeſt :
Yes Nightingales anſwere Dawes.

   Mar.   Why appeare you with this ridiculous bold-   40
neſſe before my Lady.

   Mal.   Be not afraid of greatneſſe : 'twas well writ.

   Ol. What meanſt thou by that *Maluolio?*

   Mal.   Some are borne great.

   Ol. Ha?   45

   Mal.   Some atcheeue greatneſſe.

   Ol. What ſayſt thou ?

   Mal.   And ſome haue greatneſſe thruſt vpon them.

   Ol.   Heauen reſtore thee.

   Mal.   Remember who commended thy yellow ſtock-   50
       ings.

   Ol. Thy yellow ſtockings *?*   52

---

30. *Commaunds*] F₁.
31. *the ſweet*] *that sweet* Rowe ii,+.
33. *thou*] Om. Voss conj.
35. *ſo,*] Om. Voss conj. (reading *God...kiſſe* as one line).
38, 39. *At...Dawes*] Prose, Cap. et seq.
38. *requeſt :*] *request !* Rowe i. *request ?* Rowe ii.

39. *Yes*] *Yes,* F₄, Rowe,+.   *Yes;* Cap. et cet.
41. *Lady.*] *Lady ?* Ff.
43. *meanſt*] Han. *meaneſt* Ff et cet.
44, 46, 48, 50, 53, 55, ending with a dash, Rowe et seq. (subs.) As quotations, Han. Cap. et seq.
52. *Thy*] *My* Lettsom, Dyce ii, Huds. Wh, ii.

---

  36. **kisse thy hand**] DEIGHTON : Compare *Othello*, II, i, 175, 'it had been better you had not kissed your three fingers so oft, which now again you are most apt to play the sir in,' *i. e.* display your courtly manners, as Malvolio here fancies he is doing.

  38, 39. **At your . . . Dawes**] DEIGHTON : What ! am I to answer the question when addressed by such as you are ? yes, I will, for nightingales sometimes answer the notes of jackdaws, and therefore I may without loss of dignity answer the question of a mere servant like Maria.

  52. **Thy yellow stockings ?**] DYCE (ed. i) : Mr W. N. Lettsom would read '*My* yellow stockings !' for Olivia had no idea that Malvolio is quoting the letter; and when he presently continues 'Go to, thou art made, if thou desirest to be so,'

Mal.   And wifh'd to fee thee croffe garter'd.   53
Ol.   Croffe garter'd?
Mal.   Go too, thou art made, if thou defir'ft to be fo.   55
Ol.   Am I made?
Mal.   If not, ler me fee thee a feruant ftill.
Ol.   Why this is verie Midfommer madneffe.   58

---

53. *And wifh'd*] *wifh'd* F$_4$, Rowe i.   **58.** *is verie*] *is a very* Theob. ii, Warb.
55. *Go too,*] *Go to,* F$_4$.   Johns. Var. '73, '78, '85, Ran.
57. *ler*] F$_1$.   *Midfommer*] F$_2$.

---

she exclaims '*Am I* made?' [Dyce adopted this conjecture in the text of his Second Edition (and therein was followed by HUDSON, WHITE (ed. ii), and CONRAD), but wisely deserted it in his Third Edition, on the true ground that the old text is 'a mere re-echoing [*sic*] by Olivia of Malvolio's words.' Lettsom's suggestion is unquestionably a happy one, as many a suggestion of his is, but I fear it verges too far toward improving Shakespeare.—ED.]

56. made] DYCE (ed. ii): Manningham in his *Diary* [see *Preface* to the present volume.—ED.] speaks of Olivia as being a 'widow'; and Mr Collier remarks that 'in Rich's novel the lady Julina, who answers to Olivia, is a widow, but in Shakespeare she never had been married. It is possible that in the form in which the comedy was performed on Feb. 2, 1601-2, she was a widow, and that the author subsequently made the change; but it is more likely, as Olivia must have been in mourning for the loss of her brother, that Manningham mistook her condition, and concluded hastily that she lamented the loss of her husband.'—*Introd. to Twelfth Night.* Mr Peacock, too, believes that Manningham has made a mistake in 'calling Olivia a widow.'—*Preface* to his translation of *Gl' Ingannati*, p. 6. But Mr Lettsom thinks very differently. On the present speech of Olivia, 'Am I made?' he observes: 'This, and Malvolio's speeches just above, show that Collier was wrong in supposing that Manningham mistook the condition of Olivia. In the play as we have it, this part has little comic power; but nothing could have been more effective than the natural astonishment of the *widow* Olivia, when she heard her steward (as she understood him) talking of her yellow stockings, her cross-gartering, and finally of her virgin state; for I have no doubt that Shakespeare originally wrote "Am I *maid?*"' [This seems to me extremely doubtful, unless Lettsom means that the present text is not that which Manningham heard. First, had Lettsom's interpretation been intended, it is likely that the phrase would have been 'Am I *a* maid?' Secondly, at the very beginning of the play, Olivia is described as a 'maid'; it would therefore cause her no surprise to be called one. Whereas she might well express utter bewilderment over the assurance that she had but to wish and her fortune would be 'made.'—ED.]

58. Midsommer madnesse] STEEVENS: ''Tis midsummer moon with you,' is a proverb in Ray's *Collection*; signifying, you are mad.—HALLIWELL 'He wyll waxe madde this mydsommer moone if you take nat good hede on hym.'—Palsgrave[p. 775, ed. 1852]. Again, 'And that your grace may see what a meer madnesse, a very mid-summer frenzy, 'tis to be melancholy, for any man that wants no monie.'—Chapman's *Revenge for Honour*,[I, i. Many other examples are added.]

Enter Seruant.

Ser. Madame, the young Gentleman of the Count   60
Orſino's is return'd, I could hardly entreate him backe : he
attends your Ladyſhips pleaſure.

Ol. Ile come to him.
Good *Maria*, let this fellow be look d too.   Where's my
Coſine *Toby*, let ſome of my people haue a ſpeciall care   65
of him, I would not haue him miſcarrie for the halfe of
my Dowry.   *exit*

Mal. Oh ho, do you come neere me now : no worſe
man then ſir *Toby* to looke to me. This concurres directly with the Letter, ſhe ſends him on purpoſe, that I may   70
appeare ſtubborne to him : for ſhe incites me to that in
the Letter. Caſt thy humble ſlough ſayes ſhe : be oppo-
ſite with a Kinſman, ſurly with ſeruants, let thy tongue
langer with arguments of ſtate, put thy ſelfe into the
tricke of ſingularity : and conſequently ſetts downe the   75
manner how : as a ſad face, a reuerend carriage, a ſlow
tongue, in the habite of ſome Sir of note, and ſo foorth .   77

60. *Count*] *Duke* Rowe, +.

63. *him.*] *him.* [Exit Ser.] Cap.

64. *too.*] *to.* F$_3$F$_4$.

65. *Coſine*] *Uncle* Rowe ii, +.
Toby,] *Toby ?* Rowe.

66. *the halfe*] *half* Theob. ii, Warb.
Johns.

67. *exit*] Exeunt Oliv. and Mar. Cap.
Scene VIII. Pope, +.

68. *Oh ho,*] Ff, Pope, Han. Cap.

Oh, ho, Rowe, Theob. i.   *Oh, oh !*
Theob. ii, Warb. Johns.   *O, ho !* Cam.

68. *now :*] *now ?* F$_4$.

69. *me.*] *me !* Rowe.

70. *Letter,*] *letter ;* Theob.

72–75. *Caſt...ſingularity*] As a quotation, Han. Cap. et seq.

74. *langer with*] *tang* Cap. Dyce ii.
twang Huds.   *tang with* Ff. et cet.

61. **entreate him backe**] For other examples of the omission of the verb with
adverbs implying motion, see ABBOTT, §§ 30, 32, 41.

66. **miscarrie**] SCHMIDT (*Lex.*) supplies many examples of the use of this word
in the sense of to come to grief or mischance.

68. **do you come neere me now:**] W. A. WRIGHT : That is, do you understand
me now ? do you know who I am ?

72, 73. **opposite**] See II, v, 140.

74. **langer**] See *Text. Notes*, and II, v, 141.

75. **consequently**] W. A. WRIGHT : That is, accordingly, in accordance therewith. Compare *King John*, IV, ii, 240 : 'Yea, without stop, didst let thy heart
consent, And consequently thy rude hand to act The deed, which both our tongues
held vile to name.' [A better definition than that given by Schmidt (*Lex.*) of 'pur-
suantly, thereafter,' which denotes sequence in time.—ED.]

77. **some Sir of note**] See Deighton's quotation at line 36, from *Othello ;* also
Wint. Tale, IV, iv, 390 : 'O heare me breath my life Before this ancient Sir.'

I haue lymde her, but it is Ioues doing, and Ioue make me   78
thankefull.   And when fhe went away now, let this Fellow be look'd too : Fellow ? not *Maluolio*, nor after my   80
degree, but Fellow.   Why euery thing adheres togither,
that no dramme of a scruple, no fcruple of a fcruple, no
obftacle, no incredulous or vnfafe circumftance : What
can be faide ? Nothing that can be, can come betweene
me, and the full profpect of my hopes.   Well Ioue, not I,   85
is the doer of this, and he is to be thanked.

Enter Toby, Fabian, and Maria.

To.   Which way is hee in the name of fanctity.   If all   88

78. *lymde*] F₂. *limde* F₃. *limd* F₄.   Rowe et seq.
lim'd Rowe.
    78, 85. *Ioues ... Ioue*] *God's ... God*
Hal. Huds.
    80. *too*] *to* Ff.
      Fellow ?] *fellow !* Rowe.
    83. *circumftance :*]   *circumftance—*

83, 84. *circumftance...Nothing*] *circumftance,—what can be said ?—nothing* Perring.
    87. Scene IX. Pope, +.
    88. *fanctity.*] *fanctity ?* Ff.

78. **lymde**] JOHNSON ; That is, I have entangled or caught her, as a bird is
caught with birdlime. [Compare, *Much Ado*, III, i, 109 : 'Shee's tane (*limed*, in
the Qto) I warrant you, We haue caught her Madame.']

78. **Ioues . . . Ioue**] See II, v, 161. R. G. WHITE with plausibility conjectured
that we should here read *Love's* and *Love.*—INNES : It may be, however, that Malvolio thought it more becoming to adopt the pagan adjurations of the court, in lieu
of his previous puritanism.

80. **Fellow ?**] JOHNSON : This word, which originally meant companion, was not
yet totally degraded to its present meaning ; and Malvolio takes it in the favourable
sense.

82. **scruple, no scruple of a scruple**] KEIGHTLEY (*N. & Qu.* IIIrd, xii, 61,
1867) : To understand this phrase, we must take the first and last 'scruple' in the
moral sense, the second as the weight, the third part of a dram.   I owe this simple
and natural explanation to J. J. A. Boase.   [This is a virtual withdrawal of the
reading : 'no scruple of an *ounce*,' in Keightley's edition.   Compare *2 Hen. IV* :
I, ii, 149 : 'But how I should be your patient to follow your prescriptions, the wise
may make some dram of a scruple, or indeed a scruple itself.']

83. **incredulous**] WALKER (*Crit.* i, 65) : This may be an erratum for *incredible ;*
yet I think not.—W. A. WRIGHT : This appears to be here used in an active sense.
Malvolio would say that nothing has occurred which would make him incredulous.
For instances of adjectives used both in the active and passive sense, see ABBOTT, § 3.

88. **sanctity**] WALKER (*Crit.* iii, 88) : Certainly *sanity ;*—the same corruption
has taken place in *Hamlet*, I, iii, early in the scene,—' on his choice depends The
sanctity and health of the whole state '; for there too *sanity* must be the right reading ; ' sanctity,' at any rate, is absurd.   Compare *heavily* and *heavenly*, *Much Ado*,
V, iii, 22. [This emendation, more sure in *Hamlet* than here, is tempting.   But Sir
Toby's next words show a connection of thought with matters religious, which

the diuels of hell be drawne in little, and Legion himſelfe
poſſeſt him, yet Ile ſpeake to him.   90

   Fab.   Heere he is, heere he is : how iſt with you ſir ?
How iſt with you man ?

   Mal.   Go off, I diſcard you : let me enioy my priuate:
go off.

   Mar.   Lo, how hollow the fiend ſpeakes within him ;   95

89. *of hell*] *in hell* Rowe, +, Cap.
Var. Ran. Steev. Var. Knt, Coll. Sta.
90. *poſſeſt*] *possess* Coll. MS.

93. *priuate*] *privacy* Rowe, +, Coll.
ii, iii (MS).

---

makes for retaining 'sanctity.'   Moreover, rather than *sanity*, should it not be
insanity ?—ED.]

  89. **drawne in little**] In a note on 'heauen would in little show,' *As You Like
It*, III, ii, 139, MALONE observes that the allusion is to a miniature portrait ; and
STEEVENS refers to 'give twenty, forty, fifty, a hundred ducats apiece for his picture
in little,'—*Hamlet*, II, ii, 383.—W. A. WRIGHT : In the present passage, the phrase
'drawn in little,' which has this technical meaning [*i. e.* in miniature], is used in the
sense of 'contracted into a small compass'; the devils being supposed, as in Milton
(*Par. Lost*, i, 789), to have the power of altering their dimensions.

  89. **Legion**] This is taken from *Mark*, v, 9 : 'And he asked him, What is thy
name ? And he answered, saying, my name is Legion ; for we are many.' Compare *Hamlet*, I, ii, 244 : 'I'll speak to it, though hell itself should gape,' etc.

  92. **How ist with you man ?**] In the CAMBRIDGE EDITION an Anonymous
critic plausibly conjectures that this speech belongs to Sir Toby. It is not likely
that Fabian put the very same question to Malvolio twice, addressing him first as
'sir,' and then as 'man'; whereas the latter address comes more naturally from
Sir Toby, Malvolio's superior in rank.—ED.

  93. **my priuate**] COLLIER (ed. ii) : 'Private' was doubtless (as the MS Corrector informs us) an error of the press for *privacie*, as it was then commonly spelt.
Shakespeare no where else uses 'private' as a substantive, unless idiomatically with
the preposition *in* before it,—'in private.'—DYCE (*Strictures*, p. 77) : Shakespeare
uses 'private' as a substantive in the sense of 'secret or confidential communication,' in *King John*, IV, iii,—'Whose private with me of the Dauphin's love,' etc.;
and Jonson uses 'private' as a substantive in the sense of 'particular interest or
safety,' *Catiline*, III, ii,—'Nor must I be unmindful of my private,' etc. Is it not,
therefore, far more probable that here 'private' is used as equivalent to *privacy* than
that the former word should be 'as the MS Corrector informs us,' a misprint for
the latter ? Indeed, I do not doubt that examples of 'private' signifying *privacy*
are to be found in other early writers, though Shakespeare's commentators, never
imagining that the old reading would be questioned, saw no necessity for searching
them out.—W. A. WRIGHT : That is, privacy. Bacon (*Essay* xxxiii, p. 141, ed.
Wright) uses 'private' as a substantive, though not exactly in the same sense :
'Besides some Spots of Ground, that any Particular Person, will Manure, for his
own Private.'

  95. **hollow**] An irritating epithet to apply to Malvolio's pompous, *ore rotundo*,
style of speaking. And of all sources, to attribute it to a fiend !—ED.

did not I tell you ? Sir *Toby*, my lady prayes you to haue   96
a care of him.

Mal.   Ah ha, does fhe fo ?

To.   Go too, go too : peace, peace, wee muft deale
gently with him : Let me alone.   How do you *Maluolio*?   100
How ift with you *?* What man, defie the diuell : confider,
he's an enemy to mankinde.

Mal.   Do you know what you fay ?

Mar.   La you, and you fpeake ill of the diuell, how
he takes it at heart.   Pray God he be not bewitch'd.   105

Fab.   Carry his water to th'wife woman.

---

98. *Ah ha,*] Ff, Rowe, Pope, Han.
Ah, ha, Cap. *Ah, ah!* Sta. *Ah, ha!*
Theob. et cet.

  99. *too, go too*] *to, go to* Ff (*goe* F₂).

100. *Let me*] *let him* Rowe, Pope,
Han.

  do you] *do you do* F₄, Rowe i.

101. *confider,*] *consider* Rowe, Pope,
Han.

104. *and`you*] Ff, Rowe, Coll. ii.   *if
you* Pope, +.   *an you* Cap. et cet.

106. *th'wife*] Ff, Rowe, +, Wh.   *the
wise* Cap. et cet.

---

98. **does she so ?**] I doubt the interrogation mark here.   Though in the form
of a question, it is spoken with an air of exultation, equivalent to ' Aha, I knew
that would happen.'—ED.

100. **do you**] Note the humorous turn which the Fourth Folio (it is hardly to
be supposed intentionally) gives to this address.—ED.

104. **La you**] This is hyphened ' La-you' in *Wint. Tale*, II, iii, 64, where there
is the following note : EARLE (§ 197) : ' La ' is that interjection which in modern
English is spelt *lo*.   It was used in Saxon times both as an emotional cry and also
as a sign of the respectful vocative. . . . In modern times, it has taken the form of
lo in literature, and it has been supposed to have something to do with the verb
to look.   In this sense it has been used in the *New Testament* to render the Greek
ἰδοὺ, that is, ' Behold !'   But the interjection ' la ' was quite independent of another
Saxon exclamation, viz. *loc*, which may with more probability be associated with
locian, to look.   The fact seems to be that the modern *lo* represents both the Saxon
interjections *la* and *loc*, and that this is one among many instances where two
Saxon words have been merged into a single one. . . . While *lo* became the literary
form of the word, *la* has still continued to exist more obscurely, at least down to a
recent date, even if it be not still in use.   *La* may be regarded as a sort of feminine
lo.   In novels of the close of the last century and the beginning of this, we see *la*
occurring for the most part as a trivial exclamation of the female characters.

104. **and you speake ill**] How far Maria outshines her companions in the
gentle art of exquisite teasing !—ED.

106. **wise woman**] DOUCE (i, 101) : Here may be a direct allusion to one of
the two ladies of this description mentioned in the following passage from Heywood's play of *The Wise Woman of Hogsdon :* ' You have heard of Mother Notting-
ham, who for her time was prettily well skill'd in casting of Waters ; and after her,
Mother Bombye.'   The several occupations of these imposters are thus described in
this play of Heywood : ' Let me see how many trades have I to live by : First, I

Mar.   Marry and it ſhall be done to morrow morning   107
if I liue.   My Lady would not looſe him for more then ile
ſay.

Mal.   How now miſtris?   110
Mar.   Oh Lord.

To.   Prethee hold thy peace, this is not the way : Doe
you not ſee you moue him? Let me alone with him.

Fa.   No way but gentleneſſe, gently, gently : the Fiend
is rough, and will not be roughly vs'd.   115

    To.   Why how now my bawcock? how doſt ẙ chuck?
Mal.   Sir.

To.   I biddy, come with me.   What man, tis not for
grauity to play at cherrie-pit with ſathan. Hang him foul 119

---

107. *and it*] *an it* Knt. (misprint?).
108. *looſe*] *loſe* F$_4$.
112. *this is*] *that is* F$_4$, Rowe,+.
113. *Let...him.*] Om. F$_3$F$_4$, Rowe i.
114. *way but*] *my* F$_3$F$_4$.
116. *bawcock*] *havock* F$_3$F$_4$, Rowe i.
117. *Sir.*] *Sir?* Theob. et seq. (subs.)

118. *I biddy,*] Ff. *Ay Biddy*, Rowe.
Ay biddy, Pope.   *Ay, biddy*, Theob.+,
Cap. Wh. i.   *Ay, Biddy*, Mal. et cet.
    biddy...me] As quotation, Coll.
iii.

119. *ſathan*] *Satan* F$_4$.

---

am a wise woman, and a fortune-teller, and under that I deale in physicke and
forespeaking, in palmistry, and recovering of things lost.   Next, I undertake to
cure madd folkes,' etc.

116. **bawcock**] MURRAY (*N. E. D.*): Adopted from the French *beau coq*, 'fine
cock,' for *bewcock*.   A colloquial or burlesque term of endearment ; equivalent to
Fine fellow, good fellow.   *Hen. V:* IV, i, 44, 'The King's a Bawcock, and a
Heart of Gold.'

118. **I biddy, come with me**] RITSON (*Remarks*, p. 66): This seems to be a
scrap of some old song, and should be printed as such. [This suggestion, Malone
said, had but little probability.   It is, however, the general opinion at present that
Ritson was right.—ED.]—MALONE : 'Come, Bid, come,' are words of endearment
used by children to chickens and other domestic fowl.—COLLIER (ed. i) : This may
be only a corruption of 'I bid ye come with me,' or 'biddy' may be meant for a
term of familiarity.   It is most likely a quotation, though no original of it has come
to light.—HALLIWELL : Sir Toby had prᴇviously addressed him with the epithets
'bawcock' and 'chuck' (chick), and now imitates the call used to chickens and
poultry.—W. A. WRIGHT : Probably the fragment of a song.

119. **cherrie-pit**] STEEVENS : 'Cherry-pit' is pitching cherry-stones into a little
hole.   Nash, speaking of the paint on ladies' faces, says : 'You may play at cherry
pit in their cheekes.'[*Pierce Penilesse*, p. 45, ed. Grosart.   As far as a mention
of the game is concerned, it makes no difference where it is played, in paint, or in
wrinkles.   A verification of Steevens's quotation, however, shows that there is no
mention by Nash of 'the paint on ladies' faces'; Nash is speaking of 'old hack-
sters in the wrinkles of whose face, yee may hide false dice, and play at cherry
pit in the dint of their cheekes.'—ED.] Again, in *The Witch of Edmonton :* 'I
have lov'd a witch ever since I play'd at cherry-pit.'[III, i.]

Colliar.   120

Mar.   Get him to fay his prayers, good fir *Toby* gette
him to pray.

Mal.   My prayers Minx.

Mar.   No I warrant you, he will not heare of godly-
neſſe.   125

Mal.   Go hang your felues all : you are ydle fhallowe
things, I am not of your element, you fhall knowe more
heereafter.   *Exit*

To.   Iſt poſsible *?*

Fa. If this were plaid vpon a ſtage now, I could con-   130
demne it as an improbable fiction.

To   His very genius hath taken the infection of the
deuice man.   133

120. *Colliar*] *Collier* F$_4$.
121. *prayers,...*Toby] F$_2$. *prayers,...*
Toby, F$_3$F$_4$, Rowe, Pope, Cam. Rlfe,
Dtn, Wh. ii. *prayers,... Toby ;* Theob.
Warb. Johns.   *prayers ;...Toby*, Var.

'73, et cet.
124. Mar.] Fab. Anon. ap. Cam.
131. *improbable*] *unprofitable* F$_3$F$_4$,
Rowe i.
133. *deuice man*] *device, man* Rowe.

119. **sathan**] W. A. WRIGHT : Satan is thus spelt everywhere in Shakespeare.
The form appears to have been derived from the Miracle Plays, for I do not find
it in the printed translations of the Bible which were in existence in Shakespeare's time.

120. **Colliar**] JOHNSON : The devil is called ' Collier' for his blackness.   ' Like
will to like, quoth the Devil to the Collier.'—STEEVENS : ' Collier' was, in our
author's time, a term of the highest reproach.   So great were the impositions practised by the venders of coal, that Greene, at the conclusion of his *Notable Discovery of Coosnage*, 1592, has published what he calls, ' *A Pleasant Discovery of the
Coosenage of Colliars.*'

123. **Minx**] W. A. WRIGHT : Of very certain meaning, but uncertain etymology.
Cotgrave gives, ' *Gadrouillette :* f. A minx, gigle, flirt, callet, Gixie ; (a fained word,
applyable to any such cattell.)'   Again, ' *Obereau :* A hobbie (Hawke ;) also, a
young minx, or little proud squall.'   It is used also for a lapdog in Udall's translation of the *Apophthegmes of Erasmus* (ed. Roberts, 1877), p. 143 : ' There ben litle
minxes, or pupees that ladies keepe in their chambers for especial iewels to playe
withall.'   In the same passage ' mynxe' is the translation of *Melitæus*.   The word
may possibly be derived from the mink or minx, the name of which is believed to
be of Swedish origin (*mænk*); and from the fur-bearing animal it may have been
transferred, on account of some fancied resemblance, to a long-haired lapdog, and
afterward applied, like puppy, puss, and vixen, to animals of a superior order.
Some, however, connect ' minx' with ' minnekin.'

127. **element**] See I, i, 31 and III, i, 58.

132. **very genius**] W. A. WRIGHT : The familiar spirit which was supposed to
govern a man's actions ; here used for the spiritual nature.   Sir Toby would say,
' The plot has taken possession of his very soul.'

Mar. Nay purſue him now, leaſt the deuice take ayre, and taint.   135

Fa. Why we ſhall make him made indeede.

Mar. The houſe will be the quieter.

To. Come, wee'l haue him in a darke room & bound. My Neece is already in the beleefe that he's mad: we may carry it thus for our pleaſure, and his pennance, til our ve-   140 ry paſtime tyred out of breath, prompt vs to haue mercy on him : at which time, we wil bring the deuice to the bar and crowne thee for a finder of madmen : but ſee, but ſee.

>   *Enter Sir Andrew.*

Fa. More matter for a May morning.   145

An. Heere's the Challenge, reade it: I warrant there's vinegar and pepper in't.

Fab. Iſt ſo ſawcy?

And. I, iſt? I warrant him : do but read.

To. Giue me.   150

---

134. *leaſt*] *leſt* F₄.
137. *will be*] *well be* F₂.
139. *beleefe*] *beleife* F₂. *belief* F₃F₄.
    he's] *he is* Johns. Var. Ran.
Mal. Steev. Var. Knt, Hal. Ktly.
144. Scene. X. Pope, +.
    Enter...] After line 145, Sta.

149. *I, iſt?*] F₂. *I, is't?* F₃F₄. *Ay, is't?* Rowe, +, Cap. Var. Mal. *Ay, is't,* Coll. Dyce, Wh. Sta. Glo. Cam. *Ay, is it,* Steev. et cet.
    read] *read it* Ktly.
150. *Giue*] *Give't* Lettsom ap. Dyce.

134, 135. take ayre, and taint] That is, exposed, and our fun, therefore, spoilt.—ED.

138. darke room] Compare *As You Like It*, III, ii, 382, 'Loue is meerely a madnesse, and, I tel you, deserues as wel a darke house and a whip, as madmen do.'

143. finder of madmen] JOHNSON : This is, I think, an allusion to the witch-finders, who were very busy.—RITSON (*Remarks*, p. 67) : 'Finders of madmen' are those who formerly acted under the writ *De Lunatico inquirendo ;* in virtue whereof they *found* the man *mad.*

145. May morning] STEEVENS : It was usual on the first of May to exhibit metrical interludes of the comic kind, as well as the morris-dance.—TOLLET (*Note appended to 1 Hen. IV.*) quotes as follows from Stowe's *Survay of London :* 'I finde also, that in the Moneth of May, the Citizens of London (of all estates) lightly in euery Parish, or sometimes two or three Parishes ioining together, had their seuerall Mayings, and did fetch May-poles, with diuers warlike shewes, with good Archers, Morice-dauncers, and other deuices for pastime all the day long : and towards the Euening, they had Stage-playes, and Bonefiers in the streets.' [p. 151, ed. 1618.]

149. warrant him] DEIGHTON : ' Him' is the person challenged, Cesario ; dative case, I give my word to him that, etc.

Youth, whatſoeuer thou art, thou art but a ſcuruy fellow.   151
    Fa.   Good, and valiant.
    To.   Wonder not, nor admire not in thy minde why I doe call
thee ſo, for I will ſhew thee no reaſon for't.   (Law
    Fa.   A good note, that keepes you from the blow of ỹ   155
    To.   Thou comſt to the Lady Oliuia, and in my ſight ſhe vſes
thee kindly : but thou lyeſt in thy throat, that is not the matter
I challenge thee for.
    Fa.   Very breefe, and to exceeding good ſence-leſſe.   159

151. [Sir Toby reads. Rowe.
153. admire not] admire F₃F₄,
Rowe i.
155. *good*] *very good* Rowe i.
156. comſt] F₂. comm'ſt F₃. com'ſt
F₄. *comest* Mal.
157. throat,] *throat;* Coll. Wh.
Dyce, Cam.

159. *and to*] Ff, Coll. Wh. Dyce,
Cam. Sta. Ktly, Rlfe. *and* Rowe et
cet. *and thereto* Lettsom. *and, too,*
Kinnear.
    good] *good*, Hal.
    ſence-leſſe.] *ſence-leſſe*, F₂. *ſenſe-*
-leffe, F₃. *ſenſe-leſs.* F₄ et seq. (*sense-*
less Cap.)

153. **nor admire not**] For the double negative, see ABBOTT, § 406, or Shakespeare *passim*.   For a triple negative, see III, i, 163.   For 'admire' used, as here,
in its Latin sense, see *Tempest*, V, i, 179 : 'I perceiue these Lords At this encounter
doe so much admire That they deuoure their reason.'

157. **lyest in thy throat**] STAUNTON (*Note on 2 Hen. IV:* I, ii, 94): 'To lie in
the throat,' an expression which is frequently met with in Shakespeare, appears to
have borne a deeper meaning than is usually ⸱upposed.   In a curious old treatise on
War and the Duello, which has escaped the researches of all the commentators,
entitled VALLO LIBRO CON*tinente appertenentie ad Capitanii*, etc. [*The Bulwark,
A Book containing whatsoever appertains to Captains, in holding and fortifying a
city with bastions, with a new kind of fire added* [? *aggioti*] *as appears by the plates,
and of divers powders*, etc. etc.], **1524**, there is a chapter in the part devoted to the
duello, which is headed ' *Della Divisione del Mentire*' [*On the Division of Giving the
Lie*], and which contains the following remarks on giving the lie :—' And observe
that an honourable man, when he gives the lie is wont to say thou dost not speak
the truth ; another will give the lie by saying thou dost lie in thy throat ; another
by saying thou liest in thy throat like a scoundrel, and yet another by saying thou
liest in thy throat like the scoundrel that thou art ; thus each phrase is in advance
of its predecessor, and differs from it ; for example, if a man should say thou liest
in thy throat like a scoundrel, it is not to be understood that his opponent is called
a scoundrel, but lies in his throat as a scoundrel would lie in like case ; and he must
not quarrel and fight as if he had been called a scoundrel ; while if the words are :
thou liest in thy throat like the scoundrel that thou art, then a quarrel and encounter
result from his having been called a scoundrel and from this "as thou art." '—
[Staunton gives merely the old Italian ; he does not translate it,—perhaps wisely.
It is open to doubt that the passage fully justifies his assertion that the 'lie in the
throat' bore a deeper meaning than is usually supposed.   We all know that 'thou
liest in thy throat' is stronger than simply 'thou liest,' and this is really all that
the quotation shows.—ED.]

159. **and to exceeding**] R. G. WHITE (ed. i): If Fabian had said, 'Very

To.I will way-lay thee going home, where if it be thy chance　160
to kill me.

Fa.　Good.

To.　*Thou kilſt me like a rogue and a villaine.*

Fa.　Still you keepe o'th windie ſide of the Law:good.

Tob.　*Fartheewell, and God haue mercie vpon one of our*　165
ſoules. He may haue mercie vpon mine, but my hope is better,
and ſo looke to thy ſelfe.　Thy friend as thou vſeſt him, & thy
ſworne enemie, Andrew Ague-cheeke.

To.　If this Letter moue him not, his legges cannot :
Ile giu't him.　　　　　　　　　　　　　　　　　　　170

Mar.　Yon may haue verie ſit occaſion fot't : he is now
in ſome commerce with my Ladie, and will by and by
depart.

To.　Go ſir *Andrew* : ſcout mee for him at the corner　174

---

161. me] *me—* Rowe, +.　*me,—*　　　165. one of] Om. F₃F₄, Rowe i.
Cap. et seq.　　　　　　　　　　　　　　169. To.] Om. Han. Cap. Coll. Wh.
　163. kilſt] F₂.　kill'ſt F₃F₄.　　　　Hal. Dyce, Cam.
　165. Fartheewell,] F₂.　Fare the　　171. *Yon...fot't*] F₁.
well, F₃.　Fare thee well, F₄.

---

brief, and to exceeding good *purpose*,' adding 'less' aside, there would have been
no obscurity found, yet no more exists now than would have existed then.

　159. **sence-lesse**] HALLIWELL : This word is to be either divided in pronunciation, or to be spoken aside.　On the stage the latter arrangement is the most effective.

　164. **o'th windie side of the Law**] W. A. WRIGHT : So that the law cannot
scent you out and track you, as a hound does the game. [Unquestionably the right
definition ; and yet, at the same time, it is possible that Fabian may be punning
upon his previous speech, where he says, 'a good note which keepes you from *the*
blow of the Law.'—ED.]

　166. **mercie vpon mine**] JOHNSON : We may read 'upon *thine*,' etc.　Yet the
passage may well enough stand without alteration.　It were much to be wished that
Shakespeare, in this, and in some other passages, had not ventured so near profaneness.—M. MASON : The present reading is more humorous than that suggested by
Johnson.　The man on whose soul he hopes that God will have mercy, is the one
that he supposes will fall in the combat ; but Sir Andrew hopes to escape unhurt,
and to have no present occasion for that blessing.　The same idea occurs in *Henry*
V. where Mrs Quickly, giving an account of Falstaff's dissolution, says, ' Now I, to
comfort him, bid him a' should not think of God ; I hoped there was no need to
trouble himself with any such thoughts yet.'

　169. **To.　If this**, etc.] These words are merely Sir Toby's remarks after he has
finished reading the letter.　'*To.*' is therefore needless and was omitted by Hanmer,
and by some of the best subsequent editors.

　172. **commerce**] That is, intercourse.　Ophelia asks Hamlet, 'Could beauty, my
lord, have better commerce than with honesty ?' III, i, 110.

　174. **scout mee**] The ethical dative ; see ABBOTT, § 220.

of the Orchard like a bum-Baylie : fo foone as euer thou   175
feeſt him, draw, and as thou draw'ſt, fweare horrible : for
t comes to paſſe oft, that a terrible oath, with a ſwaggering accent ſharpely twang'd off, giues manhoode more
approbation, then euer proofe it felfe would haue earn'd
him.　Away.   180
    And.　Nay let me alone for fwearing.   *Exit*
    To.　Now will not I deliuer his Letter : for the behaui-
our of the yong Gentleman, giues him out to be of good
capacity, and breeding : his employment betweene his
Lord and my Neece, confirmes no leſſe.　Therefore, this   185
Letter being fo excellently ignorant, will breed no terror
in the youth : he will finde it comes from a Clodde-pole.
But ſir, I will deliuer his Challenge by word of mouth ;
fet vpon *Ague-cheeke* a notable report of valor, and driue
the Gentleman (as I know his youth will aptly receiue it)   190
into a moſt hideous opinion of his rage, skill, furie, and
impetuoſitie.This will fo fright them both, that they wil
kill one another by the looke, like Cockatrices.   193

---

175. *bum-Baylie*] *bum-Baily* Ff.
bum-bailiff Theob. *bum-bailie* Knt.
  176. *draw'ſt*] *drawest* Coll. Wh. i,
Hal. Dyce, Cam.
    horrible] *horribly* Ff, Rowe,+,
Cap. Var. Ran. Coll. iii.
  177. *t*] F₁.

179. *earn'd*] *earned* Var. '03, et seq.
182. *his*] *this* F₃F₄, Rowe i.
184. *employment*] *imployment* F₄.
185, 195. *Neece*] F₃F₄. *Neice* F₂.
187. *finde it*] *find that it* F₃F₄,
Rowe,+.
193. Scene XI. Pope,+.

---

  175. **bum-Baylie**] Johnson (*Dict.*) : A bailiff of the meanest kind, one that is
employed in arrests.—Murray (*N. E. D.*) : The bailiff that is close at the debtor's
back, or that catches him in the rear.　Compare the French equivalent *pousse-cul.*
  176. **sweare horrible**] For adjectives used as adverbs, see Abbott, § I.
  179. **approbation**] Schmidt (*Lex.*) : That is, attestation.
  193. **Cockatrices**] Murray (*N. E. D.*) : Middle English *cocatris, -ice*, adopted
from Old French *cocatris*, masculine, corresponding to Provençal *calcatriz*, Italian
calcatrice, feminine representative of the Latin *calcātrix, calcātrīcem*, apparently a
mediæval rendering of the Greek ἰχνεύμων, ichnumon.　This last meant literally
'tracker, trace out, hunter out,' formed on ἰχνεύ-ειν to track, trace out, hunt out,
formed on ἴχνος track, footstep.　Latin *calcātrix* is feminine agent-substantive of
calcāre, originally 'to tread,' in mediæval Latin 'to tread on the heels of, track,
trace out' (formed on *caix, calcem*, heel).　Thus *calcātrix* came to render *ichneumon.* (Prof. Thor Sundby, *Brunetto Latino's Livnet og Skrifter*, Kjöbenhavn,
1869, p. 142–4.)　In Old French the word was partially popularized, as seen by
the phonetic change of the original *calc-* through *caulc* to *cauc-, coc-*, and *chauc-,
choc-.*
  The sense-history of this word is exceedingly curious.　The Ichneumon, an

[**193. kill one another by the looke, like Cockatrices**]

Egyptian quadruped, said to devour reptiles and crocodiles' eggs (which it searches for in the sand), is called by Pliny, VIII. 24 (35), § 88, the mortal enemy of the aspis and the crocodile. As to the latter, he tells that when the crocodile is asleep or dozing with its jaws open, the ichneumon darts down its throat, and destroys it by gnawing through its belly; a tale originating, partly at least, in the habits of the bird *trochilus*, as mentioned by Herodotus. . . . From an early period, Western writers entertained the notion that this ichneumon was amphibious or aquatic; the immediate followers of Pliny appear to have identified it with the Otter. Pliny's tale is repeated by Solinus and Isidore; in the text of Solinus known to Ammianus Marcellinus (about A. D. 400) the animal is called *enhydros*, the second kind of ichneumons; while Isidore appears to make two distinct animals, the Ichneumon and the Enhydros, 'a little beast so-called because it lives in the water, and mostly in the Nile.' But the Greek ἐνυδρίς was not only the *otter*, but also a *water-snake = hydrus;* and the latter was the only sense in which *enhydris* had been used by Pliny. Later compilers took this to be the sense of *enhydrus, -os,* in Solinus and Isidore, and the crocodile's enemy was now described as a ' water-snake ' or ' fish.' . . . Meanwhile also the Latinized name calcatrix comes into view. It is found, along with the transformed description, in the version of the story (*circa* 1263) by Brunetto Latino in *Li Livre dou Tresor,* where it is said ' then comes another fish which is named *hydrus,* that is *cocatris,* and enters within his body '; further, ' and you must know that cokatrix, albeit he is born in the water, and within the Nile, he is not at all a fish, but is a water-serpent.' . . . The *cocatris = ichneumon = enhydris = hydrus,* having thus been transformed into an aquatic reptile, living in the Nile, other writers proceeded to identify it with the crocodile itself. The *Bestiaire divin* of Guillaume le Normand (*circa* 1210) makes *coquatrix* the crocodile, and *ydrus* his enemy. . . . And in later French, as well as in other Romanic languages, ' crocodile' became, at least, one of the recognized meanings of *cocatrix*. . . . In English the confusion with *crocodile* hardly appears, except once or twice as a literalism of translation. Here, *cocatrice* appears from the first as the equivalent of Latin *basiliscus* or *regulus* equivalent to Basilisk. It was thus used . . . by Wyclif and his followers to translate *regulus* (Isaiah, xi. 8; xiv. 29; lix. 5) and *basiliscus* (Ps. xc. [i.] 13) of the Vulgate. In the former of these (also in Jer. viii. 17) it was retained in the 16–17th cent. versions; but in the revised text of 1885, it has been changed to *basilisk.* The history of this further transition of sense is still obscure; but it is to be noticed that *cocatrice* translates French *basilicoc,* and that *coc* is apparently a connecting link. But some traditional notions of the ichneumon as the enemy of the *aspis* (which appeared later in the well-known statement that the only animal which could kill the basilisk was the *mustela* or weasel) were probably contributory, as well as the mediæval confusion, under the name *regulus,* of the basilisk (*rex serpentium*) with the trochilus (*rex avium,* Old French *roytelet,* in modern French *roitelet,* ' wren '). Further etymological speculation, in France or England, working upon the syllable *coc, coq,* in *basili-coc, coc-atris,* probably also associating the crested basilisk with the crested bird, and mingling with it vague notions of the crocodile's eggs, buried in the sand, and producing a tiny reptile, originated the well-known notion of ' a serpent hatched by a venomous reptile from a cock's (*i. e. basili-cock's* or *cok-adrill's*) egg,' embodied in the heraldic monster, half cock, half serpent.

[Its definition is] 1. A serpent, identified with the Basilisk, fabulously said to kill by its mere glance, and to be hatched from a cock's egg.

Enter Oliuia and Uiola.

*Fab.*Heere he comes with your Neece, giue them way   195
till he take leaue, and prefently after him.

To. I will meditate the while vpon fome horrid meffage
for a Challenge.

Ol. I haue faid too much vnto a hart of ftone,
And laid mine honour too vnchary on't :   200

---

194. Enter...] After line 198, Coll.   199. *I haue*] *I've* Pope, +, Dyce ii,
195. *way*] *away* F$_4$.   iii.
198. *Challenge.*] *Challenge.* Exeunt.   200. *on't*] Ff, Rowe, Pope, Han.
Ff.   Knt, Coll. Wh. i, Rlfe. *out* Theob. et cet.

---

194. **Enter...**] In the Folios and Quartos the entrances are frequently set down, for the benefit of the prompter, some lines in advance of the actual entrance of the actors.

200. **laid . . . vnchary on't**] CAPELL (p. 150): 'Lay'd out' is *exposed*. (W. A. WRIGHT: It rather means *expended*.)—DOUCE (i, 103): Theobald's substitution of *out* is unnecessary. The old text simply means, I have *placed* my honour too incautiously *upon* a heart of stone.—DYCE (*Few Notes*, p. 76): I must exclaim against their [*i. e.* Douce, Knight, and Collier] thrusting back into the text an obvious error of the press. The misprint of 'on't' for *out* is common enough. So the Qto 1640 of Fletcher's *Bloody Brother*, IV, i, has,—'Princes may pick their suffering nobles on't, And one by one employ them to the block,' etc.—where the other old copies have, as the sense requires, '*out*.' So, too, in Fletcher and Shakespeare's *Two Noble Kinsmen*, I, iv, the Qto 1634 has 'Y'are ont of breath,' where the Second Folio (the play is not in the first) gives '*out*.' With the passage of Shakespeare now under consideration, compare the following lines by a nameless dramatist: 'Keepe her from the Serpent, let her not gad To euerie Gossips congregation, For there is blushing modestie *laide out*,' etc.—*Euerie Woman in her Humour*, 1609, sig. H3. —COLLIER (ed. ii): Mr Dyce, who is too apt to justify one corruption by another, argues in favour of *out*, and shows by divers instances that the word may have been misprinted; it is unquestionable that 'to lay *out*' is a very common expression; but so is 'to lay *on't*,' and as it affords a distinct meaning, is repeated in all early editions, and is unamended by the MS Corrector, we prefer to make Olivia say poetically that she has laid her honour on a heart of stone, as it were, on an altar, than prosaically to observe merely that she has incautiously laid *out* her honour.—DYCE (ed. ii): Alas for Mr Collier's *reasoning!* The explanation which he gives of his text ought alone to have convinced him that 'on't' was a misprint. Olivia might perhaps talk with propriety of 'laying her *love* on a heart of stone'; but with no propriety could she talk of 'laying her HONOUR on a heart of stone.' The genuine lection, 'And laid mine honour too unchary out,' means 'And have been more prodigal in expressing and giving proofs of my affection than was strictly consistent with my honour.'—W. A. WRIGHT: 'Unchary' is unsparingly, lavishly. The word etymologically signifies heedlessly, carelessly; but that Shakespeare understood it in the other sense is evident from *Hamlet*, I, iii, 36: 'The chariest maid is prodigal enough, If she unmask her beauty to the moon'; where 'chariest' and 'prodigal' are contrasted. Theobald's change is at once justified and rendered

There's fomething in me that reproues my fault :   201
But fuch a head-ftrong potent fault it is,
That it but mockes reproofe.

   Vio.   With the fame hauiour that your paffion beares,
Goes on my Mafters greefes.   205

   Ol.   Heere, weare this Iewell for me, tis my picture :
Refufe it not, it hath no tongue, to vex you :
And I befeech you come againe to morrow.
What fhall you aske of me that Ile deny,
That honour (fau'd) may vpon asking giue.   210

   Uio.   Nothing but this, your true loue for my mafter.

   Ol.   How with mine honor may I giue him that,
Which I haue giuen to you.

   Vio.   I will acquit you.

   Ol.   Well, come againe to morrow : far-thee-well,   215

---

202. *it is,*] *it is :* F$_2$F$_3$.

204. *hauiour*] *'haviour* Theob. +.

204, 205. *that your...greefes*] Separate line, Cap. conj.

205. *Goes...greefes*] Ff (*griefs* F$_3$F$_4$). *Goes...grief* Rowe, +, Cap. Var. Hal. Cam. Dyce ii, iii, Ktly, Rlfe, Huds. Wh. ii.   *Go...griefs* Mal. et cet.

210. *That honour (fau'd)*]   *That*

(*honour fav'd*) F$_3$F$_4$, Rowe i, Johns. Coll. Ktly.   *That honour sav'd* Pope, Theob. Warb. Johns. Cam.

210. *may*] *I may* Ktly.

    giue.] *give ?* F$_4$.

211. *this, your*] *this ; your* Coll. Wh. ii.   *this,—your* Dyce.   *this ;— your* Cam.

213. *you.*] *you ?* Ff.

---

necessary by this meaning of 'unchary.' In *Wint. Tale*, IV, iv, 160, ' He tells her something That makes her blood look out'; the Folios read 'on't' as here.— DEIGHTON : For 'laid out' compare *Cym.* II, iii, 92 : ' You lay out too much pains For purchasing but trouble.'—SCHMIDT (*Gesammelte Abhandlungen*, p. 327) : That is, I have thereon wagered my honour too incautiously, I have set it too carelessly on the hazard. That 'lay' has this meaning must be familiar to every commentator ; it occurs again in the last line of this same scene : ' I dare lay any money, 'twill be nothing yet.' The change which the editors have adopted : 'laid *out*,' is, possibly, quite un-Shakespearian ; in place of the fignifcation which it is said that ' lay out' bears, namely, *to expose*, Shakespeare elsewhere uses the phrase 'to lay open,' and Dyce, in order to justify the change, is obliged to take refuge in a quotation from *Every Woman in her Humour*. If the Folio had *ont* it would be possible to conjecture a misprint for *out*, but ' on't,' with an apostrophe, would be set up by no negligent compositor instead of *out*. [The fact that in *The Winter's Tale*,(IV, iv, 186, of this ed.) and elsewhere, *out* has been misprinted *on't*, with the apostrophe, seems to demand Theobald's change. Schmidt's interpretation is to me by no means the true one, albeit Rolfe inclines to accept it.—ED.]

   206. **Iewell**] JOHNSON : This does not properly signify a single gem, but any precious ornament or superfluity.—W. A. WRIGHT : From the Old French *joiel*, *joel*, or *jouel*, a diminutive of *joie*, which is the Latin *gaudium*.

A Fiend like thee might beare my foule to hell.   216
          Enter Toby and Fabian.

To. Gentleman, God faue thee.

Vio. And you fir.

To. That defence thou haft, betake the too't : of what   220
nature the wrongs are thou haft done him, I knowe not :
but thy intercepter full of defpight, bloody as the Hunter, attends thee at the Orchard end : difmount thy tucke,
be yare in thy preparation, for thy affaylant is quick, skilfull, and deadly.   225

Vio. You miftake fir I am fure, no man hath any quarrell to me : my remembrance is very free and cleere from
any image of offence done to any man.

To. You'l finde it otherwife I affure you : therefore, if
you hold your life at any price, betake you to your gard :   230
for your oppofite hath in him what youth, ftrength, skill,
and wrath, can furnifh man withall.   232

---

216. *Fiend*] *friend* Grey (so quoted, i, 234).

    hell.] *hell.* Exit. Ff. Scene XII. Pope, +.

220. *the too't*] *thee too't* F_2. *thee to't* F_3F_4.

221. *him,*] *him ;* F_2.

222. *intercepter*] *intercepter,* Pope. *interpreter,* Warb. (corrected in MS) Johns.

223. *Orchard end*] *orchard-end* Theob. +, Dyce, Cam. Sta.

226. *fir I am fure,*] F_2. *fir, I am fure,* F_3F_4 (*ame* F_4), Cap. *Sir, I am sure* Rowe, Pope, Han. *Sir, I am sure;* Knt, Wh. i, Dyce i, Sta. *Sir; I am sure,* Theob. et cet.

230. *gard*] *guard* F_3F_4.

232. *man*] *a man* F_3F_4, Rowe, Pope, Han.

---

220. **defence thou hast**] For the construction, see I, v, 99.

222, 223. **bloody as the Hunter**] CAPELL (*Gloss.* s. v. *lethe*) : A term us'd by Hunters to signify the blood shed by a deer at its fall, with which it is still a custom to mark those who come in at the death.

223. **dismount thy tucke**] W. A. WRIGHT : In plain English, draw thy sword. The hangers or straps by which the rapier was attached to the sword-belt are called in the affected language of Osric the ' carriages ' (*Hamlet*, V, i, 158), and Sir Toby's ' dismount ' is in keeping with this phraseology. A tuck was a small rapier. Cotgrave gives, ' *Verdun*, m. The little Rapier, called a Tucke.' The word comes to us from the French *estoc*, which Cotgrave defines as ' The stocke, trunke, or bodie of a tree, . . . also, a Rapier, or tucke.' In Florio's *Worlde of Wordes*, 1598, we find, ' Stocco, a truncheon, a tuck, a short sword, an arming sword.'

224. **yare**] That is, ready, nimble. See, if need be, notes on *Temp.* I, i, 8.

226, 227. **quarrell to me**] Compare *Much Ado*, II, i, 226, ' The Lady Beatrice hath a quarrell to you '; or ABBOTT (§ 187) for examples of the various uses of *to*, without verbs of motion ; here ' to ' means *against*.

232. **withall**] ABBOTT (§ 196) : This emphatic form of *with* is used for *with* after the object, at the end of a sentence.

Vio. I pray you fir what is he?   233

To. He is knight dubb'd with vnhatch'd Rapier, and
on carpet confideration, but he is a diuell in priuate brall,   235

234. *knight*] *knight*, Theob. *a knight*   Cap. Var. Ran. Steev. Var. Wh. i,
Coll. MS, Wh. i, Walker, Coll. iii.   Dyce ii, iii.
     vnhatch'd] *unhack'd* Pope, +,   235. *brall*] *brawl* F₃F₄.

234. **vnhatch'd**] MALONE: It appears from Cotgrave's definition of '*Hacher*.
To hacke, shread, slice; hew, chop, ... also, to hatch a hilt,' that *hatch* was a technical term. Perhaps we ought to read,—'with *an hatched* rapier,' *i. e.* with a rapier,
the hilt of which was engraved and ornamented. Our author, however, might have
used 'unhatch'd' in the sense of *unhacked;* and therefore I have made no change.
—DYCE (*Remarks*, p. 76): In Shirley's *Love in a Maze*, II, ii, we find: 'Thy
hair is fine as gold, thy chin is hatch'd With silver,' etc. '*i. e.*' says Gifford, 'ornamented with a white or silvery beard. This ... explains the passage in *Tro. &
Cress.*[I, iii], "As venerable Nester hatch'd in silver," on which the commentators
have wasted so many words. Literally, to *hatch* is to inlay [originally, I believe,
to cut, engrave, mark with lines]; metaphorically, it is to adorn, to beautify, with
silver, gold, etc. [also to colour or stain].'Shirley's *Works*, ii, 301.   That the
word *hatch* was particularly applied to the ornamenting of weapons, might be shown
from many examples besides the following: 'Who first shall wound through others
armes, his blood appearing fresh, Shall win this sword, siluerd, and hatcht.'Chapman's *Iliads of Homer*, b. xxiii, p. 324. 'Dote on my horse well trapp'd, my sword
well hatch'd.'Beaumont & Fletcher, *Bonduca*, II, ii. '*Hatching* is to silver or gild
the hilt and pomell of a sword or hanger.'R. Holme, *Ac. of Armory*, 1688, b. iii,
p. 91. Now, since *hatch* was a very common technical term for the ornamenting of
weapons, is there any probability that Shakespeare would have employed the
expression 'un*hatched* rapier' in the sense of '*unhacked* rapier'? Surely not. An
'*unhatched* rapier' could only mean 'an unornamented rapier'; which does not
suit the context, for carpet-knights were most likely to have the ceremony performed
with a highly ornamented sword. .... I am therefore strongly inclined to agree with
those commentators who have supposed that the right reading is '*unhacked* rapier.'
[STAUNTON, however, agrees with Malone in thinking that we ought to read '*an
hatched* rapier,' which is indeed, if emendation be necessary, plausible; the words
might be readily confused in the compositor's ear. As for the spelling, we find
'retchlesse' for *reckless* in *The Marriage of Witt and Wisdome*, 1579, p. 54, ed.
Shakespeare Society. Thus here, though I should be loath to alter the text, I think
that 'unhatch'd' bears the meaning of *unhacked.*—ED.]

235. **on carpet consideration**] CAPELL (p. 150): The 'unhack'd rapier' was
lay'd on most unmercifully about the time of this play; and for making something
too free with this profusion of *carpet* knighthoods, divers poets and players are said
to have been lay'd by the heels, and, among the rest, Ben Jonson. A most small
matter serv'd at that time of day for the exercise of even greater severities, so that
'tis wonder the expressions of this passage drew none upon Shakespeare: Middleton
the poet, for a well-intention'd play of his writing, call'd *A Game at Chess*, but
which gave offence to the Spaniard, got himself into prison; where he lay some
time (says a MS that has been seen by the editor), but was at last discharg'd upon
presenting the petition that follows: 'A harmless game, coin'd only for delight,
Was play'd betwixt the black house and the white: The white house wan; yet still

foules and bodies hath he diuorc'd three, and his incenſe-   236
ment at this moment is ſo implacable, that ſatisfaction
can be none, but by pangs of death and ſepulcher : Hob,
nob , is his word : giu't or take't.

    Vio. I will returne againe into the houſe, and deſire   240
ſome conduct of the Lady. I am no fighter, I haue heard

---

236. *diuorc'd three,*] *divorc'd ; three*   239. *nob*] *nod* Rowe ii, Pope.
F₄.   241. *fighter,*] *fighter.* Rowe.

---

the black doth brag She had the power to put me in the bag : Use but your royal
hand, 'twill set me free ; 'Tis but removing of a man, that's—me.'—REED : In
Francis Markham's *Booke of Honour*, 1625, p. 71, we have the following account
of *Carpet Knights :* ' Near vnto these in degree, (but not in qualitie, for these are
truly (for the most part) vertuous and worthie) is that ranke of Knights which are
called *Carpet-Knights,* being men who are by the Princes Grace and favour made
Knights at home and in the time of peace by the imposition or laying on of the
King's sword, having by some special service done to the common-wealth, or for
some other particular vertues made known to the sovereign, as also for the dignitie
of their births, and in recompense of noble and famous actions done by their ancestors, deserved this great title and dignitie.'   He then enumerates the several orders
of men on whom this honour was usually conferred, and adds : ' these of the vulgar
or common sort, are called *Carpet-Knights,* because (for the most part) they receiue
their honour from the King's hand in the Court, and vpon Carpets, and such like
Ornaments belonging to the King's State and Greatnesse ; which howsoever a curious envie may wrest to an ill sense, yet questionlesse there is no shadow of disgrace
belonging unto it, for it is an honour as perfect as any honour whatsoever, and the
services and merits for which it is conferred, as worthy and well deserving both of
the King and country, as that which hath wounds and scarres for his witnesse.'—
STEEVENS : In Baret's *Alvearie,* 1580, [the following definition is given of ' *Bos
ad præsepe.* A Prouerbe to be applied agaynst] those which doe not exercise themselues with some honest affaires ; but serue abhominable and filthy idleñesse, and
as we vse to call them carpet knightes.' B. ante O.[956].—W. A. WRIGHT : By
employing the term ' consideration' Sir Toby implies that Sir Andrew's honours had
been purchased. [Burton (*Anat,* Part I, Sect. 2, Memb. 2, Subs. 2) speaks contemptuously of Carpet Knights.—ED.]

    238. **can be none**] For ' can ' see ' Is best,' III, iii, 45. For ' none,' see
' she'll none,' I, iii, 100.

    238, 239. **Hob, nob**] MURRAY (*N. E. D.* s. v. *Hab*) : Known in the phrases
hab nab, hab or nab from *circa* 1550. Conjectured to represent some part of the
verb *Have,* presumably the present subjunctive, Old English *hæbbe,* early southern
Middle English *habbe,* in conjunction with the corresponding negative form Old
Eng. *næbbe,* Mid. Eng. *nabbe ;* the alternative phrase *habbe he, nabbe he,* equivalent
to ' have he or have he not,' accounts fairly for the sense, and answers phonolog-
ically ; but there is a long gap in the history, between the general disappearance of
the *habbe* forms of the verb in Mid. Eng. and the first examples of *hab nab.* [Of
this *hab nab,* Dr Murray (*s. v. Hob-nob*) thinks that ' Hob nob ' is in origin apparently a variant, and quotes the present line ; where Shakespeare really gives the
meaning which he himself attached to it, namely, ' giu 't or take 't.']

of fome kinde of men, that put quarrells purpofely on o-   242
thers, to tafte their valour : belike this is a man of that
quirke.

To. Sir, no : his indignation deriues it felfe out of a ve-   245
ry computent iniurie, therefore get you on, and giue him
his defire. Backe you shall not to the houfe, vnleffe you
vndertake that with me, which with as much fafetie you
might anfwer him : therefore on, or ftrippe your fword
ftarke naked : for meddle you muft that's certain, or for-   250
fweare to weare iron about you.

Vio. This is as vnciuill as ftrange. I befeech you doe
me this courteous office, as to know of the Knight what
my offence to him is : it is fomething of my negligence,
nothing of my purpofe.   255

To. *I* will doe fo. Signiour *Fabian*, ftay you by this
Gentleman, till my returne.   *Exit Toby.*

Vio. Pray you fir, do you know of this matter ?

Fab. I know the knight is incenft againft you, euen to
a mortall arbitrement, but nothing of the circumftance   260
more.

---

243. *tafte*] *test* Coll. conj.
245. *Sir, no :*] *No, Sir, no :* Han.
    deriues] *drives* F₄, Rowe, Pope.
246. *computent*] *competent* F₄, Rowe
et seq.
    him] Om. F₃F₄.
249. *him :*] *him ?* F₂. *to him ;* Han.

249. *or*] *and* Han. Om. Coll. MS.
    your fword] *you of sword* Anon.
ap. Cam.
252. *as vnciuill*] *an uncivil* Cap.
(corrected in Errata), Var. '73.
253. *office, as to*] *office, to* Cap.

---

241. **conduct**] Compare, ' Come, bitter conduct, come, unsavory guide '—*Rom.
& Jul.* V, iii, 116.

243. **to taste**] That is, to test. See III, i, **79**.

244. **quirke**] That is, caprice. Cotgrave has : ' *Scotin :* m. ine : f. Difficult,
intricate, obscure, full of quirkes and quiddities.'

246. **computent**] I am by no means certain that this word should be discarded
for the Fourth Folio's 'competent.' Had Shakespeare ever used the verb *compute*,
there would be no question as to 'computent'; Murray (*N. E. D.*) gives no
examples of it earlier than 1631.—ED.

250. **meddle you must**] MALONE : Afterwards, Sir Andrew says—' Pox on't,
I'll not meddle with him.' The vulgar yet say, ' I'll neither meddle nor make
with it.'

253. **this courteous office, as to know**] ABBOTT (§ 280) : We now use only
such with *as*, and only *that* with *which*. Since, however, *such* was frequently used
with *which*, naturally *that* [in the present case *this*] was also used with *as* used for
which. [See also lines 263, 264 below : ' Nothing of that wonderful promise . . . as
you are like,' etc.]

Vio. I befeech you what manner of man is he?   262

Fab. Nothing of that wonderfull promife to read him
by his forme, as you are like to finde him in the proofe of
his valour. He is indeede fir, the moft skilfull, bloudy, &   265
fatall oppofite that you could pofsibly haue found in anie
part of Illyria : will you walke towards him, I will make
your peace with him, if I can.

Vio. I fhall bee much bound to you for't : I am one,
that had rather go with fir Prieft, then fir knight : I care   270
not who knowes fo much of my mettle.   *Exeunt.*

        Enter Toby and Andrew.   272

262. *you what*] *you, what* F$_3$F$_4$.   Dyce, Sta. Huds.   Act IV, iv. Irving.
263. *promife to*] *promife, to* Cap.   The Street adjoining Olivia's
267. *Illyria*] *Illirya* F$_4$.   Garden. Dyce, Sta. Huds.
   him,] *him ?* F$_4$.   272. Andrew] *Andrew hanging back.*
272. Scene XIII. Pope, +. Scene V.   Coll. ii (MS).

270. sir Priest] JOHNSON : He that has taken his first degree at the University
is in the academical style called *Dominus*, and in common language was termed *Sir*.
[See notes on ' Sir Topas,' IV, ii, 4.]

271. mettle] SCHMIDT (*Lex.*) : Constitutional disposition, character, temper.
So also in V, i, 337.

271, 272. Exeunt. Enter Toby and Andrew.] CAPELL (p. 150) : This ' Exeunt' appears to be wrong from Sir Toby's pointing to them at line 281 : ' Fabian
can scarce hold him yonder'; indeed the action is hurt by it ; the effect is lost of
the gestures and looks of both parties under their separation.—DYCE disagrees with
Capell to such an extent that he here begins the Fifth Scene, in ' the Street adjoining Olivia's garden,' and comments thereon as follows : Sir Toby, before going out,
has desired Fabian to ' stay by this gentleman' (Viola) till his return from talking
with Sir Andrew ; a little after, Fabian says to Viola, ' will you *walk towards him*'
(sir Andrew)? and accordingly *makes his exit with her*. Sir Toby now enters
accompanied by Sir Andrew ; and though the Folio does not mark a new scene, it is certain that, previous to the entrance of the two knights, the audience of Shakespeare's
days (who had no painted movable scenery before their eyes) were to *suppose* a
change of scene. Presently Antonio enters, draws his sword in defence of Viola
(whom he mistakes for Sebastian), and is arrested by the Officers ; and from the
speech of the First Officer, in V, i, 64, we learn distinctly where his arrest took
place : ' Here *in the streets*, desperate of shame and state, In private brabble did we
apprehend him.'—Sir Andrew, then, was waiting for the pretended page ' at the corner of the orchard,' line 174, ' at the orchard-end,' line 223,—that is, in the street at
the extremity of Olivia's orchard or garden ; there Sir Toby had joined him ; and
thither Fabian and Viola walk. I may add that the rather unsatisfactory stage-
arrangements here were in a certain degree forced upon Shakespeare ; he found it
necessary to get rid of Viola while Sir Toby was terrifying Sir Andrew with an account
of his antagonist's ferocity. (Since writing the above, I have examined a modern
acting copy of the play ; in it the scene is changed here from ' *A Room in Olivia's
house*' to ' Olivia's garden.')—MARSHALL : In the acting-edition of this play, as pre-

To. Why man hee s a verie diuell, I haue not feen fuch   273
a firago : I had a paffe with him, rapier, fcabberd, and all :

274. *firago*] Ff, Var. '21, Coll. Dyce,   *virago* Rowe et cet.
Cam. Sta. Ktly, Rlfe, Huds. Wh. ii.   274. *fcabberd*] *fcabber'd* F₂.

---

pared for the Lyceum Theatre, Scene iv. of Act IV. commences here, the place being
The Orchard End.   There can be no doubt that a change of scene is necessary
here.—CAMBRIDGE EDITORS : The Fourth Scene is continued in the Folios, and as,
in all other instances throughout the play, the beginning of each scene is accurately
marked, we have thought it best to follow them in this.   According to the Folios,
Fabian and Viola leave the stage just as Sir Toby and Sir Andrew enter, and, not
meeting them, may be supposed to return to the place appointed in lines 239, 240
[lines 256, 257 of the present text.—ED.] Capell, contrary to the directions of
the Folios, keeps Fabian and Viola on the stage.   They are, indeed, all the
while within sight of Sir Toby, as appears from lines 268, 269 [*i. e.* 280, 281 of
present text], but not necessarily visible to the audience.   The comic effect would,
no doubt, be heightened if Fabian were seen using all his efforts to prevent Viola
from running away, but this is scarcely a sufficient reason for deserting our only
authority. [On a stage like Shakespeare's, which made such a constant demand
on the imagination,—where merely a grey veil thrown over the head made the
wearer invisible to his fellow-actors,—it is conceivable that the two couples
might have obeyed the stage-directions of the Folios, when at *Exeunt* they
retired a few paces, and *Re-entered* by advancing, and all the while have remained
but a few paces apart, in full sight of each other and yet be supposed to be beyond
earshot ; as Toby left Viola he was supposed to have made his exit, and to have
re-entered as he joined Andrew.   Dyce reminds us that Shakespeare's audience
had to *suppose* a change of scene, owing to the lack of painted scenery, and yet,
at the same time, talks of 'streets' and 'orchards,'—as though these streets and
orchards were portrayed before the eyes of Shakespeare's audience.   Shakespeare's
audience heard only the text, and believed whatever was told them.   If they were
told that Antonio was arrested in the street they so accepted it, though, for all that
their eyes actually saw, he was arrested in what at one time they had been told was
Olivia's chamber.   I agree entirely with Capell that the two groups—Andrew and
Toby, Viola and Fabian—were both, at the same moment, on Shakespeare's stage
at least, in sight of each other and of the audience.   *Possibly,* Sir Toby's assertion that 'Fabian can scarce hold him yonder' (interpreted as depicting Viola's
attempts to run away), is become the pernicious source of the conversion of
Viola's exquisite bearing throughout, into low farce.   But it must be borne in
mind that Sir Toby's description of Fabian's struggles with Viola (which Sir
Andrew could have seen for himself, but he was too limp to perceive anything but
his own peril) was as veracious as that Viola had given him the stuck in, with rapier,
scabbard, and all.—ED.]

274. **firago**] JOHNSON : 'Virago' cannot be properly used here, unless we suppose Sir Toby to mean, I never saw one that had so much the look of a woman with
the prowess of a man.—STEEVENS : A *virago* always means a female warrior, or, in
low language, a scold, or turbulent woman.   In Heywood's *Golden Age*, 1611,
Jupiter enters 'like a nymph or virago'; and says, 'I may pass for a bona-roba, a
rounceval, a virago, or a good manly lass.' [II, i, p. 30, ed. Shakespeare Soc.]   If

and he giues me the ſtucke in with ſuch a mortall motion   275
that it is ineuitable : and on the anſwer, he payes you as

275. *ſtucke in*] *stuck—in* Johns.   Sing.
stuck-in Cap. Var. Mal. Steev. Var.   276. *ineuitable*] *invitable* F$_4$.
Wh. i, Sta. Dyce ii, iii, Ktly.   *Stuckin*   *you*] *your* F$_2$.

Shakespeare (who knew Viola to be a woman, though Sir Toby did not) has made
no blunder, Dr Johnson has supplied the only obvious meaning of the word.
'Firago' may, however, be a ludicrous word of Shakespeare's coinage.—MALONE :
Why may not the meaning be more simple, 'I have never seen the most furious
woman so obstreperous and violent as he is'? I do not conceive that 'firago' is a
word of Shakespeare's coinage, but a common corruption for *virago*, like *fagaries*
for vagaries.—RITSON (p. 65) : The word 'virago' is certainly inapplicable to a
man, a blustering, hectoring fellow, as Sir Toby means to represent Viola ; for he
cannot possibly entertain any suspicion of her sex ; but it is no otherwise so, than
rounceval is to a woman [see the foregoing quotation from Heywood], meaning a
terrible fighting blade ; from Roncesvalles, the famous scene of the fabulous combat
with the Saracens.—COLLIER : It may be spelt 'firago' perhaps with allusion to the
word 'devil' in the preceding part of the sentence.—W. A. WRIGHT : Sir Toby's
corruption of *virago*, or else a word of his own coinage. If 'fire-eater' had been
in existence at the time, 'firago' might be a hybrid between this and 'virago.'
['Firago' seems far more expressive than the tame 'virago'; there is in it a suggestion of *fire, fury, fiend, ferocious*, all combined.—ED.]

275. **stucke in**] STEEVENS : The 'stuck' is a corrupted abbreviation of the
Stoccata, an Italian term in fencing. So in *The Returne from Parnassus*, 1606 :
'I, heare is a fellow, Iudicio, that carryed the deadly stock-[ado] in his pen.'[I, ii,
p. 87, ed. Macray.] Again, Marston's *Second Part of Antonio and Mellida*, 1602 :
'I would passe on him with a mortall stocke'[I, iii. See *Rom. & Jul.* III, i, 79 :
'Alla stoccata carries it away.' I think Capell erred in joining 'stuck' and 'in'
with a hyphen ; 'in,' I believe, qualifies 'give,' that is, 'gives me the stuck home,'
and probably it was so understood by Dr Johnson, who placed after 'stuck' not a
hyphen, but a dash. Possibly, Sir Toby uttered the 'in' after 'stuck' with great
emphasis, accompanied with a manual illustration on the breast of Sir Andrew which
was well devised to reduce him to abject terror. What the 'stuck' or stoccata is we
learn from *Vincentio Saviolo his Practise*, 1595 : 'let the scholler obserue the same
time in going backe as the teacher shall, . . . and let him lifte vp his other hand with
his ward on high, that he be not stricken on the face with the mandritta, or in the
belly with the thrust or stoccata. Wherefore at the selfe same time that the scholler
shall deliuer the foresaide stoccata to the teacher, the teacher shall yeelde and
shrinke with his bodye, and beate the stoccata outward on the left side.'—p. 9,
verso.—ED.]

276. **ineuitable**] That is, what Shakespeare calls, in *Othello*, 'unshunnable.'
—ED.

276. **on the answer**] Thus, Vincentio Saviolo *his Practise :* 'As the Scholler
parteth in the counter time, hee must in the same instant breake the stoccata with
his lefte hande, and aunswere againe with the other : also the Maister, to make his
scholler quicke and readye, shall vse to aunswere him in the same time that his
scholler deliuereth his stoccata,' etc., p. 17.—ED.

276. **he payes you**] MALONE : That is, he hits you.

furely, as your feete hits the ground they ftep on. They   277
fay, he has bin Fencer to the Sophy.

And.   Pox on't, Ile not meddle with him.

To.   I but he will not now be pacified,   280
Fabian can fcarfe hold him yonder.

An   Plague on't, and I thought he had beene valiant,
and fo cunning in Fence, I'de haue feene him damn'd ere
I'de haue challeng'd him. Let him let the matter flip, and
Ile giue him my horfe, gray Capilet.   285

To.   Ile make the motion : ftand heere, make a good
fhew on't, this fhall end without the perdition of foules,
marry Ile ride your horfe as well as I ride you.

               Enter Fabian and Viola.

I haue his horfe to take vp the quarrell, I haue perfwaded   290
him the youths a diuell.

Fa.   He is as horribly conceited of him : and pants, &
lookes pale, as if a Beare were at his heeles.

To.   There's no remedie fir, he will fight with you for's
oath fake : marrie hee hath bette r bethought him of his   295
quarrell, and hee findes that now fcarfe to bee worth tal-

277. *hits*] Ff. *hit* Rowe et seq.
278. *bin*] *been* Ff.
279. *Ile*] ile F$_2$. *I'le* F$_3$F$_4$.
280. Prose, Cap. et seq.
281. *yonder*] Om. Rowe.
282. *and I*] *if I* Pope, Han. *an I* Theob. et seq.
285. *him*] *you* Anon. ap. Cam. *Capilet*] *Capulet* Dyce, Huds.
287. *foules,*] *fouls ;* F$_4$, Rowe:
288. [Aside. Theob.
289. Viola.] *Viola unwillingly.* Coll. MS.
290. *I...quarrell*] Separate line, Sta. [To Fabian. Rowe. Aside,

Cap.
290. *take vp*] *make up* Anon. ap. Cam.
291. *youths*] *youth's* F$_3$F$_4$.
292, 293. [Aside. Cap.
292. *as horribly*] *horribly* Rowe, Pope, Han.
294. To.] To. [to Viola.] Cap. *for's*] *for his* Mal. Steev. Var. Knt.
295. *oath fake*] *oath's sake* Cap. Coll. ii. *oath-sake* Dyce. *hath*] *had* Theob. ii, Warb. Johns. Var. Ran.
296. *fcarfe to bee*] *to be scarce* Cap. conj.

278. **Sophy**] See II, v, 169.
285. **Capilet**] W. A. WRIGHT : 'Capul' was a north-country word for a horse, and possibly 'capilet' may be a diminutive of this. MURRAY (*N. E. D.* s. v. *Caple, capul*) gives a quotation from *Land Cokaygne*, as early as *circa* 1290 : 'Hors, no capil, kowe, no ox,' which adds probability to Wright's suggestion.
290. **to take vp**] See *As You Like It*, V, iv, 100 : 'I knew when seuen Iustices could not take vp a Quarrell.'
292. **horribly conceited**] MALONE : That is, he has as horrid an idea or conception of him. [Compare *Othello*, III, iii, 174: 'From one, that so imperfectly conceits.']

king of : therefore draw for the fupportance of his vowe,   297
he protefts he will not hurt you.

Vio.   Pray God defend me : a little thing would make
me tell them how much I lacke of a man.   300

Fab.   Giue ground if you fee him furious.

To.   Come fir *Andrew*, there's no remedie, the Gentleman will for his honors fake haue one bowt with you:
he cannot by the Duello auoide it : but hee has promifed
me, as he is a Gentleman and a Soldiour, he will not hurt   305
you.   Come on, too't.

And.   Pray God he keepe his oath.

Enter Antonio.

Vio.   I do affure you tis againft my will.   309

297. *vowe,*] *vow ;* Cap.

299. Vio.] Vio. [Aside.] Cap.

302. To.] To. [Go to Andrew.] Coll.
MS. ap. Cam.

306. [They draw. Rowe.

307. [draws. Cap.

307. Scene XIV. Pope, +.

308. Enter...] After line 309, Dyce,
Cam. Sta. Enter...draws, and runs
between. (after line 309) Cap.

309. [to Sir And. draws. Cap.

---

297. **supportance**] That is, maintaining or upholding. SCHMIDT (*Lex.*) furnishes an example of its use literally, as a support, or prop : 'Give some supportance
to the bending twigs.'—*Rich. II :* III, iv, 32.

304. **by the Duello**] The earliest example of the use of this form, given by
MURRAY (*N. E. D.*) is from *Love's Lab. L.* I, ii, 185, so that one might almost
attribute its introduction to Shakespeare. 'Duellum,' an adoption from the mediæval
Latin, *duellum* (an ancient form of Latin *bellum*), dates from 1284. 'Duel' is
found in Coryat's *Crudities,* 1611.   For 'duelling, as a practice, having its code of
laws,' Murray quotes Tomkis, *Albumazar,* 1615 : 'Understand'st thou well nice
points of duel ? . . . by strict laws of duel I am excus'd To fight on disadvantage.'—
IV, vii.

309. **I do, etc.**] SPEDDING (*Fraser's Maga.* Aug. 1865, p. 266) : That the
humours of the duelling scene will ever be brought back within the text of Shakespeare, and the limits of *becoming* mirth, is more than we can hope. Managers can
hardly be expected to sacrifice a piece of farce, which always makes the audience
very merry, though Shakespeare has evidently taken pains to preserve Viola from
the ridiculous attitude in which it places her, and she can never be seen as she was
meant to be until it is reformed. . . . Viola, it must be remembered, has to sustain
the part of a young gentleman, who must not seem to be afraid of a drawn sword,
or unused to handle one.   If she cannot contrive to avoid the fight handsomely, the
resource she looks to is not flight but confession,—a confession of her disguise.
'Pray God defend me,' she says to herself when it is coming to extremity, 'a little
thing would make me,'—not, take to my heels,—but '*tell them* how much I lack of a
man.'   How she would have done it we do not know ; but we may be sure she
would have known how to do it gracefully and without loss of feminine dignity.
But being a person of great feminine (though not masculine) courage, of remark-

Ant.   Put vp your ſword : if this yong Gentleman   310
Haue done offence, I take the fault on me :
If you offend him, I for him defie you.
   To.   You ſir ? Why, what are you ?
   Ant.   One ſir, that for his loue dares yet do more
Then you haue heard him brag to you he will.   315
   To.   Nay,if you be an vndertaker, I am for you.

312. [Drawing. Rowe.   316. [Draws. Rowe.

able composure and presence of mind and ready wit, she reserves that for the last
extremity ; hoping by judgement, gentleness, pacific bearing, and intervention of
Providence, to avoid the necessity of so inconvenient a disclosure.   Of the attempts
to run away, and the dragging back and pushing on by main force, it is not enough
to say that there is no trace in the original text ; they are inconsistent with it.   For
up to the very last, when there seemed to be no chance of escape left, the only evidence she had given of the fear which she had such good right to feel, was ' panting
and looking pale.'   And even when she is obliged to draw her sword, or prepare to
draw it (for it is doubtful whether Shakespeare intended to expose her to so severe a
trial as the actual crossing of weapons), her words are still calm, and such as any
gentleman might have used—' I do assure you, 'tis against my will.'   Indeed, from
the beginning to the end of the adventure she neither does nor says anything (her
complexion and the beating of her heart excepted) that would have misbecome a
well-behaved, peaceful young gentleman, who disliked to be drawn by a bully into a
brawl.   She acts throughout with discretion, intelligence, and a collected judgement.
. . . She goes forward to the place where the danger is ; and there is not the slightest
indication that she is either pushed or pulled ; so far, therefore, she has contrived to
perform her part without betraying more than had appeared before in her countenance
and behaviour.   And when it comes at last to a crisis, in which she *must* either have
disgraced her man's apparel or betrayed her secret, the sudden appearance of Antonio
rescues her from the indignity.   Now we submit that this struggle between woman's
fear and woman's courage, wit, and self-respect,—gently, gracefully, bravely, and
successfully carried through under very trying circumstances,—is much finer comedy,
as well as much more in harmony with the sentiment of the play, than the mere
terrors and perplexities of a young woman frightened out of her wits at the idea of
a naked sword,—though executed to perfection.   The inward sinking of the heart
may be made visible enough to the audience without any display of unseemly terror.
[These brave words of Spedding cannot be too thoroughly digested.   A reluctance
to engage in a street brawl, with an unknown ruffian, for no known cause, cannot be,
in any age, attributed in a gentleman to cowardice.   It seems to me that Shakespeare has taken special pains to guard Viola from all imputation of pusillanimity.
—ED.]

316. **an vndertaker**] TYRWHITT : At the meeting of the parliament in 1614,
there appears to have been a very general persuasion, or jealousy at least, that the
King had been induced to call a parliament at that time, by certain persons who had
undertaken, through their influence in the House of Commons, to carry things
according to his Majesty's wishes.   These persons were immediately stigmatized
with the invidious name of *undertakers ;* and the idea was so unpopular that the

EnterOfficers.   317

Fab. O good fir *Toby* hold: heere come the Officers.

To. Ile be with you anon.

Vio. Pray fir, put your fword vp if you pleafe.   320

And. Marry will I fir : and for that I promis'd you Ile
be as good as my word. Hee will beare you eafily, and
raines well.

1.Off. This is the man, do thy Office.

2 Off. *Anthonio*, I arreft thee at the fuit of Count *Orfino*   325

An. You do miftake me fir.

1.Off. No fir, no iot : I know your fauour well :
Though now you haue no fea-cap on your head :   328

317. Enter...] After line 323, Dyce,
Sta. Coll. iii.
    Officers.] Officer. F₄.
319. [to Antonio. Cap.
320. [To Sir And. Rowe.
    fword] *word* F₄, Rowe.

323. *raines*] *rains* F₄. *reins* Rowe.
325. Anthonio...*fuit*] One line, Cap.
Mal. Steev. Var. Knt, Coll. Wh. i,
Dyce, Sta. Ktly.
    Count] *Duke* Rowe, +.

King thought it necessary to deny positively (how truly is another question) that
there had been any such *undertaking*. Sir Francis Bacon also (then attorney-general) made an artful, apologetical speech in the House of Commons upon the same
subject : 'when the house (according to the title of the speech) was in great heat,
and much troubled about the undertakers.'—RITSON : 'Undertakers' were persons
employed by the King's purveyors to take up provisions for the royal household, and
were no doubt exceedingly odious. But still, I think, the speaker intends a quibble ;
the simple meaning of the word being one who undertakes, or takes up the quarrel
or business of another.—M. MASON : I am of Ritson's opinion. DYCE (*Gloss.*)
also adopts it.—W. A. WRIGHT : In the Authorised Version of Isaiah xxxviii, 14,
'Undertake for us' signifies 'Be surety for us.' There is no reason to suppose that
Sir Toby uses it with any more contempt than is naturally felt for a meddlesome person. At the beginning of the 17th century, it signified what we should now call a
'contractor,' and Bacon in his speech in the House of Commons concerning the
Undertaker says : 'I had heard of Undertakings in several kinds. There were
Undertakers for the plantations of Derry and Coleraine in Ireland, the better to
command and bridle those parts. There were, not long ago, some Undertakers for
the north-west passage ; and now there are some Undertakers for the project of dyed
and dressed cloths.'—*Life and Letters*, ed. Spedding, v, 43. [Inasmuch as we now
know that this play was acted in 1601-2, a meaning attached to 'undertakers' in
1614 can hardly carry much weight ; and yet that the term was an opprobrious one at
least five years earlier we learn from Ben Jonson's *Dedication* to *The Silent Woman*,
1609, where he says that he would rather be 'freed in my fame by the authority of a
judge than the credit of an undertaker,' that is, he would prefer the vindication of such
men as Sir Francis Stuart than the applause of men, the iniquity of whose nature, he
says further on, he hated. The 'undertakers' in the parliament of 1614 were probably so called because the name was already disgraceful, or, as Tyrwhitt says,
'invidious.'—ED.]

Take him away, he knowes I know him well.

   Ant. I muſt obey. This comes with ſeeking you :   330
But there's no remedie, I ſhall anſwer it :
What will you do : now my neceſſitie
Makes me to aske you for my purſe. It greeues mee
Much more, for what I cannot do for you,
Then what befals my ſelfe : you ſtand amaz'd,   335
But be of comfort.

   2 Off. Come ſir away.

   Ant. I muſt entreat of you ſome of that money.

   Vio. What money ſir ?

For the fayre kindneſſe you haue ſhew'd me heere,   340
And part being prompted by your preſent trouble,
Out of my leane and low ability
Ile lend you ſomething : my hauing is not much,
Ile make diuiſion of my preſent with you :
Hold, there's halfe my Coffer.   345

   Ant. Will you deny me now,
Iſt poſſible that my deſerts to you   347

---

330. *obey.*] *obey.* [To Viola.] Coll.
Cap.

332, 333. *do :...purſe.*] *do,...purſe ?*
Dyce. Sta. Cam. Rlfe.   *doe ?...purſe.*
Ff, Rowe et cet.

334. *more, for*] *more ; for* F₄, Rowe.
more for Coll. Dyce, Sta. Cam.

336. *But be*] *Be* F₃F₄.

337–339. *Come ... ſir ?*] Two lines,
ending *you...ſir ?* (reading *money back.*)

337. *away*] *come away* Ktly.
341. *part being*] *part, being* Cap.
343. *hauing*] *Having* Theob. Warb.
Johns.

   much,] *much ;* Theob.
345. *there's*] *there is* Han. Steev. Var.
Knt, Hal.

346. *now,*] *now ?* F₃F₄.

---

328. **sea-cap**] HALLIWELL quotes the following note from Fairholt : The 'sea-cap' of the Shakespearian era appears to have been generally composed of fur, as appears from Ammon's curious book *De omnibus Illiberalibus sive Mechanicis Artibus*, 1574.

330. **with seeking you**] For examples of a similar use of *with*, see ABBOTT, § 193, p. 128.

341. **And part**] That is, partly. See *Othello*, V, ii, 363 : 'This wretch hath part confest his Villany.'

343. **my hauing**] That is, possession. See *As You Like It*, III, ii, 362 : 'for simply your having in beard is a yonger brothers revenew.' Schmidt's *Lex.* furnishes many examples.

344. **diuision of my present**] After 'present,' money or store is understood. For examples of adjectives used for nouns, see ABBOTT, § 5, p. 20.

345. **Hold**] WALKER (*Crit.* iii, 88) and ABBOTT (§ 512, p. 424) would make this a separate interjectional line ; retaining 'there's' of the Folio.

Can l*a*cke perſwaſion. Do not tempt my miſery,
Leaſt that it make me ſo vnſound a man
As to vpbraid you with thoſe kindneſſes
That I haue done for you.
Vio. I know of none,
Nor know I you by voyce, or any feature:
I hate ingratitude more in a man,
Then lying, vainneſſe, babling drunkenneſſe,
Or any taint of vice, whoſe ſtrong corruption
Inhabites our fraile blood.
Ant. Oh heauens themſelues.
2.*Off.* Come ſir, I pray you go.
Ant. Let me ſpeake a little. This youth that you ſee
I ſnatch'd one halfe out of the iawes of death, (heere,

348. *lacke*] F_1.
perſwaſion.] *perſuaſion?* Ff.
349. *Leaſt*] *Left* F_4.
352. *none,*] *none.* Ff.
355. *lying, vainneſſe, babling drunkenneſſe*] Ff, Rowe i, +, Cap. Var. Ran. Mal. *lying vainness, babbling drunkenness* Rowe ii (ap. Cam.), Coll. Sing. Ktly, Cam. ii. *lying, vainness, babbling, drunkenness* Steev. et cet.
358. *heauens*] *Heav'ns* Rowe, +.
359. *pray you go*] *pray you* Lloyd ap. Cam.
360. *ſpeake*] *but speak* Han.
360, 361. *a little...heere,*] Separate line (reading *Why, this youth*) Han.
361. *death,*] *death;* Theob.

349. **Least that**] For the construction, see I, ii, 53.

355. **lying, vainnesse, babling drunkennesse**] COLLIER: 'Lying' and 'babbling' are not to be taken as substantives, but as participial adjectives. [See *Text. Notes.*]—W. A. WRIGHT: The reading of Rowe, ed. ii. appears to be the best. In Steevens's arrangement there is no sequence or climax in the four things which are stigmatised as vices, and it is better to take the words in pairs, with an adjective and substantive in each pair.—DEIGHTON: There seems to me a cumulative force which is lost by adopting Rowe's reading. [In my copy of Rowe ii. there is a faint battered comma after 'lying,' which may well have disappeared in subsequent impressions. Steevens was absurdly wrong in placing a comma after 'babbling.' I much prefer to take the words in pairs, as Collier and Wright suggest.—ED.]

355. **vainnesse**] This, SCHMIDT (*Lex.*) defines as 'falseness'; W. A. WRIGHT as 'boastfulness.' Schmidt overlooked the tautology in 'lying falseness.'

359. **Come sir, etc.**] WALKER (*Crit.* iii, 89): Arrange, perhaps,—'Come, sir, I pray go. (Not "I pray *you* go." Yet I doubt) Let me speak a little | This youth, that you see here, | I snatch'd one half,' etc. [If these sentences were properly pronounced on the stage, no human ear could detect these divisions which Walker recommends.—ED.]—K. ELZE (p. 184): The words 'a little,' besides spoiling the metre, impress the reader as ridiculously superfluous, and have probably slipped from their original place, which was in the second half of the preceding line. I suspect the original wording to have been somewhat as follows: 'Come, sir, I pray you go. *Tarry a little* | *And* let me speak. This youth that you see here, | ' etc.

Releeu'd him with such fanctitie of loue ;   362
And to his image, which me thought did promife
Moſt venerable worth, did I deuotion.
　　1.*Off*.　What's that to vs, the time goes by : Away.   365
　　Ant.　But oh, how vilde an idoll proues this God :
Thou haſt *Sebaſtian* done good feature, ſhame.
In Nature, there's no blemiſh but the minde :
None can be call'd deform'd, but the vnkinde.
Vertue is beauty, but the beauteous euill   370

362. *loue ;*] Ff, Han. Cam. Huds.
love, Rowe, +, Glo. *love,*— Cap. et cet.
363. *his*] *this* Walker, Huds.
me thought] *methought* Rowe.
364. *venerable*] *veritable* Coll. ii, iii
(MS).
365. *vs,*] Ff. Rowe i. *us ?* Rowe ii.

366. *vilde*] F₂F₃. *vild* F₄, Rowe,
Knt. *vile* Pope.
　　God :] *god :* F₂F₃. *God !* F₄.
367. *feature, ſhame*] F₂. *feature
ſhame,* F₃F₄.
370. *beauteous euill*] *beauteous-evil*
Mal. Steev. Var. Dyce, Sta.

362. **such sanctitie of loue ;**] CAPELL placed a dash after 'love,' as an incomplete sentence. WALKER was so impressed with this incompleteness that he says (*Crit.* iii, 89) 'a line seems to have dropped out after "love," for the only meaning which (as the passage stands) "such" can possibly have, is inadmissible. I would read and point : " I snatch'd one half out of the jaws of death ; | Reliev'd him ; with such sanctity of love [a line omitted] And to *this* image, which methought did promise," etc. The emendation of *this* for "his" I have also proposed [in *Crit.* ii, 222], where see other instances of the confusion between these two words.'—HUDSON : The context, I think, fairly requires the sense of *all* instead of 'such.' *Much* might more easily be misprinted 'such,' but is not strong enough for the place. The occurrence of 'idol' in the last line shows Walker's emendation, 'this,' to be right. Antonio does not mean that he has been worshipping an image of the supposed Sebastian, but that what he has taken for something divine turns out to be but a hollow image.—W. A. WRIGHT : For 'such,' in this sense, compare *Cymbeline*, V, v, 44 : ' Your daughter, whom she bore in hand to love With such integrity, she did confess Was as a scorpion in her sight.'

364. **venerable**] COLLIER (ed. ii) : No doubt 'worth' is 'venerable,' but what Antonio means is '*veritable* worth,' and such is the word substituted, most fitly, by the MS Corrector. Antonio apprehended that he had found Sebastian's worth mere ingratitude and falsehood. The word was either misheard or misprinted.—DYCE (ed. ii) : But the context ('devotion,' 'idol,' 'god') is decisive against [this] alteration.　[The use of 'devotion' alone is decisive.—ED.]

367. **feature, shame**] Although, in general, I set no great value on the punctuation of the compositors of the Folio, yet, now and then, it is noteworthy. The comma after 'feature' seems to have been really placed with a purpose ; possibly, to indicate that 'feature' means *the whole exterior*, as Touchstone asks Audrey, ' does my simple feature content you ?' and that the voice must not run on, and, absorbing an *s* from 'shame,' convert the phrase into 'feature*s* shame.'—ED.

369. **the vnkinde**] That is, unnatural. Thus, *Lear*, III, iv, 73 : 'Nothing could have subdued nature To such a lowness but his unkind daughters.'

370. **beauteous euill**] A combination similar to 'proper false,' in II, ii, 31.

Are empty trunkes, ore-flourifh'd by the deuill.   371

   1. *Off.*   The man growes mad, away with him :

Come, come fir.

    Ant.   Leade me on.   *Exit*

    Vio.   Me thinkes his words do from fuch pafsion flye   375

That he beleeues himfelfe, fo do not I :

Proue true imagination, oh proue ttue,

That I deere brother, be now tane for you.

    To.   Come hither Knight, come hither *Fabian :* Weel

whifper ore a couplet or two of moft fage fawes.   380

    Vio.   He nam'd *Sebaftian* : I my brother know

Yet liuing in my glaffe : euen fuch, and fo

In fauour was my Brother, and he went   383

372, 373. Prose, Mal. Dyce, Cam. Ktly, Rlfe, Wh. ii.

372. *The*] *Surely the* Han.

373. *Come*] 2.O. *Come* Cap.

375. [Aside. Ed. conj.

     Me thinkes] *Methinks* F₄.

376. *himfelfe,*] *himself ;* Rowe ii.

377. *ttue*] F₁.

378. *tane*] *ta'en* Rowe.

379. *Weel*] *Well* Ff.

379, 380. Two lines of verse (reading, *We'll whisper o'er a couplet of sage saws*) Voss conj.

380. [converse apart. Cap.

381. [Aside. Ed. conj.

---

371. empty trunkes] STEEVENS : In the time of Shakespeare, trunks, which are now deposited in lumber-rooms, or other obscure places, were part of the furniture of apartments in which company was received. I have seen more than one of these, as old as the time of our poet. They were richly ornamented on the top and sides with scroll-work, emblematical devices, etc.

376. so do not I] JOHNSON : This, I believe, means, I do not yet believe myself, when, from this accident, I gather hope of my brother's life.—W. A. WRIGHT : Viola was not so confident in her belief that Sebastian lived, as Antonio was that she was Sebastian.—DEIGHTON : His words appear to be born of such strong feeling that the man believes what he says, viz.: that he knew me before and rescued me from the sea ; but I do not believe with him, *i. e.* I know that his belief is a mistaken one. [This man has faith in what he says, which I have not.—ED.]

380. a couplet or two of most sage sawes] DEIGHTON : Said in ridicule of Antonio's moralising and Viola's soliloquising. [That it was said in ridicule of Antonio is, I think, clear ; Antonio's last lines ran in couplets. But I cannot think it refers to Viola, who surely must have spoken aside.—ED.]

381, 382. know Yet liuing] For the construction, see I, v, 299.

382. liuing in my glasse] STEEVENS : I suppose Viola means : ' As often as I behold myself in my glass, I think I see my brother alive '; *i. e.* I acknowledge that his resemblance *survives* in the reflection of my own figure.—DEIGHTON : It seems to me to mean rather ' I know my brother to be mirrored to the life in my person, in myself who am the glass '; compare *Hamlet*, III, i, 161, ' The glass of fashion,' said of Hamlet, whose person reflected the highest fashion. [I do not doubt that Deighton is correct.—ED.]

Still in this fafhion, colour, ornament,
For him I imitate : Oh if it proue,   385
Tempefts are kinde, and falt waues frefh in loue.

To.   A very difhoneft paltry boy, and more a coward
then a Hare, his difhonefty appeares, in leauing his frend
heere in neceffity, and denying him: and for his coward-
fhip aske *Fabian*.   390

Fab.   A Coward, a moft deuout Coward, religious in
it.

And.   Slid Ile after him againe, and beate him.

To.   Do, cuffe him foundly, but neuer draw thy fword

And.   And I do not.   395

Fab.   Come, let's fee the euent.

To.   I dare lay any money, twill be nothing yet.   *Exit*   397

Actus Quartus, Scæna prima.

Enter Sebaftian and Clowne.   2

Clo.   Will you make me beleeue, that I am not fent for
you ?

Seb.   Go too, go too, thou art a foolifh fellow,   5
Let me be cleere of thee.

385. *Oh*] *So* Becket, Coll. conj.
386. *loue.*] *love.* Exit. Ff.
387. To.] Yob. F₄.
388. *Hare,*] *Hare :* F₃F₄.
391. *a moft*] Om. Han.
393. *Slid*] *'Slid* F₃F₄.   *Od's lid* Han.
394. *Do,*] *Do :* Coll. Dyce, Sta. Cam.
neuer] *ne'er* Han.
draw] Om. F₃F₄, Rowe i.

395. *And*] *If* Pope, Han. *An* Theob. et seq.
not.] *not,*— Theob. et seq.
[Exit Sir And. Theob.
396. *let's*] *let us* Han.
397. *any*] Om. Han.
Exit.] Exeunt. Rowe.
The Street. Rowe.   ...before
Olivia's House. Cap.
5. *too*] *to* Ff.
5, 6. Prose, Wh. i.

---

385. **if it proue**] For other instances of the omission of *so*, see ABBOTT, § 64.

391, 392. **religious in it**] DEIGHTON : One who seems positively to worship cowardice. [Is it not rather, one who practises it religiously ?—ED.]

393. **Slid**] See II, v, 34.

1. **Scæna prima**] MARSHALL : In [Irving's] acting-edition, this scene forms part of the preceding one.

3. **Will you**] The French *veux-tu.*

5. **Go too, go too**] According to Bartlett's *Concordance*, this exclamation is used eighteen or nineteen times in these plays ; and, of course, with varying shades of

Clo. Well held out yſaith : No, I do not know you,		7
nor I am not ſent to you by my Lady, to bid you come
ſpeake with her : nor your name is not Maſter *Ceſario*,
nor this is not my noſe neyther : Nothing that is ſo, is ſo.		10
Seb. I prethee vent thy folly ſome-where elſe, thou
know'ſt not me.
Clo. Vent my folly : He has heard that word of ſome
great man, and now applyes it to a foole. Vent my fol-
ly : I am affraid this great lubber the World will proue a		15

11, 12. *thou … me.*] Separate line, Cap.
11. *ſome-where*] F₂. ſomewhere F₃F₄.
14, 15. *folly :*] folly ! F₄.
15. *great lubber the World*] Ff, Rowe, +, Cap. Var. Ran. Mal. Steev. Sta.

great lubberly world Coll. MS. Huds.
great lubberly word Douce, Badham, Wh. *great lubber, the world,* Var. '03 et cet. *great lubber, for all the world* Bulloch.

meaning, but in the majority of cases it expresses impatience. We reverse the action and say ' Come, come.'—ED.

7. Well held out] An artful way of implying that much of this contest has been carried on before Sebastian and Feste enter.—ED.

13. Vent my folly] CAPELL (p. 151) : ' Vent' is a mercantile word and in use with citizens, and suggests the Clown's reflection about the ' world' in line 15.— REED : This affected word seems to have been in use in Shakespeare's time.— HUNTER (i, 409) : We have here Shakespeare ridiculing affectations in language. Jonson, in his *Volpone*, fights by his side in respect of this word : ' Pray you what news, sirs, vents our climate ?'—II, i. [It is strange to find Hunter supporting Reed in the supposition that Shakespeare here ridicules the use of ' vent.' Both must have known that Shakespeare himself (as ROLFE points out) uses the word many times. Two years before this play was written, Jaques says of Touch-stone, in *As You Like It*, II, vii, 43 : ' He hath strange places cram'd With obser-uation, the which he vents In mangled forms.' See, too, Kent's use of the word in the first Scene of *King Lear*. Feste was on the alert to ridicule any expression or any action of Sebastian, to ' check at any feather'; and the contempt, implied by the phrase, stung him.—ED.]

15. great lubber the World] JOHNSON : That is, affectation and foppery will overspread the world.—DOUCE : A typographical corruption seems to have crept into this place from similitude of sound ; but a very slight alteration will restore the sense. The clown is speaking of ' vent' as an affected word ; we should therefore read : ' this great *lubberly word* will prove,' etc., *i. e.* will turn out to be cockney language.—KNIGHT quotes Douce, and then pertinently asks : ' But is the little word " vent" a great lubberly word ?' He then continues, ' The Clown is tolerably consequential in his thoughts ; and, if there were any precise meaning in his fear that the world would prove a cockney, we do not see how he brings the matter in. May not the speech be spoken aside, " I am afraid the world will prove this great lubber (Sebastian) a cockney "—a foolish fellow ? Such an inversion is not uncom-mon.'—COLLIER (ed. ii) : The MS Corrector reads ' *lubberly* world.' Shakespeare uses the word ' lubberly' in *Mer. Wives*, V, v, and it is very possible that *lubberly*

Cockney : I prethee now vngird thy ftrangenes, and tell   16
_____

was misheard 'lubber the.'—BADHAM (p. 284) : The coherency of this passage is
none of the closest ; for what has the state of the world at large to do with Sebastian using a choice expression ? [Hereupon Badham, not knowing, of course, that
he had been anticipated by Douce, proposes with 'certainty' that the phrase is the
'great *lubberly word*,' whereof the meaning is] that this imposing word will probably turn out to be no proof that the person using it is an adept in courtly phrase,—
that Sebastian, when his single borrowed bravery of language is used, will show the
weakness of his own wit.—HALLIWELL : The meaning of this passage appears to
be, I am afraid the whole of the large world will be infected with foppery and
affectation, in other words, will prove a cockney.—R. G. WHITE, also, not knowing that he had been anticipated by both Douce and Badham, adopted 'lubberly
word,' asking in his First Edition whether 'there can be a doubt that *lubberly word*
was mistaken for "lubber yᵉ world"?' 'This correction,' he adds, 'was made by
the present editor before he knew of the existence of Collier's MS Corrector,' but
he should have known of Douce, whose emendation was made in 1807. In his
Second Edition, White's note reads : '*lubberly word :* that is, *vent*, which, in the
sense of utter, was affectedly used in S.'s day. [Was it affectation in Kent to say to
Lear, 'While I can vent clamour from my throat '?—ED.] The clown fears it will
prove a cockney ; that is, petted and adopted. But with any interpretation the
passage is doubtful.'—STAUNTON : The point of this is not apparent. . . . Omitting
the adjective 'great,' which may have been caught by the compositor from the line
above, Douce's emendation probably gives us what the poet wrote.—DYCE (ed. ii) :
I can hardly believe that Shakespeare would have made the Clown speak of 'vent'
as a 'great lubberly word'; and I doubt much if 'great lubberly' could signify either
'imposing' or 'pretentious,' as Badham and R. G. White respectively gloss the
expression.—H. H. S. CROFT (*Gloss.* p. 471) : A clue to the true explanation of
this sentence will undoubtedly be found in the repetition by the Clown of the word
'vent,' which evidently struck him as something new fangled and unaccustomed, its
'strangeness' appeared to him a mark of affectation, of *mignardise*, such that the
'great man,' the great (unknown) lubber, 'the world' (the *on dit*), from whom
Sebastian had borrowed it, must necessarily turn out to be some effeminate, dainty fellow, in short, a 'cockney.' [Feste says, I think, in effect : If terms used by great ones
are to be applied to fools, and on every petty occasion (just as he himself afterwards
uses 'vent'), I am afraid that the world, great lubber as it is, will turn out, after all,
to be nothing but a milksop. When Edgar in *Lear* speaks of the affected evasions
of mankind in misnaming its vices, he calls it 'the excellent foppery of the world.'
Thus here, if the affected misapplications of terms becomes widespread, it will show
that the world is nothing but a foppish cockney.—ED.]

16. **Cockney**] MURRAY (*N. E. D.*) : Middle English *coken-ey, -ay*, apparently
equivalent to *coken* of cocks + *ey, ay* (Old English *æg*) egg ; literally 'cocks' egg.'
This derivation satisfies the form : *ey, ay* (*ai*), are regular Mid. Eng. forms of *egg*,
rhyming with the same words (*day*, etc.) as *cokenay* itself ; *coken* genitive plural is
as in *clerken coueitise*, *P. Pl.* B. iv, 119, and in many similar instances ; the use of
the gen. pl. is as in German *hühnerei*, fowls' egg, *hahnenei*, cocks' egg. [The
first sense of the word is given as :] An egg : the egg of the common fowl, hen's
egg ; or perhaps one of the small or mis-shapen eggs occasionally laid by fowls, still
popularly called in some parts 'cocks' eggs,' in German *hahneneier*. Thus, 1362,

me what I ſhall vent to my Lady? Shall I vent to hir that   17
thou art comming?

Seb.   I prethee fooliſh greeke depart from me, there's
money for thee, if you tarry longer, I ſhall giue worſe   20
paiment.

---

17. *Lady ?*] F₂. *Lady :* F₃. *Lady ;*
F₄, Rowe.

17, 18. *that thou*] *that that* F₂.

19–21. *I ... paiment.*] Three lines,
ending *me ;...longer,...payment.* Cap. et
seq.

19. *greeke*] F₂. *Greek* F₃. *Greek*

F₄. *grig* or *gleeker* Anon. ap. Cam.

19. *me,*] *me ;* Theob.

20. *thee,*] *thee.* F₄.

I ſhall] *I'll* or *'Shall* Walker
(*Vers.* 237).

worſe] *worser* Anon. ap. Cam.

Langland, *Piers Ploughman*, A. vii, 272, 'And I sigge, bi my soule, I haue no salt
Bacon, Ne no Cokeneyes, bi Crist, Colopus to maken.' Again, 1562, J. Heywood,
Prov. & Epigr. (1867), 36, ' Men say He that comth euery daie, shall haue a cock-
naie. He that comth now and then, shall haue a fatte hen,' etc. . . . [Of this first
sense] the meaning appears to be established by the first quotation ; the constituents
of a Collop were precisely bacon and an egg. This meaning also completely
explains the quotation from Heywood. . . . To account for the appellation, we might
suppose *coken-ay* to be originally a child's name for an egg ; but as *cocks' eggs* . . . are
at the present day applied in popular speech or dialect to small or malformed eggs, it
is not improbable that this was originally the specific sense of *cokenay*. The old
notion that such eggs produced a serpent is well known [see ' cockatrices,' III, iv,
195] ; but no trace of this appears in the popular use of *cokenay.* [The second
sense of the word, Murray gives as] ' A child that sucketh long,' ' a nestle-cock,'
' a mother's darling'; ' a cockered child, pet, minion'; ' a child tenderly brought
up'; hence, a squeamish or effeminate fellow, a ' milksop.' . . . The application of
either a child's word for an egg, or of the name of a small or mis-shapen egg, as a
humorous or derisive appellation for a ' child sucking long,' a ' nestle-cock,' a ' milksop,' obviously explains itself. . . . An apparent parallel is the French word *coco,*
' child's name for an egg, also a term of endearment applied to children, and of
derision applied to men : *mon petit coco, quel grand coco !*'

19. **greeke**] THEOBALD (Nichols, *Illust.* ii, 357) : I suspect it should rather be
' foolish *geck,*' *i. e.* gull, buffoon. [Hanmer has this emendation in his text ; probably, it occurred to him independently. There is no means of knowing whether or
not he derived it from Theobald.]—UPTON (*Remarks on Three Plays of Jonson,*
p. 48) : *Pergraecari,* in Plautus is to spend the hours in mirth, wine, and banquets.
Hence the proverb, ' As merry as a Greek.' Sebastian calls the clown ' foolish
Greek ' for his unseasonable mirth.—COLLIER : This is in reference to the Clown's
jocularity. ' Merry Greek ' was a well understood expression. Mathew Mery-
greeke is a character in Udall's *Ralph Roister Doister.*—HALLIWELL : Terms, like
Greek or Trojan, were employed in familiar language, in a variety of senses which
can be distinguished only by the context. Nash, *Have with you to Saffron Walden,*
1596 : ' A rare ingenuous odde merry Greeke, who (as I haue heard) hath translated
my *Piers Pennilesse* into the *Macaronicall* tongue.' [p. 47, ed. Grosart. Both
Warburton (*ad. loc.*) and Douce (i, 152) here interpret ' Greek ' as equivalent to
pander ; corresponding to the Clown, Pompey, in *Meas. for Meas.* Sebastian sup-

Clo.   By my troth thou haſt an open hand:theſe Wiſe-   22
men that giue fooles money, get themſelues a good report, after foureteene yeares purchaſe.

        Enter Andrew, Toby, and Fabian.   25
   And.   Now ſir, haue I met you again : ther's for you.
   Seb.   Why there's for thee, and there, and there,
Are all the people mad ?
   To   Hold ſir, or Ile throw your dagger ore the houſe.   29

22, 23. *Wiſe-men*] Ff.   *wise   men*
Rowe et seq.
  23, 24, *report,*] Ff, Cap.   *report—*
Sta. Cam.   *report* Rowe et cet.
  24. *after*] *at a* Anon. ap. Cam.
  26. *again :*] *again ?* F$_4$.
     ther's] F$_1$.
     [Striking Seb.   Rowe.

27, 28. Prose, F$_4$, Rowe, +.
    and there, and there,] *and there,*
and there, and there : Cap. Dyce ii, iii,
Huds.
    [Beating Sir And.   Rowe.
  29. *dagger*] *danger* Var. '85 (misprint).

---

poses Feste to be such a character, because of his solicitations to visit his mistress,
—an interpretation not to be lightly discarded.—ED.]

  23, 24. **report, after foureteene yeares purchase**] HEATH (p. 192) : That is,
purchase a good report at a very extravagant price.—TOLLET : Perhaps 'fourteen
years' purchase' was, in Shakespeare's time, the highest price for land.   Bacon's
Essay on Usury mentions sixteen years' purchase.   'I will not give more than
according to fifteen years' purchase,' said a dying usurer to a clergyman who advised
him to study for a purchase of the kingdom of heaven.—REED : Sir Josiah Child,
Discourse on Trade, says, '*certainly* anno 1621, the current price of lands in England was *twelve* years' purchase ; and so I have been assured by many ancient men
whom I have questioned particularly as to this matter ; and I find it so by purchases
made about that time by my own relations and acquaintance.'   Sir Thomas Culpep-
per, senior, who wrote in 1621, affirms, 'that land was then at twelve years'
purchase.'—COLLIER : The meaning may be, that they do not obtain a good report
by such means until after the lapse of much time and longer experience of their
liberality than the Clown had had.   On the other hand [Tollet's argument is plaus-
ible].—STAUNTON : That is, After the *rate* of fourteen years' purchase.   The current price of land when this play was written appears to have been twelve years'
purchase ; so, buying character of fools was a bad bargain.—W. A. WRIGHT : The
Folios put a comma at 'report,' meaning probably the same as Staunton, who
marked it with a dash, to indicate that what follows is said aside, or in a different
tone.   [The marketable value of land, or its so-called *purchase*, was computed to be
the sum of its annual rentals, or the total return from it, for a certain number of
years.]

  27. **and there, and there,**] It would be shocking and disgraceful if Sir Andrew
were not beaten according to metre.   CAPELL therefore pitilessly gave him a fourth
blow ; and DYCE, equally ruthless, did the same ; because 'the words had evidently
been omitted in the Folio by a mistake which is not unfrequent when such repetitions
occur.'   Can zeal for metre further go ?—ED.

Clo.   This will I tell my Lady ſtraight, I would not be   30
in ſome of your coats for two pence.

To.   Come on ſir, hold.

An.   Nay let him alone, Ile go another way to worke
with him : Ile haue an action of Battery againſt him, if
there be a ny law in Illyria : though I ſtroke him firſt, yet   35
it's no matter for that.

Seb.   Let go thy hand.

To.   Come ſir, I will not let you go.   Come my yong
ſouldier put vp your yron : you are well fleſh'd :   Come
on.   40

Seb.   I will be free from thee.   What wouldſt y̆ now ?
If thou dar'ſt tempt me further, draw thy ſword.   42

---

31. *two pence*] *two-pence* F₃F₄, Cap.
Coll.

[Exit Clown. Rowe.
32. *Come on ſir,*] F₂F₄.   *Come on,
ſir,* F₃.   *Come, sir,* Ran.   *Come off,
sir ;* Anon. ap. Cam.
[Holding Seb. Rowe.
33. *alone,*] *alone ;* Coll. Dyce, Cam.
35. *be*] *he* F₂.
though] *tho* F₄.

35. *ſtroke*] F₂. *ſtrook* F₃. Cap. *ſtruck*
F₄.
35, 36. *yet...that*] *Yet...that.* (Separate line) F₄, Rowe.
38–40. *Come ſir,...on*] Three lines,
ending *sir,...ſouldier...on.* Walker (*Crit.*
i, 17).
41. [Wrenches from him, and draws.
Cap.
42. *further*] *farther* Coll.

---

34. **action of Battery**] CASTLE (p. 109. See III, ii, 15) : Here Aguecheek
mistakes the law, which is that a person who assaults another first cannot bring an
action for the beating he gets from his provocation.   This was the law in Shakespeare's time, though, as I have said, in Anne's reign the judges allowed an action
to be brought where excessive violence was used.   Thus, if a woman pushed a man,
he was not entitled to knock her down with a cudgel.   But I do not think these two
allusions (see III, ii, 15), both of which are doubtfully, if not wrongfully, used,
can put this play amongst the legal class. [Has not Castle slightly misapprehended
the passage ?   There is no ignorance of the law on Sir Andrew's part.   He
acknowledges that, inasmuch as he struck Sebastian first, he has no right of action,
yet, 'no matter for that,' he is going to have his action of battery all the same ;
though the law is dead against him he is nevertheless going to appeal to it.   I can
perceive no 'mistake' of Sir Andrew's here.—ED.]

39. **flesh'd**] BRADLEY (*N. E. D.*) : FLESH, *v.* I. *trans.* To reward (a hawk or
hound) with a portion of the game killed, in order to excite his eagerness in the
chase.   Hence, in wider sense, to render (an animal) eager for prey by the taste of
blood.   2. To initiate in or inure to bloodshed or warfare.

42. **draw thy sword**] COLLIER : Here the modern editors insert 'Draws' as a
stage-direction ; but it is very clear from what Sir Toby last says, 'Come my young
soldier, put up your iron,' etc., that Sebastian had already drawn his sword.   It was
drawn at the time when Sir Toby had threatened to throw Sebastian's 'dagger o'er
the house.'—BADHAM does not agree with Collier in thinking that all this speech
is addressed to Sebastian ; he says (p. 281) that the words 'put up your sword

To. What, what? Nay then I muſt haue an Ounce or   43
two of this malapert blood from you.

                    Enter Oliuia.   45

Ol. Hold *Toby*, on thy life I charge thee hold.
To. Madam.
Ol. Will it be euer thus? Vngracious wretch,
Fit for the Mountaines, and the barbarous Caues,
Where manners nere were preach'd : out of my ſight.   50
Be not offended, deere *Ceſario* :
Rudesbey be gone. I prethee gentle friend,   52

44. [They draw and fight. Rowe.   *ſight!* Dyce.
45. Scene II. Pope, +.   51. Ceſario:] Ceſario. F₃F₄.
47. *Madam.*] *Madam?* Theob. *Mad-*   52. *Rudesbey*] F₂.   *Rudesby* F₃F₄ et
am— Coll. Dyce.   seq. *Rude spy* Procter.
50. nere] *ne're* Ff.   *gone.*] gone. [Exeunt Sir T. and
   preach'd : ... ſight.] *preach'd !...*   Sir A. Rowe.

[*sic*] ; you are well fleshed,' ' should be bracketed, as addressed to Sir Andrew.'
[I agree with Badham that the command, 'put up your iron,' is addressed to Sir
Andrew, who, seeing that Sebastian was safely held by Sir Toby, and that he had
no danger to apprehend, had drawn his blade, against Sir Toby's express injunction
at the close of the preceding scene. Sir Toby knew well that if Sir Andrew had
his sword drawn and Sebastian should wrench himself free, Sebastian would make
quick work of the ' manakin '; therefore he intended to hold Sebastian long enough
to divert the latter's indignation from Sir Andrew to himself, wherein he succeeded.
' You are well flesh'd ' is also addressed to Sir Andrew and intended to flatter him
into quiet by intimating that as a victor he has tasted enough blood. Sebastian at
the first attack had laid his hand upon his dagger. This dagger-hand Toby held
fast. As soon as Sebastian had thrown off Sir Toby, he draws his sword with the
words, ' What wouldst thou now?'—ED.]

   44. malapert] Cotgrave gives : '*Marmiton : m.* A Scullion, or kitchin boy ; also,
a greasie, or slouenly knaue ; and, a saucie, malapert, or knauish fellow.'

   52. Rudesbey] HALLIWELL : ' And as he which is ceremonious may be thought
to be a dissembler, so he which is not so, may be taken to be a clowne, a rudesby,
or a contemner of others.'—Guazzo, *Ciuile Conuersation.* [p. 77, 78.]—FITZEDWARD
HALL (*Modern English*, p. 272, *Note* on ' tricksy ' in *The Vicar of Wakefield*) :
The formation of *tricksy* is observable ; the word exemplifying the rare suffix *-sy*,
which, perhaps, consists of *s* euphonically prefixed to the adjectival *-y* of *roomy*, for
instance. *Tricksy* is, then, *trick* + *sy*. . . . Again, as a friend suggests to me, *doxy*,
instead of being referable to the Danish *dukke* [see *Wint. Tale*, IV, iv, 346], may
have started from the vernacular *ducky*, and so consist of *duck* + *s* + *y*. But we are
not yet at the end of words presumably embodying a euphonic *s*. [In the following
list, each word is followed by the page and volume of the work wherein it occurs ;
to save space these are here omitted] : *Idlesby, Lewdsby, Rigsby, Sneaksby, Suresby,*
and *Rudesby*, which is used twice by Shakespeare [See *Tam. of the Shr.* III, ii, 10].
' You are a rudesby yourself,' writes, in 1774, Mrs Catherine Clive, in *The Private
Correspondence of David Garrick*, etc., i, 604. Here we have annexed to adjectives

Let thy fayre wifedome, not thy pafsion fway   53
In this vnciuill, and vniuft extent
Againft thy peace.   Go with me to my houfe,   55
And heare thou there how many fruitleffe prankes
This Ruffian hath botch'd vp, that thou thereby
Mayft fmile at this : Thou fhalt not choofe but goe :
Do not denie, befhrew his foule for mee,
He ftarted one poore heart of mine, in thee.   60

---

56. *heare*] *here* F₄.   60. *mine,*] *mine* F₄.
58. *Mayft*] *Maift* Ff.

---

and substantives, *s*, with *-by;* unless some one proves the existence of the termination *-sby*. And what is this *-by*? Some have seen *boy* in it. The old spelling
rudesbey suggests no solution.

54. vnciuill] Evidently suggested by the terms in which she has just character-
ised Toby's conduct as 'fit for mountains and barbarous caves.'—ED.

54. vniust extent] JOHNSON : 'Extent' is, in law, a writ of execution, whereby
goods are seized for the King. It is therefore taken here for violence in general.
[See *As You Like It*, III, i, 18, of this ed. where the use of 'extent,' as a legal term,
is discussed. Of course, it has no tinge of legal phraseology in the present passage.]

57. botch'd vp] HEATH (p. 193) : This is a metaphor taken from the employment of a botcher, who set patches on old worn-out cloaths. The sense is, How
many fruitless pranks this ruffian hath been obliged to make satisfaction for, at the
expense of his fortune and reputation.—W. A. WRIGHT : That is, patched up
clumsily. This does not refer to the patching up of quarrels which Sir Toby's
conduct had bred, but to the awkwardly contrived tricks he was constantly playing.
[Possibly this was also Warburton's interpretation when he conjectured *hatched*
up.—*Notes & Qu.* VIIIth, iii, 203.]

58. choose but goe] ABBOTT (§ 353, p. 254) : The obvious and grammatical
construction is 'thou shalt not choose anything except (to) go'; but probably (contrary to Mätzner's view, iii, 18) the explanation of the omission is, that Shakespeare
mentally supplies 'shall,' 'can,' etc. 'Thou shalt not choose anything else, but
(shalt) go.'

60. one poore heart of mine] JOHNSON : I know not whether there be not an
ambiguity intended between 'heart ' and *hart*. The sense, however, is easy enough.
'He that offends thee, attacks one of my hearts'; or, as the ancients expressed it,
'half my heart.'—MALONE : The equivoque suggested by Dr Johnson was, I have
no doubt, intended. 'Heart' in our author's time was frequently written *hart;* and
Shakespeare delights in playing on these words. [Had both Dr Johnson and Malone
forgotten the 22nd line of the first scene of this play?—ED.]—WHITER (p. 96) :
I am persuaded that no quibble was here intended ; but that the equivocal word
suggested to the unconscious Poet a term which was allied to one of its significations.
—STAUNTON : The hunter's technical phrase 'started,' might have convinced Dr
Johnson that the poet was playing on the word. [I prefer Whiter's mode of express-
ing it. It is not a quibble, nor even a play on the words ; these imply consciousness, or, at least, intention ; but I believe that it was an unconscious adoption by
Olivia of both significations of the word.—ED.]

Seb.   What rellifh is in this? How runs the ftreame?
Or I am mad, or elfe this is a dreame :
Let fancie ftill my fenfe in Lethe fteepe,
If it be thus to dreame, ftill let me fleepe.

   *Ol.*Nay come I prethee, would thoud'ft be rul'd by me   65
   Seb.   Madam, I will.
   Ol.   O fay fo, and fo be.   *Exeunt*   67

Scæna Secunda.

Enter Maria and Clowne.   2

Mar.   Nay, I prethee put on this gown, & this beard,
make him beleeue thou art fir *Topas* the Curate, doe it
quickly.   Ile call fir *Toby* the whilft.   5

65. *I prethee*] *I pray* Pope, +.
1. Scene III. Pope, +.
Olivia's House. Rowe.

4, 5. *Curate...quickly*] *Curat...quikly*
F_4.
5. *whilft*] *whil'ft* F_3F_4.
[Exit M. Theob.

---

61. **rellish is in this?**] JOHNSON : How does this taste? What judgement am
I to make of it?

64. **If it be thus . . . let me sleepe**] STAUNTON : This speech recalls that of
Antipholus of Syracuse, under similar circumstances of bewilderment ; *Com. of Err.*
II, ii, 214.

65. **I prethee**] WALKER (*Crit.* i, 78) : Read *I pray* [*sic* Pope] ; the other is too
rugged for a rhyming couplet.

67. **and so be**] GERVINUS (trans. Bunnett, i, 603) : [Sebastian], drawn into the
quarrel with the squires, at one stroke gives back the blows due, and proves to Olivia
that he would know how to free her from her dissolute guests. The charm exercised
by a nature at once so fresh and so victorious, Olivia is not alone to experience. The
poet has taken care that the instinctive feeling of the Countess should not be construed into womanly weakness ; for men of strong nature entirely share it with her.
The rough captain, Antonio, is attracted to this youth by just as blind an impulse of
pleasure and love, he loiters about him, in spite of the danger to which he exposes
himself in the adverse town, for his sake he takes delight in this danger, he bestows
his love upon him without retention or restraint ; he himself calls it witchcraft, which
drew him to the joyous dexterous youth.

4. **sir Topas**] See III, iv, 270, ' sir Priest.'—STEEVENS : The name Sir Topas
is taken from Chaucer. [Would it not have been more correct to say, it is found in
Chaucer?—ED.]—NARES : *Dominus*, the academical title of a bachelor of arts, was
usually rendered by *Sir* in English, at the Universities ; so that a bachelor, who in
the books stood *Dominus* Brown, was in conversation called *Sir* Brown. This was
in use in some Colleges even in my memory.—PERCY (quoted by Halliwell) : *Sir*
seems to have been a title formerly appropriated to such of the inferior clergy as
were only *Readers* of the service, and not admitted to be preachers, and therefore

Clo.   Well, Ile put it on, and I will diffemble my felfe   6

6. *diffemble*] *deffemble* F$_4$.

___

were held in the lowest estimation; as appears from a remarkable passage in Machell's MS Collections for the History of Westmoreland and Cumberland, preserved in the Dean and Chapter's Library at Carlisle. The reverend Thomas Machell lived temp. Car. II. Speaking of the little chapel of Martindale, the writer says, 'There is little remarkable within or about it but a neat churchyard, which by the peculiar care of the old Reader, *Sir* Richard, is kept clean, and as neat as a bowling-green. Within the limits of myne own memory all *Readers* in Chapels were called *Sirs*, and of old have been writ so ; whence, I suppose, such of the laity as received the noble order of knighthood being called *Sir's* too, for distinction sake had *Knight* writ after them ; which had been superfluous, if the title *Sir* had been peculiar to them.'—DOUCE (quoted by Halliwell) : The question whether priests were formerly knights in consequence of being called *sir* remains to be decided. Examples that those of the *lower* class were so called are very numerous ; and hence it may be fairly inferred that *they* at least were not knights, nor is there perhaps a single instance of the order of knighthood being conferred upon ecclesiastics of any degree. Having casually, however, met with a note in Dyer's *Reports* (p. 216 B.), which seems at first view not only to contain some authority for the custom of *knighting priests* by abbots, in consequence of a charter granted to the Abbot of Reading for that purpose, but likewise the opinion of two learned judges, founded thereupon, that *priests were anciently knights*, I have been induced to enter a little more fully upon this discussion, and to examine the validity of those opinions. [The curious reader is referred to the solid folio page in Halliwell, devoted to this examination, wherein the validity of the judges' opinion is learnedly disproved. The discussion thus concludes :] Having thus, I trust, refuted the opinion that the title of ' Sir' was given to priests in consequence of their being *knights*, I shall venture to account for it in another manner. This custom then was most probably borrowed from the French, amongst whom the title *Domnus* is often appropriated to ecclesiastics, more particularly to the Benedictines, Carthusians, and Cistercians. It appears to have been originally a title of honour and respect, and was, perhaps, at first, in this kingdom as in France, applied to particular orders, and afterwards became general as well among the secular as among the regular clergy. The reason of preferring *Domnus* to *Dominus* was that the latter belonged to the Supreme Being, and the other was considered as a subordinate title, according to an old verse :—
Cœlestem Dominum, terrestrem dicito Domnum. Hence *Dom, Damp, Dan, Sire,* and, lastly, *Sir ;* for authorities are not wanting to show that all these titles were given to ecclesiastics. [Did Shakespeare choose this name by design ? Reginald Scot, in his *Discoverie of Witchcraft* (Sixt Chap. p. 294, ed. 1584), speaking of the virtues imparted to precious stones, says that ' a topase healeth the lunatike person of his passion of lunacie.' This reference I owe to my son, H. H. F., Jr. —ED.]

6. **dissemble my selfe**} MALONE : That is, disguise myself.—STEEVENS : Shakespeare has here stumbled on a Latinism ; thus, Ovid : ' Achilles Veste virum longa dissimulatus erat.'—[*Ars Amat.* I, 689.]—KNIGHT : Writers do not *stumble* upon nice shades of meaning. [Which is hardly fair to Steevens, who, I believe, meant no disparagement to Shakespeare, but merely that Shakespeare had, without knowing it, used a classic Latin phrase.—ED.]

in't, and I would I were the firſt that euer diſſembled in   7
in ſuch a gowne.   I am not tall enough to become the
funĉtion well, nor leane enough to bee thought a good
Student : but to be ſaid an honeſt man and a good houſ-   10
keeper goes as fairely, as to ſay, a carefull man, & a great

---

8. *gowne*] *gown*.   [Putting it on]
Coll. MS.
    tall] *fat* Farmer, Var. '03, '13,
'21, Sing. Ktly.

10. *Studient*] F₁.
11. *carefull*] *graceful* Han. Warb.
Cap.

---

8. not tall enough] TYRWHITT : This cannot be right.   The word wanted
should be part of the description of 'a careful man.'   I should have no objection
to read,—*pale*.—STEEVENS : 'Not tall enough,' perhaps means 'not of sufficient
height to overlook a pulpit.'   Dr Farmer would read *fat* instead of ' tall,' the
former of these epithets, in his opinion, being referable to the following words—
' a good housekeeper.'—STAUNTON : ' Tall ' in its ancient sense of *robust, stout,
personable*, offers quite sufficient contrast to 'lean' of the following line.—HUTSON
(p. 491) : From what Feste says here, it may perhaps be inferred that diminutive
size, or insignificant appearance, or even ludicrous physical disproportion had helped
to keep him from becoming a clergyman.   We know that jesters were greatly aided
in their calling by some grotesque feature, or oddity of manner, or peculiarity of
voice, and that dwarfs in mediæval times were a favourite ornament of courts. . . .
These considerations, the language Feste uses here, and the fact that we find him
with the clerical education and without the clerical office, make it very probable that
he was thick-set and of low stature, and so undignified in general appearance as to
preclude him from receiving holy orders.   [I am afraid that Hutson's ingenious theory
is, at this point, founded on a mistaken interpretation of ' tall.'   See I, iii, 21.   Is it
not possible to interpret Feste's words as anything but disparaging to his own personal appearance?   He was not portly enough on the one hand, nor lean enough on
the other, with the inference that in every other walk in life, but that of a parson, he
was exactly right.—ED.]

   10. Studient] W. A. WRIGHT : Also thus spelt in *Mer. Wives*, III, i, 38, where
Justice Shallow says, ' keepe a Gamester from the dice, and a good Studient from his
booke, and it is wonderful.'   It may be that in both these passages the mis-spelling
is intentional, for in *Love's Lab. Lost*, II, i, 64 ; III, i, 36, the word is in its usual
form.   [As far as the compositor is concerned, I think the spelling is intentional.   It
is possible that it represented a not unusual pronunciation.   WALKER (*Vers.* 156)
quotes from Middleton's *Old Law*, I, i,[p. 8, ed. Dyce] : ' Evander . . . has hit the
law That all our predecessive students Have miss'd unto their shame,' and then
remarks, ' Read *studients*, as the word is often written.   Perhaps Dyce has corrected
the passage in his Middleton.[No.—ED.]Compare the Italian *studiente* (they
have *studente* also ; was "studiente" then the prevailing form?) and the French
étudiant.'   See ' Dexteriously,' I, v, 58 ; 'iealious,' IV, iii, 30.—ED.]

   10. to be said] See ABBOTT (§ 200, p. 134) for examples of ' to be said' used
for *to be called.*

   11. carefull man] WARBURTON : This refers to what went before, ' I am not tall
enough,' etc.; it is plain then that Shakespeare wrote : ' as to say, a *graceful* man,'
i. e. comely.   CAPELL (p. 151) justifies his adoption of this emendation by the fact

ſcholler.　The Competitors enter.　　　　　　　　　12

Enter Toby.

To.　Ioue bleſſe thee M. Parſon.

Clo.　*Bonos dies* ſir *Toby*: for as the old hermit of *Prage*　　15
that neuer ſaw pen and inke, very wittily ſayd to a Neece
of King *Gorbodacke*, that that is, is : ſo I being M.Parſon,
am M. Parſon ; for what is that, but that? and is, but is?

To.　To him ſir *Topas*.

Clow.　What hoa, I ſay, Peace in this priſon.　　　　20

To.　The knaue counterfets well : a good knaue.

Maluolio within.　　22

---

13. Enter ...] Enter ... and Maria.
Theob.
　14. *Ioue*] *God* Hal. Huds.
　14, 17, 18, etc. *M.*] Ff. *Mr.* Rowe,
+, Cap. *master* Var. '73 et seq.
　15-18. Mnemonic lines, Warb.
　15. Prage] Prauge F₄. *Prague* Rowe.
　16. *Neece*] Ff, Rowe. *neice* Pope, +.
niece Johns.
　17. Gorbodacke] F₂F₄. Gorbodack
F₃, Rowe. *Gorboduck* Pope, +. *Gorboduc* Cap. et seq.

17. *that that*] *that* F₄.
　that that is, is] As a quotation,
Cap.
　18. *that,...is ?*] 'that' but 'that,' and
'is' but 'is'? Cam. Wh. ii.
　that ?] Ff, Rowe, +, Var. Knt,
Coll. Sta. *that,* Dyce. *that ;* Cap. et cet.
　19. [Opening a door. Coll. MS.
　20. *ſay,*] say,— Theob. say, [rap-
ping at an inner Door] Cap.
　[In a counterfeit voice. Han.
　21, 3c. [Aside. Cap.

---

that 'careful' ' has no relation whatever to the word with which it ought to have
some, namely—" tall." ' '—STEEVENS : A 'careful' man, I believe, means a man
who has such a regard for his character, as to entitle him to ordination. [Steevens
alone appears to have perceived that these lines refer to Sir Topas. Feste says, in
effect, that though in bodily shape he may be unfit to impersonate Sir Topas, yet if
he be called an honest man and a good housekeeper it will be quite enough to make
him fairly represent a careful man and a great scholar like the Curate.—ED.]

　12. **Competitors**] M. MASON : That is, confederates, or associates. 'Com-
petitor' is used in the same sense in *Richard III :* IV, iv, 506 : 'every hour more
competitors flock to their aid.'

　15. **hermit of Prage**] DOUCE : Not the celebrated heresiarch Jerome of Prague,
but another of that name born likewise at Prague, and called *the hermit of Camal-
doli* in Prague.—W. A. WRIGHT : But this is treating the Clown's nonsense too
seriously. No one has attempted to identify the niece of King Gorboduc.

　17. **King Gorbodacke**] HALLIWELL : ' The opinion of things is the measure of
their value, as was wisely said of a neece of King Gorbudukes. Know then, that
if another then the coronet had recived this script, he would not perchance have
valued it so highly.'—Suckling's *Letters*, 1659, [vol. ii, p. 219, ed. Hazlitt, 1892,
where in a footnote to 'king' it is said that the 'old copy has, and perhaps Suckling
wrote, *queene.*' Not many of Suckling's letters have been preserved, but in these
few Shakespeare is quoted familiarly several times. Of course, this 'niece' is a
purely fictitious character, and undoubtedly Suckling had in mind this very speech
of Feste, but I suppose changed it for amusement to '*Queen* Gorboduc.'—ED.]

Mal. Who cals there?   23

Clo. Sir *Topas* the Curate, who comes to viſit *Maluo-*
lio the Lunaticke.   25

Mal. Sir *Topas*, ſir *Topas*, good ſir *Topas* goe to my
Ladie.

Clo. Out hyperbolicall fiend, how vexeſt thou this
man? Talkeſt thou nothing but of Ladies?

Tob. Well ſaid M. Parſon.   30

Mal. Sir *Topas*, neuer was man thus wronged, good
ſir *Topas* do not thinke I am mad : they haue layde mee
heere in hideous darkneſſe.

Clo. Fye, thou diſhoneſt ſathan: I call thee by the
moſt modeſt termes, for I am one of thoſe gentle ones,   35
that will vſe the diuell himſelfe with curteſie : ſayſt thou
that houſe is darke?   37

---

24. [This and all that follows from the Clown, in a counterfeit voice. Han.

29. *Talkeſt...Ladies*?] Separate line, Pope ii, +, Var. '73.

nothing but of] *of nothing but of* Theob. i. *of nothing but* Theob. ii, Warb. Johns. Var. '73.

34. *ſathan*] Pope, +. *Sathan* Ff,

Rowe, Han. Cap. Knt. *Satan* Wh. Dyce, Cam.

36. *ſayſt*] F₂. *ſay'ſt* F₃F₄, Rowe, +, Cap. Var. Mal. Steev. Var. Knt. *sayest* Dyce, Cam.

37. *that*] *this* Mason. Ran. Dyce conj. *that this* Hal. *the* or *that the* Anon. ap. Cam. *that'* Ed. conj.

---

34. **sathan**] For the spelling, see III, iv, 119.

35. **modest**] See I, iii, 11.

36. **will**] That is, wish to.

37. **that house**] Both MASON (p. 119) and DYCE (ed. ii) conjectured '*this* house.' HALLIWELL reads 'that this house,' and says that *this* seems to be essential. Probably there is an absorption of *the* in the final *t* of 'that.' But Feste was not within the room; he was probably looking into it through a window or through a door ajar. In Rowe's frontispiece, the earliest illustration of the play, it is a door.—ED.

37. **house is darke**] MALONE: The Clown gives this pompous appellation ['house'] to the small room in which Malvolio, we may suppose, was confined, to exasperate him.—HALLIWELL: 'A darkened room' was sometimes called a darkhouse. 'A sprite apering to Jhon and him, when they sate upon division of the lands, in likeness of a bere, and therewith Peter fell out of his wits, and was tyed in a dark house and beat out his brains against a post, and Jhon stabed himself all on St. Marks dai.'—*MS Ashmol.* 236. 'In the beginning, therefore, of the cure, if neither age, nor state of the bodie, nor time of the yeare do let it, you must cut the veine of the hams or of the ankles. . . . Afterward you must place the sicke in a darke house, which is moderately warme.'—Barrough's *Method of Physick*, 1624. [Rosalind says, 'Love is merely a madness and deserves as well a dark house and a whip as madmen do.' If Feste used the word 'house' to exasperate Malvolio, as

Mal.   As hell fir *Topas.*   38
Clo.   Why it hath bay Windowes tranſparant as bari-
cadoes, and the cleere ſtores toward the South north, are   40

---

39. *bay*] *bow* Ran. conj.
40. *cleere ſtores*] *cleare ſtones* F₂. *clear
ſtones* F₃F₄, Rowe, +, Cap. Var. Ran.
Mal. Steev. Var.   *clear stories* or *clear-
-stories* Blakeway, Var. '21, Knt, Coll.
Wh. i, Dyce, Sta. Ktly.   *clearstores*
Cam. i, Rlfe. *clere-storeys* Huds. *clear-*

stories Cam. ii, Wh. ii.
    40. *toward*] Ff, Dyce, Cam. Wh. ii.
towards Rowe et cet.
    South north] *South North* F₂F₄,
Rowe, +. *south north* Cam. *South-
-North* F₃, Theob. et cet.

Malone says, his intention failed; Malvolio adopts it, when he asserts that 'this
house is as darke as ignorance.'—ED.

    39. bay Windowes] MALONE: See Minshieu's *Dict.* s. v. : '*Baywindow*,
Because it is builded in manner of a Baie or rode for shippes, that is, round.'

    39, 40. baricadoes] MURRAY (*N. E. D.*): An adaptation of the French *barri-
cade*, or Spanish *barricada*, formed from French *barrique* or Spanish *barrica* a cask,
the first street *barricades* in Paris being composed of casks filled with earth, paving-
stones, etc. ['*Faire vne Barriquade*, to make a defence of barrels and pales for the
shot.'—Hollyband's *French Dict.* 1593.—ED.]

    40. cleere stores] See *Text. Notes.*—MURRAY (*N. E. D.* s. v. *Clerestory*) : Com-
monly believed to be formed on *clere*, CLEAR + STORY, stage of a building, 'floor'
of a house. (*Clere* must here have meant 'light, lighted,' since the sense of 'free,
unobstructed' did not yet exist.) This assumed derivation is strengthened by the
parallel *blind-story*, although this may have been a later formation in imitation of
clere-story. The great difficulty is the non-appearance of *story* in the sense required
before *circa* 1600, and the absence of all trace of it in any sense in the 14th, 15th,
and chief part of the 16th century. At the same time there is a solitary instance of
storys in Robert of Gloucester (1724), 181, which may mean 'elevated structure' or
'fortified place.' The substantive *estorie* in Old French had no such sense, but the
past participle *estoré* meant 'built, constructed, founded, established, instituted, fortified, furnished, fitted out,' whence a substantive with the sense 'erection, fortifica-
tion' might perhaps arise. [Its sense is :]The upper part of the nave, choir, and
transepts of a cathedral or other large church, lying above the triforium (or if there
is no triforium, immediately over the arches of the nave, etc.), and containing a
series of windows, clear of the roofs of the aisles, admitting light to the central
parts of the building. [HUNTER'S is the solitary voice raised in defence of the
reading of the Second Folio, 'cleare stones.' To read 'clear-stories' is, he thinks],
'a case of great editorial misjudgement. For, in the first place, what have clerestories to do with the cell in which Malvolio was confined; and, in the second,
clerestory was a term in the time of Shakespeare of very rare occurrence. What
Shakespeare wrote was unquestionably "clear stones," and if it is said that this is a
contradiction, it is answered that Shakespeare meant to make the Clown speak in
that manner, as is manifest in the whole of what he says. Stones are clear just as
there is a point of the compass which may be called the south-north or as ebony is
lustrous.'—W. A. WRIGHT: 'Clear stones' is not even sensible nonsense. [If the
authorities had been reversed, and 'clear stones' had been the text of the First
Folio, it would have been accepted, I think, as Feste's nonsense, and as intelligible
as the Vapians passing the Equinoctial of Queubus. But our highest authority reads

as luftrous as Ebony : and yet complaineft thou of ob-   41
ftruction ?

Mal. I am not mad fir *Topas*, I fay to you this houfe is
darke.

Clo. Madman thou erreft : I fay there is no darkneffe   45
but ignorance, in which thou art more puzel'd then the
Ægyptians in their fogge.

Mal. I fay this houfe is as darke as Ignorance, thogh
Ignorance were as darke as hell; and I fay there was neuer man thus abus'd, I am no more madde then you are,   50
make the triall of it in any conftant queftion.

Clo. What is the opinion of *Pythagoras* concerning
Wilde-fowle?   53

45. *Madman*] F$_2$. *Madam* F$_3$. *Mad*
man F$_4$. *Mad-man* Rowe.

49. *and*] *an* F$_4$.

51. *conftant*] *consistent* Coll. MS. ap·
Cam.

53. *Wilde-fowle*] *Wild-foule* F$_4$.

'clear stores' (where only an *i* or a *y* may have dropped out), and we must
make the best of it. One slight plea can be urged in its favour, and this is that
'clerestories' suggest a church—a befitting place wherein to exorcise an evil
spirit, and designed still further to worry Malvolio. Hunter weakened his argument when he asked what clerestories have to do with Malvolio's cell.?—quite as
much as clear stones, or, as Dyce says, 'bay windows.' All is pure nonsense.—ED.]

47. **Ægyptians in their fogge**] Thus, in *Exodus*, x, 21 : And the Lord said
unto Moses, Stretch out thine hand toward heaven, that there may be darkness over
the land of Egypt, even darkness which may be felt. And Moses stretched forth his
hand toward heaven ; and there was thick darkness in all the land of Egypt three
days. They saw not one another, neither rose any from his place for three days.

51. **constant question**] JOHNSON : A settled, a determinate, a regular question.
—MALONE : Rather, in any regular conversation, for so generally Shakespeare uses
the word 'question.' [Compare Hamlet's test of madness (III, iv, 141), 'bring me
to the test, And I the matter will re-word, which madness Would gambol from.'
Here Malvolio means any consecutive discussion, or, as W. A. WRIGHT expresses it,
'any regularly conducted formal conversation or discussion.' It may be doubted that
either test would be accepted as final by mental pathologists of the present day.]—
BUCKNILL (*Mad Folk*, 325) : The idea of testing the existence of insanity by questions on the doctrine of transmigration, may find its counterpart in more than one
recent legal investigation, in which it has been argued by very learned counsel, and
maintained by very eminent physicians, that because an educated gentleman retains
some knowledge of his previous acquirements, it is impossible he can be insane.

52. **Pythagoras**] WALKER (*Crit.* i, 152) finds herein one of the many instances
of Ovid's influence on Shakespeare. [In the account of the doctrines of Pythagoras
in *Metam.* xv, Shakespeare might have read, '—Parcite, vaticinor, cognatas caede
nefanda Exturbare animas.'—ll. 173–175 ; again, 'quoniam non corpora solum,
Verum etiam volucres animae sumus, inque ferinas Possumus ire domos, pecu-
dumque in pectora condi.'—ll. 456–458. But these doctrines were familiarly known ;
there is no need to suppose that Shakespeare went to the original.—ED.]

Mal. That the foule of our grandam, might happily
inhabite a bird. 55

Clo. What thinkſt thou of his opinion ?

Mal. I thinke nobly of the foule, and no way aproue
his opinion.

Clo. Fare thee well : remaine thou ſtill in darkeneſſe,
thou ſhalt hold th'opinion of *Pythagoras*, ere I will allow 60
of thy wits, and feare to kill a Woodcocke, leſt thou diſ-
poſſeſſe the foule of thy grandam. Fare thee well.

Mal. Sir *Topas*, ſir *Topas*.

Tob. My moſt exquiſite ſir *Topas*.

Clo. Nay I am for all waters. 65

---

54. *happily*] Ff, Rowe, +. *haply* Han.
Cap. et seq.
56. *thinkſt*] *thinkest* Var. '03 et seq.
59. *darkeneſſe,*] *darkness ;* Rowe.
60. *th'*] *the* Johns. et seq.
61. *wits,*] *wits ;* Theob. et seq.
62. *foule*] *houſe* Ff, Rowe, Pope,

62. [Closing the door. Coll. MS.
63. Topas.] *Topas,*— Wh. i, Dyce.
64–73. [Aside. Cap.
65. [This in his own voice. Han.
waters] *wanters* or *ventures* Anon.
ap. Cam.

---

53. **Wilde-fowle**] THEOBALD (*Nichols,* ii, 357) : I do not know whether it is
reasonable to call our Poet's fools and clowns to any account ? But should not the
question have been—'concerning *the soul*'? ['Hands off !' is the first thought which
rises in the heart and murmurs from the tongue when any phrase is in question, not
alone of Feste but, of all Shakespeare's Dogberrys and Clowns. Were it not for
this, Theobald's emendation would be worthy of consideration. Malvolio does not
reply directly to the question. Feste asks about a wild-fowl and Malvolio replies
about the soul.—ED.]

60. **allow**] See 'allow,' I, ii, 64.

61. **Woodcocke**] A proverbially silly bird. See II, v, 83.

62. **soule**] See *Text. Notes* for a sophistication of the Ff.

62. **Fare thee well**] BUCKNILL (*Mad Folk,* 323) : This interview represents a
caricature of the idea that madness is occasioned by demoniacal possession and is cura-
ble by priestly exorcism. The idea was not merely a vulgar one in Shakespeare's time,
but was maintained even long afterward by the learned and the pious. More than a
trace of it, indeed, remains to the present day in Canon LXXII. of the Church,
which provides that no Minister without the license of the Bishop of the Diocese
shall 'attempt, upon any pretence whatever, either of possession or obsession, by
fasting and prayer, to cast out any devil or devils, under pain of the imputation of
imposture or cosenage, and deposition from the ministry.'

65. **I am for all waters**] MR SMITH (ap. Grey, i, 235) : That is, a cloak for
all kinds of knavery ; taken from the Italian proverb, Tu hai mantello d'ogni acqua.
Thou hast a cloak for all waters.—JOHNSON : I rather think this expression borrowed
from sportsmen, and relating to the qualifications of a complete spaniel.—CAPELL
(p. 151) : The expression—*fish in all waters,* is alluded to in what is given the
Clown ; his meaning—that he could put on all characters.—M. MASON (p. 120) :
The word *water,* as used by jewellers, denotes the colour and the lustre of diamonds

Mar. Thou mightſt haue done this without thy berd   66
and gowne, he ſees thee not.

To. To him in thine owne voyce, and bring me word
how thou findſt him : I would we were well ridde of this
knauery. If he may bee conueniently deliuer'd, I would   70
he were, for I am now ſo farre in offence with my Niece,
that I cannot purſue with any ſafety this ſport the vppeſhot. Come by and by to my Chamber.   *Exit*   73

66. *berd*] *beard* Ff.
67. *gowne*,] *gown ;* Theob.
69. *findſt*] *findest* Var. '03 et seq.
   well] *all* Ff, Rowe, +. *all well*
Coll. MS.
71. *Niece*] *Neece* Ff. *Neice* Rowe,

Pope, Theob. Han. Warb.
72. *ſport the*] *sport to the* Rowe et
seq. *sport'* *the* Ed. conj.
72, 73. *vppeſhot.*] *up-ſhot* Ff.
73. *Chamber*] *Champer* F₂.
   Exit.] Exit with Maria. Theob.

---

and pearls, and from thence is applied, though with less propriety, to the colour
and hue of other precious stones. I think that Shakespeare in this place alludes to
this sense of the word ' water.' The Clown is complimented by Sir Toby for per-
sonating Sir Topaz so exquisitely, to which he replies, that he can put on all colours,
alluding to the word Topaz, which is the name of a jewel, and was also that of the
curate.—MALONE : That is, I can turn my hand to anything ; I can assume any
character I please ; like a fish, I can swim equally well in all waters.—HALLIWELL :
According to Heywood, one of the phrases applicable to a drunkard was ' one that
can relish all waters,' that is, drink anything. . . . Another conjecture is that the
proverbial phrase originated from a passage in *Isaiah*,—' Blessed are ye that sow
beside all waters.'—STAUNTON : A metaphor borrowed, perhaps, from the tavern :
' Hee is first broken to the sea in the Herring-man's Skiffe or Cock-boate, where
having learned *to brooke all waters*, and drinke as he can out of a tarrie canne,' etc.
—Nashe's *Lenten Stuffe*, p. 27. The literal meaning of ' I am for all waters,' was,
undoubtedly, ' I am ready for any drink.' The cant term for potations, in Shakespeare's time, was *waters ;* and to ' breathe in your *watering*,' *1 Hen. IV* : II, v,
meant to take breath while drinking. See Taylor's, The Water-Poet, ' Drinke and
welcome, or the famous history of the most part of Drinkes in use in Greate Brit-
aine and Ireland ; with an especial Declaration of the Potency, Vertue, and Operation of our English Ale : with a description of all sorts of *Waters*,' etc. [What-
ever the origin of the phrase, be it to fish in all waters, or to swim in all waters, or
to drink all liquors, I think that Malone's interpretation is the true one : that Feste
means he can turn his hand to anything.—ED.]

66. **berd**] Possibly, a phonetic spelling, indicating a pronunciation like our
bared, the past participle of *bare*. J. P. Kemble was ridiculed for retaining this old
pronunciation, which, however, he supposed to be the same as *bird*.—ED.

70. **If he may . . . I would**] For a similar irregularity in the sequence of tenses,
see *As You Like It*, I, ii, 175, ' we wil make it our suite to the Duke, that the
wrastling might not go forward'; or ABBOTT, § 370.

72, 73. **vppeshot**.] W. A. WRIGHT : That is, the decisive shot, a term in
archery, as the ' up-cast ' or final throw, was used in the game of bowls. Compare
Hamlet, V, ii, 371 [of this ed.], ' And, in this upshot, purposes mistook Fall'n on
the inventors' heads.'

Clo. Hey Robin, iolly Robin, tell me how thy Lady
does.   75
Mal. Foole.
Clo. My Lady is vnkind, *perdie.*
Mal. Foole.
Clo. Alas why is ſhe ſo?
Mal. Foole, I ſay.   80
Clo. She loues another.   Who calles, ha?
Mal. Good foole, as euer thou wilt deſerue well at
my hand, helpe me to a Candle, and pen, inke, and paper: 83

Scene IV. Pope, +.   76, 78, 80, 100. *Foole.... Foole....*
74. [Singing. Rowe.   *ſay....* Topas.] *Fool,—... Fool,—...*
74, 75. Two lines, as verse. Cap. et   *say,—... Topas,—* Theob. et seq.
seq. *Hey, jolly Robin, tell to me How*   77. *perdie.*] *perdy.* Cap. et seq.
does thy lady do? Farmer.   81. *another.*] *another—* Rowe et
74. *thy*] *my* Rowe ii, +.   seq.

74. **Hey Robin, etc.**] PERCY (i, 196, ed. 1844): This song has been recovered
from an ancient MS of Dr Harrington's, at Bath. . . . The volume seems to have been
written in the reign of Henry VIII.; . . . this song is there attributed to Sir Thomas
Wyatt; but the discerning reader will probably judge it to belong to a more obsolete writer. The MS is strictly followed, except to mark the changes of the dialogue
by inverted commas. The first stanza appears to be defective, and it should seem
that a line is wanting, unless the four first words were lengthened in the tune. 'A
Robyn, | Jolly Robyn, | Tell me how they leman doeth, | And thou shalt knowe of
myn. ‖ "My lady is unkynde perde." | Alack! why is she so? | "She loveth an
other better than me; | And yet she will say no."' [There are four more stanzas.]—
SINGER (ed. ii): The air to which this song was sung is to be found in *The Cithern
Schoole* by Anthony Holborne, 1597. [The only ancient music for this song which
I can find is that given by NAYLOR (p. 190), who couples with it the air given at
line 122 *post*. His remark is: 'Here are two relics of music for the Clown, prob-
ably of the same period as [*Farewell, Dear Heart,* II, iii, 101]:—

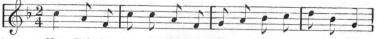

Hey, Rob - in, jol - ly Rob - in, Tell me how thy   la - dy does,

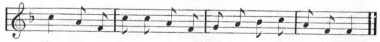

Hey, Rob - in, jol - ly Rob - in, tell me how thy   la - dy does.

77. **perdie**] A corruption of *par Dieu*. See *Hamlet*, III, ii, 282, where, in the
First Folio, it is also spelt as here, and also in modern editions changed to *perdy*.
82, 83. **as euer ... helpe me**] ABBOTT (§ 275, p. 189): The *so* is omitted after
as in adjurations; thus here, 'As ever thou wilt ... (so) help me,' etc., where *as*
means 'in which degree,' and *so* 'in that degree.'

as I am a Gentleman, I will liue to bee thankefull to thee
for't.   85

  Clo. M. *Maluolio?*

  Mal. I good Foole.

  Clo. Alas ſir, how fell you beſides your fiue witts?

  Mall. Foole, there was neuer man ſo notoriouſlie a—
bus'd : I am as well in my wits (foole) as thou art.   90

  Clo. But as well : then you are mad indeede, if you be
no better in your wits then a foole.

  Mal. They haue heere propertied me : keepe mee in   93

86. *M.*] *Mr.* Rowe, +, Cap. *Master* Var. '73 et seq.
  Maluolio *?*] Malvolio ; F₄. *Malvolio!* Rowe. *Malvilio!* Han. ii (misprint).
88. *Alas*] *Alaſs* F₃F₄.
  beſides] *beside* Cap. conj. Var.
'73, '78, '85, Ran.
91. *well :*] *well!* Rowe, +. *well?* Cap. et seq.
  you are] *thou art* Rowe ii, +.
93. *heere*] Om. Pope, Han.
  keepe] *they keep* Han.

84. **I will liue to bee thankefull**] ABBOTT (§ 319, p. 227) : The 'will' refers, not to 'live,' but to 'live-to-be-thankful,' and the sentence means, 'I *purpose* in my future life to prove my thankfulness.'

88. **beſides**] Compare *Much Ado,* V, i, 141, 'Dost thou weare thy wit by thy side? *Claudio.* Neuer did any so, though verie many haue been beside their wit.' SCHMIDT (*Lex.*) furnishes many examples of this use of *beside* and *besides* as a preposition, meaning *out of.*

88. **fiue witts**] MALONE : The 'wits,' Dr Johnson observes, were reckoned five, in analogy to the five senses. From Stephen Hawes's poem, called *Graunde Amoure,* ch. xxiv, ed. 1554, it appears that the 'five wits' were :—'common wit, imagination, fantasy, estimation, and memory.' 'Wit' in our author's time was the general term for the intellectual power. ['Wit,' both in its old and in its modern sense, is used in *Much Ado.* The *Index* to that play in this ed. furnishes examples. Compare, *Sonn.* 141 : 'But my five wits nor my five senses can Dissuade one foolish heart from loving thee,' etc., where the senses and the wits are regarded as distinct. DR SKEAT has kindly called my attention to the fact that the wits, although not specified, are enumerated as five in Langland's *Vision of Piers Ploughman,*—circa 1362–1380,—Passus i, line 15, Text B.—ED.]

89. **notoriouslie**] That is, egregiously. Malvolio seems fond of the high-sounding word. In the last scene at the end of the play (line 347) he tells the Countess that she has done him 'notorious wrong,' and a few lines further on, he says he has been made a 'most notorious gecke and gull.' He infects even the Countess ; she acknowledges that he has been 'notoriously abus'd.'—ED.

93. **heere propertied me**] JOHNSON : That is, they have taken possession of me, as of a man unable to look to himself.—COLLIER : It may be doubted whether Shakespeare had not some allusion to the 'properties' (as they were then, and are still, called) of a theatre, which, when out of use, were thrust into some dark loft or lumber-room.—DYCE (*Remarks,* p. 78) : There is certainly no allusion here to theatrical 'properties,'—no more than there is in the following passages : 'Your

darkeneſſe, ſend Miniſters to me, Aſſes, and doe all they
can to face me out of my wits.   95

   Clo. Aduiſe you what you ſay : the Miniſter is heere.
Maluolio, Maluolio, thy wittes the heauens reſtore : endeauour thy ſelfe to ſleepe, and leaue thy vaine bibble
babble.

   Mal. Sir *Topas.*   100

---

94. *Aſſes,*] *asses !* Coll.   96–98. [All this in a counterfeit
                                 voice. Han.

---

grace shall pardon me ; I will not back ; I am too high-born to be propertied, To
be a secondary at control, Or useful serving-man and instrument, To any sovereign
state throughout the world.'—*King John*, V, ii, 79 ; 'his large fortune, Upon his
good and gracious nature hanging, Subdues and properties to his love and tendance
All sorts of hearts.'—*Timon*, I, i, 55.—STAUNTON : It here bears the same meaning,—that, apparently, of circumscribed, restricted, appropriated,—as in *King John*
[just quoted].—ABBOTT (§ 290, p. 201), in a list of verbs formed from nouns, gives
' propertied ' as meaning ' treat as a tool.'—W. A. WRIGHT : That is, treated me
as a property or thing to be used for a particular purpose, as if I had no will of my
own. Compare *King John* [as above. Dyce's quotation from *Timon* is not, I
fear, exactly parallel. In spite of the majority in favour of what is essentially
Dr Johnson's interpretation, I cannot but think that Collier's suggestion is not
to be lightly discarded. No one seems to have considered the force of the ' here.'
Had the phrase been simply ' they have propertied me,' Dr Johnson's explanation
would be probable, but Malvolio says, ' they have here propertied me,'—'here,' as
he once before said, ' in hideous darkness.' It is in that particular place that they
have propertied him, not propertied him in general. In view of this locative emphasis,
the quotation from *King John* is hardly parallel : Lewis's contrast is between a
sovereign and a serving-man. If we bear in mind the frequency of Shakespeare's
allusions to the stage, Collier's interpretation, coupled with the ' here,' will seem, I
think, not improbable.—ED.]

   95. **face me out of my wits**] W. A. WRIGHT : That is, to cheat me out of my
wits by sheer impudence. See V, i, 89.

   97, 98. **endeauour thy selfe**] See ABBOTT (§ 296, p. 208) for other verbs now
used intransitively but used by Shakespeare reflexively.

   98, 99. **bibble babble**] See HUNTER's note in *Appendix, Date of Composition.*
Compare ' there is no tiddle taddle nor pibble pabble in Pompey's camp.'—*Hen. V :*
IV, i, 71.—HALLIWELL : Thus, ' Whan the peres are gone ; they are but dyble dable.
I marvell ye can abyd suche byble bable.'—Bale's *Kynge Johan,* [p. 7, ed. Camden
Soc.] ' Go to, come hether ; I will forgive thee, if thou wilt become an honest man,
and cast idlenes, slouthfulnes, and thy bible bable aside.'—Florio's *Second Frutes,*
1591. ' What is logicke but the high waie to wrangling, contayning in it a world of
bibble-babble ?'—*An Amond for a Parrat,* n. d.—W. A. WRIGHT : See Latimer
(*Sermons*, p. 507, Parker Soc. ed.) : ' I speak of faithful prayer ; for in time past we
took bibbling babbling for prayer, when it was nothing less.' [Thus, Cotgrave,
' *Bavasse : f.* An idle tale, vaine tatle, bible-bable.' See also WHEATLEY's Dict.
of *Reduplicated Words.* The number of these examples (and I have given only a

Clo. Maintaine no words with him good fellow.   101
Who I fir, not I fir. God buy you good fir Topas : Marry Amen. I will fir, I will.

Mal. Foole, foole, foole I fay.

Clo. Alas fir be patient. What fay you fir, I am fhent   105
for fpeaking to you.

Mal. Good foole, helpe me to fome light, and fome
paper, I tell thee I am as well in my wittes, as any man in
Illyria.

Clo. Well-a-day, that you were fir.   110

---

101. [In the counterfeit voice. Han.
102. [This in his own voice. Han.
    Who I fir] *Who I, sir,* Rowe,
Pope, Han. *Who, I, sir ?* Theob. et seq.
    buy you] *b' w' you* Pope, +, Cap.
Var. Mal. Steev. *b' wi' you* Var. '03 et
seq.
102, 103. *Topas :...Amen.*] *Topas—
Marry, amen.—* Theob. et seq. (except
Cam.)

102, 103. *Marry Amen*] To be
spoken in the counterfeit voice. Han.
    103. *I will.*] *I will fir.* Ff, Rowe,
Pope, Han.
    104. *fay.*] Ff, Rowe, +. *say !* Coll.
say,— Cap. et cet.
    105. *you fir,*] F_2F_4. *you, sir,* Rowe i.
you, fir ? F_3, Rowe ii et seq.
    108. *paper,*] F_2F_4. *Paper.* F_3. *paper;*
Rowe.

---

selection) is of importance, showing, as it does, that Shakespeare did not, of necessity, take these words from Darrel's account of the disturbances in the Starchy
household.—ED.]

101. **Maintaine no words with him**] JOHNSON : Here the Clown in the dark
acts two persons, and counterfeits, by variation of voice, a dialogue between himself and Sir Topas.—'I will, sir, I will' is spoken after a pause, as if, in the meantime, Sir Topas had whispered.

102. **God buy you**] WALKER (*Vers.* 227) : *God be with you* is in fact *God b'
wi' you ;* sometimes a trisyllable, sometimes contracted into a disyllable ;—now
Good-bye. (Query, whether the substitution of *good* for *God* was not the work of the
Puritans, who may have considered the familiar use of God's name in the common
form of leave-taking as irreverent ? I suggest this merely as a *may-be.*) This form is
variously written in the Folio and in old editions of our other dramatists ; sometimes
it is in full, even when the metre requires contraction ; at others, *God b' wi' ye,
God be wy you, God bwy, God buy,* etc. I have noticed the form *God b' wi' you* as
late as Smollett (*Roderick Random*, chap. iii.) : 'B'wye, old gentleman'; if not
later.

105. **shent**] STEEVENS (Note on *Hamlet*, III, ii, 381) : To shend is to reprove
harshly, to treat with rough language.—W. A. WRIGHT (Note on *Coriolanus*, V,
ii, 91) : The original meaning of the word is 'to disgrace, put to shame,' from the
Anglo-Saxon *scenden*. In the earlier Wicliffite translation of *1 Samuel*, xx, 34,
instead of what in the Authorised Version is 'because his father had done him
shame,' we find 'forthi that his fader hadde shent hym.'

110. **Well-a-day**] EARLE (§ 200) : *Wa* has a history much like *la*. [See III,
iv, 104.] It has changed its form in modern English to *wo.* 'Wo,' in the *New
Testament,* as *Rev.* viii, 13, stands for the Greek interjection οὐαί and the Latin *vae.*
In the same way it is used in many passages in which the interjectional character is

Mal. By this hand I am : good foole, fome inke, pa-   111
per, and light : and conuey what I will fet downe to my
Lady : it fhall aduantage thee more, then euer the bearing of Letter did.

Clo. I will help you too't. But tel me true, are you not   115
mad indeed, or do you but counterfeit.

Mal. Beleeue me I am not, I tell thee true.

Clo. Nay, Ile nere beleeue a madman till I fee his brains
I will fetch you light, and paper, and inke.

Mal. Foole, Ile requite it in the higheft degree :   120
I prethee be goue.

Clo. I am gone fir, and anon fir,   122

115. *too't.*] *to't.* Rowe.
116. *indeed,*] *indeed?* Steev. et seq.
   counterfeit.] *counterfeit?* Ff.
117. *me I am not,*] *me, I am not,* Ff,
Rowe i. *me, I am not:* Rowe ii et seq.
118. *Ile*] F₂. *I'le* F₃. *I'e* F₄.

118. *nere*] *ne'er* Ff.
   madman] *mad-man* Rowe, +.
120, 121. Prose, Rann et seq.
121. *goue*] F₁.
122. [Singing. Rowe.
122–129. Twelve lines, Cap. et seq.

---

distinct. This word must be distinguished from *woe*, which is a substantive. For
instance, in the phrase ' weal and woe.' The fact is, that there were two distinct
old words, namely, the interjective *wa* and the substantive *woh*, genitive *woges*,
which meant depravity, wickedness, misery. Often as these have been blended, it
would be convenient to observe the distinction, which is still practically valid, by a
several orthography, writing the interjection *wo*, and the substantive *woe*. This
interjection was compounded with [*la*] into the forms *wala* and *welawa*,—a frequent
exclamation in Chaucer, and one which, before it disappeared, was modified into the
feebler form of *wellaway*. A still more degenerate variety of this form was *well-a-
day*. Pathetic cries have a certain disposition to implicate the present time, as in
woe worth the day!

  115, 116. **are you not mad indeed**] JOHNSON : If he was not mad, what did he
counterfeit by declaring that he was not mad? The fool, who meant to insult him,
I think, asks, ' are you mad, or do you but counterfeit?' That is, ' You look like a
madman, you talk like a madman. Is your madness real, or have you any secret
design in it?' This, to a man in poor Malvolio's state, was a severe taunt.—M.
MASON (p. 120) : Malvolio had assured the Clown that he was as well in his senses
as any man in Illyria ; and the Clown in reply asks him this provoking question :
' Is it true that you are not really mad?' that is, that you are really in your right
senses, or do you only pretend to be so?—MALONE : The words ' do you but counterfeit?' surely mean, ' do you but counterfeit madness,' or, in other words, ' assume
the appearance of a madman, though not one.' Our author ought, I think, to have
written either ' are you *mad* indeed, *or* do you but counterfeit?' or else ' are you
not mad indeed, *and* do you but counterfeit?' But I do not suspect any corruption.
—W. A. WRIGHT : The question in its present form is equivalent to ' you are mad,
are you not?'

  122. **I am gone, sir, etc.**] FARMER : We have here another old catch ; appar-

Ile be with you againe : 123
In a trice, like to the old vice,

124. *In a*] *With a* Coll. ii (MS). 124. *like to*] *Like* Coll. MS.

ently, I think, not of Shakespeare.—DYCE (ed. ii, p. 383) : It is probably an old
song, somewhat altered by our poet.—NAYLOR (p. 190) gives the following air (see
line 74, above) :

I'm gone, sir, and a-non, sir, I'll be with you a-gain, sir.

124. **old**] This does not refer, I think, to age, or to the Vice of aforetimes, but is
the good humoured 'old,' and implies a sneaking regard.—ED .

124. **old vice**] JOHNSON : The 'vice' was the fool of the old moralities. Some
traces of this character are still preserved in puppet-shows, and by country mummers.
—NARES (s. v. *Iniquity*) : The established buffoon in the old moralities. He was
grotesquely dressed in a cap with ass`s ears, a long coat, and a dagger of lath ; one
of his chief employments was to make sport with the devil, leaping on his back and
belabouring him with his dagger of lath, till he made him roar. The devil, however, always carried him off in the end. The morality of which representation
clearly was, that sin, which has the wit and courage to make very merry with the
devil, and is allowed by him to take great liberties, must finally become his prey.—
COLLIER (*Hist. of Dram. Poetry*, ii, 188, ed. 1879) : Regarding the Vice, Douce
was of opinion that the name was derived from the nature of the character ; and certain it is that he is represented most wicked by design, and never good but by accident. Malone tells us that 'the principle employment of the Vice was to belabour
the Devil'; but although he was frequently so engaged, he had also other and
higher duties. He figured now and then in the religious plays of a later date, and
in *The Life and Death of Mary Magdalen*, 1567, he performed the part of her
lover, under the name of Infidelity, before her conversion ; in *King Darius*, 1565,
he also acted a prominent part, by his own evil impulses, under the name of
Iniquity, without any prompting from the representative of the principle of evil.
Such was the general style of the Vice ; and as Iniquity he is spoken of by Shakespeare (*Rich. III :* III, i.) and Ben Jonson (*Staple of News*, Second Intermean).
The Vice and Iniquity seem, however, sometimes to have been distinct persons ; and
he was not unfrequently called by the name of particular vices ; thus, in *Lusty
Juventus*, the Vice performs the part of Hypocrisy ; in *Common Conditions*, he is
called Conditions ; in *Like will to Like*, he is named Nichol New-fangle ; in *The
Trial of Treasure*, his part is that of Inclination ; in *All for Money*, he is called
Sin ; in *Tom Tyler and his Wife*, Desire ; and in *Appius and Virginia*, Haphazard.
Gifford designates the Vice 'the buffoon of the old Mysteries and Moralities,' as if
he had figured in the Miracle-plays represented at Chester, York, and elsewhere ;
Malone, also, speaks of him as the 'constant attendant' of the Devil in 'the
ancient religious plays?' The fact is that the Vice was wholly unknown in our
'religious plays,' which have hitherto gone by the name of 'Mysteries,' and to
which Gifford and Malone refer. *The Life and Repentance of Mary Magdalen* and
King Darius, already mentioned as containing the character of the Vice, were not
written until after the reign of Mary. The same remark will apply to the *Interlude*

[124. like to the old vice]

of Queen Hester, 1561, which differs from other religious plays, inasmuch as the Vice there is a court jester and servant, and is named Hardy-dardy. With regard to 'Moralities,' it is certainly true that in the ancient Moral-plays characters of gross buffoonery and vicious propensities were inserted for the amusement and instruction of the audience ; but, although we hear of 'the fool' in Medwall's Interlude, performed before Henry VIII. in 1516, such a character seems very rarely to have been specifically called 'the Vice' anterior to the Reformation. On the external appearance of the Vice, Douce has observed, that 'being generally dressed in a fool's habit,' he was gradually and undistinguishably blended with the domestic fool ; and there is every probability that such was the result. Ben Jonson, in his *The Devil is an Ass*, alludes to this very circumstance, when he is speaking of the fools of old kept in the houses of nobility and gentry :—'Fifty years agone and six, When every great man had his Vice stand by him In his long coat, shaking his wooden dagger.'—Act I. sc. i. The Vice here spoken of was the domestic fool of the nobility about the year 1560 ; to whom also Puttenham, in his *Arte of English Poesie* (1589, p. 69), alludes, under the terms 'buffoon or vice of plays.' In the second Intermean of his *Staple of News*, Ben Jonson tells us that the Vice sometimes wore 'a juggler's jerken with false skirts' ; and though Douce is unquestionably correct when he states that the Vice was 'generally dressed in a fool's habit,' he did not by any means constantly wear the parti-coloured habiliments of an idiot ; he was sometimes required to act a gallant, and now and then to assume the disguise of virtues it suited his purpose to personate. In *The Life and Repentance of Mary Magdalen*, he several times changes his apparel for the sake of deception. In *The Trial of Treasure*, 1567, he was not only provided, as was customary, with his wooden dagger, but in order to render him more ridiculous, with a pair of spectacles (no doubt of a preposterous size), which he is desired by one of the characters to put on. The 'long coat' worn by the Vice, according to the preceding quotation from Ben Jonson's *Devil is an Ass*, was doubtless that dress which, Douce informs us, belonged 'to the idiot or natural fool,' often of a mischievous and malignant disposition ; and it affords another link of connection between the Vice and the domestic fool. . . . The Vice, like the fool, was often furnished with a dagger of lath, and it was not unusual that it should be gilt. Just preceding the mention of the 'juggler's jerkin' by Ben Jonson, as part of the dress of the Vice, is an allusion to the ludicrous mode in which poetical justice was not unfrequently done to him at the conclusion of a Moral. Tattle observes, 'but there is never a fiend to carry him away' ; and in the first Intermean of the same play, Mirth leads us to suppose, that it was a very common termination of the adventures of the Vice, for him to be carried off to hell on the back of the devil : 'he would carry away the Vice on his back, quick to hell, in every play where he came.' In *The Longer thou livest the more Fool thou art*, and in *Like will to Like*, the Vice is disposed of nearly in this summary manner ; in the first, Confusion carries him to the devil, and in the last, Lucifer bears him off to the infernal regions on his shoulders. In *King Darius*, the Vice runs to hell of his own accord, to escape from Constancy, Equity, and Charity. According to Bishop Harsnet, the Vice was in the habit of riding and beating the devil at other times than when he was thus hurried against his will to punishment. [In Drummond of Hawthornden's Conversations with Ben Jonson, there occurs the following item : 'A play of his, upon which he was accused, The Divell is ane Ass ; according to *Comedia Vetus*, in England the Divell was brought in either with

your neede to fuftaine.   125
Who with dagger of lath, in his rage and his wrath,
        cries ah ha, to the diuell :
Like a mad lad, paire thy nayles dad,
        Adieu good man diuell.   *Exit*   129

---

127. *ah ha,*] *ah, ah,* Rowe i.   *ah
ha!* Rowe ii et seq.
   128. *dad,*] *Dad,* Ff.   *dad;* Dyce,
Cam.
   129. *good man diuell*] *good man
Divell* F$_2$. *good man Devil* F$_3$F$_4$. *good
Man Devil* Rowe i.   *good man Drivel*

Rowe ii,+, Ran. Steev. Var. Harness,
Walker, Coll. ii, iii (MS), Dyce, Cam. i,
Sta. *goodman Devil* Cap. Var. '73, '78,
'21, Mal. Wh. Glo. Cam. ii.   *goodman
Civil* or *good man, be civil* Anon. ap.
Cam.

---

one Vice or other : the play done the Divel carried away the Vice, he brings in the
Divel so overcome with the wickedness of this age that thought himself ane Ass.'
—p. 28, ed. Sh. Soc.—ED.]
   128. paire thy nayles dad] MALONE : The Devil was supposed from choice to
keep his nails always unpared, and therefore to pare them was an affront.   So, in
Camden's *Remaines,* 1615 : ' I will follow mine own minde, and mine old trade ;
Who shall let me ? the divel's nailes are unparde.'—FARMER : I know not whether
this line should not be thrown into a question : ' pare thy nails, dad ?'   In *Hen. V :*
IV, iv, 76, we meet again ' this roaring devil i' th' old play, that every one may pare
his nails with a wooden dagger.'
   129. good man diuell] JOHNSON : This line has neither rhyme nor meaning.
I cannot but suspect that the fool translates Malvolio's name, and says : ' Adieu,
goodman *mean-evil.*'—M. MASON (p. 120) : I believe, with Johnson, that this is an
allusion to Malvolio's name, but not in his reading, which destroys the metre.
Read—' Adieu, good *mean-evil,*' that is, *good Malvolio,* literally translated.—
MALONE : The last two lines of this song have, I think, been misunderstood.
They are not addressed in the first instance to Malvolio, but are quoted by the
Clown, as the words ' ah, ha !' are, as the usual address in the old Moralities to the
Devil.   We have in *The Merry Wives,* ' No *man* means evil but the *devil,*' [V, ii,
15] ; and in *Much Ado,* ' God's a good man,' [III, v, 37.   A recurrence of the
same word, instead of a rhyme, is hardly a sufficient reason for a change, especially in a song like this, which is sung by Feste in the mere exuberance of his high
spirits.   If the words apply to Malvolio, however vaguely, well and good ; too close
an application was hardly to be desired.   To imply that Malvolio is the Devil in a
play, is to imply that Feste himself is the Vice,—hardly a more creditable character.
For Feste's purpose, it is sufficient that the Song, taking up Malvolio's last words,
ends with bidding him adieu.—ED.]

Scæna Tertia.

Enter Sebaſtian.   2
This is the ayre, that is the glorious Sunne,
This pearle ſhe gaue me, I do feel't, and ſee't,
And though tis wonder that enwraps me thus,   5
Yet 'tis not madneſſe. Where's *Anthonio* then,
I could not finde him at the Elephant,
Yet there he was, and there I found this credite,
That he did range the towne to ſeeke me out,
His councell now might do me golden ſeruice,   10

---

1. Scene V. Pope, +.
    Another Apartment in Olivia's
House. Theob. Olivia's Garden. Cap.
3, 4. *Sunne,...ſee't,*] F₂F₃. *Sunne,...
ſee't.* F₄, Rowe, Pope, Han. *sun ;...
ſee't.* Theob. Warb. Johns. *sun ;...ſee't ;*

Cap. et seq.
6. *then,*] *then ?* Ff.
8. *credite*] F₂. *current* Han. *credited*
M. Mason, Ktly.   *credit* F₃F₄ et cet.
writ Cartwright.
9. *out,*] *out.* Rowe.

---

1. Scæna Tertia] MARSHALL : In [Irving's] acting-edition, this scene is the
first scene of Act V.

5. wonder that enwraps me] For other instances where Shakespeare uses this
figure, see the note in this ed. on ' I am so attired in wonder,' *Much Ado*, IV, i, 152.
It is frequent in the *Psalms ;* thus, ' Let them be clothed with shame and dishonour
that magnify themselves against me.'—xxxv, 26.

8. credite] THEOBALD : That is, I found it justified, credibly vouched. Whether
' credit ' will easily carry this meaning, I am doubtful.   The expression seems
obscure ; I very much suspect that the poet wrote *credent*.   Thus, in *Wint. Tale :*
' Then 'tis very credent Thou may'st cojoin with something.' [I, ii, 142.]—WAR-
BURTON : That is, account, information.   CAPELL (p. 152) accepts Theobald's definition, but discards his emendation, together with Warburton's definition, which, he
says, is ' making any thing of any thing.'—STEEVENS : Robertson, speaking of
some memorandums included in the Letters to Mary, Queen of Scots, observes,
that they were not ' the credit of the bearer '; *i. e.* points concerning which the
Queen had given him verbal instructions, or information.   ' Credit,' therefore, might
have been the prevalent term for *oral intelligence.*—COLLIER : The meaning of
Sebastian merely is, that he had not been able to find Antonio at the Elephant,
where, however, he had been, and where he (Sebastian) found this ' credit,' or
belief, that Antonio had gone to seek Sebastian.—SINGER (ed. ii) : I find in a letter
from Elizabeth to Sir Nicholas Throckmorton among the Conway Papers,—' This
beror came from you with great spede. . . . We have heard his credit and fynd your
carefulness and diligence very great.'—W. A. WRIGHT : That is, this opinion in
which people believed, this current belief.   ' Credit ' is used in just the same sense
as ' trust ' in line 17.   [The almost technical use of ' credit,' when applied to a messenger, seems to be uncalled for here, where no messenger is mentioned.   I think
the simpler explanation of Collier and of Wright is to be preferred.—ED.]

For though my foule difputes well with my fence,   11
That this may be fome error, but no madneffe,
Yet doth this accident and flood of Fortune,
So farre exceed all inftance, all difcourfe,
That I am readie to diftruft mine eyes,   15
And wrangle with my reafon that perfwades me
To any other truft, but that I am mad,
Or elfe the Ladies mad; yet if 'twere fo,
She could not fway her houfe, command her followers,
Take, and giue backe affayres, and their difpatch,   20

---

11. *fence*] *fenfe* Ff.
12. *madneffe,*]   *madness;*   Theob.
Warb. Johns. Cap.
13. *flood*] *floud* F₃F₄.

17. *I am*] *I'm* Pope, +, Dyce ii, iii.
18. *Ladies*] *lady's* Rowe.
20. *affayres, and their difpatch*] *and her affairs dispatch* Cartwright.

---

14. **instance**] That is, example. Compare 'Wise saws and mordern instances,' in Jaques's 'Seven Ages.'

14. **discourse**] MURRAY (*N. E. D.*), under the second sense of this word, quotes Dr Johnson's definition of it: 'The act of the understanding, by which it passes from premises to conclusions,' and then adds : 'reasoning, thought, ratiocination ; faculty of reasoning, reason, rationality'; which adequately explains Sebastian's present use. Hamlet's 'discourse of reason,' I, ii, 150, Murray treats as a phrase, and gives an example of its use, as early as 1413. In *Othello*, IV, ii, 182, where Desdemona says 'in discourse of thought,' I ventured, with much hesitation, to suggest that Shakespeare might have used 'discourse' in its derivative Latin sense, equivalent to *range*, and I still think that such an interpretation will remove some difficulties where 'discourse' is limited by another substantive.—ED.

17. **trust**] JOHNSON : That is, to any other belief, or confidence, to any other fixed opinion.

20. **Take, and giue backe affayres, and their dispatch**] COLLIER (ed. ii) reads, in accordance with his MS Corrector, '. . . and thus dispatch affairs'; and remarks : *Thus* was misprinted 'their,' and the other words became accidentally displaced, so that although the meaning might be evident, the construction of the sentence was altogether deranged.—DYCE (ed. ii) : No editor, as far as I know, has questioned this very questionable line.—Qy. '. . . and *them* dispatch'?—Here Mr Collier's MS Corrector makes a violent alteration.—W. A. WRIGHT : The verbs and substantives must be distributed here as in *Wint. Tale*, III, ii, 164, 165 : 'Though I with death and with Reward did threaten and encourage him.' And in *Macbeth*, I, iii, 60 : 'Speak then to me, who neither beg nor fear Your favours nor your hate.' In the present passage 'take' goes with 'affairs' and 'give back' with 'their dispatch.' The phrase is thus equivalent to 'take a business in hand and discharge it.'—DEIGHTON : 'Take and give back ' is equivalent to 'administer,' 'attend to,' by receiving reports from her steward and passing orders upon them ; and 'see to,' or some such verb, is easily supplied from 'take and give back.' [Wright's explanation is, I think, the true one ; with it, the line ceases to be 'questionable.' The line is an example of what CORSON has named 'respective

With fuch a fmooth, difcreet, and ftable bearing   21
As I perceiue fhe do's : there's fomething in't
That is deceiueable.   But heere the Lady comes.

Enter Oliuia, and Prieſt.

Ol. Blame not this hafte of mine : if you meane well   25
Now go with me, and with this holy man
Into the Chantry by : there before him,
And vnderneath that confecrated roofe,
Plight me the full affurance of your faith,
That my moft iealious, and too doubtfull foule   30

21. *ſtable bearing*] *ſtable-bearing* Ff,   *comes the lady* Steev. Var. '03, '13.
Rowe i.   30. *.iealious*] *jealous* Ff.
    23. *the Lady comes*] *she comes* Pope, +.

---

construction,' of which there are many instances in Shakespeare ; thus, Touchstone
(*As You Like It*, V, iv, 61, 62) says, 'to sweare and to forsweare, according as
marriage binds and blood breakes,' where 'sweare' goes with 'binds' and 'forsweare' with 'breaks.'   Again, a notable instance, in *Hamlet*, III, i, 151 : 'The
courtier's, scholar's, soldier's, eye, tongue, sword.'   This is not to be confounded
with a chiasm, or *criss-cross* construction, as in *Mer. of Ven.* III, i, 57, where Shylock says 'warmed and cooled by the same Winter and Summer'; and again in
'land rats and water rats, water thieves and land thieves.'—ED.]

    23. **deceiueable**] That is, deceptive or deceitful.   WALKER (*Crit.* i, 183), on
'adjectives in -*able* and -*ible*, both positive and negative ones, which are frequently
used in an active sense,' gives the following examples of 'deceivable':—Bacon,
Essay on Deformity,—'therefore, it is good to consider of deformity, not as a sign
which is more deceiveable, but as a cause which seldom faileth of the effect.'   Sidney, *Arcadia*, B. ii, p. 179, l. 29,—'this colour of mine, which she (in the deceivable style of affection) would entitle beautiful.'   Bunyan, *Holy War*, ed. 1791,
p. 21,—'Diabolus—made this further deceivable speech to them, saying,' etc.   And
p. 40, ult. margin,—'Very deceivable language.'—RUSHTON (*Lex. Scripta*, p. 29) :
In the ancient statutes the words 'deceivable' and 'deceitful' are synonyms ; for
example, the 43rd Elizabeth, cap. x., speaks first of deceitful things as 'subtil
sleights and untruths'; and afterwards, referring to the same 'subtil sleights and
untruths,' speaks of them as deceivable things.   [See *Rich. II:* II, iii, 84, 'Show
me thy humble heart and not thy knee, Whose duty is deceivable and false.']

    27. **Chantry**] MURRAY (*N. E. D.*) : 3. An endowment for the maintenance of
one or more priests to sing daily mass for the souls of the founders or others specified by them.   b. A chapel, altar, or part of a church so endowed.   [It is to the
latter that Olivia refers.—ED.]

    27. **by**] That is, near, at hand.   Thus, *Rich. III:* I, ii, 234, 'What ! I . . . to
take her With curses in her mouth, tears in her eyes, The bleeding witness of her
hatred by.'

    30. **iealious**] In the First Folio 'jealous' is thus uniformly spelt in *Othello*, and
even in cases, like the present, where a trisyllable is not needed.   'It is noticeable,'
says WALKER (*Vers.* p. 156), 'that "jealous" or "jealious," as a trisyllable,

May liue at peace.   He fhall conceale it,   31
Whiles you are willing it shall come to note,
What time we will our celebration keepe
According to my birth, what do you fay ?

   Seb.   Ile follow this good man, and go with you,   35
And hauing fworne truth, euer will be true.

   *Ol.*Then lead the way good father,& heauens fo fhine,
That they may fairely note this acte of mine.   *Exeunt.*

                        Finis Actus Quartus.   39

31. *May liue*] *May henceforth live* Han.   *heav'n* Rowe i.   *and heav'ns* Rowe ii, Theob. Warb. Johns.   *heav'ns* Pope, Han.   *and heavens* F₂ et cet.

32. *Whiles*] *While* Wh.

34. *birth,*] *birth.* Rowe.

37. *& heauens*] *& heaven* F₃F₄.   *and*

39. Quartus.] Quarti. Ff.

---

occurs, with scarcely an exception, at the end of lines.' Probably, it was pronounced indifferently as a disyllable or as a trisyllable, but even when a disyllable, the pronunciation was possibly *jealyous.*   The successful but illiterate Manager, Henslowe, whose spelling is generally extremely phonetic, records in his Diary (*Sh. Soc.* p. 29), the receipts from a play which he calls ' the gelyous comodey,'— probably a play founded on some tale of jealousy.   WALKER (*Crit.* iii, 18), in a note on ' Lay by all nicety and prolixious blushes,' *Meas. for Meas.* II, iv, 162, says, ' Compare the old forms *stupendious* (the common people even now say *tremendious*), *robustious,* e. g. *Hamlet,* III, ii, 10 ; *Hen. V:* III, vii, 159 ; and Drayton, *Moses,* B. ii, p. 154.   Other similar forms : *superbious,* and even *splendidious.*' See ' Dexteriously,' I, v, 58 ; ' studient,' IV, ii, 10.—ED.

   31. He shall conceale it] WALKER (*Vers.* 154) : Certainly not conceāl ; perhaps something has dropped out.—KEIGHTLEY (*Expositor,* p. 180) : This line is imperfect.   In my Edition I added *still* (printed, or perhaps written, *till*), and we might also read *closely* or *truly,* i. e. faithfully.   We might also end the line with ' whiles,' and begin the next with *That ;* as *while* and *whiles that* occur in Chaucer, Golding, and others.   [See *Text. Notes* for HANMER'S remedy for the metre, which is seldom defective to the ear when there is a break in the line.—ED.]

   32. Whiles] That is, until.   See III, ii, 10.—GOULD (p. 21) : There should be a colon after ' willing ': the passage as at present printed [*i. e.* with no punctuation after ' willing '] is nonsense.   [It is to be feared that this remark reveals Gould's misapprehension of ' Whiles.'—ED.]

   33. What time] See I, v, 150.

   33. celebration] That is, the marriage ceremony.   For the ceremony of betrothal which here takes place in the Chantry, see Douce's elaborate note on ' contract,' V, i, 167.

   37. heauens so shine, etc.] STEEVENS : Alluding perhaps to a superstitious supposition, the memory of which is still preserved in a proverbial saying : ' Happy is the bride upon whom the sun shines.'   [This note has been quoted by more than one editor.   But to impute to the refined Olivia such a meteorological aspiration is unworthy.   She merely echoes a similar prayer uttered by Friar Laurence in *Rom. & Jul.* II, vi, 1, ' So smile the heavens upon this holy act, That after hours with sorrow chide us not.'—ED.]

Actus Quintus. Scena Prima.

Enter Clowne and Fabian. 2

Fab. Now as thou lou'ft me, let me fee his Letter.

Clo. Good M. *Fabian,* grant me another requeft.

Fab. Any thing. 5

Clo. Do not defire to fee this Letter.

Fab. This is to giue a dogge, and in recompence defire my dogge againe.

Enter Duke, Uiola, Curio, and Lords.

Duke. Belong you to the Lady *Oliuia,* friends? 10

Clo. I fir, we are fome of her trappings.

Duke. I know thee well : how doeft thou my good Fellow? 13

The Street. Pope. Before Olivia's House. Cap.

3. *his*] *this* Ff, Rowe, Pope, Han. Cap.

4. *M.*] *Mr.* Rowe, +, Cap. *master* Var. '73 et seq.

7. *This*] *That* Var. '78, '85, Ran. Mal. Steev. Var. Sta.

9. Curio, and Lords.] and Attendants. Cap.

12. *doeft*] *do'ft* F₃F₄.

2. **Enter Clowne**] HUTSON (p. 493) : It seems to me that it is not without significance that the jester is made to open the last three acts of the play. It is to show, as it were, the growing spirit of mirth and mistake, misconception and mischief, blundering and confusion, as in a masquerade, which appertains to the season of revels from which the play takes its name. To make this the more apparent, the personification of the spirit of mischief-making, the jester Feste, is thus made prominent, opening the Third Act with Viola, the Fourth with Sebastian, and the Fifth with Fabian.

7. **to giue a dogge**, etc.] B. NICHOLSON (*N. & Qu.* VIIth, iv, 185) : The singularity and definiteness of the comparison, made when no dog was in question, together with this, that the giving and reclaiming of the dog run not on all fours with the asking for and denial of the letter, all gave me the impression that there is here a reference to some contemporary anecdote. In Manningham's *Diary*, on March 26, 1602/3, two days after the queen's death, occurs the following : 'Mr. Francis Curle told me howe one Dr Bullein, the Queenes kinsman, had a dog which he doted on, soe much that the Queene understanding of it requested he would graunt hir one desyre, and he should have what soever she would aske. Shee demaunded his dogge ; he gave it, and " Nowe, Madame," quoth he, " you promised to give me my desyre." " I will," quothe she. " Then I pray you give me my dog againe." '[p. 148, ed. Camden Soc.] The knowledge and acumen of my friend Miss Emma Phipson, author of *The Animal Lore of Shakespeare's Time*, first directed my attention to this illustration and explanation of the passage. It is, therefore, in her name, and not in my own, that I write this.

Clo. Truely fir, the better for my foes, and the worfe
for my friends.   15
    Du. Iuft the contrary : the better for thy friends.
    Clo. No fir, the worfe.
    Du. How can that be?
    Clo. Marry fir, they praife me, and make an affe of me,
now my foes tell me plainly, I am an Affe : fo that by my   20
foes fir, I profit in the knowledge of my felfe, and by my
friends I am abufed : fo that conclufions to be as kiffes, if   22

16. *better*] *bettee* F₄.	*that, conclusion to be asked, is* Theob.
22. *that conclufions to be as kiffes*]	Warb. *the conclusion to be asked is* Han.

19. **and make**] That is, and thereby indirectly make an ass of me.

22. **so that conclusions to be as kisses, etc.**] That is, 'conclusions *being* as kisses.' See II, ii, 8.—WARBURTON : What monstrous absurdity have we here? The Clown is affecting to argue seriously and in form. I imagine the Poet wrote : So that, conclusion to be *asked, is, i. e.* so that the conclusion I have to demand of you is this, if your four, etc. He had in the preceding words been inferring some *premises*, and now comes to the *conclusion* very *logically;* you grant me, says he, the premises ; I now ask you to grant the conclusion.—JOHNSON : Though I do not discover much ratiocination in the Clown's discourse, yet, methinks, I can find some glimpse of a meaning in his observation, that 'the conclusion is as kisses.' For, says he, 'if four negatives make two affirmatives, the conclusion is as kisses ; that is, the conclusion follows by the conjunction of two negatives, which by 'kissing' and embracing, coalesce into one, and make an affirmative. What the *four* negatives are I do not know. I read, 'So that conclusions be as kisses.'—HEATH (p. 193) : Men often ask premises, and sometimes even beg them, as Mr Warburton well knows, but no man ever asked a conclusion. This is always inferred as a thing of right and necessity. Such stuff as this could never fall from the pen of Shakespeare. The common reading being evidently absurd and corrupt, I may be allowed to guess that our poet wrote, 'So that conclusions *follow as kisses*,' that is, close on each other's heels. As to what follows, 'if your four negatives make your two affirmatives,' I suppose it is one of those absurdities commonly put into the mouths of clowns or jesters, which make a part of their character, and seems intended to ridicule the formal solemnity of the men of science. In any other view it is quite beside the purpose of the argument.—CAPELL (p. 152) : That is, so that to make conclusions follow as thick as kisses do often ; for this speaker had just made a conclusion, and that properly, from something he had premis'd ; and now affects to draw it a second time from premisings that have nothing to do with it, and thrown in only for laughing ; and these laughable premises he fetches from a grammatical dogma, that two negatives make an affirmative.—FARMER : One cannot but wonder that this passage should have perplexed the Commentators. In *Lust's Dominion*, the Queen says to the Moor : 'Come, let's kiss. *Eleazar.* Away, away ! *Queen.* No, no says ay ; and twice away says stay.' [I, i.] Sir Philip Sidney has enlarged upon this thought in the sixty-third sonnet of his *Astrophel and Stella.*—COLERIDGE (p. 122) : Surely Warburton could never have wooed by kisses and won, or he would not have flounder-flatted so just and humorous, nor less pleasing than

your foure negatiues make your two affirmatiues, why   23
then the worfe for my friends, and the better for my foes.

    Du. Why this is excellent.   25

    Clo. By my troth fir, no : though it pleafe you to be
one of my friends.

    Du. Thou fhalt not be the worfe for me, there's gold.

    Clo. But that it would be double dealing fir, I would
you could make it another.   30

    Du. O you giue me ill counfell.

    Clo. Put your grace in your pocket fir, for this once,
and let your flefh and blood obey it.

    Du. Well, I will be fo much a finner to be a double
dealer : there's another.   35

---

24. *for my friends*] *of my friends* F₃F₄.

28. [Giving money. Coll. ii (MS), Dyce ii. Giving it. Coll. iii.

29. *double dealing*] *double-dealing* Rowe et seq.

30. *you could*] *could* Rowe i.

33. *obey*] *sway* Warb. conj. (MS *N. & Qu.* VIII, iii, 203.)

34, 35. *double dealer*] *double-dealer* Rowe et seq.

35. [Giving more money. Coll. ii (MS). Giving it. Coll. iii.

---

humorous, an image into so profound a nihility. In the name of love and wonder, do not four kisses make a double affirmative? The humour lies in the whispered ' No !' and the inviting ' Don't !' with which the maiden's kisses are accompanied, and thence compared to negatives, which by repetition constitute an affirmative.—CAMBRIDGE EDITORS : The meaning seems to be nothing more recondite than this : as in the syllogism it takes two premises to make one conclusion, so it takes two people to make one kiss.—W. A. WRIGHT : In the Clown's argument, the affirmative conclusion follows the negative premises, as kisses follow upon refusal. [Feste has only two negatives, namely : (*a.*) my friends by indirection, do not make me wise ; (*b.*) my foes plainly do not make me out to be wise ; but these two negatives will furnish only one affirmative,—and he needs two affirmatives, namely : (*c.*) the worse for my friends, and (*d.*) the better for my foes. These affirmatives are gained if conclusions are like kisses, because if *two* lips say 'no' *twice* it is plainly equivalent to *four* negatives, because twice two are four ; and these four negatives will supply the two needed affirmatives. Q. E. D.—ED.]

    23. your] Thus, Hamlet says, 'your worm is your only emperor for diet, your fat king and your lean beggar is but variable service.' For other examples see, if need be, ABBOTT, § 221.

    25. excellent] C. C. CLARKE (p. 418) : Ay, it is the excellent philosophy of a sweet and happy-tempered fellow, whose good-humoured jokes have a fund of true wisdom in their playfullest utterances, and who is not merely a professional jester, but a most delightful associate.

    32. your grace] In order to emphasize the double meaning of 'grace,' as a title of the Duke, and ' grace' in the theological sense, R. G. WHITE (ed. i) prints the phrase in quotation marks : ' your Grace.' ' Flesh and blood is again theological and equivalent to ' the natural man.' ' It' in ' obey it' refers, of course, to ' ill counsel.'

Clo. *Primo, fecundo, tertio,* is a good play, and the olde   36
faying is, the third payes for all : the triplex fir, is a good
tripping meafure, or the belles of S. *Bennet* fir, may put
you in minde, one, two, three.

Du. You can foole no more money out of mee at this   40
throw: if you will let your Lady know I am here to fpeak
with her, and bring her along with you, it may awake my
bounty further.

Clo. Marry fir, lullaby to your bountie till I come a-   44

---

36. Primo, fecundo, tertio] Not Italics, Cam.

37. *triplex*] *triplet* Johns. Coll. ii
(MS). In Italics, Cap.

38. *or*] *as* Han. Mason, Ran. Huds.
S.] *St.* Rowe. *saint* Cap.

39. *minde,*] *mind ;* Steev. et seq.

---

34. **so . . . to be**] For a similar omission of *as* after 'so,' see II, ii, 11.

37. **triplex**] That is, triple time in music, where each bar is divided into three
equal parts. JOHNSON and COLLIER'S MS Corrector, however, changed it to *triplet*,
a quite different thing. 'Triplet, a group of three notes, played in the usual time
of two similar ones.'—HILES, *Mus. Dict.* Collier adopted *triplet* in his Second
Edition, but returned to 'triplex' in his Third.—ED.

38. **or**] DYCE (ed. ii) : Hanmer's alteration is perhaps right.

38. **the belles of S. Bennet**] JOHNSON : When in this play Shakespeare mentioned the 'bed of Ware,' he recollected that the scene was in Illyria, and added
'in England'; but his sense of the same impropriety could not restrain him from
the bells of St. Bennet.—STEEVENS : Shakespeare's improprieties and anachronisms
are surely venial in comparison with those of contemporary writers. Lodge, in his
True Tragedies of Marius and Sylla, 1594, has mentioned *the razors of Palermo*
and *St. Paul's steeple.* Stanyhurst, the translator of four books of Virgil, in 1582,
compares Choroebus to a *bedlamite,* says old Priam girded on his *Morglay* [p. 60,
ed. Arber], and makes Dido tell Æneas, 'yf yeet soom progenye from me Had
crawld, by the fatherd, if a *cockney* dandiprat hopthumb.'[p. 106, ed. Arber.]—
HALLIWELL : Although this notice is not a positive anachronism, as á church dedicated to this Saint might be supposed in any part of Europe, there can be little
doubt but that the poet was thinking of his own country. In the absence of certain
information respecting which of the several churches in London dedicated to St.
Bennet was famous for its bells, conjecture points to St. Bennet's, Paul's Wharf, one
of the many churches destroyed in the Great Fire.—W. A. WRIGHT : The allusion
is, perhaps, to some old rhyme which has been lost ; or it may be to the real bells
of [the church mentioned by Halliwell].

41. **throw**] DYCE (*Gloss.*) : Here perhaps 'throw' is used with a quibble,—the
word meaning both 'a throw of the dice' and 'time' (the latter signification being
common in our earliest poets).

44. **lullaby**] HALLIWELL (*Sh. Soc. Papers,* iii, 35) : This is sufficiently unusual
as a verb to justify an example. 'Yet by accident the unmanag'd appetite . . . doth
dul the quicker spirits . . . makes the head totter, *lullabees* the scences,' etc.—*The
Optick Glasse of Hvmers,* 1639, p. 19.—DYCE (*Few Notes,* 77) added another :
'Sweet sound that all mens sences *lullabieth.*'—Anthony Copley's *Fig for Fortune,*

gen. I go fir, but I would not haue you to thinke, that		45
my defire of hauing is the finne of couetoufneffe : but as
you fay fir, let your bounty take a nappe, I will awake it
anon.						*Exit*

Enter Anthonio and Officers.

Vio. Here comes the man fir, that did refcue mee.		50
Du.   That face of his I do remember well,
yet when I faw it laft, it was befmear'd
As blacke as Vulcan, in the fmoake of warre :
A bawbling Veffell was he Captaine of,
For fhallow draught and bulke vnprizable,		55

---

49. Scene II. Pope, +.
 Enter...] After line 50, Dyce,
Cam. Sta.
 54. *bawbling Veffell*] *bauble-vessel*

Ktly conj.
 54. *he*] *the* F₄.
 55. *vnprizable*] *unprisable* Gould.

1596, p. 59.—J. E. SPINGARN (*N. & Qu.* VIIIth, v, 283) adds a third : ' That old acquaintance, now strangely saluted with a new remembrance, is neither *lullabied* with thy sweet Papp, nor scarre-crowed with thy sower hatchet.'—Harvey's *Pierce's Supererogation*, pt. ii, p. 69, ed. 1593.—HALLIWELL : The word ' lullaby ' in the text may, however, possibly be a substantive, the construction in that case being,— let there be a lullaby to your bounty.

   54. **bawbling**] DYCE (*Gloss.*) : Trifling, insignificant, contemptible.

   55. **vnprizable**] JOHNSON (*Dict.*) : Not valued ; not of estimation. [Johnson's definition applies to this passage alone ; he did not notice the only other passage where the word occurs in Shakespeare : ' Your ring may be stolen, too ; so your brace of unprizable estimations : the one is but frail and the other casual.'—*Cymbeline*, I, iv, 99.]—DYCE (*Gloss.*) : Not of estimation, of small account. [' Unprizable ' in *Cym.* Dyce defines as ' inestimable, priceless,' and adds : ' Coles may be cited as illustrating the double meaning of this word : " Unprisable, *inaestimabilis.*" " Inaestimabilis, *Inestimable, not to be valued, also of no value.*" ' SCHMIDT (*Lex.*) also notes the two opposite meanings.—ABBOTT (§ 3) : This means ' not able to be made a prize of, captured.'—W. A. WRIGHT : That is, invaluable, inestimable.   Johnson and others take it in the sense of valueless, as being beneath price ; but shallow draught is not necessarily a defect in a ship, and it was probably by means of this quality combined with its small size which enabled it to move quickly, that the captain could attack a much larger vessel with advantage, just as the small English ships made such ' scathful grapple ' with the unwieldy floating batteries of the Spanish Armada.   Cotgrave gives ' Impreciable. . . . vnprisable, vnualuable.'   Abbott's interpretation is extremely doubtful.—DEIGHTON : That is, of little importance, worth.   The tone of the Duke is contemptuous as to the vessel in comparison with the ' noble bottoms ' of his own fleet, and so more complimentary to the skill and valour of the captain.—INNES : Most probably this means worthless, of no value.   The Duke would hardly have used the contemptuous term ' bawbling ' if he were going to call the same ship ' invaluable ' in the next breath. [THE CENTURY DICTIONARY thus justly defines the word : ' Incapable of being

With which fuch fcathfull grapple did he make,   56
With the moft noble bottome of our Fleete,
That very enuy, and the tongue of loffe
Cride fame and honor on him: What's the matter?

   1 *Offi.*   *Orfino,* this is that *Anthonio*   60
That tooke the *Phœnix,* and her fraught from *Candy,*
And this is he that did the *Tiger* boord,
When your yong Nephew *Titus* loft his legge ;
Heere in the ftreets, defperate of fhame and ftate,
In priuate brabble did we apprehend him.   65

59. *Cride*] *Cride'* F$_2$.   *Cri'd* F$_3$F$_4$.   63. *legge ;*] *leg.* Coll.
62. *boord*] *board* Rowe.   65. *brabble*] *brawle* Gould.

---

prized or of having its value estimated, as being either below valuation or above or
beyond valuation.'   Hence it follows that the meaning can be determined only by
the context, which, in the present passage, is, I think, in favour of 'valueless.'
Thus 'unvalued' is also used by Shakespeare with opposite meanings.   In *Hamlet,*
I, iii, 19, Laertes says of Hamlet, 'He may not as unvalued persons do, Carve for
himself'; where 'unvalued' means common, ordinary.   In *Richard III :* I, iv, 27,
Clarence describes the sight, in his dream, of 'heaps of pearls, Inestimable stones,
unvalued jewels,' where 'unvalued' means uncommon, extraordinary.—ED.]

   56. scathfull] STEEVENS : That is, destructive.—HALLIWELL : The substantive
scathe, harm, loss, damage, is very common.   A North country proverb says, ' One
doth the scathe, another hath the scorn.'   'So did they beat, from off their native
bounds, Spain's mighty fleet with cannons' scathful wounds.'—Niccols' *England's
Eliza, Mirr. Mag.,* p. 833, 1610.

   57. bottome] Thus, in *Mer. of Ven.* I, i, 47, Anthonio says, ' My ventures are
not in one bottome trusted, Nor to one place.'   It is still in common use.

   58. tongue of losse] That is, the voice of those who had lost their vessels.

   60. Orsino] The undeniable abruptness of this address is softened by an Anonymous conjecture, recorded in the Cam. Ed., of ' Signior Orsino,' or ' Noble Orsino.'

   61. fraught] That is, freight, a word Shakespeare does not use.   MURRAY (*N.
E. D.*), however, records 'freight' as a ship-load, in Arnolde's *Chronicle,* 1502.   As
a verb, who can forget in *Macbeth,* 'Give sorrow words; the grief that does not
speak Whispers the o'erfraught heart, and bids it break '?—ED.

   61. Candy] That is, Candia, now Crete.

   62. the Tiger] Again, in *Macbeth,* I, iii, 7, 'Her husband's to Aleppo gone,
master o' the Tiger.'—W. A. WRIGHT : A common name for a vessel in Shakespeare's day, and, if we may trust Virgil (*Æn.* x, 166), even in the days of Æneas.

   64. desperate of shame and state] JOHNSON : That is, unattentive to his character or his condition, like a desperate man.—DEIGHTON : Schmidt (*Lex.*) takes
' state ' as equivalent to danger, or dangerous position, but the point emphasized seems
to be his disreputable character, not his recklessness of danger.

   65. brabble] W. A. WRIGHT : That is, brawl, quarrel.   See Gossen, *Schoole
of Abuse* (ed. Arber), p. 26 : 'Terpandrus, when he had ended the brabbles at
Lacedæmon, neyther pyped Rogero nor Turkelony.'   Cotgrave has ' Noise : f. A
brabble, brawle, debate, wrangle, squabble,' etc.

Uio. He did me kindneſſe ſir, drew on my ſide,   66
But in concluſion put ſtrange ſpeech vpon me,
I know not what 'twas, but diſtraction.

  D*u.* Notable Pyrate, thou ſalt-water Theefe,
What fooliſh boldneſſe brought thee to their mercies,   70
Whom thou in termes ſo bloudie, and ſo deere
Haſt made thine enemies?

  Ant. *Orſino:* Noble ſir,
Be pleas'd that I ſhake off theſe names you giue mee:
Anthonio neuer yet was Theefe, or Pyrate,   75
Though I confeſſe, on baſe and ground enough
Orſino's enemie. A witchcraft drew me hither:
That moſt ingratefull boy there by your ſide,
From the rude ſeas enrag'd and foamy mouth
Did I redeeme: a wracke paſt hope he was: 80
His life I gaue him, and did thereto adde

---

66. *did*] *shew'd* Cap. (corrected to *did*, Errata).

73. Orſino: *Noble ſir*] *Noble Sir, Orſino* Han.

76. *on baſe and*] *and on base* Mal. conj. (withdrawn).

78. *ingratefull*] *ungrateful* F₄, Rowe, +, Var. Ran. Hal.

79. *ſeas*] *sea's* Rowe ii.
foamy] *fomy* F₄.

80. *wracke*] F₂. *wrack* F₃F₄, Rowe, Knt, Wh. *wreck* Pope et cet.

---

68. distraction] That is, madness.

69. **Pyrate, thou ſalt-water Theefe**] Thus, Shylock says, 'There be land-rats and water-rats, water-thieves and land-thieves, I mean pirates.' I, iii, 20.— DEIGHTON: Middleton, *The Phœnix,* I, ii, 57, speaks of 'a gallant salt-thief.'

70. **their mercies**] For other examples of *their* used in its old signification, as a genitive, where we should use *of those,* see ABBOTT, § 219.

71. **deere**] I think this use of 'dear' comes under the second sense, given by MURRAY (*N. E. D.*), of the Second division (*a²*) of the adjective, and defined 'hard, severe, heavy, grievous; fell, dire'; as in the following examples: *Richard II:* I, iii, 151, 'The datelesse limit of thy deere exile'; *Sonnet* 37, 'I, made lame by Fortunes dearest spight'; *Timon,* V, i, 231, 'What other meanes is left vnto vs In our deere perill'; and, possibly, in Hamlet's 'Would I had met my dearest foe in heauen,' etc., I, ii, 180.

77. **witchcraft**] W. A. WRIGHT: Falstaff attributed his attachment to Poins to the same cause. See *1 Hen. IV:* II, ii, 18, 'I have forsworn his [Poins's] company hourly any time this two and twenty years, and yet I am bewitched with the rogue's company. If the rascal have not given me medicines to make me love him, I'll be hanged; it could not be else; I have drunk medicines.'

78. **ingratefull**] This form is used by Shakespeare, or his compositors, twice as often as *ungrateful.*

80. **wracke**] A phonetic spelling, as regards the sound of the vowel, and uniformly so spelled in the Folio.

My loue without retention, or reſtraint,   82
All his in dedication.   For his ſake,
Did I expoſe my ſelfe (pure for his loue)
Into the danger of this aduerſe Towne,   85
Drew to defend him, when he was beſet :
Where being apprehended, his falſe cunning
(Not meaning to partake with me in danger)
Taught him to face me out of his acquaintance,
And grew a twentie yeeres remoued thing   90
While one would winke : denide me mine owne purſe,
Which I had recommended to his vſe,
Not halfe an houre before.
   Vio.   How can this be ?
   Du.   When came he to this Towne ?   95
   Ant.   To day my Lord : and for three months before,
No *intrim*, not a minutes vacancie,
Both day and night did we keepe companie.
        Enter Oliuia and attendants.
   Du.   Heere comes the Counteſſe, now heauen walkes   100
      on earth :
But for thee fellow, fellow thy words are madneſſe,
Three monthes this youth hath tended vpon mee,   103

83. *All his*] *All this* Ff, Rowe, Pope.
  in] *is* F₃F₄.
84. *for*] *of* F₃F₄.
90. *twentie yeeres remoued*] Ff, Rowe,
+, Cam. Wh. ii.   *twenty-years-removed*
Cap. et cet.
91. *me*] *be* F₃F₄.
95. *he*] *you* Han.   *ye* Dyce ii, iii.
96. *months*] *monthes* F₂.
97, in parenthesis, Theob. et seq.
(except Coll. Hal. Cam.)

97. intrim] interim Ff.
99. Scene III. Pope, +.
99. Enter...] After line 104, Dyce,
Sta.
102. *fellow, fellow*] Ff. *fellow ; fel-low*, Rowe, Pope, Han. Var. '21, Coll.
i, ii, Hal. Cam. Ktly.   *fellow,—fellow*,
Dyce, Sta. Rlfe.   *fellow, fellow*, Theob.
et cet.   *fellow,* Gould.
103. *monthes*] F₂.

83. dedication] That is, in the dedication of my love, it was entirely his.—ED.
84. pure] For examples of adjectives used as adverbs, see ABBOTT, § 1.
89. face me out] See IV, ii, 95.
102. for thee] That is, as regards thee.   Thus, *Wint. Tale*, III, ii, 45, 'For
Honor, 'Tis a deriuatiue from me to mine'; again, *Lear*, II, ii, 114, 'For you,
Edmund, whose virtue,' etc.   For other examples, see ABBOTT, § 149.   For the
punctuation after 'fellow,' I prefer Dyce's.—ED.
103. Three monthes] Is it not strange that there is any one now-a-days who
can imagine that he is keener-sighted than Shakespeare ?   And yet there are critics

But more of that anon.   Take him afide.

Ol.   What would my Lord, but that he may not haue,   105
Wherein *Oliuia* may feeme feruiceable *?*
Cefario, you do not keepe promife with me.

Vio.   Madam:

Du.   Gracious *Oliuia*.

Ol.   What do you fay *Cefario* ? Good my Lord.   110

Uio.   My Lord would fpeake, my dutie hufhes me.

Ol.   If it be ought to the old tune my Lord,
It is as fat and fulfome to mine eare
As howling after Muficke.

Du.   Still fo cruell ?   115

Ol.   Still fo conftant Lord.

Du.   What to peruerfeneffe *?* you vnciuill Ladie
To whofe ingrate, and vnaufpicious Altars
My foule the faithfull'ft offrings haue breath'd out
That ere deuotion tender'd.   What fhall I do ?   120

Ol.   Euen what it pleafe my Lord, that fhal becom him

Du.   Why fhould I not, (had I the heart to do it)   122

---

104. [Go back. Coll. MS ap. Cam.
107. *do not*] *don't* Pope, Han.
108. *Madam :*] *Madam.* Ff.   *Madam !* Theob.   *Madam ?* Cap.
109. Oliuia] *Olivia,*— Theob. et seq.
110. *Lord.*] *Lord*— Rowe et seq.
111. *me.*] *me :* F₄.
112. *ought*] *aught* Theob. ii, Warb. Johns. Mal. et seq.
113. *fat*] *flat* Warb. Han. Cap. Ran.
115. *Still*] *Still, still* Cap.

115. *cruell*] *cruel, Lady* Daniel.
116. *fo conftant Lord*] *Lord, so conftant* Han.   *so constant* K. Elze.
   Lord] *my Lord* F₃F₄, Rowe i.
117. *What*] *What !* Steev. Var. Knt, Wh. i, Hal. Ktly.
   to] Om. Gould.
119. *haue*] Ff, Rowe.   *has* Pope, +.   *hath* Cap. et seq.
122. *do it*] *do't* Pope, +.

---

who think that Shakespeare, in this lapse of three months, committed an oversight, which, hidden from him, is patent to them. Orsino said 'three months,' and Shakespeare intended that his auditors should believe that Orsino told the truth, and they do believe it when they listen to the play.—ED.

105. **but that he**] That is, omitting that which he may not have, namely, her love.

110. **Good my Lord.**] Probably accompanied by a gesture to the Duke to keep silent and let Cesario speak.—ED.

113. **fat and fulsome**] WARBURTON'S 'flat' suggestion beguiled even Capell.—JOHNSON : 'Fat' means dull ; so we say a fat-headed fellow.—HALLIWELL : 'Fat and fulsome' implies here the excess of satiety, and, hence, unbearable, absolutely nauseous.—W. A. WRIGHT : Both words properly apply to the sense of taste, but are here referred to that of hearing.

119. **offrings haue**] 'Have' is plural by attraction ; and is rather more likely to be due to the compositor's ear than to Shakespeare's.—ED.

Like to th'Egyptian theefe, at point of death   123
Kill what I loue : (a fauage iealoufie,
That fometime fauours nobly) but heare me this :   125
Since you to non-regardance caft my faith,
And that I partly know the inftrument   127

123. *th' Egyptian*] Pope, +, Dyce ii,
iii. *the Egyptian* Ff (*Ægyptian* F₄),
Rowe et cet.

  theefe,... death] Ff, Rowe, +,
Var. '73. *thief...death*, Coll. Dyce. Cam.
Sta. Wh. ii. *thief,...death*, Cap. et cet.

 124, 125. *loue : (a ... nobly)*] F₂F₃.

love ? (a...nobly) F₄. *love ? a...nobly;*
Rowe, +, Coll. Dyce. Cam. Sta. Wh.
ii. (subs.) *love ; a...nobly ?* Cap. et cet.

 125. *heare me*] *hear* Pope, Han.

 126. *non-regardance*]   *none-regard-
ance* F₃F₄.

123. **Egyptian theefe**] THEOBALD points out that Shakespeare derived this
reference from the story of *Theagenes and Chariclea* in the *Ethiopica* of Heliodorus,
and gives the following argument : This Egyptian thief was Thyamis, a native of
Memphis, and the head of a band of robbers.   Theagenes and Chariclea falling into
their hands, Thyamis fell desperately in love with Chariclea, and would have married her.   Soon after, a stronger body of robbers coming down upon Thyamis's
party, he was in such fears for his mistress, that he had her shut into a cave with
his treasure.   It was customary with those barbarians, when they despaired of their
own safety, first to make away with those whom they held dear, and desired for
companions in the next life.   Thyamis, therefore, benetted round with his enemies,
raging with love, jealousy, and anger, went to his cave ; and calling aloud in the
Egyptian tongue, so soon as he heard himself answered towards the cave's mouth
by a Grecian, making to the person by the direction of her voice, he caught her by
the hair with his left hand, and (supposing her to be Chariclea) with his right hand
plunged his sword into her breast.—MALONE : There was an English translation
of Heliodorus by Thomas Underdowne.—W. A. WRIGHT : It was licensed to
Francis Coldocke in 1568–9 ; a copy, without date, is in the Bodleian Library.
Another edition appeared in 1587, and Shakespeare may very well have read it, as
it was a popular book.   [W. THEOBALD (*Baconiana*, p. 460, Feb. 1895) dissents
from the opinion that the present reference is to the *Ethiopica*, and asserts that the
allusion is derived from a story, given by Herodotus, ii, 121, of two burglars,
brothers, who were caught in a trap in their attempt to break into the royal treasury,
whereupon, to escape identification, one brother, in Mr Theobald's language, ' removed the head' of the other.   But the learned critic, faithful to the spirit of his
Society, has so nebulous an idea of what he attacks that he confounds the characters,
and imagines that Theagenes is the Egyptian robber ; his views, therefore, in the
present instance cannot be distinguished, it is to be feared, from the general conclusions aimed at by his associates of the *Bacon Society*.—ED.]

126. **non-regardance**] We find in *Ven. & Ad.* 521, ' Say, for non-payment
that the debt should double'; in *Wint. Tale*, I, ii, 305 (of this ed.), ' Whereof the
execution did cry out Against the non-performance.'   These two instances together
with the present are the only ones where Shakespeare uses this awkward negative.
—ED.

127. **And that**] ABBOTT (§ 285, p. 195) gives ' that' as here equivalent to *if
that ;* and again in *Wint. Tale*, I, ii, 103, ' and that with vs You did continue
fault.'   In both of these instances, and doubtless in others, it seems to have escaped

That fcrewes me from my true place in your fauour :   128
Liue you the Marble-brefted Tirant ftill.
But this your Minion, whom I know you loue,   130
And whom, by heauen I fweare, I tender deerely,
Him will I teare out of that cruell eye,
Where he fits crowned in his mafters fpight.
Come boy with me, my thoughts are ripe in mifchiefe :
Ile facrifice the Lambe that I do loue,   135
To fpight a Rauens heart within a Doue.
    Uio. And I moft iocund, apt, and willinglie,
To do you reft, a thoufand deaths would dye.
    Ol. Where goes *Cefario ?*
    Vio. After him I loue.   140
More then I loue thefe eyes, more then my life,
More by all mores, then ere I fhall loue wife.
If I do feigne, you witneffes aboue
Punifh my life, for tainting of my loue.
    Ol. Aye me detefted, how am I beguil'd?   145

128. *fauour :*] *favour*, Cap. et seq.
129. *brefted*] *breafted* F₃F₄.
133. *mafters*] F₂F₃. *Mafter* F₄.
135. *loue,*] *love.* Cap. (Corrected in Errata).
136. [Duke going. Theob.
138. [following. Theob.

145. *Aye me detefted,*] *Ay me detefted,* F₄. *Ay me, detefted!* Rowe,+, Var. Ran. Cam. Dyce ii, iii. *Ah me detefted!* Cap. *Ah me! detefted?* Coll. *Aye me, detefted!* Dyce i. *Ah me, detefted!* Var. '85 et cet.

---

notice (it certainly escaped mine, in *The Wint. Tale*) that the *if* is already expressed by *and*, which, in a modern edition, might with advantage be printed *an*.—ED.

128. **screwes**] STEEVENS : So in *Macbeth*, I, vii, 74 : 'But screw your courage to the sticking place.' [See *Wint. Tale*, I, ii, 482 : 'he sweares As he had seen't, or beene an Instrument To vice you to't'; where Staunton appositely refers to the present passage.]

131. **tender**] DYCE (*Gloss.*) : To have consideration for, to look upon with kindness or affection. Thus, 'Tender yourself more dearly,' *Hamlet*, I, iii, 107.

137. **apt, and willinglie**] Many similar instances where, of two adverbs, only the latter has the adverbial termination, are to be found in WALKER (*Crit.* i, 218), ABBOTT (§ 397), and SCHMIDT (*Lex.* 6, p. 1419). W. A. WRIGHT considers 'jocund' in this line as also an adverb; but I rather prefer to regard it as an adjective. 'Apt,' of course, means ready ; just as the Duke says : 'I am most apt t'embrace your offer.'—line 335, below.—ED.

144. **for tainting of my loue**] 'Tainting,' as a verbal noun, is properly followed by ' of.' The full form would be, ' for the tainting of my love.' See 'for the better increasing your folly,' I, v, 76 ; also 'With viewing of the Towne.' III, iii, 47.

145. **detested**] WALKER (*Crit.* ii, 311) : See what precedes. In the writers of that age *detest* is used in the sense which as then it still retained from its original,

*Uio.*Who does beguile you? who does do you wrong?   146
  Ol.   Haſt thou forgot thy ſelfe *?* Is it ſo long?
Call forth the holy Father.
  Du.   Come, away.
  Ol.   Whether my Lord? *Ceſario*, Husband, ſtay.   150
  D*u*.   Husband?
  Ol.   I Husband. Can he that deny?
  D*u*.   Her husband, ſirrah?
  Vio.   No my Lord, not I.
  Ol.   Alas, it is the baſeneſſe of thy feare,   155
That makes thee ſtrangle thy propriety :
Feare not *Ceſario*, take thy fortunes vp,
Be that thou know'ſt thou art, and then thou art   158

---

146. *does*] *do's* F₃F₄.
148. [Exit an Att. Cap.

149. [To Viola. Theob.
150. *Whether*] *Whither* Ff.

---

detestari, being indicative of something spoken, not an affection of the mind ; compare *attest, protest*, which still retain their etymological meaning.   Bacon, *Advancement of Learning*, Bk. ii., speaking of secrecy in matters of government,—' Again, the wisdom of antiquity . . . in the description of torments and pains, next unto the crime of rebellion . . . doth detest the offence of facility.'   So understand *Cym.* II., near the end,—' I'll write against them, Detest them, curse them.'   In *All's Well*, III, v, it means, perhaps, *renounce* (and so in *Twelfth Night*, above),—' 'Tis a hard bondage, to become the wife Of a detesting lord.'   Compare the circumstances. *Ant. & Cleop.* IV, xii, ' Since Cleopatra died, I have liv'd in such dishonour, that the gods Detest my baseness'; *cry out against*.   *Mid. N. D.* III, ii, 462 [where this note is given substantially.—Ed.], ' That I may backe to Athens by day-light, From these that my poore companie detest.'   Sidney, *Arcadia*, Bk. ii, p. 188, l. 33,— ' each bewailing the other, and more dying in the other than in himself ; cursing their own hands for doing, and their breasts for not sooner suffering ; detesting their unfortunately-spent time in having served so ungrateful a tyrant,' etc.   And so understand Milton, *History of England*, Bk. vi, p. 315,—' for though he seems to have had no hand in the death of Ironside, but detested the fact, and bringing the murderers . . . forth, . . . delivered them to deserved punishment,' etc.   An invective against avarice, which occurs in Dubartas, i, v, p. 45, col. 1, is entitled, in a marginal note, ' Detestation of Avarice for her execrable and dangerous effects.' [Walker has undoubtedly suggested a meaning in Shakespeare's use of *detest* whereby force may be added to certain passages.—MURRAY (*N. E. D.*) gives examples, extending from 1533 to Swift, in 1745, of the meaning : ' To curse, calling God to witness ; to express abhorrence of, denounce, execrate,' but quotes none from Shakespeare.—Ed.]

146. **does do**] See III, i, 114 ; or ABBOTT, § 303, p. 215.

156. **propriety**] HALLIWELL : This seems to be here used in the sense of property in one's self, individuality.   ' Strangle thy propriety,' that is, destroy or suppress thy individuality, deny your identity.

As great as that thou fear'ſt.

Enter Prieſt.   160

O welcome Father :

Father, I charge thee by thy reuerence

Heere to vnfold, though lately we intended

To keepe in darkeneſſe, what occaſion now

Reueales before 'tis ripe : what thou doſt know   165

Hath newly paſt, betweene this youth, and me.

   Prieſt. A Contract of eternall bond of loue,   167

---

159. *that*] Om. F₃F₄.

160. Enter...] After line 161, Cap.

161. *Father :*] Father. Rowe. *fa-ther !* Cap.

163-165. *though...ripe :*] (*though...*

ripe) Pope et seq. (except Cam.)

165. *doſt*] doeſt F₂. *do'ſt* F₃F₄.

167. *of eternall*] *and eternal* Mal. conj.(withdrawn). Coll. ii, iii (MS), Dyce ii. iii, Huds.

158, 159. know'st thou art . : . thou fear'st] That is, be my husband, and then thou art socially equal to 'that thou fear'st,' *i. e.* the Duke.

165. ripe :] Of course, the colon here is wrong ; the clause 'though lately we intended . . . before 'tis ripe,' is merely parenthetical.

167. Contract] DOUCE (i, 108) : By this 'Contract' [see IV, iii, 27–29] is meant a *betrothing, affiancing,* or *promise of future marriage,* anciently distinguished by the name of *espousals,* a term which was for a long time confounded with *matrimony,* and at length came exclusively to denote it. The form of betrothing at church, in this country, has not been handed down to us in any of its ancient ecclesiastical service books ; but it is to be remembered that Shakespeare is here making use of foreign materials, and the ceremony is preserved in a few of the French and Italian rituals. The custom of betrothing appears to have been known in ancient times to almost all the civilised nations among whom marriage was considered as a sacred engagement. Our northern ancestors were well acquainted with it. . . . The length of time between espousals and marriage was uncertain, and governed by the convenience of the parties ; it generally extended to a few months. . . . Vincent de Beauvais, a writer of the 13th century, in his *Speculum historiale,* lib. ix, c. 70, has defined *espousals* to be *a contract of future marriage,* made either by a simple promise, by earnest or security given, by a ring, or by an oath. During the same period, and the following centuries, we may trace several other modes of betrothing : I. The interchangement of rings. Thus, in Chaucer's *Troylus and Cryseyde,* Bk. III, st. 189 : 'Soon after this thei spak of sondry thynges As fel to purpose of this aventure ; And pleyynge entrechan*g*eden hire rynges, Of whiche I kan nought tellen no scripture.' When espousals took place at church, rings were also interchanged. . . . In the life of St. Leobard, who is said to have flourished about the year 580, written by Gregory of Tours, he gives a ring, a kiss, and a pair of shoes to his affianced. The ring and shoes were a symbol of securing the lady's hands and feet in the trammels of conjugal obedience ; but the ring of itself was sufficient to confirm the contract. In the *Miracles of the Virgin Mary,* compiled in the twelfth century by a French monk, there is a story of a young man, who, falling in love with an image of the Virgin, inadvertently placed on one of its fingers a ring which he had received of his mistress, accompanying the gift with the most tender language of respect and

Confirm'd by mutuall ioynder of your hands,   168
Attefted by the holy clofe of lippes,
Strengthned by enterchangement of your rings,   170

190. *enterchangement*] *interchangement* Mal. et seq.

affection. A miracle instantly took place, and the ring remained immoveable. The
young man, greatly alarmed for the consequences of his rashness, consulted his
friends, who advised him by all means to devote himself to the service of the
Madonna. His love for his former mistress prevailing over their remonstrances, he
married her; but on the wedding night the newly betrothed lady appeared to
him, and urged her claim with so many dreadful menaces that the poor man felt
himself compelled to abandon his bride, and that very night to retire privately
to a hermitage, where he became a monk for the rest of his life. . . . The giving
of rings was likewise a *pledge of love* in cases where no marriage could possibly happen. In a romance by Raimond Vidal, a Provençal poet of the thirteenth
century, a knight devotes himself to the service of a lady, who promises him a kiss
in a year's time when she shall be married. They ratify the contract by an exchange
of rings. . . . No instance has occurred where rings were interchanged at a marriage.
II. The kiss that was mutually given. III. The joining of hands. IV. The testimony of witnesses. That of the priest alone was generally sufficient, though we
often find many other persons attending the ceremony. The words 'there before
him' and 'he shall conceal it' sufficiently demonstrate that betrothing, and not
marriage, is intended [by Olivia]; in the latter the presence of the priest alone
would not have sufficed. . . . The ceremony, generally speaking, was performed by
the priest demanding of the parties if they had entered into a contract with any
other person, or made a vow of chastity or religion. . . . Then this oath was administered : 'You swear by God and his holy saints herein, and by the saints of Paradise, that you take this woman, whose name is N., to wife within forty days, if holy
church will permit.' The priest then joined their hands, and said, 'And thus you
affiance yourselves'; to which the parties answered, 'Yes, sir.' They then received
a suitable exhortation on the nature and design of marriage and an injunction to
live piously and chastely till that event should take place. They were not permitted,
at least by the church, to reside in the same house, but were nevertheless regarded
as man and wife; this will account for Olivia's calling Cesario 'husband'; and
when she speaks of 'keeping celebration according to her birth,' it alludes to *future
marriage.* This took place in a reasonable time after betrothing, but was seldom
protracted in modern times beyond forty days. . . . The desuetude of espousals in
England seems to have given rise to the action at law for damages in breach of
promise of marriage.

167. **Contract of**] DYCE adopts Malone's withdrawn conjecture, on the ground
that 'the transcriber's or compositor's eye rested on the 'of' which occurs later in
the line. [Dyce, and Walker also, not infrequently offer this explanation. Were it
said that the latter 'of' had been influenced by the impression left in the mind by
the former 'of,' the explanation would be comprehensible, but when the process is
reversed, and that which is not leaves a deeper impression than that which is, then
it is not easy for Dyce to take with him the present—ED.]

168. **ioynder**] ABBOTT (§ 443, p. 325): Perhaps this comes from the French
joindre.—W. A. WRIGHT: The word does not occur again, but Shakespeare has
'rejoindure' in *Tro. & Cress.* IV, iv, 48.

And all the Ceremonie of this compact   171
Seal'd in my function, by my teftimony :
Since when, my watch hath told me, toward my graue
I haue trauail'd but two houres.
    Du.   O thou diffembling Cub : what wilt thou be   175
When time hath fow'd a grizzle on thy cafe ?

174. *trauail'd*] *travell'd* F₃F₄.   176. *on thy cafe*] *upon thee* Ktly conj.
                                            (*N. & Qu.* I, vii, 44).

    171. Ceremonie] STAUNTON (*Note* on *All's Well*, II, iii, 185) : It has never, that we are aware, been noticed that Shakespeare usually pronounces *cere* in *ceremony, ceremonies, ceremonials*, (but not in *ceremonious, ceremoniously,*) as a mono-syllable, like *cere-cloth, cerement*. Thus, in *Mer. Wives*, IV, vi, 'To give our hearts united ceremony.' Again, in *Mid. N. D.*, V, i, 'Not sorting with a nuptial ceremony.' Again, in *Jul. Cæs.* I, i, 'If you do find them deckt with ceremonies,' and, II, ii, 'Cæsar, I never stood on ceremonies.' [This selection of examples is hardly judicious, inasmuch as, in each instance, the word in question comes at the close of the line, where a certain license is always allowed. WALKER, also, noticed this same contraction ; he observes (*Crit.* ii, 73) in connection with the passage now before us : It appears,—although the present passage would not alone be sufficient to prove it, inasmuch as the *y* [Walker refers to the modern spelling] might per-haps be elided, though this elision, perhaps I might add every other (except *th'* and the like), is uncommon in Shakespeare,—that 'ceremony' and 'ceremonious' were pronounced by our ancient poets,—very frequently at least,—*cer' mony* and *cer' monous.* [LETTSOM, in a footnote, says that 'some of the writers quoted by Walker seem to have even pronounced *cermny, cermnous.*' If Shakespeare used this unpleasing pro-nunciation, which I greatly doubt, I should prefer Staunton's *cere* to Walker's *cer*. —ED.]
    171. compact] According to SCHMIDT (*Lex.*) this word has the accent on the last syllable everywhere in Shakespeare, except in *1 Hen. VI :* V, iv, 163 : 'And therefore take this compact of a truce.' W. A. WRIGHT remarks, hereupon, that this would help to shew, if evidence were wanting, that the play is not Shakespeare's.
    172. in my function] W. A. WRIGHT : That is, in the discharge of my office, which seems to have been that of Olivia's private chaplain. See IV, iii, 27.
    176. case] SIR F. MADDEN (*N. & Qu.* Ist, vi, 469), after stating that in a copy of F₁, belonging to Mr Henry Foss, 'cafe' is printed 'cafe,' remarks that this proves 'beyond doubt that the word in question should be *face*, but by transposition of the letters became *cafe*, and was then altered into "case." '—CAMBRIDGE EDITORS : In Capell's copy of F₁ the reading is plainly 'case.' [The reading 'cafe' is equally plain in the F₁ of the present ED.]—HALLIWELL : That is, the skin. 'There are brought also into Scotland out of these ilands great store of sheepes felles, oxe hides, gotes skinnes, and cases of martirnes dried in the sunne.'—Holinshed's *Description of Scotland*, p. 18. The fox's skin was technically termed the *case*. 'And if the Lyons skinne doe faile, Then with the Foxes case assaile.'—Florio's *Second Frutes*, 1591. [It is needless to go afield for authorities. No better exam-ple can be offered than the pun which Shakespeare puts into the mouth of the Shep-herd's son in *Wint. Tale*, IV, iv, 901, where he says to Autolycus : 'though my case be a pittifull one, I hope I shall not be flayd out of it.'—ED.]

Or will not elfe thy craft fo quickely grow,   177
That thine owne trip fhall be thine ouerthrow :
Farewell, and take her, but direƈt thy feete,
Where thou, and I (henceforth) may neuer meet.   180
    Vio. My Lord, I do proteft.
    Ol. O do not fweare,
Hold little faith, though thou haft too much feare.

            Enter Sir Andrew.

    And. For the loue of God a Surgeon, fend one pre-   185
fently to fir *Toby*.
    Ol. What's the matter ?
    And. H'as broke my head a-croffe, and has giuen Sir
Toby a bloody Coxcombe too : for the loue of God your
helpe, I had rather then forty pound I were at homc.   190
    Ol. Who has done this fir *Andrew* ?
    And. The Counts Gentleman, one *Cefario*: we tooke
him for a Coward, but hee's the verie diuell incardinatc.
    Du. My Gentleman *Cefario* ?
    And. Odd's lifelings heere he is : you broke my head   195

178. *ouerthrow :*] *ouerthrow ?* Ff.
  180. *I (henceforth)*] *(I henceforth)* F_3F_4.
  181. *proteft.*] *protest—* Rowe et seq.
  183. *Hold*] *How* Ff, Rowe.
    though] *tho* F_4.
    Scene IV. Pope, +.
  184. *Enter…*] *Enter…with his Head broke.* Rowe.
  185. *Surgeon,*] Ff, Rowe, +. *surgeon !* Dyce, Cam. Sta. *surgeon ;* Cap. et cet.
    fend] *and* F_3F_4, Rowe i. *and send* Rowe ii, +, Var. '73, '78, Ran. Dyce ii, iii.
  188. *H'as*] *He has* Mal. Steev. Var. '21, Knt, Coll. Hal. Wh. Cam. Rlfe.

Has Dyce i. *'Has* Dyce ii, iii.
  188. *a-croffe*] *across* Cap. et seq.
    has] Om. F_3F_4, Rowe, +. *h'as* Cap. *'has* Dyce ii, iii.
  189. *too*] *to* F_2.
  190. *helpe,*] *help !* Coll. Dyce, Cam. *help.* Pope et cet.
    homc] F_1.
  192. *Counts*] *Duke's* Han.
  193. *diuell*] *Divell* F_2. *Devill* F_3. *Devil* F_4.
    incardinatc] F_1. *incarnate* Rowe, Pope, Han.
  195. *Odd's*] Ff, Hal. *'Od's* Dyce, Cam. Rlfe. *Od's* Rowe et cet.
    is :] *is.* Johns. *is !* Dyce, Sta.

---

183. **Hold little faith**] See Abbott (§ 86) for examples where 'a' is omitted ; on p. 62 the present passage is quoted, and Abbott remarks that 'a' is omitted before *little*, where we commonly place it in the sense of *some*.

190. **forty pound**] W. A. Wright : Sir Andrew was willing to spend twenty times as much upon his safety as upon his accomplishments. See II, iii, 23.

193. **incardinatc**] Rowe supposed this to be a blunder of the compositor, instead of Sir Andrew.

195. **Odd's lifelings**] See II, v, 34.

for nothing, and that that I did, I was fet on to do't by fir   196
Toby.

Vio. Why do you fpeake to me, I neuer hurt you :
you drew your fword vpon me without caufe,
But I befpake you faire, and hurt you not.   200

Enter Toby and Clowne.

And. If a bloody coxcombe be a hurt, you haue hurt
me : I thinke you fet nothing by a bloody Coxecombe.
Heere comes fir *Toby* halting, you fhall heare more: but if
he had not beene in drinke, hee would haue tickel'd you   205
other gates then he did.

Du. How now Gentleman? how ift with you ?

To. That's all one, has hurt me, and there's th'end on't: 208

---

198. *me,*] F$_2$F$_4$, Rowe i. *me* F$_3$. *me ?*
Rowe ii et seq.

201. Enter...] Enter Sir Toby, drunk,
led by the Clown (After line 203)
Cap. After line 206, Dyce.

204. *halting,*] *halting :* Wh. Cam.
halting,— Dyce, Sta.

206. *other gates*] Ff. *other-gates*
Rowe, +. *othergates* Cap. et seq.

208. *one,*] *one ;* Cap. et seq.

has] Ff, Dyce i, Cam. *h' as*
Rowe, Cap. Sta. *'has* Dyce ii, iii. *he
has* Pope et cet.

th'end] *an end* F$_3$F$_4$, Rowe, +.

---

200. bespake] The force of this *be-* seems merely to render transitive the intransitive verb, *speak.* Here it means simply to address. MURRAY (*N. E. D. s. v.* 6)
quotes the same phrase from Marlowe, *Edward II :* I, iv, ' My gentle lord, bespeak
these nobles fair.' Of course, in ' I will bespeak our dyet,' III, iii, 45, the word
bears a different meaning.

203. set nothing by] W. A. WRIGHT : That is, do not regard. See *Ecclesiasticus,*
xxvi, 28 : ' Men of understanding that are not set by.'

206. other gates] See II, v, 3.—ABBOTT (§ 25, p. 35) : That is, in another
gate or fashion. [For ' gate,' signifying way, manner, method, see BRADLEY
N. E. D. s. v. *Gate, sb.*², III. NARES quotes, ' When Hudibras, about to enter
Upon an othergates adventure,'—P. I, C. iii, l. 42, and CARR (*Craven Dialect*)
quotes another form of the word, used by Scott : ' I myself must be your Majesty's
Chamberlain and bring you to your apartments in other guise than would be my
desire.'—*Quentin Durward,* iii, p. 3. HALLIWELL gives, as a corruption, a word
' which occurs in a vernacular Cheshire proverb ': ' I have otherguess fish to fry than
snigs (eels) without butter,' but the CENTURY DICTIONARY gives ' otherguess ' in a
quotation from Smollett's *Roderick Random,* and from Charles Reade ; it is still
current, or was current some years ago, among the farmer folk of New England.
—ED.]

208. has hurt] It is possible that there is here an elision both of the *e* in *He,*
and of the *h* in *has ;* just as we find it in line 188, above ; but it is unlikely. Sir
Toby's speech is thick, and plain ' has ' was probably his best utterance. At the
same time, the omission of the nominative is common before *has, is,* etc. See line
302, below ; or ABBOTT, § 400.—ED.

Sot, didſt ſee Dicke Surgeon, ſot?

   Clo. O he's drunke ſir *Toby* an houre agone : his eyes   210
were ſet at eight i'th morning.

   To. Then he's a Rogue, and a paſſy meaſures panyn : I   212

---

209. *didſt*] *did'ſt thou* F₃F₄, Rowe i.

210. *ſir* Toby] *ſir above* F₂F₃. *ſir, above* F₄, Rowe, Pope, Han. *sir Toby, above* Theob. Warb. Johns. Ran.

211. *ſet*] Om. F₃F₄.

212. *Rogue, and a paſſy meaſures panyn :*] Cam. i, Glo. *Rogue after a paſſy meaſures Pavin :* Ff, Rowe. *rogue, and a past-measure Painim.* Pope, +. *rogue, and a past-measure paynim :* Cap. *rogue, and a passy-measure pavin :* Var. '73, '78. *rogue :—and after a passy-measure or a pavin,* Ran. *rogue. After a passy-measure or a pavin* Var. '85,

Steev. Var. '03, '13. *rogue, and a passy-measures pavin :* Mal. Knt, Coll. i, iii, Sing. Dyce, Hal. Ktly, Hunter, Del. Rlfe. Dtn. *rogue, and a passy measures pavin ;* Var. '21, Cam. ii, Cla. Symons. *rogue. After a passy-measures pavin ;* Harness. *rogue, and a passing-measures pavin.* Coll. ii (MS). *rogue and a passy measures paynim ;* Wh. i (*panym* ed. ii), Huds. *rogue, after a passy-measure's pavin ;* Sta. *rogue, and 'a passes measure, paynim !* Daniel. *rogue and a passy-measures pavon.* Kinnear.

---

212. **a passy measures panyn**] STEEVENS : This may mean 'a pavin danced out of tune.' Sir Toby might call the surgeon by this title, because he was drunk 'at a time when he should have been sober,' and in a condition to attend on the wounded knight. This dance is mentioned in Gosson's *Schoole of Abuse*, 1579, among other dances : 'Thinke you that those miracles [the effects of music] coulde bee wrought with playing of Daunces, Dumpes, Pauins, Galiardes, Measures Fancyes, or new streynes?'[p. 26, ed. Arber].—TYRWHITT : Ben Jonson, in *The Alchemist*, calls it a Spanish dance : 'your Spanish pavin the best dance.'[IV, ii, p. 138, ed. Gifford. Ford also thus terms it : 'I have seen an ass and a mule trot the Spanish pavin with better grace,' I, ii, vol. i, p. 121, ed. Dyce, quoted by Steevens] ; but it seems to have come originally from Padua, and should rather be written *pavane*, as a corruption of *paduana*. A dance of that name (*saltatio paduana*) occurs in an old writer, quoted by the annotator on Rabelais, b. v, c. 30. —SIR J. HAWKINS : The *pavan*, from *pavo* a peacock, is a grave and majestic dance. The method of dancing it was anciently by gentlemen dressed in a cap and sword, by those of the long robe in their gowns, by princes in their man- tles, and by ladies in gowns with long trains, the motion whereof in the dance resembled that of a peacock's tail. This dance is supposed to have been invented by the Spaniards, and its figure is given, with the characters for the steps, in the *Orchesographia* of Thoinet Arbeau. Of the *passamezzo* little is to be said, except that it was a favourite air in the days of Queen Elizabeth. Ligon, in his *History of Barbadoes*, mentions a *passamezzo* galliard, which in the year 1647, a Padre in that island played to him on the lute ; the very same, he says, with an air of that kind which in Shakespeare's *Henry IV.* was originally played to Sir John Falstaff and Doll Tearsheet, by Sneak, the musician. This little anecdote Ligon might have by tradition ; but his conclusion, that because it was played in a dramatic representation of *Henry IV.*, it must be as ancient as his time is very idle and injudicious. 'Passy- measure' is, therefore, undoubtedly a corruption of *passamezzo.*—TYRWHITT : With the help of Sir John Hawkins's explanation, I think I now see the meaning of this passage. [With the help of the Second Folio] I should imagine the following regu-

[212. a passy measures panyn]

lation of the whole speech would not be far from the truth: 'After a passy-measure or a pavin, I hate a drunken rogue,' *i. e.* next to a passy-measure or a pavin, etc. It is in character that Sir Toby should express a strong dislike of *serious dances*, such as the *passamezzo* and the *pavan* are described to be.—MALONE: From what has been stated, I think it is manifest that Sir Toby means only by this expression, that the surgeon is a rogue, and a grave solemn coxcomb. [This explanation DYCE (*Gloss.*) adopts.] It is one of Shakespeare's unrivalled excellences, that his characters are always consistent. Even in drunkenness they preserve the traits which distinguished them when sober. Sir Toby, in the first Act of the play, shewed himself well acquainted with the various kinds of the dance.—BOSWELL: It is surely rather ludicrous to see four sober commentators gravely endeavouring to ascertain the correct meaning of what Sir Toby says when he is drunk.—DOUCE: Spanish pavans are mentioned by Brantôme in his *Dames illustres*, who adds that he had seen it danced by Francis I. and his sister, the celebrated Margaret of Navarre, and also by Mary, Queen of Scots. In an old MS collection of lessons for the virginals, there is one called: 'Dr Bull's melancholy pavin.'—KNIGHT: The humour lies in Sir Toby's calling 'Dick surgeon' *by the names* of the solemn dances which he abhors, confounding the two.—COLLIER (ed. i): The pavin, or peacock dance, was a slow heavy movement, such as a drunken man, like 'Dick surgeon,' might be supposed to execute in his intoxication.—IBID. (*Shakespeare Society's Papers*, i, 24): The difficulty here, with all the commentators, is to understand why 'Dick surgeon' is called 'a passy-measures pavin'; having become intoxicated, of course he has *passed* the ordinary *measures* of discretion in his cups; but the word 'pavin' also requires further explanation. I was not aware, until very recently, that there was in Shakespeare's time a well-known dance, called 'the *passing measure* pavin'; and it is to this that Sir Toby alludes. 'Dick surgeon' has *passed* his *measures* in getting drunk, and these words instantly bring 'pavin' to the knight's mind. I have before me a list of thirteen dances in MS of the time with curious descriptions of the figures belonging to them, and the first of these is 'the passinge measure pavyon,' which is thus explained, I do not say how intelligibly to modern professors: '*The passinge measure Pavyon.* 2 singles and a double forward, and 2 singles syde. Reprynce back.' HALLIWELL quotes many of these preceding notes, and adds very many examples where the word pavan or pavin is introduced.—CROFT (*Glossary* to Elyot's *Gouernour, s. v.* 'Pauion'): This dance, more usually spelt *pavane*, was so called from the Latin, 'pavo,' notwithstanding that M. Littré, who suggests that such a derivation would give *pavone* rather than *pavane*, considers the origin uncertain. But as the dance was undoubtedly introduced into France from some other country, either Spain or Italy, in which the peacock is called *pavon* and *pavone* respectively, it requires no very violent assumption to suppose that the name by which the dance was popularly known, was adopted and Gallicised without any attention being paid to the strict rules of etymology. . . . With regard to the origin of the name, even if we reject M. Compan's explanation that the positions occupied by the dancers suggested a comparison with the circle of a peacock's tail when fully extended, yet from the picturesque description of the dance handed down to us by Arbeau, we can form some idea of the magnificent spectacle presented to the eyes of the spectators, and it requires no great effort of the imagination to see in the long trains and flowing robes, and the stately movements of the wearers, a resemblance to a group of peacocks, strutting on a hate a drunken rogue.   213

 Ol. Away with him? Who hath made this hauocke
with them?   215

 And. Ile helpe you ſir *Toby*, becauſe we'll be dreſt together.

 To. Will you helpe an Aſſe-head, and a coxcombe, &   218

---

214. *him?*] *him:* Rowe ii et seq.   '21, Coll. Glo. Cam. Sta. Ktly. *help,—*
(subs.)   Hal. Dyce, Sta.
  218. *helpe an*] *help?—An* Mal. Var.

---

lawn, and exhibiting with conscious pride all the splendour of their natural plumes.
This at any rate seems to be the view taken by the authors of the *Dictionary of the
Spanish Academy*, where we find Pavana defined as 'Especie de danza Española,
que se executa con mucha gravidád, seriedád y mesúra, y en que los movimientos
son mui pausados : por lo que se le dió este nombre con alusion à los movimientos
y ostentacion del Pavo real.' . . . [This present passage from *Twelfth Night*] is by no
means free from obscurity, but in order to render it intelligible, we must adopt the
rule 'res pro personâ,' and take *pavin* for a musician or player of *pavanes.*—R. G.
WHITE adheres in his Second Edition to *paynim*, with the remark that the passage
'seems after all a mere drunken effort to say, with drunken bombast, a passing
measure (that is, egregious) paynim.'—W. A. WRIGHT : It is most likely that *pavin*
is the right reading, and that 'panyn' is a misprint for 'pauyn.' . . . Richardson
quotes from Sidney's *Arcadia*, b. 3,[p. 329, ed. 1598] : 'An with that turning vp his
mustachoes, and marching as if he would begin a pauen, he went toward Zelmane.'
From this it appears that the pavin was danced with a slow and stately step, as is
indicated by the epithet 'passy measures,' a corruption of *passamezzo.* . . . But the
question now arises, if a pavin was a grave and stately dance, and the epithet 'passy
measures' describes the step used in dancing it, what does Sir Toby mean in so
calling the surgeon? It is not necessary always to find meaning in what a drunken
man says, but Malone's interpretation is probably not far wrong. Sir Toby might
also possibly refer to the slow pace of the surgeon in coming to attend him.—
NAYLOR (p. 114) : Morley (*Practical Music*, 1597) instances two particular dances
which were commonly associated together : *Pavans* and *Galliards*, the first of these,
he says, is for 'grave' dancing, having three 'strains,' each containing 8, 12, or 16
semibreves (two beats in a bar), which are each repeated. . . . (P. 134)The only
Pavan mentioned by Shakespeare is the *Passy measures pavin* or Passamĕso, or
Pass e mezzo, which is the earliest form of the word. . . . (P. 135)The Passamezzo
tune has a similar construction [Naylor gives the notes in his Appendix] to the
ordinary pavan, *i. e.* it consists of regular 'strains,' which in their turn contain a
certain *even* number of semibreves or 'bars.' In the case given, the strains consist
of *eight* bars each. This must be borne in mind in Sir Toby's speech. Toby being
only moderately sober, naturally feels indignant at the doctor's indiscretions in the
same kind ; and the Clown's remark about the latter's eyes brings this fantastic comparison into his head. The doctor's eyes were 'set at eight,' and so is a Pavan 'set
at eight.' It is easy to see Sir Toby's musical gifts asserting themselves, confused
recollections reeling across his brain of that old rule in Morley about the right number of semibreves in a strain, 'fewer than *eight* I have not seen in any Pavan.'

a knaue : a thin fac'd knaue, a gull ?

   Ol.   Get him to bed, and let his hurt be look'd too.   220

               Enter Sebaſtian.

   Seb.   I am ſorry Madam I haue hurt your kinſman:

But had it beene the brother of my blood,

I muſt haue done no leſſe with wit and ſafety.

You throw a ſtrange regard vpon me, and by that   225

I do perceiue it hath offended you :

Pardon me (ſweet one) euen for the vowes   227

219. *a knaue :*] *a knave,—* Dyce. [Exe. Clo. To. & And. Rowe.

220. *too*] *to* Ff.   Scene V. Pope, +.

222. *I am*] *I'm* Dyce ii, iii.   *kinſman*] *Uncle* Rowe ii, Pope, Han.

225. [All stand in amaze. Theob. All start. Coll. MS.

225. *You throw*] Sep. line, Walker (*Crit.* iii, 89).

   vpon me, and by that] *on me, by which* Pope, +.   *on me ; by that* Voss, Lettsom, Huds.

225, 226. *by that...you :*] One line, Cap. Var. '78. '85, Ran. Mal. Steev. Var. Hal.

[To me, Naylor's admirable explanation carries instant conviction. It is, of course, assumed that 'panyn' is a misprint for *pavin.*—ED.]

   218. helpe an Asse-head] MALONE : I believe Sir Toby means to apply all these epithets either to the surgeon or Sebastian ; and have pointed the passage accordingly.—STEEVENS : As I cannot help thinking that Sir Toby, out of humour with himself, means to discharge these reproaches on the officious Sir Andrew, who needs the surgeon's *help,* I have left the passage as I found it. [Malone has the right punctuation and a wrong interpretation. Steevens the wrong punctuation and a right interpretation. Sir Toby addresses Sir Andrew, who has just offered to help him, with ' Will *you* help?—an Ass-head,' etc.—ED.]

   219. thin fac'd knaue] W. A. WRIGHT : Like Master Slender in the *Merry Wives* (i, iv, 22), who had 'a little wee face,' and between whom and Sir Andrew there are many points of resemblance. The Bastard Faulconbridge, in *King John* (I, i), makes merry over his brother's thin face.

   219. gull] See III, ii, 69.

   221. Enter Sebastian] Drummond of Hawthornden records the remark of Ben Jonson that ' He had ane intention to have made a play like Plautus Amphitruo, but left it of, for that he could never find two so like others that he could persuade the spectators they were one.'—p. 29, ed. Shakespeare Society.—ED.

   225. You throw] WALKER (*Crit.* iii, 89) arranges these two words in a separate line ; but adds, 'though even this is awkward.'—LETTSOM (Footnote) : Read,— ' You throw a strange regard *on* me ; by that,' etc. *And* is wretchedly flat here ; it probably crept in from the line above. [Lettsom did not know that more than forty years previously VOSS (p. 625) had proposed the same reading. Voss was not, however, always equally happy. On the same page as that just given, his proposal to read *vow,* instead of 'vows,' in line 227, so as to rhyme with 'ago,' makes us pause in wonder over his pronunciation of either word. There can be no harm in printing ' You throw' as a separate line, if an actor could properly indicate it on the stage.—ED.]

We made each other, but fo late ago.   228
   Du.   One face, one voice, one habit, and two perfons,
A naturall Perfpectiue, that is, and is not.   230

---

230. *naturall*] *nat'ral* Pope, +.   230. *Perfpectiue*] *pèrspective* Dyce.

228; **so late ago**] ABBOTT (§ 411, p. 297): This seems to be a combination of
' *so lately* ' and ' *so* short a time *ago.*'

230. **A naturall Perfpectiue**] For the accent ' pérspective,' see ABBOTT's list
(§ 492) of words where the accent is nearer the beginning than with us.   Compare
' Like perspectives which rightly gazed upon Show nothing but confusion, eyed
awry Distinguish forms.' (—*Richard II :* II, ii, 18), where the two following notes
are given : WARBURTON : Amongst *mathematical* recreations, there is one in *optics*,
in which a figure is drawn, wherein all the rules of *perspective* are *inverted :* so that,
if held in the same position with those pictures which are drawn according to the
rules of *perspective*, it can present nothing but confusion : and to be seen in form,
and under a regular appearance, it must be looked upon from a contrary station ;
or, as Shakespeare says, ' eyed awry.' —TOLLET : Dr Plot's *History of Staffordshire,*
p. 391, explains this perspective, or odd kind of ' pictures upon an indented board,
which, if held directly, you only perceive a confused piece of work ; but, if
obliquely, you see the intended person's picture. [Hereupon follows the explanation
of their manufacture, which is of no importance here. On the present passage
Tollet has the following :] This may be explained by a book called *Humane Indus-
try,* 1661, p. 76 : ' It is a pretty art that in a pleated paper and table furrowed or
indented, men make one picture to represent several faces—that being viewed from
one place or standing, did shew the head of a Spaniard, and from another, the head
of an ass.'   ' A picture of a chancellor of France presented to the common beholder
a multitude of little faces ; but if one did look on it through a perspective, there
appeared only the single pourtraicture of the chancellor himself.'   Thus, that which
is, is not, or in a different position appears like another thing.—CAPELL (p. 152) :
' Perspective ' is—reflection ; this last enterer [Sebastian] (says he [the Duke]) is
surely a reflection of the other, an appearance of nature's forming that seems a body
and is none.—JOHNSON : A ' perspective ' seems to be taken for shows exhibited
through a glass with such lights as make the pictures really protuberant. The
Duke therefore says, that nature has here exhibited such a show, where shadows
seem realities ; where that which *is not* appears like that which *is.*—DOUCE : The
several kinds of perspective glasses used in Shakespeare's time, may be found
collected together in Scot's *Discoverie of Witchcraft,* 1584, Bk. xiii, ch. 19. They
cannot be exceeded in number by any modern optician's shop in England. It is to be
observed that a ' perspective ' formerly meant a glass that assisted sight in any way.
—HALLIWELL : Shakespeare probably here means a simple mirror, such as either a
looking-glass, or the natural mirror of water and other substances ; or, perhaps,
a mirror thus made by nature, which really is a reflected substance, but is merely a
shadow, when considered in reference to its being a mirror. [The passage in Scot's
Discovery of Witchcraft referred to by Douce is quite curious enough to reprint :
' But the woonderous devises, and miraculous sights and conceipts made and conteined in glasse, doo farre exceed all other ; whereto the art perspective is verie
necessarie. For it sheweth the illusions of them, whose experiments be seene in
diverse sorts of glasses ; as in the hallowe, the plaine, the embossed, the columnarie,

Seb.   Anthonio: O my deere *Anthonio,*   231
How haue the houres rack'd, and tortur'd me,
Since I haue loſt thee ?

   Ant.   Sebaſlian are you ?

   Seb.   Fear'ſt thou that *Anthonio*?   235

   Ant.   How haue you made diuiſion of your ſelfe,
An apple cleft in two, is not more twin
Then theſe two creatures.   Which is *Sebaſlian*?   238

---

231. Anthonio :] Anthonio, Ff. *An-*   ii. *Feared you* Pope.
tonio! Coll.   236. *your ſelfe,*] *your self?* Rowe ii.
    Anthonio,] Anthonio ! Ff.   237. *apple*] *ample* F_3F_4.
235. *Fear'ſt thou*] *Fear'd thou* Rowe

---

the pyramidate or piked, the turbinall, the bounched, the round, the cornerd, the
inversed, the eversed, the massie, the regular, the irregular, the coloured and cleare
glasses : for you may have glasses so made, as what image or favour soever you
print in your imagination, you shall thinke you see the same therein.   Others are so
framed, as therein one may see what others doo in places far distant ; others,
wherby you shall see men hanging in the aire ; others, whereby you may perceive
men flieng in the aire ; others, wherin you may see one comming, & another going ;
others, where one image shall seeme to be one hundred, etc.   There be glasses also,
wherin one man may see another mans image, and not his owne ; others, to make manie
similitudes ; others, to make none at all.   Others, contrarie to the use of all glasses, make
the right side turne to the right, and the left side to the left ; others, that burne
before and behind ; others, that represent not the images received within them, but
cast them farre off in the aire, appearing like aierie images, and by the collection
of sunne beames, with great force setteth fier (verie farre off) in everie thing that
may be burned.   There be cleare glasses that make great things seeme little, things
farre off to be at hand ; and that which is neere, to be far off ; such things as are
over us, to seeme under us ; and those that are under us, to be above us.   There
are some glasses also, that represent things in diverse colours, & them most gorgeous,
speciallie any white thing.   Finally, the thing most worthie of admiration concerning these glasses, is, that the lesser glass dooth lessen the shape : but how big so
ever it be, it maketh the shape no bigger than it is.   And therfore *Augustine*
thinketh some hidden mysterie to be therein. . . . I thinke not but *Pharaos* magicians
had better experience than I for those and such like devices.   And (as *Pompanacius*
saith) it is most true, that some of these feats have been accounted saints, some
other witches.   And therefore I saie, that the pope maketh rich witches, saints ;
and burneth the poore witches.'—p. 222, ed. 1583 ; p. 258, ed. Nicholson.   It
would have been cruel to have omitted this last gem.   With such an embarrassment of wealth, it is not surprising that the commentators found some difficulty in
furnishing an exact definition of 'perspective,' or of specifying the particular kind
to which the Duke refers ; possibly, it is that 'to make manie similitudes.'   For my
part, it is quite sufficient to assume that by '*natural* perspective' Orsino means that
an effect has been produced by nature which is usually produced by art.—ED.]

   235. **Fear'st thou**] Sebastian misinterprets the expression of astonishment in
Anthonio's face.

Ol. Moſt wonderfull.

Seb. Do I ſtand there ? I neuer had a brother :   240
Nor can there be that Deity in my nature
Of heere, and euery where. I had a ſiſter,
Whom the blinde waues and ſurges haue deuour'd :
Of charity, what kinne are you to me ?
What Countreyman? What name? What Parentage ?   245
    Uio. Of *Meſſaline* : *Sebaſtian* was my Father,
Such a *Sebaſtian* was my brother too :
So went he ſuited to his watery tombe :
If ſpirits can aſſume both forme and ſuite,
You come to fright vs.   250
    Seb. A ſpirit I am indeed,
But am in that dimenſion groſſely clad,
Which from the wombe I did participate.
Were you a woman, as the reſt goes euen,   254

---

241. *that*] *a* Ff, Rowe, Pope, Han.
244. [To Viola. Rowe.
    kinne] *kin* F₃F₄.
245. *Countreyman*] Ff.
246. Meſſaline :] *Metelin ;* Han.

247. *too*] *to* F₂.
248. *watery*] *waťry* Pope, +. *watry*
Cap.
254. *goes*] *goe* F₂. *go* F₃F₄, Rowe,
Pope.

---

242. **heere, and euery where**] ABBOTT (§ 77, p. 56) connects these words by
hyphens, and considers the whole phrase to be used as a noun, meaning ' the divine
attribute of ubiquity.'

243. **blinde**] That is, pitiless ; inasmuch as they could not see the loveliness they
were destroying.

244. **Of charity**] See ABBOTT (§ 169) for other examples of ' of ' used in appeals
to signify *out of*.

245. **What Countreyman**] ABBOTT (§ 423) suggests that such phrases as ' Your
sovereignty of reason,' *Hamlet*, I, iv, 73 ; ' My better part of man,' *Macbeth*, V,
viii, 18, etc., are perhaps illustrated by the present phrase, which stands for ' a man
of what country ?'

248. **So . . . suited**] That is, in such a suit of clothes. So also ' suit ' in the
next line.

252. **dimension**] That is, bodily shape. See I, v, 259.

253. **Which**] The force of the ' in ' in the preceding line extends to this
' Which '; but see ABBOTT (§ 200) for the ' omission of the preposition after some
verbs which can be easily regarded as transitive.'

253. **participate**] SCHMIDT (*Lex.*) : That is, have in common with others.—
DEIGHTON : Not, I think, as Schmidt explains it, but acquired at my birth as a
portion of that which constitutes me, the other portion being my soul. [I prefer
Deighton's explanation.—ED.]

254. **as the rest goes euen**] W. A. WRIGHT : That is, as the rest accords,
agrees. See *Cymb.* I, iv, 47 : ' I was then a young traveller ; rather shunned to go
even with what I heard, than in my every action to be guided by others' experiences.'

I fhould my teares let fall vpon your cheeke,   255
And fay, thrice welcome drowned *Viola.*

    Vio. My father had a moale vpon his brow.

    Seb. And fo had mine.

    Vio. And dide that day when *Viola* from her birth
Had numbred thirteene yeares.   260

    Seb. O that record is liuely in my foule,
He finifhed indeed his mortall acte
That day that made my fifter thirteene yeares.

    Vio. If nothing lets to make vs happie both,
But this my mafculine vfurp'd attyre :   265
Do not embrace me, till each circumftance,
Of place, time, fortune, do co-here and iumpe   267

---

256. *And*] *As* Cap. (In Errata corrected to *And*).
    thrice...Viola.] As a quotation,
Theob.

257. *moale*] *Moat* F$_4$, Rowe i. *mole*
Rowe ii.

257. *brow.*] *brow,*— Dyce, Huds.

259. *dide*] *di'd* Ff.

261. *foule,*] *soul !* Cap.

264. *lets*] *letts* Rowe. *let's* Johns.

265. *attyre :*] *attire,* Cap.

267. *co-here*] *cohere* F$_3$F$_4$.

---

261. **record**] For instances of the shifting of the accent from the first syllable in
the verb to the second syllable in the noun, see WALKER (*Vers.* 133), or ABBOTT
(§ 490). The noun occurs twice in the *Sonnets* with the accent on the first syllable :
'The living record of your memory.'—55, 8 ; 'Of thee, thy record never can be
missed.'—122, 8. In the very next *Sonnet* (123, 11) it is accented on the last :
'For thy records and what we see doth lie.'

264. **lets to make**] That is, prevents. For this meaning of 'let' see Shakespeare *passim.* For the construction of the infinitive, 'to make,' see I, v, 299.

265. **masculine vsurp'd**] WALKER (*Crit.* i, 33) treats this as a compound
epithet, *masculine-usurp'd,* and adds the remark : 'A contorted phrase, perhaps,
but Shakespearian.' The contortion lies, I think, wholly in Walker's hyphen. The
phrase is not compound ; the attire was both masculine and usurped. Men do not
usurp their own clothes. For 'usurp' in the sense of 'counterfeit,' see I, v, 186.
—ED.

267. **co-here**] Malvolio says 'everything adheres together' (III, iv, 81), that is,
each circumstance fits another circumstance, like links in a chain, so that the whole
story hangs together. Here Viola speaks of time and place and fortune as all
cohering ; that is, each one must agree with the other two and form one consistent
story.—ED.

267. **iumpe**] HALLIWELL gives examples, drawn from many sources, of the
use of 'jump' as a verb, meaning to agree ; but a *Concordance* would have furnished as many from Shakespeare. It is used as an adverb in the Qtos of *Hamlet,*
I, v, 65 : 'Thus twice before, and jump at this dead hour.' Again, Iago says :
'My wife must . . . draw the Moor apart And bring him jumpe, where he may Cassio
find.' II, ii, 419.

That I am *Viola*, which to confirme,   268
Ile bring you to a Captaine in this Towne,
Where lye my maiden weeds : by whofe gentle helpe,   270
I was preferu'd to ferue this Noble Count :
All the occurrence of my fortune fince
Hath beene betweene this Lady, and this Lord.
   Seb.   So comes it Lady, you haue beene miftooke :
But Nature to her bias drew in that.   275

268. Viola,] *Viola ;* Rowe.
269. *Captaine*] *captain's* Coll. MS.
Wh. i, Ktly.
270. *maiden weeds*] *maids weeds*
Theob. Warb. Johns. Cap. Var. '73,
'78, Dyce ii, iii, Huds. Coll. iii. *maid-
-weeds* Walker (*Crit.* iii, 90).
271. *preferu'd*] *preferred* Theob.

Han. Ran. Dyce ii, iii, Huds.
271. *Count*] *Duke* Rowe, +.
272, 273. *occurrence ... Hath*] *occur-
ents...Have* Han. Mal. conj.
273. *this Lord*] *his Lord* F_3F_4.
274. [To Oli. Rowe.
275. *drew*] *true* Coll. MS.

270. **Where**] W. A. WRIGHT : 'Where' is here used loosely for 'At whose
house,' or refers immediately to 'town.' [With this explanation, *captain's* of Collier's MS Corrector is needless.]

270. **maiden weeds**] See *Text. Notes* for Theobald's and Walker's correction
of the metre.—STAUNTON : Perhaps the prosody of this line is more effectually
corrected by adding than subtracting a syllable : '*he* by whose gentle help,' etc.
[The grammar may be improved, but it is difficult to see how the prosody is 'more
effectually corrected' by adding a syllable to a line already too long. Shakespeare
constantly uses 'weeds' in the sense of 'garments.' Cordelia says to Kent :
'Be better suited ; These weeds are memories of those worser hours,' etc. The
Prince says to Claudio, in *Much Ado :* 'Come let us hence, and put on other
weeds,' etc.—ED.]

271. **preseru'd**] THEOBALD : I suspect, from the similitude in the two words,
'preserv'd' and 'serve' (a sameness of sound, which Shakespeare would, probably,
have avoided), the copyists, or men at press, committed a slight mistake. When
the Captain and Viola first appear upon the stage, she says to him, 'I'll serve this
Duke, Thou shalt present me,' etc. I, therefore, believe the author wrote : 'I was
preferred to serve,' etc.—WALKER (*Crit.* iii, 90) : Read *preferr'd*, as sound and
sense both require. [Walker finds the opposite mistake of 'prefer' for *preserve* in
1 Hen. VI : III, i, 110.]—STAUNTON : Theobald's emendation is an undeniable
improvement, and is almost verified by the passage which he quotes. [And yet in
the text neither of his First nor of his Second Edition did Staunton adopt it. In
a modernised text I should unhesitatingly adopt *preferr'd*.—ED.]

272. **occurrence**] HANMER'S change to *occurrents* is extremely plausible, but is
checked by the 'Hath' in the next line, which, however, Hanmer did not scruple
to change into *Have*. W. A. WRIGHT calls attention to *Macbeth*, I, vii, 11, where
the Folio has 'ingredience' for *ingredients*.

274. **mistooke**] See ABBOTT (§ 343) for many curtailed forms of past participles,
such as 'mistook' for *mistaken ;* 'wrote' for *written*, etc.

275. **Nature to her bias drew**] A simile taken from the game of bowls, wherein
the term 'bias' may be either an oblique line (which hardly applies here) or the

You would haue bin contra&ted to a Maid,   276
Nor are you therein (by my life) deceiu'd,
You are betroth'd both to a maid and man.

   Du.   Be not amaz'd, right noble is his blood :
If this be fo, as yet the glaffe feemes true,   280
I fhall haue fhare in this moft happy wracke,
Boy, thou haft faide to me a thoufand times,
Thou neuer fhould'ft loue woman like to me.

   Vio.   And all thofe fayings, will I ouer fweare,
And all thofe fwearings keepe as true in foule,   285
As doth that Orbed Continent, the fire,
That feuers day from night.   287

276. *bin*] *been* Ff.
279. *amaz'd,*] *amaz'd :* Pope.
   blood] *bloud* F₃.
281. *wracke,*] *wrack,* F₃F₄. *wreck.*
Rowe.
282. [To Viola. Rowe.
283. *fhould'ft*] *fhoulft* F₂.
284. *fayings,*] *sayings* Rowe.

284. *ouer fweare*] *over-fweare* Ff.
286. *Continent, the fire,*] Ff, Rowe i.
continent the fire, Theob. Warb. Johns.
continent, the fire Coll. Sta. *continent
the fire* Rowe ii et cet.
286, 287. *fire ... feuers*] *fires ... fever*
Sing. Hal. Ktly.

---

lead wherewith the bowls were loaded on one side to give them a thwart action,
which by a player is to be either counteracted or used. ' To draw to a bias' seems
to have been a phrase (and it may be so to this day,—I speak under correction)
which means that the line was true to the direction imparted by the bias. Thus, in
the present passage, Nature obeyed her bias. Sebastian is happy in the thought
that nature prompted Olivia to fall in love with the reflection of himself, as she saw
it in his twin sister, Viola.—ED.

   280. **as yet the glasse seemes true**] ABBOTT (§ 110, p. 78; placing the
phrase in parenthesis, and printing : ' as, yet, the' etc.) : The Duke has called the
appearance of the twins 'a natural perspective that is and is not,' *i. e.* a *glass* that
produces an optical delusion of two persons instead of one. He now says : ' if
they are two, brother and sister (*and indeed*, spite of my incredulity, the perspective
or glass seems to be no delusion), then I shall,' etc. The curious introduction of
the ' wreck' suggests that the *glass* called up the thought of the 'pilot's glass'
(*All's Well*, II, i, 168). [Is the introduction of ' wreck' so 'curious'? Is it not a
natural reference to the wreck suffered by both brother and sister, which in its event
is most happy ? Yet Abbott is certainly correct in his good suggestion of the mental
connection between ' glass' and ' wreck.'—ED.]

   286, 287. **Orbed Continent, the fire, That,** etc.] SINGER : The allusion is to
Genesis, I, 14. This leads us to the correction of *fires* for ' fire,' as required by the
plural ' swearings,' as well as clearness of construction. [' And God said, Let there
be lights in the firmament of the heaven to divide the day from the night; and let
them be for signs, and for seasons, and for days, and for years.'—*Genesis*, I, 14.]
—W. A. WRIGHT : It is doubtful whether by ' orbed continent' is to be understood
the sun itself, which is called ' orbed' from its globular shape (compare ' the orbed
earth,' *Lover's Complaint*, 25), or the vaulted firmament which contains the orbs or

Du.   Giue me thy hand,   288
And let me fee thee in thy womans weedes.

Uio.   The Captaine that did bring me firft on fhore   290
Hath my Maides garments : he vpon fome Action
Is now in durance, at *Maluolio's* fuite,
A Gentleman, and follower of my Ladies.

Ol.   He fhall inlarge him : fetch *Maluolio* hither,
And yet alas, now I remember me,   295
They fay poore Gentleman, he's much diftract.

  Enter Clowne with a Letter, and Fabian.
A moft extracting frenfie of mine owne   298

---

292. *Is*] *s* F₄.
293. *Ladies*] *Lady's* Rowe.
294. *inlarge*] Cap. *enlarge* Ff et cet.
297. Enter...] After line 299, Coll.
      Clowne] the Clowne Ff.
      and Fabian] Om. Cap.

Scene VI. Pope, +.
      298. *extracting*] *exacting* Ff, Rowe,
Sing. Ktly.   *distracting* Han. Coll. ii,
iii (MS), Huds.   *exciting* Cartwright.
engrossing Kinnear.

---

spheres of the celestial bodies, ' the fire,' in this case, being the sun.   It appears to
be commonly assumed that the former view is the correct one ; but as Shakespeare
(*Coriolanus*, I, iv, 39) makes Coriolanus swear ' by the fires of heaven,' that is, the
stars and other heavenly bodies, it seems more natural to take ' fire,' in the present
passage, as metaphorically used for the sun and not the element, fire ; in which case,
' orbed continent' must mean the firmament.   But there is almost as much to be said
in favour of one view as of the other.—DEIGHTON : The objection [to the construction which considers ' the fire' as in apposition to ' that orbed continent'] is merely
that ' keep' would be used transitively in the clause ' And all,' etc., and intransitively in the clause which is compared with it, [*i. e.* ' that orbed continent, the fire,
That severs,' etc., keeps (*i. e.* on in its orbit)].   Compare Marlowe *2 Tamburlaine*,
II, iv, 2 : ' The golden ball of heaven's eternal fire,' which supports this interpretation.   [Inasmuch as Shakespeare almost invariably uses ' continent' in its Latin
sense, I prefer to consider the phrase ' orbed continent, the fire' as meaning ' the
sphere which contains, or keeps, the fire (*i. e.* the sun) that severs,' etc.—ED.]

294. **inlarge**] That is, set him at liberty.   Thus, *Hen. V :* II, ii, 57 : ' We'll yet
enlarge that man, Though Cambridge, Scroop, and Grey . . . Would have him
punish'd.'

295. **I remember me**] W. A. WRIGHT : Thus, in the Prayer-Book Version of
Psalm xxii, 27 : ' All the ends of the world shall remember themselves.'

296. **distract**] See WALKER (*Crit.* ii, 324) for a long list of ' forms of past tenses
and participles, from verbs ending in *t*, and also (though less numerous) in *d*, where
the present remains unaltered'; such as *waft, heat, start*, etc.   See I, i, 31 ; or
ABBOTT, § 342.

298. **extracting**] WARBURTON : That is, a frenzy that drew me away from everything but its own object.—MALONE : Thus, in *The Historie of Hamblet*, 1608, sig.
C, [3 *verso.*—W. A. WRIGHT] : ' To try if men of great account bee extract out of
their wits.'—STEEVENS : William de Wyrcester, speaking of Henry VI., says : ' ita

From my remembrance, clearly banifht his.

How does he fi rah ?   300

*Cl.*Truely Madam, he holds *Belzebub* at the ftaues end as
well as a man in his cafe may do : has heere writ a letter to
you, I fhould haue giuen't you to day morning. But as a
madmans Epiftles are no Gofpels, fo it skilles not much
when they are deliuer'd.   305

 Ol. Open't, and read it.

 Clo. Looke then to be well edified, when the Foole
deliuers the Madman. *By the Lord Madam.*

 Ol. How now, art thou mad ?

 Clo. No Madam, I do but reade madneffe : and your   310

299. *banifht*] *banifh* Ff.
301. *Truely*] *Truly* F₃F₄.
302. *has*] Ff, Wh. i, Dyce i, Cam.
H' as Rowe, +, Cap. Var. Ran. Sta. *'has*
Dyce ii, iii, Wh. ii. *he has* Mal. et cet.
303. *giuen' t*] Ff, Rowe, +, Cap. Var.
Dyce, Sta. Cam. *given it* Mal. et cet.
304. *madmans*] *mad mans* F₃F₄,
Rowe. *mad-man's* Pope.

306. *Open' t*] *Open it* Mal. Steev.
Var. Knt, Coll. Hal.
308. *Madman*] *Madam* F₄.
 [Reads. Rowe. Reads very
loud. Coll. iii.
 Madam.] *Madam,*— Theob. et
seq.
309. *art thou*] *art* Pope, +.
310. *and*] *an* Pope et seq.

quod extractus a mente videbatur.'—RITSON (*Remarks*, p. 67) : 'If dr. Warburton
had considered his explanation a single moment he would undoubtedly have given it
right, *i. e.* a frenzy that *drew* every object but one *out* of my memory.' HUNTER
(i, 411) prefers the reading of the Second Folio, '"A most exacting frenzy," a
frenzy that exacted from me all attention, all my thoughts and time ; far better than
"extracting," which seems to have got in from the "distract" of the line above.'—
R. G. WHITE (ed. i) : In Shakespeare's day 'extracting' was used in a sense similar to that of *distracting*.—LETTSOM (*ap.* Dyce, ed. ii) : [If it be as R. G. White
says] how does it happen that nobody has produced a second instance of it ? why
did Malone and Steevens attempt to defend the old text by two quotations that are
nothing to the purpose ? I infer that they had nothing better to produce. At any
rate it is impossible that Shakespeare could have written 'extracting' in the sense
of *distracting* in this line, when he had written 'distract' in the line above. He
would either have placed *distracting* here, or employed a word in no manner connected with 'distract,' or referring to it. Perhaps 'extracting' is a mere printer's
blunder for *enchanting*. At III, i, 114, we have 'After the last enchantment you
did here.'—The COWDEN-CLARKES : To our minds, there is a playful and bewitch-
ing effect in Olivia's change of the first syllable of the slightly varying word, with,
mayhap, a half-smiling, half-tender emphasis in her tone and a momentary glance
towards her new-trothed husband, as she utters the significant confession. [War-
burton's or Ritson's interpretation seems to be adequate.—ED.]

 302. **has**] See *Text. Notes ;* and line 208, above.

 304. **Epistles are no Gospels**] DEIGHTON : An allusion to the portions of the
epistles and gospels in the sacred canon appointed to be read in the service of the
Church.

Ladyſhip wil! haue it as it ought to bee, you muſt allow   311
Vox.

Ol.   Prethee reade i'thy right wits.

Clo.   So I do Madona : but to reade his right wits, is to
reade thus : therefore, perpend my Princeſſe, and giue   315
eare.

Ol.   Read it you, ſirrah.

Fab. Reads.   By the Lord Madam, you wrong me, and
the world ſhall know it : Though you haue put mee into
darkeneſſe, and giuen your drunken Coſine rule ouer me,   320
yet haue I the benefit of my ſenſes as well as your Ladie-
ſhip.   I haue your owne letter, that induced mee to the
ſemblance I put on ; with the which I doubt not, but to
do my ſelfe much right, or you much ſhame : thinke of
me as you pleaſe.   I leaue my duty a little vnthought of,   325
and ſpeake out of my iniury.   *The madly vs'd Maluolio.*

Ol.   Did he write this *?*

Clo.   I Madame.

Du.   This ſauours not much of diſtraƈtion.

Ol.   See him deliuer'd *Fabian*, bring him hither :   330

---

312. Vox] *oaths* Mason. *folks—* or *volks—* Bulloch.

313. *reade*] *read it* F₃F₄, Rowe,+.

314. *Madona*] *Madonna* Var. '78, Mal. et seq.

317. [To Fabian. Rowe.

320. *Coſine*] *Cozen* F₂F₃. *Coz n* F₄.

Uncle Rowe ii₅+.

321. *the benefit*] *benefit* F₃F₄, Rowe, Pope, Han.

326. madly vs'd] *madly-us'd* Var. '73 et seq. (subs.)

330. [Exit Fabian. Cap.

---

312. **Vox**] HEATH : This word hath absolutely no meaning. Perhaps we should read, ' you must allow *for't* '; that is, you must make the proper allowances for the condition he is in.—CAPELL (i, 152) : The Clown had enter'd upon his reading in a very extravagant manner, and tells his lady who checks him for't, that *voice* and tone must be granted him if she'd have it read right.—RITSON (*Remarks*, p. 68) : That is, you must allow me the full and proper use of my *voice*. She had just checked him for bawling too loud, which he tells her is the right method of reading a madman's letter. [Both Capell and Ritson anticipate Malone's interpretation, albeit to Malone is given the sole credit.]

314. **his right wits**] JOHNSON (*Var.* 1785) : To read his *wits right* is to read thus. To represent his present state of mind, is to read a madman's letter, as I now do, like a madman.

315, 316. **therefore, perpend my Princesse, and giue eare**] WALKER (*Crit.* iii, 138) : Perhaps from a tragedy ; though dramatic scraps seem to be hardly in the Clown's way.

325. **I leaue my duty, etc.**] DEIGHTON : An allusion to the subscription of duty at the end of letters to a superior.

My Lord, ſo pleaſe you, theſe things further thought on,   331
To thinke me as well a ſiſter, as a wife,
One day ſhall crowne th'alliance on't, ſo pleaſe you,
Heere at my houſe, and at my proper coſt.

　　Du.   Madam, I am moſt apt t'embrace your offer :   335
Your Maſter quits you : and for your ſeruice done him,
So much againſt the mettle of your ſex,
So farre beneath your ſoft and tender bree ding,
And ſince you call'd me Maſter, for ſo long :
Heere is my hand, you ſhall from this time bee   340
your Maſters Miſtris.

　　Ol.   A ſiſter, you are ſhe.   342

331–335. Transposed to follow 342,
Gould.

　　333. *th'alliance*] Ff, Rowe, +, Dyce
ii, iii.   *the alliance ;* Coll. ii.   *the
alliance* Cap. et cet.

　　　　on't, ſo] *an't so* Heath, Ran.
Hal.   *and, so* Coll. ii (MS).   *on's, so*
Dyce ii, iii, Huds.

　　335. *t'embrace*] Ff, Rowe, +, Coll.
Wh. i, Dyce ii, iii.   *to embrace* Cap.
et cet.

　　336. [To Viola. Rowe.

　　337. *mettle*] *metal* F₄, Rowe, +, Var.

'73, '78, '85.
　　338. *breeding,*]   *breeding.*   Pope.
breeding ; Theob.

　　339. *long :*] *long,* Pope et seq.

　　341, 342. *Miſtris.   Ol.   A ſiſter, you
are ſhe.*] *mistress, and his sister she.*
Han.

　　342. Om. Var. '85.

　　　　ſiſter,] Ff, Rowe, Pope. *sister,—*
Theob. +. *sister :—* Coll. *sister ?—* Cap.
et cet.

　　　　ſhe] *to me* Gould.

---

　　331. **these things further thought on**] DEIGHTON supposes that there is here
a reference to 'the business about Malvolio.' I think that Olivia refers rather to a
further consideration of all that has just occurred, her betrothal to Sebastian, the
revelation that Viola is Sebastian's sister, the Duke's inchoate betrothal to Viola by
pledging his hand, etc. The purpose of the nominative absolute here is to express
a condition precedent, and is equivalent to ' if in the further .deliberation of these
matters, you think me,' etc.—ED.

　　333. **th'alliance on't**] HEATH (p. 194) : The word ' on't,' in this place, is mere
nonsense. I doubt not the poet wrote : ' an't, so please you.'—JOHNSON : This is
well conjectured ; but ' on't ' may relate to the double character of sister and wife.—
DYCE (ed. ii) : ' On't ' is plainly a mistake for *on's, i. e.* on us, equivalent to *of us.*
[I see no need of change.   Olivia assumes that her own marriage is certain, and,
with commendable haste, wishes to silence the Duke's importunities for ever, by
marrying him to Viola ; she therefore says that if the Duke thinks as well of her for
a sister (which he can be only by marrying Viola) as he thought of her for a wife,
the family alliance (' the alliance on't ') shall be, by a double marriage, crowned on
one and the same day.—ED.]

　　334. **proper**] That is, own.

　　335. **apt**] That is, ready ; as in line 137, above.

　　336. **quits**] That is, releases.

　　337. **mettle**] That is, disposition ; as in III, iv, 271.

Enter Maluolio.   343

Du. Is this the Madman?

Ol. I my Lord, this fame : How now *Maluolio*?   345

Mal. Madam, you haue done me wrong,
Notorious wrong.

Ol. Haue I *Maluolio*? No.

Mal. Lady you haue, pray you perufe that **Letter.**
You muft not now denie it is your hand,   350
Write from it if you can, in hand, or phrafe,
Or fay, tis not your feale, not your inuention :
You can fay none of this.   Well, grant it then,
And tell me in the modeftie of honor,
Why you haue giuen me fuch cleare lights of **fauour,**   355
Bad me come fmiling, and croffe-garter'd **to you,**
To put on yellow ftockings, and to frowne
Vpon fir *Toby*, and the lighter people :
And acting this in an obedient hope,   359

Scene VII. Pope, +.

343. Enter...] Re-enter Fab. with
Malv. Cap.

344, 346. *Is this ... me wrong*] As
two lines, ending *fame ... me wrong*
Cap. Mal. et seq.

344. *Madman*] Mad man F₃F₄.

346, 347. One line, Theob. Warb.

Johns.

349. *haue,*] *have ;* Rowe ii.

352. *feale, not*] F₂F₃, Cap. Knt,
Hal. Dyce, Cam. Rlfe. *feal, nor* F₄,
Rowe et cet.

356. *Bad*] *Bade* Johns.

359. *And acting*] *And, acting* Cap.
hope,] *hope ?* F₄.

---

342. **A sister**] CAPELL (i, 152) : The manner in which Olivia is made to take
cognisance of her mistaken Cesario is both proper and delicate ; intimating that she
would have more than a sister's love for her from remembrance of what had passed :
yet is this beauty sunk in the Oxford copy [*i. e.* Hanmer] by a proceeding as violent
as improper. [See *Text. Note,* 341, 342.]

343. **Enter Maluolio**] COLLIER (ed. ii) : The MS Corrector adds : ' with straw
about him, as from prison.' This has been the practice in modern times, and it
shows how old was the stage-tradition, for the sake of comic effect.—DYCE (*Few
Notes*, p. 77) : I well remember that, when *Twelfth Night* was revived at Edinburgh
many years ago, Terry, who then acted Malvolio (and acted it much better than any
one I have since seen in the part), had ' straw about him,' on his release from durance.
[In a footnote, Dyce adds :] That revival is immortalised by Sir Walter Scott :
' Flora Mac-Ivor bore a most striking resemblance to her brother Fergus ; so much
so, that they might have played Viola and Sebastian with the same exquisite effect
produced by the appearance of Mrs Henry Siddons and her brother [William
Murray] in those characters.'—*Waverley*, i, 317.

345, 346. **How now . . . wrong**] For metre's sake WALKER (*Vers.* 174) would
read ' *Ma' am, you've* (or more properly *y' have*).'

351. **from it**] That is, differently. See I, v, 189.

358. **lighter**] JOHNSON : People of less dignity or importance.

Why haue you fuffer'd me to be imprifon'd,   360
Kept in a darke houfe, vifited by the Prieft,
And made the moft notorious gecke and gull,
That ere inuention plaid on ? Tell me why ?
    Ol.   Alas *Maluolio,* this is not my writing,
Though I confeffe much like the Charracter :   365
But out of queftion, tis *Marias* hand.
And now I do bethinke me, it was fhee
Firft told me thou waft mad ; then cam'ft in fmiling,
And in fuch formes, which heere were prefuppos'd
Vpon thee in the Letter : prethee be content,   370
This practice hath moft fhrewdly paft vpon thee :
But when we know the grounds, and authors of it,
Thou fhalt be both the Plaintiffe and the Iudge   373

---

362. *and gull*] *or gull* Ff, Rowe, Pope, Han.

  363. *ere*] *e' er* Rowe.
    me] *we* Knt (misprint).
    why ?] *why.* Mal. et seq.

368. *then cam'ft in*] *then cam' st thou* Theob. +. *thou cam' st in* Ran. Coll. ii,

iii (MS), Wh. Dyce ii, iii, Huds. *then cam' st thou in* Ktly.

  369. *formes, which*] *forms, as* Ktly conj.

    prefuppos' d] *preimposed* Coll. ii, iii (MS).

---

362. **gecke**] JOHNSON : A fool.—STEEVENS : So, in *Cymbeline,* V, iv, 67 : 'And to become the geck and scorn O'th' other's villainy.'—BRADLEY (*N. E. D.*) : Apparently adopted from Low German *geck,* equivalent to Dutch *gek.* A fool, simpleton ; one who is befooled or derided, a dupe.

368. **then cam'st**] MALONE : That is, then *that thou* cam'st in smiling.— STEEVENS : I believe the lady means only what she has clearly expressed : ' then thou camest in smiling '; not *that* she had been informed of this circumstance by Maria. Maria's account, in short, was justified by the subsequent appearance of Malvolio. ABBOTT (§§ 400, 401) gives examples of the omission of the personal pronouns. ' The inflection of the second person singular allows the nominative to be readily understood, and therefore justifies its omission.' See I, v, 147 ; II, iii, 28, 112.

369. **presuppos'd**] WARBURTON : For *imposed.*—STEEVENS : It rather seems to mean previously pointed out for thy imitation ; or such as it was supposed thou wouldst assume after thou hadst read the letter. The *supposition* was *previous* to *the act.*

370. **Vpon thee**] FLEAY (Ingleby, *The Man,* ii, 83) : Read : ' *Here* in the letter.' ' Upon thee ' has been mistakenly picked up from the next line by the compositor. [For a compositor, while setting up one line, to ' pick up ' two words from the end of a future line is a feat of malicious legerdemain which cannot be too severely reprehended. By this emendation *here* is repeated within four words : ' *here* were presuppos'd *here* in the letter.' Does the context warrant this unusual emphasis ?—ED.]

371. **past vpon thee**] See III, i, 43.

Of thine owne caufe.

   Fab. Good Madam heare me fpeake,   375
And let no quarrell, nor no braule to come,
Taint the condition of this prefent houre,
Which I haue wondred at. In hope it fhall not,
Moft freely I confeffe my felfe, and *Toby*
Set this deuice againft *Maluolio* heere,   380
Vpon fome ftubborne and vncourteous parts
We had conceiu'd againft him. *Maria* writ
The Letter, at fir *Tobyes* great importance,
In recompence whereof, he hath married her :
How with a fportfull malice it was follow'd,   385
May rather plucke on laughter then reuenge,
If that the iniuries be iuftly weigh'd,
That haue on both fides paft.
   Ol. Alas poore Foole, how haue they baffel'd thee *?*   389

---

375. *heare*] *here* F$_2$.

379. *confeffe my felfe*] *confess, my-self* Theob. et seq.

   Toby] *Sir Toby* Theob. Warb. Johns.

382. *againft*] *in* Tyrwhitt, Ran. Dyce

ii, iii, Huds. Wh. ii.

388, 389. *That...Foole*,] One line, Walker.

389. *Foole*] *Fool* F$_4$. *Soul* Coll. ii, iii (MS). *Tool* Anon. ap. Cam.

   thee ?] *thee !* Han.

---

376. **let . . . to come**] ABBOTT (§ 349, p. 250) quotes this line as an illustration of the insertion of 'to' after 'let,' both in the sense of *suffer* and in that of *hinder*. [See I, v, 299.] Here it is in the sense of *suffer*. [It is to be feared that Abbott has here overlooked the construction of 'Taint' in the next line, which would have shown him that 'to come' has no connection whatever with 'let,' but means '*no future* brawl.'—ED.]

380–382. **Set this . . . against him**] ABBOTT (§ 244, p. 165) : We must either explain thus : 'Set this device against Malvolio here (*which device*), Upon some stubborn and discourteous parts, We had conceived against him,' or suppose (more probably), that there is some confusion between 'conceiving enmity' and 'disliking parts.' [The latter supposition is, I think, to be preferred. Dyce and others adopt Tyrwhitt's emendation of 'We had conceived *in* him,' instead of 'against him,' which, as W. A. WRIGHT says, 'no doubt gives an easier sense.'—ED.]

381. **Vpon some stubborne,** etc.] That is, in consequence of some stubborn, etc. Compare, 'When he shal heare she dyed vpon his words.'—*Much Ado,* IV, i, 232.

383. **sir Tobyes**] W. A. WRIGHT : Fabian appears to have invented this to screen Maria.

383. **importance**] STEEVENS : That is, importunacy, importunement.

384. **he hath married her**] W. A. WRIGHT : Though a short time before he was hopelessly drunk, and sent off to bed to get his wounds healed.

387. **If that**] See I, ii, 52.

389. **poore Foole**] There is a long and interesting discussion of this phrase in

Clo. Why fome are borne great, fome atchieue great-   390
neffe, and fome haue greatneffe throwne vpon them.   I
was one fir, in this Enterlude, one fir *Topas* fir, but that's
all one : By the Lotd Foole, I am not mad : but do you remember, Madam, why laugh you at fuch a barren rafcall,
and you fmile not he's gag'd : and thus the whirlegigge   395
of time, brings in his reuenges.

390, 391. *fome ... them*] As a quotation, Theob.

391. *throwne*] *thrust* Theob. +, Coll.
ii (MS).

392. *Enterlude*] *Interlude* Rowe.

393. *By ... mad*] As a quotation,
Theob.

     Lotd] F₁.

393-395. *remember, Madam...gag'd*]

remember, Madam,—'why ... gagg'd.'
Theob. +, Cap. Ran. *remember ? 'Madam,...gagg'd'* Mal. et seq.

395. *and*] *an* Pope et seq.

     whirlegigge] *whirle-gigge* F₂F₃.
whirl-gigg F₄, Rowe, +.   *whirligig*
Cap.

396. *time,*] *time* Rowe.

Lear, V, iii, 306 (of this edition) ; the larger share of it is, of course, taken up
with the application of the phrase to Cordelia ; there is a general agreement that it
is one of endearment, or, as in the present passage, of compassion.   WALKER, in a
chapter (*Crit.* ii, 297) on the 'confusion of *f* and long *s*,' quotes the present passage, as a possible instance of that confusion, with the remark : ' I have sometimes
thought that Olivia would not have called Malvolio by such a disparaging title, under
the actual circumstances, but I much doubt.'   COLLIER'S MS Corrector substituted
soul for 'foole,' and Collier adopted the change, because, as he says, 'Olivia could
never mean to insult Malvolio, but to compassionate him.'—DYCE (ed. ii) : Mr
Collier adopted *soul* in the very face of the following passages of Shakespeare, which
demonstrate that ' poor fool' was neither more nor less than a sort of term of endearment : ' Yea, my lord ; I thank it [my heart], *poor fool*, it keeps on the windy side
of care.'—*Much Ado*, II, i ; ' the *poor* dappled *fools*,' etc.—*As You Like It*, II, i ;
' So many weeks ere the *poor fools* will yean,' etc.—*3 Hen. VI :* II, v ; '*poor* venomous *fool*, Be angry and dispatch.'—*Ant. & Cleop.* V, ii ; ' The *poor fool* prays her
that he may depart,' etc.—*Ven. & Ad.* 578, [and *Lear*, V, iii, 306].

     389. **baffel'd**] MURRAY (*N. E. D.*) : Etymology, and even immediate source,
uncertain.   Cotgrave gives : ' Baffoüé : m. ée : f. Hoodwinked, also, deceiued, also,
besmeared, also, baffled, disgraced, vnworthily handled, iniuriously vsed, reuiled,
reproched.'

     391. **throwne**] DYCE (ed. i) : Qy. is 'thrown' (instead of *thrust*) an oversight
of the author ? or an error of the scribe or printer ?—STAUNTON : We believe it to
be neither one nor the other, but a purposed variation common to Shakespeare in
cases of repetition, possibly from his knowing, by professional experience, the difficulty of quoting with perfect accuracy.—W. A. WRIGHT : It is more likely that
Shakespeare was quite indifferent in the matter, for in *All's Well*, V, iii, 313, where
Helena reads from a written letter, she varies from the same document as given
in III, ii. [See ' her great P's,' II, v, 88.]

     395. **whirlegigge**] HALLIWELL : ' Whyrlegyge, chyldys game.'—*Prompt. Parv.*
[In Shakespeare a ' gig ' is a top.   Holofernes says to Moth : ' Thou disputest like
an infant ; go, whip thy gig.'—*Love's Lab. L.* V, i, 70.]

Mal. Ile be reueng'd on the whole packe of you ?		397
Ol. He hath bene moſt notoriouſly abus'd.
Du. Purſue him, and entreate him to a peace :
He hath not told vs of the Captaine yet,		400
When that is knowne, and golden time conuents
A ſolemne Combination ſhall be made
Of our deere ſoules. Meane time ſweet ſiſter,
We will not part from hence. *Ceſario* come
(For ſo you ſhall be while you are a man:)		405
But when in other habites you are ſeene,
Orſino's Miſtris, and his fancies Queene.		*Exeunt*

Clowne ſings.		408

---

397. *you ?*] *you.* Ff. *you.* [Exit]	Han.
Rowe.				408. ſings] Sings to pipe and tabor.
401. *conuents*] *convenes* Quincy MS.	Coll. MS. Epilogistic Song by the
403. *Meane time*] *In the mean time*	Clown. Hal.

---

397. HAZLITT (p. 264) : If poor Malvolio's treatment is a little hard, poetical justice is done in the uneasiness which Olivia suffers on account of her mistaken attachment to Cesario, as her insensibility to the violence of the Duke's passion is atoned for by the discovery of Viola's concealed love of him.

399. **peace**] BOAS (p. 324) : We scarcely share the Duke's trust that Malvolio may be entreated to a peace. The self-love of natures such as his cannot be humbled by outward defeat. He belongs to the stiff-necked generation, which learns nothing and forgets nothing.

401. **conuents**] STEEVENS : Perhaps we should read, *consents.* To 'convent,' however, is to assemble ; and therefore, the count may mean, when the happy hour *calls us* again *together.*—DOUCE : That is, shall serve, agree, be convenient. [DYCE (*Gloss.*) quotes this definition without dissent.]—HALLIWELL : That is, calls, summons us.—W. A. WRIGHT : There is no evidence for the meaning 'agrees, is suitable,' though the analogy of 'convenient' may have been in Shakespeare's mind. From 'convent,' to summon, the transition is easy to the following passage in Beaumont & Fletcher, *The Knight of Malta,* I, iii, where 'conventing' signifies 'meeting by summons': ''Tis well. Our next occasion of conventing Are these two gentlemen.'

403. **sister**] This line lacks a syllable, unless 'dear' be pronounced *de-ar.* WALKER (*Vers.* 209) thought that possibly 'sister' may have been, in one or two passages, a trisyllable. One of these passages is in *As You Like It,* IV, iii, 91 : 'Like a ripe sister'; another is in the present line. 'Can Shakespeare,' he asks, 'have written *sister-in-law* by anticipation? It is well known that words sometimes drop out at the end of a line in the Folio. Yet this seems harsh.' 'Harsh' is not strong enough.—ED.

407. **fancies**] That is, love ; see I, i, 17.

408. **Clowne sings**] WARBURTON : This wretched stuff not Shakespeare's, but the Players !—CAPELL : Either this song was one then in vogue, which he who per-

[408. Clowne sings.]

sonated the Clown (Mr Kemp, perhaps) might be famous for singing; or else, the
composition of him, the said Clown, and so lug'd into the play, without rime or
reason; or if indeed Shakespeare's writing,—of which it has small appearance,—
a thing idly drop'd from him upon some other occasion, and recommended by the air
it was set to; for to the play it has no relation; nor is it suitable to the person 'tis
given to, who is a wag and no fool, and therefore cannot with any propriety be made
the retailer of so much nonsense as is contain'd in this song. . . . The concluding
stanza is made to epilogize, is intelligible, and something in character, for its connection with those that preceed it is a meer badinage: But what connection there is,
or what propriety, in the burden of the stanza's, it will be hard to discover; unless
we shall be pleas'd to admit, that the sorrows of life, and the troubles which attend
it throughout, are alluded-to in the words of the burden.—FARMER: Here again we
have an old song, scarcely worth correction.—STEEVENS: It is scarce credible that,
after Shakespeare had cleared his stage, he should exhibit his Clown afresh, and with
so poor a recommendation as this song, which is utterly unconnected with the subject
of the preceding comedy. I do not hesitate to call the nonsensical ditty before us,
some buffoon actor's composition, which was accidentally tacked to the prompter's
copy of *Twelfth Night*, having been casually subjoined to it for the diversion, or at
the call, of the lowest order of spectators.—KNIGHT: We hold this song to be the
most philosophical Clown's song upon record: and a treatise might be written upon
its wisdom. It is the history of a life, from the condition of 'a little tiny boy,'
through 'man's estate,' to decaying age,—'when I come unto my bed'; and the
conclusion is, that what is true of the individual is true of the species, and what was
of yesterday was of generations long past away,—for 'A great while ago the world
begun.'—STAUNTON: It is to be regretted, perhaps, that this 'nonsensical ditty,' as
Steevens terms it, has not been long since degraded to the footnotes. It was evidently one of those jigs, with which it was the rude custom of the Clown to gratify
the groundlings upon the conclusion of a play. These absurd compositions, intended
only as a vehicle for buffoonery, were usually improvisations of the singer, tagged to
some popular ballad-burden,—or the first lines of various songs strung together in
ludicrous juxtaposition, at the end of each of which, the performer indulged in
hideous grimace, and a grotesque sort of 'Jump Jim Crow' dance.—R. G. WHITE
(ed. ii): This clown was a singing clown; a functioner on Shakespeare's stage
whose position was as clearly defined as that of the singing chambermaid is on our
own. This song was one of those with which he was in the habit of amusing the
groundlings. It is none of Shakespeare's.—CHAPPELL (p. 225): This song is still
sung on the stage to this tune. It has no other authority than theatrical tradition.—
HALLIWELL: It may be doubted whether it be really the original which was used in
Shakespeare's own time.

When that I was a   lit-tle ti-ny boy, With a heigh   ho! the wind and the rain, A

When that I was and a little tine boy,
  with hey, ho, the winde and the raine: 410
A foolifh thing was but a toy,
  for the raine it raineth euery day.   412

409. and a] *an a* Theob. i. *a* Theob. 409. tine] *tiny* Rowe ii et seq.
ii, Warb. Johns. Var. '73.

409. **When that**] See I, ii, 52.

409. **and a**] ABBOTT (§§ 95, 96) explains this as an emphatic use for *also, even,* and *that too.* It may be so, but I prefer to consider it as a meaningless redundant expression, not uncommon in old ballads, where some syllables are needed to complete the measure. Thus in *The Fair Flower of Northumberland:* 'She's gane down to her father's stable, Oh my dear, and my love that she wan.'—*Child's Ballads,* i, 116.

409. **tine**] SKEAT (*Athenæum*, 21 July, 1900): The word *tiny* has never been satisfactorily explained. I believe I have made three discoveries about it, of which only the last has been hitherto noticed.   1. It was originally never spelt with a final *-y*, but only with a final *-e.*   2. It was originally a substantive.   3. It is seldom (if ever) used in any old writer without the word *little* preceding it. That is, the correct old phrase was 'a little tine,' the word 'tinè' being properly disyllabic, as at present, though it was sometimes actually treated as a monosyllable. It occurs four times in Shakespeare. In each instance it is spelt with a final *e* in the First Folio; but it is used as an adjective. The four references are: [The present passage]; 'any pretty little tine kickshaws,'—*2 Hen. IV:* V, i, 29; 'my little tyne thief,'—*id.* V, iii, 60; 'a little tyne wit,'—*Lear,* III, ii, 274. In the two following instances it is also an adjective: 'Littell tine child' and 'littell tyne child,' in a Coventry pageant printed by Sharp; see note to *Coventry Mysteries,* ed. Halliwell, p. 414. So also in 'a litill tyne egg,'—*Wars of Alexander,* ed. Skeat, l. 507. But the following examples show that it was once a *substantive.* In the first instance the

But when I came to mans eſtate,   413
 with hey ho, &c.
Gainſt Knaues and Theeues men ſhut their gate,   415
 for the raine, &c.

But when I came alas to wiue,
 with hey ho,&c.
By ſwaggering could I neuer thriue,
 for the raine, &c.   420

<hr>

414, 418. hey ho,] hey, ho, Ff.
415. Gainſt] 'Gainſt F₃F₄.
Knaues and Theeues] *knave and*

thief Farmer, Ran. Steev. Huds.
417. alas] *at last* Rowe, Pope.

<hr>

spelling is late and incorrect : 'Thou hast striken the Lord of Learne A litle tinye aboue the knee.'—Percy *Folio MS*, j, 192, l. 272. 'he was constreynd A lytyll tyne abak to make abew retret.'—Lydgate, *Assembly of the Gods*, l. 1063. 'A lytyll tyne his ey castyng hym besyde.'—*The same*, l. 1283. 'Sir, I pray you a lytyll tyne stande backe.'—Skelton, *Garlande of Laurell*, l. 505. 'For when prouender prickt them a little tine.'—Heywood, *Dialogues*, etc., sig. D., *Works*, ed. 1598. Heywood certainly considered it as a monosyllable, for he rhymes it with 'fine' (as quoted in the last edition of Nares) : 'Freendes, I perceyve the ants tale (more false than fine) Makth you your owne shadowes to dread, as it weare, To prosede in war ; but stey a litle tine.'—Heywood, *Spider and Flie*, 1556. This is enough to show that the correct old phrase was 'a little tine,' with the sense 'a little bit'; and that the word *tine* was originally a substantive, as well as originally disyllabic, and should in modern English have been represented by *tinee*, not by *tiny*. For the adjectival use we have the exact parallel in 'a bit bread' or 'a bit paper'; in 'his wee bit ingle' in Burns ; and in 'the bit callant' in Scott. See *N. E. Dict.* under 'Bit,' § 9. As to the suffix *ee*, it is tolerably common, as in *feoffee, guarantee, patentee, committee*, and the rest ; it invariably represents the French pp. masculine suffix *-é*, or the feminine suffix *-ée*. Hence it is certain that *tinee* is a word of French origin. Only one such word is known, viz., the Old French *tinee*, feminine, meaning 'the content of a vessel called a *tine*.' Mistral's *Provençal Dict.* gives *tinado*, translated by 'cuvée'; and it must be remembered that *tinado* is feminine, and represents a late Latin form *tinata*. Properly speaking, a *tine* was a huge vat of vast dimensions, but its size varied almost indefinitely. The nearest English equivalent is 'tubful'; but tubs are of all sizes. Thus Torriano, *Ital. Dict.*, prudently defines *tina* as 'any great tun, stand, wooden vat, tub, tray, or bowl'; so that, after all, it might come down to the size of 'a bowl.' But the very fact that a *tine* was usually a large tub, and a *tinee* was a large tubful, made it necessary, when the size intended was small, to prefix the word *little*. This was safe, because a *little tinee* was necessarily the contents of a small tine, and meant no more than a little quantity or a little bit. It easily became vague, because the substantive *tine* (used once by Chaucer) was little understood.

415. **Knaues and Theeues**] FARMER : This must evidently be, *knave and thief*. When I was a boy, my folly and mischievous actions were little regarded ; but when I came to manhood, men shut their gates against me, as a *knave and a*

But when I came vnto my beds,   421
    with hey ho, &c.
With toſpottes ſtill had drunken heades,
    for the raine, &c.

A great while ago the world begon,   425
    hey ho, &c.
But that's all one, our Play is done,
    and wee'l ſtriue to pleaſe you euery day.   428

FINIS.

421–423. beds ... heades] *bed ... head*
Han. Ran. Steev. Var. Knt, Coll. Wh.
Hal. Dyce, Ktly, Huds.
  422. hey ho] hey, ho F_2F_4. he, ho F_3.
  423. toſpottes] Toſpots Ff. *Toss-
pots* Rowe ii.
    ſtill had] *I had* Han. *still I*

had Coll. ii, iii (MS).
  423. drunken] *broken* Anon. ap.
Cam.
  425. begon] F_2. be-gon F_3 begone
F_4. *begun* Rowe.
  426. hey ho,] with hey, ho, Ff.
  428. [Exit. Rowe.

---

thief.—DYCE (ed. ii) : Farmer required greater precision of language than is to be
looked for in such a composition.

  421. my beds] HALLIWELL: 'It is said among the folkes heere, that if a man
die in his infanſy, hee hath onely broke his fast in this world. If in his youth, hee
hath left us at dinner. That it is bedde time with a man at three score and tenne.'—
Overbury's *New and Choiſe Characters*, 1615. [*Newes from the lower end of the
Table*, ed. 1627.]

  428. wee'l striue to please you euery day.] WEISS (p. 204) : When the play
is over, the Duke plighted to his page, Olivia rightly married to the wrong man, and
the whole romantic ravel of sentiment begins to be attached to the serious conditions
of life, Feste is left alone upon the stage. Then he sings a song which conveys to us
his feeling of the world's impartiality ; all things proceed according to law ; nobody
is humoured ; people must abide the consequences of their actions, 'for the rain it
raineth every day.' A 'little tiny boy' may have his toy ; but a man must guard
against knavery and thieving ; marriage itself cannot be sweetened by swaggering ;
whoso drinks with 'toss-pots' will get a 'drunken head'; it is a very old world,
and began so long ago that no change in its habits can be looked for. The grave
insinuation of this song is touched with the vague, soft bloom of the play. As the
noises of the land come over sea well-tempered to the ears of islanders, so the
world's fierce, implacable roar reaches us in the song, sifted through an air that
hangs full of the Duke's dreams, of Viola's pensive love, of the hours which music
flattered. The note is hardly more presageful than the cricket's stir in the late
silence of a summer. How gracious has Shakespeare been to mankind in this
play ! He could not do otherwise than leave Feste all alone to pronounce its bene-
diction. [It is delightful to find a reader, since Knight, on whom the charm of
this song is not lost.—ED.]

APPENDIX

APPENDIX

THE TEXT

THE excellent state of the TEXT of this play has been noticed in the *Preface* to the present volume. Indeed, its excellence has been so taken for granted that beyond, possibly, the remark that the play is to be found only in the Folio, COLLIER, DYCE, SINGER, STAUNTON, HALLIWELL, HUDSON, W. A. WRIGHT, and DEIGHTON make no reference to it. KNIGHT remarks that, 'with the exception of a few mani-'fest typographical errors, the original copy is remarkably correct.'

DATE OF COMPOSITION

THE discovery of Manningham's *Diary*, announced by COLLIER, in 1831,* dis-proved all dates previously proposed for the *Composition* of the present play. Man-ningham witnessed a performance of *Twelfth Night* on 'Feb. 2, 1601'; inasmuch as the new year then began on the 25th day of March, this February, instead of being the last month of 1601, is, according to our present reckoning, the second month of 1602. This date is the latest limit, therefore, before which this play must have been written. Those who believe that in the list given by Meres all the plays are mentioned which had, at that time, been written by Shakespeare, find in the date of *Wits Commonwealth*, 1598, an earliest limit. This space of four years is again diminished by those who believe that in Maria's comparison of Mal-volio's smiles to 'the new map' (III, ii, 79, 80), a direct allusion is made to a map published in 1599–1600. Hereby the term is narrowed to about three years,—close enough to satisfy all but the most exacting, especially when we remember that two or three other plays must be also therein included.

The subject has been dealt with in a general way in the *Preface* to the present volume. The notes by Editors and Critics, on the question, which have been deemed worthy of preservation, are to be found on the following pages,—all notes written before the discovery of Manningham's *Diary* have been omitted, albeit the dates for which they pleaded will be found in the recapitulation at the close :—

COLLIER (*Hist. of Eng. Dram. Poetry*, 1831, i, 327) : This comedy was indis-putably written before 1602, for in February of that year it was an established play, and so much liked that it was chosen for performance at the Reader's Feast on Can-dlemas day, at the Inn of Court to which the author of this Diary belonged—most likely the Middle Temple, which at that date was famous for its costly entertain-ments. [Here follows, published for the first time, the extract from Manningham's *Diary*, given in the *Preface* to the present volume. Collier read one sentence erron-eously ; instead of 'prescribing his gesture in smiling, his apparaile, etc.,' he read,

---

* *Hist. of Eng. Dram. Poetry*, i, 327. See *Preface* to the present volume.

'prescribing his gestures, inscribing his apparaile, etc.'   Collier then proceeds :] At this date, we may conclude with tolerable safety that *Twelfth Night* had been recently brought out at the Black-friars Theatre, and that its excellence and success had induced the managers of the Reader's Feast to select it for performance, as part of the entertainment on that occasion.   There is no reason to suppose that any of Shakespeare's productions were represented for the first time anywhere but at a theatre.   The *Comedy of Errors*, noticed in the preceding extract, was no doubt also Shakespeare's work mentioned by Meres in 1598, and not the old *History of Error* performed at Hampton Court in 1576–7.

HUNTER (1845, i, 380) agrees with Steevens that there is an allusion to *Twelfth Night* in *Every Man Out of his Humour*, and as Jonson's play was performed in 1599, to this year he assigns the present play, and finds additional evidence in the publication in this year of Harsnet's *Discovery of the fraudulent practices of John Darrel*, etc.   The connection which Hunter detects between Shakespeare and Harsnet is, I think, of the slightest.   The fraudulent practices of John Darrell consisted in driving out by exhortation and prayer several devils which infested the household of Nicholas Starkey or Starchy.   Hunter gives from Harsnet a full account of the proceedings, which is interesting as a report by a layman of a case of hysteria (often called now-a-days 'Spiritualism'; indeed, Starchy's children manifested many of the symptoms presented by a modern 'spiritualist medium').   It is narrated, that when the Bible was brought in 'they shouted in a scoffing manner " Bible-bable, '" Bible-bable," continuing this cry for some time.   This was accompanied by strange 'and supernatural whooping, so loud that the house and ground shook again.' Another account of the affair relates the same circumstance : 'When we called for 'a bible, they fell a laughing at it, and said, " Reach them the bibble-babble, bibble- '"babble."'   It is in the use of this phrase that Hunter finds one of the filaments connecting Harsnet's *Discovery* with *Twelfth Night*.   When Sir Topas is exorcising the spirit from the lunatic Malvolio (IV, ii, 98), he tells him to leave his 'vain bibble- 'babble,' and the recurrence of these words would be striking were not the phrase so common.   Fluellen, in *Henry V*, gives it a Welsh pronunciation : 'pibble-pabble.' The second circumstance pointing to Harsnet is the phrase 'the lady of the Strachy,' which Hunter conjectures was introduced by Shakespeare 'on account of its near 'resemblance to the name of *Starchy*, and as a kind of intimation early in the play 'that the audience might expect something on what was at the time a topic of no 'small public interest.'

W. W. LLOYD (Singer's *Second Edition*, 1856, p. 489) : In the year 1600 the puritanical city magistrates obtained an order from the Privy Council restricting stage performances, which whether enforced or not must have been an interruption and an inconvenience.   It has been thought that some retaliation is apparent in the portrait of the sour mar-mirth Malvolio, who, according to Maria, is 'sometimes a 'sort of a puritan.'   If such were intended it is good humoured and gentle enough, and of a very different tone to the satire of Ben Jonson on the same class, so far as I have had the perseverance to read.

CHAPPELL (1856?, p. 209) : Inasmuch as the tune of 'O mistress mine' is to be found in print in 1599, [see *Note*, II, iii, 42], it proves either that *Twelfth Night* was written in or before that year, or that, in accordance with the then prevailing custom, 'O mistress mine' was an old song, introduced into the play.   [The music, which was not given in the *Commentary* at II, iii, 42, is here copied from Chappell :]

BATHURST (1857, p. 88): *Twelfth Night* is in the perfect, or middle, style of metre [*i. e.* where there is entire boldness and freedom], with rather a leaning to the older unbroken. In one speech, seven lines out of twenty-one have double endings. Except the priest's speech near the end, no passage of enumeration (like that about Dr Pinch, or Hamlet's on grief), no monosyllables at the end, a little continued rhyme; verses somewhat broken, but often not (chiefly at the end of speeches, which in *The Two Gentlemen of Verona, e. g.* they scarcely ever are), but not broken, in general, to much effect. The speeches sometimes consist of, oftener end in, rhymes, very naturally. I must have drowned my book 'Deeper than did ever plummet sound,' if this play had been his last, or *The Winters' Tale* had been written in 1604, as was once believed.

[In 'The Order of Shakspere's Plays,' by F. J. FURNIVALL, *Twelfth Night* is placed in the *Second Period* (? 1595–1601), and in the *Third Group* of 'Sunny- or 'Sweet-time Comedies,' with *Much Ado* and *As You Like It* as companions.—ED.]

—FLEAY (*Shakespeare Manual*, 1876, p. 227): In order to examine into the question of the date of *Twelfth Night*, it is first necessary to consider the structure of the plot. There are two distinct plots in it, as in *Troylus and Cressida* there are three. In Shakespeare's usual practice, where there are two plots, as in *Lear*, they are, even when derived from distinct sources, so interwoven that it is impossible to disentangle one of them and present it separately. But this is not the case in [*Twelfth Night* and *Troylus and Cressida*]. Just as the story of Troylus' love is separable from that of Ajax's pride and Achilles' wrath, so is the story of Viola, the Duke and Olivia, separable from that of Malvolio, Sir Toby and Maria. Wherever this is the case, one of three conclusions must be drawn: either the play has been written at two periods (as I think this is the case here); or by two authors, which is not the case here; or it is an inferior piece of work, which is also not the case here. The characters that belong to what I consider the early part of the play are, the Duke, Sebastian, Antonio, Viola, Olivia, Curio, Valentine, and the Captain. The part of the play in which they enter is I, i, ii, iv, v (part); II, i, ii, iv; III, i (part), iii, iv (part); IV, i (part), iii; V, i. This can be cut out so as to make a play of itself entirely independent of the other characters, which is the infallible sign of priority of composition.

This part of the play is full of the young, fresh, clear poetry of Shakespeare's early time, the time of *The Midsummer Night's Dream*, his first period. The other part is that of the man of the world, the satirist; kindly and good humoured, but still the satirist. All this latter part is added by Shakespeare himself; it is from the same mint as Falstaff and his companions, the same as Pistol and Parolles. For the play of *All's Well that Ends Well* in like manner divides into two parts. ... In both these plays, too, the early part has been revised; and *All's Well* has been nearly rewritten, so that the old play has been broken up, and only pieces of it can be recognised as boulders imbedded in the later strata; in *Twelfth Night*, the stratification has not been disturbed; only the surface has been denuded and scratched a little, and some new material has been deposited here and there.

The first indication I have found of this date is in II, iv, 4, where Viola was evidently intended to be the singer. [Fleay's remarks are given in the Commentary on the line; see also II, iv, 59, for another explanation. No second indication is offered to us, other than the learned critic's personal certainty. He continues:] The character in style is not pronounced enough to fix the date of any portion. I feel certain myself that the prose part is of the same time as *As You Like It* and *Much Ado about Nothing;* and that the verse part is a revision of earlier work done quite at the beginning of the Second Period; but for this I rely rather on the many subtle undefinable links between it and other plays of that date than on such broad facts as we have here room for. ... The part of *Twelfth Night* that contains the Viola story comprehends nearly all the verse part; and as there is none of the Malvolio and Aguecheek part in verse except 17 lines of V, i, 280–323 [these figures are given as they stand in Mr Fleay's text. They must be wrong, but 'metrical tests' are of such airy substance that I dare not meddle, lest the whole fabric fall. —ED.], we may take the rhyme-ratio of the whole play (minus these 17 lines) or 112 : 876 – 17, or 112 : 859, or 1 : 7.5, as that required for our purpose. But it is impossible in those cases where an author has partly rewritten his early sketch, as is clearly the case in these two plays, to ascertain what part of the early work has been *cancelled;* and therefore we must not press the rhyme-ratio too strictly. . . . In the present plays I am quite content to find that the results I arrive at from totally different reasoning are entirely confirmed by the rhyme-test; and on all grounds alike I conclude that the original draft of the story of Viola was made about the date of 1594.—IBID. (*Introd. to Shakespearian Study,* 1877, p. 25): I believe this part of the play [*i. e.* the Viola story] was written in 1595. . . . Duke in this play is synonymous with Count, as it is with Emperor in the *Two Gentlemen of Verona,* and with King in *Love's Labour's Lost.* Shakespeare does not commit this mistake in plays written after 1595.—(P. 114.)If any part of it is of the earlier date, it was revised and rewritten at the later [*i. e.* in 1601].

IBID. (*Life and Work,* etc., 1886, p. 219): The date of *Twelfth Night* lies between Marston's *Malcontent* (1602) (of Malevole, in which play Malvolio is clearly a caricature) and *What You Will* (1602), by the same author. This adoption of the name of his play seems to have induced Shakespeare to replace it by the now universally adopted title. The appellation 'Rudesby' (IV, i, 55) is from Chapman's *Sir Giles Goosecap* (1601). Several minor points have been already noticed under the previous play of *All's Well,* [such as the misprint of ' Violenta' for *Viola* in F$_1$, I, v, 167; the name ' Capilet,' III, iv, 285; and the allusion to the ' Puritans']. In this play, as in that, I believe that the earlier written scenes have been incorporated. It is only in similar cases that we find such contradictions as that between the three months' sojourn of Viola at the Count's court (V, i), and the three days' acquaintance with the Duke in I, iv. In II, iv, there are palpable signs of alteration, and III, i, 151–168, and V, i, 135–154, are surely of early date. [I can see no reason for assigning these passages to an early date except that they recall the impassioned style of *Romeo and Juliet,*—but this impassioned style is here needed, and any author, not to mention Shakespeare, would have instinctively adopted it; they are the two places where the play rises to the height of tragic love, and any language set to a lower key would have been cold and lifeless.—ED.] Moreover, the singular agreement of the plot with the *Comedy of Errors* in the likeness of the twins, and with *The Gentlemen of Verona,* or rather with *Apolonius and Silla,* whence part of that play was derived, point to a likelihood that the first conceptions of these plays were not far apart in time. I think the early portions were written in 1593, like those of the preceding play. For the change from Duke (I, i–iv) to Count in the rest of the play compare *The Gentlemen of Verona.*

HALLIWELL-PHILLIPPS (*Outlines,* etc., 1882, p. 264): This comedy was certainly written not very long before the performance at the Middle Temple, as may be gathered from the use Shakespeare has made of the song: 'Farewell, dear love,' a ballad which had first appeared in the previous year in the *Booke of Ayres* composed by Robert Jones, London, 1601. Jones does not profess to be the author of the words of this song, for he observes,—' If the ditties mislike thee, 'tis my fault that ' was so bold to publish the private contentments of divers gentlemen without their ' consents, though, I hope, not against their wils'; but there is every reason to believe that the ditty referred to in *Twelfth Night* was first published in this work, a collection of new, not of old songs.

CANON AINGER (*Eng. Illust. Maga.,* March, 1884, p. 372): It is easy to be wise after the event [*i. e.* the discovery of Manningham's *Diary.*—ED.], but I think that the soundest criticism of the present day would have dated [*Twelfth Night*] somewhere in the interval between 1600 and 1605. The versification separates it from the earlier of Shakespeare's comedies, and there is no sign in the play of that dominion of the graver mind, that oppression under the riddles of the world and life, that colours so markedly the later comedies of *The Tempest* and *The Winter's Tale.* . . . It had most likely been produced for the first time on Twelfth-night, a few weeks only before its performance at the Middle Temple, and to have owed its title to that circumstance.

To recapitulate :—

THEOBALD	1604
TYRWHITT, STEEVENS, RANN, MALONE (1790), HARNESS	1614
CHALMERS	1613
MALONE (1821)	1607
HUNTER	1599
KNIGHT . . . . either	1600 or 1601
COLLIER . . . . end of 1600, or beginning of 1601
DYCE, DEIGHTON . . . . most probably about 1600
SINGER (ed. ii), R. G. WHITE . . . . . . 1599 or 1600
BATHURST	1602
HALLIWELL . . . . 1599, 1600, or 1601
STAUNTON, HUDSON . . . . . between 1598 and 1602
FLEAY, FURNIVALL, STOKES, ROLFE	1601
W. A. WRIGHT . . . . performed for the first time, probably on Twelfth-night, early in 1601–2
INNES . . . . not earlier than 1601

SOURCE OF THE PLOT

THE earliest writer to give attention to the sources whence Shakespeare derived the plots of his plays is GERARD LANGBAINE, in his *Account of the English Dramatick Poets* (Oxford, 1691), where, in reference to *Twelfth Night*, he remarks, ' I ' know not whence this Play was taken ; but the Resemblance of *Sebastian* to his ' Sister *Viola*, and her change of Habit, occasioning so many mistakes, was doubt-' less first borrowed (not only by *Shakespear*, but all our succeeding Poets) from ' *Plautus*, who has made use of it in several Plays, as *Amphitruo, Mænechmi*,' etc.

In 1753 there appeared, ' *Shakespeare Illustrated : or the Novels and Histories,* ' *on which the Plays of Shakespear are Founded,* etc. By the Author of the Female ' Quixote, [Mrs Charlotte Lennox].' In this work (vol. i, p. 197) an incomplete translation of *The Thirty-sixth Novel* of Bandello is given, and a claim made for it as the source of the plot of *Twelfth Night*. With the ' Observations on the ' Use Shakespear has made ' of this novel we are not here concerned ; they are uniformly to Shakespear's disparagement ; according to Mrs Lennox, there is scarcely an incident which is not treated more skilfully by Bandello than by Shakespear ; she ' wonders ' that the latter ' should borrow so many incidents, and yet task his ' invention to make those incidents unnatural and absurd ' ; and concludes her ' observations ' with the remark that *Twelfth Night* is ' full of such absurdities,' as the devotion of Antonio to Sebastian, 'which might have been avoided had the 'characters as well as the action been the same with the novel.'

The next contributor to the subject is CAPELL, who (vol. i, p. 69) thinks that, to all appearance, the foundation of the serious part of *Twelfth Night* lies in a novel of Belle-Forest (vol. iv, p. 201) entitled : 'Comme vne fille Romaine se vestant en 'page seruist long temps vn sien amy sans estre cogneuē, & depuis l'eust à mary, 'auec autres discours.' 'This novel is itself taken from Bandello, and must be 'accounted the source 'till some English novel appears, built (perhaps) upon that 'French one, but approaching nearer to Shakespeare's comedy.'

With Bandello and Belle-Forest, as the sources of the present plot, the Shake-spearian world was content until COLLIER announced the discovery of a story which so closely resembled *Twelfth Night* that it has been held, ever since, with more or less confidence, to be the material which Shakespeare moulded into his Comedy. The title of the story is *Apolonius and Silla*, and is the second in a collection, whereof the full title is: *Riche his Farewell | to Militarie profession : con | teining verie pleasaunt discourses | fit for a peaceable tyme. | Gathered together for the onely delight of | the courteous Gentlewomen bothe | of England and Irelande, | For whose onely pleasure thei were collected together, | And unto whom thei are directed and dedi-cated | by Barnabe Riche, Gentleman.* | Imprinted at London by Robart Walley, 1581.

The announcement of the discovery of this book was made by Collier in 1820 (*Poetical Decameron*, vol. ii, p. 134), but in literary circles Riche's collection may have been known some years earlier. BOSWELL remarks (*Variorum, 1821*, vol. xi, p. 321) that he found *Apolonius and Silla* 'pointed out [as the source of *Twelfth* 'Night*] in a very modest and respectful letter to [Malone] in the year 1806, by Mr 'Octavius Gilchrist of Stamford.' Collier's *Decameron* is made up of conversations between three friends,—a plan which prohibited the reproduction of the whole novel ; wherefore only those extracts were there given which yielded the closest parallels to Shakespeare's play.

In the *Variorum of 1821*, Boswell reprinted the whole of Riche's story, omitting only a few unimportant paragraphs of introduction. It was again reprinted in *Shakespeare's Library*, 1843 ; and in 1846, Collier reprinted and edited the whole of Riche's book for *The Shakespeare Society*.

From the expression 'Gathered together' in the title, it is to be inferred that Riche was merely the collector of these 'pleasaunt discourses' and not the author. For *Apolonius and Silla*, it has been supposed that he went to Bandello, but I think it is tolerably certain that for this story his authority was Bandello's translator, Belle-Forest, albeit he has changed every name, and represents Olivia (Julina) as a widow. It is certainly possible that SHAKESPEARE had read Riche's *Farewell to a Militarie profession*, but that he used *Apolonius and Silla* in the composition of *Twelfth Night*, I greatly doubt. There is a coarse, unrefined atmosphere through-out Riche's story, whereof there is, of course, not the smallest trace in SHAKE-SPEARE'S comedy.

The reprint which follows is taken from Collier's edition for *The Shakespeare Society*. At times, under the pretence of preaching morality, Riche indulges in unsavory remarks ; these and other coarsenesses have all been omitted, where possi-ble, and I have sedulously avoided all intimation of the omission :—

OF APOLONIUS AND SILLA.

THE ARGUMENT OF THE SECOND HISTORIE.

Apolonius Duke, havyng spent a yeres service in the warres against the Turke, returning homeward with his companie by sea, was driven by force of weather to the Ile of Cypres, where he was well receivcd by Pontus, gouvernour of the same ile, with whom Silla, daughter to Pontus, fell so straungely in love, that after Apolonius was departed to Constantinople, Silla, with one man, followed, and commyng to Constantinople, she served Apolonius in the habite of a manne, and after many prety accidentes falling out, she was knowne to Apolonius, who, in requitall of her love, maried her. [Hereupon follows a page and a half of commonplace moralising on the vagaries of love.]

During the tyme that the famous citie of Constantinople remained in the handes of Christians, emongst many other noble menne that kepte their abidyng in that florishyng citie, there was one whose name was Apolonius, a worthie duke, who beyng but a verie yong man, and even then newe come to his possessions, whiche were verie greate, levied a mightie bande of menne at his owne proper charges, with whom he served againste the Turke duryng the space of one whole yere: in whiche tyme, although it were very shorte, this yong Duke so behaved hym self, as well by prowesse and valiaunce shewed with his owne handes, as otherwise by his wisdome and liberalitie used towardes his souldiors, that all the worlde was filled with the fame of this noble Duke. When he had thus spent one yeares service, he caused his trompet to sounde a retraite, and gatheryng his companie together, and imbarkyng theim selves, he sette saile, holdyng his course towardes Constantinople: but, beeyng uppon the sea, by the extreamitie of a tempest whiche sodainly fell, his fleete was desevered, some one waie, and some another; but he hymself recovered the Isle of Cypres, where he was worthily received by Pontus, duke and gouvernour of the same ile, with whom he lodged while his shippes were newe repairyng.

This Pontus, that was lorde and governour of this famous Ile, was an auncient duke, and had twoo children, a soonne and a daughter: his soonne was named Silvio, of whom hereafter we shall have further occasion to speake; but at this instant he was in the partes of Africa, servyng in the warres.

The daughter her name was Silla, whose beautie was so peerelesse, that she had the soveraintie emongest all other dames, as well for her beautie as for the noblenesse of hir birthe. This Silla, having heard of the worthinesse of Apolonius, this yong Duke, who besides his beautie and good graces had a certaine naturall allurement, that beeyng now in his companie in her father's courte, she was so strangely attached with the love of Apolonius, that there was nothyng might content her but his presence and sweete sight; and although she sawe no maner of hope to attaine to that she moste desired, knowyng Apolonius to be but a geaste, and readie to take the benefite of the next winde, and to departe into a straunge countrey, whereby she was bereved of all possibillitie ever to see hym againe, and therefore strived with herself to leave her fondenesse, but all in vaine; it would not bee, but, like the foule whiche is once limed, the more she striveth, the faster she tieth her self. So Silla was now constrained, perforce her will, to yeeld to love, wherefore, from tyme to tyme, she used so greate familiaritie with hym as her honour might well permitte, and fedde him with suche amourous baites as the modestie of a maide could reasonably afforde; whiche when she perceived did take but small effecte, feelyng herself so muche out raged with the extreamitie of her passion, by the onely countenaunce that she bestowed uppon Apolonius, it might have been well perceiv~d that the verie eyes pleaded unto hym for pitie and remorse. But Apolonius, commyng but lately from out the feelde from the chasyng of his enemies, and his furie not yet throughly desolved, nor purged from his stomacke, gave no regarde to those amourous entisementes, whiche, by reason of his youth, he had not been acquainted with all. But his minde ranne more to heare his pilotes bryng newes of a merie winde to serve his turne to Constantinople, whiche in the ende came very prosperously ; and givyng Duke Pontus hartie thankes for his greate entertaynment, takying his leave of hymself and the Ladie Silla, his daughter, departed with his companie, and with a happie gaale arived at his desired porte. Gentlewomen, accordyng to my promise, I will here, for brevities sake, omit to make repetition of the long and dolorous discourse recorded by Silla for this sodaine departure of her Apolonius, knowyng you to bee as tenderly hearted as Silla her self, whereby you maie the better conjecture the furie of her fever. But Silla, the further that she sawe herself bereved of all hope ever any more to see her beloved Apolonius, so muche the more contagious were her passions, and made the greater speede to execute that she had premeditated in her mynde, which was this. Emongest many servants that did attend uppon her, there was one whose name was Pedro, who had a long tyme waited upon her in her chamber, wherby she was well assured of his fidelitie and trust : to that Pedro therefore she bewraied first the fervencie of her love borne to Apolonius, conjuring hym in the name of the goddes of love herself, and bindyng hym by the duetie that a servante ought to have, that tendereth his mistresse safetie and good likyng, and desiryng hym, with teares tricklyng doune her cheekes, that he would give his consent to aide and assiste her in that she had determined, whiche was for that she was fully resolved to goe to Constantinople, where she might againe take the vewe of her beloved Apolonius, that he, accordyng to the trust she had reposed in hym, would not refuse to give his consent, secretly to convaie her from out her father's courte, accordyng as she should give hym direction, and also to make hym self pertaker of her journey, and to waite upon her till she had seen the ende of her determination.

Pedro, perceivyng with what vehemencie his ladie and mistresse had made request unto hym, albeeit he sawe many perilles and doubtes dependyng in her pretence, notwithstandyng, gave his consent to be at her disposition, promisyng her to further her with his beste advice, and to be readie to obeye whatsoever she would please to commaunde him. The match beyng thus agreed upon, and all thynges prepared in a readinesse for their departure, it happened there was a gallie of Constantinople readie to departe, whiche Pedro understandyng, came to the captaine, desiryng him to have passage for hymself and for a poore maide that was his sister, whiche were bounde to Constantinople uppon certaine urgent affaires : to whiche request the captaine graunted, willyng hym to prepare aborde with all speede, because the winde served him presently to departe.

Pedro now commyng to his mistres, and tellyng her how he had handeled the matter with the captaine, she likyng verie well of the devise, disguisyng herself into verie simple atyre, stole awaie from out her father's court, and came with Pedro, whom now she calleth brother, aboarde the galleye, where all thynges beyng in readinesse, and the winde servyng verie well, thei launched forthe with their oares, and set saile. When thei were at the sea, the captaine of the galleye, takyng the vewe of Silla, perceivyng her singular beautie, he was better pleased in beholdyng

of her face then in takyng the height either of the sunne or starre, and thinkyng
her, by the homelinesse of her apparell, to be but some simple maiden, calling her
into his cabin, he beganne to breake with her, after the sea fashion, desiryng her
to use his owne cabin for her better ease, and duryng the tyme that she remained
at the sea, she should not want a bedde. Silla, not beyng acquainted with any
suche talke, blusshed for shame, but beyng stroke into a greate feare, moste
humbly desired the captaine that for that present he would depart. The captaine
was contented so farre to satisfie her request, and departed out, leavyng her alone
in his cabin.

Silla, beyng alone by her self, drue oute her knife, and, fallyng upon her knees,
desired God to receive her soule, continuyng a long and pitifull reconciliation to
God, in the middest whereof there sodainely fell a wonderfull storme, the terrour
whereof was suche, that there was no man but did thinke the seas would presently
have swallowed them: the billowes so sodainly arose with the rage of the winde,
that thei were all glad to fall to heaving out of water, for otherwise their feeble
gallie had never bin able to have brooked the seas. This storme continued all that
daie and the next night; and thei beeyng driven to put romer before the winde, to
keepe the gallie a hed the billowe, were driven uppon the maine shore, where the
gallie brake all to peeces: there was every man providyng to save his own life;
some gat upon hatches, boordes, and casks, and were driven with the waves to and
fro; but the greatest nomber were drouned, amongst the whiche Pedro was one;
but Silla her self beyng in the caben, as you have heard, tooke holde of a cheste
that was the captaines, the whiche, by the onely providence of God, brought her
safe to the shore, the whiche when she had recovered, not knowyng what was
become of Pedro her manne, she deemed that bothe he and all the rest had been
drouned, for that she sawe no bodie uppon the shore but her self. Wherefore, when
she had a while made greate lamentations, complainyng her mishappes, she beganne
in the ende to comforte herself with the hope that she had to see her Appolonius,
and found suche meanes that she brake open the chest that brought her to lande,
wherin she found good store of coine, and sondrie sutes of apparell that were the
captaines. And now, to prevent a nomber of injuries that might bee proffered to a
woman that was lefte in her case, she determined to leave her owne apparell, and
to sort her self into some of those sutes, that, beyng taken for a man, she might
passe through the countrie in the better safetie: and, as she changed her apparell,
she thought it likewise convenient to change her name; wherefore, not readily hap-
penyng of any other, she called her self Silvio, by the name of her owne brother,
whom you have heard spoken of before.

In this maner she travailed to Constantinople, where she inquired out the palace
of the Duke Apolonius; and thinking herself now to be bothe fitte and able to
plaie the servyngman, she presented herself to the Duke, cravyng his service. The
Duke, verie willyng to give succour unto strangers, perceivyng him to bee a proper
smogue yong man, gave hym entertainment. Silla thought her self now more then
satisfied for all the casualties that had happened unto her in her journey, that she
might at her pleasure take but the vew of the Duke Apolonius, and above the reste
of his servantes was verie diligent and attendaunt uppon hym; the whiche the Duke
percevyng, beganne likewise to growe into good likyng with the diligence of his
man, and therefore made hym one of his chamber: who but Silvio then was moste
neare aboute hym, in helpyng of hym to make hym readie in a mornyng, in the set-
tyng of his ruffes, in the keepyng of his chamber? Silvio pleased his maister so

well, that above all the reste of his servantes aboute hym he had the greatest credite, and the Duke put him moste in trust.

At this verie instaunt there was remainyng in the citie a noble Dame, a widowe [see III, iv, 56, and *Note.*—ED.], whose housebande was but lately deceased, one of the noblest men that were in the partes of Grecia, who left his lady and wife large possessions and greate livinges. This ladies name was called Julina, who, besides the aboundance of her wealth and the greatnesse of her revenues, had likewise the soveraigntie of all the dames of Constantinople for her beautie. To this Ladie Julina Apolonius became an earnest suter; and, accordyng to the maner of woers, besides faire woordes, sorrowfull sighes, and piteous countenaunces, there must bee sendyng of lovyng letters, chaines, bracelettes, brouches, rynges, tablets, gemmes, juels, and presentes, I knowe not what. So my Duke, who in the tyme that he remained in the Ile of Cypres had no skill at all in the arte of love, although it were more then half proffered unto hym, was now become a scholler in love's schoole, and had alreadie learned his first lesson; that is, to speake pitifully, to looke ruthfully, to promise largely, to serve diligently, and to please carefully: now he was learnyng his seconde lesson; that is, to reward liberally, to give bountifully, to present willyngly, and to write lovyngly. Thus Apolonius was so busied in his newe studie, that I warrant you there was no man that could chalenge hym for plaiyng the truant, he followed his profession with so good a will: and who must bee the messenger to carrie the tokens and love letters to the Ladie Julina, but Silvio, his manne: in hym the Duke reposed his onely confidence to goe betweene hym and his ladie.

Now, gentilwomen, doe you thinke there could have been a greater torment devised, wherewith to afflicte the harte of Silla, then her self to bee made the instrumente to woorke her owne mishapp, and to plaie the atturney in a cause that made so muche againste her self? But Silla, altogether desirous to please her maister, cared nothyng at all to offende herself, followed his businesse with so good a will, as if it had been in her owne preferment.

Julina, now havyng many tymes taken the gaze of this yong youth, Silvio, perceivyng hym to bee of suche excellente perfecte grace, was so intangeled with the often sight of this sweete temptation, that she fell into as greate a likyng with the man as the maister was with herself; and on a tyme, Silvio beyng sent from his maister with a message to the Ladie Julina, as he beganne very earnestly to solicit in his maister's behalfe, Julina, interruptyng hym in his tale, saied: Silvio, it is enough that you have saied for your maister; from henceforthe, either speake for your selfe, or saie nothyng at all. Silla, abashed to heare these wordes, began in her minde to accuse the blindnesse of Love, that Julina, neglectyng the good will of so noble a Duke, would preferre her love unto suche a one, as nature it self had denaied to recompense her likyng.

And now, for a tyme leavyng matters dependyng as you have heard, it fell out that the right Silvio indeede (whom you have heard spoken of before, the brother of Silla) was come to his father's courte into the Ile of Cypres; where, understanding that his sister was departed in maner as you have heard, conjectured that the very occasion did proceade of some liking had betwene Pedro her man (that was missyng with her) and herself: but Silvio, who loved his sister as dearly as his owne life, and the rather for that, as she was his naturall sister, bothe by father and mother, so the one of theim was so like the other in countenaunce and favour, that there was no man able to descerne the one from the other by their faces, savyng by their aparell, the one beyng a man, the other a woman.

Silvio, therefore, vowed to his father, not onely to seeke out his sister Silla, but also to revenge the villanie whiche he conceived in Pedro for the carriyng awaie of his sister; and thus departyng, havyng travailed through many cities and tounes, without hearyng any maner of newes of those he wente to seeke for, at the laste he arrived at Constantinople, where as he was walkyrg in an evenyng for his owne recreation, on a pleasaunte greene yarde, without the walles of the citie, he fortuned to meete with the Ladie Julina, who likewise had been abroad to take the aire; and as she sodainly caste her eyes uppon Silvio, thinkyng hym to bee her olde acquaintaunce, by reason thei were so like one another, as you have heard before, saied unto hym, Sir Silvio, if your haste be not the greater, I praie you, let me have a little talke with you, seyng I have so luckely mette you in this place.

Silvio, wonderyng to heare hym self so rightlie named, beyng but a straunger, not of above twoo daies continuance in the citie, verie courteouslie came towardes her, desirous to heare what she would saie.

Julina, commaunding her traine somthyng to stande backe, saied as followeth: Seyng my good will and frendly love hath been the onely cause to make me so prodigall to offer that I see is so lightly rejected, it maketh me to thinke that men bee of this condition, rather to desire those thynges whiche thei can not come by, then to esteeme or value of that whiche bothe largely and liberallie is offered unto theim: but if the liberalitie of my proffer hath made to seme lesse the value of the thing that I ment to present, it is but in your owne conceipt, consideryng how many noble men there hath been here before, and be yet at this present, whiche hath bothe served, sued, and moste humbly intreated, to attaine to that, whiche to you of myself I have freely offred, and I perceive is despised, or at the least verie lightly regarded.

Silvio, wonderyng at these woordes, but more amazed that she could so rightlie call hym by his name, could not tell what to make of her speeches, assuryng hym self that she was deceived and did mistake hym, did thinke, notwithstandyng, it had been a poincte of great simplicite, if he should forsake that whiche Fortune had so favourably proffered unto hym, perceivyng by her traine that she was some ladie of great honour, and vewyng the perfection of her beautie and the excellencie of her grace and countenaunce, did thinke it unpossible that she should be despised, and therefore aunswered thus:

Madame, if before this tyme I have seemed to forgett my self, in neglectyng your courtesie whiche so liberally you have ment unto me, please it you to pardon what is paste, and from this daie forewardes Silvio remaineth readie preste to make suche reasonable amendes as his abilitie may any waies permit, or as it shall please you to commaunde.

Julina, the gladdest woman that might bee to heare these joyfull newes, saied: Then, my Silvio, see you faile not to morrowe at night to suppe with me at my owne house, where I will discourse farther with you what amendes you shall make me: to whiche request Silvio gave his glad consente, and thus thei departed, verie well pleased. And as Julina did thinke the tyme verie long till she had reapte the fruite of her desire, so Silvio he wishte for harvest before corne could growe, thinkyng the tyme as long till he sawe how matters would fall out; but, not knowyng what ladie she might bee, he presently (before Julina was out of sight) demaunded of one that was walkyng by, what she was, and how she was called? who satisfied Silvio in every poincte, and also in what parte of the toune her house did stande, whereby he might enquire it out.

Silvio, thus departing to his lodging, passed the night with verie unquiet sleapes, and the nexte mornyng his mynde ran so muche of his supper, that he never cared neither for his breakfast nor dinner ; and the daie, to his seemyng, passed awaie so slowlie, that he had thought the statelie steedes had been tired that drawe the chariot of the sunne, or els some other Josua had commaunded them againe to stande, and wished that Phaeton had been there with a whippe.

Julina, on the other side, she had thought the clocke setter had plaied the knave, the daie came no faster forewardes : but sixe a clocke beeyng once stroken, recovered comforte to bothe parties ; and Silvio, hastenyng hymself to the pallace of Julina, wherby her he was frendly welcomed, and a sumpteous supper beeyng made readie, furnished with sondrie sortes of delicate dishes, thei satte them doune, passyng the supper tyme with amorous lokes, lovyng countenaunces, and secret glaunces conveighed from the one to the other, whiche did better satisfie them then the feedyng of their daintie dishes.

Supper tyme beeyng thus spent, Julina did thinke it verie unfitly if she should tourne Silvio to goe seeke his lodgyng in an evenyng, desired hym therefore that he would take a bedde in her house for that night ; and, bringyng hym up into a faire chamber that was verie richely furnished, she founde suche meanes, that when all the reste of her household servauntes were a bedde and quiet, she came her self to beare Silvio companie. The mornyng approchyng, Julina tooke her leave, and conveighed her self into her owne chamber ; and when it was faire daie light, Silvio, makyng hym self readie, departed likewise about his affaires in the toune, debatyng with hymself how thynges had happened, beyng well assured that Julina had mistaken him ; and, therefore, for feare of further evilles, determined to come no more there, but tooke his journey towardes other places in the partes of Grecia, to see if he could learne any tidynges of his sister Silla.

The Duke Apolonius, havyng made a long sute and never a whit the nerer of his purpose, came to Julina to crave her direct aunswere, either to accept of hym and of suche conditions as he proffered unto her, or els to give hym his laste farewell.

Julina, as you have heard, had taken an earnest penie of another, whom she had thought had been Silvio, the Duke's man, was at a controversie in her self what she might doe : one while she thought, seyng her her occasion served so fitt, to crave the Duke s good will, for the mariyng of his manne ; then againe, she could not tell what displeasure the Duke would conceive, in that she should seeme to preferre his man before hymself, did thinke it therefore beste to conceale the matter, till she might speake with Silvio, to use his opinion how these matters should be handled : and hereupon resolvyng herself, desiryng the Duke to pardon her speeches, saied as followeth.

Sir Duke, for that from this tyme forwardes I am no longer of myself, havyng given my full power and authoritie over to another, whose wife I now remaine by faithfull vowe and promise : and albeit I knowe the worlde will wonder when thei shall understande the fondnesse of my choice, yet I trust you yourself will nothyng dislike with me, sithe I have ment no other thing then the satisfiyng of myne owne contentation and likyng.

The Duke, hearyng these woordes, aunswered : Madam, I must then content my self, although against my wil, having the lawe in your owne handes to like of whom you liste, and to make choise where it pleaseth you.

Julina, givyng the Duke greate thankes, that would content himself with suche pacience, desired hym likewise to give his free consent, and good will to the partie whom she had chosen to be her housebande.

Naie, surely, madam, (quoth the Duke) I will never give my consent that any other man shall enjoye you then myself; I have made too greate accompt of you, then so lightly to passe you awaie with my good will. But seeyng it lieth not in me to let you, havyng (as you saie) made your owne choise, so from hence forwardes I leave you to your owne likyng, alwaies willyng you well, and thus will take my leave.

The Duke departed towardes his owne house, verie sorrowfull that Julina had thus served hym: but in the meane space that the Duke had remained in the house of Julina, some of his servantes fell into talke and conference with the servantes of Julina; where, debatyng betwene them of the likelihood of the mariage betweene the Duke and the ladie, one of the servantes of Julina saied, that he never sawe his ladie and mistres use so good countenaunce to the Duke hym self, as she had doen to Silvio his manne; and began to report with what familiaritie and courtesie she had received hym, feasted hym, and lodged hym, and that, in his opinion, Silvio was like to speede before the Duke, or any other that were suters.

This tale was quickly brought to the Duke hymself, who, makyng better inquirie in the matter, founde it to be true that was reported; and, better consideryng of the woordes whiche Julina had used towardes hymself, was verie well assured that it could bee no other then his owne manne, that had thrust his nose so farre out of joynte: wherefore, without any further respect, caused hym to be thrust into a dongeon, where he was kept prisoner in a verie pitifull plight.

Poore Silvio, havyng gotte intelligence by some of his fellowes what was the cause that the Duke his maister did beare suche displeasure unto hym, devised all the meanes he could, as well by meditation by his fellowes, as otherwise by petitions and supplications to the Duke, that he would suspende his judgemente till perfecte proofe were had in the matter, and then, if any maner of thyng did fall out againste hym, wherby the Duke had cause to take any greef, he would confesse hym self worthie not onely of imprisonmente, but also of moste vile and shamefull death. With these pititions he daiely plied the Duke, but all in vaine; for the Duke thought he had made so good proofe, that he was throughlie confirmed in his opinion against his man.

But the Ladie Julina, wonderyng what made Silvio that he was so slacke in his visitation, and why he absented hym self so long from her presence, beganne to thinke that all was not well; but in the ende, perceivyng her self to bee with child, fearyng to become quite banckroute of her honour, did thinke it more then tyme to seeke out a father, and made suche secret searche and diligent enquirie, that she learned the truthe how Silvio was kepte in prison by the Duke his maister; and mindyng to finde a present remedie, as well for the love she bare to Silvio, as for the maintenaunce of her credite and estimation, she speedily hasted to the pallace of the Duke, to whom she saied as followeth.

Sir Duke, it maie bee that you will thinke my commyng to your house in this sorte doeth somethyng passe the limites of modestie, the whiche I protest, before God, proceadeth of this desire, that the worlde should knowe how justly I seke meanes to maintaine my honour. But to the ende I seeme not tedious with prolixitie of woordes, nor to use other then direct circumstances, knowe, sir, that the love I beare to my onely beloved Silvio, whom I doe esteeme more then all the jewelles in the worlde, whose personage I regard more then my owne life, is the onely cause of my attempted journey, beseechyng you, that all the whole displeasure, whiche I understand you have conceived against hym, maie be imputed unto my charge, and that it would please you lovingly to deale with him, whom of myself I have chosen, rather for the satisfaction of mine honest likyng, than for the vaine preheminences or honourable dignities looked after by ambicious myndes.

The Duke, having heard this discourse, caused Silvio presently to be sent for, and to be brought before hym, to whom he saied : Had it not been sufficient for thee, when I had reposed myself in thy fidelitie and the trustinesse of thy service, that thou shouldest so traiterously deale with me, but since that tyme hast not spared still to abuse me with so many forgeries and perjured protestations, not onely hatefull unto me, whose simplicitie thou thinkest to bee suche, that by the plotte of thy pleasaunt tongue thou wouldest make me beleeve a manifest untrothe ; but moste habominable bee thy doynges in the presence and sight of God, that hast not spared to blaspheme his holy name by callyng hym to bee a witnesse to maintaine thy leasynges, and so detestably wouldest forsweare thyself in a matter that is so openly knowne.

Poore Silvio, whose innocencie was suche that he might lawfully sweare, seing Julina to be there in place, aunswered thus.

Moste noble Duke, well understandyng your conceived greefe, moste humbly I beseche you paciently to heare my excuse, not mindyng therby to aggravate or heape up youre wrathe and displeasure, protestyng, before God, that there is nothyng in the worlde whiche I regarde so muche, or dooe esteeme so deare, as your good grace and favour ; but desirous that your grace should know my innocencie, and to cleare my self of suche impositions, wherewith I knowe I am wrongfully accused, whiche, as I understande, should be in the practisyng of the Ladie Julina, who standeth here in place, whose acquitaunce for my better discharge now I moste humbly crave, protestyng, before the Almightie God, that neither in thought, worde, nor deede, I have not otherwise used my self then accordyng to the bonde and duetie of a servante, that is bothe willyng and desirous to further his maister's sutes ; which if I have otherwise saied then that is true, you, Madame Julina, who can verie well deside the depthes of all this doubte, I moste humbly beseche you to certifie a trothe, if I have in any thyng missaied, or have other wise spoken then is right and just.

Julina, havyng heard this discourse whiche Silvio had made, perceivyng that he stoode in greate awe of the Duke's displeasure, aunswered thus : Thinke not, my Silvio, that my commyng hither is to accuse you of any misdemeanour towardes your maister, so I dooe not denaie but in all suche imbassages wherein towardes me you have been imployed, you have used the office of a faithfull and trustie messenger, neither am I ashamed to confesse, that the first daie that mine eyes did beholde the singular behaviour, the notable curtesie, and other innumerable giftes wherewith my Silvio is endued, but that beyonde all measure my harte was so inflamed, that impossible it was for me to quenche the fervente love, or extinguishe the least parte of my conceived torment, before I had bewraied the same unto hym, and of my owne motion craved his promised faithe and loialtie of marriage ; and now is the tyme to manifest the same unto the worldle whiche hath been doen before God and betwene ourselves, knowyng that it is not needefull to keepe secret that whiche is neither evill doen nor hurtfull to any persone. Therefore (as I saied before) Silvio is my housbande by plited faithe, whom I hope to obtaine without offence or displeasure of any one, trustyng that there is no manne that will so farre forget hymself as to restraine that whiche God hath left at libertie for every wight, or that will seeke by crueltie to force ladies to marrie, otherwise then accordyng to their owne likyng. Feare not then, my Silvio, to keepe your faith and promise whiche you have made unto me ; and as for the reste, I doubte not thynges will so fall out as you shall have no maner of cause to complaine.

Silvio, amased to heare these woordes, for that Julina by her speeche seemed to confirme that whiche he moste of all desired to bee quite of, saied : Who would have thought that a ladie of so greate honour and reputation would her self bee the embassadour of a thyng so prejuditiall and uncomely for her estate !   What plighted promises be these whiche bee spoken of ? altogether ignoraunt unto me, whiche if it bee otherwise then I have saied, you sacred goddes consume me straight with flash-yng flames of fire.   But what woordes might I use to give credite to the truthe and innocencie of my cause ?   Ah, Madame Julina ! I desire no other testimonie then your owne, I desire no other testimonie then your owne honestie and vertue, think-yng that you will not so muche blemishe the brightnesse of your honour, knowyng that a woman is, or should be, the image of curtesie, continencie, and shamfastnesse, from the whiche so sone as she stoopeth, and leaveth the office of her duetie and modestie, besides the degraduation of her honour, she thrusteth her self into the pitte of perpetuall infamie.   And as I can not thinke you would so farre forgette yourself by the refusall of a noble Duke, to dimme the light of your renowne and glorie, whiche hetherto you have maintained emongest the beste and noblest ladies, by suche a one as I knowe my self to bee, too farre unworthie your degree and callyng, so moste humbly I beseche you to confesse a trothe, whereto tendeth those vowes and promises you speake of, whiche speeches bee so obscure unto mee, as I knowe not for my life how I might understande them.

Julina, somethyng nipped with these speeches, saied : And what is the matter, that now you make so little accompte of your Julina ? that, beeyng my housband in deede, have the face to denaie me, to whom thou art contracted by so many solemne othes ?   What ! arte thou ashamed to have me to thy wife ?   How muche oughtest thou rather to be ashamed to breake thy promised faithe, and to have despised the holie and dreadfull name of God ? but that tyme constraineth me to laye open that whiche shame rather willeth I should dissemble and keepe secret, behold me then here, Silvio, whom thou haste gotten with childe ; who, if thou bee of suche hon-estie, as I trust for all this I shall finde, then the thyng is doen without prejudice, or any hurte to my conscience, consideryng that by the professed faithe thou diddest accoumpte me for thy wife, and I received thee for my spouse and loyall housbande, swearyng by the Almightie God that no other then you have made the conquest and triumphe of my chastitie, whereof I crave no other witnesse then yourself and mine owne conscience.

Silvio, half in a chafe, saied.   What lawe is able to restraine the foolishe indis-cretion of a woman that yeeldeth herself to her owne desires ? what shame is able to bridle or withdrawe her from her mynd and madnesse, or with what snaffell is it possible to holde her backe from the execution of her filthinesse ? but what abhom-ination is this, that a ladie of suche a house should so forget the greatnesse of her estate, the aliaunce whereof she is descended, the nobilitie of her deceased hous-bande, and maketh no conscience to shame and slaunder her self with suche a one as I am, beyng so farre unfit and unseemely for her degree ! but how horrible is it to heare the name of God so defaced, that wee make no more accompt but for the maintenaunce of our mischifes, we feare no whit at all to forsweare his holy name, as though he were not in all his dealinges mooste righteous, true, and juste, and will not onely laie open our leasinges to the worlde, but will likewise punishe the same with mooste sharp and bitter scourges.

Julina, not able to indure hym to proceede any farther in his sermon, was alreadie surprised with a vehement greefe, began bitterly to crie out, utteryng these speeches followyng.

Alas! is it possible that the soveraigne justice of God can abide a mischiefe so greate and cursed? why maie I not now suffer death, rather than the infamie whiche I see to wander before myne eyes? Oh, happie, and more then right happie, had I bin, if inconstant fortune had not devised this treason, where in I am surprised and caught! Am I thus become to be intangled with snares, and in the handes of hym who will openly deprive me of my fame, by makyng me a common fable to al posteritie in tyme to come? Ah, traitour, and discourtious wretche! is this the recompence of the honest and firme amitie which I have borne thee? wherein have I deserved this discourtesie? by loving thee more then thou art able to deserve? Is it I, arrant theefe! is it I, uppon whom thou thinkest to worke thy mischives? doest thou think me no better worth, but that thou maiest prodigally waste my honour at thy pleasure? didest thou dare to adventure uppon me, having thy conscience wounded with so deadly a treason? Ah, unhappie, and, above all other, most unhappie!

Here withall her teares so gushed doune her cheekes, that she was not able to open her mouth to use any farther speeche.

The Duke, who stood by all this while and heard this whole discourse, was wonderfully moved with compassion towardes Julina, knowyng that from her infancie she had ever so honourably used herself, that there was no man able to detect her of any misdemeanour, otherwise then beseemed a ladie of her estate : wherefore, beyng fully resolved that Silvio, his man, had committed this villanie against her, in a greate furie, drawyng his rapier, he saied unto Silvio :

How canst thou, arrant theefe! shewe thy self so cruell and carelesse to suche as doe thee honour? Hast thou so little regard of suche a noble ladie, as humbleth herself to suche a villaine as thou art, who, without any respecte either of her renowne or noble estate, canst be content to seeke the wracke and utter ruine of her honour? But frame thyself to make such satisfaction as she requireth, although I knowe, unworthie wretche, that thou art not able to make her the least parte of amendes, or I sweare by God that thou shalt not escape the death which I will minister to thee with my owne handes, and therefore advise thee well what thou doest.

Silvio, havyng heard this sharpe sentence, fell doune on his knees before the Duke, cravyng for mercie, desiryng that he might be suffered to speake with the Ladie Julina aparte, promising to satisfie her accordyng to her owne contentation.

Well, (quoth the Duke) I take thy worde ; and therewithall I advise thee that thou performe thy promis, or otherwise I protest, before God, I will make thee suche an example to the worlde, that all traitours shall tremble for feare how they doe seeke the dishonouryng of ladies.

But now Julina had conceived so greate greefe againste Silvio, that there was muche a dooe to perswade her to talke with hym ; but remembryng her owne case, desirous to heare what excuse he could make, in the ende she agreed, and beyng brought into a place severally by themselves, Silvio beganne with a piteous voice to saie as followeth.

I knowe not, madame, of whom I might make complaint, whether of you or of my self, or rather of Fortune, whiche hath conducted and brought us both into so greate adversitie. I see that you receive greate wrong, and I am condemned againste all right ; you in perill to abide the brute of spightfull tongues, and I in daunger to loose the thing that I moste desire ; and although I could alledge many reasons to prove my saiynges true, yet I referre my self to the experience and bountie of your minde.   And here with all loosing his garmentes doune to his stomacke, shewed Julina his breastes, saiyng : Loe, Madame ! behold here the partie whom you have chalenged to bee the father of your childe.   See, I am a woman, the daughter of a noble Duke, who, onely for the love of him whom you so lightly have shaken off have forsaken my father, abandoned my countreie, and, in maner as you see, an become a servyng-man, satisfiyng myself but with the onely sight of my Apolonius. And now, Madame, if my passion were not vehement, and my tormentes without comparison, I would wish that my fained greefes might be laughed to scorne, and my desembled paines to be rewarded with floutes : but my love beyng pure, my travaile continuall, and my greefes endlesse, I trust, madame, you will not onely excuse me of crime, but also pitie my distresse, the which, I protest, I would still have kept secrete, if my fortune would so have permitted.

Julina did now thinke her self to be in a worse case then ever she was before, for now she knewe not whom to chalenge to be the father of her child ; wherfore, when she had told the Duke the very certaintie of the discourse which Silvio had made unto her, she departed to her owne house, with suche greefe and sorrowe, that she purposed never to come out of her owne doores againe alive, to be a wonder and mocking stocke to the worlde.

But the Duke, more amased to heare this straunge discourse of Silvio, came unto him, whom when he had vewed with better consideration, perceived indeede that it was Silla, the daughter of Duke Pontus, and imbracing her in his armes, he saied.

Oh, the braunche of all vertue, and the flowre of curtesie it self ! pardon me, I beseche you, of all suche discourtesies as I have ignorantlie committed towardes you, desiring you that without farther memorie of auncient greefes, you will accept of me, who is more joyfull and better contented with your presence, then if the whole worlde were at my commaundement.   Where hath there ever been founde suche liberalitie in a lover, whiche havyng been trained up and nourished emongest the delicacies and banquettes of the courte, accompanied with traines of many faire and noble ladies, living in pleasure and in the middest of delightes, would so prod- igallie adventure your self, neither fearing mishapps, nor misliking to take suche paines as I knowe you have not been accustomed unto ?   O, liberalitie never heard of before !   O, facte that can never bee sufficiently rewarded !   O, true love moste pure and unfained !   Here with all sendyng for the moste artificiall woorkmen, he provided for her sondrie sutes of sumpteous apparell, and the marriage daie appoincted, whiche was celebrated with great triumphe through the whole citie of Constantinople, every one prasing the noblenesse of the Duke ; but so many as did behold the excellent beautie of Silla gave her the praise above all the rest of the ladies in the troupe.

The matter seemed so wonderfull and straunge, that the brute was spreade throughout all the partes of Grecia, in so muche that it came to the hearyng of Silvio ; who, as you have heard, remained in those partes to enquire of his sister : he beyng the gladdest manne in the worlde, hasted to Constantinople, where, com- ming to his sister, he was joyfullie receved, and moste lovynglie welcomed, and entertained of the Duke his brother in lawe.   After he had remained there twoo or three daies, the Duke revealed unto Silvio the whole discourse how it happened betweene his sister and the Ladie Julina, and how his sister was chalenged for get-tyng a woman with childe.   Silvio, blushyng with these woordes, was striken with greate remorse to make Julina amendes, understanding her to bee a noble ladie, and was lefte defamed to the worlde through his default : he therefore bewraied the whole circumstaunce to the Duke, whereof the Duke beyng verie joyfull, immediatelie repaired with Silvio to the house of Julina, whom thei founde in her chamber in greate lamentation and mournyng.   To whom the Duke saied : Take courage, madam, for beholde here a gentilman that will not sticke bothe to father your child and to take you for his wife ; no inferiour persone, but the sonne and heire of a noble Duke, worthie of your estate and dignitie.

Julina, seyng Silvio in place, did know very well that he was the father of her childe, and was so ravished with joye, that she knewe not whether she were awake, or in some dreame.   Silvio, imbracyng her in his armes, cravyng forgivenesse of all that was past, concluded with her the marriage daie, which was presently accomplished with greate joye and contentation to all parties.   And thus, Silvio havyng attained a noble wife, and Silla, his sister, her desired housband, thei passed the residue of their daies with suche delight as those that have accomplished the perfection of their felicities.

In Manningham's Diary it is stated that *Twelfth Night* is 'most like and neere 'to that in Italian called *Inganni*.'   HUNTER (i, 391) found that there are two Italian comedies, bearing that title, by two separate authors, one of whom was Nicolo Secchi, whose play was printed at Florence in 1562, and the other was Curzio Gonzaga, whose *Inganni* was printed at Venice in 1592.   There is a third, but of a date later than *Twelfth Night ;* it needs, therefore, no attention.

Gonzaga's play I have not seen, but from Hunter's brief description it cannot vary greatly from Secchi's.   'In both,' says Hunter, there is ' a brother and a sister, ' the latter clothed in man's attire, and bearing to each other so near a resemblance ' as to produce entertaining embarrassments, which is the pivot on which the main ' incidents of the serious part of *Twelfth Night* turn.   The name assumed by the ' lady in disguise in Gonzaga's play is *Cesare*, which will be easily admitted to have ' suggested the name *Cesario* in Shakespeare.   Beyond this, however, the resem- ' blance is not striking.'

HUNTER gives the date of the first edition of Secchi's *Inganni* as 1562.   The title-page, however, refers to an earlier date as that of its performance.   My copy bears the date 1582 ; I suppose that there was no change in the editions of different years, beyond the corrections of old typographical errors and the addition of new ones, albeit on the title-page they were always said to be corrected *con summa diligenza*.   The title-page of the copy now before me is as follows :—GL' INGANNI | COMEDIA | DEL SIGNOR N. S. | Recitata in Milano l'anno 1547. dinanzi | alla Maestà del Re Filippo. | *Nvovamente Ristampata,* | *& con summa diligenza corretta.* | In Venetia, | Appresso Bernardo Giunti, e Fratelli. MDLXXXII.

The *Prologue* is as follows :—

GL' INGANNI, OR DECEITS

' Anselmo, a Genoese merchant, who traded to the Levant, left his wife in Genoa with his two children, one a boy called Fortunato and a girl named Genevra.   After he had endured for four years the longing for his wife and family, he returned home to see them, and wishing to leave again he took them with him, and when they were on board ship, he clad both the children for greater convenience in short clothes, so that the girl appeared like a boy : and on the voyage to Soria he was taken by Corsairs and carried to Natolia, where he remained as a slave for fourteen years : his children had a different fortune : inasmuch as the boy was sold several times : but last of all in this city, which on this occasion shall be Naples, and at present he is servant to Dorotea, a courtesan, who lives there at that little door. The mother and Genevra, after various accidents, were bought by M. Massimo Caraccioli, who lives at that door : but by the advice of her mother, who has now been dead for six years, Genevra has changed her name and is called Ruberto, and, as her mother when alive had counselled her, she always passed herself off as a boy, in the belief that by this means she could better guard her honour. Fortunato and Ruberto, by the information of their mother, know that they are brother and sister. M. Massimo has a son, called Gostanzo, and a daughter called Portia. Gostanzo is in love with Dorotea, the courtesan, to whom Fortunato is servant : Portia, his sister, is in love with Ruberto, although she is a girl, because she had always been held to be a boy. Ruberto, the girl, unable to respond to the caresses of Portia, has, under cover of night, substituted for herself her brother Fortunato, with the result that Portia is now expecting every day to be confined. On the other hand, Ruberto, as a girl and enamoured of her master Gostanzo, experiences double anxiety, one due to the love which torments her, and the other to the fear that Portia's plight should be discovered. Massimo, the father of Portia and Gostanzo, has perceived the condition of his daughter, and has sent to Genoa to inquire into the parentage of Ruberto, in order that if the youth prove of low birth and unfit to be the husband of his daughter, whom he believes has been beguiled by him, he will have him put to death. But from what I have understood, the father of the twins, who has escaped from the Turks, ought to-day to be returned with the messenger, and I think that everything will be arranged. Be attentive, and because you have no supper here, there have been prepared for you some viands of laughter, partially to satisfy your hunger. You shall have a brave soldier who will not allow you to become wearied, and an old Doctor,—both of them in love with the Courtesan, Dorotea, who skins them alive. Do not stir, I hear a noise.'

Beyond the circumstance, which we learn from this Prologue, that there is some 'cross wooing,' this plot reveals nothing which affords any indication that Shakespeare had ever used it or even seen it. There is one short dialogue wherein COLLIER finds a parallel to Cesario's acknowledgement to the Duke that the woman with whom he was in love resembled the Duke himself. It is where Ruberto (Viola) tells Gostanzo (Orsino) that she knows a young girl who is much in love with him. '*Gostanzo.* Where is she? *Ruberto.* Near you. *Gost.* How shall I get to her ? *Rub.* As you would come to me. *Gost.* How do you know that she loves me ? *Rub.* Because she often talks to me of her love. *Gost.* Do I know her ? *Rub.* As well as you know me. *Gost.* Is she young ? *Rub.* Of my age. *Gost.* And loves me ? *Rub.* Adores you. *Gost.* Have I ever seen her ? *Rub.* As often as you have seen me.'

The 'brave soldier,' to whom the Prologue referred, has a servant named Straccia. From the similarity of sound, COLLIER supposes that, in some way, wherein imagination must take a wild flight, this servant's name became converted into 'the lady 'of the Strachy.'

T. L. PEACOCK (*Preface* to Translation of *Gl' Ingannati*), speaking of the *Inganni*, says that 'much of this comedy is borrowed, in parts closely translated, 'from the *Asinaria* of Plautus. Cleaereta, the mother ; Philenium, the daughter ;

'Argyrippus, the lover; are reproduced in Gillitta, Dorotea, and Gostanzo.' He specifies parallel scenes in the two comedies. The 'brave soldier,' to whom the Prologue to the *Inganni* referred, is insulted and fleeced by Giletta and her daughter, Dorotea, and, after being thrust into the street, and the door barred against him, besieges the house. This incident Peacock regards as similar to Thraso's attack on the house of Thais in Terence's *Eunuchus*, IV, vii.

HUNTER did not even find quite as much as Collier, in the *Inganni*, to indicate that Shakespeare had derived from it any portion of his plot. In his search after this Italian comedy he was led, however, to the knowledge of another play, which, he asserted, was 'beyond question' the Italian source of the plot of *Twelfth Night*. This is a comedy the title of which is *Gl' Ingannati*. A general account of this play is given in the *Preface* to the present volume. The scenes in which the four principal characters are chiefly concerned have been translated by T. L. PEACOCK, and a connecting outline of the rest is added. The original has no stage-directions; these have been, here and there, supplied by the Translator. Peacock's translation is, substantially, as follows:—

DRAMATIS PERSONÆ

Gherardo Foiani, *father of Isabella.*
Virginio Bellenzini, *father of Lelia and Fabrizio.*
Flaminio de' Carandini, *in love with Isabella.*
Fabrizio, *son of Virginio.*
Messer Piero, *a pedant, tutor of Fabrizio.*
L'Agiato } *rival hotel-keepers.*
Fruella }
Giglio, *a Spaniard.*
Spela, *servant of Gherardo.*
Scatizza, *servant of Virginio.*
Crivello, *servant of Flaminio.*
Stragualcia, *servant of Fabrizio.*
Lelia, *daughter of Virginio, disguised as a page, under the name of Fabio.*
Isabella, *daughter of Gherardo.*
Clementia, *nurse of Lelia.*
Pasquella, *housekeeper of Gherardo.*
Cittina, *a girl, daughter of Clementia.*
The Scene is in Modena.

GL' INGANNATI—THE DECEIVED

ACT I.—SCENE.—*A Street, with the house of Virginio. Virginio and Gherardo.* [Virginio, an old merchant, has two children, a son and a daughter, Fabrizio and Lelia. He has lost his property and his son in the sack of Rome, May, 1527, when his daughter had just finished her thirteenth year. The comedy being performed in the Carnival of 1531, the girl is in her seventeenth year. Another old man, Gherardo, who is wealthy, wishes to marry her, and the father assents, provided the maiden is willing. Gherardo thinks that the father's will ought to be sufficient, and that it only rests with him to make his daughter do as he pleases.]

SCENE.—*Virginio* and *Clementia.* [Virginio having shortly before gone on business to Bologna, in company with a Messer Buonaparte and others, has left Lelia in a convent with her Aunt Camilla, and now, in the intention of her marriage, desires Lelia's nurse, Clementia, to go to the convent to bring her home. Clementia must first go to mass.]

SCENE.—*A Street, with the house of Flaminio. Lelia, afterwards Clementia.*

Lelia (*in male apparel*). It is great boldness in me, that, knowing the licentious customs of these wild youths of Modena, I should venture abroad alone at this early hour. What would become of me, if any one of them should suspect my sex? But the cause is my love for the cruel and ungrateful Flaminio. Oh, what a fate is mine! I love one who hates me. I serve one who does not know me; and, for more bitter grief, I aid him in his love for another, without any other hope than that of satiating my eyes with his sight. Thus far all has gone well; but now, what can I do? My father is returned. Flaminio is come to live in the town. I can scarcely hope to continue here without being discovered; and if it should be so, my reputation will be blighted for ever, and I shall become a byword in the city. Therefore I have come forth at this hour to consult my nurse, whom, from the window I have seen coming this way. But I will first see if she knows me in this dress.

[*Clementia enters.*

Clementia. In good faith, Flaminio must be returned to Modena; for I see his door open. Oh! if Lelia knew it, it would appear to her a thousand years till she came back to her father's house. But who is this young coxcomb that keeps crossing before me, backward and forward? What do you mean by it? Take yourself off, or I will show you how I like such chaps.—*Lelia.* Good morning, good mother.

Clem. I seem to know the boy. Tell me, where can I have seen you?

Lelia. You pretend not to know me, eh? Come a little nearer, nearer still; on this side. Now?

Clem. Is it possible? Can you be Lelia? Oh, misery of my life! What does this mean, my child?—*Lelia.* Oh! if you cry out in this way, I must go.

Clem. Is this the honour you do to your father, to your house, to yourself, to me, who have brought you up? Come in instantly. You shall not be seen in this dress.

Lelia. Pray have a little patience.—*Clem.* Are you not ashamed to be seen so?

Lelia. Am I the first? I have seen women in Rome go in this way by hundreds.

Clem. They must have been vile women.

Lelia. Oh, among so many vile, may there not have been one good one?

Clem. Why do you go so? Why have you left the convent? Oh, if your father knew it, he would kill you.

Lelia. He would end my misery. Do you think I value life?

Clem. But why do you go so? Tell me.

Lelia. Listen, and you shall hear. You will then know how great is my affliction,—why I have left the convent,—why I go thus attired, and what I wish you to do in the matter. But step more aside, lest any one should pass who may recognise me, seeing me talking with you.—*Clem.* You kill me with impatience.

Lelia. You know that after the terrible sack of Rome, my father, having lost everything, and, together with his property, my brother Fabrizio, in order not to be alone in his house, took me from the service of the Signora Marchesana, with whom he had placed me, and, constrained by necessity, we returned to our house in Modena to live on the little that remained to us here. You know, also, that my father, having been considered a friend of the Count Guido Rangon, was not well looked on by many.

Clem. Why do you tell me what I know better than you? I know, too, for what reason you left the city, to live at our farm of Fontanile, and that I went with you.

Lelia. You know, also, how bitter were my feelings at that time; not only remote from all thoughts of love, but almost from all human thought, considering that, having been a captive among soldiers, I could not, however purely and becomingly I might live, escape malicious remark. And you know how often you scolded me for my melancholy, and exhorted me to lead a more cheerful life.

Clem. If I know it, why do you tell it to me? Go on.

Lelia. Because it is necessary to remind you of all this, that you may understand what follows. It happened at this time that Flaminio Carandini, from having been attached to the same party as ourselves, formed an intimate friendship with my father, came daily to our house, began to admire me secretly, then took to sighing and casting down his eyes. By degrees I took increasing pleasure in his manners and conversation, not, however, even dreaming of love. But his continuous visits, and sighs, and signs of admiration at last made me aware that he was not a little taken with me, and I, who had never felt love before, deeming him worthy of my dearest thoughts, became in love with him so strongly that I had no longer any delight but in seeing him.—*Clem.* Much of this also I knew.

Lelia. You know, too, that when the Spanish soldiers left Rome my father went thither to see if any of our property remained, but, still more, to see if he could learn any news of my brother. He sent me to Mirandola, to stay, till his return, with my Aunt Giovanna. With what grief I separated from my dear Flaminio you may well say, who so often dried my tears. I remained a year at Mirandola, and on my father's return I came back to Modena, more than ever enamoured of him who was my first love, and thinking still that he loved me as before.

Clem. Oh, insanity! How many Modenese have you found constant in love of one for a year? One month to one, another month to another, is the extent of their devotion.

Lelia. I met him, and he hardly remembered me, any more than if he had never seen me. But the worst of it is, that he has set his heart on Isabella, the daughter of Gherardo Foiani, who is not only very beautiful, but the only child of her father, if the crazy old fellow does not marry again.

Clem. He thinks himself certain of having you, and says that your father has promised you to him. But all this does not explain to me why you have left the convent, and go about in male apparel.

Lelia. The old fellow certainly shall not have me. But my father, after his return from Rome, having business at Bologna, placed me, as I would not return to Mirandola, in the convent with my cousin Amabile. I found, that among these reverend mothers and sisters, love was the principal subject of conversation. I therefore felt emboldened to open my heart to Amabile. She pitied me, and found means to bring Flaminio, who was then living out of the town, in a palazzo near the convent, several times to speak with her and with others, where I, concealed behind curtains, might feast my eyes on seeing him and my ears with hearing him. One day, I heard him lamenting the death of a page, whose good service he highly praised, saying how glad he would be if he could find such another. It immediately occurred to me, that I would try to supply the vacant place, and consulting with Sister Amabile, she encouraged me, instructed me how to proceed, and fitted me with some new clothes, which she had had made, in order that she might, as others do, go out in disguise about her own affairs. So one morning early, I left the convent in this attire, and went to Flaminio's palazzo. There I waited till Flaminio came out; and Fortune be praised, he no sooner saw me, than he asked me most courteously, what I wanted and whence I came.

Clem. Is it possible that you did not fall dead with shame?

Lelia. Far from it indeed. Love bore me up. I answered frankly, that I was from Rome, and that, being poor, I was seeking service. He examined me several times from head to foot so earnestly, that I was almost afraid he would know me. He then said that if I pleased to stay with him, he would receive me willingly and treat me well; and I answered that I would gladly do so.

Clem. And what good do you expect from this mad proceeding?

Lelia. The good of seeing him, hearing him, talking with him, learning his secrets, seeing his companions, and being sure that if he is not mine, he is not another's.

Clem. In what way do you serve him?

Lelia. As his page in all honesty. And in this fortnight that I have served him, I have become so much in favour, that I almost think appearing in my true dress would revive his love.

Clem. What will people say when this shall be known?

Lelia. Who will know it, if you do not tell it? Now what I want you to do is this: that, as my father returned yesterday, and may perhaps send for me, you would prevent his doing so for four or five days, and at the end of this time I will return. You may say that I am gone to Roverino with Sister Amabile.

Clem. And why all this?

Lelia. Flaminio, as I have already told you, is enamoured of Isabella Foiani; and he often sends me to her with letters and messages. She, taking me for a young man, has fallen madly in love with me, and makes me the most passionate advances. I pretend that I will not love her, unless she can so manage as to bring Flaminio's pursuit of her to an end; and I hope that in three or four days he will be brought to give her up.

Clem. Your father has sent me for you, and I insist on your coming to my house, and I will send for your clothes. If you do not come home with me, I will tell your father all about you.

Lelia. Then I will go where neither you nor he shall ever see me again. I can say no more now, for I hear Flaminio call me. Expect me at your house in an hour. Remember that I call myself Fabio degl' Alberini.—I come, Signor.—Adieu Clementia. [*Exit* Lelia.

Clem. In good faith, she has seen Gherardo coming, and has run away. I must not tell her father for the present, and she must not remain where she is. I will wait till I see her again.

SCENE.—*Gherardo, Spela,* and *Clementia.* [In this scene, *Clementia* makes sport of the old lover, treating him as a sprightly youth. He swallows the flattery, and echoes it in rapturous speeches, while his servant, *Spela,* in a series of asides, exhausts on his folly the whole vocabulary of anger and contempt.]

SCENE.—*Spela* and *Scatizza.* [*Spela,* at first alone, soliloquises in ridicule of his master. *Scatizza,* the servant of Virginio, who had been to fetch Lelia from the convent, enters in great wrath, having been laughed at by the nuns, who told him all sorts of contradictory stories respecting her; by which he is so bewildered that he does not know what to say to Virginio.]

ACT II.—*The Street, with the house of Flaminio. Enter Lelia (as Fabio) and Flaminio.*

Flaminio. It is a strange thing, Fabio, that I have not yet been able to extract a kind answer from this cruel, this ungrateful Isabella, and yet by her always receiving you graciously and by giving you willing audience I am led to think that she does not altogether hate me. Assuredly, I never did anything, that I know, to displease her ; you may judge, from her conversation, if she has any cause to complain of me. Repeat to me what she said yesterday, when you went to her with that letter.

Lelia. I have repeated it to you twenty times.

Flam. Oh repeat it to me once more. What can it matter to you ?

Lelia. It matters to me this, that it is disagreeable to you, and is, therefore, painful to me, as your servant, who seek only to please you ; perhaps these answers may make you vexed with me.

Flam. No, my dear Fabio ; I love you as a brother ; I know you wish me well, and I will never be wanting to you, as time shall show. But repeat to me what she said.

Lelia. Have I not told you? That the greatest pleasure you can do her is to let her alone ; to think no more of her, because she has fixed her heart elsewhere ; that she has no eyes to look on you ; that you lose your time in following her, and will find yourself at last with your hands full of wind.

Flam. And does it appear to you, Fabio, that she says these things from her heart, or, rather, that she has taken some offence with me? For at one time she showed me favour, and I cannot believe she wishes me ill, while she accepts my letters and my messages. I am disposed to follow her till death. Do you not think that I am in the right, Fabio?

Lelia. No, signor.—*Flam.* Why?—*Lelia.* Because, if I were in your place, I should expect her to receive my service as a grace and an honour. To a young man like you, noble, virtuous, elegant, handsome, can ladies worthy of you, be wanting ? Do as I would do, signor ; leave her ; and attach yourself to some one who will love you as you deserve. Such will be easily found, and perhaps as handsome as she is. Have you never yet found one in this country who loved you ?

Flam. Indeed I have, and especially one, who is named Lelia, and to whom, I have often thought I see a striking likeness in you ; the most beautiful, the most accomplished, the best mannered young girl in this town ; who would think herself happy, if I would show her even a little favour ; rich and well received at court. We were lovers nearly a year, and she showed me a thousand favours ; but she went to Mirandola, and my fate made me enamoured of Isabella, who has been as cruel to me as Lelia was gracious.

Lelia. Master, you deserve to suffer. If you do not value one who loves you, it is fitting that one you love should not value you.—*Flam.* What do you mean?

Lelia. If you first loved this poor girl, and if she loved and still loves you, why have you abandoned her to follow another? Ah, Signor Flaminio ! you do a great wrong, a greater than I know if God can pardon.

Flam. You are a child, Fabio. You do not know the force of love. I cannot help myself. I must love and adore Isabella. I cannot, may not, will not think of any but her. Therefore, go to her again ; speak with her ; and try to draw dexterously from her, what is the cause that she will not see me.—*Lelia.* You will lose your time.—*Flam.* It pleases me so to lose it.—*Lelia.* You will accomplish nothing. —*Flam.* Patience.—*Lelia.* Pray let her go.—*Flam.* I cannot. Go, as I bid you.—

Lelia. I will go, but— *Flam.* Return with the answer immediately. Meanwhile I will go in.—*Lelia.* When time serves, I will not fail.—*Flam.* Do this, and it will be well for you. [*Exit* Flaminio.

Lelia. He is gone in good time, here is Pasquella coming to look for me.

[*Enter* Pasquella.

Pasquella. I do not think there is in the world a greater trouble or a greater annoyance, than to serve a young woman like my mistress, who has neither mother nor sisters to look after her, and who has fallen all at once into such a passion of love, that she has no rest night or day, but runs about the house, now up stairs, now down, now to one window, now to another, as if she had quicksilver in her feet. Oh, I have been young and I have been in love; but I gave myself some repose. If she had fallen in love, now, with a man of note, and of fitting years; but she has taken to doting on a boy, who, I think, could hardly tie the points of his doublet, if he had not some one to help him; and every day, and all day, she sends me to look for him, as if I had nothing to do at home. But here he is, happily.—Good day to you, Fabio. I was seeking you, my charmer.

Lelia. And a thousand crowns to you, Pasquella. How does your fair mistress?

Pasqu. And how can you suppose she does? Wastes away in tears and lamentations, because all this morning you have not been near her house.

Lelia. She would not have me there before day break. I have something to do at home. I have a master to serve.

Pasqu. Your master always wishes you to go there; and my mistress entreats you to come, for her father is not at home, and she has something of importance to tell you.

Lelia. Tell her she must get rid of Flaminio, or I shall ruin myself by obeying her.—*Pasqu.* Come and tell her so yourself.—*Lelia.* I have something else to do, I tell you.—*Pasqu.* It is but to go, and return as soon as you please.—*Lelia.* I will not go. Go and tell her so.—*Pasqu.* You will not?—*Lelia.* No, I say. Do you not hear?—*Pasqu.* In very, very truth, Fabio, Fabio, you are too proud; you are young; you do not know your own good; these good looks will not last for ever; you will not always have such rosy cheeks, such ruby lips; when your beard grows, you will not be the pretty pet you are now. Then you will repent your folly. Just tell me how many are there in this city who would not think the love of Isabella the choicest gift of heaven.

Lelia. Then let her give it to them, and let me alone who do not care for it.

Pasqu. Marry, how true it is, that boys have no brains! O dear, dear Fabio, pray come, and come soon, or she will send me for you again, and will not believe that I have delivered her message.—*Lelia.* Well, Pasquella, go home. I did but jest. I will come.—*Pasqu.* When, my jewel?—*Lelia.* Soon.—*Pasqu.* How soon? —*Lelia.* Immediately; go.—*Pasqu.* I shall expect you at the door.—*Lelia.* Yes, yes.—*Pasqu.* If you do not come, I shall be very angry.

SCENE.—*A street with two hotels and the house of* Gherardo. *Enter Giglio (a Spaniard) and Pasquella.* [Giglio, who is in love with Isabella, and longs for an opportunity of speaking to her without witnesses, tries to cajole Pasquella into admitting him to the house, and promises her a rosary, with which he is to return in the evening. She does not intend to admit him, but thinks to trick him out of the rosary. He does not intend to give her the rosary, but thinks to delude her by the promise of it.]

SCENE.—*The Street with the house of Flaminio. Enter Flaminio and Crivello.*

Flaminio. You have not been to look for Fabio, and he does not come. I do not know what to think of his delay.

Crivello. I was going and you called me back. How am I to blame?

Flam. Go now, and if he is still in the house of Isabella, wait till he comes out, and send him home instantly.

Criv. How shall I know if he is there or not? You would not have me knock and inquire?

Flam. I have not a servant worth his salt, but Fabio. Heaven grant me favour to reward him!—What are you muttering, blockhead? Is it not true?

Criv. What would you have me say? Of course I say, yes. Fabio is good; Fabio is handsome; Fabio serves well; Fabio with you; Fabio with your lady; Fabio does everything; Fabio is everything. But—

Flam. What do you mean by but—?

Criv. He is too much trusted; he is a stranger, and some day he may disappear, with something worth taking.

Flam. I wish the rest of you were as trustworthy. Yonder is Scatizza. Ask him if he has seen Fabio; and come to me at the bank of the Porini. [*Exeunt.*

SCENE.—[Spela soliloquizes on the folly of Gherardo, who had sent him to buy a bottle of perfume; and some young men in the shop, understanding for whom it was wanted, had told him he had better buy a box of assafœtida.]

SCENE.—*The Street with the hotels, and with the house of* Gherardo.

[Crivello and Scatizza are talking of keeping carnival at the expense of their masters, when Gherardo's door opens, and they stand back. Lelia and Isabella enter from the house of Gherardo.]—*Lelia.* Remember what you have promised me. —*Isabella.* And do you remember to return to me. One word more.—*Lelia.* What more?—*Isab.* Listen.—*Lelia.* I attend.—*Isab.* No one is here?—*Lelia.* Not a living soul.—*Isab.* Come nearer. I wish— *Lelia.* What do you wish?—*Isab.* I wish that you would return after dinner, when my father will be out.—*Lelia.* I will; but if my master passes this way, close the window, and retire.—*Isab.* If I do not, may you never love me.—*Lelia.* Adieu. Now return into the house.—*Isab.* I would have a favour from you.—*Lelia.* What?—*Isab.* Come a little within.—*Lelia.* We shall be seen.—*Scatizza* [*aside*]. She has kissed him.—*Crivello* [*aside*]. I had rather have lost a hundred crowns than not to have seen this kiss. What will my master do when he knows it?—*Scat.* [*aside*]. Oh, the devil! You won't tell him? —*Isab.* Pardon me. Your too great beauty, and the too great love I bear you, have impelled me to this. You will think it hardly becoming the modesty of a maid, but God knows, I could not resist.

Lelia. I ask no excuses, signora. I know too well what extreme love has led me to.—*Isab.* To what?—*Lelia.* To deceiving my master, which is not well.— *Isab.* Ill fortune come to him!—*Lelia.* It is late. I must go home. Remain in peace.—*Isab.* I give myself to you.

Lelia. I am yours. [*Isabella goes in.*] I am sorry for her, and I wish I were well out of this intrigue. I will consult my nurse, Clementia; but here comes Flaminio.—*Criv.* [*aside*]. Scatizza, my master told me to go to him at the bank of the Porini. I will carry him this good news. If he does not believe me, I shall call you to witness.—*Scat.* I will not fail you; but if you take my advice, you will keep quiet, and then you will always have this rod in pickle for Fabio, to make him do as you please.

Criv. I tell you I hate him. He has ruined me.—*Scat.* Take your own way.

SCENE.—*The street, with the house of* Flaminio.

Flaminio. Is it possible, that I can be so far out of myself, have so little self-esteem, as to love, in her own despite, one who hates me, despises me, will not even condescend to look at me? Am I so vile, of so little account, that I cannot free myself from this shame, this torment? But here is Fabio. Well, what have you done?—*Lelia.* Nothing.—*Flam.* Why have you been so long away?—*Lelia.* I have delayed, because I waited to speak with Isabella.—*Flam.* And why have you not spoken to her?—*Lelia.* She would not listen to me; and if you would act in my way, you would take another course; for by all that I can so far understand, she is most obstinately resolved to do nothing to please you.—*Flam.* Why, even now, as I passed her house, she rose and disappeared from the window, with as much anger and fury as if she had seen some hideous and horrible thing.

Lelia. Let her go, I tell you. Is it possible that in all this city there is no other who merits your love as much as she does?

Flam. I would it were not so. I fear this has been the cause of my misfortune; for I loved very warmly that Lelia Bellenzini, of whom I have spoken; and I fear Isabella thinks this love still lasts, and on that account will not see me; but I will give Isabella to understand that I love Lelia no longer; rather that I hate her, and cannot bear to hear her named, and will pledge my faith never to go where she may be. Tell Isabella this as strongly as you can.—*Lelia.* Oh, me!—*Flam.* What has come over you? What do you feel?—*Lelia.* Oh, me!—*Flam.* Lean on me. Have you any pain?—*Lelia.* Suddenly. In the heart.—*Flam.* Go in. Apply warm cloths to your side. I will follow immediately, and, if necessary, will send for a doctor to feel your pulse and prescribe a remedy. Give me your arm. You are pale and cold. Lean on me. Gently, gently. [*Leads her into the house and returns.*] To what are we not subject! I would not, for all I am worth, that anything should happen to him, for there never was in the world a more diligent and well-mannered servant, nor one more cordially attached to his master.

[Flaminio *goes off, and* Lelia *returns.*

Lelia. Oh, wretched Lelia! Now you have heard from the mouth of this ungrateful Flaminio how well he loves you. Why do you lose your time in following one so false and so cruel? All your former love, your favours, and your prayers were thrown away. Now your stratagems are unavailing. Oh, unhappy me! Refused, rejected, spurned, hated! Why do I serve him, who repels me? Why do I ask him, who denies me? Why do I follow him, who flies me? Why do I love him, who hates me? Ah, Flaminio! Nothing pleases him but Isabella. He desires nothing but Isabella. Let him have her. Let him keep her. I must leave him, or I shall die. I will serve him no longer in this dress. I will never again come in his way since he holds me in such deadly hatred. I will go to Clementia, who expects me, and with her I will determine on the course of my future life.

SCENE.—*Enter Flaminio and Crivello.*

Crivello. And if it is not so, cut out my tongue, and hang me up by the neck.

Flaminio. How long since?—*Criv.* When you sent me to look for him.—*Flam.* Tell me again how it was, for he denies having been able to speak with her.

Criv. You will do well to make him confess it. I tell you, that, watching about the house to see if he were there, I saw him come out; and as he was going away, Isabella called him back into the doorway. They looked round to see if any one were near, and not seeing any one, they kissed each other.—*Flam.* How was it that they did not see you?—*Criv.* I was ensconced under the opposite portico.—*Flam.*

How then did you see them?—*Criv.* By peeping in the nick of time, when they saw nothing but each other.—*Flam.* And he kissed her?—*Criv.* I do not know whether he kissed her, or she kissed him; but I am sure that one kissed the other. —*Flam.* Be sure that you saw clearly, and do not come by and by to say that it seemed so; for this is a great matter that you tell me of. How did you see it?— *Criv.* Watching with open eyes, and having nothing to do but to see.—*Flam.* If this be true, you have killed me.—*Criv.* This is true. She called him back; she embraced him; she kissed him. If this is to kill you, you are dead.—*Flam.* It is no wonder that the traitor denied having been there. I know now why he counselled me to give her up; that he might have her himself. If I do not take such vengeance as shall be a warning to all traitorous servants, may I never be esteemed a man. But I will not believe you without better evidence. You are ill-disposed to Fabio, and wish to get rid of him; but, by the eternal heaven! I will make you tell the truth, or I will kill you. You saw them kissing?

Criv. I did.—*Flam.* He kissed her?—*Criv.* Or she him. Or both.—*Flam.* How often?—*Criv.* Twice.—*Flam.* Where?—*Criv.* In the entry of her house.— *Flam.* You lie in your throat. You said in the doorway.—*Criv.* Just inside the doorway.—*Flam.* Tell the truth.—*Criv.* I am very sorry to have told it.—*Flam.* It was true?—*Criv.* Yes; and I have a witness.—*Flam.* Who?—*Criv.* Virginio's man, Scatizza.—*Flam.* Did he see it?—*Criv.* As I did.—*Flam.* And if he does not confess it?—*Criv.* Kill me.—*Flam.* I will.—*Criv.* And if he does confess it? —*Flam.* I will kill both.—*Criv.* Oh, the devil! What for?—*Flam.* Not you. Isabella and Fabio.—*Criv.* And burn down the house, with Pasquella and every one in it.—*Flam.* Let us look for Scatizza. I will pay them. I will take such revenge as all the land shall ring of.

ACT III.—*The street with the hotels and the house of* Gherardo. [Messer Piero, who had been before in Modena, points out some of its remarkable places to Fabrizio, who had been taken from it too young to remember it. Stragualcia is a hungry fellow, who is clamorous for his dinner.]

SCENE.—*Enter L' Agiato, Fruella, Piero, Fabrizio, and Stragualcia.* [L' Agiato and Fruella, two rival hotel-keepers, quarrel for the patronage of the new comers.]

L' Agiato. Oh, Signors, this is the hotel; lodge at *The Looking-glass,*—at *The Looking-glass!*

Fruella. Welcome, Signors; I have lodged you before. Do you not remember your Fruella? The only hotel for gentlemen of your degree.

L' Agia. You shall have good apartments, a good fire, excellent beds, white crisp sheets; everything you can ask for.

Fru. I will give you the best wine of Lombardy; partridges, home-made sausages, pigeons, pullets; and whatever else you may desire.

L' Agia. I will give you veal sweet-breads, Bologna sausages, Mountain wine, all sorts of delicate fare.

Fru. I will give you fewer delicacies and more substantials. You will live at a fixed rate. At *The Looking-glass* you will be charged even for candles.

Stragualcia. Master, let us put up here. This seems best.

L' Agia. If you wish to lodge well, lodge at *The Looking-glass.* You would not have it said that you lodged at *The Madman.*

Fru. My *Madman* is a hundred thousand times better than your *Looking-glass.*

Piero. *Speculum prudentia significat, justa illud nostri Catonis, Nosce teipsum.* You understand, Fabrizio?—*Fabr.* I understand.—*Fru.* See who has most guests, you or I.—*L'Agia.* See who has most men of note.—*Fru.* See where they are best treated.—*L'Agia.* See where there are most delicacies.—*Strag.* Delicacies, delicacies, delicacies ! Give me substance. Delicacies are for the Florentines.— *L'Agia.* They all lodge with me.—*Fru.* They did ; but for the last three years they have come to me.—*L'Agia.* My man, give me the trunk, it seems to gall your shoulder.—*Strag.* Never mind my shoulder, I want to fill my stomach.—*Fru.* Here are a couple of capons, just ready. They are for you.—*Strag.* They will do for a first course.—*L'Agia.* Look at this ham.—*Piero.* Not bad.—*Fru.* Who understands wine ?—*Strag.* I do ; better than the French.—*Fru.* See if this pleases you. If not, you may try ten other sorts.—*Strag.* Fruella, you are the prince of hosts. Taste this, master. This is good. Carry in the trunk.—*Piero.* Wait a little. What have you to say ?—*L'Agia.* I say that gentlemen do not care for heavy meats, but for what is light, good, and delicate.—*Strag.* He would be an excellent nurse in a hospital.—*Piero.* Do not be uncivil. What will you give us ?—*L'Agia.* You have only to command.—*Fru.* Where there is plenty a man may eat little or much as he pleases ; but where there is little, and the appetite grows with eating, he can only finish his dinner with bread.—*Strag.* You are wiser than the statutes. I have never seen a landlord so much to my mind.—*Fru.* Go into the kitchen, brother ; there you will see.—*Piero. Omnis repletio mala, panis autem pessima.*

Strag. [*aside*]. Paltry pedant ! One of these days I must crack his skull.

L'Agia. Come in, gentlemen. It is not good to stand in the cold.

Fabr. We are not so chilly.—*Fru.* You must know, gentlemen, this hotel of *The Looking-glass* used to be the best in Lombardy ; but since I have opened this of *The Madman*, it does not lodge ten persons in a year, and my sign has a greater reputation throughout the world than any other hostelry whatever. The French come here in flocks, and all the Germans that pass this way.—*L'Agia.* That's not true. The Germans go to *The Pig.*—*Fru.* The Milanese come here.—*Piero.* Where do the Neapolitans lodge ?—*Fru.* With me.—*L'Agia.* The greater part of them lodge at *The Cupid.*—*Fru.* Many with me.—*Fabr.* Where does the Duke of Malfi ?—*Fru.* Sometimes at my house, sometimes at his, sometimes at *The Sword*, sometimes at *The Cupid.*—*Piero.* Where do the Romans lodge ; we are from Rome. —*L'Agia.* With me.—*Fru.* That's not true. He does not lodge a Roman in a year, except two or three old cardinals, who keep to him from habit. All the rest come to *The Madman.*

Strag. I would not go from here unless I were dragged away. Master, there are so many pots and pipkins about the fire, so many soups, so many sauces, so many spits turning with partridges and capons, such an odour of stews and ragouts, such a display of pies and tarts, that, if the whole court of Rome were to come here to keep Carnival there would be enough and to spare.—*Fabr.* Have you been drinking ?—*Strag.* And such wine !—*Piero. Variorum ciborum commistio pessimam generat digestionem.*

Strag. Bus asinorum ; buorum, castronorum, tatte, batte, pecoronibus,—the devil take all pedants ! Let us go in here, master.—*Fabr.* Messer Piero, what shall we do ?—*Piero. Etiam atque etiam cogitandum.*—*Strag.* [*aside*]. I can hardly keep my hands off him.—*Piero.* I think, Fabrizio, we have not much money.

Strag. Master, I have just seen the host's daughter, as beautiful as an angel.

Piero. Well, let us put up here. Your father, if we find him, will pay the reckoning.—*Strag.* I will go into the kitchen, taste everything there, drink two or three cups of wine, fall asleep by a good fire, and the devil take economy.—*L'Agia.*

Remember, Fruella. You have played me too many tricks. One day we must try which head is hardest.—*Fru.* Whenever you please. I am all ready to crack your skull.

SCENE.—*The Street, with the house of Virginio. Enter Virginio and Clementia.*

Virginio. These are the manners you have taught her ! This is the honour she does me ! Have I for this escaped so many misfortunes, to see my property without an heir, my house broken up, my daughter disgraced ; to become the talk of the town ; not dare to lift up my head ; to be pointed at by boys ; to be laughed at by old men ; to be put into a comedy by *The Intronati ;* to be made an example in novels ; to be an eternal scandal with all the ladies of the land ? For if one knows it, in three hours the whole city knows it. Disgraced, unhappy, miserable father ! I have lived too long. What can I think of ? What can I do ?

Clementia. You will do well to make as little fuss about it as you can, and to take the quietest means you can, to bring your daughter home, before the town knows anything about it. May that Sister Novellante Ciancini have no more breath in her body than I have faith that Lelia goes dressed as a man. Don't encourage their evil speaking. They want to make her a nun, and that you will leave her all your property.

Virg. Sister Novellante told the truth. She told me, besides, that Lelia is living as a page with a gentleman of this city, who does not know that she is not a boy.

Clem. I don't believe it. — *Virg.* Neither do I, that he does not know that she is not a boy.—*Clem.* That's not what I mean. — *Virg.* It's what I mean. But what else could I expect when I entrusted her bringing up to you?—*Clem.* Rather, what could you expect, when you wanted to marry her to a man old enough to be her grandfather ? — *Virg.* Let me catch her, and I will drag her home by the hair. I have a description of her dress ; I'll find her ; that's enough.—*Clem.* Take your own way. I'll lose no more time in washing a coal. [*Exeunt.*

SCENE.—*Enter Fabrizio and Fruella.*

Fabrizio. While my two servants are sleeping, I will walk about to see the city. When they get up, tell them to come toward the piazza.

Fruella. Assuredly, young gentleman, if I had not seen you put on these clothes, I should have taken you for the page of a gentleman of this town, who dresses like you all in white, and is so like you that he appears to be your very self.—*Fabr.* Perhaps I may have a brother.—*Fru.* It may be so.—*Fabr.* Tell my tutor to inquire for he knows whom.—*Fru.* Trust to me. [*Exit.*

Pasquella [*who enters*]. Good faith, there he is ! I was afraid I should have to search the city before I found you. My mistress says you must come to her as soon as you can on a matter of great importance to both of you.—*Fabr.* Who is your mistress?—*Pasqu.* As if you didn't know.—*Fabr.* I know neither her nor you.— *Pasqu.* Don't be vexed, Fabio dear.—*Fabr.* That's not my name. You're under some mistake.—*Pasqu.* No, no, Fabio. You know there are few girls in this country as rich and as beautiful and I wish you would make an end of the business ; for going backward and forward day after day, taking messages and bringing messages, only sets folk talking without any good to you and with little credit to her.

Fabr. [*aside*]. What can this mean ? Either the woman is crazy, or she takes me for some one else. But I'll see what will come of it. Let us go, then.

Pasqu. Dear me, I think I hear people in the house. Stay here a minute. I'll see if Isabella is alone, and I will make a sign to you if the coast is clear. [*Exit.*

Fabr. I'll see the end of this mystery. Perhaps this is the servant of some light o' love and a scheme to get money out of me. I will stand aside a little, to see who goes in or out of the house, and judge what sort of a lady she may be.

Scene.—*Enter Gherardo, Virginio, and Pasquella.*

Gherardo. Pardon me. If this is so, I renounce her. If Lelia has done this, it must be, not merely because she will not have me, but because she has taken somebody else.—*Virginio.* Don't believe it, Gherardo. I pray you, do not spoil what has been done.—*Gher.* And I pray you to say no more about it.—*Virg.* Surely, you will not be wanting to your word.

Gher. Yes, where there has been a wanting in deed. Besides, you do not know if you can recover her. You are selling a bird in the bush. I heard your talk with Clementia.

Virg. If I do not recover her, I can't give her to you. But if I do recover her, will you not have her? And that immediately?

Gher. Virginio, I had the most honourable wife in Modena. And I have a daughter who is a dove. How can I bring into my house one who has run away from her father, and gone, heaven knows where, in man's clothes? Whom should I find to marry my daughter?

Virg. After a few days, nothing will be thought of it. And I think no one knows it, but just ourselves.

Gher. The whole town will be full of it.—*Virg.* No, no.—*Gher.* How long is it since she ran away?—*Virg.* Yesterday, or this morning.—*Gker.* Who knows that she is still in Modena?—*Virg.* I know it.—*Gher.* Find her, and we'll talk it over again.—*Virg.* Do you promise to take her?—*Gher.* I'll see.—*Virg.* Say yes.— *Gher.* I'll not say yes; but— *Virg.* Come, say it freely.—*Gher.* Soft. What are you doing here, Pasquella? What is Isabella about?—*Pasquella.* Kneeling before her altar.—*Gher.* Blessings on her! A daughter who is always at her devotions is something to be proud of.

Pasqu. Ay, indeed. She fasts every fast day, and repeats the prayers of the day, like a little saint.—*Gher.* She resembles that blessed soul, her mother.

Virg. Oh, Gherardo! Gherardo! Here she is of whom we have been speaking. She seems to be hiding or running away because she has seen me. Let's go after her.—*Gher.* Take care you don't make a mistake. Perhaps it's not she.—*Virg.* Who wouldn't know her? And haven't I all the signs which Sister Novellante gave me?—*Pasqu.* Things look squally. I'll take myself off. [*Exit.*

Enter Fabrizio.

Virg. So, my fine miss, do you think this a befitting costume for you? This is the honour you confer on my house. This is the content you give to a poor old man. Would I had been dead before you were born; you were born only to disgrace me, to bury me alive. And you, Gherardo, what say you of your betrothed? Is she not a credit to you?—*Gher.* No betrothed of mine.—*Virg.* Shameless minx! What would become of you, if this good man here should reject you for a wife? But he overlooks your follies, and is willing to take you.—*Gher.* Soft, soft.—*Virg.* Go into the house, hussy!—*Fabr.* Old man, have you no sons, friends or relatives in the city, whose duty it is to take care of you?

Virg. What an answer? What do you mean?

Fabr. I am wondering that being so much in need of a doctor you are allowed to be at large, when you ought to be locked up and in a strait-waistcoat.

Virg. 'Tis you that ought to be locked up, and you shall be, if I don't kill you on the spot, as I have a mind to.

Fabr. You insult me, because, perhaps, you think me a foreigner. But I am a Modenese, and of as good a family as you.

Virg. [*aside to Gherardo*]. Gherardo, take her into your house. Don't let her be seen in this fashion.—*Gher.* No, no ; do you take her home.

Virg. Just listen to me a minute, but keep an eye on her that she doesn't run away. [*They talk apart.*

Fabr. I have seen madmen before now, but such a madman as this old fellow I never saw going at large. What a comical mania, to imagine that young men are girls. I wouldn't for a thousand crowns, have missed this fun, to make a story of, for evenings in carnival. Here they come again. I'll humour their foolery, just to see what will come of it.—*Virg.* Come here.—*Fabr.* What do you want, old man? —*Virg.* You worthless hussy, you !—*Fabr.* Don't be abusive ; I'll not stand it.— *Virg.* Brazen face !—*Fabr.* Ha ! ha ! ha ! ha !—*Gher.* Let him speak. Don't you see how angry he is? Do as he bids you.

Fabr. What's his anger to me? What's he to me, or you either?

Virg. You'll kill me before my time.

Fabr. Die when you please ; you've lived too long already.

Gher. Don't use such language, dear little daughter ; don't speak so to your father, dear little sissy.

Fabr. Let the two old doves go ahead ; they're both crazy on one subject. What a go, it is ! Ha ! ha ! ha ! ha !—*Virg.* Are you still laughing at me?—*Fabr.* You're an old fool.—*Gher.* [*aside*]. I am afraid the poor girl has lost her wits.

Virg. I thought so from the first, when I saw with how little patience she received me. Pray take her into your house. I cannot take her to my own, without making myself a spectacle to the whole town.

Fabr. [*aside*]. What are they consulting about now, these two old dotard brothers of Melchisedech ?

Virg. [*aside*]. Let us coax her indoors, and as soon as she is within, lock her up in a chamber with your daughter.—*Gher.* Be it so.

Virg. Come hither, daughter mine, I'll no longer be angry with you. I pardon everything. Only behave well in future.—*Fabr.* Many thanks.—*Gher.* Behave like a good daughter, do.—*Fabr.* The other chimes in with the same tune.—*Gher.* Go in, then, like a good girl.—*Virg.* Go in, my daughter.—*Gher.* This house is your own. You are to be my wife.—*Fabr.* Your wife and his daughter? Ha ! ha ! ha !—*Gher.* My daughter will be glad of your company.—*Fabr.* Your daughter, eh? Very good. I'll go in.—*Virg.* Gherardo, now that we have her safe, lock her up with your daughter, while I send for her clothes.

Gher. Pasquella, call Isabella, and bring the key of her room. [*Exeunt.*

ACT IV.—*Enter Piero and Stragualcia.*

Piero. You ought to have fifty bastinadoes, to teach you to keep him company when he goes out, and not to get drunk and sleep as you have done, and let him go about alone.

Stragualcia. And you ought to be loaded with birch and broom, sulphur, pitch, and gunpowder, and set on fire to teach you not to be what you are.—*Piero.* Sot, sot !—*Strag.* Pedant, pedant !—*Piero.* Let me find your master.—*Strag.* Let me find his father.—*Piero.* What can you say of me to his father?—*Strag.* And what can you say of me ?—*Piero.* That you are a knave, a rogue, a rascal, a sluggard, a coward, a drunkard. That's what I can say.—*Strag.* And I can say that you are a thief, a gambler, a slanderer, a cheat, a sharper, a boaster, a blockhead, an imposter, an ignoramus, a traitor, a profligate. That's what I can say.—*Piero*. Well, we are both known.—*Strag*. True.—*Piero*. No more words. I will not place myself on a footing with you.—*Strag*. Oh, to be sure ; you have all the nobility of the Maremma. I am better born than you. What are you, but the son of a muleteer? This upstart, because he can say *cujus masculini*, thinks he may set his foot on every man's neck.

Piero. Naked and poor goest thou, Philosophy.* To what have poor letters come ! Into the mouth of an ass.

Strag. You'll be the ass presently. I'll lay a load of wood on your shoulders.

Piero. For the sake of your own shoulders, let me alone, base groom, poltroon, arch-poltroon.

Strag. Pedant, pedant, arch-pedant ! What can be said worse than pedant? Can there be a viler, baser, more rubbishy race? They go about puffed up like bladders because they are called *Messer* This, *Maestro* That.

Piero. You speak like what you are. Either you shall leave this service or I will.

Strag. Who would have you in his house or at his table, except my young master, who is better than bread.

Piero. Many would be glad of me. No more words. Go to the hotel, take care of your master's property. By and by we'll have a reckoning.

Strag. Yes, we will indeed have a reckoning, and you shall pay it.

Piero. Fruella told me Fabrizio was gone toward the Piazza. I will follow him.   [*Exit*.

Strag. If I did not now and then make head against this fellow, there would be no living with him. He has no more courage than a rabbit. When I brave him, he is soon silenced ; if I were once to knock under to him, he would lead me the life of a galley-slave.   [*Exit*.

SCENE.—*Enter Gherardo, Virginio, and Messer Piero.*

Gherardo. I will endow her as you desire ; and if you do not find your son, you will add a thousand gold florins.—*Virginio*. Be it so.—*Piero*. I am much deceived or I have seen this gentleman before.—*Virg*. What are you looking at, good sir ?— *Piero*. Certainly, this is my old master. Do you know in this town one Signor Virginio Bellenzini ?—*Virg*. I know him well. He has no better friend than I am.— *Piero*. Assuredly you are he. *Salve, patronorum optime.*

Virg. Are you Messer Pietro de' Pagliaricci, my son's tutor?—*Piero*. I am indeed.—*Virg*. Oh, my son ! Woe is me ! What news do you bring of him? Where did you leave him? Where did he die? Those traitors murdered him,— those Jews, those dogs ! Oh, my son ! my greatest blessing in the world ! Tell me about him, dear master.

Piero. Do not weep, sir, for heaven's sake. Your son is alive and well.

Gher. If this is true, I lose the thousand florins. Take care, Virginio, that this is not a cheat.

Piero. Your son, in the sack of Rome, was a prisoner of one Captain Orteca ; and because the Captain had two comrades who might claim their share, he sent us secretly to Siena ; then, fearing that the Sienese might take him and set your son at liberty, he took us to a castle of the Signor di Piombino, fixed our ransom at a thousand ducats, and made us write for that amount.—*Virg*. Was my son ill-treated?

Piero. No, they treated him like a gentleman. We received no answers to our

---

* ' Povera e nuda vai, Filosofia.'—*Petrarca*, p. 1, s. 7.—*Trans.*

letters.—*Virg.* Go on.—*Piero.* At Corregia, the Captain was killed, the Court took possession of his property and set us at liberty.—*Virg.* And where is my son?—*Piero.* Nearer than you suppose.—*Virg.* In Modena?—*Piero.* At the hotel of *The Madman.*—*Gher.* The thousand florins are gone; but it suffices to have her. I am rich enough without them.

Virg. I die with impatience to embrace him. Come, master.

Piero. But what of Lelia?—*Virg.* She is grown into a fine young woman. Has my son advanced in learning?—*Piero.* He has not wasted his time.—*Virg.* Call him out. Don't tell him. Let me see if he will know me.—*Piero.* He went out a little while ago. I will see if he is returned.   [*Exeunt.*

SCENE.—*Enter Virginio, Gherardo, Piero, and Stragualcia, afterwards Fruella.*

Piero. Stragualcia, ho, Stragualcia, has Fabrizio returned?—*Stragualcia.* Not yet. —*Piero.* Come here. Speak to your old master. This is Signor Virginio.—*Strag.* Has your anger passed off?—*Piero.* You know I am never long angry with you.— *Strag.* All's well then. Is this our master's father?—*Piero.* It is.—*Strag.* Oh, worthy master. You are found just in time to pay our bill at *The Madman.*— *Piero.* This has been a good servant to your son.—*Strag.* 'Has been' only.— *Piero.* And still is.—*Virg.* I shall take care of all who have been faithful companions to my son.—*Strag.* You can take care of me with little trouble.—*Virg.* Demand. —*Strag.* Settle me as a waiter with this host, who is the best companion in the world, the best provided, the most knowing of any host I have ever seen. I think there is no other paradise on earth.—*Virg.* Have you breakfasted?—*Strag.* Somewhat.—*Virg.* What have you eaten?—*Strag.* A brace of partridges, six thrushes, a capon, a little veal, with only two jugs of wine.—*Virg.* Fruella, give him whatever he wants, and leave the payment to me.—*Strag.* Signor Virginio, you have reason to thank the Master, who loves your son better than his own eyes.—*Virg.* Heaven be bountiful to him.—*Strag.* It concerns you first, and heaven afterward.—*Gher.* I must leave you for a while. I have some business at home.—*Virg.* Take care that Lelia does not get away.—*Gher.* That's what I am going for.—*Virg.* She is yours. I give her to you. Arrange matters to your mind.   [*Exeunt.*

SCENE.—*Enter Gherardo, Lelia, and Clementia.*

Gherardo. One cannot have things all one's own way. Patience. But how is this? Here is Lelia! That careless Pasquella has let her escape.

Lelia. Does it not really seem to you, Clementia, that Fortune makes me her sport?—*Clementia.* Be of good cheer. I'll find some means to content you. But come in and change your dress. You must not be seen so.

Gher. I will salute her, however, and learn how she has got out. Good day to you, Lelia, my sweet spouse. Who opened the door for you? Pasquella, eh? I am glad you have gone to your nurse's house; but to let yourself be seen in this dress does little honour to you or to me.

Lelia. To whom are you speaking? What Lelia? I am not Lelia.

Gher. Oho, a little while ago, when your father and I locked you in with my daughter Isabella, didn't you confess that you were Lelia? And now you think I don't know you! Go, my dear wife, and change your dress.

Lelia. God send you as much of a wife, as I have a fancy for you as a husband.
                [*Exit.*

Clem. Go home, Gherardo. All women like pranks, some one kind, some another. This is a very innocent one. Still, such little amusements are not to be talked about.

Gher. No one shall hear of it from me. But how did she escape from my house, where I had locked her up with Isabella?—*Clem.* Locked up whom?—*Gher.* Lelia; this very Lelia.—*Clem.* You're mistaken. She has not left my side to-day; just for pastime she put on these clothes, as girls will do, and asked me if she didn't look well in them.

Gher. You want to make me see double. I tell you I locked her up with Isabella.—*Clem.* Where have you just come from?—*Gher.* From the hotel of *The Madman.*—*Clem.* Did you drink?—*Gher.* A little.—*Clem.* Now go to bed, and sleep it off.—*Gher.* Let me see Lelia for a moment before I go, that I may give her a piece of good news. Her brother is returned safe and sound, and her father is waiting for him at the hotel.—*Clem.* I hasten to tell her.—*Gher.* And I to blow up Pasquella, for letting her escape.   [*Exeunt.*

SCENE.—*Enter Pasquella.* [Pasquella who had known Lelia only as Fabio, and did not know what the two old men had meant by calling the supposed Lelia, whom they had delivered to her charge, a girl, has nevertheless, obeyed orders in locking up Fabrizio with Isabella, and now delivers an untranslateable soliloquy. Giglio enters, and Pasquella, seeing him approach, retires within the court-yard, through the grated door of which a dialogue is carried on. Giglio wishes to gain admission to Gherardo's house without giving Pasquella the rosary he promised her. He shows it to her, but withholds it on pretence that it needs repairs. She, however, wishes to get the rosary, and give him nothing in return. She pretends to doubt its genuineness and prevails on him to let her count the beads. As soon as she has it, she cries out that the chickens are loose and that she cannot open the gate until she has got them all in. Giglio declares that he sees no fowls, and that she is fooling him. She laughs at him; he expostulates, implores, threatens to break down the door, set fire to the house, to burn everything in it, herself included. In the midst of his wrath, he sees Gherardo approaching, and then runs away. Gherardo enters] :—

Gherardo. What were you doing at the gate with that Spaniard?—*Pasquella.* He was making a great noise about a rosary. I couldn't make out what he wanted. —*Gher.* Oh, you've executed your trust well. I could find it in my heart to break all your bones.—*Pas.* For what?—*Gher.* Because you have let Lelia escape. I told you to keep her locked in.—*Pas.* She is locked in.—*Gher.* I admire your impudence. She is not. I have just left her with her nurse, Clementia.—*Pas.* And I have just left her where you ordered her to be kept. She never went away. The chamber has been kept locked.—*Gher.* Where is the key? Give it to me. If she is not there you shall pay for it.   [*Exit.*

Enter Flaminio. Flaminio. Pasquella, how long is it since my Fabio was here? —*Pas.* Why?—*Flam.* Because he is a traitor, and I'll punish him; and because Isabella has left me for him. Fine honour to a lady in her position, to fall in love with a page! Tell her she will repent; and as for him,—I carry this dagger for him.—*Pas.* While the dog barks, the wolf feeds.—*Flam.* You will see.   [*Exit.*

Enter Gherardo. Gher. Oh me! to what am I come! Oh, traitor, Virginio! Oh Heaven! what shall I do!

Pas. What is the matter, master?—*Gher.* Who is he that is with my daughter? —*Pas.* He? Why you told me that it was Virginio's daughter.

[Gherardo has discovered the betrothal, and gives vent to his rage in untranslateable terms.]

SCENE.—*Enter Gherardo, Virginio, and Messer Piero.*

Piero. I wonder he has not returned to the hotel. I do not know what to make of

Dr Keller gives a synopsis of each of the five acts of *Paedantius*, but as it supplies none of the speeches of the hero, or of any other character, it is not here reprinted.

ENGLISH CRITICISM

HAZLITT (p. 293) : If we were to part with any of the author's comedies, it should be this. Yet we should be loth to part with Don Adriano de Armado, that mighty potentate of nonsense, or his page, that handful of wit ; with Nathaniel the curate, or Holofernes the school-master, and their dispute after dinner on 'the 'golden cadences of poesy'; with Costard the clown, or Dull the constable. Biron is too accomplished a character to be lost to the world, and yet he could not appear without his fellow courtiers and the King : and if we were to leave out the ladies, the gentlemen would have no mistresses. So that we believe we may let the whole play stand as it is, and we shall hardly venture to 'set a mark of reprobation on it.' Still we have some objections to the style, which we think savours more of the pedantic spirit of Shakespeare's time than of his own genius; more of controversial divinity, and the logic of Peter Lombard, than of the inspiration of the Muse. It transports us quite as much to the manners of the court, and the quirks of courts of law, as to the scenes of nature or the fairy-land of his own imagination. Shakespeare has set himself to imitate the tone of polite conversation then prevailing among the fair, the witty, and the learned, and he has imitated it but too faithfully. It is as if the hand of Titian had been employed to give grace to the curls of a full-bottomed periwig, or Raphael had attempted to give expression to the tapestry figures in the House of Lords. Shakespeare has put an excellent description of this fashionable jargon into the mouth of the critical Holofernes 'as too picked, too 'spruce, too affected, too odd, as it were, too peregrinate, as I may call it'; and nothing can be more marked than the difference when he breaks loose from the trammels he had imposed on himself, 'as light as bird from brake,' and speaks in his own person.

CHARLES ARMITAGE BROWN (p. 249) : Whether this comedy was ever popular, or merely admired by the few, may be doubted ; but it was formed to be acceptable to the gentry of the time ; and it was played before the Queen, with additions to its first appearance. This fact may account for the unequal division of the acts. It is a comedy of conversation, and exhibits every mode of speech, from ignorance, pedantry, and affected euphony, up to elegant discourse, and the grandest eloquence. . . . So completely is it a comedy of conversation that majesty itself is a companionable gentleman ; and we mix among the groups of lords and ladies, or with Costard and Holofernes, finding ourselves equally at home. . . . Objections are made to the poverty of the fable, and to the want of invention in its management. But the author would have defeated his own purpose, had he admitted an intricacy of plot, or placed his characters in situations to call forth the stronger passions. Satirical as it is, the entire feeling is good-humour. A reader who can enter into the spirit of it, will find sufficient interest to keep his attention on the alert. As to the charge of a want of dramatic invention, where the four lovers follow each other to the same spot, where three of them read their love-sonnets, and hide themselves, by turns, among the trees, possibly that may be considered of little weight. Three of the lovers are so artificial, that each must needs pen a sonnet to his lady, not only because it was out of his power to speak to her, but it was the fashion to pen sonnets : and each must sigh her name in a grove, because such had been, time out of mind, the lover's humour. At any rate, the amusing discovery at the last, and Biron's eloquent poetry, make ample amends.

If Shakespeare had not assured us this young Ferdinand was King of Navarre, I could not have believed it ; he is so unlike a King. He never pleads his sacred anointment, nor threatens with his royal displeasure, nor receives flattery from great men of his own making ; nor can he despise Costard, the clown. His wit allows him to sport a jest, his good-temper to take one from others; and at all times he is superior to playing the monarch over his associates. Longaville and Dumain are as much Kings of the conversation as himself. A weariness of courtly pleasure, the fashion, the idleness of their days, give these youths a butterfly-notion of being book-worms. Scholars they will be, and learned ones, and that at the end of three years. . . . Biron, whose ascendant mind cannot but convince their common-sense, has no control over their folly. Rousseau was not the first to ' reason against read- ' ing '; Biron was before him, and he speaks some things which hard spellers in a closet should con over betimes. . . . Holofernes stalks about with the ghost of a head ; vanity was his Judith. . . . Moth, not too young to join with the best effect in their full-blown talk, though old enough to laugh at it ; a character the poet has introduced to prove the absurdity of men's priding themselves in their deformities of language. . . . On his other characters, those of well-educated society, Shake- speare bestows his own easy-flowing, expressive language, steeped in the imagina- tion, not begrimed in affectation. Thus was the satire directed towards the ladies and gentlemen of his time ; holding forth to them the choice, either to be ranked among the silly pedants, and laughed at by children like Moth, or among their superiors. The principal character is Biron, whose properties by turns, are eloquence and mocking gibes ; the latter are keenly reprobated, and, in promise, corrected by Rosaline. When free from that fault, which, on the stage among fictitious persons, is harmlessly delightful, but, away from it, meets with none but ' shallow laughing ' hearers,' and is at the painful expense of the party ridiculed, he is beyond common praise ; nor is there throughout Shakespeare a strain of eloquence equal to Biron's near the end of the fourth Act, beginning with, ' Have at you then, affection's men ' at arms !'

THOMAS CAMPBELL : In this play there is a tenuity of incident that has pre- vented its popularity. The characters are rather playfully sketched than strongly delineated, or well discriminated. Biron is the witty hero of the king's courtiers, as Rosaline is the heroine of the princess's ladies. But the whole play is such a riot of wit, that one is at a loss to understand who were intended to be the wittiest per- sonages. Dull, methinks, shows himself to be the most sensible person in the play when he says that he understood not the jargon which the other characters had been uttering. But still, what with Biron and Holofernes, nobody could wish *Love's Labour's Lost* to be forgotten.

HALLAM (ii, 386) : *Love's Labour's Lost* is generally placed, I believe, at the bottom of the list. There is indeed little interest in the fable, if we can say that there is any fable at all ; but there are beautiful coruscations of fancy, more original conception of character than in *The Comedy of Errors*, more lively humour than in the *Gentlemen of Verona*, more symptoms of Shakespeare's future powers as a comic writer than in either. Much that is here but imperfectly developed came forth again in his later plays, especially in *As You Like It* and *Much Ado about Nothing*.

W. W. LLOYD (*Singer's Edition. Critical Essay*, 1856, p. 325): Of all the plays of Shakespeare, *Love's Labour's Lost* is perhaps that which bears most the appearance of being a definite satire on his contemporaries. Some traces of individual satire have been challenged, but not more than have seemed traceable in other plays; it is in the agreement in general colour, and in detailed manners of the follies exhibited, with those which were rife under Elizabeth, that we trace 'the form and 'pressure' of her time. In truth, there seems, to a reader of the present day, to be the essential weakness in the execution of the play, that it contains too much of the very faults it would expose; he becomes weary of the quaint verbalism, the strained affectation of phraseological acuteness, the slowness of the action, either retarded by distinctions and divisions of refinement entirely, or when it should become most lively and excited, losing itself in the crosspaths and byeways of indirect and sophistical contrivance,—the sacrifice of plainness and simplicity, not infrequently involving loss of true sensitive consideration for the claims and feelings of others. The mirror, I suspect, reflects the age too truthfully,—at least a certain class of its faults; and the social exaggerations in language and demeanour, true as they are to general human nature, are still not at present so abundant in these forms, as to prepare us to relish a still more concentrated version on the stage. It seems supererogatory for the dramatist to set such whims and motives in action, and to conduct them elaborately to their catastrophe, when we turn away from them at the first instance with disgust, and cannot have patience to sympathise with them so strongly as is requisite, if we would completely understand them. It was otherwise, no doubt, in the days of yore. ... (P. 331): It has been conjectured with much show of probability that Shakespeare, at the age of twelve, may have been among the multitudes attracted to Kenilworth, in 1575, a few miles only from Stratford, to witness the gorgeous and fantastic reception of Elizabeth by Leicester, at that time a sanguine and encouraged suitor. The Queen arrived a huntress, like the Princess of the play, and was greeted by the gods of mythology and symbolical moralities. . . . The Queen herself, in her reply to the Lady of the Lake, seems to have set the example of banter; and it was completed by the representative of Orion 'on a dolphin's back,' whose speech had got dissolved in the wine he had drunk, and who with frankness that reminds of Biron, tore off his mask and swore 'He was none of Arion, not he; but honest Harry Goldingham.' Incidents like these were no doubt frequent in those days of complimentary masks and shows, and Shakespeare might have gathered his moral of plain-dealing from any; but I would prefer recognising, in the drama of the masking lovers, the early impressions of the costly fête that was, to the potent Lord of Warwickshire, a work of wooing,—a labour of love, and that his renunciation of his hopes, not many months later, made memorable as a wooing in vain,—Love's Labour's Lost.

CHARLES BATHURST (p. 13): Much rhyme. Alternate rhymes. Very unbroken, unless in one place. Few double endings. Some rough, long lines; and some long, but regular; as quotations, not in the dialogue; both Alexandrine and seven-foot. A speech wholly of trisyllabic lines. Here are two instances of weak endings: II, i, 179, and 'In pruning me? When shall you hear that I Will praise 'a hand, a foot, a face, an eye.'—IV, iii, 189. The comic parts of the play are not to my purpose. They are exceedingly good, and show great force, and knowledge of human nature, for a play so early in his series. There are four fools, or dull persons in it, completely discriminated from each other. The parts in verse are certainly too much loaded with conceits and ideas of some sort; and the subject of the play leads to that. It is like a French play, a play of conversation, rather than a drama. The speeches are either too long, or else there is too much of the short dialogue of repartee, common in those times.

J. A. HERAUD (p. 40): This comedy and the tragedy of *Hamlet* had the same birth-year; but the former was printed earlier. The same elements belong to both; each, in its own way, is philosophical and critical, and dependent rather on the dialogue than the story. They are both scholastic dramas, replete with the learning of the time, and bear marks of their author having been a diligent student. In *Love's Labour's Lost* there is an ostentatious display of classical lore. The spirit of the whole is a desire to represent the manners of the Elizabethan epoch in the costume of the Middle Ages. What has been called 'the whimsical determination in 'which the drama is founded' is in perfect harmony with that costume, and with the history of 'the Courts of Love,' which had so much interest for the kings and knights of chivalry. But the real subject is the triumph of Protestant principle over vows of celibacy and other similar absurdities in the institutions that the Reformation had superseded; and in connection with this, the illustration of the characteristics then beginning. . . . The same moral is enforced in a still sterner manner in *Measure for Measure*, written full fourteen years later. The reader who desires to mark the steps of the author's improvement, and to identify the same mind in both works, will do well to compare the two plays. In the latter, the poet has put off the student, and taken on the statesman; the State is substitute for the Academe, as the arena for the display of the dramatic fable. We shall best find, however, the characteristics of the Elizabethan period in the academical aspects; simply because they were the result of an educational process, partly carried on through the medium of the pulpit, and partly through that of the press. The schoolmaster and the curate are accordingly intruded into the play, and exhibited in contrast with the uninstructed constable. The concurrence of such opposite characters on the same plane doubtless serves intentionally to indicate the stage of transition into which the era was then passing. Connected with this point is the peculiar diction of the play. . . . The coxcomb Spaniard, Armado, and his precocious page, Moth, with the clown, Costard, —all equally 'draw out the thread of their verbosity finer than the staple of their 'argument.' And even so does the play itself, which has scarcely any argument of action, but abundance of dialogue teeming with verbal affectations, and devoted mainly to their exposure. There is no incident, no situation, no interest of any kind;—the whole play is, literally and exclusively, 'a play on words.' While looking upon all this from the absurd side, the dramatist is, nevertheless, careful to suggest to the thoughtful student of his work, by means of some beautiful poetry, aphoristic sentences, and other finely artistic devices, that above these negative instances, when exhausted, there will be found to preside an affirmative and prior principle, which is indeed the spirit of the age, whereby the 'Providence which shapes our 'ends, rough-hew them how we will,' is conducting and guiding the world in its progresses to 'a consummation devoutly to be wished.' A philosophical, nay, a pious, design and purpose lies at the bottom of all the whimsicalities that misrepresent what they should embody;—in so doing, however, not especially singular; since the most serious and grave solemnities must also needs fall infinitely short of the verities they symbolize. Nor has Shakespeare left this very curious Aristophanic drama without its Chorus. It is the witty Biron who fills that office ; whose shafts are not directed against the euphuism of the time, but against the attempted aceticism which the progress and catastrophe of the play are destined to explode. . . . Here [in 'It is *religion* to be thus forsworn,' IV, iii, 382], indeed, is a justification for Luther and his broken vows. The very genius of the Reformation inspires this drama. The wife is enthroned instead of the vestal ; and the married man cares no longer for the song of the cuckoo, or the menace of horns. Biron who utters these sayings is himself a convertite. . . . The composition of this play, if duly considered, may serve to dissipate many errors regarding the qualities of mind needful to a man's becoming a dramatist. First and foremost, we find in this comedy a reliance in the poetic capacity. There is no extraneous action, no borrowed story, but the very materials of it are made out of the poet's own mind ; he trusts, not to his fable, but to his own wit and fancy. The logic of wit and the conceits of fancy are its twin-factors. . . . While, therefore, the play is purely a creation out of nothing, the dia-logue presents itself as a scholastic laboratory, where phrases are passed off for thoughts, and verbal exaggeration must be accepted for humour. It is not on the business of the stage, rapidity or complication of action, or the interest of the story, that the poet depends,—these would have all been alien to the spirit, design, and purpose of the work ; but on the activity of the thought, the intellectual combination of ideas, and the logical juxtaposition of verbal signs. He had faith that out of these an effective play could be generated ; and it was so. . . . In the Boyet and Biron, however, we recognise *rôles* requiring a courtier's acquaintance with things courtly, and a certain amount of worldly knowledge ; while in Costard, Moth, and Dull we perceive a dramatic art scarcely excelled in the poet's more mature produc-tions. So early had he perceived that law of dramatic composition, by which the highest was to be brought into sympathy with the lowest intellects, through inter-mediation of such characters as Roderigo in *Othello* and the Fool in *Lear*. If our calculation be correct, *Love's Labour's Lost* was the product of Shakespeare's twenty-fourth year. . . . The play is an organism; and as such is remarkably elabo-rate ; as any one will discover who examines the manner in which the fourth and fifth acts are constructed, and the artifices with which the various discoveries are prepared for ; but the elaboration is carried to excess ; four lovers and four ladies encumber the scene, and make a development needful, that prolongs the treatment beyond the limits of patient attention. In the course of his dramatic practice, Shake-speare was taught a wiser economy, and also learned the advantage of adding to his own idealities an historic or romantic action, as a convenient body for their stage-manifestation. But it was the Soul that gave Form to the body, not the body that prescribed Laws to the Soul.

E. DOWDEN (p. 62) : *Love's Labour's Lost* is a satirical extravaganza embody-ing Shakspere's criticism upon contemporary fashions and foibles in speech, in manners, and in literature. This probably more than any other of the plays of Shakspere suffers through lapse of time. Fantastical speech, pedantic learning, extravagant love hyperbole, frigid fervours in poetry, against each of these, with the brightness and vivacity of youth, confident in the success of its cause, Shakspere directs the light artillery of his wit. Being young and clever, he is absolutely devoid of respect for nonsense, whether it be dainty, affected nonsense, or grave unconscious nonsense. But over and above this, there is a serious intention in the play. It is a protest against youthful schemes of shaping life according to notions rather than according to reality, a protest against idealising away the facts of life. The play is chiefly interesting as containing Shakspere's confession of faith with respect to the true principles of self-culture. . . . The play is Shakspere's declaration in favour of the fact as it is. Here, he says, we are with such appetites and passions. Let us in any scheme of self-developement get *that* fact acknowledged at all events. Otherwise, we shall quickly enough betray ourselves as arrant fools, fit to be flouted by women, and needing to learn from them a portion of their directness, practicality, and good sense.

And yet the Princess, and Rosaline, and Maria, have not the entire advantage on their side. It is well to be practical ; but to be practical, and also to have a capacity for ideas is better. Berowne, the exponent of Shakspere's own thought, who entered into the youthful, idealistic project of his friends with a satisfactory assurance that the time would come when the entire dream-structure would tumble ridiculously about the ears of them all,—Berowne is yet a larger nature than the Princess or Rosaline. *His* good sense is the good sense of a thinker and of a man of action. When he is most flouted and bemocked, we yet acknowledge him victorious and master ; and Rosaline will confess the fact by and by.

In the midst of merriment and nonsense comes a sudden and grievous incursion of fact full of pain. The father of the Princess is dead. All the world is not mirth,—' this side is Hiems, Winter, this Ver, the Spring.' . . . Let us get hold of the realities of human nature and human life, Shakspere would say, and let us found upon these realities, and not upon the mist or the air, our schemes of individual and social advancement. Not that Shakspere is hostile to culture ; but he knows that a perfect education must include the culture, through actual experience, of the senses and of the affections.

IBID. (*Shakespeariana*, ii, 204, May, 1885) : Probably the first play of Shakespeare, in which he worked out ideas of his own, not following in the steps of a predecessor, is *Love's Labour's Lost*. It is throughout a piece of homage, half-serious, half-playful, to the influence of women. It tells us that the best school in which to study is the school of life, and that to rouse and quicken all our faculties, so that we may learn brightly the lessons of that school, we chiefly need the inspiration of love. The play looks as if it were Shakespeare's mirthful reply to the sneers and slights of some of his fellow-dramatists, who had come up to town from the University, well-read in the classical literature supposed in those Renaissance days to be the sole source of true culture, and who were indignant that a young fellow from Stratford, who had at best picked up a little irregular schooling, ' small Latin ' and less Greek,' from a country pedagogue, should aspire to the career of a dramatic poet. If Shakespeare were not a graduate of Oxford or Cambridge, he was something better,—he had graduated in the school of life ; he had looked about him with quick, observant eyes ; he had thought and felt ; he had struggled, sported, loved ; he had laughed at Stratford Dogberrys, had perhaps broken open the lodge and killed the deer of the Stratford Mr Justice Shallow ; and if he had not kissed the keeper's daughter (which is far from improbable), he had certainly kissed Anne Hathaway to his heart's content. And now in *Love's Labour's Lost*, while all the affectations of mock dignity and pedantry, and spurious learning, and fantastical refinement are laughed to scorn with a young man's light and vigorous laughter, Shakespeare comes forward to maintain that our best school-masters are life and love, and he adds, half-playfully, half-seriously, that if we wish to say our lesson brightly and well, we must first go and learn it from a woman.

F. J. FURNIVALL (*Leopold Ed. Introduction*, p. xxiv) enumerates the following features of this play :—(1) Shakspere started with the notion that mistaken identity was the best device for getting fun in comedy; he relied on it in the ladies' changed masks here, as later in *Much Ado* ; in the two sets of twins in his *Errors* ; in Puck's putting the juice in the wrong man's eyes in *Mid. N. Dream* ; in Sly in *The Shrew*, etc.; and it is indeed in all his comedies in some form or other;—(2) his obscurity (or difficulty) of expression is with him from his start, ' *King.* The extreme parts of ' time extremely form All causes to the purpose of his speed; And often, at his very ' loose, decides That which long process could not arbitrate.'—V, ii, 813. (3) He brings his Stratford out-door life and greenery, his Stratford countrymen's rough sub-play, on to the London boards, . . . (4) he re-writes the characters and incidents of this play, . . . (5) the ' college of witcrackers ' (*Much Ado*, V, iv) here overdo their quips, and tire one with them ; (6) Shakspere makes the young nobles behave like overgrown school-boys when teaching Moth,—this want of dignity, . . . is a mark of very early work. (7) Rosaline's making Berowne wait for a year may have been taken from Chaucer's *Parliament of Foules*, where the lady (or eagle representing her) insists on a year's delay before she chooses which of her three lovers she will have. (8) The best speech in the play is, of course, Berowne's on the effect of love in opening men's eyes and making the world new to them. How true it is, every lover since can bear witness ; but still there is a chaffiness about it, very different to the humility and earnestness of the lovers who follow Berowne in Shakspere, except his second self, Benedick.

HALLIWELL-PHILLIPPS (*Memoranda*, p. 17) : Tofte's lines [See Malone, *Date of Composition*], viewed in connection with the other early notices of the comedy, serve to show that *Love's Labour's Lost* was a popular play during the life-time of the author, when perhaps its satire was best appreciated. Towards the close of the following century, it had so completely fallen in general estimation that Collier, who, although an opponent of the drama, was not an indiscriminate censurer of Shakespeare, says that here the ' poet plays the fool egregiously, for the whole play ' is a very silly one.' * . . . A complete appreciation of *Love's Labour's Lost* was reserved for the present century, several modern psychological critics of eminence having successfully vindicated its title to a position amongst the very best productions of the great dramatist.

A. C. SWINBURNE (p. 46) : The example afforded by *The Comedy of Errors* would suffice to show that rhyme, however inadequate for tragic use, is by no means a bad instrument for romantic comedy. In another of Shakespeare's earliest works, which might almost be described as a lyrical farce, rhyme plays also a great part ; but the finest passage, the real crown and flower of *Love's Labour's Lost*, is the praise or apology of love spoken by Biron in blank verse. This is worthy of Marlowe for dignity and sweetness, but has also the grace of a light and radiant fancy enamoured of itself, begotten between thought and mirth, a child-god with grave lips and laughing eyes, whose inspiration is nothing akin to Marlowe's. In this as

* *Short View of the Immorality and Profaneness of the English Stage*, 1699, p. 125.

in the overture of the play and in its closing scene, but especially in the noble passage which winds up for a year the courtship of Biron and Rosaline, the spirit which informs the speech of the poet is finer of touch and deeper of tone than in the sweetest of the serious interludes of *The Comedy of Errors*. The play is in the main a lighter thing, and more wayward and capricious in build, more formless and fantastic in plot, more incomposite altogether than that first heir of Shakespeare's comic invention, which on its own ground is perfect in its consistency, blameless in composition and coherence; while in *Love's Labour's Lost* the fancy for the most part runs wild as the wind, and the structure of the story is as that of a house of clouds which the wind builds and unbuilds at pleasure. Here we find a very riot of rhymes, wild and wanton in their half-grown grace as a troop of 'young satyrs, 'tender-hoofed and ruddy-horned'; during certain scenes we seem almost to stand again by the cradle of new-born comedy, and hear the first lisping and laughing accents run over from her baby lips in bubbling rhyme; but when the note changes we recognise the speech of gods. For the first time in our literature the higher key of poetic or romantic comedy is finely touched to a fine issue. The divine instrument fashioned by Marlowe for tragic purposes alone has found at once its new sweet use in the hands of Shakespeare. The way is prepared for *As You Like It* and *The Tempest*; the language is discovered which well befit the lips of Rosalind and Miranda.

WALTER PATER (*Macmillan's Magazine*, December, 1885, p. 90) : Play is often that about which people are most serious; and the humorist may observe how, under all love of playthings, there is almost always hidden an appreciation of something really engaging and delightful. This is true always of the toys of children; it is often true of the playthings of grown-up people, their vanities, their fopperies even—the cynic would add their pursuit of fame and their lighter loves. Certainly, this is true without exception of the playthings of a past age, which to those who succeed it are always full of pensive interest—old manners, old dresses, old houses. For what is called fashion in these matters occupies, in each age, much of the care of many of the most discerning people, furnishing them with a kind of mirror of their real inward refinements, and their capacity for selection. Such modes or fashions are, at their best, an example of the artistic predominance of form over matter; of the manner of the doing of it over the thing done; and have a beauty of their own. It is so with that old euphuism of the Elizabethan age—that pride of dainty language and curious expression, which it is very easy to ridicule, which often made itself ridiculous, but which had below it a real sense of fitness and nicety; and which, as we see in this very play, and still more clearly in the Sonnets, had some fascination for the young Shakspere himself. It is this foppery of delicate language, this fashionable plaything of his time, with which Shakspere is occupied in *Love's Labour's Lost*. He shows us the manner in all its stages; passing from the grotesque and vulgar pedantry of Holofernes, through the extravagant but polished caricature of Armado, to become the peculiar characteristic of a real though still quaint poetry in Biron himself—still chargeable, even at his best, with just a little affectation. As Shakspere laughs broadly at it in Holofernes or Armado, he is the analyst of its curious charm in Biron; and this analysis involves a delicate raillery by Shakspere himself at his own chosen manner.

This 'foppery' of Shakspere's day had, then, its really delightful side, a quality in no sense 'affected,' by which it satisfies a real instinct in our minds—the fancy so many of us have for an exquisite and curious skill in the use of words. Biron is the perfect flower of this manner—' A man of fire-new words, fashion's own knight' —as he describes Armado, in terms which are really applicable to himself. In him this manner blends with a true gallantry of nature, and an affectionate complaisance and grace. He has at times some of its extravagance or caricature also, but the shades of expression by which he passes from this to the 'golden cadence' of Shakspere's own chosen verse, are so fine, that it is sometimes difficult to trace them. What is a vulgarity in Holofernes, and a caricature in Armado, refines itself in him into the expression of a nature truly and inwardly bent upon a form of deli-cate perfection, and is accompanied by a real insight into the laws which determine what is exquisite in language, and their root in the nature of things. He can appre-ciate quite the opposite style—' In russet yeas, and honest kersey noes'; he knows the first law of pathos, that—' Honest plain words best suit the ear of grief.' He delights in his own rapidity of intuition; and, in harmony with the half-sensuous philosophy of the Sonnets, exalts, a little scornfully, in many memorable expres-sions, the judgement of the senses, above all slower, more toilsome means of knowl-edge, scorning some who fail to see things only because they are so clear—' So ere ' you find where light in darkness lies, Your light grows dark by losing of your ' eyes'—as with some German commentators on Shakspere. Appealing always to actual sensation from men's affected theories, he might seem to despise learning; as, indeed, he has taken up his deep studies partly in play, and demands always the profit of learning in renewed enjoyment; yet he surprises us from time to time by intuitions which can come only from a deep experience and power of observation; and men listen to him, old and young, in spite of themselves. He is quickly im-pressible to the slightest clouding of the spirits in social intercourse, and has his moments of extreme seriousness; his trial-task may well be, as Rosaline puts it— ' To enforce the pained impotent to smile.' But still, through all, he is true to his chosen manner; that gloss of dainty language is a second nature with him; even at his best he is not without a certain artifice; the trick of playing on words never deserts him; and Shakspere, in whose own genius there is an element of this very quality, shows us in this graceful, and, as it seems, studied, portrait, his enjoyment of it.

As happens with every true dramatist, Shakspere is for the most part hidden behind the persons of his creation. Yet there are certain of his characters in which we feel that there is something of self-portraiture. And it is not so much in his grander, more subtle and ingenious creations that we feel this—in Hamlet and King Lear—as in those slighter and more spontaneously developed figures, who, while far from playing principal parts, are yet distinguished by a certain peculiar happi-ness and delicate ease in the drawing of them—figures which possess, above all, that winning attractiveness which there is no man but would willingly exercise, and which resemble those works of art which, though not meant to be very great or im-posing, are yet wrought of the choicest material. Mercutio, in *Romeo and Juliet*, belongs to this group of Shakspere's characters—versatile, mercurial people, such as make good actors, and in whom the ' Nimble spirits of the arteries,' the finer but still merely animal elements of great wit, predominate. A careful delineation of little, characteristic traits seems to mark them out as the characters of his predilec-tion; and it is hard not to identify him with these more than with others. Biron, in *Love's Labour's Lost*, is perhaps the most striking member of this group. In this character, which is never quite in touch with, never quite on a perfect level of understanding with the other persons of the play, we see, perhaps, a reflex of

Shakspere himself, when he has just become able to stand aside from and estimate the first period of his poetry.

T. R. PRICE (*Shakespeariana*, 1890, vol. vii, p. 82) : In tracing the characters of Longaville and Dumain, Shakespeare, forsaking the country-side recollections of his boyhood, draws from the gay young lords that he watched lounging in the theatres of London or ruffling through the streets. Just as Maria and Katherine stood to the Princess, so Longaville and Dumain stand to the King. This almost mechanical symmetry of construction is one of the chief marks of Shakespeare's youthful workmanship. The groups balance against each other, three against three, like the dancers in a country dance, or like the clauses in one of Armado's sentences. There is in the dramatic work of the young Shakespeare, the same too-elaborate accuracy of grouping as in the artistic work of the young Raphael. But in spite of the artificial groups, the separate figures are sharply defined, each made fully individual. Longaville, for example, is full of dramatic life. He is tall and big, stubborn, a little disposed to be gruff and overbearing. When the King brings forward his plan of the new life, the life from which women are to be excluded, and all given up to study and meditation, Longaville not only goes into the scheme with boisterous energy, but he is rude and contemptuous toward Biron's scruples. He is proud of his own dull wit in devising against women the penalty of cutting out their tongues, and he indulges in cheap jests against their love of talk. He is rather coarse in his own tastes, and proposes to get great fun out of the society of Costard and Armado. Such men like to have creatures near them that they can make the butts of their clumsy wit. When he goes with the King to meet the Princess and her ladies, he falls, in spite of his vows, dead in love with Maria, whom he had met once before in Normandy. But although Maria remembers him, he, duller and less observant than the lady, fails to recognise Maria, and in questioning Boyet about her he shows the same quick temper and bad manners that he had shown before in talking with Biron. Unused to self-control, he makes no struggle to keep his vow, nor to conquer his love. He plies his poor brains to make a poem in her honour, and he shows in his stiff and ungainly verses, which parody the fashionable poetry of Shakespeare's time, his own poverty of thought and badness of taste. After reciting his own poem with complacency, he detects his friend Dumain in the same act of perjury. He in turn is detected by the King. He shows no shame in being discovered; he that was first in urging the vow against women is again the first in breaking it. In all he is headstrong and impetuous, Disguised as a Russian, he goes masquerading with the King, and he is cheated by the ladies into making love by mistake to Katharine. In the wit-duel of the maskers he is not sharp nor nimble enough to hold his own; he has to bear from Katharine hard jests at his clumsiness, his rustic ways of talking, and his lack of polite conversation. When the pageant begins, he joins in cutting jokes at Holofernes and Armado, but here, too, he is always second-rate and second-hand in his wit, catching the thought from others, and weighing it down by his own heaviness. Yet, as it often happens, the big, handsome, dull-witted soldier wins by his honest devotion the love of the gentle and refined woman. He courts his Maria with fervour and with success. He sends her gifts of pearls and sheets of verses. The pearls, may be, make amends for the verses. He wins the love of his Maria. We see the tall, good-looking, stupid fellow, for the last time ere the curtain falls for ever, smiling with delight under the caressing compliments of his lady love.

Dumain is as different from his friend Longaville as Katharine is from Maria. He is small and beardless, youthful and insignificant in appearance. He is gentler and deeper of nature, far less strenuous and masterful. He takes the King's vows with great sincerity and even solemnity of mood, and he reproaches Biron with the worldliness of his views of life. He is full of sentiment, and so eager to love somebody that when he sees Katharine, in spite of her red face and pockmarks, he falls at once in love with her. He sees in her all physical perfections, sends her rich presents, and writes her verses. His poetry is utterly unlike Longaville's ; instead of being court poetry it is pastoral ; instead of being full of fashionable conceits it is full of natural beauty and tender sentiment. Yet although he loves so deeply, he feels the shame of breaking his vow against women, and appeals to Biron to find excuse and justification for the purpose. When he joins the rest in scoffing at Holofernes and Armado, his jesting is, as he tells us, only to hide his heartache. He is quicker of wit than Longaville, and makes some pretty speeches and some good puns. There is a soft, modern pathos in his last appeal to Katharine : ' But what ' to me, my love, but what to me ?' But the sentimental lover is apt to be the unsuccessful one ; there is a weak vein in Dumain's character that excites not love but ridicule in the worldly-minded Katharine. She utters a parting jest at his lack of beard and his lack of vigor ; and she goes leaving her lover almost hopeless. But sentiment has its consolations as well as dangers. In a few weeks we can believe that Dumain was as deeply in love with some one else as he had been with Katharine.

SIR EDWARD STRACHEY (*Atlantic Monthly*, January, 1893, p. 108) : The ladies in the play, as in nature, are at first inclined to make fun of the serious ardour of their admirers, till the whole scene becomes a tilting-match or tournament of wits, in which,—again with truth to nature,—the ladies get the better, and the men confess themselves ' beaten with pure scoff.' But love is becoming lord of all with the ladies, too. Another transition is marked when the princess exclaims, ' We are wise ' girls to mock our lovers so !' Then come the tidings of the death of her father. In a moment the electric spark crystallizes that life of fun and joyousness. The generous and noble-minded youths and maidens become dignified men and women, and turn to the duties of real life, though agreeing that the new is still to be linked with the old. If the poet had told us the real ending, he would have called the play *Love's Labour's Won*, and so anticipated the answer to a still vexed question of Dr Dryasdust. . . .

Love's Labour's Lost is remarkable for its careful accuracy of thought and word even in its fun, and indicates how much Shakespeare must, in the days of his earliest compositions, have studied the logical use of language, even when he is employing it to express the most fanciful conceits or the most soaring imaginations. The play is full of instances of this careful composition, with its regular balance of thoughts, words, and rhymes in the successive lines. This use of language is perfect in its kind ; yet how different it is from that of *The Tempest, Othello*, or *Hamlet !* Surely the difference between the youthful and the mature genius is plain enough.

W. J. COURTHOPE (vol. iv, p. 84) : *Love's Labour's Lost* may, in fact, be regarded as a study of absurdity in the abuse of language, intentional or unintentional, by all orders of society, from the courtier to the clown. Lyly's euphuistic manner is partly imitated as in itself a species of comic wit, and partly ridiculed as an exhibition of human folly ; the various examples of courtly, scholastic, and rustic pedantry are contrasted with each other in the nicest gradations. In each form of speech, however, the influence of *Euphues* is apparent. The chivalrous idea of gallantry, inherited from the Courts of Love, and modified by Lyly, animates the combats of wit between Biron on the one side, and Boyet and the ladies on the other; the love sonnets resemble some of Shakespeare's own in the euphuistic extravagance of their metaphor; while the logical and verbal conceits, which Lyly had brought into fashion are illustrated in Biron's speech [in IV, iii, 1–9].

Euphues' ridiculous precision is amusingly hit off in Don Armado, who, with his page Moth, is, I think, certainly an improved version of Sir Tophas and his page, Epiton, in Lyly's *Endymion*. The lofty gravity, with which the Spaniard proclaims his passion for the stolid Jaquenetta, is a curious anticipation,—though the absurdity takes a different form,—of Don Quixote and his Dulcinea.

In *Love's Labour's Lost* the underplot is brought into great prominence. Don Armado is the pivot on which it turns, but many other characters revolve round him, of whom perhaps, the most notable is Holofernes, the schoolmaster, a person reflecting in a ridiculous form the conceit of the schoolmen of the Universities. There is considerable humour in the dialogue between this pedant, his admirer, Sir Nathaniel, the curate, and Dull, the constable. [IV, ii, 40–94].

GERMAN CRITICISM *

H. ULRICI (1847, vol. ii, p. 86): The inner and ideal centre upon which this graceful play turns,—in the light, playful movement of its humour,—is the significant contrast between the fresh reality of life which ever renews its youth, and the abstract, dry and dead, study of philosophy. This contrast, when, in absolute strictness, it completely separates the two sides that belong to one another, at once contains an untruth which equally affects both sides, deprives both of their claim of right, and leads them into folly and into contradiction with themselves. That philosophy which disregards all reality and seeks to bring itself within itself, either succeeds in entombing itself in the barren sand of a shallow, absurd, and pedantic learning, or else,—overcome by the fascinations of youthful life,—it becomes untrue to itself, turns into its opposite, and is justly derided as mere affectation and empty pretence. One of these results is exhibited in the case of the learned Curate, Sir Nathaniel, and the Schoolmaster, Holofernes, two starched representatives of the retailers of learned trifles, and in the pompous, bombastic Spanish Knight, a very Don Quixote in high-flown phraseology; the other is exhibited in the fate of the King and his associates. Owing to their capricious endeavour to gain knowledge and to study philosophy, by living an entirely secluded life, they at once fall into all the frivolities and follies of love; in spite of their oaths and vows of fraternity, nature and living reality assert themselves and win an easy victory. And yet the victory of false wisdom is in reality nothing more than a victory of folly over folly. For nature and reality, taken by themselves are only changing pictures, transient phenomena, to interpret which correctly is the task of the inquiring mind. When they are not rightly understood, when the *ethical* relations forming their substance are not recognised, then life itself degenerates into a mere semblance, all the activity and pleasure in life become mere play and frivolity; without the seriousness of this recognition, love

---

* Much of German comment on this play has been incorporated in the preceding pages in the Commentary, by the side of English Commentators.—ED.

is mere tinsel, while talent, intelligence, and culture become mere vain wit and an empty play of thoughts. This recognition is not, however, attained by communities for philosophical study and discussions, but by serious self-examination, by the exercise of self-control and the curbing of one's own lusts and desires, by seclusion only in this sense and for this end. This, therefore, is imposed upon the Prince and his companions by their ladies as a punishment for their arrogance. The fine and ever correct judgement of noble women is here as triumphant as their great talent for social wit and refined intrigue. The moral of the piece may be said to be contained in the speech of the Princess where she condemns the King to a twelvemonth's fast and strict seclusion, in the sense intimated above, and again in the words of Rosaline, in which she makes it a condition to the vain Biron,—a man who boasts of the power of his mind and wit in social intercourse,—that, to win her love he shall for a twelvemonth, from day to day, visit 'the speechless sick' and 'converse with groaning 'wretches,' and, in order to exercise all the powers of his wit, demands of him 'to force the pained impotent to smile.' The end of the comedy thus, to a certain extent, returns to where it began : both sides of the contrast out of which it arose prove themselves untenable in their one-sided exclusiveness : the highest delight and pleasure of existence, all wit and all talents are mere vanity without the earnestness and depth of the thoughtful mind which apprehends the essence of life ; but study and philosophy, also, are pure folly when kept quite apart from real life. It is the same contrast as that between Spring and Winter, Cuckoo and Owl : if separate from one another they would lead either to excessive luxuriousness or to a state of deadly torpidity ; but they are not separate and are not intended to be separate, their constant change in rising out of and passing over one into the other, in short, their mutual inter-action produces *true* life.

This deeper significance of the merry piece, with its fine irony and harmless satire is, of course, not expressed in didactic breadth, but only intimated in a playful manner. Shakespeare was too well aware that it was not the business of the drama to preach morals and that to give pedantic emphasis to the serious ethical relations would not only injure the effect of the comic, but absolutely destroy it. And yet it is only the above-described contrast from which the whole is conceived, and upon which its deeper significance rests, that explains why Shakespeare furnished the main action,—the bearers of which are the King and the Princess with their knights and ladies,—with the ludicrous subordinate figures of Sir Nathaniel, Holofernes, Don Armado, and Dull, etc., and with a series of intermezzos which apparently stand in no sort of connection with it. These obviously form an essential part of the whole, and with the addition of the satirical element is, at the same time, intended to place its significance in a still clearer light. For there can scarcely be any doubt that the piece contains a satirical tendency. . . .

(Page 90) : For wherever Shakespeare, in his comedies, allows the interference of the satirical element, he surrounds it with such an abundance of wit and jest, that it is, so to say, lost in their midst ; this is evidently done to rid it of its offensive sting, and to lessen the impression of deliberateness. The reason of the poet's having given the whole such a bright colouring, is, that when regarded from without, the piece appears to be but an insignificant play of jest and joke, but a merry rivalry of wit and banter among the dramatic personages.

Dr G. G. Gervinus (1849–50, vol. i, p. 228) : From this over-abundance of droll and laughter-loving personages, of wits and caricatures, the comedy gives the idea of an excessively jocular play ; nevertheless, every one on reading it feels a certain want of ease, and on account of this very excess, cannot enjoy the comic effect. In structure and management of subject, it is indisputably one of the weakest of the poet's pieces ; yet one divines a deeper merit than is readily perceived, and which is with difficulty unfolded. . . . The poet, who scarcely ever aspired after the equivocal merit of inventing his stories himself, seems according to this [historical fact, recorded in Monstrelet] to have himself devised the matter, which suffers from a striking lack of action and characterisation. The whole turns upon a clever interchange of wit and asceticism, jest and earnest ; the shallow characters are forms of mind, rather proceeding from the cultivation of the head than the will ; throughout there are affected jests, high-sounding and often empty words, but no action, and, notwithstanding, one feels that this deficiency is no unintentional error, but that there is an object in view. There is a motley mixture of fantastic and strange characters, which for the most part betray no healthy groundwork of nature, and yet the poet himself is so sensible of this, that we might trust him to have had his reason for placing them together, a reason worth our while to seek. And indeed we find, on closer inspection, that this piece has a more profound character, in which Shakespeare's capable mind already unfolds its power; we perceive in this, the first of his plays, in which he, as subsequently is ever the case, has had one single moral aim in view, an aim that here lies even far less concealed than in others of his works.

(Page 236): Whoever reads the comic scenes 'the civil war of wits' between Boyet and his ladies, between Biron and Rosaline, between Mercutio and Romeo, Benedick and Beatrice, and others, scenes, which in *Love's Labour's Lost* for the first time occur in more decided form and in far greater abundance than elsewhere, whoever attentively reads and compares them, will readily see that they rest upon a common human basis, and at the same time upon a conventional one as to time and place. They hinge especially on the play and perversion of words ; and this is the foundation for wit common in every age. Even in the present day we have but to analyze the wit amongst jovial men, to find that it always proceeds from punning and quibbling. That which in Shakespeare then is the conventional peculiarity, is the determined form in which this word-wit appears. This form was cultivated among the English people as an established custom, which invested jocose conversation with the character of a regular battle. They snatch a word, a sentence, from the mouth of an adversary whom they wish to provoke, and turn and pervert it into a weapon against him; he parries the thrust and strikes back, espying a similar weakness in his enemy's ward ; the longer the battle is sustained, the better ; he who can do no more is vanquished. In this piece of Shakespeare's, Armado names this war of words an *argument*; it is clearly designated as like a game at tennis, where the words are hurled, caught, and thrown back again ; where he loses, who allows the word, like the ball, to fall; this war of wit is compared to a battle, that between Boyet and Biron, for example, to a sea-fight. The manner in which wit and satire thus wage war, is by no means Shakespeare's property ; it is universally found on the English stage, and is transferred to it directly from life. What we know of Shakespeare's social life reveals to us this same kind of jesting in his personal intercourse. Tradition speaks of Shakespeare as 'a handsome, well-shaped 'man, very good company, and of a very ready and pleasant and smooth wit.'

G. Sarrazin (*Sh. Jahrbuch*, xxxi, 1895, p. 210): There is much in the composition and characterisation of this comedy which recalls the *Commedia dell' arte* with its typical figures. Costard resembles the Peasant Bertolino (Pedrolino) with his mother wit ; Jaquenetta is like Colombine, who in Italian pantomimes is wont to be the wife or sweetheart of Pedrolino (Pierros). Don Armado affords a kinship with the *Miles Gloriosus*, who is nearly allied to the Captain Spavento or Captain Matamoros. The schoolmaster Holofernes corresponds to the Pedant of Italian comedies. Biron and his companions are almost identical with the typical *Amorosi* (Flavio, Leandro). The sonorous, almost pompous sentences, the stichomythia [*i. e.* conversation in alternate lines], the Sonnets,—all these border more on Italian, or, at least, on Romance taste. It is possible that Lyly may have had herein some influence, but it will not account for all. At all events, the piece may be most easily accounted for, if it be considered as the fruit of that sojourn in Italy which has been conjectured. But it is a fruit ripened in English air : in spite of French material, in spite of the imitation of Italian art, the whole atmosphere is downright English.

The poet knew right well how to adapt his scenes to an English presentation. By his poetic fancy, the Princess of Fame is transformed into the glorious Queen of England. Of the real French princess he retained only those traits which were flattering to Elizabeth : her beauty, her grace, her wit. In other respects, the Princess is such as the Queen of England appeared, or, at least, such as she wished to appear. Just as it is represented in the drama, she was wont to take her favourites by surprise and to be entertained with masques, plays, dancing, and hunting. When, in the year 1590, she was on a visit to an uncle of the Lord of Southampton, in Coudray, she shot three deer, The reserve of the Princess toward the wooing of the King is evidently a compliment designed for the Queen, in so far as she is compared to the chaste moon (IV, iii, 247). The poetic imagination of the poet has depicted the court of the King of Navarre like the domain of an English Lord. He placed the stately park somewhere in the south of England where grows the sycamore, and imagined it dotted with cornfields and meadows, where bloom daisies pied and violets blue and lady-smocks all silver-white, and where are grassy plots with green geese feeding.

GEORGE BRANDES (p. 54): Shakespeare had not yet attained the maturity and detachment of mind which could enable him to rise high above the follies he attacks, and to sweep them aside with full authority. He buries himself in them, circumstantially demonstrates their absurdities, and is still too inexperienced to realise how he thereby inflicts upon the spectator and the reader the full burden of their tediousness. It is very characteristic of Elizabeth's taste that, even in 1598, she could still take pleasure in the play. All this fencing with words appealed to her quick intelligence ; while, with the unabashed sensuousness characteristic of the daughter of Henry VIII. and Anne Boleyn, she found entertainment in the playwright's freedom of speech, even, no doubt, in the equivocal badinage between Boyet and Maria.

FRENCH CRITICISM

FRANÇOIS-VICTOR HUGO (vol. vi, p. 41) : But the case was different in England. There, the blue-stocking gathering was not a club merely tolerated, it was a powerful society ; it was not, as in France, confined to certain aristocratic residences, it entered the castles of royalty as into its home ; it did not give tiny evening parties in tiny parlors, it held its grand levees in the palaces of Windsor, Greenwich, Westminster; it was no cabal, it was camarilla; it did not pout at the Court, it governed it; for it had at its head, not Madame la marquise de Rambouillet, but Her Majesty Elizabeth, the Queen.

Picture a learned woman having for a pen-knife a sword and the globe for a paper-weight, ruling not over kitchens but over an empire, directing not a household but society, and giving her orders, not to an Abigail but, to a people. To this blue-stocking, who wears the garter of Edward III., accord all the feminine caprices which Molière has denounced,—the lackadaisical manners of Cathos, the prudery of Arsinoë, the vanity of Belise, the affectation of Armande, and the violence of Philaminte, and magnify them all with the formidable haughtiness of the Tudors. Picture to yourself this really learned woman, this queen who addresses the ambassador of France in French, the Venetian envoy in Italian, the nuntio of the Empire in German, the parliamentarian of Spain in Castilian, and the representative of Poland in Latin; this sovereign lady who translated Plato, Isocrates, Euripides, Xenophon, Plutarch, Sallust, Horace, Boëthius, Seneca, with the same hand that signed the death-warrant of Mary Queen of Scots; picture her as seated not among the Vadiuses and Trissotins, as in Molière, but served on bended knee by the most youthful and handsomest of Clitandres, and enthroned amid adulations and incense, in a never ending apotheosis.

Such was the opponent that the author of *Love's Labour's Lost* had to face. Do not suppose that I exaggerate in attributing to Queen Elizabeth all the whims which our great Poquelin distributed among his *precieuses*. It is curious to note with what minuteness history confirms the justice of this comparison. All the affectations which the poet of the *Femmes Savantes* has rallied, all the false theories which he scoffed at in the salon of Chrysale, all the excentricities which he whipped over the shoulders of poor Mascarille were boldly patronised by the all-powerful daughter of Henry VIII.—The 'chart of tenderness,' so sumptuously traced by Mlle de Scudéry, was but a degenerate copy of the affected map of the world licensed by Elizabeth; in this model map, the capital of the land of Passion was designated, not as an open town but, as a strong impenetrable fortress; with her sovereign pen, Elizabeth had blotted out the Castle of *Petits-Soins*, destroyed the hamlet of *Billets-Doux*, and, on this side of the river of *Inclination*, she had planted the pillars of Hercules of a universe of gallantry. Woe to the fool-hardiness which should dare to overstep these unalterable bounds! It would instantly hear the thunderous rumblings of imperial anger. . . .

(Page 45): In thus preaching to all the renunciation of the flesh, Elizabeth was conforming to a thoroughly selfish prejudice; she would not permit to others a happiness forbidden to her. What despair was hers when the marriage between her and the Duc d'Anjou was broken off. For forbidden joys she had sighed all her life in vain; a husband, a family, a home! Ah, what transports, had she only had a son! what intoxication of joy! She would not then have had to bequeath her crown to the son of her rival, Mary. . . . Whenever one of her immediate courtiers married, it was to her like the opening of a half closed wound. She flew into a passion; she swore; she scolded the couple when affianced who thus reminded her that she was an old maid; she scolded them when married, because they thus reproached her for not being a mother. Thus it was that with a monkish fanaticism she propagated the mystic religion of the *precieuses*. Not content to be its priestess, she wished to be its idol. Her courtiers extolled her as divine; she

made a show of loving me ; then, I know not wherefore, she showed herself altogether averse to me and contrary to my desires, so that, an she be at the door or the window, whenas I pass through the street, she withdraweth indoors, so soon as she seeth me, and will no longer hearken to my letters or messages. Yesterday, more by token, I sent my page to see an he might avail to speak with her ; but he hath never returned to render me an answer, so that I find myself bereaved at once of my mistress and of a good and most engaging servant. Had he returned and brought me news that she still persisted in her wonted obduracy, I was resolved to importune her no longer, but to seek me another lady, to whom my service should be more acceptable, since, to tell the truth, meseemeth a great folly to ensue one who shunneth me, to love one who loveth me not, and to seek one who will none of me.'
'You may take your oath of that,' rejoined Pippa. 'A fine thing, indeed ! Certes, for my part, I would not be so fond as to love one who wished me not well. But tell me, an it please you ; if Nicuola yet wished you well, nay, loved you more than ever, what would you say thereof? Think you she would deserve to be loved of you?' 'Indeed,' replied the young man, 'she would deserve that I should love her even as myself. But it may not be as you say, for that she must certainly be despited against me, inasmuch as she wrote to me again and again after her return to Jesi and I took no manner heed of her, nor know I where she is, so long is it since I saw her.' 'Nay, for that matter,' rejoined Pippa, 'I know you have seen her innumerable times in the last few days and have spoken very familiarly with her.' Whereupon quoth Lattanzio, 'Dame Pippa, you are mistaken in this.' And she, 'Nay, I am not mistaken, for that in good sooth I should know what I say and speak not to the wind. But harkye, an it were as I tell you and I caused you see for yourself that Nicuola loveth you more than ever, what would you do? And if she had been in your house and had served you and had done that which every least servant must do and had never been known of you, what would you think? Nay, make not such a show of wonderment, for the thing is e'en as I say. And so you may see I have told you the truth, I am ready to certify you thereof in such wise that you shall say as I say. But first answer me ; if Nicuola had done as I tell you, what would she deserve?' 'You tell me fables and dreams,' answered Lattanzio, 'but, if this were true, I know not what to say, save that it would behoove me love her infinitely and make her mistress of myself.' Quoth Pippa, 'It is well,' and calling Nicuola, bade her bring with her the page's clothes which she had worn.

Accordingly, Nicuola, who had heard all, took up the clothes and presented herself, all rosy in the face, before her nurse and her lover ; whereupon quoth Pippa, 'Here, Lattanzio, is your Nicuola ; here is your Romolo ; here is your so much desired page, who hath abidden with you and hath for your love exposed herself to exceeding great risk of her honour and her life. Here is she who, scorning all the world, hath recked of you only ; and withal you have never known her in all this time.' With this she told the whole story of Nicuola's turning page, adding, 'Now what say you?' Lattanzio abode as one half beside himself and stared at Nicuola, himseeming he dreamed, nor knew not what to say, hearing she had abidden with him, clad as a boy. However, he presently recovered himself somewhat and bethinking of the cruelty of Catella, than whom Nicuola was far fairer, and considering the latter's devotion and the risk to which she had exposed herself for excess of love, he said, well-nigh weeping, 'Nicuola, I will not presently enter upon the labyrinth of vain excuses ; but, an you be of such mind as Dame Pippa affirmeth, I will take you to wife, whenas you will.' Nicuola, who desired nothing in the world more than this, could scarce contain herself for joy, and casting herself at his feet, replied to him on this wise, saying, 'My Lord, since you, of your favour, deign to take me for yours, here am I at your service, for that myself and my pleasure will still be yours in everything.' With this, Lattanzio drew a ring from his finger and espoused her to his lawful wife in the presence of Pippa, saying, 'So our affairs may be ordered with the more repute and honour, I will, as soon as I have dined, go speak with your father and demand you of him to wife.' Then, having taken order for that which he purposed to do, Lattanzio departed and went to dinner; after which he set out to visit Nicuola's father, whilst she herself went home with Pippa to meet Messer Ambrogio, by whom she was joyfully received.

Meanwhile, Paolo, as soon as he had dined, went forth the inn and made, all alone, for Catella's house. When he reached the head of the street, he saw Gerardo come out of the house and go I know not whither. Scarce was he gone when Catella showed herself at the window and saw Paolo; whereupon, thinking him her Romolo, she beckoned to him to enter, as soon as he was near the door, and he accordingly entered the house, resolved to certify himself what this meant. Catella in a trice came down the stairs and embracing him, kissed him, for that she believed him to be Romolo; then, 'Dear my life,' quoth she, 'and ultimate end of all my thoughts, thou makest thyself over-scarce. Marry, I told thee my mind two days agone, and that I would have none other than thyself to husband.' Therewith she bade the maid watch for my lord's return and advise her thereof, what while she fell to kissing Paolo and bespeaking him with the softest of words. He, being nowise dull-witted and perceiving that she mistook him for another, feigned himself fallen well nigh dumb for excess of love and kissed her again and again, sighing the while. Then, 'My soul,' quoth she, 'I would fain have thee rid thyself of yonder master of thine, so we may be together whenassoever it liketh us.' And he, 'Let that not trouble you, for I will e'en find means to do without him.' 'Ay do thou, my life,' rejoined Catella. While they were thus holding amorous discourse, Gerardo came home and entered the house. As he passed the door of the chamber where the two lovers had seated themselves on a bench to talk, he heard folk within and to say 'Who is there?' and to open the chamber-door with a thrust of his foot were one and the same thing. When he saw Paolo with his daughter, he mistook him for Nicuola, of whom, as has been already said, he was sore enamoured; wherefore the anger forsaking him into which he had entered, thinking a man to be with Catella, he stared at Paolo, and the more he eyed him, the more was he stablished in his opinion that it was Nicuola. Catella was half-dead at her father's appearance, and Paolo trembled all over; but, when they saw the old man stand fast, without saying aught, they awaited the result with better courage. As hath already been said, Paolo and Nicuola his sister were so alike that it was exceeding uneath for whoso was most familiar with them to discern which of them was the male and which the female; wherefore Gerardo, after he had considered Paolo with the utmost wonderment, abode certain, knowing Ambrogio's son to be lost, that Nicuola had clad herself as a man and said to Paolo, 'Nicuola, Nicuola, wert thou not who thou art, I warrant thee I had played thee and Catella an ill trick'; then, turning to his daughter, he bade her go aloft and leave Nicuola there, for that he would bear the latter better company than she. Catella accordingly departed, herseeming she had thitherto come off good cheap, since her father had nowise chidden nor beaten her, but knew not nor might divine to what end he called Romolo Nicuola. Catella being gone, 'Dear my Nicuola,' quoth Gerardo, 'what habit is this in which I see thee?' How can Ambrogio thy father suffer thee go thus alone? What camest thou to do here? Camest thou belike to see how I order the house and how I live? It is two days since I spoke with thy father and prayed him be pleased to resolve me an he would e'en give me thee to wife or not. Marry, I assure thee thou shalt have a good time with me and I will leave thee the governance of the house.' What while Paolo said to himself, 'I have e'en been twice mistaken to-day for some one else. This old fellow's daughter thinketh I am a certain Romolo, and he himself taketh me for my sister.' Then said Gerardo, 'Nicuola, dost thou answer me nothing?' and offered to kiss her; but Paolo pushed him away, 'An you will aught, speak with my father and let me go, for I came hither I know not how.' Whereupon the old man answered, 'Ay, ay, begone; I will speak with thy father and make an end of the matter.'

Paolo accordingly went away and repairing to his father's house, there found Lattanzio, who had presently sought Nicuola in marriage and to whom Ambrogio, knowing him for a rich and noble youth, had promised her. When Paolo entered, Lattanzio, seeing him, abode dumbfounded, and but that at that moment Ambrogio caused him touch his daughter's hand, he had taken him for Nicuola. The joy which Ambrogio felt at the coming of Paolo, whom he accounted dead, was beyond measure and description, more by token that he had not only recovered his son, but had honourably married his daughter. Great was the rejoicing and many the caresses which passed between the four; then, the collation being brought, behold, in came Gerardo, who seeing Nicuola seated by Lattanzio and Paolo, whom he thought to be Nicuola, speaking with his father, cried, well-nigh beside himself, 'God aid me! I know not if I sleep nor what I do!' and clasping his hands, abode all full of wonderment. Paolo, to whom Catella's savoury kisses had been supremely grateful, told his father he would do him a favour to marry him with Gerardo's daughter, and Ambrogio, knowing that the match could not but be a good one, thereupon told Gerardo how he had married Nicuola to Lattanzio and prayed him consent to give Catella to Paolo to wife. Accordingly, this match also was concluded and so, out of all hope, Ambrogio found himself to have recovered his son rich and well married and to have, to boot, honourably established his daughter. Meanwhile, Paolo let fetch his gear from the hostelry and keeping two serving-men for himself, requited the others in such wise that they avouched themselves content. All were full of joy, except Gerardo, who would fain have had Nicuola; however, in the end he resigned himself to his lot; whilst the two lovers and their wives applied to give themselves a good time, and yet live merrily to this day.

In the Second Book of Sir Philip Sidney's *Arcadia*, Pyrocles and Philoclea pass the promise of marriage, and at the request of the lovely damsel, the 'Princesse of his Heart,' Pyrocles tells the story of his recent adventures, and among them the pathetic and tragic story of Zelmane, as follows :*—But the next morning, we (having striven with the Sunnes earlinesse) were scarcely beyond the prospect of the high turrets of that building, when there overtooke us a young Gentleman, for so he seemed to us, but indeede (sweet Ladie) it was the faire *Zelmane*, *Plexirtus* daughter; whom unconsulting affection (unfortunately borne to me-wards) had made borrowe so much of her naturall modestie, as to leave her more-decent rayments, and taking occasion of *Andromanas* tumultuous pursuing us, had apparelled her selfe like a page, with a pitifull crueltie cutting off her golden haire, leaving nothing,

---

* Book II, p. 186, ed. 1598.

but the short curles, to cover that noble head, but that she ware upon it a faire head-peece, a shield at her backe, and a launce in her hand, els disarmed. Her apparell of white, wrought upon with broken knots, her horse, faire and lustie, which she rid so, as might shew a fearefull boldnes, daring to doo that, which she knew that she knew not how to doo : and the sweetnesse of her countenance did give such a grace to what she did, that it did make handsome the unhandsomnesse, and make the eye force the minde to beleeve, that there was a praise in that unskilfulnesse. But she straight approached me, and with fewe words (which borrowed the helpe of her countenance to make themselves understood) she desired me to accept her into my service : telling me she was a noblemans sonne of *Iberia*, her name *Daiphantus*, who having seen what I had done in that court, had stolne from her father, to follow me. I enquired the particularities of the maner of *Andromanas* following me, which by her I understood, she hiding nothing (but her sexe) from me. And still me thought I had seene that face, but the great alteration of her fortune, made her far distant from my memorie : but liking verie well the yong Gentleman (such I tooke her to be) admitted this *Daiphantus* about me, who well shewed there is no service like his, that serves because he loves. For though born of Princes blood, brought up with tenderest education, unapt to service (because a woman) and full of thoughts (because in a strange estate), yet Love enjoyned such diligence, that no apprentice, no, no bondslave could ever be by feare more readie at all commandements, then that yong Princesse was. How often (alas) did her eyes say unto me, that they loved? and yet (I not looking for such a matter) had not my conceipt open to understand them ; how often would she come creeping to me, betweene gladnesse to be neare me, & feare to offend me? Truly, I remember, that then I marvailed to see her receive my commandements with sighes, and yet do them with cheereful-nesse : sometimes answering me in such riddles, as I then thought a childish inex-perience : but since returning to my remembrance they have come more cleere unto my knowledge : and pardon me (onely deare Lady) that I use many words : for her affection to me deserves of me an affectionate speach.

[Poor Zelmane did not long survive. Finding death near she revealed herself to Pyrocles in a most touching interview and breathed her last in his arms.—ED.]

In Peele's *Sir Clyomon and Sir Clamydes*, 1599, Neronis, the daughter of the King of the Strange Marshes, disguises herself as a page, and attends on her lover, Sir Clyomon, acting as his squire, and messenger to the court of his father, the King of Denmark.

It is, however, needless to gather the dramas wherein the heroine disguises her-self in order to be near her lover, as Dunlop * justly remarks this feature is ' one of ' the most common incidents in the Italian novels and our early British drama. ' Besides *Twelfth Night* and *The Two Gentlemen of Verona*, it is the foundation of ' Beaumont and Fletcher's *Philaster*, Shirley's *Grateful Servant, School of Compli-*' *ment, Maid's Revenge*, etc.'

DUNLOP † observes that the ' rudiments of Bandello's story may be found in ' Cinthio.' From the synopsis which he proceeds to give, it is evident that he refers to the *Eighth Novel* of the *Fifth Decade* of the *Hecatommithi*. It is somewhat diffi-cult to comprehend what Dunlop means by ' rudiments.' In Cinthio's story there are twins, a shipwreck, a scattered family, and a boy disguised as a girl, and a girl

---

* *History of Fiction*, p. 274, 3rd ed. London, 1845.
† *Ibid.*, p. 274, 3rd ed. 1845.

disguised as a boy, and both disguises assumed in pursuit of an illicit love, which in the boy's case was successful, and when the father of the young girl, whom the boy has disgraced starts forth to avenge his daughter he meets the disguised sister, and mistaking her for her brother casts her into prison.

If these be rudiments, then is Dunlop right. But we now know that Bandello took his story not from Cinthio, but from the *Ingannati*.

TICKNOR (ii, 11), in an account of the four Comedias of Lope de Rueda (who flourished between 1544 and 1567), says that the 'first of them, *Los Engaños*,— ' "Frauds,"—contains the story of a daughter of Verginio, who has escaped from 'the convent where she was to be educated, and is serving as a page to Marcelo, 'who had once been her lover, and who had left her because he believed himself to 'have been ill treated. Clavela, the lady to whom Marcelo now devotes himself, 'falls in love with the fair page, somewhat as Olivia does in *Twelfth Night*, and this 'brings in several effective scenes and situations. But a twin-brother of the lady-'page returns home after a considerable absence, so like her, that he proves the other 'Sosia, who, first producing great confusion and trouble, at last marries Clavela, and 'leaves his sister to her original lover.'

KLEIN (ix, 159) proves that *Los Engannos* of Lope de Rueda is a translation of *Gl' Ingannati*. In the edition of 1567 it bore the title *Comedia de los Engaña-dos*, an exact translation of the Italian title. Here and there Rueda had shifted the scenes and changed the names, the nurse Clemencia was changed to Julietta, etc., but in the plot and progress of the story he remained faithful to his original.

In a review (*Sh. Jahrbuch*, 1895, xxxi, 414) of Dr Bahlsen's edition of Fletch-er's *Rule a Wife and have a Wife*, it is said that Dr Bahlsen had detected a note-worthy similarity between *Twelfth Night* and an anonymous Spanish drama called, *La Española en Florencia*. I can find no notice of this play either in TICKNOR, or in the volumes of KLEIN devoted to the *Spanish Drama*. ALBERT R. FREY (*New York Sh. Soc.*, Paper No. 3, p. 27) says that 'in the *Comedias nuevas escogidas* '(1659) it [*La Española en Florencia*] is ascribed to Calderon, a fact which would 'settle the dispute, did not Barrera deny that he is the author. Rivadeneyra ascribes 'it to Lope de Vega, under the title of *Burlas Veras*, while Chorley, in a manuscript 'note in his *Catálogo*, states that it is not written in Lope's style and cannot be his.'

CRITICISMS

SAMUEL PEPYS (*Centurie of Prayse*, p. 316) : *September 11* (1661).—Walking through Lincoln's Inn Fields observed at the Opera a new play 'Twelfth Night,' was acted there, and the King there ; so I, against my own mind and resolution, could not forbear to go in, which did make the play seem a burthen to me, and I took no pleasure at all in it.

January 6 (1662-3).—After dinner to the Duke's House, and there saw 'Twelfth Night' acted well, though it be but a silly play, and not related at all to the name or day.

January 20 (1668).—To the Duke of York's house and saw 'Twelfth Night,' as it is now revived; but, I think, one of the weakest plays that ever I saw on the stage.

DOWNES (1662, p. 32) : Twelfth Night, or what you will; wrote by Mr Shake-spear, had mighty success by its well performance : *Sir Toby Belch*, by Mr *Better-ton; Sir Andrew Ague-cheek* by Mr *Harris; Fool* by Mr *Underhill; Malvolio*, the Steward, by Mr *Lovel; Olivia* by Miss *Ann Gibbs:* All the parts being justly acted crown'd the Play. Note, It was got up on purpose to be acted on Twelfth Night.

JOHNSON (1765) : This play is in the graver part elegant and easy, and in some of the lighter scenes exquisitely humorous. *Ague-cheek* is drawn with great pro-priety, but his character is, in a great measure, that of natural fatuity, and is there-fore not the proper prey of a satirist. The soliloquy of *Malvolio* is truly comick ; he is betrayed to ridicule merely by his pride. The marriage of *Olivia*, and the succeeding perplexity, though well enough contrived to divert on the stage, wants credibility, and fails to produce the proper instruction required in the drama, as it exhibits no just picture of life.

A. W. SCHLEGEL (1811, ii, 174) : This comedy unites the entertainment of an intrigue, contrived with great ingenuity, to the richest fund of comic characters and situations, and the beauteous colours of an ethereal poetry. In most of his plays Shakespeare treats love more as an affair of the imagination than the heart ; but here we are particularly reminded by him that, in his language, the same word, *fancy*, signified both fancy and love. The love of the music-enraptured Duke to Olivia is not merely a fancy, but an imagination ; Viola appears at first to fall arbi-trarily in love with the Duke, whom she serves as a page, although she afterwards touches the tenderest chords of feeling ; the proud Olivia is entangled by the modest and insinuating messenger of the Duke, in whom she is far from suspecting a dis-guised rival, and at last, by a second deception, takes the brother for the sister. To these, which I might call ideal follies, a contrast is formed by the undisguised absurdities to which the entertaining tricks of the ludicrous persons of the piece give rise, in like manner under pretence of love.... These [comic] scenes are as admirably conceived and significant as they are laughable.

W. HAZLITT (*Characters*, etc., 1817, p. 255) : This is justly considered as one of the most delightful of Shakespear's comedies. It is full of sweetness and pleas-antry. It is perhaps too good-natured for comedy. It has little satire, and no spleen. It aims at the ludicrous rather than the ridiculous. It makes us laugh at the follies of mankind, not despise them, and still less bear any ill-will towards them. Shake-spear's comic genius resembles the bee rather in its power of extracting sweets from weeds or poisons than in leaving a sting behind it. He gives the most amusing exaggeration of the prevailing foibles of his characters, but in a way that they them-selves, instead of being offended at, would almost join in to humour ; he rather contrives opportunities for them to show themselves off in the happiest lights, than renders them contemptible in the perverse construction of the wit or malice of others. ... (P. 257) : Shakespear's comedy is of a pastoral and poetical cast. Folly is indigenous to the soil, and shoots out with native, happy, unchecked luxuriance. Absurdity has every encouragement afforded it ; and nonsense has room to flourish in. Nothing is stunted by the churlish, icy hand of indifference or severity. The poet runs riot in a conceit, and idolizes a quibble. His whole object is to turn the meanest or rudest objects to a pleasurable account. The relish which he has of a pun, or of the quaint humour of a low character, does not interfere with the delight with which he describes a beautiful image or the most refined love.

HALLAM (1839, iii, 560) : The general style [of *Twelfth Night*] resembles, in my judgement, that of *Much Ado about Nothing*, which is referred with probability to the year 1600. *Twelfth Night*, notwithstanding some very beautiful passages, and the humorous absurdity of Malvolio, has not the coruscations of wit and spirit of character that distinguish the excellent comedy it seems to have immediately followed ; nor is the plot nearly so well constructed. Viola would be more interesting, if she had not indelicately, as well as unfairly towards Olivia, determined to win the Duke's heart before she had seen him. The part of Sebastian has all that improbability which belongs to mistaken identity, without the comic effect for the sake of which that is forgiven in Plautus and in *The Comedy of Errors*.

GERVINUS (1850, p. 429) : The Duke's mind, wholly filled with his love for Olivia, seems stirred by deep sentiments of the most sacred tenderness and truth. Sunk in melancholy, he avoids all noisy society ; the chase and every other employment is a burden to him ; 'unstaid and skittish' in everything, he seems prompted by the desire to compensate for this variability by the firm constancy of his love. To nurture this love with the most delicate and strongest aliments is his sole business ; he courts therefore the solitude of nature, and surrounds himself with music. He attracts the Clown from the Countess's house, that with his full-sounding voice he may sing to him songs of hopeless unrequited love. A tender poetic soul, the Duke with delicate feeling has made his favourite poetry the popular song of the spinning-room, which is more exquisite and simple in its touching power than aught that lyric art has created in the erotic style ; he revels even to satiety in the enjoyment of these heart-felt tunes, which are like an echo to the heart. This proneness to go to extremes in his love, in his melancholy, and in all inclinations which are congenital to and in accordance with his ruling passion, is expressed in all that the Duke says and does. . . . He calls his love more noble than the world ; he compares it to the insatiable sea ; no other love, least of all that of a woman, is like his ; he makes a show of it everywhere, by messengers, before musicians, and companions, and even the sailors know the story of it. But this very inclination to exaggeration induces us to look more closely into the genuineness of this most genuine love. It almost seems as if the Duke were more in love with his love, than with his mistress ; as if like Romeo with Rosalind he rather speculated in thought over his fruitless passion, than felt it actually in his heart ; as if his love were rather a production of his fancy than a genuine feeling. It startles us, that just that which in a paroxysm of self-loving commendation he said of his own love compared to the love of a woman, he himself contradicts in a calm thoughtful moment, when he says to Viola that the fancies of men are more giddy than women's are, more longing, but yet more wavering, sooner lost and worn. Thus it is with his own. To give an air of importance to their love, to pride themselves and to presume upon it, is in truth the habit or, rather, the bad habit of men. Viola tells him, what is just his case, that men make more words about their love, that they say more, swear more, but their shows are more than will, for they prove much in their vows, but little in their love. Olivia must feel this throughout the urgent suit of the Duke ; she calls his love heresy, and turns coldly away from his seeming favour. She sees him send to her, and she hears of his longing, but she does not see him bestirring himself in his own cause, she hears a claim advanced, but she finds no desert unless it be that of higher rank ; and it is this very superiority in the Duke which she disdains. Must she not have remotely gathered even from his messages the refined conceit of her princely suitor, with which he presumes upon his love : ' it *can* give no place, it *can* bide no denay.' Must she not despise this very tone of rank, in which he bids Cesario tell her that he prizes not a quantity of dirty lands and values not her fortune ? Must not all this sound in her ears as if the Duke meant that nothing might and could be lacking to him and his love, as if he grounded his pretensions rather upon his princely rank than upon the high nature of his love ? In other instances she is far removed from coldness and contempt, something in the very nature of the Duke must have provoked her proud disdain, and we shall feel that he indeed gave her good cause for this.

That the aim and object of desire are missed by this self-reflection on love, by this melancholy tarrying upon an undefined yearning, by this too tender nurture of a self-pleasing passion, and by the languid inactivity which it produces, are shown by Orsino's example ; and the poet has not neglected to make this lesson still more forcible by a striking contrast. The Fool no less than Olivia, has seen through the Duke's disease, and he tells him of an excellent remedy : ' I would have men of such constancy,' he says, ' put to sea that their business might be everything, and their intent everywhere; for that's it, that always makes a good voyage of nothing.' Thus those natures which, forgetful of all else, become absorbed in one constant affection, he would drive into the very element of adventure, that they might forget their ponderings upon one intent, that in a natural course of life they might be delivered from the hard service of one idol, that that freshness might be restored to them which permits a man even in matters of love to reach his aim more quickly and easily, while the weak votaries of love forfeit their end.

BATHURST (1857, p. 89) : It is a pity Shakespeare could not have written more plays in such verse as this has. It contains the most beautiful description of music ('It came o'er my ear'), and it might so describe itself. As to the ideas, they are delightfully clear, though never prosaic. There is a disposition to excursiveness, and most beautiful ; or rather, perhaps, such excursiveness springs naturally from the character of the two principal personages, who are made for each other ; and of their condition of mind, being in love. This is the play of which love is peculiarly the subject; not *Romeo and Juliet*, where the love is mere commonplace love. Even a sovereign Prince is brought in, merely to be in love. Shakespeare makes him express very strongly that love of music, which the poet himself felt most strongly, as we often see elsewhere. . . . *Twelfth Night* is the play which Shakespeare wrote most at his ease, and in which the characters, whether serious or comic, seem to be most at their ease too. They do not appear to be taken out of their places to form a drama ; though there is a sufficient amount of interest in the story.

HALLIWELL (1857, p. 247) : The genius displayed in the works of Shakespeare is of so transcendent a character, an editor is placed at this disadvantage, that, in the progress of his labours, the consideration of each successive drama unfolds so much of wonderful art, the tendency of his criticism is liable on each occasion to be influenced unduly in the estimate of the one under consideration, impressed by those newly discovered excellencies which ever attend a diligent study of a Shakespearian drama ; but making every allowance for an enthusiasm resulting from a recent examination of the beauties of the following play, it may fairly be estimated as the chief monument of the author's genius for comedy, and the most perfect composition of the kind in the English or in any other language. In this, as in some other plays, Shakespeare exhibits the wonderful power of his dramatic art by reconciling the introduction of the most fascinating poetry with the action of characters whose discourse is replete with buffoonery ; so that, when the curtain falls, our admiration is divided between the serious and comic portions of the drama. . . . Sir Toby Belch is a genuine English humourist of the old school, and his butt, Sir Andrew Aguecheek, is perhaps still more richly comic, always enjoying a joke, and never understanding it.

F. KREYSSIG (1862, iii, 268) : On these simple foundations, Shakespeare erected the exquisite, graceful structure of the most perfect of his comedies, and at the same time, by the most complete scheme and by a rarely full range of characters, he drew the attention from external circumstances and concentrated it on the inner life of the action, and by giving an absolute unity of interest he breathed into it all the true dramatic soul. That saying of Goethe : ' That in every finished work of Shakespeare there could be found a central idea,' here finds its justification in fullest measure. Let it be supposed that Shakespeare had set himself the task to show, within the limit of one treatment, like a recapitulation, every combination of comedies in one single comedy, and it would not be difficult to prove that in *Twelfth Night* the task had been successfully accomplished. Just consider, for a moment, the three wooers who aspire to the fair Olivia's hand, observe Olivia's relation to Viola, and enlarge this series of enamoured situations by glancing at Maria's victorious campaign against the bibulous Knight, and we shall have a shaded series, tolerably complete, of amourous folly or foolish amourousness in an ascending scale from the wooing of a charming woman by a feeble-minded, senseless ninnyhammer, on through the self-seeking of inane puffed-up stupidity and of downright shrewd intriguing, up to the fantastic youthful follies of natures, noble and gifted, to be sure, but untried and still ignorant of their own quality. And inasmuch as it is not Shakespeare's wont to base the action of his comedies on the requirements of frivolous wit or even of malicious slander, thus in this play we do not fail to hear the lovely ground-tone, which at first softly sounding, at last rises triumphantly above the chaos of clashing tones, and in the most delightful way harmonises all discords ; I mean the portrayal of deep and true love in sound healthy natures. Then at the close this victory puts an end to all mistakes within and without, and leaves us in a mood of serene and joyous peace, an emotion which it is the aim of true comedy to produce, just as the subsidence of passion into a manly resignation is that of tragedy.

T. KENNY (1864, p. 199) : The grace and vigour of Shakespeare's genius are frequently observable throughout the whole of the incidents of the play ; but we cannot class this work among his highest achievements, and the admiration with which we regard it is by no means free from any qualification. There is much of extravagance and improbability in the development of its more romantic incidents, and it thus frequently becomes less purely creative and less absolutely truthful than less striking productions of the poet's genius. The treatment of the story is sometimes manifestly melodramatic, as, for instance, in the appearance of Antonio, and his arrest by the officers; and, we think we may add, in the hurried and strange marriage contract between Olivia and Sebastian. The disguise of Viola is one of those artifices which are only possible in the large domain of poetry; and the freedom of poetry itself seems somewhat abused in the representation of the supposed complete likeness between her and her brother. The merely comic business of the play is more naturally executed. Many people will probably regard the misadventures of the befooled and infatuated Malvolio as its most vigorous and amusing episode. But we cannot help thinking that the punishment to which the vanity of Malvolio is exposed, is somewhat coarse and excessive. In spite of the bad character which he bears in his very name, there is nothing in his conduct, as far as we can see, to justify the unscrupulous persecution of his tormentors. The poet himself, when the pressure of dramatic necessity is removed, seeks to treat this incident in his usual easy temper; but we doubt whether such an outrageous practical joke could ever be forgotten or forgiven by its victim. We confess that, as exemplifications of Shakespeare's wonderful comic power, we prefer to this humiliation and discomfiture of Malvolio the scenes in which Sir Toby and Sir Andrew make the welkin ring to the echo of their uproarious merriment. It is often in lighter sketches of this description that the hand of Shakespeare is most distinguishable and most inimitable; and this triumphant protest against the pretensions of a narrow and jealous austerity will no doubt last as long as social humour forms one of the elements of human life:—' Dost thou think, because thou art virtuous, there shall be no more cakes and ale?' We find in *Twelfth Night* no striking indication of Shakespeare's power in the delineation of character. Such a display was, perhaps, hardly compatible with the general predominance of the lighter romantic element throughout the whole work. The passion of the Duke for Olivia is neither very deep nor very dramatic. It is merely dreamy, restless, longing, and enthralling desire. It is the offspring of a mood which, we cannot help thinking, was specially familiar to the poet himself; and it seems directly akin to the state of feeling which he has revealed in his Sonnets. We do not believe, however, that he required for its delineation the light of a personal experience. His airy imagination, aided by his general human sensibility, enabled him truly to reproduce this, and perhaps all other conceivable passions; and it may be that it was when his fancy was most disengaged, it was most readily and vividly creative. Neither Viola nor Olivia can be ranked among his finest female characters. The former has a difficult and a somewhat unnatural part to sustain; and although she fills it with considerable brilliancy and spirit, she scarcely enlists our strongest sympathies in her favour. The allusion, however, to her untold love is one of the bright passages in Shakespeare's drama, and will for ever form for tender hearts a cherished remembrance. The character of Olivia suffers much more from the perplexities or temptations to which she becomes exposed, and she certainly fails to display, amidst those trials, the highest maidenly purity and refinement. *Twelfth Night* is, we think, on the whole, one of the bright, fanciful, and varied productions of Shakespeare's less earnest dramatic mood; but it possesses neither complete imagination nor complete natural truthfulness; and it seems to us to be more or less deficient throughout in consistency, in harmony, in the depth and firmness of touch, which distinguish the finer creations of his genius.

E. Montégut (1867, iii, 361): *Twelfth Night* is a masquerade, slightly grotesque, as befits a play whereof the title recalls one of those festivals which were most dear to the jocund humour of our forbears. This festival was the day whereon in every family a king for the nonce was crowned after he had been chosen by lot, sometimes it fell to a child to be the ruler over the whole family, again a servant was crowned by his master, for the moment it was the world turned upside down, a rational hierarchy topsy-turvy, authority created by chance, and the more grotesque the surprise, the merrier the festival. You have seen it all depicted on the canvas of the jocose and powerful Jordaens, this jolly festival and its king with a large red face, his glass in his hand and his crown on his head, his fat and fair Flemish women excited by beer, good cheer, good health, and good humour ; and their plump children so tempting to the taste of the Brillat-Savarin of cannibalism. In grotesqueness, *Twelfth Night* does not yield to the picture by Jordaens, and assuredly no caricature from the brush of this robust and popular master can match, either in comic power or as a reproduction of ancient manners, the characters of Uncle Toby and his comrades and the picture of their nocturnal drinking bouts. The whole episode of the wild orgy of Toby and of the crotchety Malvolio is drawn incomparably to the life ; Shakespeare has there, so to speak, surpassed himself, for he has there shown himself a consummate master of a species of composition which has been many a time denied to him, namely, comedy. That Shakespeare, in the comedy of fancy, of caprice, of adventure, is without a peer is acknowledged by every one ; but he has been gravely reproached with not being able to stand a comparison with those masters who draw their resources exclusively from those faculties whence alone true comedy springs ; in a word, with not being sufficiently in his comedies exclusively comic. The episodes of Sir Toby and Malvolio correct this judgement of error ; Rabelais is not more of a buffoon, and Molière not more exclusively comic than Shakespeare in these two episodes.

The sentimental and romantic portions of the play are stamped with that inimitable grace which especially characterises Shakespeare ; but even here this comedy remains faithful to its title of *Twelfth Night ;* for ambiguity still reigns sovereign mistress there, and treats the real world under its double form, the reality of nature and that of society, like a carnival farce. The characters instigated by their whims or the spitefulness of chance are deceived as to condition and sex and become involved in an imbroglio of charming and dangerous complications. Beneath the real piece, another can be read at the will of the reader, just as by certain artifices one image may be seen beneath another image, and herein lies the delicate point of this charming work for which that famous saying appears to have been expressly written : ' Glide, mortals, bear not heavily.' A surly reader or a stern critic might say that this poetic Viola is merely an amiable adventuress. And her brother, Sebastian, her living mirror, so charming that the friendships which he inspires cling to him like lichens on a rock—is he not too womanish ? in sooth, he needed but the whim of donning woman's clothes to become *una feminuccia*, as the Italians say in their expressive diminutives. Of the Countess Olivia, with her singular mistakes, may we not also have some doubts ? We might suspect that Toby, with his unmannerly perverted wit, who knew his world and fathomed his niece, was not far wrong when he said she was a ' Cataian,' herein alluding to that land of Cathay whence came, with the Italian renaissance, and that princess Angelique through whom Medor was made happy and Roland desperate, all the magicians, sorceresses, enchantresses, and sirens who ruled all hearts in the chivalric literature of the sixteenth century. But, hush ! youth, grace, beauty, with all their dreams, their illusions and their charms, enwrap these adventures. We are here in fairyland ;

why should we try to discover the real nature of these personages? They are the children of the imagination, of caprice, graceful fairies, sylphs and imps, *piccolini stregoni*.

In Shakespeare's plays philosophy is rarely lacking; is there then a philosophy in this poetic masquerade? Ay, there is one here, and to its fullest depth. In two words it is: we are all, in varying degrees, insane; for we are all the slaves of our defects, which are genuine chronic follies, or else we are the victims of dreams which attack us like follies at an acute stage. Man is held in leash by his imagination, which deceives him even to the extent of reversing the normal conditions of nature and the laws of reality. An image, ordinary but true, of man in every station is this silly Malvolio, whose folly unavowed and secretly cherished, bursts forth on a frivolous pretext. Malvolio is, no question, a fool, but this sly waiting woman who ensnares him by an all-revealing strategem, is she herself exempt from the folly of which she accuses Malvolio? and if the steward believes himself beloved by his mistress, does she not pursue the same ambitious dream of making a match with Sir Toby, who, however degraded and drunken, is at least a gentleman and the uncle of Olivia? It is the same dream under very different conditions which Viola pursues,—a dream which would never have come true, if luck had not extricated her from the *cul de sac* whither her temerity had led her. What is to be said of Olivia but that her imagination, suddenly smitten, could go so far astray as to stifle in her the instinct which should have revealed to her that Viola was of her own sex? The friendship of Antonio for Sebastian,—a friendship which involves him in perils so easily foreseen,—is a sentiment exactly twin with the love of Olivia for Cesario-Viola. All dream, all are mad, and differ from another only in the kind of their madness,—some have a graceful and poetic madness, others a madness grotesque and trivial. And after all, some of these dreams come true. Must we ascribe the honour of success to the good sense of the happy ones who see their secret desires crowned? Ah no, we must ascribe it to nature. We all dream,—it is a condition of humanity; but in this multitude of dreams, Nature accepts only certain ones which are in harmony with grace, with poesy, and with beauty; for Nature is essentially platonic, and thrusts aside as a revolt and a sin, every dream wherein ugliness intrudes. Hence it is that Viola's secret dream comes true, while Malvolio's is condemned to remain for ever a grotesque chimera. Very humble indeed should all of us be, for we are only a little less mad than our neighbours; it is Nature alone who is our arbiter and decides which of us she wishes to pose as sages, and which of us she intends to retain in the rank of fools.

H. I. RUGGLES (1870, p. 15): The organic idea [which is 'Man in his relations to Pleasure and Pastime.' See note on 'Title.'—ED.] will give form to the characters, incidents, metaphors, diction, and phraseology of the piece. This idea is but another name for the law which forms the moral basis of the play, and which is illustrated both in its observance and in its infraction, that is, by one or more characters that are the direct representatives of it, and by others that embody the different phases and degrees of error which arise from its violation. In *Twelfth Night*, this fundamental law is that rule of reason which prescribes the standard of excellence, and declares that the highest beauty is virtue or grace (which always implies the presence of temperance and decorum); that genius,—comprising all natural gifts and propensities, but more particularly when applied to the mind, wit, imagination, and invention,—must be subordinated to the judgement, and that pleasure, whether of the sense or imagination, must be restrained from excess. The observance of this rule will be evinced in grace and elegance of mind and deportment, and in gentleness and generosity of sentiment; such a character is Viola. The grossest infractions of the rule, on the other hand, will be personated by those whose low tastes, intemperate habits, exuberant humour, or rude jests, violate all decorum,—such as Sir Toby and his companions,—or by such as are the dupes of their imaginations, through inordinate vanity, as Malvolio; while characters more complex will be found in those who, like Orsino and Olivia, are marked by grace and gentility both inborn and acquired, but who, grounding their affections upon mere external beauty, are devoid of all restraints in the indulgence of their fancies and passions.

(P. 39): This comedy is pervaded with the spirit of literature and gentility. It is lifted above the working-day world into a sphere of ease, culture, and good-breeding. Its characters are votaries of pleasure in different degrees, from the lowest gratification of the sense up to the more refined pleasures derived from the exercise of the imagination, which, after all, are but the pleasures of the sense at second-hand. Beside the air of elegance it possesses, it is filled to the brim and overflowing with the spirit that seeks to enjoy this world without one thought or aspiration beyond. It jumps the hereafter entirely. Every scene of it glows with the warmth and sunshine of physical enjoyment. It places before us the sensual man, with his fondness for cheer, his cakes and ale, his delights of the eye and ear, his pleasure in pastime and sport, his high estimation of a good leg and a good voice, in short, of all that can gratify the sense, win favour, or conduce to worldly advantage.

F. J. FURNIVALL (*The Leopold Shakspere*, 1877, Introd. p. lix.): Still one of the comedies of Shakspere's bright, sweet time. True, that we have to change Rosalind's rippling laugh for the drunken catches and bibulous drollery of Sir Toby and his comrade, and Touchstone for the Clown; but the leading note of the play is fun, as if Shakspere had been able to throw off all thought of melancholy, and had devised Malvolio to help his friends 'fleet the time carelessly,' as they did in the golden world. Still though, as ever in the comedies, except *The Merry Wives*, there's the shadow of death and distress across the sunshine, Olivia's father and brother just dead, Viola and Sebastian just rescued from one death, Viola threatened with another, and Antonio held a pirate and liable to death. And still the lesson is, as in *As You Like It*, 'Sweet are the uses of adversity'; out of their trouble all the lovers come into happiness, into wedlock. The play at first sight is far less striking and interesting than *Much Ado* and *As You Like It*. No brilliant Beatrice or Benedick catches the eye, no sad Rosalind leaping into life and joyousness at the touch of assured love. The self-conceited Malvolio is brought to the front, the drunkards and Clown come next; none of these touches any heart; and it's not till we look past them, that we feel the beauty of the characters who stand in half-light behind. Then we become conscious of a quiet harmony of colour and form that makes a picture full of charm, that grows on you as you study it, and becomes one of the possessions of your life.

A. C. SWINBURNE (*A Study of Shakespeare*, 1880, p. 155): All true Pantagruelians will always, or at least as long as may be permitted by the Society for the Suppression of Vice, cherish with an especial regard the comedy in which Shakespeare also has shown himself as surely the loving as he would surely have been the beloved disciple of that insuppressible divine, the immortal and most reverend vicar of Meudon. Two only among the mighty men who lived and wrote and died within the century which gave birth to Shakespeare were found worthy of so great an honour at his hands as the double homage of citation and imitation ; these two, naturally and properly enough, were François Rabelais and Christopher Marlowe. We cannot but recognise on what far travels in what good company ' Feste the jester ' had but lately been, on that night of ' very gracious fooling ' when he was pleased to enlighten the· unforgetful mind of Sir Andrew as to the history of Pigrogromitus, and of the Vapians passing the equinoctial of Queubus. At what precise degree of latitude and longitude between the blessed islands of Medamothy and Papimania this equinoctial may intersect the Sporades of the outer ocean, is a problem on the solution of which the energy of those many modern sons of Aguecheek who have undertaken the task of writing about and about the text and the history of Shakespeare might be expended with an unusually reasonable hope and expectation of arriving at an exceptionally profitable end.

Even apart from their sunny identity of spirit and bright sweet brotherhood of style, the two comedies of *Twelfth Night* and *As You Like It* would stand forth confessed as the common offspring of the same spiritual period by force and by right of the trace or badge they proudly and professedly bear in common, as of a recent touch from the ripe and rich and radiant influence of Rabelais. No better and no fuller vindication of his happy memory could be afforded than by the evident fact that the two comedies which bear the imprint of his sign manual are among all Shakespeare's works as signally remarkable for the cleanliness as for the richness of their humour. Here is the right royal seal of Pantagruel, clean-cut and clearly stamped, and unincrusted with any flake of dirt from the dubious finger of Panurge. In the comic parts of those plays in which the humour is rank and fragrant that exhales from the lips of Lucio, of Boult, or of Thersites, there is no trace or glimpse of Rabelais. From him Shakespeare has learnt nothing and borrowed nothing that was not wise and good and sweet and clean and pure. All the more honour, undoubtedly to Shakespeare, that he could borrow nothing else ; but assuredly, also, all the more honour to Rabelais, that he had enough of this to lend.

WILH. OECHELHÄUSER (*Einführungen in Shakespeare's Bühnen-Dramen*, 1885, 2te Aufl. ii, 378) : The closing scene of this comedy presents an especial difficulty. Whenever I have seen it on the stage under the most diverse arrangements, and in greater or less completeness, I have been always impressed by its unsatisfactory conclusion ; it invariably left the audience cold and unmoved. Here, beyond anywhere else, we miss, in the original, all stage-directions ; unquestionably there has been here committed to mimetic art and to by-play, a large and significant share of the interpretation of the poet's intentions and of filling out the dialogue in its production on the stage. But when we make the attempt, which is unavoidable in any arrangement, to supply our own stage-directions, we find, in the apportionment of the various interests, which are combined in that final scene, that there is an inherent obstruction to any satisfactory conclusion. The resolution of the comic episode of Malvolio, which is itself interrupted by the time consumed in summoning Malvolio, thrusts itself intolerably upon the two loving couples who, *post tot discrimina rerum*, have just reached the threshold of their joyous freedom which must now remain, through this new incident, unsettled in the balance. Our emotion demands that at the conclusion the solution of all the complications ending in the happiness of these couples thus happily brought together, shall sound forth full and joyously. Instead thereof, in the original, the riddle of the twin brother and sister is brought close up to a clear solution ; then, when the excitement of both couples is at fullest bent, they must needs become mere spectators of the ending of a comic episode, which at such a moment cannot but be to them utterly uninteresting, nay, to every one of them except to Olivia, the beginning of it was utterly unknown. During the temporary interruption, caused by summoning Malvolio, a dialogue between the duke and Olivia is interjected, but it is so short that it cannot charm back again the former emotion, nor does it lead to a conclusion. Hereupon, follows another long interruption while Malvolio's case is finished off, and then all of a sudden, after Orsino has addressed six lines to Olivia and to Viola, the play ends. . . . (P. 379) : I cannot but believe that I have discovered an effective solution without disturbing Shakespeare's arrangement of the final scene, to wit :—as soon as Sebastian has recognised Viola, and her own secret has perforce been revealed, I represent Viola as leaving the stage, and then, at the conclusion of Malvolio's case (which affords abundant time for dressing) she re-enters in her *maiden weeds*. Accordingly, merely by the addition of three or four lines of my own, I have so combined the dialogues of the lovers (which now are given before, during, and after Malvolio's episode) as to form a conclusion whereby a spectator, after the comic episode is finished, can again adapt his emotion to the tone of the main action and resume its solution with unabated interest.

[The lines just referred to are inserted after V, i, 256, and are as follows : *Viola (gently putting aside the arms of Sebastian who is about to embrace her)*. Embrace me not, until Cesario stands Confessed as Viola. Let us delay A moment on the threshhold of our joy. (*She hastens away, throwing a tender glance on her brother and the duke.*) *Sebastian*. Too much of joy ! Olivia and Viola ! (*He embraces Olivia.*) —Ed.]

When the chief character, about whom the complications are woven the thickest, namely Viola, thus absents herself, and from such a natural and urgent motive, the intensity of the immediate interest in the three characters remaining on the stage, Olivia, Orsino, and Sebastian, is relaxed ; hence the insertion of Malvolio's scene really ceases to jar. Moreover, the reappearance of Viola in her woman's dress cannot fail greatly to deepen the impression of the final scene ; on the other hand, the sight of a duke embracing a page suggests no illusion. This way of ending the play seems so manifest that, at first glance, it is not easy to comprehend why the poet did not make use of it, especially since in the original the duke says to Viola, ' Give me thy hand And let me see thee in thy woman's weeds.'

A closer examination, however, reveals how skilfully Shakespeare dealt with his materials. On *his* stage the female characters were played by boys ; in this case, the woman's weeds would have disturbed the illusion, by no means would they have heightened it. Here we have another instance, out of many, of the necessity, in dealing with the old dramas, of keeping constantly before us the difference between the ancient stage and our own. A mechanical reproduction might not infrequently exert at the present time an effect directly opposite to that which it would have had in the sixteenth century. And *to attain the corresponding effect* is really the ideal aim of reproductions.

HERMANN CONRAD (*Preuss. Jahrbücher*, Juli, 1887, p. 28) : That which determines the artistic unity of two plots is solely their thorough, organic combination ;

one must be material and one must be personal. On the one hand, one act must influence the course of the others ; on the other hand, the actors, especially the chief actors, must have a prominent part in both plots,—so that our interest in both is centralised in one person. If this central character is at the same time the hero of one plot, all the better ; but at any rate, he must be a prominent personage between the two heroes, who should be as much as possible involved in the action of the two plots, so that both may be equally entangled in the net.

This organic unity of the two very different plots may be readily exemplified in *The Merchant of Venice:* Bassanio's eagerness to win Portia is the inducement to sign the fateful bond ; it is only on the score of this contract that Bassanio can enter Belmont as a wooer, and the Jew can plot to execute his revenge on the hated Antonio, and again, in turn, had not Bassanio won Portia, Antonio would have waited for a rescuer in vain. Both plots, that in Belmont and that in Venice, grew as though from one germ, out of the bond, ran for a time independently side by side, in order to be reunited in the Trial scene, in which all the chief actors of both plots are brought together. The personal centre of both plots, the ligature between the two heroes, Shylock and Portia, is Bassanio, a chief actor in one, while his whole soul is, at the same time, absorbed in the other.

What Bassanio is for the organic unity of *The Merchant of Venice*, Olivia is for *Twelfth Night*. In neither of the two plots is she the chief character, but merely a very prominent one ; to win her hand is the main spring of one, whereby a chance is given to Viola to reveal her feminine advantages, as it is also of the other, which involves Malvolio's humiliation. How important she is to the establishment of the artistic whole will be noted if we were to put another character in her place as the aim of Malvolio's ambition. Should the aspirations of the Steward extend beyond the house of his mistress, his discomfiture elsewhere follows, and the artistic unity of the plot is lost as well as our own interest, and, in fact, we have enclosed two comedies in one frame. To guard against the impression that we have here a mere unity of persons, there is the unity of place ; there are only six short scenes, secondary components of the composition, and one chief scene (II, iv) which are not laid in Olivia's house. Through this arrangement not only do the actors in both plots come in continuous touch with each other, but the plots themselves define each other and interlace. Just as the haughty Olivia excites the aspirations of the narrow prosaic Malvolio, so Viola is brought down from romantic heights to common daily life by the episode of the duel, which also serves to reveal the pusillanimity of Sir Andrew. Malvolio's mad presumption was fostered by the favoured position which his liberal unsuspicious mistress gave him near her person ; and his hopes were nourished by the persistent rejection to which even such a brilliant wooer as the Duke had to submit. And never could Sir Toby have kindled in Sir Andrew's soul such murderous designs had not Viola been the messenger of love from a powerful rival. Sebastian, too, could not have won Olivia until he had proved his valour on the two foolish knights.

➤ CANON AINGER (*Shakespeare in the Middle Temple. Eng. Illust. Maga.*, March, 1884, p. 371) : But besides the three days of feasting alternating with the readings, there were two special festivals during the Reader's year of office [at the Middle Temple], at which solemn revels were performed for the entertainment of the judges and serjeants belonging to the society. These took place on All Saints' Day, and on the feast of the Purification, February 2nd. Much ceremony (and it is in this sense that the word *solemn* is to be taken) was observed on these occasions. A few days before, two 'ancient Barristers' had carried the invitation to the judges and serjeants, and on their taking their places in hall on the Grand day, two other barristers waited on them with 'basins and ewers of sweet water for the washing of their hands, and two other like ancient barristers with towels.' The Readers, bearing white staves, ushered in the dinner, preceded by minstrels. The dinner itself was carried in by young gentlemen under the Bar—the students. After dinner, the distinguished guests, again escorted by the Readers, withdrew to the Temple Gardens, or other retirement, while the hall was cleansed and prepared for the festivities that were to ensue. On their return, still with great solemnity, the gentlemen of the Inn trod a measure, then one of the Readers called upon one of the 'gentlemen of the Bar to give the Judges a song,' the rest of the company joining in chorus ; and after a procession, in which bowls of Ipocras were offered to the judges by the students—the hall was gradually vacated, the readers ushering their distinguished guests down the hall to the court gate, where they took their leave of them.

This was the portion of the revel at which the members of the Inn personally assisted. But after dinner, before the dance and song began, the performance of a stage-play seems to have taken place. In the corresponding account of the revels at the Inner Temple, which in their general arrangements were identical with those of the sister Inn, Dugdale writes, 'First the solemn Revels (*after Dinner and the Play ended*) are begun by the whole House.' At the Middle Temple we are equally well assured that the play was not forgotten. There is a curious list, supplied by Dugdale, of the officers and servants in the pay of the Middle Temple, in which the professional actors, performing on these occasions, are mentioned. The list includes the steward, the chief butler, the chief cook, the panyerman, the four 'puisne butlers,' the porter, the gardener, the second cook, the turnspits, the two washpots, the laundress, and the porter : 'the musick, their yearly entertainment, besides their diurnal pay for service'; and the catalogue is completed by the following entry :— 'The stage-players on the two Grand Days—for each play 10*l.*' 'But of late,' adds Dugdale, writing some sixty years after the date of Manningham's diary, 'these are doubled, and receive forty pounds a play.' Perhaps he meant £40 for the two occasions.

On the Grand day, then, of Feb. 2nd, 1602, the Feast of the Purification, a play was represented after the usual custom, by professional actors. Mr John Manningham had borne his share of the duties required from young gentlemen under the Bar. He had helped to carry the bread and meat to the high table ; he had danced in the measure, and joined in the chorus, and offered the spiced wine to the judges. But he had also enjoyed the treat of a theatrical performance by real professionals.

(Page 373) : Moreover, as there can be little doubt, Shakespeare was also among the actors on the occasion. The company who played *Twelfth Night* was that of the Lord Chamberlain's servants, acting at the Globe Theatre on Bankside. We have an authentic list of the players composing that company. Two of them, John Hemings and Henry Condell, who edited the First Collected Edition of Shakespeare's plays, prefixed to that edition the 'names of the Principal actors in all these plays.' This list of twenty-six names is headed with Shakespeare's, not perhaps as the most distinguished actor, but in homage to the famous dramatist. Next in order comes the great tragedian, Richard Burbage, the Hamlet, and Lear, and Othello, and Richard III. of the company—whose claims to that position no one seems to have disputed. But we know something of Shakespeare's line as an actor, and he was giving a 'taste of his quality' in several plays of his own and others just before and just after this performance at the Middle Temple. He had acted in *Every Man in his Humour* in 1598; had played old Adam in *As You Like It*, probably in 1600; and was soon to play the Ghost in his own *Hamlet*. He was in the full tide of his career as actor in the winter of 1601-2. As author of the play he was surely not excluded from the cast when it was acted (as seems probable) before the queen a few weeks earlier, and on this important occasion of a Reader's feast at the Temple.

What did he play? The characters which we know to have been assigned to him in other dramas suggest that broad comedy and the *rôle of jeune premier* were alike out of his line. Characters of an age past middle life—characters of dignity and with a certain pathetic interest—seem to have suited him best. We cannot think of him as cast for Sebastian. At eight and thirty he would have hardly suited for the 'double' of the young and beautiful Viola. Toby, Andrew, and the clown, are all out of the question. Was it Malvolio that he took—supposing Burbage to have declined it? Perhaps Burbage created the character. The best tragedians in modern times have not scorned the part. John Kemble, we know, occasionally took it: and in our own time we have seen it admirably played by Mr Phelps. Tragedians have discovered what Lamb acutely points out, that Malvolio 'is not essentially ludicrous. He becomes comic but by accident.' The character is, in fact, on the border land between the serious and the humorous, and supplies the sombre element that is needed to set off the comic interest.

It would indeed be curious if, failing Malvolio, the character of Orsino was sustained by its author; curious if it had fallen to him to utter the lines long ago pointed out as so appropriate to his own matrimonial fortunes [II, iv, 35-44].

Had the great poet's own affection 'held the bent' in that gay and wicked city of London? Was he reminded, with no touch of an unquiet conscience, of Ann Shakespeare (*née* Hathaway), patiently bearing her widowed lot, a matron now of five and forty, in far-off Stratford? Or had ten years of the prosaic realities of an actor's life rubbed off some of the gilt of sentiment, and as he lounged at the side-scenes was he considering rather about those hundred and seven acres of arable land in the parish of Old Stratford that he was to buy of William and John Combe in the May following?

Of author, actors, and acting, John Manningham tells us not a word. What an opportunity—for *us*, at least—was then lost! What would we not have given for any criticism by a gentleman of taste and intelligence of a play of Shakespeare's performed by the Lord Chamberlain's servants! Did John Manningham smile on occasion of these solemn festivities, when Sir Andrew exclaimed, 'I am a fellow of the strangest mind in the world! I delight in masques and revels sometimes altogether!' Did he recognise something of his own pleasant manner-of-the-world's contempt for Puritanism in the character of Malvolio, and the practical joking to which that decorous personage was subjected? The conjuring of the evil spirit out of poor Malvolio by that heartless impostor, the Puritan curate, Sir Topas, we are sure must have delighted the young gallants of the Temple, and have brought the play to an end amid boundless merriment.

And so the curtain falls, alike on Shakespeare's play, and on our glimpse of the festivities at an Inn of Court nearly three hundred years ago—

> 'Our revels now are ended : these our actors
> Are melted into air—into thin air.'

The judges have paced down the hall, and taken water at the Temple stairs, or coach in the Strand : the lights are out, and Mr Manningham and his chamber-fellow, Mr Curle, are on their way to their single room, humming to one another in the vein of sentiment that follows hard upon revelling, ' O, mistress mine, where are you roaming ?' or the Clown's jig at parting : ' When that I was and a little tiny boy,' etc.

The John Manningham of this fragment of diary is a very real person indeed. The very miscellaneousness of its contents shows us many sides of him, and enables us to know him as he was. Whether he is telling stories of Sir Thomas More, on his way down to Westminster ; or complaining in good set terms that the last preacher at the Temple Church would not take the trouble to make himself heard ; or quoting a friend's improper remark respecting the ancients of the honourable society (the barristers of oldest standing, that is to say), that ' if you put a case in the first books of the law to them, you may presume they have forgotten it ; if in the new bookes, you may doubt whether they have read it '—in each and all we feel we are in contact with a once living piece of humanity, and through no other relic of that famous Elizabethan age are we brought nearer, it seems to me, to Shakespeare and his fellow-actors. There are echoes or premonitions of the Shakespearian manner scattered throughout the diary, moreover, that fall very pleasantly on the ear. He tells, for example, the following anecdote of Marston the dramatist :—

' John Marston the last Christmas he danced with Alderman More's daughter, a Spaniard born. Fell into a strange commendacion of her witt and beauty. When he had done, shee thought to pay him home, and told him she thought he was a poet. "'Tis true," said he, "for poets fayne and lye, and soe dyd I when I commended your beauty, for you are exceeding foule." '

Is it merely coincidence, that we here recall a passage of arms between Touch-stone and Audrey ? ' The truest poetry is the most feigning ; and lovers are given to poetry ; and what they swear in poetry, may be said as lovers, they do feign.' It is likely enough that the extravagance of young lovers' sonnets, made to their mistress's eyebrow, was a stock-jest in many shapes in that era of exuberant flattery. There is a more solemn and beautiful echo of a Shakespearian thought in a citation made by Manningham from some divine or moralist unknown :—' Wee come first unwitting, weeping and crying into a world of woe, and shall we not weep and cry when we knowe it ?' It was not till three or four years later that poor mad Lear repeated the thought in those marvellous lines :—

> ' Thou must be patient : we came crying hither.
> Thou know'st, the first time that we smell the air
> We waul and cry—I will preach to thee, mark me !
> When we are born, we cry that we are come
> To this great stage of fools.'

And, finally, of the Middle Temple Hall—the bricks, as Jack Cade would have said,—' are alive at this day to testify it.' The exterior, Mr Halliwell-Phillipps tells us, ' has undergone numerous changes since the time of Shakespeare, the old louvre having long been removed, the principal entrance or porch rebuilt, and the whole exposed to a series of repairs and alterations. The main features of the interior, however, bear practically the same appearance they originally presented. It is true that some of the minor accessories are of modern date, but the beautiful oaken screen and the elegant wood-carved roof suffice to convey to us an exact idea of the room in which the humours of Malvolio delighted an Elizabethan audience.' Long may it stand unchanged, though the buildings that surround it are rapidly being transformed under the hand of the restorer.

VIOLA

MRS JAMESON (1833, i, 243) : As the innate dignity of Perdita in *The Winter's Tale* pierces through her rustic disguise, so the exquisite refinement of Viola triumphs over her masculine attire. Viola is, perhaps, in a degree less elevated and refined than Perdita, but with a touch of sentiment more profound and heart-stirring ; she is 'deep-learned in the lore of love,'—at least theoretically,—and speaks as masterly on the subject as Perdita does of flowers. . . .

We are left to infer (for so it is hinted in the first scene) that the Duke—who, with his accomplishments and his personal attractions, his taste for music, his chivalrous tenderness, and his unrequited love, is really a very fascinating and poetical personage, though a little passionate and fantastic—had already made some impression on Viola's imagination ; and, when she comes to play the confidante, and to be loaded with favours and kindness in her assumed character, that she should be touched by a passion made up of pity, admiration, gratitude, and tenderness, does not, I think, in any way detract from the genuine sweetness and delicacy of her character, for '*she never told her love.*'

Now all this, as the critic wisely observes, may not present a very just picture of life ; and it may also fail to impart any moral lesson for the especial profit of well-bred young ladies : but is it not in truth and in nature ? Did it ever fail to charm or to interest, to seize on the coldest fancy, to touch the most insensible heart ? . . .

What beautiful propriety in the distinction drawn between Rosalind and Viola ! The wild sweetness, the frolic humour which sports free and unblamed amid the shades of Ardennes, would ill become Viola, whose playfulness is assumed as part of her disguise as a court-page, and is guarded by the strictest delicacy. She has not, like Rosalind, a saucy enjoyment in her own incognito ; her disguise does not sit so easily upon her ; her heart does not beat freely under it.

The feminine cowardice of Viola, which will not allow her even to affect a courage becoming her attire,—her horror at the idea of drawing a sword,—is very natural and characteristic ; and produces a most humorous effect, even at the very moment it charms and interests us.

Contrasted with the deep, silent, patient love of Viola for the Duke, we have the lady-like wilfulness of Olivia ; and her sudden passion, or rather fancy, for the disguised page takes so beautiful a colouring of poetry and sentiment that we do not think her forward. Olivia is like a princess of romance, and has all the privileges of one ; she is, like Portia, high-born and high-bred, mistress over her servants—but not, like Portia, 'queen o'er herself.' She has never in her life been opposed ; the first contradiction, therefore, rouses all the woman in her, and turns a caprice into a headlong passion. . . .

The distance of rank which separates the Countess from the youthful page—the real sex of Viola—the dignified elegance of Olivia's deportment, except where passion gets the better of her pride—her consistent coldness towards the Duke— the description of that 'smooth, discreet, and stable bearing' with which she rules her household—her generous care for her steward Malvolio, in the midst of her own distress,—all these circumstances raise Olivia in our fancy, and render her caprice for the page a source of amusement and interest, not a subject of reproach. *Twelfth Night* is a genuine comedy—a perpetual spring of the gayest and the sweetest fancies. In artificial society men and women are divided into castes and classes, and it is rarely that extremes in character or manners can approximate. To blend into one harmonious picture the utmost grace and refinement of sentiment and the broadest effects of humour, the most poignant wit and the most indulgent benignity, in short, to bring before us in the same scene Viola and Olivia, with Malvolio and Sir Toby, belonged only to Nature and to Shakespeare.

A woman's affections, however strong, are sentiments when they run smooth ; and become passions only when opposed.

In Juliet and Helena [in *All's Well that Ends Well*], love is depicted as a passion, properly so called ; that is, a natural impulse throbbing in the heart's blood, and mingling with the very sources of life ;—a sentiment more or less modified by the imagination ; a strong abiding principle and motive, excited by resistance, acting upon the will, animating all the other faculties, and again influenced by them. This is the most complex aspect of love, and in these two characters it is depicted in colours at once the most various, the most intense, and the most brilliant.

In Viola and Perdita, love, being less complex, appears more refined ; more a sentiment than a passion,—a compound of impulse and fancy, while the reflective powers and moral energies are more faintly developed.

SIR EDWARD RUSSELL (*Fortnightly*, 1 Sept. 1884, p. 405) : Upon Viola's character, MISS ELLEN TERRY'S sweet and happy idiosyncrasy has wrought an exquisite modification. Viola undoubtedly lies in most of our minds as an extremely sentimental person. The impression being chiefly derived from the speech, 'She never told her love.' In order to conform to this conception it was necessary to suppress any exuberant gaiety in those passages in which Viola is tickled by the thought that she, a woman, is about to be loved as a man by Olivia. Those who see Miss Terry in the part will be convinced by the most irresistible of demonstrations that Viola was rather one of those thoroughly healthy and happy young women, who, while fraught with the capacity for loving and certain to be true in love, will scarcely pine grievously under their own love-troubles, or regard those of any ordinary woman as likely to be fatal. It is not very seriously of herself that she tells the story about concealment feeding on the damask cheek. She will not play patience on a monument unless the smiling at grief be very genuine. She feels the pathos of the story. Her frame quivers as she tells it to Orsino with lowered head, and his head presses upon hers in mere brotherly sympathy. But Viola is hearty though not heart-whole, and Miss Terry persuades us readily that the true Viola is one from whose gentle nature gaiety is not likely to be permanently estranged.

JOSEPH KNIGHT (1893, p. 205) : There are two conceptions of Viola, either of which is defensible. There is the sentimental view, which links the character with Bellario or Euphrasia in the *Philaster* of Beaumont and Fletcher and other similar personages of the early drama ; and there is the more realistic view, which makes her assumption of masculine attire something of a madcap freak. The latter view is that taken by Miss Neilson. It is fully borne out by the text. Viola falls in love with the Duke in the three months during which she is his confidante and messenger. It is absurd to suppose that love for a man she has never seen could have led her to the first assumption of masculine attire. The words, moreover, spoken to her by Olivia show that she put on, with Rosalind, a 'swashing and a martial outside.' Olivia charges her with having been saucy, and tells her she 'began rudely.' Viola's address to Maria, 'No, good swabber, I am to hull here a little longer,' affords no especial proof of timidity of demeanour. It is only, then, in her graver moments, and when in presence of her lord, that Viola shows the sentimental aspect of her character. Like the Di Vernon of Scott, she can melt into tenderness, but her general mood is one of almost saucy defiance. Miss Neilson presents this character to the life. She has every physical qualification for the part, and looks surprisingly attractive in her Grecian costume. She enjoys thoroughly the confusion her assumption of manly dress creates, and her delight when she finds herself taken for a man by Olivia is infectious. Not less happy is she in the more serious passages, the grace and delicacy of the play being, so far as the scenes in which she plays are concerned, fully preserved.

W. WINTER (1895, iii, 24): Yet Malvolio is not the central image in the comedy, to the exclusion of Viola. If the humour crystallises around him, the tender loveliness, the poetic beauty, the ardent, unselfish emotion, the exquisite glee and radiant grace crystallise around her. Viola is Shakespeare's ideal of the patient idolatry and devoted, silent self-sacrifice of perfect love. Viola makes no attempt to win; spreads no lure; resorts to no subterfuge. In such cases the advance is usually made by woman. It is so made by Rosalind, for example, a character commonly, and erroneously, named as the perfection of abstract poetical spirituality and refinement. It is not made by Viola. She loves, and she is simply herself, and she will submit, without a murmur, to any sorrow that may await her. 'She never told her love.' Rosalind is a woman. Viola is a poem. Rosalind is human. Viola is human, too, but also she is celestial. Disguised as a boy, she will follow the fortunes of her lord, and she will even plead his cause, as a lover, with the beautiful woman who has captured his physical longing and languishing, sentimental fancy. A woman, under such circumstances, commonly hates her rival with the bitterness of death. Viola never harbours hate, never speaks one word of antagonism or malice. She does not assume that Orsino is her property because she happens to love him, or that he is in any way responsible for the condition of her feelings, or that Olivia is reprehensible because she has fascinated him. There is no selfishness in her love, because there is no selfishness in her nature. Her desire to see the face of Olivia is the pathetic desire to know what it is that has charmed the man whom she worships, and, through her simulated glee, when she does see it, shines the touching consciousness that the beauty of Olivia might well inspire any man's devotion. Nothing could be more fervent and generous than the candour and enthusiasm with which she recognises that beauty, and pleads with it for compassion upon a suffering worshipper. She knows Orsino's sorrows by her own, and pities him and would help him if she could. That is true love, which desires not its own happiness, but the happiness of its object, and which feels, without any conscious knowledge, that itself is the perfection of human attainment, and that it may be better to lose than to win. Shakespeare has incarnated that lovely spirit in a person of equal loveliness, and has inspired it with the exuberant glee that is possible only to perfect innocence. Viola is as gay as she is gentle, and as guileless and simple as she is generous and sincere. The poet has emphasised his meaning, furthermore, by the expedient of contrast between the two women. Olivia,—self-absorbed, ostentatious in her mourning, acquisitive and voracious in her love, self-willed in her conduct, conventional in her character, physically very beautiful, but spiritually insignificant,—while she is precisely the sort of woman for whom men go wild, serves but to throw the immeasurable superiority of Viola into stronger relief. . . .

(P. 43): After the action of the piece has opened, several comical situations are devised for Viola, together with several situations of serious perplexity, which mostly tend to create a comic effect for the auditor. In those situations Viola's gleeful spirit is liberated,—her irrepressible hilarity, on being expected to play the part of a masculine lover, and her feminine consternation, when confronted with the necessity of combat, being artfully contrasted, for the sake of humorous results. The true note of the character, however, is serious. Viola is a woman of deep sensibility, and that way MISS REHAN comprehended and reproduced her,—permitting a wistful sadness to glimmer through the gauze of kindly vivacity with which, otherwise, her bright and gentle figure is artfully swathed. That was the pervading beauty of the impersonation. Those frolic scenes in which Viola participated are consonant with MISS REHAN'S propensity for mirth and with her faculty for comic action. She rejoiced in them and she made the listener rejoice in them. But the underlying cause of her success in them was the profound sincerity of her feeling,—over which her glee was seen to play, as moonlight plays upon the rippling surface of the ocean depth. In that embodiment, more than in any assumption of character previously presented by her, she relied upon a soft and gentle poetry of condition, discarding strong emphasis, whether of colour, demeanour, or speech. Her action was exceedingly delicate, and if at any moment she became conspicuous in a scene it was as the consequence of dramatic necessity, not of self-assertion. Lovely reserve and aristocratic distinction blended in the performance, and dignified and endeared it. The melody of Shakespeare's verse,—especially in the passage of Viola's renunciation,—fell from her lips in a strain of fluent sweetness that enhanced its beauty and deepened the pathos of its tender significance. In such tones the heart speaks, and not simply the warmth of an excited mind, and so the incommunicable something that the soul knows of love and sorrow finds an utterance, if not an intelligible expression. Subtlety of perception naturally accompanies deep feeling. Viola, when, as Cesario, she has captured the fancy of Olivia, although she may view that ludicrous dilemma archly, and even with a spice of innocent mischief, feels a woman's sympathy with the emotions of her sex, and her conduct toward Olivia is refined and considerate. MISS REHAN was admirably true to the Shakespearian ideal in that particular, as also she was in expressing the large generosity of Viola toward Olivia's beauty. It is only a woman intrinsically noble who can be just toward her prosperous rival in matters of the heart. MISS REHAN, in her embodiment of Viola, obeyed the fine artistic impulse to make no effort. Her elocution was at its best,—concealing premeditation, and flowing, as the brook flows, with continuous music and spontaneous, accidental variation. . . . Her witchery in Viola did not consist in her action,—although that was appropriate, dignified, symmetrical, expressive, and winning,—but in her assumption and preservation of a sweet, resigned patience; not despairing, not lachrymose,—a gentle, wistful aspect and state of romantic melancholy, veiled but not concealed beneath an outward guise of buoyant, careless joy.

MALVOLIO

CHARLES LAMB (1823?, ii, 369): The part of Malvolio was performed by Bensley with a richness and a dignity of which (to judge from some recent castings of that character) the very tradition must be worn out from the stage. No manager in these days would have dreamed of giving it to Mr Baddeley or Mr Parsons; when Bensley was occasionally absent from the theatre, John Kemble thought it no derogation to succeed to the part. Malvolio is not essentially ludicrous. He becomes comic but by accident. He is cold, austere, repelling; but dignified, consistent, and, for what appears, rather of an over-stretched morality. Maria describes him as a sort of Puritan; and he might have worn his gold chain with honour in one of our old round-head families, in the service of a Lambert or a Lady Fairfax. But his morality and manners are misplaced in Illyria. He is opposed to the proper *levities* of the piece, and falls in the unequal contest. Still his pride, or his gravity, (call it which you will,) is inherent and native to the man, not mock or affected, which latter only are the fit objects to excite laughter. His quality is at the best unlovely, but neither buffoon nor contemptible. His bearing is lofty, a little above his station, but probably not much above his deserts. We see no reason why he should not have been brave, honourable, accomplished. His careless committal of the ring to the ground (which he was commissioned to restore to Cesario) bespeaks a generosity of birth and feeling. His dialect on all occasions is that of a gentleman and a man of education. We must not confound him with the eternal, old, low steward of comedy. He is the master of the household to a great princess; a dignity probably conferred upon him for other respects than age or length of service. Olivia, at the first indication of his supposed madness, declares that she ' would not have him miscarry for half of her dowry.' Does this look as if the character was meant to appear little or insignificant? Once, indeed, she accuses him to his face,—of what?—of being ' sick of self-love,'—but with a gentleness and considerateness which could not have been if she had not thought that this particular infirmity shaded some virtues. His rebuke to the knight and his sottish revellers is sensible and spirited; and when we take into consideration the unprotected condition of his mistress, and the strict regard with which her state of real or dissembled mourning would draw the eyes of the world upon her house-affairs, Malvolio might feel the honour of the family in some sort in his keeping; as it appears not that Olivia had any more brothers or kinsmen to look to it,—for Sir Toby had dropped all such nice respects at the buttery-hatch. That Malvolio was meant to be represented as possessing estimable qualities, the expression of the Duke, in his anxiety to have him reconciled, almost infers: ' Pursue him and entreat him to a peace.' Even in his abused state of chains and darkness, a sort of greatness seems never to desert him. He argues highly and well with the supposed Sir Topas, and philosophises gallantly upon his straw. There must have been some shadow of worth about the man; he must have been something more than a mere vapour,—a thing of straw, or Jack in office,—before Fabian and Maria could have ventured sending him upon a courting errand to Olivia. There was some consonancy (as he would say) in the undertaking, or the jest would have been too bold even for that house of misrule.

Bensley, accordingly, threw over the part an air of Spanish loftiness. He looked, spake, and moved like an old Castilian. He was starch, spruce, opinionated, but his superstructure of pride seemed bottomed upon a sense of worth.

There was something in it beyond the coxcomb. He was big and swelling, but you could not be sure it was hollow. You might wish to see it taken down, but you felt that it was upon an elevation. He was magnificent from the outset; but when the decent sobrieties of the character began to give way, and the poison of self-love, in his conceit of the Countess's affection, gradually to work, you would have thought that the hero of La Mancha in person stood before you. How he went smiling to himself! With what ineffable carelessness would he twirl his gold chain! What a dream it was! You were infected with the illusion, and did not wish that it should be removed. You had no room for laughter. If an unseasonable reflection of morality obtruded itself, it was a deep sense of the pitiable infirmity of man's nature, that can lay him open to such frenzies; but, in truth, you rather admired than pitied the lunacy while it lasted; you felt that an hour of such mistake was worth an age with the eyes open. Who would not wish to live but for a day in the conceit of such a lady's love as Olivia? Why, the Duke would have given his principality but for a quarter of a minute, sleeping or waking, to have been so deluded. The man seemed to tread upon air, to taste manna, to walk with his head in the clouds, to mate Hyperion. O shake not the castles of his pride; endure yet for a season bright moments of confidence; 'stand still, ye watches of the element,' that Malvolio may be still in fancy fair Olivia's lord!—but fate and retribution say 'no.' I hear the mischievous titter of Maria,—the witty taunts of Sir Toby,—the still more insupportable triumph of the foolish knight,—the counterfeit Sir Topas is unmasked,—and 'thus the whirligig of time,' as the true clown hath it, 'brings in his revenges.' I confess that I never saw the catastrophe of this character, while Bensley played it, without a kind of tragic interest.

HUNTER (1845, i, 381): Though in other plays of Shakespeare we have indirect and sarcastical remarks on the opinions or practices by which the Puritan party in the Reformed Church of England were distinguished, casually introduced, it is in this play that we have his grand attack upon them; that here in fact there is a systematic design of holding them up to ridicule, and of exposing to public odium what appeared to him the dark features of the Puritan character. Not only does this appear in particular expressions and passages in the play, but to those who are acquainted with the representations which their enemies made of the Puritan character, it will appear sufficiently evident that Shakespeare intended to make Malvolio an abstract of that character, to exhibit in him all the worst features, and to combine them with others which were simply ridiculous. The character which his mistress gives him is that he is 'sad and civil,' and that he 'suits as a servant with her fortune,' in her state of affliction. This shows that, previously to the introduction into his mind of the fantastic notions which afterwards possessed him, it was intended that he should be of a formal, grave, and solemn demeanour, and, as to his attire, dressed with a Quaker-like plainness, which would heighten the comic effect when afterwards he decked himself with all manner of finery when he sought to please, as he supposed, his mistress. As we proceed we find that he is a person not moved to cheerfulness by any innocent jest; he casts a malign look on every person and everything around him; he seeks to depreciate everything and everybody; even Feste, the poor innocent domestic fool, who plays his part admirably, is not too far removed below the line of a rational jealousy to be free from the effects of his malign disposition: 'I saw him put down the other day by an ordinary fool.' At the same time he has a most inordinate conceit of himself, 'sick of self-love;' and, without possessing any of the qualities by which a generous ambition may and does effect its designs, he aims at objects which he ought to have regarded as without the range of his desires, even so far as to seek to possess himself of the hand and fortune of his mistress. Under a show of humility he hides a proud and tyrannical heart; in what he says of Sir Toby he shows the petty tyranny which he will exercise when the golden opportunity shall arrive. He begrudges any little service to any one, even that belonging to the office which he holds; and when there is anything in which he is employed, where he has the chance of smoothening or roughening asperities, or when he has to form a judgement on what he witnesses, he invariably takes the unkinder part, and shows at the same time that he has pleasure in taking it. His first introduction to the audience is with the remark which he makes, ' Yes, and shall do till the pangs of death shake him ;' and he makes his final exit exclaiming, ' I'll be revenged on the whole pack of you.' Such is Malvolio, who thus answers to his name, and who is perhaps one of the most finished characters drawn by Shakespeare, or any other·dramatist. As the representative of a class, however, it is overcharged with what is unamiable. It was no part of the object of Shakespeare to soften or to mix those redeeming features which were to be found in the Puritan character. His object was to hold up the Puritan to aversion ; and the moment he entered, the spectators would perceive by his attire the kind of person brought before them, or, if that were not sufficient, there was no mistaking the words of Maria : ' Sometimes he is a kind of Puritan.'

In Malvolio's general character the intention was to make the Puritan odious ; in the strategem of which he is the victim to make him ridiculous. It seems as if it were originally the poet's intention to deliver him up into the hands of Falstaff. Sir Toby is corpulent and witty, needy, dishonest, shifting, drunken, and ' much a liar,' with all Falstaff's address in extricating himself from a difficulty. Several of his expressions are quite in the Falstaff vein. Strip Falstaff, in short, of his military character and court brocade, and send him from the taverns of London to a well-replenished hall in the country, and we have the character of Sir Toby. In his companion Sir Andrew we have Slender again under a new name, even to the trick of *quoting*, the main characteristic of Slender. A stroke or two may be perceived, just sufficient to discriminate them, but such strokes, if such exist, are few; so few that there can be hardly a doubt that the poet's original intention, or perhaps a suggestion made to him, was that the Puritan should be delivered up into the hands of Falstaff. Falstaff's æra was, however, too decidedly fixed, and this rendered it expedient to invent a new name, and perhaps to introduce certain new features into the character.

HENRY GILES (1868, p. 177) : I pass now to the fool *sentimental*. I am not sure, however, that we should make the sentimental a distinct species of fool, since every man is at one time or other in the sentimental condition, and some men are never out of it. In youth we hardly call it folly ; but there are those who escape it in youth, on whom it comes with obstinate perverseness when youth is over. Victims there are who are verdant, poor fellows, all their lives ; sensitive perennial plants, susceptible evergreens in the gardens of the romantic. But *love* is the soul of sentiment ; and no man can be secure against love. A man may escape it six days in the week, but, as the great Shandy asserts, fall over head and ears into it on Saturday night. Wisdom, ·strength, and valour, love breaks down ; imperial ambition and the most sovereign command it humbles ; it turns the miser into a spendthrift, and charms the cynic into song. . . . Malvolio is even such a weak brother, and with such indulgence must he be treated. We may pity him,—in some measure respect him,—but we *must* laugh at him. He is an excellent specimen of the sentimental fool, and we must enjoy him. He makes very extraordinary grimaces. Men in love generally do, if you could but see them. He cuts very strange antics ; and while the fit is on him, he is in the highest degree amusing. That he is the victim of a plot is true ; and before he loves the great lady, he is made to fancy the great lady loves him. But no innately modest man can be made the victim of such a plot. Yet, if we could see every man as we see Malvolio, we might see enough to laugh at ; if we could hear men's inward whisperings as we hear his, we might hear soliloquies which would be more self-confident and more self-admiring. Malvolio in this is no singular phenomenon ; he is only the *fool-part* of masculine vanity exposed ; but men laugh at him as sincerely as if that fool-part had no concern with themselves. We wonder that Malvolio should be deceived as he was. But Malvolio had been already told that he was a wondrous proper man. If Olivia was great, was she not also a woman ? And though she was mistress and he servant, ' did not the lady of the Strachy marry the yeoman of the wardrobe '? And so the visions of hope grow into blissful brightness by the interpretations of vanity. Beguiled into absurd dec- orations, he disports away in his yellow stockings and his cross-garters. He does the amiable, but not bewitchingly ; smiling fantastically, he minces out his horrid phrases, his whining interjections, and murmurs, as with the music of a raven's song, ' Sweet lady ! ho ! ho !' The sweet lady only thought him *mad*. But others do of themselves what Malvolio only did from prompting, and are more thorough fools by instinct than he was by instruction.

WILLIAM ARCHER (*Macmillan's Maga.*, August, 1884, p. 275) : I confess that Malvolio has always been to me one of the most puzzling of Shakespeare's creations. The theory, so popular with German, and with some English, commentators, which makes of him a satirical type of the Puritan as Shakespeare conceived him, will not hold ground for a moment. It is founded on one or two detached speeches wrested from their context. Maria says of him that ' he is sometimes a kind of a Puritan,' only to say in the next breath that ' the devil a Puritan ' is he ; and when Sir Andrew expresses a desire to beat him, Sir Toby derisively asks, ' What, for being a Puritan ? Thy exquisite reason, dear knight.' Is it likely that Shakespeare was himself guilty of the stupidity which even Sir Toby ridicules in his gull ? . . . There is nothing of the typical Puritan in Malvolio. He carries out his lady's orders in remonstrating with her kinsman for making her house a noisy tavern, and by so doing he draws down upon himself the vengeance of the leagued spirits of misrule. If it be Puri- tanism to do his duty as a man of sense and a faithful steward in attempting to put a stop to drunken ribaldry, then the poet seems rather to eulogise than to satirise Puri- tanism. On the other hand, his misfortunes, so far as he himself is responsible for them, spring from defects by no means characteristically Puritan. Spiritual pride is the besetting sin of the 'unco guid'; it is physical vanity which leads Malvolio so readily to swallow his tormentors' bait. A scorn, real or affected, for the things of this life is the mark of the Puritan ; Malvolio, however little taste he may have for the gross ' cakes and ale ' of the boon companions, has not the slightest desire to conceal his worldliness beneath a mask of other-wordliness. But such argument is futile. No one who reads the play without a preconceived theory can find in Mal- volio the smallest trace of the zealot. All that can by any stretch of language be called Puritanism in his conduct redounds entirely to his honour. To me it seems that Shakespeare, in drawing him, had not so clear an idea as usual of the precise phase of character he wished to represent. He was more concerned to obtain comic effects than to create a consistent, closely-observed type. We do not *know* Malvolio as we know Polonius, Jaques, Mercutio, Dogberry. This may be a mere personal impression, but I seem to trace in the commentators something of the uncertainty which has always troubled me with reference to his character. The very fact that he has been so misinterpreted proves that. There is a certain vagueness in his charac- terisation. . . . If I may hazard a theory, I should say that he is not a Puritan, but a Philistine. The radical defect of his nature is a lack of that sense of humour which is the safety-valve of all our little insanities, preventing even the most expansive egoism from altogether over-inflating us. He takes himself and the world too seriously. He has no intuition for the incongruous and grotesque, to put the drag upon his egoistic fantasy, ' sick of self-love.' His face, not only smileless itself, but contemptuous of mirth in others, has acted as a damper upon the humour of the sprightly Maria and the jovial Sir Toby ; he has taken a set pleasure in putting the poor Clown out of countenance by receiving his quips with a stolid gravity. Hence the rancour of the humorists against a fundamentally antagonistic nature ; hence, perhaps, their whim of making him crown his absurdities by a forced smile, a grimace more incongruous with his pompous personality than even cross-garters or yellow stockings. He is a being, in short, to whom the world, with all its shows and forms, is intensely real and profoundly respectable. He has no sense of its littleness, its evanescence, without which he can have no true sense of its greatness and its mystery. In common life this absorption in the shows of things manifests itself in a deficient feeling for proportion and contrast. He has no sense of humour,— that is the head and front of his offending. That his punishment, strictly considered, is excessive, to the point of barbarity, cannot, I think, be doubted ; but the air of the fairy tale interpenetrates the farce, and we do not demand a strict apportionment of justice either poetical or practical. It is certain that no sense of painful injustice has generally been found to interfere with the pleasure to be derived from the play.

SIR EDWARD RUSSELL (*Fortnightly*, 1 Sept. 1884, p. 403) : Lean, lank, with self-occupied visage, and formal, peaked Spanish beard ; dressed in close garb of black striped with yellow, and holding a steward's wand, in the lightness of which there is something of fantastic symbolism, [IRVING'S Malvolio] steps on the stage with nose in air and eyes half shut, as if with singular and moody contemplation. He is visibly possessed of pride, of manners, and of intelligence. His pride, though intense, is not diseased, until the poison-dish of imagined love has been presented to him and has begun its work. Irving's gait ; his abstraction of gaze, qualified by a polite observance of his lady, and a suspicious vigilance over his fellows in her service and her turbulent relations and followers ; his sublime encounter with the Fool ; his sententious observations on everything in general, and the infinite gravity yet imaginative airiness of his movements, carry the Malvolio of Shakespeare to a higher point of effect, probably, than it has ever before reached on the stage. . . . I do not wish, as Coleridge said, to flounder-flat a humorous image, but there is no evading certain results of the genuinely humanistic as opposed to the entirely humor- istic rendering of certain of Shakespeare's characters. The gaunt and sombre steward is not, and is not likely to be, a purely amusing character. Even his tormentors at one point relent a little at the thought that they may carry their cruel joke too far, and for the nineteenth century it is carried too far to be entirely funny. Malvolio in the dark hole uttering sage, conscientious words to prove to the false Sir Topas that he is not mad, becomes a pathetic figure. The language evidently requires to be delivered with all Mr Irving's serious and significant earnestness.

W. WINTER (*Shadows of the Stage*, 1895, iii, 22) : People laugh at Malvolio, but they miss the meaning of him if they are not made to think as well as to laugh. For Malvolio is a person of serious individuality ; a capable person, and one of ruminant mind and austere temperament. The mirth that is derived from him is derived by devices of mischief,—as when a sportive boy decorates a marble statue with a stovepipe hat. No plight can be more laughable than that of the pompous ass whose pomposity is made the direct means of his ridiculous disgrace. Malvolio falls into that plight and becomes ludicrously absurd, but his discomfiture is due to one of the chronic frailties of human nature, a frailty which, in him and by means of him, it is the purpose of the poet kindly and humorously to expose and rebuke. Malvolio would be a farce part, and nothing more, if he were simply a silly coxcomb, cajoled and teased by a pert chambermaid. He is manifestly intended for the image of overweening self-love, of opinionated self-conceit, of narrow-minded, strutting, consequential complacency. 'Go off !' he cries, 'I discard you. I am not of your element.' The world contains many creatures that have within themselves, more or less modified, the potentiality of Malvolio's disease. Shakespeare has covered him with confusion and laughter, making him the butt not only of the worldly, rubicund, rollicking, masterful Sir Toby, but of lean and silly Sir Andrew, with his thimbleful of brains, and of the quaint, jocose Clown, and the comic serving-man, Fabian, and the shallow, prattling, skittish Maria. The spreading of the snare and the capture of the victim are deliciously droll, and when all the contributary parts are well acted the resultant effect of perfect mirth is inevitable. But Shakespeare has also covered with confusion and swept away, upon an irresistible tide of contemptuous laughter, the vicious infirmity of self-conceit.

J. W. HALES (*Contemporary Rev.*, Jan. 1895, p. 65) : Thus Shakespeare took no part in the Puritan-baiting that became a favourite dramatic pastime. And this for-bearance is to be accounted for not only by the general fairness and comprehensive sympathy of his nature,—by his splendid incapacity to believe ill of a large section of his fellow-creatures and his fellow-Englishmen,—by his innate repugnance to mere abuse and vilification, but also by the fact, that at Stratford he was brought into such close and intimate contact and acquaintance with so many specimens, public and private, of the Puritan breed. Annoyed and vexed as he might some-times be, and often undoubtedly was, by the self-complacency and omniscience and final judgements of these persons, trying as it must have been to hear some 'chosen vessels' pour out their wrath on the stage and all connected with it, as we can scarcely doubt he sometimes did, yet he was never made unjust or truculent. . . . Their acrimony might well seem to him somewhat oblivious of the real spirit of Christianity, and their opinions sadly wanting in breadth of view and in a real knowledge of the subjects on which they delivered themselves with such assurance ; but he had a profound respect for the uprightness of their intentions and their genu-ine sincerity, and the substantial goodness of their hearts and lives. Happily, to show that we do not speak quite without book, we are able to give a very suggestive illustration of the attitude of Shakespeare in his private life towards the Puritan divines who from time to time favoured Stratford with a visit. In the Chamberlain's accounts for 1614 is to be found this remarkable entry : ' *Item, for one quart of sack and one quart of claret wine, given to a Preacher at the New Place*, xxd.' By way of explanation, we must point out that it was customary for the Corporations of towns, at least in Warwickshire and Leicestershire, to pay distinguished visitors the compliment of sending them a present, generally of wine, to the house, public or private, where they were staying. When Sir Thomas Lucy, or Sir Fulke or Sir Edward Greville came into Stratford, this little attention was usually shown them. And, with the growth of Puritanism, the same civility was often extended to the itinerant lecturers. Evidently one of these gentlemen was, in 1614, the guest of Shakespeare ; and together, perhaps assisted by a neighbour or two who dropped in, they discussed a bottle of sack and a bottle of claret, supplemented, it may be suspected, by other bottles from the cellar of New Place. There, in the parlour or in the garden by the bowling-green, they sat hobnobbing, the preacher and the actor and playwright. . . . Both host and guest must have been the better for such intercourse,—the more catholic and human. But probably the guest derived the greater advantage from it ; his ideas of the drama must have been illuminated and enlarged ; and he must have realised that there were other ways of benefiting the world besides pulpit ministrations, that comedies and tragedies might do excellent service no less than his own expositions and discourses, and that of the author of them it might be said,—if the guest was fortunate enough to have read *Much Ado about Nothing*,—' the man doth fear God, howsoever it seems not in him by some large jests that he will make.' When Shakespeare made Sir Toby ask that immortal question :—' Dost thou think, because thou art virtuous, there shall be no more cakes and ale ?' he had probably in his mind the local headquarters of Puritanism, that very Banbury from which in later life his guest, or guests, probably came. Assuredly that was precisely the question then needing to be put to the overbearing zealots who threatened by their intolerance to make life intolerable ; and we may venture to hope that that well-timed remonstrance was not without some influence in assuaging the fanatical temper of that age as well as of ages since. At all events, it is pleasant to know that at New Place itself some of the 'virtuous' enjoyed their ' cakes and ale.'

CLEMENT SCOTT (1896, p. 272) : The entrance of Mr Irving as Malvolio was, as usual, eagerly expected. As the self-conceited steward, with an air of disgust and disdain for every one but himself, he looked like some grey and crafty old fox, and was scarcely recognised. Every word that fell from his lips was attentively listened to, every gesture was faithfully scanned. There were roars of laughter, of course, when the old man disturbed the revellers in his dressing-gown and night-cap. The scene with the latter, if too deliberate and a trifle too slow in utterance, was, of course, one of the acting features of the play, and it was noticed that Mr Irving in the later scenes, after Malvolio's cruel imprisonment as a madman, worked up his indignation to almost tragic importance. The line, ' I'll be revenged on the whole pack of you !' was spoken as an exit with the concentrated hate and ungovernable vehemence of a Shylock.

———

FESTE

H. ULRICI (1847, ii, 7) : The contrast most carefully worked out is that between the Fool by profession and the involuntary fools, Malvolio, Sir Andrew, and Sir Toby. While the latter, in their own conceit and foolishness, unconsciously draw the cap and bells over their own ears, the former, in his self-adapted mental garb of motley colours, moves with inimitable adroitness, and pins the lappets of his wit to the back of all the other characters. The meaning of the poem is, so to say, centred in him. He alone, in full consciousness, contemplates life as a merry Twelfth Night, in which every one has, in fact, only to play his allotted part to the greatest possible amusement of himself and others. He does not wish to be more nor less than a fool in the great mad-house of the world; on this account he has an unconquerable aversion to all starched common-sense and calculating plans, to that hollow unmeaning gravity which cannot understand a joke, because it fancies its proudly-adopted dignity thereby injured, and which is never able to rise above the petty, selfish interests of its own dear self; this accounts for his dislike of Malvolio. Again, he alone has respect for his cap and bells, for he is aware that fun and laughter, joke and jest are the seasoning of life, and that there is more depth and sense in humorous folly like his own, than in the sour-mindedness of so-called sensible people, who are in reality devoid of true sense, because the poetry of life, all the higher interests of man which extend beyond common prose, are unintelligible to them.

G. G. GERVINUS (1850, p. 438): No other of Shakespeare's fools is so conscious of his superiority as Feste. He says it, indeed, too often, and he shows still oftener that his foolish wisdom is in fact no folly, that it is a mistake to call him a fool, that the cowl does not make the monk, that his brain is not so motley as his dress. The poet has not in this play brought the words and actions of the Fool into relation with the one main idea of the piece, but he has opposed him rather to the separate characters in separate expressions. It is in this play that the instructive passage occurs, which designates the fool's difficult office as demanding that he should 'observe their mood on whom he jests, the quality of the persons, and the time, and check at every feather that comes before his eye;' this is exactly the part which Shakespeare has made the Fool here play. He is fit for anything; he lives with each after his own fashion, knowing their weaknesses, considering their nature, carefully adapting himself to the mood of the moment. When any one, Viola or the Duke, wishes to speak with his mistress, he knows how to beg gracefully; when he sings to the melancholy Duke, he refuses recompense; he deprecates expressly the idea of his begging being construed into covetousness. He boasts of being a good householder, but, in the dissolute society of the Knights, he himself is also somewhat mad; yet not so mad as to allow their bloody quarrels to pass unpunished. He knows how to discriminate between persons as well as between time and place. With natural, fresh, free natures, such as Sebastian and Viola, he is at once on a friendly footing. On the other hand, he punishes Malvolio for the contempt with which he speaks of him and his profession. He joins in playing him the trick which is to cure his self-conceit, and he tells him this, with impressive warning, in case of repetition. To Sir Andrew he talks glaring nonsense which enchants him; he knows that he passes for no fox with the coarse Sir Toby, the more craftily and easily he watches Maria, as she lays her bait for the churl of 'most weak *pia mater*'; and he praises her as the most witty of her sex, if she can wean him from drinking. To his mistress Olivia he is faithfully devoted, as one belonging to her house; he condemns the extravagance of her incipient melancholy; he distinctly designates the affair between her and the Duke as foolish; he promotes the connection with Viola and Sebastian. He keenly penetrates the Duke's changeable disposition, and bitingly, although good-naturedly, upbraids him with it; at the same time he tells him of a remedy which exactly gives a key to the inward condition of the lover's character. If the Fool be cleverly played, it can be, therefore, a guide through the most important points of this comedy.

F. KREYSSIG (1862, iii, 286) : In Feste, who is far more deeply involved in the plot than Touchstone, or any others of his class (except, perhaps, the Fool in *Lear*), we have the accomplished Fool, the allowed Merryman, in the full exercise of his skill ; but, in accordance with the innocent and joyous character of the comedy, without the stinging satire which we feel so keenly in *As You Like It*. On the contrary, it is his aim by ingenious jokes and harmless teasings to add spice to the flagging entertainment, and, at the same time, he is at full liberty accurately to gauge the characters about him, and as opportunity gives benefit to proffer jestingly to them his opinion of them ; even this, however, he does with the greatest prudence ; and (which is noteworthy) he speaks ill of no one behind the back. Thus it is that he is become perfect in his difficult position, and well deserves Viola's praise : 'This fellow is wise enough to play the fool,' etc., III, i, 60. In this sense he may well say to Olivia : ' *Cucullus non facit monachum*, I wear not motley in my brain.' Of course he is placed in the sharpest contrast to Malvolio, the personification of insipid arrogance. It would, indeed, be a radical defect in that insufferable pedant if he could take a joke ; if he did not invariably regard bird-bolts as cannon-bullets as soon as ever they hit his worthy person. . . . It is against this principle, therefore, of which Malvolio is the representative, and against this principle alone that Feste makes an earnest front. His remarks about the changeable taffeta of the Duke's doublet, and about Olivia's weak mourning for her brother, are purely good humoured ; he never elsewhere indulges his satire against classes or ranks, unless it be where he compares husbands and fools to pilchards and herrings. But when it comes to flouting the arrogant pietistic steward, who would banish cakes and ale and witty foolery, then he marshalls all his talents, and, when donning the gown of ' Sir Mathias,' * permits himself to utter the first and only sharp thrust at earnest and dangerous people : ' I would I were the first that ever dissembled in such a gown.' The passage is all the more striking, inasmuch as the whole disguise, as Maria afterwards remarks, is needless. It may be incidentally remarked, that throughout the conjuration scene the Fool imitates the unctuous tone of the Puritanic divines, whereas the priest, to whom Olivia entrusts her fate, is to be regarded clearly as a Catholic monk ; a further indication of Shakespeare's almost instinctive repugnance to the whole canting and pietistic Puritanical movement which, shortly after his death, proscribed his masterpieces, together with all other sports of merry England, and to whose folly it is to be ascribed that only by wading through the slough of the demoralised comedy of the Restoration, could England find the way to return to her Shakespeare.

H. I. RUGGLES (1870, p. 34) : Among the other characters, all of whom are absorbed in the pursuit of their own ends, stands idly the wise, cool-headed jester, Feste. He reads the minds of all, penetrates their designs, and sees clearly in what

---

* A fresh instance of the unwisdom (to give it the mildest possible name) wherein even the best of Germans (among whom Kreyssig is assuredly pre-eminent) will indulge in changing at pleasure the names of Shakespeare's *dramatis personæ*. In the present instance, what point is gained by changing ' Sir Topas ' to *Sir Mathias ?*
—ED.

'admirable fooling' they all are. A respecter of times and persons, he adapts himself to all in turn. The incoherent jargon with which he tickles the ears of the silly Sir Andrew, who thinks it 'the best fooling when all's done,' becomes keen and logical satire in his colloquies with the cultivated Duke. He is aware 'that foolery does walk about the orb, like the sun; it shines everywhere,' and this truth gives him a high regard for his own profession. Fool as he is, he 'wears no motley in his brain,' but is a serious, thoughtful man. His 'practice is as full of labour as a wise man's art.' He puts forth all his professional ability to roast Malvolio, not only because between them there is the natural aversion which must exist between the intolerant and the all-tolerant, but more particularly because Malvolio sought to discredit him and his vocation with his mistress. His concluding remark, as he exults over the mortified steward, 'thus doth the whirligig of time bring in his revenges,' is more philosophic than would befit the mouth of any other personage in the play.

C. W. Hutson (1875, p. 480): Feste's versatility and his reminiscences of scholastic training make one suspect that he must have been educated for the Church and have ruined his prospects by some wild prank. . . . (Page 489) : This sad strain ['Come away, come away, death,' etc.], sung evidently with taste and feeling by our Feste, to please the Duke so well, helps to point us to the real character of the jester. The true significance of the great dramatist's putting this wailing dirge into the Clown's mouth seems to me to be that he wishes to indicate his conception of the character as that of one whose culture and native gifts have both been overborne by some imperious and ineradicable foibles, aided by the force of circumstances. Capacity for thought . . . and capacity for sentiment, still manifested by his musical ability and the power with which he evidently rendered this song, indicate versatility of mind and character. To this we must add the histrionic capacity afterwards shown when he deceives Malvolio by feigned voice and style into mistaking him for the Parson. This versatility might have borne better fruit than the life of a great lady's jester but for the large developement of certain lower tastes and passions, which one cannot help noting in Feste, and also the opportune opening for him in the new profession, when his lively pranks shut him off from the clerical career for which he seems to have been originally destined.

John Weiss (1876, p. 198): Of all Shakespeare's clowns, Feste is the best endowed with a many-sided mirth, as, indeed, he should be, to pass lightly through the mingled romance and roystering of the play and favour all its moods. The sentiment of the Duke is as inebriated as the revelling which Malvolio provokes. Olivia's protracted grief for her brother is as carefully cosseted by her, as if on purpose to give the Clown an opportunity. All the characters, noble and common, have some weakness which he intuitively rallies. The charm of the comedy lies in these unsubstantial moods of the chief personages which consort with the more substantial whims and appetites of the others. The only sobriety is vested in the Clown; for all his freaks have a consistent disposition. So the lovely poetry of the mock mourners alternates with the tipsy prose of the genuine fleshly fellows. Their hearty caterwauling penetrates to Olivia's fond seclusion, and breaks up her brooding. Feste is everywhere at home. When he plays the [part of Sir Topas, he replies to Sir Toby's congratulation], 'Nay, I am for all waters,'—that is, for topaz, diamond, gems of the first water, all many-coloured facets I'll reflect. . . . The Clown is not only quaint, droll, full of banter, sly with sense, like clowns in the other plays, but he is the most ebullient with spirits of them all, ready for the next freak, to dissemble himself in the curate's gown and carry on two voices with Malvolio in the prison, or to carouse with the two knights till daybreak, and delight them with manufacturing burlesques. . . . (Page 202) : Though Shakespeare empties all his own love for pure fun into this Clown, he makes of him the only cool and consistent character in the play, and thus conveys to us his conviction of the superiority of an observer who has wit, humour, repartee, burlesquing, and buffoonery at command ; for none but wise men can make such fools of themselves. Such a fine composition is apt to be misunderstood by the single-gifted and prosaic people ; but this only piques the bells to their happiest jingle ; and a man is never more convinced of the divine origin of his buffooning talent than when the didactic souls reject it as heresy. All Shakespeare's clowns brandish this fine bauble ; their bells swing in a Sabbath air, and summon us to a service of wisdom. Feste has no passion to fondle and no chances to lie in wait for except those which can help his foolery to walk over everybody like the sun. Even when he seems to be wheedling money out of the Duke and Viola, he is only in sport with the weakness which purse-holders have to fee, to conciliate, to enjoy a prospect of grandeur. His perfectly dispassionate temper is sagacity itself. It discerns the solemn fickleness of the principal personages. They are all treated with amusing impartiality ; and it is in the spirit of the kosmos itself which does not stand in awe of anybody. It seems, indeed, as if the function of fool, and the striking toleration which has always invested it, was developed by Nature for protection of those of her creatures who are exposed to flattery and liable to be damaged by it. Not for shallow amusement have rich and titled persons harboured jesters, who always play the part of the slave of Pyrrhus, at proper intervals to remind them that they are mortal. All men secretly prefer to know the truth ; but the pampered people cannot bear to sit in the full draught of it. Its benefit must, however, be in some way conveyed to them. Bluff Kent is banished for saying to Lear, in plainest Saxon, what the Fool kept insinuating with impunity. Therefore no genuine court has been complete without its fool. . . . Feste bandies words with Viola and makes her submit to delicate insolences ; her distinguished air cannot abate him. He pretends to wish to be convinced by Malvolio that the latter is sane, but concludes that he will never believe a madman till he can see his brains. Feste keeps his own head on a level keel as the sparkling ripples of his drollery go by. Shakespeare's intention is conspicuous in him to make all the clowns the critics of all the other personages, and kept in the pay of their creator.

AGUECHEEK

Lamb (1823?, ii, 373) : Few now remember Dodd. What an Aguecheek the stage lost in him ! Lovegrove, who came nearest to the old actors, revived the character some few seasons ago, and made it sufficiently grotesque ; but Dodd was *it*, as it came out of Nature's hands. It might be said to remain *in puris naturalibus*. In expressing slowness of apprehension, this actor surpassed all others. You could see the first dawn of an idea stealing slowly over his countenance, climbing up by little and little, with a painful process, till it cleared up at last to the fulness of a twilight conception,—its highest meridian. He seemed to keep back his intellect, as some have had the power to retard their pulsation. The balloon takes less time in filling than it took to cover the expansion of his broad moony face over all its quarters with expression. A glimmer of understanding would appear in a corner of his eye, and for lack of fuel go out again. A part of his forehead would catch a little intelligence, and be a long time in communicating it to the remainder.

LATER PERFORMANCES

HALLIWELL (*Works*, 1857, vii, 246) : *Twelfth Night*, the perfection of English comedy, and the most fascinating drama in the language, could not have failed in success as an acting play, and there is sufficient evidence to show that it was appreciated at an early period as one of the author's most popular creations. There is not only the testimony of Manningham in its favour, . . . but Leonard Digges, in the verses describing the most attractive of Shakespeare's acting dramas, expressly alludes to the estimation in which the character of Malvolio was held by the frequenters of the theatre :—'The cock-pit, galleries, boxes, all are full, To hear Malvolio, that cross-garter'd gull.' * Nor was *Twelfth Night* held in less esteem by the sovereign and the court. It was performed before James I. long after there had ceased to be any attraction from its novelty, as appears from the following entry in a MS preserved at the Audit Office :—'To John Heminges, etc., upon a warrant dated 20 April, 1618, for presenting two severall playes before his Majesty, on Easter Monday, Twelfte Night, the play soe called, and on Easter Tuesday, the Winters Tale, xx. *li.*' A few years afterwards, it seems to have been acted under the title of Malvolio :—'At Candlemas, Malvolio was acted at court by the King's servants,'—Herbert's Diary, 1622–3. *Twelfth Night* was also occasionally acted after the Restoration of Charles II. . . . Charles Burnaby, in the preface to his comedy entitled, Love Betray'd, or the Agreeable Disappointment, Lond. 1703, asserts that he has taken part of the tale, and about fifty lines, from Shakespeare's *Twelfth Night*. These obligations are so trifling, Burnaby's comedy can scarcely be admitted into the list of Shakespearian alterations, but it is curious as an evidence of the liberty permitted in those days to be taken with the works of the great dramatist.

GENEST records fifteen or sixteen revivals of *Twelfth Night* between 1663 and 1813, but gives no more than the names of the actors. In November, 1820, it was acted at Covent Garden seventeen times, 'degraded,' says Genest (ix, 99), 'to an opera'; 'it was a wretched piece of business,' he adds, 'but as it is not printed, it is impossible to point out the quantum of its demerits.'

---

* These lines are to be found in some *Commendatory verses* prefixed to the *Poems Written by Wil. Shakes-peare. Gent.* 1640. Immediately preceding the two lines quoted above by Halliwell, we find, 'let but Beatrice And Benedicke be seene, loe in a trice'; then follows, 'The Cockpit, Galleries, Boxes, all are full, To heare Maluoglio, that crosse garter'd Gull.' The line, 'The Cockpit, Galleries, Boxes, all are full,' appears to be amphibious ; it applies both to Beatrice and Benedicke, and to Malvolio.—ED.

COSTUME, ETC.

In LUDWIG TIECK's Novel, *Der junge Tischlermeister*, the Baron Elsheim devises a performance of *Twelfth Night* at his castle as a festivity for his mother's birthday. The play is analysed scene by scene, and descriptions given of the costumes. Especial importance is attached to the construction of the stage, which has greater length than depth, and whereof a main feature is two short flights of steps, one on each side, leading to an upper, inner, and smaller stage. The acting of the amateurs is duly depicted, and the whole novel is entertaining, but written as it was in 1836, and as a protest against the French theatre then in fashion, there is nothing in it which I have deemed necessary, in these days of scenic splendour and of antiquarian fidelity, to transfer to these pages. It is sufficient to call the student's attention to it as a story very well worth reading for its own sake.

KNIGHT: *Twelfth Night* is amongst the most perplexing of Shakspere's plays to the sticklers for accuracy of costume. The period of action is undefined. The scene is laid in Illyria, whilst the names of the *Dramatis Personæ* are a mixture of Span- ish, Italian, and English. The best mode of reconciling the discrepancies arising from so many conflicting circumstances appears to be the assumption, first, that Duke Orsino is a Venetian governor of that portion of Dalmatia which was all of the ancient Illyria remaining under the dominion of the republic at the commencement of the seventeenth century, and that his attendants, Valentine, Curio, etc., as well as Olivia, Malvolio, and Maria, are also Venetians; and, secondly, that Sir Toby and Sir Andrew are English residents; the former a maternal uncle to Olivia,—her father, a Venetian Count, having married Sir Toby's sister. If this be allowed, and there is nothing that we can perceive in the play to prevent it, there is no impropriety in dressing the above-named characters in the Venetian and English costume of Shakspere's own time, and the two sea-captains and Sebastian in the very picturesque habits of 'Chimariot, Illyrian, and dark Suliote.' Viola might, therefore, by assuming the *national* male dress, be more readily mistaken for her brother, as it is absurd to suppose that she could otherwise, by accident, light upon a fac-simile of the suit he appears in; and any manifest difference, either in form or colour, would tend to destroy the illusion. We leave the decision, however, to our readers, at the same time referring those who think with us to our [remarks on Costume in] *The Merchant of Venice* [pp. 386, et seq. in this Ed.] and *Othello* [pp. 405, et seq. *ib.*] for the Venetian and English costume of the commencement of the seventeenth century, and confine our pictorial illustrations to the dress of a woman of Mitylene from the *Habiti Antiche e Moderni* of Cæsare Vecellio. The embroidered jacket and greaves, 'the snowy camisa and the shaggy capote' of the Greek captains have become almost as familiar to our sight as a frock-coat, Welling- ton boots, and trousers.

EDWARD W. GODWIN, F. S. A. (*The Architect*, 24 April, 1875): Although the action of *Twelfth Night* is described as taking place in a city of 'Illyria,' there are but few words in the text which give anything like a Dalmatian complexion. If we accept Illyria, we have a city or sea-port of the Venetian Republic, under the local government of a duke. Two passages,—one referring to the arrest of Antonio, the other to the Count's galleys and a sea-fight in which they were engaged,—are almost the only things, apart from the proper names, which could interfere with the action if we preferred to remove it to England, for the spirit of this play as compared with the other Italian plays is thoroughly English. The time of the action is that of the production of the work, between 1598 and 1602. There are in all, eighteen scenes, including four in Olivia's garden and two at the sea-coast; this reduces the architectural scenes to twelve, from which, setting aside the repetitions, we have :—1. An interior in the COUNT'S palace. 2. An interior in OLIVIA's house. 3. A street before OLIVIA's house. 4. Another street. It is quite possible to treat this play for the modern stage as I have already treated some others,—that is to say, dividing it into acts, each containing one set scene, as thus :—

Act   I. OLIVIA's house,—an interior. (I, iii, v; II, iii.)
Act II. The Count ORSINO's palace,—an interior. (II, ii, iv.)
Act III. OLIVIA's house,—exterior and garden, with a garden-house. (II, v;
        III, i, ii, iv; IV, ii.)
Act IV. The street before OLIVIA's house. (IV, i, iii; V.)

The sea-coast scenes and those in the COUNT'S palace, not here included, may be described, so far as they relate to the plot, either by the characters or in a prologue, or the coast scenes may be retained in their entirety where there is a good proscenium, and acted before the curtain or act-drop, which should then, of course, be painted for the purpose.

The architecture of the palace of Orsino and of Olivia's house may be Renaissance or Gothic or both. We have no special locality or town to consider, and, therefore, we cannot strictly follow any old examples. Our business in *Twelfth Night* is to compose or design the architecture in harmony with that which obtained in a Venetian town on the eastern coast of the Adriatic about the year 1600. This is the work of an architect as well as of an antiquary, and there are various ways of doing it; but there is more than this, for in planning the scenes it is necessary that the architect should understand something of the requirements of the stage, and of the *business* of the action, or the best design in the world may result in failure. Stage management, or the 'business,' as it is technically called, is one of the colours on which the dramatic picture depends; scenery is another; costume another; and the choicest tints, the high lights, the jewels of the picture are to be found,—or should be found,—in the expression of the actor's voice, face, and figure. But the *whole* batch of colours and tints must be as one in their treatment, if we wish to see a play rendered fitly. For one man to design an interior for Olivia's house with no control of or understanding as to the stage management; another to arrange the business of the action in total ignorace of the inner arrangement of an Italian mansion, or of the uses of its several parts; for one to paint the walls knowing nothing of the colours of the costume; another to design the dresses utterly indifferent to the colours of his background; are the happy-go-lucky processes usually employed on the English stage, and any success that may result from the adoption of such ways and means must necessarily be of the nature of a fluke. If we really want to progress in these matters, the first step is to accept the dictum of Macready :—*No actor should be a manager.* This strikes at the very root of the compound system of ignorance, mystery, envy, and egotism under which the dramatic and histrionic arts languish, flickering up now and then by the special help of some exceptional individual with, I will not say false, but misleading brightness.

The *Costume* need not detain us long. VECELLIO will still be a faithful servant to us if we only treat him properly. The text, too, refers to a number of interesting details.   We are told that Sir Toby is dressed in a rough country style, having on his feet strapped boots, and Sir Andrew has a weakness for dark crimson (damask) stockings.   In I, v, we see one of *the uses* of the lady's veil which occurs so frequently in the illustrations of Vecellio.   The steward Malvolio has a gold or silver-gilt chain, a 'branched velvet' gown (*i. e.* one with a broad branch pattern), a watch, rich jewels, and yellow stockings cross-gartered, although in the beginning of the action his stockings, trunk hose, and doublet would probably have been black.   Besides this, we have a doublet of changeable taffeta, cheveril or kid gloves, and miniature portraits worn as jewels.

WILH. BOLIN (*Jahrbuch d. d. Sh.-Gesellschaft*, 1889, xxiv, 151): We divide *Twelfth Night* into four Acts, whereof only the second demands a change of scene. Our first Act lies at the edge of a grove near the castle of Olivia; the other three are in her garden, which is converted only once into a room at the Duke's. . . . Malvolio is locked up in a cellar of the castle, with a cellar-window open to the garden.

E. K[ILIAN?] (*Jahrbuch d. d. Sh.-Gesellschaft*, 1894, xxix, xxx, 288): The scenic arrangements were greatly simplified at the performances at Carlsruh in 1893, inasmuch as Olivia's garden was so arranged that it served for the performance of the whole first Act.   It represented a park in front of Olivia's villa; this park bordered on the public highway (from lower left to upper right) which led from the sea-coast to the town.   On the left Olivia's mansion extended obliquely into the stage. From an open gallery in the first story, two flights of steps, one on each side, led down into the garden.   Between these flights of steps, under the gallery, there was the entrance to a cellar-like apartment, wherein in the fourth Act Malvolio was confined.   On the right, opposite to the mansion, there was a slight elevation, on which stood a marble table, surrounded with shrubbery and statues; here Sir Toby and Sir Andrew were convivial; on the left, in front, screened by the front of the mansion, was a quiet, retired little spot adapted to the scene between Viola and Olivia. Through the trees of the park was a distant view of the sea.

The first four scenes of the first Act are played consecutively on this stage, as is likewise done by the Meiningen troup.   But Valentine's words at the opening of the fourth scene, where he says, 'he hath known you but three days,' etc., have to be changed into 'He hardly knows you, and already you are no stranger.'   It is self-evident that the opening scene of the play is to be accepted as a serenade by the duke before the windows of his mistress.   On this stage the fifth scene of the first Act, as has been said, can be also played without further change.   At the conclusion of the fourth scene Viola goes up the steps into the house, the duke makes his exit on the right.   Maria and Feste advance from left lower entrance; then Olivia and Malvolio, returning from a walk in the garden, advance from the back.   When Maria reappears to announce Viola's visit, she descends the steps from the house. It is assumed that Viola has been told to await in the house Olivia's return from a walk in the park.   Maria's first words must be slightly changed: 'Madam, there is *in the house* a young gentleman,' etc.   In the same way Sir Toby's and Malvolio's references to 'the gate' must be suitably changed.

The second Act opens with the same stage by moonlight and begins with the carouse of the two Squires [*sic*] and the Clown.   Then for the fourth scene it is changed to a room in Orsino's palace.   Viola's monologue (II, ii) is introduced at the opening of this scene, in accordance with OECHELHÄUSER'S suggestion; apart from other grounds, this monologue is much more appropriate and excites more sympathy when delivered under these circumstances than if it were spoken in the street. The song 'Come away, come away, death' is sung by Viola, who, in this scene, is most properly alone with the duke. The following scene with Malvolio, with which the Act closes, is again in Olivia's park.

This same stage-setting remains unchanged in the last three Acts. The fifth Act has some slight changes in order to bring it in accord with the final scene. As suggested by OECHELHÄUSER, whose exposition in reference hereto merits unqualified assent, Viola hastens from the stage when the duke has expressed the wish to see her in her maiden weeds, in order to reappear just before the close in her own garments. The play then ends with the oaths of fidelity between Orsino and Viola, which have been transposed so as to be very last.

THE following are the Costumes of some of the principal characters, selected from a list of twenty-two, embracing every character in the play, set forth in *Shakespearian Costumes. With Illustrations of the whole of the Characters in each Play, in correct costume, compiled from authentic Sources, as given by* Montfaucon, Royall MSS, Holbein, Zuccaro, Strutt, etc. *Drawn by* Robert L. Bööcke, London, Samuel Miller, 1889 :—

ORSINO.—Doublet made in white brocaded and crimson brocaded silk, fitting close to the figure; to which is joined a full skirt made in white silk, trimmed with a band of crimson and gold brocaded silk. Puffed sleeves. Surtout of blue satin brocaded with gold, made with full puffed half-sleeves, and ornamented with a deep collar and broad facings of ermine. Lace ruffle round the neck. Orders and badges. Jewelled sword-belt. Slash trunks. Silk tights. Blue satin shoes.

SEBASTIAN.—Vest of amber silk richly embroidered with gold, double breasted and wrapped round the waist by a sash of crimson silk; over which is a jewelled belt. Slashed sleeves, showing the under-sleeves of white cambric. Short Greek jacket of blue velvet, embroidered with gold and silver thread, and trimmed with epaulets. White cambric or satin knickerbockers. Silk stockings. Greaves of crimson silk embroidered with gold. Shoes. Red cloth fez.

VIOLA.—*As Cesario (Second Dress)*: Doublet of pink silk, trimmed with a basque, cut in tabs and ornamented with braces of blue silk. Full sleeves, slashed blue and pink, and trimmed with an epaulet. Pink silk short cloak, lined with blue. Pink silk trunks. Blue silk tights. Low shoes. Sugar-loaf hat, trimmed with a feather. Sword. NOTE.—According to some authors, Viola, being the sister of Sebastian, would assume her brother's dress in her disguise. Therefore, if Viola wears this costume, Sebastian must also wear it.

VIOLA (*First Dress*).—Dress of puce coloured silk, made with a pointed body, open V-shape at the neck, and trimmed with revers. Holbein sleeves, lined with cream silk, open, and showing full under-sleeves of cream silk. Lace ruffle. Full skirt, forming a demi-train. Low hat, forming a point in front, and trimmed with an ostrich-tip plume.

OLIVIA.—Train dress in black velvet or silk. The skirt is full, pleated in at the waist, and forms a demi-train. Pointed body, cut low at the neck, and trimmed with a Medicis collar. Tight-fitting sleeves, with short hanging sleeves, loose from the shoulder. Jewelled girdle. Large lace veil.

MARIA.—Costume in two shades of cashmere. High body, cut open at the neck, trimmed with a high linen collar, and ornamented with a plastron, laced.

Puffed basque. Coat sleeves, trimmed with puffed epaulets. Short full skirt.
White muslin apron. Stockings to match the dress. Low pointed shoes, ornamented with ribbon bows.

Sir Toby Belch.—Leather jerkin, fastened round the waist with a belt. Surtout of brown cloth, made with full short sleeves of blue and brown cloth, and
under-sleeves of brown. Slashed trunks of blue and brown cloth. Russet brown
silk tights. Lace ruffle. High boots.

Sir Andrew Aguecheek.—Pointed doublet of blue silk, slashed with white,
made with full sleeves trimmed with puffed epaulets. Short cape in amber brocaded
satin, lined with white silk. Slasked trunks in pink and blue silk, tied to the
doublet with silk bows. Pink silk tights tied over the knee with silk garters. Low
shoes. Silk hat trimmed with a plume.

Malvolio.—Doublet of light brown silk, quilted or latticed with gold braid.
Pink silk sleeves, puffed at the shoulder, and slashed with brown. Trunks slashed
to match. Brown silk tights, cross-gartered. Lace ruffle and cuffs. Low shoes.

TIME ANALYSIS

P. A. Daniel (*New Shakspere Soc. Trans.*, 1877–9, p. **173**) : Day i. *Act* I, i.
introduces us to Orsino and his love-suit to Olivia. *Scene* ii. Viola, who has been
quite recently rescued from shipwreck, resolves to enter the Duke's service, disguised as a boy. *Scene* iii. makes us acquainted with Sir Toby, Sir Andrew, and
Maria. These scenes may all be supposed to take place on one and the same day.

An *interval* of three days.

Day 2. *Act* I, iv. Viola as Cesario is already in high favour with the Duke.
'He hath known you,' says Valentine, '*but three days*, and already you are no
stranger.' This speech marks an interval of three days between this and the preceding scenes. *Scene* v. At Olivia's house. Olivia requests Cesario to come again
to-morrow. *Act* II, i. Sebastian arrives, and, from his speeches, we judge that he is
still in the first agony of his grief for the loss of his sister. *Scene* ii. Malvolio
delivers the ring. *Scene* iii. Sir Toby, Sir Andrew, and Feste carouse. Maria persuades Sir Toby 'to be patient for *to-night*,' for 'since the youth of the Count's
was *to-day* with my lady, she is much out of quiet.' So ends Day No. 2, Sir Toby
retiring to burn some sack ; for ''tis too late to go to bed now.'

Day 3. From this point to the end of the play all is but matter for *one* May
morning.

The time represented by this Play is three days, with an interval of three days
between the first and second.

> Day i. Act I, i–iii.
> > *Interval* of three days.
> " 2. Act I, iv and v ; Act II, i–iii.
> " 3. Act II, iv and v ; Acts III, IV, and V.

There remains to notice in Act V. a statement inconsistent with the plot of the
Play as revealed in the previous scenes. Viola and Sebastian both suffered the same

shipwreck, and when they arrive in Illyria it is evident that but very few days can have elapsed since their escape. Yet, when Antonio is brought before the Duke in Act V, he asserts that Sebastian has been in his company for *three months*. It might indeed be said that this inconsistency is merely imaginary, and is founded on too strict an interpretation of the dialogue in Act I, ii, and Act II, i ; but the Duke makes a similar assertion with regard to Viola, '*Three months* this youth hath tended upon me.' And this is in absolute contradiction to Valentine's speech on the second day of the action (I, iv), where he says that the Duke 'hath known you [Viola] *but three days.*'

SUNDRY TRANSLATIONS OF

'*Come away, come away death*,' etc.—II, iv, 60.

J. J. ESCHENBURG (Strasburg, 1778) :—

> Komm hinweg, komm hinweg, Tod,
>   In dunkle Cypressen verschleuss mich !
> Flieh hinweg, flieh hinweg, Hauch,
>   Ein grausames Mädchen erwürgt mich.
> Mein Leichentuch, mit Laub besteckt,
>   Bereitet !
>   Die Liebe hat zur Bahre mich
>   Geleitet.
>
> Keine Blum', o ! keine Blum' streu
>   Je Wohlgeruch auf meinen Sarg hin !
> Nicht ein Freund, nicht ein Freund geh
>   Hin zu meinem Leichnam, und klag' ihn !
> Begrabt mich, tausendfält'gen Schmerz
>   Zu sparen,
> Hin, wo Verliebte nichts von mir
>   Erfahren.

JOHANN HEINRICH VOSS (Leipzig, 1818) :—

> Komm hinweg, komm hinweg, Tod !
> Mit traurigem Schleier umlegt mich !
>   Flieh im Hauch, flieh im Hauch, Noth !
> Ein grausames Mädchen erschlägt mich !
> Im weissen Tuch voll Immergrün
>   Denkt meiner.
> Ob mancher starb, so treu dahin
>   Schied keiner.
>
>   Keine Blum, keine Blum süss,
> Streut mir auf den dunkelen Sarg hin !
>   Kein Gesell, kein Gesell grüss'
> Ach Staub mir, wo Erde verbarg ihn.

Zu sparen so viel tausend Schmerz,
Leg, Freund, mich
Geheim, wo kein treuliebend Herz
Beweint mich.

J. G. v. HERDER (1826, *Shakespear-Museum*, p. 79) :—

Süsser Tod, süsser Tod, komm,
Komm, senk mich nieder ins kühle Grab !
Brich, o Herz, brich, o Herz fromm,
Stirb fromm der süssen Tyrannin ab !
Mein Gruftgewand schneeweiss und rein,
Legt es fertig !
Kein Braüt'gam hüllte je sich drein
So fröhlich.

Keine Blum', keine Blum' süss
Sollt ihr auf'n schwarzen Sarg mir streun !
Keine Trän', keine Trän' fliess',
Wo sanft wird ruhn mein Totenbein !
Ach tausend, tausend Seufzer schwer—
Nein—ihr Meinen,
Legt hin mich, wo kein Liebender
Kommt weinen.

AUGUST WILHELM VON SCHLEGEL (Berlin, 1826) :—

Komm herbey, komm herbey, Tod !
Und versenk' in Cypressen den Leib.
Lass mich frey, lass mich frey, Noth !
Mich erschlägt ein holdseliges Weib.
Mit Rosmarin mein Leichenhemd,
O bestellt es !
Ob Lieb ans Herz mir tödlich kömmt,
Treu' hält es.

Keine Blum', keine Blum' süss
Sey gestreut auf den schwärzlichen Sarg.
Keine Seel', keine Seel', grüss'
Mein Gebein, wo die Erd' es verbarg.
Und Ach und Weh zu wenden ab,
Bergt alleine
Mich, wo kein Treuer wall' ans Grab,
Und weine.

FRANZ DINGELSTEDT (Hildburghausen, 1868) :—

Erlös mich, Tod, von meiner Pein
Und bett' mich in Cypressen !
Mich schlägt die Herzallerliebste mein,
Dieweil sie mich vergessen.

Mit Rosmarin mein Grab bestreu',
    Darin ich lieg' in Frieden ;
Kein Liebender ist je so treu
      Geschieden !

Meinen Sarg kein Kränzlein zieren soll,
    Nicht zu Häupten, noch zu Füssen ;
Kein Freund, kein Freund soll trauervoll
    Die kalte Asche grüssen.
Und dass mir Niemand folgen thu',
    Wenn ich bestattet werde ;
Mein schweres Leid deckt schweigend zu
      Die Erde !

Otto Gildemeister (Leipzig, 1869) :—

Komm mit, O Tod, komm mit zur Gruft,
Und Trauerkrepp legt auf den Schragen !
Flieh, Lebensluft, flieh, Lebensluft !
Ein' schöne Jungfrau hat mich erschlagen.
Mein Leichenhemd mit Eiben dran,
O, lasst es kommen ;
Nie hat ein so getreuer Mann
Den Tod genommen.

Keine Blume nicht, keine Blume süss
Streut mir auf meine schwarze Decke !
Kein Freund auch nicht, kein Freund begrüss'
Mein' arme Leich' an der Kirchhofsecke.
Um tausend, tausend Seufzer zu sparen,
Versenkt mich alleine,
Dass kein Verliebter mein Grab gewahre
Und um mich weine !

L. von Kobell (*Deutsche Revue*, Berlin, June, 1892) :—

Komm' herbei, komm' herbei, Tod,
Bett' im Cypressenschrein den Leib,
Flieh', Atem, flieh' meine Not,
Mir brach das Herz ein schönes Weib.
Mein Leichentuch schafft schnell herbei,
Weiss wie Schnee,
Das Einzige, das mir bleibt treu,
Das teilt mein Weh !

Keine Blum', keine Blum' süss,
Sei mir gestreut auf den Sarg,
Kein Freund, kein Freund grüss',
Wo die Erde mich barg.
Viel tausend Seufzer zu wenden ab,
Legt mich alleine,
Dass kein Treuliebender auf meinem Grab
Mitleidig weine.

M. Le Tourneur (Paris, 1783) : —

> Viens, ô mort, viens ;
> Qu'on me couche sous un triste Cyprès ;
> Fuis, éteins-toi, souffle de ma vie.
> Une beauté cruelle m'a donné la mort.
> Semez de feuillage mon drap funèbre,
> Préparez-le.
> Jamais homme ne fit dans la mort un rôle aussi sincère.
> Que l'est le mien.
>
> Point de fleur, pas une douce fleur
> Sur mon triste cercueil.
> Point d'ami, pas un seul ami
> Qui salue ma tombe infortunée.
> Pour épargner mille & mille soupirs,
> Ah ! placez-moi dans un lieu ignoré,
> Où l'amant fidèle & mélancolique ne trouve jamais mon tombeau.
> Pour l'arroser de ses larmes.

François-Victor Hugo (Paris, 1864) : —

> Arrive, arrive, ô mort,
> Et que je sois couché sous un triste cyprès !
> Envole-toi, envole-toi, haleine,
> Je suis tué par une belle fille cruelle ;
> Mon linceul blanc, tout décoré d'if,
> Oh ! préparez-le.
> Dans la scène de la mort nul si vraiment
> Ne joua son rôle.
>
> Que pas une fleur, pas une fleur embaumée
> Ne soit semée sur mon noir cercueil.
> Que pas un ami, pas un ami ne salue
> Mon pauvre corps, là où seront jetés mes os.
> Pour m'épargner mille et mille sanglots,
> Oh ! mettez-moi quelque part
> Où un triste amant ne puisse trouver ma tombe
> Pour y pleurer !

Émile Montégut (Paris, 1867) : —

> Viens, ô mort, viens,
> Et dans une bière de triste cyprès, couche-moi.
> Envole-toi, envole-toi, souffle de vie,
> Je suis tué par une cruelle belle fille.
> Mon blanc linceul, semé de if,
> Oh prépare-le !
> Jamais amant plus sincère ne représenta
> La scène de sa mort.

Que pas une fleur, pas une douce fleur,
Soit jetée sur mon noir cercueil ;
Que pas un ami, pas un ami ne visite
Mon pauvre corps, là où mes os seront jetés.
Pour épargner mille et mille soupirs
Couchez-moi, oh ! couchez-moi,
Là où nul triste et fidèle amant ne puisse trouver mon tombeau
Pour y pleurer.

BENJAMIN LAROCHE (Paris, Cinquième Édition, 1869) :—

O trépas ! viens fermer mes yeux !
Couchez dans le cyprès ma dépouille mortelle.
Mon âme, envolez-vous aux cieux !
J'expire sous les coups d'une beauté cruelle.
Oh ! préparez mon blanc linceul !
Que l'if funèbre le décore.
Mon trépas, nul ne le déplore ;

Pas une fleur sur mon cercueil !
Nul ami ne suivra mon deuil.
Que je sois inhumé sans gloire
Dans quelque vallon écarté,
Où nul amant ne soit tenté
D'offrir des pleurs à ma mémoire.

MAURICE BOUCHOR (Paris, 1896) :—

Fuis, mon âme, fuis ! Je meurs sous les traits
De la plus cruelle des vierges.
Viens, ô Mort ! qu'on m'étende, à la lueur des cierges,
Dans un cercueil de noir cyprès.
Qu'on m'ensevelisse loin d'elle
Dans le blême linceul, couvert de branches d'if,
Qui, partageant mon sort, ami sûr, mais tardif,
Du moins me restera fidèle.

Que pas une fleur, une pauvre fleur
Sur ma tombe ne soit semée ;
Pour moi que nul ami, que nulle voix aimée
N'ait des paroles de douleur.
Que je sois seul avec mes peines,
Et laissez au désert blanchir mes ossements,
De peur que sur ma tombe, hélas ! les vrais amants
Ne versent trop de larmes vaines.

GIULIO CARCANO (Milano, 1881) :—

T'appressa, o morte ; vieni, t'affretta,
Dentro al cipresso posar desio :
Fugge l'estremo respiro mio,

Muojo, fanciulla crudel, per te !
Bianco lenzuolo, di fronde ornato
S'appresti a me.

Nè un fior soave, nè un solo fiore
Altri cosparga sul cener muto ;
Nè d'un amico sul freddo suol.
Sotto una gleba dormire io possa
Ignota al sol,
Nè sosti a piangere su quella fossa
Amante in duol.

JAIME CLARK (Madrid, 1873) :—

Ven á mí, ven á mí, cruda muerte ;
De cipreses mi tumba cercad.
Huye, aliento, que es fuerza perderte,
Ya que en ella no encuentro piedad.
Preparad mi sepultura
Yerta y fria :
No hubo nunca fe tan pura
Cual la mia.

Ni una flor, ni una flor candorosa
Engalane mi negro ataud ;
Ni un amigo, ni una alma piedosa
Pulse triste en mi huesa el laud.
Cerradla y borrad su huella ;
Nunca errante
Acuda á llorar en ella
Fiel amante.

LIFE AND DEATH OF THE MERRY DEUILL OF EDMONTON

WHILE these last pages are going through the press, I have been so fortunate as to obtain from London a reprint, in 1819, of this book, and am thus enabled to verify Steevens's quotation. It is not a play, and has very little to tell of Peter Fabell, the Merry Devil of Edmonton, which fully accounts for its absence from the *Shakespeariana* in the various libraries. It is merely a collection of coarse stories, twenty-one in number, whereof only five concern Peter Fabell ; the remainder consist of low, and, generally, disgusting, practical jokes of Smug, the Smith. On p. 24 is to be found Steevens's quotation : 'honest *Smug* loued . . . to bee mad merry amongst a mad company of his bare-chind boone companions, his little wanton wagtailes, his sweet and twenties, his pretty pinchineyed pigsnies, etc., as hee himselfe used commonly to call them.' This, I think, decisively confirms the interpretation of 'sweet and twenty' as a term of endearment. The small volume of fifty-two pages is signed 'Tho. Brewer,' who, I am very sure, did not write that truly delightful little comedy, *The Merry Devil of Edmonton*. See II, iii, 54, and *Note*, where an unfilled line luckily gives the chance to insert in the electrotype plate a reference to the present page.

PLAN OF THE WORK, Etc.

IN this Edition the attempt is made to give, in the shape of TEXTUAL NOTES, on the same page with the Text, all the VARIOUS READINGS of *Twelfth Night*, from the Second Folio down to the latest critical Edition of the play; then, as COMMENTARY, follow the Notes which the Editor has thought worthy of insertion, not only for the purpose of elucidating the text, but at times as illustrations of the History of Shakespearian criticism. In the APPENDIX will be found criticisms and discussions, which on the score of length could not be conveniently included in the *Commentary*.

LIST OF EDITIONS COLLATED IN THE TEXTUAL NOTES

THE SECOND FOLIO	[F₂]		1632

THE SECOND FOLIO ..	.. ..	[F$_2$] ..	.. 1632
THE THIRD FOLIO ..	.. ..	[F$_3$] ..	.. 1664
THE FOURTH FOLIO ..	.. ..	[F$_4$] ..	.. 1685
N. ROWE (First Edition)	.. .. ..	[Rowe i] ..	.. 1709
N. ROWE (Second Edition) ..	.. .. ..	[Rowe ii] ..	.. 1714
A. POPE (First Edition)	.. .. ..	[Pope i] ..	.. 1723
A. POPE (Second Edition) ..	.. .. ..	[Pope ii] ..	.. 1728
L. THEOBALD (First Edition)	.. ..	[Theob. i] .	.. 1733
L. THEOBALD (Second Edition)	.. ..	[Theob. ii] .	.. 1740
SIR T. HANMER	.. .. ..	[Han.] ..	.. 1744
W. WARBURTON	.. .. ..	[Warb.] ..	.. 1747
E. CAPELL	.. .. ..	[Cap.] ..	(?) 1761
DR JOHNSON	.. .. ..	[Johns.] ..	.. 1765
JOHNSON and STEEVENS	.. .. ..	[Var. '73] ..	.. 1793
JOHNSON and STEEVENS	.. .. ..	[Var. '78] ..	.. 1778
JOHNSON and STEEVENS	.. .. ..	[Var. '85] ..	.. 1785
J. RANN..	.. .. ..	[Ran.] ..	.. 1787
E. MALONE	.. .. ..	[Mal.] ..	.. 1790
GEO. STEEVENS.. ..	.. .. ..	[Steev.] ..	.. 1793
REED'S STEEVENS	.. .. ..	[Var. '03] ..	.. 1803
REED'S STEEVENS	.. .. ..	[Var. '13] ..	.. 1813
BOSWELL'S MALONE ..	.. .. ..	[Var.] ..	.. 1821
C. KNIGHT	.. .. ..	[Knt.] ..	(?) 1840
J. P. COLLIER (First Edition)..	.. ..	[Coll. i] ..	.. 1842
J. O. HALLIWELL (Folio Edition)	.. ..	[Hal.] ..	.. 1856
S. W. SINGER (Second Edition)	.. ..	[Sing. ii] ..	.. 1856
A. DYCE (First Edition)	.. ..	[Dyce i] ..	.. 1857
H. STAUNTON	.. ..	[Sta.] ..	.. 1857
J. P. COLLIER (Second Edition)	.. ..	[Coll. ii] ..	.. 1858
R. G. WHITE (First Edition)..	.. ..	[Wh. i] ..	.. 1858
CAMBRIDGE (First Edition, W. G. CLARK and W. A. WRIGHT)		[Cam.] ..	.. 1863
T. KEIGHTLEY..	.. ..	[Ktly.] ..	.. 1864
A. DYCE (Second Edition) ..	.. ..	[Dyce ii] ..	.. 1866

A. Dyce (Third Edition)   ..   ..   [Dyce iii]   1875
J. P. Collier (Third Edition)   ..   ..   ..   [Coll. iii]   1877
W. J. Rolfe   ..   ..   [Rlfe.]   1879
H. N. Hudson . .   ..   [Huds.]   1880
R. G. White (Second Edition)   ..   ..   ..   [Wh. ii]   1883
W. A. Wright (*Clarendon Press Series*)   ..   ..   [Wrt.]   1885
K. Deighton   ..   ..   [Dtn.]   1889
Cambridge (Second Edition, W. A. Wright)   ..   [Cam.]   1891

W. Harness   1830
Globe Edition (Clark and Wright)   ..   ..   [Glo.]   1864
N. Delius   ..   ..   [Del.]   Elberfeld, 1869
Rev. John Hunter (*Longman's Series*)   1870
F. A. Marshall (*Henry Irving Edition*)   1888
W. & R. Chambers   1895
Arthur D. Innes (*The Warwick Shakespeare*)   1895
Elizabeth Lee (*Blackie's Junior School Shakespeare*)   1895
A. Wilson Verity (*The Pitt Press Shakespeare for Schools*)

4th ed. Cambridge, 1895
R. F. Cholmeley (*Arnold's School Shakespeare*) ..   ..   n. d.
Israel Gollancz   ..   ..   n. d.

These last eleven editions I have not collated beyond referring to them in disputed passages, and recording, here and there in the Commentary, the views of their editors.

Within the last twenty-five years,—indeed, since the appearance, in 1864, of *The Globe Edition*,—the text of Shakespeare is become so settled that to collate, word for word, the text of editions which have appeared within this term, would be a very fruitless task. When, however, within recent years an Editor revises his text in a Second or a Third Edition, the case is different; it then becomes interesting to mark the effect of maturer judgement.

The present Text is that of the First Folio of 1623. Every word, I might say almost every letter, has been collated with the original.

In the Textual Notes the symbol Ff indicates the agreement of the *Second, Third*, and *Fourth Folios*.

I have not called attention to every little misprint in the Folio. The *Textual Notes* will show, if need be, that they are misprints by the agreement of all the Editors in their corrections.

Nor is notice taken of the first Editor who adopted the modern spelling, or substituted commas for parentheses, or changed ? to !.

The sign + indicates the agreement of Rowe, Pope, Theobald, Hanmer, Warburton, and Johnson; hereafter this symbol will include the *Variorum of 1773.*

When Warburton precedes Hanmer in the *Textual Notes*, it indicates that Hanmer has followed a suggestion of Warburton's.

The words *et cet.* after any reading indicate that it is the reading of *all other* editions.

The words *et seq.* indicate the agreement of all subsequent editions.

The abbreviation (*subs.*) indicates that the reading is *substantially* given, and that immaterial variations in spelling, punctuation, or stage-directions are disregarded.

When *Var.* precedes *Steev.* or *Mal.* it includes the *Variorums* of 1773, 1778, and 1785; when it follows *Steev.* or *Mal.* it includes the *Variorums* of 1803, 1813, and 1821.

An Emendation or Correction given in the *Commentary* is not repeated in the *Textual Notes*, unless it has been adopted by an Editor in his Text; nor is *conj.* added in the *Textual Notes* to the name of the proposer of the conjecture unless the conjecture happens to be that of an Editor, in which case its omission would lead to the inference that such was the reading of his text.

Coll. MS refers to COLLIER'S copy of the Second Folio bearing in its margin manuscript annotations.

In citing plays or quoting from them, the Acts, Scenes, and Lines of *The Globe Edition* are followed, unless otherwise noted. Of course, all references to *Twelfth Night* refer to the present text.

LIST OF BOOKS

To economise space in the foregoing pages, as a general rule merely the name of an author has been given, followed, in parentheses, by the number of volume and page.

In the following LIST, arranged alphabetically, enough of the full titles is set forth to serve the purposes of either identification or reference.

Be it understood that this List contains only those books wherefrom quotations have been taken at first hand. It does not include those which have been consulted or used in verifying references; were these included the List would be many times longer.

E. A. ABBOTT : *Shakespearian Grammar*	London, 1870
ALFRED AINGER : *Shakespeare in the Middle Temple* (English Illustrated Magazine, March).	" 1884
C. ANDREWS : *Lives of Twelve Bad Women*	" 1897
W. ARCHER : *Macmillan's Magazine*, August	" 1884
JOHN AUBREY : *Brief Lives*, etc., 1669 (ed. CLARK)	Oxford, 1898
C. BADHAM : *Text of Shakespeare* (Cambridge Essays)	1856
S. BAILEY : *Received Text of Shakespeare*	London, 1862
MATTEO BANDELLO, trans. by JOHN PAYNE (Villon Soc.)	" 1890
BARET'S *Alvearie*	" 1580
J. D. BARNETT : *Notes on Twelfth Night*	" 1895
J. BARTLETT : *Concordance*	" 1894
C. BATHURST : *Differences of Shakespeare's Versification*, etc.	" 1857
BATMAN VPPON BARTHOLOME, *De Proprietatibus Rerum*	" 1582
T. S. BAYNES : *Shakespearian Glossaries* (Edin. Rev., July)	1869

ANDREW BECKET : *Shakespeare's Himself Again* .. .. London, 1815
FRANÇOIS DE BELLE-FOREST : *Histoires Tragiques,* etc. .. Lyon, 1578
BLACKWOOD'S *Magazine,* August.. 1853
F. S. BOAS : *Shakespeare and his Predecessors* .. .. .. London, 1896
F. BODENSTEDT : *Shakespeare's Dramatische Werke* .. .. Leipzig, 1867
MAURICE BOUCHOR : *Les Chansons de Shakespeare* .. .. Paris, 1896
FRANCIS BOWEN : *Gleanings from a Literary Life* .. .. New York, 1880
E. C. BREWER : *Reader's Handbook* 1888
THOS. BREWER : *Life and Death of the Merry Deuill of Edmonton* (Reprint, 1819) .. .. London, 1631
C. ELLIOT BROWNE : *Athenæum,* June 1874
J. C. BUCKNILL : *Mad Folk of Shakespeare* (2nd edition) .. " 1867
J. BULLOCH : *Studies of the Text of Shakespeare* .. .. " 1878
E. CAPELL : *Notes,* etc. .. .. " 1779
GIULIO CARCANO : *Opere di Shakespeare* .. .. Milano, 1881
R. CARTWRIGHT : *New Readings in Shakespeare* .. .. London, 1866
E. J. CASTLE : *Shakespeare, Bacon, Johnson, and Greene* .. " 1897
G. CHALMERS : *Supplemental Apology,* etc. .. .. .. " 1799
W. & R. CHAMBERS : *Book of Days* 1863
W. CHAPPELL : *Popular Music of the Olden Time* .. .. " n. d.
F. J. CHILD : *English and Scottish Ballads* .. .. .. Boston, 1882
G. B. CHURCHILL : *Shakespeare Jahrbuch.* .. .. Weimar, 1898
JAIME CLARK : *Obras de Shakespeare* .. .. Madrid, n. d.
C. C. CLARKE : *Shakespeare Characters.*. .. .. .. London, 1863
HARTLEY COLERIDGE : *Essays and Marginalia* .. .. " 1851
S. T. COLERIDGE : *Notes and Lectures* .. .. .. " 1849
E. COLES : *English Dictionary* .. .. " 1732
J. P. COLLIER : *Poetical Decameron* .. .. " 1820
" *History of English Dramatic Poetry* .. .. " 1831
J. CHURTON COLLINS : *Essays and Studies* .. .. .. " 1895
HERMANN CONRAD : *Preussische Jahrbücher,* July .. .. Berlin, 1887
C. H. COOTE : *Shakspere's New Map in Twelfth Night* .. London, 1878
COTGRAVE : *Dictionarie of the French and English Tongues..* " 1632
H. H. S. CROFT : Elyot's *Gouernour* .. .. " 1883
J. CROFT : *Annotations on Shakespeare* .. .. .. York, 1810
HELKIAH CROOKE : *Microcosmographia,* etc. .. .. London, 1615
JOSEPH CROSBY : *American Bibliopolist,* June .. .. New York, 1875
P. A. DANIEL : *Notes and Emendations* .. .. .. London, 1870
T. DE QUINCEY : *Biography of Shakespeare* (Works, vol. xv). Edinburgh, 1863
EDUARD and OTTO DEVRIENT : *Deutscher Bühnen and Familien Shakespeare* .. .. Leipzig, 1873
F. DOUCE : *Illustrations of Shakespeare,* etc. .. .. .. London, 1807
DOWNES'S *Roscius Anglicanus* (Reprint, 1789) .. .. " 1662
J. DUNLOP : *History of Fiction* (Third Edition) .. .. " 1845
A. DYCE : *Remarks on Collier's and Knight's Editions* .. " 1844
" *Few Notes,* etc. .. .. " 1853
" *Strictures on Collier's New Edition* .. .. .. " 1859
J. EARLE : *Philology of the English Tongue* .. .. .. Oxford, 1879
J. EASTWOOD and W. A. WRIGHT : *Bible Word-Book* .. London, 1866

Edinburgh Review, April 1856
T. EDWARDS : *Canons of Criticism* .. .. London, 1765
KARL ELZE : *Notes on Elizabethan Dramatists* .. .. Halle, 1889
J. J. ESCHENBURG : *Der H. Dreykönigsabend oder Was ihr*
 wollt .. .. Strassburg, 1778
R. FARMER : *On the Learning of Shakespeare* .. .. .. London, 1767
JACOB FEIS : *Shakespeare and Montaigne* .. .. .. " 1884
F. G. FLEAY : *Shakespeare Manual* .. .. " 1876
 " *Introduction to Shakespearian Study* .. .. " 1877
 " *Life and Work of Shakespeare* .. .. .. " 1886
 " *History of the Stage,* 1559–1642 .. .. " 1890
W. FRANZ : *Shakespeare-Grammatik* .. .. Halle, 1898
A. R. FREY : *Shakespeare and alleged Spanish Prototypes*
 (New York Shakespeare Society) .. .. New York, 1886
F. J. FURNIVALL : *Introduction* to The Leopold Shakspere .. London, 1877
RUDOLPH GENÉE : *Klassische Frauenbilder* .. .. .. Berlin, 1884
P. GENEST : *The English Stage,* 1660–1830 .. .. .. Bath, 1832
J. GERARDE : *The Herball,* etc. .. .. London, 1633
G. G. GERVINUS : *Shakespeare* (3te Aufl.) .. .. .. Leipzig, 1862
OTTO GILDEMEISTER : *Was ihr wollt,* Uebersetzt von .. .. " 1869
HENRY GILES : *Human Life in Shakespeare* .. .. .. Boston, 1868
EDW. W. GODWIN : *The Architect,* April .. .. .. London, 1875
ARTHUR GOLDING : *The. XV. Booke of P. Ouidius Naso,* etc. " 1567
G. GOULD : *Corrigenda,* etc. .. .. " 1884
H. GREEN : *Shakespeare and the Emblem Writers* .. .. " 1870
Z. GREY : *Critical, Historical, and Explanatory Notes* .. " 1754
MRS GRIFFITHS : *Morality of Shakespeare's Dramas,* etc. .. " 1775
M. STEPHEN GUAZZO : *The ciuile Conuersation of* (trans. by
 G. pettie and Barth. Young) .. .. " 1586
J. W. HALES : *Contemporary Review,* January .. .. " 1895
FITZEDWARD HALL : *Modern English* .. .. " 1873
H. HALLAM : *Literature of Europe* .. .. " 1839
J. O. HALLIWELL-PHILLIPPS : *Outlines of the Life of Shake-*
 speare .. .. Brighton, 1882
J. O. HALLIWELL-PHILLIPPS : *Dictionary of Misprints* .. " 1887
HAYDN'S *Dictionary of Dates* 1886
WILLIAM HAZLITT : *Characters of Shakespeare's Plays* .. London, 1817
BENJAMIN HEATH : *Revisal of Shakespeare's Text* .. .. " 1765
JAMES HENRY : *Æneidea* .. .. Dublin, 1879
J. G. HERR : *Notes on the Text of Shakespeare* .. .. Philadelphia, 1879
JULIUS HEUSSER : *Der Coupletreim in Shakespeare* (Shake-
 speare Jahrbuch, xxviii) .. .. Weimar, 1893
J. HILES : *Dictionary of Musical Forms,* etc. .. .. .. London, 1871
C. HOLLYBAND : *A Dictionarie, French and English* .. .. " 1593
FRANÇOIS-VICTOR HUGO : *Œuvres Complètes de Shakespeare* .. Paris, 1868
LEIGH HUNT : *Wit and Humour* .. .. London, 1846
JOSEPH HUNTER : *New Illustrations of Shakespeare,* etc. .. " 1845
C. W. HUTSON : *Three of Shakespeare's Merry Men* (Southern
 Magazine, May) .. .. Baltimore, 1875

C. M. Ingleby: *Shakespeare, the Man and the Book* . . . . London, 1877
Mrs Jameson: *Characteristics of Women*, etc. . . . . " 1833
T. Keightley: *The Shakespeare Expositor* . . . . . . " 1867
T. Kenny: *Life and Genius of Shakespeare* . . . . . . " 1864
W. Kenrick: *Review of Johnson's Shakespeare* . . . . " 1865
J. L. Klein: *Geschichte des Dramas* . . . . . . Leipzig, 1872
Joseph Knight: *Theatrical Notes* . . . . . . London, 1893
F. Kreyssig: *Vorlesungen über Shakespeare* . . . . Berlin, 1862
Charles Lamb: *Works* . . . . London, 1870
Gerard Langbaine: *Account of English Dramatic Poets* . . Oxford, 1691
Sydney Lee: *A Life of Shakespeare* . . . . . . London, 1898
Mrs Lennox: *Shakespear Illustrated*, etc. . . . . " 1753
M. Le Tourneur; *Shakespeare traduit de l' Anglais* . . . . Paris, 1781
W. W. Lloyd: *Critical Essays* (Singer's Second Edition) . . London, 1856
D. H. Madden: *Diary of Master William Silence* . . . . " 1897
G. P. Marsh: *Lectures on the English Language* . . . . New York, 1860
J. Monck Mason: *Comments on the last edition* [Var. 1778]
    of Shakespeare . . . . London, 1785
E. A. Meredith: *Note on some Emendations, etc.* (Transac. of
    The Literary and Historical Society of Quebec, vol. i) . . Quebec, 1863
Max Moltke: *Shakespear-Museum* . . . . . . Leipzig, 1871
E. Montégut: *Œuvres Complètes de Shakespeare* . . . . Paris, 1867
Nares: *Glossary* (ed. Halliwell and Wright) . . . . London, 1867
E. W. Naylor: *Shakespeare and Music* . . . . . . " 1896
New Shakspere Society (Transactions) . . . . . . " 1877–9
John Nichols: *Literary Illustrations*, etc. . . . . . . " 1817
W. Oechelhäuser: *Einführungen in Shakespeare's Dramen*
    (2te Aufl.) . . . . Minden, 1885
J. G. Orger: *Critical Notes on Shakespeare's Comedies* . . London, n. d.
Sir Thomas Overburye: *A Wife*, etc. . . . . . . " 1627
Palsgrave: *L'Éclaircissement de la Langue Française*, 1530 Paris, 1852
T. L. Peacock: *The Deceived*, etc. . . . . . . London, 1862
T. Percy: *Reliques of Ancient English Poetry* . . . . " 1765
Sir Philip Perring: *Hard Knots in Shakespeare* (2nd Ed.) " 1886
Promptorium Parvulorum (ed. Way, Cam. Soc.) . . . . " 1865
Puttenham: *Arte of English Poesie*, 1589 (ed. Arber).
J. P. Quincy: *MS Corrections from a Copy of the Fourth Folio* Boston, 1854
B. W. Richardson: *Shakspere and the Pia Mater* (The
    Asclepiad, vol. v., No. 20) . . . . . . London, 1888
Locke Richardson: *Shakespeare Studies* . . . . New York, 1897
Barnabe Riche: *Apolonius and Silla*, 1581 (ed. Shakespeare
    Society).
J. Ritson: *Remarks, Critical and Illustrative* . . . . London, 1783
    " *Quip Modest* . . . . " 1788
    " *Cursory Criticism* . . . . . . " 1792
H. J. Ruggles: *Method of Shakespeare as an Artist* . . New York, 1870
W. L. Rushton: *Shakespeare's Testamentary Language* . . London, 1869
Sir Edward Russell: *Fortnightly*, September . . . . " 1884
W. B. Rye: *England as seen by Foreigners*, etc. . . . . " 1865

Il Sacrificio Comedia de gli Intronati. Celebrato ne i gavo-chi di vno Carneuale in Siena. Di nuouo corretta, & ristampata .. .. In Venegia, 1585

G. SARRAZIN: *Zur Chronologie von Shakespeare's Dichtungen*
(Jahrbuch, xxxii) .. .. Weimar, 1896
Saturday Review, July .. .. London, 1884
VINCENTIO SAVIOLO: *his Practise* .. .. " 1595
A. W. VON SCHLEGEL: *Lectures* (trans. by J. BLACK) .. " 1815
SCHLEGEL *und* TIECK: *Shakspear's Dramatische Werke* .. Berlin, 1833
A. SCHMIDT: *Was ihr wollt (Uebersetzt von* SCHLEGEL. *Durch-gesehen, eingeleitet, und erläutert)* .. .. Berlin, 1869
CLEMENT SCOTT: *From 'The Bells' to 'King Arthur'* .. London, 1896
SIGNOR N. S[ECCHI]: *Gl' Inganni. Comedia del Recitata in Milano l' anno 1547. dinanzi all Maestà del Re Filippo. Nvovamente ristampata & con somma diligenza cor-retta* .. .. In Venegia, 1582
E. H. SEYMOUR: *Remarks, Critical, Conjectural*, etc. .. London, 1805
P. B. SHELLEY: *Works*, etc. .. .. Boston, 1857
SIR PHILIP SIDNEY: *Arcadia* .. .. London, 1598
S. W. SINGER: *Shakespeare Vindicated*, etc. .. .. .. " 1853
W. W. SKEAT: *Etymological Dictionary* .. .. .. Oxford, 1882
A. SKOTTOWE: *Life of Shakespeare*, etc. .. .. .. London, 1824
R. A. SMALL: *Stage Quarrell between Jonson and the Poet-asters*, etc. .. .. Breslau, 1899
ADMIRAL SMYTH: *Sailor's Wordbook* .. .. London, 1867
J. SPEDDING: *Fraser's Magazine*, August .. .. .. " 1865
R. M. SPENCE: *Notes and Queries.*
H. P. STOKES: *Chronological Order of Shakespeare's Plays* .. " 1878
COL. HENRY STRACHEY: *Il Sarto Risarcito. The Lady of the Strachy* (Privately Printed) .. .. Guildford, 1898
A. C. SWINBURNE: *A Study of Shakespeare* .. .. .. London, 1880
NICOLAUS SYLLACIUS: *De Insulis Meridiani atque Indici Maris nuper Inventis*, 1494 (Reprint, with Introduction by J. L[ENOX]) .. .. New York, 1860
W. THEOBALD: *On the Classical Attainments of the Author of Shakespeare's Plays* (Baconiana, February) .. .. London, 1895
G. TICKNOR: *History of Spanish Literature* .. .. .. Boston, 1854
T. TYRWHITT: *Observations and Conjectures*, etc. .. .. London, 1766
H. ULRICI: *Shakespeare's Dramatic Art*, 1839 (trans. by L. DORA SCHMITZ, Bohn's ed.) .. .. " 1876
J. UPTON: *Critical Observations on Shakespeare* .. .. " 1746
" *Remarks on Three Plays of Jonson* .. .. " 1749
J. H. VOSS: *Was ihr wollt* .. .. Leipzig, 1818
W. S. WALKER: *Shakespeare's Versification* .. .. .. London, 1854
" *Critical Examination of the Text*, etc. .. " 1859
A. W. WARD: *History of English Dramatic Literature* .. " 1875
T. WARTON: *History of English Poetry* .. .. .. " 1775
J. WEISS: *Wit, Humour, and Shakespeare* .. .. .. Boston, 1876

H. Wellesley : *Stray Notes*, etc. .. .. London, 1865

H. B. Wheatley : *Dictionary of Reduplicated Words* .. " 1866

R. G. White : *Shakespeare's Scholar* .. .. New York, 1854

W. Whiter : *Specimen of a Commentary on Shakespeare* .. London, 1794

F. Willughby : *Ornithology* .. .. " 1768

W. Winter : *Shadows of the Stage* .. .. New York, 1895

INDEX

TWELFTH NIGHT
A SUPPLEMENTARY BIBLIOGRAPHY
[1901 - 1966]

PRINTED IN THE UNITED STATES OF AMERICA
by SENTRY PRESS, NEW YORK, N. Y. 10019

A BIBLIOGRAPHY FOR

TWELFTH NIGHT

A Supplement Continuing the one Prepared for the

Original Variorum Edition of 1901

[1901-1966]

by

Louis Marder, Editor of *The Shakespeare Newsletter*

University of Illinois at Chicago Circle

As in previous bibliographies in this series, the items have been selected for their suggestiveness. The finding of at least one item in the particular area of research into which one is delving will undoubtedly lead to other items of the same kind.

If any important articles have been omitted, the oversight is regretted. However, the references that are listed will contain footnotes and bibliographies that will lead to further studies supplementing those that are here contained. Some 1964 items have been included.

Needless to say, with over 1000 books, editions, articles, and reviews on Shakespeare being written annually, any bibliography of Shakespeare becomes obsolete the moment it appears in print. To supplement this bibliography from previous compilations a short list of earlier bibliograpies is appended below.

For references subsequent to publication of this list, researchers are recommended to consult the survey articles and bibliographies contained in the *Shakespeare Quarterly,* the *Shakespeare Jahrbuch, The Publications of the Modern Language Association (PMLA), Studies in Philology, Modern Humanities Research Association, The Year's Work in English Studies, Shakespeare Survey,* and *Studies in English Literature. The Shakespeare Newsletter [SNL]* contains classified bibliographies from time to time.

[III]

Since most biographies include references to, or analyses of, plays, references in my "Bibliography of Shakespeare Biographies" (about 130 are listed) may profitably be consulted [*SNL,* XI:8 (May 1961), 20-21]. For additional bibliographical sources my "Bibliography of Shakespearean Bibliographies" should also prove useful [*SNL,* XII-3 (May 1962), 24-25]. The 400th Anniversary Commemorative issue of *SNL* [XIV:2-3 (April-May 1964)] contains a list of Shakespeareana in print as well as a list of almost 550 doctoral dissertations. Both *SNL* and *Abstracts of English Studies* regularly contain digests of Shakespeareana.

To past bibliographers the compiler is eternally grateful.

TABLE OF ABBREVIATIONS

AI—American Imago

DA—Dissertation Abstracts

DD—Doctoral Dissertation

DuR—Dublin Review

E&S—Essays and Studies by Members of the English Association

EA—Études Anglaises

EIC—Essays in Criticism

EIE—English Institute Essays

EJ—English Journal

ELH—Journal of English Literary History

EM—English Miscellany

ES—English Studies

ETJ—Educational Theatre Journal

Expl.—Explicator

Hud R—Hudson Review

HJ—Hibbert Journal

JEGP—Journal of English and Germanic Philology

KR—Kenyon Review

L&P—Literature and Psychology

MLN—Modern Language Notes

MLQ—Modern Language Quarterly

MP—Modern Philology

MQ—Midwest Quarterly

N&Q—Notes and Queries

Neophil—Neophilologus

PMLA—Publications of the Modern Language Association

PQ—Philological Quarterly

PsR—Psychoanalytic Review

QR—Quarterly Review

QJR—Quarterly Journal of Speech

RES—Review of English Studies

RN—Renaissance News

SAB—Shakespeare Association Bulletin

SEL—Studies in English Literature

SJ and Sh Jb—Shakespeare Jahrbuch

SNL—The Shakespeare Newsletter

SP—Studies in Philology

SQ—Shakespeare Quarterly

SR—Sewanee Review

SS—Shakespeare Survey

TLS—(London) Times Literary Supplement

UTQ—University of Toronto Quarterly

UTSE—University of Texas Studies in English

YR—Yale Review

Less frequently cited periodicals are fully identified.

REPRODUCTIONS OF THE ORIGINAL FOLIO EDITIONS OF
SHAKESPEARE

[Works] *Mr. William Shakespeare's Comedies, Histories, and Tragedies,* being a reproduction in facsimile of the first folio edition, 1623, from the Chatsworth Copy [Intro. and census by Sidney Lee.] Clarendon Press, Oxford, 1902. First Folio.

[Works] *Mr. William Shakespeare's Comedies, Histories, and Tragedies,* faithfully reproduced in facsimile from the edition of 1623. Methuen, London, 1910. First Folio.

Bartlett, Henrietta C. *Mr. William Shakespeare: Original and Early Editions of His Quartos and Folios.,* New Haven, Yale University Press, 1923.

The Winter's Tale (a Facsimile of the first folio text). Wilson, J. D., introduction. London and New York, 1928.

[Works] *Mr. William Shakespeare's Comedies, Histories, and Tragedies* A facsimile edition of 1623 prepared by Helge Kökeritz, Yale University Press, 1954. First Folio.

[Works] *Mr. William Shakespeare's Comedies, Histories, and Tragedies,* faithfully reproduced in facsimile from the edition of 1632. Methuen, London, 1909. 2nd Folio.

[Works] *Mr. William Shakespeare's Comedies, Histories, and Tragedies,* faithfully reproduced in facsimile from the edition of 1664. Methuen London, 1905. 3rd Folio.

[Works] *Mr. William Shakespeare's Comedies, Histories, and Tragedies,* faithfully reproduced from the edition of 1685. Methuen, London, 1904. 4th Folio.

A PARTIAL LIST OF BIBLIOGRAPHICAL SOURCES

Jaggard, William. *Shakespeare Bibliography.* Stratford-Upon-Avon, 1911, pp. 478.-482.

Tannenbaum, Samuel A. Annual Bibliographies in *The Shakespeare Association Bulletin,* 1924-49.

Ebisch, Walter and Levin L. Schucking. *A Shakespeare Bibliography.* Oxford at the Clarendon Press, 1931, pp. 223-4. *Supplement for the Years 1930-35,* (1937), pp. 79-80.

The Cambridge Bibliography of English Literature. Ed. by F. W. Bateson. Cambridge at the University Press, 1940, pp. 564-5.

The Shakespeare Quarterly. Annual Bibliographies, 1950-65. Ed. by Robert W. Dent.

The Cambridge Bibliography of English Literature. Genl. Ed. F. W. Bateson. Supplement Vol. V. Ed. by George Watson, Cambridge University Press, 1957, p. 267.

Smith, Gordon Ross. *A Classified Shakespeare Bibliography, 1936-1958*. The Pennsylvania State University Press, University Park, Pa., 1963.

Shakespeare: An Excerpt From the General Catalogue of Printed Books in the British Museum, Published by the Trustees of the British Museum, London, 1964, Cols. 318-23. Contains 317 Folio columns of references to Shakespeareana.

Berman, Ronald. *A Reader's Guide to Shakespeare's Plays: A Discursive Bibliography*. Chicago, 1965, pp. 78-81.

A REPRESENTATIVE LIST OF MODERN EDITIONS OF THE PLAY

Furnivall, F. J., Editor. *Works of Shakespeare*. with Intro. in *The Leopold Shakespeare,* 1904.

Works. Stratford Town Edition. Stratford-on-Avon, Shakespeare Head Press, 1904-07.

Luce, Morton, Ed. *Twelfth Night*. London, 1906 (1929). (The Arden edition)

Twelfth Night ed. by G. B. Harrison and F. H. Pritchard. London, 1925.

Twelfth Night, or *What You Will,* ed. for Syndics of Cambridge Univ. Press by John Dover Wilson and A. Quiller-Couch, 1930, pp. xxix - 193. (The New Cambridge Shakespeare)

Kittredge, George Lyman, ed. *The Complete Works of Shakespeare*. Boston, 1936.

Parrot, Thomas Marc. Editor. *Shakespeare, Twenty-three Plays and the Sonnets*. New York, 1938. With notes by Robert S. Telfer and Edward Hubler (in later editions)

Farjeon, H., ed. *The Works of Shakespeare*. New York, 1939-40.

Twelfth Night, ed. George L. Kittredge, 1941, pp. x-190.

Sixteen Plays of Shakespeare, ed. George L. Kittredge, N. Y., 1946, pp. 351-384, Notes, 385-425.

Twelfth Night: or, *What You Will,* Ed. Mark Eccles, 1948, pp. vi-87.

Cambell, Oscar James, ed. *The Living Shakespeare*. New York, 1949.

Craig, Hardin, ed. *The Complete Works of Shakespeare*. Chicago, 1951.

Downer, Alan S., ed. *William Shakespeare. Five Plays: Hamlet, King Lear, Henry IV (Part I), Much Ado About Nothing, The Tempest*. New York, 1951.

Alexander, Peter, ed. *William Shakespeare: The Complete Works*. New York, 1952.

Sisson, Chearles Jasper, ed. *William Shakespeare: The Complete Works*. New York, 1953.

Twelfth Night, ed. Charles T. Prouty, Baltimore, 1958, pp. 121. (The Pelican Shakespeare)

Twelfth Night, ed. Sir Arthur Quiller-Couch and John Dover Wilson, Cambridge Pocket Shakespeare, 1958, pp. 100.

Harrison, G. B., ed. *Shakespeare: The Complete Works.* New York, 1958.

Twelfth Night, ed. by Francis Fergusson and Charles Jasper Sisson. With a Modern Commentary by E. Martin Browne, New York, 1959, pp. 191. (The Laurel Shakespeare)

Twelfth Night, edd. Louis B. Wright and Virginia A. LaMar. New York, 1961, pp. xliv - 101. (The Folger Shakespeare Library General Reader's Shakespeare)

Ward, A. C., ed. *Twelfth Night or What You Will,* London, 1962, pp. xcvi + 181.

Campbell, Oscar J., with Alfred Rothschild and Stuart Vaughan. *Twelfth Night,* N. Y., 1964, (The Bantam Shakespeare.)

CRITICAL STUDIES

Adams, Joseph Quincy. *A Life of William Shakespeare,* New York, 1925. *passim.*

Akrigg, G. P. V. *"Twelfth Night* at the Middle Temple," SQ, IX(1958), 422-424.

Alexander, Peter. *Shakespeare's Life and Art.* London, 1939, pp. 134-138.

Allen, Percy. "Montaigne and *Twelfth Night,"* TLS, Sept. 18, 1937, p. 675.

————.*Shakespeare and Chapman as Topical Dramatists: Being a further Study of Elizabethan Dramatic Origins and Imitations,* London, 1929, *passim.*

Anon. "Actaeon: Myth and Moralising," *N&Q,* 175 (1938), 74-76.

Archer, William. "The Two *Twelfth Nights,"* Fortnightly Review, CX (1918).

Armstrong, T. Percy. "Patience on a Monument," *N&Q,* 176 (1939), 10-11. See also letter by G. C. L., *Ibid.,* p. 11.

Bache, William B. "Levels of Perception in *Twelfth Night",* Ball State Teachers College Forum, Autumn 1964, pp. 56-58.

Bachrach, A. G. H. "The Icicle on the Dutchman's Beard," *ES,* XLV (1964), 97-104.

Baldwin, Thomas W. *On Act and Scene Division in the Shakespeare First Folio.* Carbondale and Edwardville, 1965, *passim.*

————."Shakespeare's Apthonian Man," *MLN,* LXV (1950) 111-112.

Barber, C. L. *Shakespeare's Festive Comedy: A Study of Dramatic Form and its Relation to Social Custom.* Princeton, 1959, *passim.*

Barnes, Richard "Shakespeare New: Shakespeare Now," *Claremont Quarterly,* (Summer 1964), 33-51.

Barnet, Sylvan. "Charles Lamb and the Tragic Malvolio," *PQ,* XXXIII (1954), 177-188.

Barton, Sir Dunbar Plunket. *Shakespeare and the Law.* New York, 1929, *passim.*

Beck, Sydney. "The Case of 'O Mistress Mine'," *Renaissance News,* VI (1953), 19-23.

Bethell, S. L. *Shakespeare and the Popular Dramatic Tradition.* London, 1948, *passim.*

de Blacam, H. " 'Who, I, Sir? Not I, Sir'," *TLS,* (Sept. 28, 1933), 652.

Blackwell, B. *Aspects of Elizabethan Imagery.* Oxford, 1929, *passim.*

Blanchard, P. G. Shakespeare's Pronunciation: A Transcription of "Twelfth Night," I. V. Cambridge, 1927, pp. 20.

Blistein, Elmer M. *Comedy in Action.* Duke U.P., 1944, pp. xvi + 146.

———. "The Object of Scorn: An Aspect of the Comic Antagonist," *Western Humanities Review,* XIV (1960), 209-222.

Boas, Louise S. "The Clown in *Twelfth Night,*" *TLS,* Sept. 12, 1952, p. 597.

Bowden, William R., "Teaching Structure in Shakespeare: *I Henry IV, Twelfth Night,* and *Hamlet,*" *CE,* XXIII (1962), 525-531.

Bradbrook, Muriel C. *Shakespeare and Elizabethan Poetry.* London, 1951.

Bradley, A. C. "Feste the Jester" in *A Miscellany.* London, 1929.

Brennecke, E., Jr. "Shakespeare's Musical Collaboration with Morley," *PMLA,* LIV (1939), 138-1449.

Brennecke, Ernest (trans) and Henry Brennecke (coll.) *Shakespeare in Germany 1590-1700.* Chicago, 1964, pp. viii + 301.

Brittin, Norman A. "The *Twelfth Night* of Shakespeare and of Professor Draper," *SQ,* VII (1956), 211-216.

Brown, Ivor. "The Orsini Story," in his *Theater* (London), 1954/55, pp. 67-71.

Brown, John Russell. "Directions for Twelfth Night," *Tulane Drama Review,* (1961), 77-88.

———. "The Interpretation of Shakespeare's Comedies: 1900-1953," *SS8,* Cambridge, 1955, pp. 1-13.

———. *Shakespeare and His Comedies.* London, 1957, pp. 162-182.

Bullough, Geoffrey, ed. *Narrative and Dramatic Sources of Shakespeare.* London and New York, 1958, Vol. II, pp. 269-72.

Camden, Carroll. "Three Notes on Shakespeare," *MLN,* LXXII (1957), 251-253. *Twelfth Night,* V.i.224.

Campbell, J. L. "Gaelic Folk Song," *TLS,* (June 27, 1958), p. 361.

Cauthen, I. B., Jr. "The Twelfth Day of December: *Twelfth Night,* II.iii.91," *SB,* II (1949), 182-185.

Chambers, E. K. "Twelfth Night," in *Shakespeare: A Survey*. London, 1925, pp. 172-180.

——. *William Shakespeare: A Study of Facts and Problems*. Oxford, 1930, Vol. I, 404-407.

Chang, Y. Z. "Who and What Were the Cathayans?" *SP*, XXXIII (1936), 203-221.

Chapman, Raymond. "The Fair-Haired Man: An Elizabethan Superstition," *N&Q*, NS, II (1955), 332. Reply by W. H. W. Sabine, *Ibid.*, p. EDG.

——. "*Twelfth Night* and the Swan Theatre," *N&Q*, 196 (1951), 468-470.

Charlton, H. B. *Shakespearian Comedy*. London, 1938. pp. 277-299, *et passim*.

——. "Shakespeare's Comedies: The Consummation," *Bulletin of the John Rylands Library*, XXI (1937), 323-351.

Choe, Jaisou. "The World of the Romantic Comedy," in *Shakespeare's Art as Order of Life*. New York, 1965, pp. 56-67.

Clark, Eva Turner. *Shakespeare's Plays in the Order of Their Writing*. London, 1930, pp. 217-230.

Coghill, N. "The Basis of Shakesperian Comedy," in *Essays and Studies*, London, 1928, pp. 1-28.

Cohen, Hennig. "Shakespeare's *Twelfth Night*, I.v. 128-130," *Explicator*, XIV (1955), item 12.

Conrad, Hermann. "Zu den Quellen von Shakespeares *Twelfth Night*," *English Studies*, XLVI (1912-13), 73-85.

Cox, Lee Sheridan, "The Riddle in *Twelfth Night*," *SQ*, XIII (1962), 360.

Craig, Hardin. *An Interpretation of Shakespeare*. New York, 1948, pp. 159-168.

Crane, Milton. "*Twelfth Night* and Shakesperian Comedy," *SQ*, VI (1955), 1-8.

Curry, John S., S. J. *Deception in Elizabethan Comedy*. Chicago, 1955, *passim*.

Daggett, W. P. "*Twelfth Night* at the Laboratory Theatre," *SAB*, II (March 1927), 5-7.

Davy, C. B. "*Twelfth Night*," in *Adelphi*, III (Nov. 1925), 445-447.

Dean-Smith, Margaret. "The First Night of *Twelfth Night*," *TLS*, Feb. 11, 1955, p. 89.

[XIII]

de Chasca, Edmund V. "Early Editions of *Gl'Ingannati*: The Problem of Overlapping Dates," *MP*, L (1952), 79-87.

del Tufo, Joseph P., S. J., "The Structure of Shakespearean Comedy," *DA*, XXII (Fordham, 1961), 4004.

De Perott, Joseph. *Noch eine eventuelle Quelle zum Heiligen Dreikönigs abend. SJ*, XLVI (1910), 118-120.

Dickens, B. "Pythagoras Concerning Wild-Fowle," *MLR*, XX (April 1925), 186.

———. "Two Queries on *Twelfth Night*," *MLR*, XXIX (Jan. 1934), 67.

Dodds, Madeleine Hope. "The First Night of *Twelfth Night*," *N&Q*, NS, III (1956), 57-59.

Downer, Alan. "Feste's Night," *CE*, XIII (1952), 258-265.

Downer, Alan S. "For Jesus' Sake Forbear: Shakespeare vs. the Modern Theater," *SQ*, XIII (1962), 219-230.

Draper, John W. "Dramatic Irony in Shakespeare's Earlier Plays," *West Virginia Univ. Philological Papers*, XII (1959), 1-11.

———. "Et in Illyria Feste," *SAB*, XVI (1941), 220-228; *Ibid.*, XVII, 25-32.

———. "The Melancholy Duke Orsino," *Bull. Inst. Hist. Medicine*, VI (1958), 1020-29.

———. "Olivia's Household," *PMLA*, XLIX (Sept. 1934), 797-806.

———. "Shakespeare's Illyria," *RES*, XVII (141), 459-460.

———. "Sir Toby's 'Cakes and Ale'," *ES*, XX (1938), 57-61.

———. The *"Twelfth Night" of Shakespeare's Audience*. Oxford Univ. Press, 1950, pp. xiii-280.

———. "The Wooing of Olivia," *Neophil*, XXIII (1937), 37-46.

Duckles, Vincent. "New Light on 'O Mistress Mine'," *Renaissance News*, VII (1955), 98-100.

Duthie, George Ian. *Shakespeare*. London, 1951, pp. 71-80.

Eckhoff, Lorentz. *Shakespeare: Spokesman of the Third Estate*. Oslo, 1954, pp. 133-137.

Empson, William. "The Elizabethan Stage," *TLS*, Dec. 10, 1954, p. 801.

Evans, G. Blakemore. "The Dovai Manuscript — Six Shakespearean Transcripts (1694-95)," *PQ*, XLI (Jan. 1962), 159-172.

Evans, Bertrand. *Shakespeare's Comedies*. Oxford, 1960, pp. 118-143.

Evans, Gareth Lloyd. "Shakespeare Memorial Theatre 1960," *International Theatre Annual*, V (1961), 154-169.

Forbes, L. "What You Will?" *SQ*, XIII (1962), 475-485.

Fraser, Russell A. *Shakespeare's Poetics in Relation to King Lear.* New York, N. Y., 1963, *passim.*

Freeman, Bernice. "The Costumes of *Love's Labour's Lost, Twelfth Night,* and *The Tempest*," *SAB*, XI (1936), 93-106.

Fripp, Edgar I. "Twelfth Night," in *Shakespeare Man and Artist,* London, 1938, pp. 559-563.

Frye, Roland Mushat. *Shakespeare and Christian Doctrine.* Princeton, 1963, *passim.*

Garvin K., H. W. Crundell, M. H. Dodds. "A Speculation About *Twelfth Night*," *N&Q,* 170 (1936), 326-328; 373; 442; 408-409.

George, J. "*Laelia* and *Twelfth Night*," *N&Q,* 194 (1949), 29-30.

Gerard, Albert. "Shipload of Fools: A Note on Twelfth Night," *ES,* XLV (1964), 109-115.

Goddard, Harold C. *The Meaning of Shakespeare.* Chicago, 1951, pp. 294-306.

Goldsmith, Robert H. *Wise Fools In Shakespeare.* Mich. State U. P., 1955.

Gollancz, Sir Israel. "Bits of Timber: Some Observations on Shakesperean Names — 'Shylock'; 'Polonius'; 'Malvolio', in *A Book of Homage to Shakespeare.* London, 1916, pp. 170-178.

Gordon, D. J. "*Twelfth Night* and Gli Ingannati, a Note," *Bol. degli Studi Inglesi in Italia,* VII (1939), 17-27.

Gordon, George "Twelfth Night," in *Shakesperian Comedy and Other Studies,* New York, 1953, *passim.*

Grace, William J. *Approaching Shakespeare.* London, 1964, *passim.*

Gray, E. McQ. "Shakespeare's *Twelfth Night,*" *NQ,* 150 (Jan 16, 1926), 44.

Greg, Walter W. *The Shakespeare First Folio: Its Bibliographical and Textual History.* Oxford, 1955, pp. 296-298.

———. "*Twelfth Night,*" *TLS,* Dec. 31, 1954, p. 853.

Hamill, H. "A Crux in II, iv, 33f," *J of the U of Bombay,* II (Nov. 1933), 14-15.

Hankins, John Erskine. *Shakespeare's Derived Imagery.* Lawrence, 1953, *passim.*

Harbage, Alfred. *As They Liked It: An Essay on Shakespeare and Morality.* New York, 1947, *passim.*

[XV]

Hardy, Barbara. *Twelfth Night*. (Notes on English Literature), Oxford, 1962, pp. viii — 47.

Harris, Frank. *The Women of Shakespeare*. London, 1911, *passim*.

Hogan, Charles Beecher. *Shakespeare in the Theatre 1701-1800: A Record of Performances in London 1701-1750*, Oxford Univ. Press, 1952, Vol. I, pp. 454-457. *Ibid*. Vol. II, (1957), 1751-1800, pp. 657-72.

Hoy, Cyrus. "Comedy, Tragedy, and Tragicomedy," *Virginia Quarterly Review*, XXXVI (1960), 105-118.

H., R. E. *"Patience on a Monument," N&Q*, 175 (1938), 441.

Hiscock, W. G. "Twelfth Day Fare, 1600-01," *TLS*, July 29, 1955, p. 429.

Hoepfner, Theodore C. "M.O.A.I. — *Twelfth Night*," *N&Q*, NS, V (1958), 193.

Holland, Norman N. "Cuckold or Counsellor in *Twefth Night*, I.v.56," *SQ*, VIII (1957), 127-129.

———. "Twelfth Night, in *The Shakespearean Imagination*. New York, 1964, pp. 180-196.

Hollander, John. "Musica Mundana and *Twelfth Night*," *Sound and Poetry, English Institute Essays*, 1956. New York, 1957, pp. 55-82.

———. "*Twelfth Night* and the Morality of Indulgence," *Sewanee Review*, LXVII (1959), 220-238.

Hoskins, Frank L. "Misalliance: A Significant Theme in Tudor and Stuart Drama," *Renaissance Papers*, U of North Carolina, 1956, pp. 72-73.

Hotson, Leslie. *The First Night of "Twelfth Night,"* New York, 1954, pp. 256. (See reviews listed in G. R. Smith's *Classified Shakespeare Bibliography* after No. B-7021.)

———. "The First Night of *Twelfth Night*," *TLS*, Jan. 21, 1955, p. 41.

———. The First Night of the '*Twelfth Night*,' " *TLS*, Jan. 23, 1959, p. 47.

———. "Manningham's 'Mid . . . . '," *TLS*, Sept. 9, 1949, p. 585.

———. "Sir Toby's 'Castiliano Vulgo'," *TLS*, Oct. 11, 1947, p. 521.

———. "*Twelfth Night*," TLS, July 12, 1947, p. 351. See letter by J. Dover Wilson, *TLS*, July 26, 1947, p. 379.

———. "*Twelfth Night*," *TLS*, March 18, 1955, p. 165.

Hulme, Hilda M. *Explorations in Shakespeare's Language: Some Problems of Word Meaning in the Dramatic Text*. New York, 1963, *passim*.

[XVI]

Hunter, Edwin R. *Shakespeare and Common Sense*. Boston, 1954, pp. 117-120, 200-203, *et passim*.

Imam, Syed Mehdi. "Studies in Shakespeare's Plays: VII. *Twelfth Night: 'The Winds of Illyria'*," *Mother India*, (March 1961), pp. 67-69; (May 1961), pp. 67-68.

Jenkins, Harold. "Shakespeare's Twelfth Night," *Rice Institute Pamphlet*, XLV (Jan., 1959), 19-42.

Kaufman, Helen Andrews. "Nicolo Secchi as a Source of *Twelfth Night*," *SQ*, V (1954), 271-280.

Keen, Frances. "The First Night of *Twelfth Night*," *TLS*, Dec. 19, 1958, p. 737.

Kenyon, J. S. "Two Notes on Shakespeare's *Twelfth Night* (III, iii, 36ff)" *P.Q.*, V (April 1926), 176-180.

Kermode, Frank. "The Mature Comedies," in *Early Shakespeare*, Stratford-upon-Avon Studies, 3, ed. by J. R. Brown and B. Harris, London, 1961, pp. 210-27.

Knight, George Wilson. "The Theme of Romantic Friendship in Shakespeare's Plays and the *Sonnets*," in *Holborn Review 71*, (October 1929), 450-60.

———. *The Shakespearean Tempest*. London, 1953, pp. 120-127. (First ed. 1932)

Kökeritz, Helge. *Shakespeare's Pronunciation*. New Haven, 1953, *passim*.

Kranidas, Thomas. "Malvolio on Decorum," *SQ*, XV (1964), 450-451.

Lawrence, W. J. *Shakespeare's Workshop*. Oxford, 1928, *passim*.

Linthicum, M. C. "Black and Yellow," *SAB*, VIII (Dec. 7, 1933), 119-20.

———. Malvolio's Cross-gartered Yellow Stockings," *MP*, XXV (August 1927), 87-93.

Luce, Morton, ed. *Rich's Apolonius and Silla, an Original of Shakespeare's Twelfth Night*. (*Shakespeare Classics*.) London, 1912.

Ludowyk, E. F. C. "Twelfth Night," in *Understanding Shakespeare*. Cambridge, 1962, pp. 198-220.

McCullen, Joseph T., Jr. "Madness and Isolation of Character in Elizabethan and Early Stuart Drama," *SP*, XLVIII (1951), 206-218.

MacKenzie, W. R. "Standing Water in *Twelfth Night*, I. 5. 158," *MLN*, XL (May 1927), 289-93.

Marder, Louis. *His Exits and His Entrances: The Story of Shakespeare's Reputation*. New York, 1963, *passim*.

[XVII]

――――. "Longhair, Egghead, and Shakespeare," *SNL*, IX (1959), 2.

Malone, Kemp. "Meaningful Fictive Names in English Literature," *Names (Journal of the American Name Society)*, V (1957), 1-13.

Manheim, Leonard F. "The Mythical Joys of Shakespeare; or, *What You Will*," in *Shakespeare Encomium* (City College Papers I), ed. by Anne Paolucci, New York, 1964, pp. 100-112.

Markels, Julian. "Shakespeare's Confluence of Tragedy and Comedy: *Twelfth Night* and *King Lear*," in *Shakespeare 400* ed. by James G. McManaway, New York, 1964, pp. 75-88.

Mendl, R. W. S. "Twelfth Night," in *Revelation in Shakespeare*. New York, 1965, pp. 112-118.

Merchant, W. Moelwyn. "Shakespeare's Theology," *Review of English Literature*, (October 1964), 72-88.

Merion, Carslyn. "*Twelfth Night*," *TLS*, March 11, 1955, p. 149.

Moore, John Robert. "Morley and 'O Mistress Mine'," *PMLA*, LIV (1939), 149-152.

Morhardt, M. "L'identification de Malvolio," in *Mercure de France*, CCVIX (April 15, 1935), 306-316.

Morris, Joseph E. "*Twelfth Night:* The Lady of Strachy," *N&Q*, 175 (1938), 347-348. See letter by H. Kendra Baker, *N&Q*, 175 (1938), 411; H. Kendra Baker, 176 (1939), 11-12; letter by Rockingham, 176 (1939), 249; W. H. Welply, 176 (1939), 48.

Mueschke, P. and J. Fleisher. "Jonsonian Elements in the Comic Underplot of *Twelfth Night*," *PMLA*, XLVIII (1933), 722-740.

Muir, Kenneth. *Shakespeare's Sources*. London, 1957. pp. 66-77.

――――. "The Sources of *Twelfth Night*," *N&Q*, NS, II (1955), 94.

Nagarajan, S. " 'What You Will': A Suggestion," *SQ*, X (1959), 61-67.

Nagler, A. M. "Atorno Atorno,' " *TLS*, May 6, 1960, p. 289.

Noble Richmond. "Feste's Epilogue Song," *TLS* (July 10, 1930), p. 576.

――――. *Shakespeare's Biblical Knowledge and Use of The Book of Common Prayer*. London, 1935, pp. 209-213.

Oyama, Toshiko. "The Language of Feste, The Clown," *Otsuka Festschrift*, 1958, pp. 379-393.

Parrott, T. M. *Shakespearean Comedy*. New York, 1949, pp. 178-190 *et passim*.

Pearce, T. M. "Shakespeare's *Twelfth Night*," II.v.5-7, *Explicator*, VII (1948), 7, item 19.

[XVIII]

Priestley, John Boynton. *The English Comic Characters,* new ed. London, 1963.

Pruvost, Rene. *"The Two Gentlemen of Verona, Twelfth Night, et Gl'Ingannati,"* EA, XIII (1960), 1-9.

Pyle, Fitzroy. *"Twelfth Night, King Lear,* and *Arcadia,"* MLR, XLIII (1948), 449-455.

Race, Sydney. "Manningham's Diary: The Case for Re-examination," *N&Q,* 199 (1954), 380-383.

———. "The First Night of *Twelfth Night,"* N&Q, II (1955), 52-55; III (1956), 423-424; comment *Ibid.,* K. B. Danks, "Dr. Hotson & Mr. Race," II (1955), 316-317.

Ralli, Augustus. *A History of Shakesperian Criticism,* 2 Vols. Oxford, 1932; New York, 1959, *passim.*

Ramage, David. "Sir Andrew Shakesface," *N&Q,* NS, III (1956), 508.

Rattray, R. G. "Aguecake," *TLS,* Oct. 5, 1946, p. 479. Comment by W. W. Greg, "Aguecake," *TLS,* Oct. 12, 1946, p. 493; letter by R. F. Rattray, *Ibid.,* Oct. 19, p. 507.

Rea, J. "Feste's Syllogisms in *Twelfth Night,"* Ball State Teachers College Forum, Autumn 1964, 59-62.

Reese, M. M. "Twelfth Night," in *Shakespeare: His World & His Work,* London, 1953, *passim.*

Righter, Anne. "Twelfth Night," in *Shakespeare and the Idea of the Play,* New York, 1962, *passim.*

Salingar, L. G. "The Design of Twelfth Night," SQ, IX (1958), 117-139.
———. "Messaline in *Twelfth Night,"* TLS, June 3, 1955, p. 301.

Saunders, J. W. "The Elizabethan Stage," *TLS,* Nov. 11, 1955, p. 680.

Schevill, James. "Bright enigma, all thy puzzles glitter," *Teachers College Record,* Ap., 1964, 591-602.

Scott, William Inglis Dunn *Shakespeare's Melancholics.* London, 1961, pp. 192.

Secchi, Nicolo. *Self Interest,* Tr. William Reymes; ed. Helen Andrews Kaufman, 1955, pp. xxix, 106.

Seiden, M. "Malvolio Reconsidered," *University of Kansas City Review,* XXVIII (1961), 105-114.

Sen Gupto, S. C. *Shakesperian Comedy.* Calcutta, India, 1950, *passim.*
———. *The Whirligig of Time.* Bombay, 1961, pp. 114-119.

[XIX]

Simonini, R. C., Jr. "The Pedant and Church in *Twelfth Night,* III.ii.80," *MLN,* LXIV (1949), 513-515.

Sisson, Charles Jasper. "Tudor Intelligence Tests: Malvolio and Real Life," *Essays on Shakespeare and Elizabethan Drama in honor of Hardin Craig,* Missouri Univ. Press, 1962, pp. 183-200.

———. "Twelfth Night," in *New Readings in Shakespeare VIII, The Comedies, The Poems.* Cambridge, 1956, p. 184-194.

Sochatoff, A. Fred. *"Twelfth Night,"* in *"Lovers Meeting": Discussions of Five Plays by Shakespeare,* Carnegie Institute of Technology, 1964, pp. 33-51.

Solem, Delmar E. "An Experimental *Twelfth Night," Southern Speech Journal,* XXIV (1959), 197-200.

Smith, Charles G. *Shakespeare's Proverb Lore.* Cambridge, 1963. See list on p. 147.

Spencer, Hazelton. "Burnaby's *Love Betrayed* and *Twelfth Night,"* in *Shakespeare Improved: The Restoration Revisions in Quarto and on Stage.* Cambridge (Mass.), 1927, 350-353.

———. "The Elizabethan 'To Board'," *MLN,* XXXXIV (December 1929), 531-2.

Spurgeon, Caroline F. E. *Shakespeare's Imagery: And What It Tells Us.* Cambridge, 1952, pp. 268-269, *et passim.*

Stauffer, Donald. *Shakespeare's World of Images: The Development of His Moral Ideas.* New York, 1949, pp. 80-83.

Summers, Joseph H. "The Masks of *Twelfth Night," Univ. of Kansas City Review,* XXII (1955), 25-32.

Summerskill, William H. J. "Aguecheek's Disease," *Lancet,* 269 (1955), 288ff.

Swander, Homer. *"Twelfth Night*: Critics, Players, and a Script," *ETJ,* XVI (1964), 114-121.

Tannenbaum, Samuel A. "Comments on Twelfth Night," *Shakesperian Scraps,* N. Y., 1933, pp. 118-128.

Taylor, Marion A. " 'He That Did the Tiger Board': a note on a note," *SQ,* XV (1964), 110-113.

Thaler, Alvin. "The Original Malvolio?" in *Shakespeare and Democracy,* 1941, chapter VI.

Thomas, H. "For 'Castiglione Voglio'," *TLS,* July 27, 1933, 512.

[XX]

———. "A Passage (I, iii, 44) in *Twelfth Night* Emended," *TLS*, May 4, 1933, 312.

Thomas, Sidney. "A Note on Shakespeare' sMotley," *SQ*, X (1959), 255.

Thomson, J. A. K. "Twelfth Night," in *Shakespeare and the Classics*, London, 1952, pp. 127-129.

Thompson, K. M. "Shakespeare's Romantic Comedies," PMLA, LXVII (1952), 1079-1093.

Tilley, orris P. "Malvolio's Yellow Stockings and Cross-Garters," *SAB*, XII (1937), 54-55.

———. "The Organic Unity of 'Twelfth Night'," *PMLA*, XXIX, N.S., XXII (1914), 550-66.

———. "Unnotated Proverbs and Proverbial Allusions in *Twelfth Night*," *PQ*, VI (July 1927), 306-11.

Tolman, Albert H. "Is Malvolio a Puritan?" *Falstaff and Other Shakesperian Topics*, London, 1925, pp. 146-51.

Trewin, J. C. *Shakespeare on the English Stage* 1900-1964. New York, 1965, *passim*.

Van Doren, Mark. *Shakespeare*, New York, 1939.

Wain, JJohn. *The Living World of Shakespeare: A Player's Guide*. New York, 1964, *passim*.

Wallace, S. A. "Getting the Fun out of *Twelfth Night*," *EJ*, XX (Sept. 1931), 562-565.

Walsh, Grosbeck, and Robert M. Pool. *Shakespeare's Knowledge of Twins and Twinning*, 1940. (Reprinted from *Southern Medicine and Surgery*.)

Webster, Margaret. *Shakespeare Today*. London, 1957, pp. 201-205.

Welsford, Enid. *The Fool*. New York, 1961. (1st ed. 1935)

West, E. "Bradleyan Reprise: On the Fool in Twelfth Night," *SAB*, XXIV (1949), 264-274.

Williams, Charles. "The Use of the Second Person in *Twelfth Night*," *English*, IX (1952/53), 125-128.

Whitaker, Virgil K. *Shakespeare's Use of Learning: An Inquiry into the Growth of His Mind and Art*. California, 1953, pp. 178-193, *et passim*.

White, Edward J. *Commentaries on the Law in Shakespeare*. St. Louis, 1913, pp. 34-41.

[XXI]

Williams, Phillip. "Mistakes In Twelfth Night and Their Resolution," *PMLA*, LXXVI (1961), 193-199.

Wiesen, Pearl. "Twelfth Night: A Stage History," *DA*, XXIII (1962), 2257-2258.

Wilson, John Dover. "Shakespeare Emendations," *TLS*, June 8, 1933, 396.

———. *"Twelfth Night* and the Gunpowder Plot," in *TLS*, June 13, 1929, 471.

Wingate, Charles E. L. "Twelfth Night," in *Shakespeare's Heroines on the Stage*, New York, 1895, pp. 81-102.

Wood, James O. "Shakespeare the Unobservant?", *SNL*, XII (1962), 49.

Wright, L. B. "A Conduct Book for Malvolio," *SP*, XXXI (1934), 115-132.

Yellowlees, Henry. "Medicine and Surgery in the 1955 Season Plays," in *More Talking of Shakespeare*, London and N. Y., 1959, pp. 172-85.

TWELFTH NIGHT–*NOTES*